The Revolutionary Left in Spain, 1914-1923

GERALD H. MEAKER

The Revolutionary Left in Spain, 1914-1923

STANFORD UNIVERSITY PRESS

1974  STANFORD, CALIFORNIA

Stanford University Press
Stanford, California
© 1974 by the Board of Trustees of the
Leland Stanford Junior University
Printed in the United States of America
ISBN 0-8047-0845-2
LC 73-80622
Published with the Assistance of the
Andrew W. Mellon Foundation

To the memory of my mother and father,
Helen and Henry Percy Meaker,
and to Charlotte

Preface

This study grew out of my general interest in revolutionary movements and ideologies of the early twentieth century, and more immediately out of a research project focused on the Spanish Anarchist response to the Bolshevik Revolution and to the Leninist concept of revolutionary strategy and tactics. My curiosity was initially aroused by what seemed to me a paradox: namely, the discrepancy between the enthusiastic reaction of Spanish workers to the Bolshevik seizure of power in Russia (which may not have been surpassed in any other European country) and the obvious numerical weakness, lack of cohesion, and political impotence of the Communist Party that emerged in Spain in the early 1920's. In view of the seriousness of social tensions in the Peninsula—greatly aggravated by the economic impact of the European war and by the mood of proletarian combativeness that swept over Spain following the Armistice—the debacle of the Communist movement posed an interesting historical problem, and one whose study, I suspected, might help to illuminate the whole character of the revolutionary Left in Spain.

My research was thus influenced by the belief that the failure of Spanish Communism in the postwar period had to be understood in the total context of an undeveloped, somewhat isolated, and ideologically retarded labor movement lagging in many respects behind its European counterparts. It appeared in particular that the Comintern's failure was closely related to one of the more distinctive aspects of Spanish labor in that period: the continuing struggle waged by two regionally separated and perennially hostile tendencies, one Bakuninist and the other Marxist, for hegemony over the working classes of the Peninsula.

It was clear that the histories of both sides of this peculiarly divided labor movement would have to be reconstructed and related to the central question I had raised, and that the unifying theme of my work would be Spanish labor's response to the Russian Revolution—that is, the rise, development, and ultimate failure of the idea of a Leninist party in Spain. Within the limits of this preoccupation I have tried to write a fairly comprehensive political and ideological history of the Spanish labor movement during the turbulent (and little-studied) decade that began with the outbreak of World War I and ended with the suppression of the parliamentary system by the military dictatorship of Primo de Rivera in 1923.

My purpose has been to bring the several elements of the revolutionary Left —Anarchosyndicalists, Socialists, and Communists—into a common narrative framework, to trace their evolution and interaction, and to clarify insofar as possible their operative ideas, their tactics, and their internal dissensions. I have tried to write a history not of the working classes per se, but of the revolutionary movements or elites that contested for supremacy among them. For I believe that one of the more immediate needs in early twentieth-century Spanish labor studies is for an integrated, conceptually unified history whose interpretive schema, whether or not one agrees with it, will at least suggest some of the numerous monographic studies that must be carried out if the field is to emerge from infancy. I have no doubt that as more Spanish labor archives —official and unofficial—are opened to scholars, and as more materials see the light of day, the picture I have presented here will be broadened, deepened, and, in all probability, modified.

That picture centers on the remarkable durability of the doctrines and attitudes underlying the Anarchosyndicalist and Socialist movements during the postwar era, and on the capacity of these two major groups to resist (even as they partially succumbed to) the challenge of the Bolshevik Revolution and to preempt the field of revolutionary politics that the Comintern sought to enter. By their very existence and continuing plausibility as revolutionary movements in the somewhat backward Spanish milieu, the two major labor subcultures would create an "ideological vacuum" (as I shall later term it) within which the first Communist effort in Spain—handicapped, to be sure, by a variety of contingent disabilities—would virtually expire.

Whereas the success of a political or social movement has a certain concreteness about it that seems to narrow somewhat the parameters of explanation, the failure of a movement to grow and to achieve the stature and influence that historical circumstances had presumably marked out for it is an inherently more nebulous matter—less satisfying to contemplate, less easily structured, and possibly more diffuse in its causes. Nevertheless, the assumption that failure as a phenomenon can be as instructive as success is necessarily the basis of the present work. For whether one is talking about Communists, Anarchosyndicalists, or Socialists, the history of the revolutionary Left in the years 1914-23 is essentially a history of failure—the failure of ideologically impassioned, doctrinaire, and resolute men to create the revolutionary movement that alone, they felt, could destroy a privileged, oligarchical social order and make possible the emergence of the egalitarian New Jerusalem they desired.

They were, as it turned out, historically premature, they were sectarian and schismatic, and, in the end, they failed; but the story of their unavailing efforts is, I believe, well worth telling, since it sheds more than a little light on a type of revolutionary mentality that has played, and may play again, a significant role in a Spain still in the throes of the transition to modernity.

This project had its origins in a doctoral dissertation carried out under the guidance of Professor Robert Wohl of the University of California at Los Angeles, a scholar and teacher whose ability to generate intellectual excitement in those around him and to inspire the undertaking of difficult tasks is unexcelled. I owe a major debt of gratitude to Professor Stanley Payne of the University of Wisconsin, who counseled me from the beginning and whose careful reading of the manuscript was of inestimable value. I wish also to express my great appreciation to Professor Edward Malefakis of the University of Michigan, who, though traveling abroad at the time, consented to read my manuscript under difficult circumstances and motivated me to rethink some of my interpretations. From my friend Professor John P. Diggins of the University of California at Irvine I received always penetrating suggestions regarding style and substance, which I am pleased to acknowledge. I would particularly like to extend my thanks to Señor Luis Portela, who invited me into his home and shared with me not only his lucid recollections of the distant era that concerned me but his good brandy and fellowship as well. To Mr. J. G. Bell of Stanford University Press I would like to express my appreciation not only for his critical insight into the structure and intent of my work but for the remarkable patience with which he awaited its completion. Mr. James Trosper, who bore the task of editing with stoic fortitude and whose suggestions improved the manuscript at innumerable points, also has my sincere thanks. For any errors of fact or interpretation the responsibility, needless to say, is entirely my own.

My thanks also go to the following persons who generously helped me at various times and in various ways (that I think each will remember) with the research involved in this book: Juan Andrade, Jordi Arquer, Professor Siegfried Bahne, José Bullejos, Professor David T. Cattell, Theodore Draper, Germinal Esgleas, Antonio García Birlán, Manuel Gómez, Jesús González Malo, Philip Jaffe, Ramón Lamoneda, Gaston Leval, Jaime Magriña, Professor Julián Marías, Professor Robert Marrast, Joaquín Maurín, Max Nomad, Andrés Saborit, Ramón Sender, Bertram Wolfe.

Finally, I would like to thank my research assistant, Ms. Lorna K. Mercer, and the following persons attached to various libraries and archives, whose helpfulness and competence greatly facilitated completion of this book: Rudolph de Jong (International Institute for Social History, Amsterdam); Don

Vicente Llorca and Amalia Lopes Valencia (Biblioteca del Ministerio de Trabajo, Madrid); Charlotte Oyer (Oviatt Library, California State University, Northridge); Walter W. Bruegger (Research Library, UCLA); Arline Paul, Gloria Linder, and Marina Tinkoff (The Hoover Institution on War, Revolution, and Peace, Stanford); and the staff of the Bibliothèque de Documentation International Contemporaine, Paris. I am grateful, finally, to Ms. Julia Farkas for her assistance in the preparation of the Index.

G. M.

Contents

The Revolutionary Left in Spain, 1914-1923

CHAPTER ONE

The Workers and the War

The most striking feature of the Spanish labor movement in the early twentieth century was its division into competing Bakuninist and Marxist factions, which were separated not only spiritually but, to a remarkable degree, geographically. Though similar to the competition between "antipolitical" and "political" labor tendencies found elsewhere, as in France or Italy, this schism in Spain between a vigorous and popular Anarchosyndicalism and a struggling Socialism was peculiarly deep and bitter, inhibiting nearly all dialogue and provoking endless recrimination. In the grip of their contrasting world views, the two movements nourished an aversion for each other that was exceeded only by their hostility toward the ruling classes. But though they often proselytized aggressively, they failed, in the main, to penetrate one another's regional bastions. The Anarchosyndicalists remained predominant in the East and South—in Catalonia, Aragon, Levante, and Andalusia—and held outposts in such places as La Coruña and Gijón. The Socialists entrenched themselves in the Center and the North—in Castile, the Basque Provinces, and Asturias—but were almost wholly unable to win converts in Catalonia, the country's major industrial center. The importance of this division, which seemed rooted in the structure of Spanish society, would be difficult to exaggerate. That the turbulent years 1914–23 witnessed only a *révolution manquée* and not a political or social transformation must be attributed largely to this seemingly irreparable schism within the proletarian ranks. Had it been possible to eliminate the sources of discord and create a unified labor movement able to exert a force proportional to its growing numerical strength, the Spanish monarchy might have succumbed a decade earlier than it did.[1]

This division within the labor movement was due mainly to the unusual power and diffusion of Anarchist ideas in the Peninsula. Whereas in other European countries Anarchism as an ideological commitment was limited to a relatively small number of intellectuals and declassés, in Spain (after its propagation by Bakunin's disciple Giuseppe Fanelli in 1868) it assumed the form of a mass movement and surrogate religion for the dispossessed, embracing by

1900 tens of thousands of peasants in Andalusia and elsewhere in the South, and sustaining groups in Barcelona and other cities.[2] Thus when Syndicalism arose in Spain in the early twentieth century, in response to essentially the same economic and sociopolitical maladies that elsewhere nourished the "direct action" response, it also arose in a country where Anarchism was already deeply entrenched. As a result, the Spanish movement emerged as a true *Anarcho-syndicalism*, an authentic and durable amalgam of Anarchist and Syndicalist impulses that was unique to Spain.[3] The Socialist movement was also influenced by the Anarchist presence, though in a contrary manner, being pushed inevitably away from direct action, insurrectionalism, terrorism, and all other methods identified with Anarchism and toward an ever greater absorption with political tactics. Thus the distance separating Syndicalism and Socialism in Spain was even greater than, for example, in France (where relations were at least diplomatically correct), and made united action extremely difficult.[4]

Although some observers have seen the strength of Anarchism and Anarcho-syndicalism in Spain as an indication of racial vitality,[5] it was also a sign of delayed evolution. Elsewhere in Europe the 1870's and 1880's saw the displacement of Bakuninism by social democracy, with its organizational and "authoritarian" preoccupations. Not so in Spain, whose labor movement lagged perhaps half a century behind the rest of Europe, suffering (as Marx said of the German movement in the 1860's) as much from the development of capitalism as from the incompleteness of that development.[6] The tempo of Spanish industrialization after the 1870's did not match that of other Western nations and failed—even in comparison with Giolittian Italy—to raise real wages substantially or give the workers positive expectations. Behind some of the highest protectionist walls in Europe, Spanish capitalists were unable to create a viable and expansive economic system. Exporting mostly raw materials and dependent on large infusions of foreign capital and expertise, Spain was, in effect, a semicolonial country, in which foreign investment in 1914 (estimated at about $800 million) was nearly half of all Spanish industrial capital. Even the war boom largely failed to modernize the economic base: the scale of industrial enterprise, especially in Catalonia, remained small and the employer class inherently petty bourgeois.[7]

The stagnation and poverty of the agricultural sector reinforced the malaise of industry and caused extensive migration from the rural areas to Barcelona, Valencia, and Bilbao, and even to relatively unindustrialized Madrid, as well as to many smaller cities. Indeed, much of the history of Spanish labor in the early twentieth century must center around what Adam Ulam has termed the "unassimilated peasant."[8] Large numbers of peasant-proletarians set the tone of the urban labor movement, both retarding and radicalizing it by their presence—by their willingness to act as strikebreakers and their susceptibility to extremist appeals. The impact of agrarian migration was heightened by a demographic revolution, which, getting under way in the late nineteenth century, caused Spain's population to rise from 18 million in 1900 to 24 million in 1930, with about 40 percent of the increase making its way to the cities. On the eve of the war perhaps half the population of the larger cities was composed of recent migrants, of whom an estimated 70 percent had been agricultural laborers. At the same time agrarian stagnation, by imposing a slow growth rate and inadequate returns upon industry, ensured that the cities could not readily absorb the hosts of displaced peasants flowing into them, so that rural migrants were not so much drawn to the cities as pushed off the land.[9]

These masses of peasants were far from homogeneous in their mentality. It is clear that peasants from the dry, "church-hating" provinces of the South and East—that is, from Valencia, Aragon, Alicante, Murcia, and Almería—brought with them an unusually harsh and millenarian temper that put a special stamp on the Catalonian labor movement, predisposing it first to the anticlerical radicalism of Alejandro Lerroux and later to Anarchosyndicalism. The Gallegans, Castilians, Leonese, and Asturians who formed the bulk of the migration into Vizcaya, by contrast, had a somewhat different temper, which, in a context featuring larger industrial units, higher literacy, and a less abrasive relationship between the clerical establishment and the masses, encouraged the migrants to respond more favorably than their Catalonian counterparts to Socialist proselytizing. Thus Barcelona and Bilbao—the two real poles of the Spanish labor movement, containing, with their hinterlands, about 50 percent of all industrial workers—were both washed by the tide of peasant migration and radicalized by it, but with rather different results, the one becoming a stronghold of Anarchosyndicalism and the other of Socialism.[10]

The evolution of the labor movement was also greatly affected by the sociopolitical realities of the Restoration system. This regime, established by Antonio Cánovas del Castillo in 1876, in the aftermath of the Carlist Wars, was a remarkable accomplishment in its time, bringing order after decades of civil conflict and providing for a constitutional monarchy in which sovereignty was shared between the king and the Cortes. The central political mechanism consisted of two monarchical parties, the Conservative and the Liberal, which alternated in power with somewhat artificial regularity and with the help of a large corps of rural bosses, or *caciques*. Because of the lack of a large, politically vigorous middle class, the Canovite system was necessarily oligarchical, resting, despite universal suffrage, on a rather narrow political foundation of agrarian interests intermeshed with banking and industrial elites.[11]

Critics had no difficulty identifying the central weakness of the system, namely, its divorce from the real life of the nation. The gap between "official" and "vital" Spain was, as Ortega y Gasset frequently affirmed, very great. Ortega expressed the cynicism of the progressive forces when he proclaimed that the Restoration system consisted only of "phantom parties that defend ghostly ideas and, assisted by the shades of newspapers, run ministries of hallucina-tion."[12] The most serious flaw was that the two major parties remained rela-tively undifferentiated in their social bases and, for a variety of reasons, were not compelled to recruit ever wider sectors of the population. The result was that the system never mobilized the bulk of the nation behind it or established its legitimacy.[13]

Though not truly democratic, the Canovite system was by no means wholly repressive. The basic liberties were acknowledged, and trade unions had ex-tensive, though not complete, freedom to operate. Efforts were even made by the major parties, though not until after 1900, to stem the rising tide of prole-tarian protest by means of social and industrial legislation.[14] These laws re-mained, however, largely dead letters since Spain was too poor to afford them and public opinion too weak to ensure their enforcement. Wages were among the lowest in Europe. In Catalonia the average industrial worker was paid 3.50 to 4 pesetas per day; skilled workers received 5 pesetas, and women rarely more than 2.50 (in 1912 one peseta equalled 19.3 cents). In the South the daily wage for agricultural laborers was 1.50 pesetas, with only about 295 working days in the year. In Madrid the living expenses for a worker's family were 23 percent higher than in Paris, whereas income was 68.33 percent lower. Wide-spread malnutrition was reflected in a high death rate of 27 per 1,000 in the the Spanish capital, as against 17 and 16 in Paris and Brussels, respectively.[15]

No less conducive to labor extremism than hunger was the completeness of the workers' isolation from middle-class life and the general powerlessness they experienced within the collusive political system of the Restoration. Like most weak governments, Restoration ministries aggravated proletarian unrest by constantly alternating between severity and laxity, so that periods of repression were often followed by intervals of conciliation and almost indiscriminate amnesty. Both major labor organizations, the Socialist Unión General del Trabajo (UGT) and the Anarchosyndicalist Confederación Nacional del Tra-bajo (CNT), despite their radical rhetoric, often acted in the capacity of pres-sure groups, seeking to establish contact with ministers or civil servants and to influence administration of the laws. But governments in this era did little to encourage such moderation, and, indeed, their frequent resort to mass arrests and excessive force almost certainly had the opposite effect.

Closely related to this problem was the general failure of liberal-democratic institutions to function properly in an underdeveloped and basically agrarian society. No other large country in the West, as Stanley Payne has pointed out, was given democratic institutions and universal suffrage at so early a stage in its civic development; and the result, inevitably, was political corruption. Al-though there was much more to Anarchosyndicalism than mere detestation of bourgeois politics, the electoral issue was one about which many workers—

long exploited by politicians of all shades—came to feel passionately and which attracted them in large numbers to the CNT while impeding Socialist efforts to recruit them to political action. The peculiar vitality of Anarchosyndicalism in Spain thus in part reflected the instinctive response of a people living "under the theory of liberal democracy and individual civic freedom but never achieving the substance of it."[16]

Anarchosyndicalism

The workers of Catalonia did not at first reveal the instinctive affinity for Anarchist doctrines that marked the small peasants and landless laborers of Andalusia. The Barcelona labor movement as an organized force dated from 1840 and had a long tradition of mutualism and cooperative endeavors. Throughout most of the nineteenth century the city's workers were relatively moderate and opportunist in labor matters, being absorbed by immediate goals and practical reforms and very little concerned with revolutionary or Anarchist ideas. The Anarchist leader Anselmo Lorenzo was convinced that the Catalan workers, if left to their natural evolution, would never have become "internationalists."[17]

The Restoration settlement of 1876 recognized the right of unionization, and serious organizational efforts were then begun by the Catalonian proletariat. It was in these early days of the restored Bourbon monarchy that most of the great Catalonian trade unions—metalworkers, construction workers, carpenters, and others—had their origins. Without exception, they stressed traditional labor goals and conventional strike tactics, as did the already established textile union, the Tres Clases de Vapor, which served as a unifying organization for all the region's trade unions. As late as 1890 the outlook for conventional trade unionism and for political participation by Catalonian workers appeared favorable. Anarchist forces were actually stronger in other parts of Spain, whereas the Tres Clases de Vapor, along with the Socialists, continued to predominate in Barcelona. But between 1890 and 1900 Anarchism, which had ebbed and flowed in the previous two decades and had conquered much of the rural South, made its first conquest of the Barcelona labor movement, virtually liquidating Socialist influence there. The foothold won would never be lost, and Anarchism in one form or another would have to be reckoned with in Barcelona down to the time of the Civil War.[18]

This growing hegemony reflected a significant change in the composition of the Barcelona labor force resulting from the immigration of large numbers of workers from the South. These newcomers, "socially irresponsible and without associative traditions," as Vicens Vives wrote, were millenarian in temper and unhappy with their lot.[19] A French observer who worked in the factories of Barcelona described the immigrants on the eve of the war as young men 15 to 25 years of age, many of them from other provinces, who form the major part of the working-class population of Barcelona; violent and passionate spirits who are quick to catch fire, *exaltés* who are always ready for action. These effervescent masses, unprotected, without intelligent principles, lacking in will, exasperated by the conditions of ... industrial labor, which are so contrary to the demands of their nature: what a prize they offer to piratical demagogues![20]

Although they came as *inconscientes*, flooding an already oversupplied labor market and often entering into employment first as strikebreakers, the immigrants were more susceptible to the preachings of Barcelona's Anarchists than were those workers who were native Catalans or who had been Catalanized by long residence. The changing composition of the labor movement in the province was reflected in the increasing use of Castilian, which the migrants could understand, in place of Catalan in labor assemblies.[21]

Other factors, as well, worked to radicalize the Catalonian labor movement. The prosperity that had marked the first decade of the Restoration finally broke in 1887, and the workers began to suffer from chronic underemployment in many industries. More important, perhaps, was the effect of the wave of Anarchist terrorism that afflicted Barcelona from 1892 to 1896 and had the unexpected consequence of producing a growing sense of identification between the Anarchists and the labor movement. In dealing with the terrorist threat, which was a new and unnerving phenomenon to them, the police proved unable to distinguish between Anarchist terrorists and legitimate trade-union leaders. All too frequently the latter were arrested, imprisoned, and even executed along with the bomb-throwers. In the face of this common martyrdom, Anarchism became increasingly identified in the mind of the masses with the sufferings and aspirations of the workers, a process aided by the general tendency of moderates to sympathize with persecuted extremists. As Vicens Vives observes, it was, in the end, bourgeois society itself that forced the Catalonian workers under the domination of the Anarchists.[22]

Inspired by the myth of the general strike, "pure" Anarchism reached its culmination in Spain in 1902–3, burning itself out in a series of strikes and in a wave of exaltation that swept over workers in all parts of the country. By 1904 the enthusiasm of the masses had evaporated, and Anarchism was virtually extinguished as a movement in Andalusia. In Catalonia the workers embarked on a "political" phase that would last about five years, large numbers of them gravitating toward the demagogic and anticlerical Radical Party of Alejandro Lerroux, which was then making its appearance in Barcelona. From about 1905 to 1910 this was the movement of greatest attractiveness to Catalonian workers, who shared its hostility to regional nationalism and responded to its radical-sounding program and to the vague promise of a future social revolution that it held out.[23]

After an interval of apathy and disillusionment among trade unionists from 1904 to 1907, a new mystique—that of revolutionary Syndicalism—invaded the Peninsula from France and prepared the way for a great revival of the Catalonian labor movement. European Anarchism had always been inherently anti-organizational, and its relations with organized labor were often marked by mutual suspicion. But the failure of individual action and of terrorist tactics convinced many leading Anarchists that an alliance with labor was essential if libertarian ideas were not to expire for lack of a social vehicle. Such Anarchist luminaries as Peter Kropotkin, Sébastien Faure, and Fernand Pelloutier began to urge their followers to penetrate the trade unions in order to prevent the workers from falling into a narrow corporativism and to keep revolutionary attitudes alive. The foremost proponent of revolutionary Syndicalist ideas in Spain was the old Anarchist printer Anselmo Lorenzo, who translated a number of French works on this question and wrote many pamphlets of his own.[24]

Nevertheless, the Barcelona workers' revival in 1907 of their defunct municipal federation, under the name Solidaridad Obrera, was an autonomous action that owed little to outsiders. The new organization described itself as a purely Syndicalist movement and conscientiously sought to remain aloof from all political tendencies. Like the French CGT, Solidaridad Obrera was in fact more Syndicalist than Anarchist and was committed to winning immediate gains for the workers. Its original manifesto had a moderate tone and made no use of revolutionary or libertarian phraseology.[25] In 1908 Solidaridad Obrera became a regional federation, embracing 112 Catalonian trade unions and municipal federations, with a total membership perhaps as high as 25,000. An apolitical policy of "pure" Syndicalism and strict devotion to the interests of workers was reaffirmed; and it seemed momentarily as though a new and more moderate era in industrial relations had dawned in Catalonia. The moderation of the new entity was first demonstrated by its reluctance to become involved in the quasi-revolutionary events of the Tragic Week of July 1909.

The Tragic Week, an outburst of rioting and church-burning triggered by popular resentment against the Moroccan War, was both an end and a beginning. Its violence broke the spell of the hopeful Renovation Movement that had arisen in the aftermath of Spain's defeat in 1898 and largely extinguished the confidence of the public and the ruling parties in the possibility of a gradual reform of the Restoration system. Doubt spread that the parliament in Madrid could ever become the unifying center of a progressive national life, and all social groups were henceforth more inclined to rely on their own particular forms of "direct action." Thus the Tragic Week was the opening gun in the social war that would increasingly dominate Spanish life in the early twentieth century; and it raised up before the privileged groups the alarming specter of a proletarian revolution. More and more, after 1909, the various social classes retreated into an absorption with private and egoistic concerns.

The very concept of the nation was weakened, and, as Gil Munilla has said, a spirit of "absolute insolidarity" ruled Spanish life.[26]

As for the labor movement, the severe and far-ranging repression carried out by the Maura government after the Tragic Week (which included the execution of the Anarchist teacher Francisco Ferrer) radicalized both Syndicalists and Socialists, creating unrest and bitterness in the ranks of labor that would not dissipate by the outbreak of the war in 1914. Within the Catalonian labor movement the ultimate beneficiaries of the Tragic Week proved to be not the Radicals, who had engineered it, but the Anarchosyndicalists. The Radicals did indeed extract some immediate electoral advantage from their role as martyrs, but the workers soon became disillusioned with Lerrouxism and with politics in general, and the drift was toward Syndicalism and a new proletarian tough-mindedness. This process was furthered by Maura's harsh measures, which caused the withdrawal of many of the more moderate trade-union leaders and induced a more bellicose attitude among those who remained.[27]

The new truculence of the Syndicalists was revealed in a regional congress held in the Salon de Bellas Artes in Barcelona from October 30 to November 1, 1910. Most of the delegates were obscure men, and Anarchist influence was relatively unobtrusive, Tomás Herreros being the most prominent libertarian present. Also well known was the Syndicalist leader José Negre. The major debate was over the proposal to turn Solidaridad Obrera from a regional into a national organization. This had been suggested even before the Tragic Week; but Maura's harsh measures lent new urgency to the task, since the Catalonian Syndicalists felt they had suffered unduly as a result of their isolation from workers in other regions of Spain. Much of the drive to create a new national organization sprang from the workers' defensive desire to protect themselves against what they perceived as an aggressive and punitive government. After intense debate, and the expression of fears by some delegates that a new national organization might conflict with the Socialist UGT, the proposal was approved 84 to 14.[28]

The founding congress of the Confederación Nacional del Trabajo, as the new organization was called, was held in Barcelona a little less than a year later (September 8–10, 1911). It represented, in reality, the convergence of two ideological currents, one Anarchist, stressing individualist and libertarian themes and often ambivalent about organizational or material goals, and the other Syndicalist, basing itself on French practice and revealing less diffidence about the need for organizational cohesion and "small gains." Although the official doctrine of the CNT remained Syndicalist up to December 1919, three basic tendencies were discernible within the organization: Anarchist, Anarchosyndicalist (this embraced the majority of militants), and "pure" Syndicalist. In 1920 a fourth tendency would emerge, that of the Communist-Syndicalists.

The agrarian-religious crisis that had nourished peasant Anarchism in the

South in the nineteenth century continued to weigh heavily on the Catalonian labor movement, encouraging Anarchosyndicalist tendencies and inhibiting Socialist efforts. The presence of masses of angry, unassimilated peasants gave a unique tone to Catalonian Syndicalism, ensuring that it would have a different spirit and follow a different evolution from, for example, the French movement. One may be sure that even without the tide of peasant migration from the arid provinces to the South, Barcelona, with its Latin labor force, small-scale industry, relatively low productivity, caste society, illiteracy, and intransigent petty bourgeoisie, would have produced a revolutionary Syndicalist movement at least as combative as the French CGT; indeed, Catalan leaders like Salvador Seguí and Juan Peiró frequently remind one of such French Syndicalists as Victor Griffuelhes or Léon Jouhaux. But by virtue of being set in the wider Iberian context, exposed to the winds of agrarian and demographic crisis that blew out of the provinces to the South, the Syndicalist movement in Catalonia emerged as something more charged, more formidable, and certainly more Anarchist than either the French variety or the Italian.[29]

At the time of the founding congress, the CNT's future appeared promising. But the autumn of 1911 was a troubled time. The parties of the Left were involved in a clamorous campaign to have the Ferrer verdict reversed and the Moroccan adventure terminated, and there was growing anger over the implacably rising cost of living. Strikes had broken out in Vizcaya, Asturias, Zaragoza, and other regions. Finally, in mid-September, a general strike—possibly triggered deliberately by the government—broke out in Bilbao and was officially, if somewhat reluctantly, sanctioned by the Socialist Party leadership. As the strike spread over much of Spain, the CNT imprudently endorsed it also, only to have the government of José Canalejas respond by closing down the organization's regional and local centers. In October 1911 a Barcelona judge declared the CNT to be an illegal organization,[30] and from 1911 to 1914 it led a clandestine existence, guided by a secret National Committee. Many militants fled abroad to avoid the severe crackdown that followed the assassination of Canalejas in November 1912, and only one major strike, involving about 100,000 workers, was carried out in this period. But the succeeding Romanones government granted an amnesty in mid-1913, and numerous leaders returned from exile to help reorganize the Confederation. Finally, in July 1914, the CNT was once again permitted to operate legally. Its membership at this time was small, perhaps about 15,000, and few would have predicted the expansion that within five years would carry it to a membership of nearly a million and make it a revolutionary threat to the regime.[31]

Socialism

The Socialist movement, like that of the Anarchists, owed its birth to a foreign emissary. Late in 1871, some three years after Fanelli had sown the seeds of Bakuninism, Paul Lafargue, Karl Marx's Spanish-speaking son-in-law, went to Spain with the object of creating a counterorganization to block Bakunin's influence in the Peninsula. Unsuccessful in Barcelona, the country's only real industrial center, he moved to Madrid. There he was able to win over a small number of militants who belonged to the International and to obtain the support of the journal *La Emancipación*, edited by José Mesa, who was the leading figure of a group that included, among others, Pablo Iglesias, José Mora, and Juan José Morato. Less than a year later Lafargue and his followers were expelled from the Madrid Section of the International and proceeded to form a "New Madrid Section," which was the precursor of the Spanish Socialist Party. Most of the recruits for the new party would come from the Asociación del Arte de Imprimir, or Printers' Union, over which Pablo Iglesias presided after 1874 and in which he refined the tactics of proletarian exclusivism with which he would later infuse Spanish Socialism.[32]

The Socialist Labor Party of Spain (Partido Socialista Obrero Español, PSOE) was formally organized on May 2, 1879, at a banquet given in a restaurant on the Calle Tetuán. The date was chosen to coincide with the Dos de Mayo—the anniversary of the revolt of the Spaniards against French troops in 1808—but with an "antipatriotic" intent. Of the 25 men who founded the Party, 20 were manual workers; and of these, 16 were printers. The ideological core of the movement consisted of Guesdist ideas transmitted to Iglesias by his colleague José Mesa, who had moved to Paris and become acquainted with Jules Guesde. If Guesdism was, as George Lichtheim says, a "caricature" of Marxism, then the Socialism of the PSOE, a blurred reflection of Guesdism, would have to be described as somewhat impoverished.[33]

Pablo Iglesias, 29 years old at this time, was no intellectual, but rather a superb organizer and a man of immense character and unbreakable will.* Pablismo was a simple faith that laid great stress on the moral superiority of the working class and on the necessity of Socialist apartness from bourgeois society. The final victory of the workers was regarded as historically inevitable but, given the backwardness of Spain, as necessarily rather remote. And though it was believed that victory could not be achieved without a violent revolution and the seizure of political power by the proletariat, this apocalyptic vision was almost entirely subordinated to Iglesias's Guesdist conviction that the daily struggle for reforms was essential and would actually strengthen the revolutionary consciousness of the workers. The struggle for "small gains" was thus based on the perhaps dubious assumption that revolutions were more likely

---

*Jaime Vera wrote of Iglesias in 1912: "Iglesias is not a fanatic, nor an exclusivist or particularist, nor a terrorist, nor an idealist, nor of a spirit juridical, sociological, or *sabio*. And from all these negative qualities, and because of them, there results a magnificent man of preaching and action, an artist of the political, a politician of the first order, in whom stands out the supreme quality of correctness." Quoted in Morato, *Pablo Iglesias*, p. 199.

to be made on full than on empty stomachs. Nor did Iglesias believe that the ballot box should be shunned, since, despite the pervasive corruption of Spanish political life, he felt that elections were an effective means of combating capitalism and strengthening proletarian solidarity during the inescapable bourgeois-democratic phase. The election of Socialist deputies and councillors, morevoer, would allow intervention in the administrative process in order to improve the workers' immediate material situation. However, ministerial participation by Socialists was to be avoided at all costs, since it would inevitably taint the Party with bourgeois influences. The heart of the Pablista creed remained, therefore, the sense of proletarian righteousness and of inevitable conflict between the workers and their bourgeois antagonists. The revolution might be deferred; Socialists might engage in parliamentary politics; tactics might be reformist and moderate; but the central metaphysic of the conflict of classes could never be called into question.[34]

Thus the issue that confronted all Socialist parties—namely, whether to "participate" or to remain in moral and political isolation from the prevailing society—was decided by Spanish Socialists in favor of the most sectarian separation and subcultural aloofness. This exclusivist mood was greatly strengthened by the almost wholly proletarian character of the Party; and it is significant that it was first challenged by one of the few middle-class intellectuals in the movement, Dr. Jaime Vera. Early in the life of the PSOE Vera came out in opposition to the Party's inflexible and sectarian tactics, especially deploring the rancorous struggles between Socialists and Republicans. Less fearful of contamination from the bourgeoisie than were his proletarian colleagues, and reluctant to see the movement remain isolated and impotent, Vera—perhaps the one doctrinally competent Marxist in the Party—advocated a liaison with the men of the left-bourgeois parties, who, it should be remembered, had more contact with the masses at this time than did the Socialists. In 1885 Iglesias and Vera debated this question. Iglesias, as one witness said, "revealed his talent as a fearsome polemicist; and Jaime Vera revealed his culture and the breadth of his *criterio*." The victory went to Iglesias, and Vera, accompanied by José Mora, "departed sorrowfully" from the Party —to which he would later return.[35] Spanish Socialism thus became still more proletarian in its spirit and even less receptive to ideas or ideological refinements.

It was understandable that Iglesias should choose as a model not the French but the German Socialist movement. For one thing, Guesdist ideas had been derived from German practice. But there was also a politico-constitutional similarity between the German and Spanish states. Restoration Spain, like Wilhelmine Germany, fell into a middle ground between the absolute autocracy of Imperial Russia and the essentially permissive atmosphere of Britain or France, with the result that neither the Leninist-conspiratorial nor the Fabian-

Jauressian approach to Socialism was suited to Spanish conditions. Somewhat like Germany before 1918, Spain presented a peculiar pattern of repressive and permissive features. On the one hand, an authoritarian state and an entrenched economic oligarchy compelled the adoption of an intransigent revolutionary ideology; on the other, the existence of a quasi-constitutional system permitted the Left some degree of political activity and discouraged the use of revolutionary *tactics*. As Iglesias instinctively recognized, a genuinely revolutionary and voluntarist Marxism in Spain, unless it were wholly clandestine, would only have invited the destruction of the Party. Yet in such a difficult milieu a purely reformist Socialism would have lacked the combative rhetoric and revolutionary vision needed to hold the movement together against the challenge posed by an arbitrary and often repressive state, by economic backwardness, and above all by the Anarchist threat from the left. Reformist tactics the Party could afford; reformist theory or rhetoric it could not. For Iglesias, the dilemma was not easily resolved. Had he been less resolute—or more realistic—he would not even have tried to build Socialism in Spain in the 1880's and 1890's; had he been more ruthless and revolutionary, he, like a Lenin or a Bordiga, would have been driven by the obstacles in his environment to advocate the creation of an elitist and centralized corps of professional revolutionaries. But he was liberal enough, despite his sectarianism, to choose instead to build a social democratic party on the German model. The result was inevitably a revolutionary-reformist ideology.[36]

All efforts to change the orientation of the Party toward cooperation with the left-bourgeois parties were turned back by the centrist leadership. In 1904, at the Amsterdam congress of the Second International, Iglesias and Antonio García Quejido helped to defeat Jaurès and the French delegates, who urged that the subcultural isolation of European Socialists be ended, and to sustain the Germans, who sponsored a resolution reaffirming the policy of noncooperation with bourgeois society. In defending the German position, Iglesias made clear his fears that collaborationist policy would fatally weaken Spanish Socialists in the face of the Anarchist challenge.[37]

In 1888, mainly at the urging of García Quejido, the PSOE formed the Unión General del Trabajo (UGT), which, in the German manner, was expected to subordinate itself to the political leadership of the Party. The fact that the UGT was founded in Barcelona and had its headquarters there for 13 years indicates that the Socialists had originally been quite concerned with the Catalonian labor movement, which was, after all, the largest in the Peninsula. But immigration into Barcelona from the "dry" provinces, along with the increasing activity of the Anarchists in the labor movement after 1890, gradually created an ambiance unfavorable to Socialist penetration. Iglesias was later accused of a lack of interest in Catalonia; but it would be nearer the truth to say that he instinctively realized that Spanish Socialism would have to change its nature fundamentally in order to attract the workers of that region. He felt, and most contemporary observers agreed, that the "spontaneity" of the Catalonian labor force posed an almost insuperable barrier to Pablismo. In 1899 the headquarters of the UGT were moved to Madrid, which was not an industrial city; and the real heartland of Spanish Socialism increasingly became the mining and industrial zones of Vizcaya and Asturias, where it gradually developed a mass following.[38]

During the early years of the twentieth century the Socialist Party did not alter its mood or its methods. It remained a proletarian sect, a subculture closed against the world and nearly as cut off from the great mass of Spanish workers—who remained unorganized—as it was from bourgeois society. Forged in the austere image of its leader, the style of the Party was serious, moralistic, and measured; and although it was often ideologically intransigent, it remained moderate in its tactics. The PSOE was, in fact, many things that Spanish workers were not, and it is less than surprising that it grew very slowly. The Anarchist and Anarchosyndicalist movements might experience vast exaltations and fluctuations of membership, but the Socialists did not care for this kind of growth, preferring to enlarge their numbers more slowly but more surely.[39]

In 1902 the Socialists approved the use of the general strike for political purposes but refused to support, and in fact condemned, an Anarchist-sponsored strike in Barcelona. Their interest continued to focus on electoral contests and political action. This was to some extent understandable, since the franchise was broadened in Spain very early, with universal suffrage coming under Práxedes Sagasta in 1890. But in view of the backwardness of the electorate, the power of caciquismo, the pervasiveness of corruption, and the machine-like alternation of the Conservative and Liberal parties, Iglesias's obsession with elections was not without its quixotic overtones. Still, the dream of the Socialists, as Morato said, was to create an electoral body so large and determined that its very existence would put an end to fraudulent electoral practices. The year 1905 was a landmark for the electoral ambitions of the Socialists: the number of the Party's municipal councillors rose from 23 to 30, and Iglesias, Francisco Largo Caballero, and Rafael García Ormaechea, by means of a subterfuge, were able for the first time to win seats on the Madrid city council.[40]

The tranquil pace and sectarian isolation of the the Socialist Party were finally disturbed by the Tragic Week. In the aftermath of the shooting of Francisco Ferrer the Party issued (September 1909) a manifesto condemning the arbitrary actions of the Maura government and announcing the Socialists' determination to defend constitutional liberties at the side of whatever "democratic force" proposed to work for the reestablishment of constitutional guarantees and for the resignation of the government. The PSOE, says Díaz del

Moral, was "galvanized" by the events of the Tragic Week and "descended from its ivory tower full of passion and vigor." The defense of civil liberties was perhaps the one thing that could alter the Party's sectarianism, since a ministerial dictatorship guided by Maura would have made its accustomed tactics impossible and undermined its raison d'être. Political liberties had to be defended or Spanish Socialism would be faced, Iglesias feared, with dissolution or with the need to adopt conspiratorial-elitist tactics. Consequently, on November 7 the Republican-Socialist Alliance was proclaimed, in order to facilitate electoral cooperation with the left-bourgeoisie. The immediate purpose of this action was simply to achieve the dismissal of Maura; but the National Committee of the PSOE quickly proposed that the alliance be continued more or less permanently with the ultimate objective of establishing a republic, the assumption being that the monarchical regime had been the "true source" of the Tragic Week. As a result of their electoral alliance with the Republicans, the Socialists were able, in the November elections, to raise the number of Socialist councillors to 40 and for the first time to win seats in two provincial parliaments. The following year Iglesias was elected as a deputy to the Cortes.[41]

One of the most significant facets of the rejuvenation of Spanish Socialism following the Tragic Week was the growing number of intellectuals who made their way into the Party, usually coming from the republican parties, which were steadily decaying in this era. Among the earliest—even preceding the Tragic Week—was the gentlemanly, university-trained Manuel Núñez de Arenas, who in 1908, at the age of 22, first entered the newly inaugurated Casa del Pueblo. Núñez de Arenas was born into the Madrid nobility and descended from a long line of magistrates and literary figures. From studies in the universities of Madrid, Bordeaux, and Lausanne he had acquired an impressive culture and scholarly interests that ranged well beyond the Socialist movement into history and literature. Deploring the doctrinal poverty of the Party, as well as the lack of contact between the working class and the world of learning, Núñez de Arenas set up the New School, which was intended to be a center for theoretical studies and for facilitating contact between workers and intellectuals.[42]

Among the other intellectuals who came into the party in this period were Luis Araquistáin, Andrés Ovejero, Julián Besteiro, Rafael Urbano, and Oscar Pérez Solís. The number of intellectuals in the Socialist movement was still remarkably small in comparison to the French and Italian parties, but the trend was clear. The question was the impact they would have on a party that had been very proletarian, insulated, and Guesdist. In general, they would prove to be a dissident element, restless in the face of the centrist platitudes of Pablismo. A few fitted in well: Besteiro became the Party's philosopher of "separation" from a corrupt bourgeois society, content to play Kautsky to

Pablo Iglesias's Bebel; Fernando de los Ríos, who joined the party in 1919, likewise accepted Pablismo, while infusing it with his own liberal and humanistic outlook. But most of the new intellectual recruits would find revolutionary-reformism lacking in the purity and logical consistency they desired.[43]

The earliest revolt against Pablista orthodoxy came around 1911–12 and took a "Revisionist" form. Núñez de Arenas was the guiding spirit of this movement, and was supported by Mariano García Cortés, then president of the Madrid Socialist Group, by Morato, and by a number of others. Where concern for principles left off and the desire for dominance began is of course impossible to say. The New School thought of itself as a Fabian Society à l'espagnole and hoped to see the Spanish party evolve in the direction of British laborism. There can be little doubt that it also hoped to become a kind of intellectual politburo for the movement. The "Revisionists" opposed the Republican-Socialist Alliance for what they felt was its revolutionary intent, fearing that absorption with overthrowing the monarchy in favor of a republic would be counterproductive. At the same time, the orthodox Pablistas, though embarking on this "opening to the right," continued to beat the rhetorical drums of class conflict and Socialist apartness. The situation was somewhat confused ideologically, and the suspicion arises that the whole contest may have had more to do with ins and outs than with the ideas of Eduard Bernstein.[44]

The revolt against the orthodox leadership of the PSOE achieved temporary success at the Congress of 1912, where it was decided to remove Pablo Iglesias from the editorship of the Party organ El Socialista, a position that was declared incompatible with his presidency. But the group around Iglesias—Largo Caballero, Besteiro, Gómez Latorre, and Andrés Saborit—mobilized their forces and took the offensive against the dissidents in the spring and summer of 1914, driving García Cortés from the presidency of the Madrid Socialist Group. The outbreak of the war found the Pablistas once more firmly in charge of the Party, and the 1915 Congress restored Iglesias's editorship of El Socialista. The outbreak of the European conflict and the violence of the social struggle it aroused in Spain strengthened the centrist leadership still more. Only the coming of the Bolshevik Revolution and the Armistice would weaken the grasp of Iglesias's followers on the levers of party control and revive in a serious form the factional strife of the prewar period—with the odd circumstance that the "Revisionists" of 1911–14 would be the "Bolsheviks" of 1919–21.[45]

In the summer of 1914 the Socialists of the UGT and the Anarchosyndicalists of the CNT formed the two main centers of the Spanish labor movement, seeking to attract to themselves the great mass of workers who were still unorganized, in independent unions, or in unions controlled by republican political forces. In reality, both Ugetistas and Cenetistas were only tiny islands in a sea of urban and rural workers, who, despite the great native intelligence that all observers conceded them, were plagued by ignorance, illiteracy, and poverty on a scale scarcely matched in Europe. Since the number of industrial workers (1,113,839) was only two-thirds the number of agricultural workers (1,700,000), the labor movement was faced with the need to wage a two-front war and to organize both urban and rural workers in order to confront the ruling classes with any hope of success. The UGT had the greater number of union members at this time, enrolling 127,804, which represented a decline from the peak year of 1913. The CNT, whose organizational labors had been almost entirely disrupted since its founding in 1911, was said to have about 15,000 members. In the Cortes there was in 1914 only one Socialist deputy.[46]

Politics was the great bone of contention between Ugetistas and Cenetistas. The latter, of course, sought to draw the workers toward political abstentionism even as the Socialists encouraged them to vote for the Party's candidates. The antipolitical bias of the Anarchosyndicalists—hatred would not be too strong a word—was a very powerful impulse and was for many the principal rallying cry. Made cynical not only by Bakuninist strictures but also by the glaring failure of universal suffrage and parliamentary politics to produce tangible benefits for the workers, they felt real animosity toward those who preached political participation. The Cenetistas also inherited the resentments generated during the bitter contests between Socialists and Anarchists in the nineteenth century, and they retained a feeling of immense moral superiority over their rivals in the labor movement, whom they held in considerable contempt.

The struggle was in large measure one between two character types. The Cenetistas were often romantic revolutionaries, inclined to be impulsive, passionate, individualistic, obsessed with questions of dignity and liberty, and above all, slightly millenarian, convinced that the revolution they sought lay just over the horizon. The Socialist leaders were, on the whole, more prudent, more patient, and more solemn. Their style was nearly always restrained and calculating. They wore neckties, used typewriters, cultivated the bureaucratic virtues, and avoided reckless undertakings. Revolution was for them serious business, and they were not to be pushed into it precipitately. What kept their ranks small in this era, however, was not so much their lack of revolutionary passion as the "authoritarian" demands they placed on the workers in terms of organizational discipline, dues-paying, and the curbing of instincts. The CNT, in contrast, soared to a vast membership in this period precisely because it catered to and even exalted the spontaneity of the Spanish worker.[47]

It is not surprising that the issue of the war and Spain's response to it should find Socialists and Cenetistas on opposite sides. Though both were committed to the primacy of the class struggle, they differed greatly in the degree of ruthlessness with which they were prepared to uphold this principle. When the

war came the Socialists—and here one sees the influence of the recently recruited intellectuals—discovered that they were, after all, westernizers who
were certain that Spain had to be democraticized before she could be socialized,
and that therefore the cause of the Allies had to be upheld. The Cenetistas, by
contrast, revealed a more profound alienation from the liberal-democratic
values of the West and were able to maintain to the end a remarkable coldness
of heart toward the Allied cause. This indifference was all the more striking
in view of the powerful support that the conservative-clerical-military forces
in Spain gave to the Central Powers, a support that inevitably pushed the
Socialists—but not the Cenetistas—in the opposite direction. Thus the war
gravely complicated the workers' search for the unity that alone would make
possible the social and political transformation they desired.

Spain and the War

The outbreak of the war in August 1914 came as no surprise to the literate
public in Spain. The European crisis touched off at Sarajevo had been followed
attentively for weeks, and Spaniards had begun to take sides even before the
fighting broke out. Some feared that Spain might be drawn into the conflict by
its agreements with France and Britain regarding the Mediterranean, but the
overwhelming majority opposed Spanish participation on either side.[48]

The war found the Spanish political system in an unprecedented state of
flux—either in dissolution or in evolution, depending on the point of view.
Since the Tragic Week two of the more dynamic political leaders, each in his
own way committed to reform, had been eliminated: Maura by the stigma of
the execution of Ferrer, and Canalejas by an assassin's hand. In 1913 the Conservative and Liberal parties each split, and it seemed evident to many that the
Canovite system would never again work in the old way. Yet the man who
inherited power in October 1913, Eduardo Dato, was entirely committed to
the system in its traditional form; at the head of a reviving and reinvigorated
country needing to progress rather than merely to survive, the new prime
minister wished only to keep things as they were. Dato was not personally
inclined to one side or the other and seemed, superficially, the right man to
keep Spain out of the war through a policy of absolute neutrality and diplomatic *immobilisme*. Yet in the face of the domestic pressures generated by the
war, his proclivity for inertia could only undermine, in the end, the static
Canovite system he wished to preserve. Spain would not intervene in the war,
but the war would intervene in Spain.[49]

Without hesitation, and conscious for once that he expressed the national
will, Dato declared Spanish neutrality on July 30 and confirmed it on August
25. Nearly all Spaniards desired this, and even the most ardent supporters of
the Allies rejected any thought of Spanish military participation. The Radical

leader Lerroux, who urged armed intervention early in the war, spoke for only a small minority of Jacobins, and even he soon ceased to pursue this theme. Spain, in fact, possessed neither the motive nor the means to participate in the war and had, indeed, many compelling reasons to stay out.[50]

Chief among these was the fact that the great majority of Spaniards failed to comprehend the purpose or the issues of the war. Few of the modern forces whose interplay produced the European conflict had yet reached maturity in the Peninsula. Modern nationalism and militarism, imperialism, capitalism, mass democracy—these demiurges of the twentieth century remained only tendencies within the confines of a slowly evolving traditional society. Despite the grave economic impact the war would have on their lives, perhaps two-thirds of the Spanish people would display an almost frivolous inattention, unable to respond to the ideological rationales of either side. Bullfights would absorb them more than battles* and it would not be the war but the Russian Revolution that finally aroused their interest.[51]

By contrast, the upper third of Spanish society soon became passionately divided over the war, which they saw not merely as a duel between empires but as an ideological struggle in which each side embodied certain principles of universal significance. The war was viewed as but an extension of the social conflict in Spain. To the "two Spains" that coexisted so rancorously, there corresponded the two Europes that contended openly and violently. The division between supporters of the Allies and of the Central Powers was not fortuitous, but reflected, with few exceptions, the division in Spain between the "forces of movement" and the "forces of order."[52] Thus the pro-German elements—by far the larger group—included the landed interests, most conservatives, some liberals, the bureaucracy, most of the military, the Church, the Carlists, and a large portion of the literate and nationalist public. The pro-Allied sector included most of the intelligentsia, the Republicans, the Radicals, the Reformists, the Socialists, the Basque and Catalan bourgeoisie, and some segments of the lower middle class. The peripheral areas of the country, especially Catalonia, were pro-Allied; the interior regions, especially Castile, tended to favor the Central Powers.[53] At bottom, the pro-German partisans identified

---

* Jean Breton quoted a pro-Allied Spaniard: "Believe me, political apathy continues to dominate Spain. The immense majority are only interested in the war as in a bull-running. And they are more interested in bull-running than in the war.... You have already seen the accounts of the prowess of the *toreros* encroach upon the [newspaper] columns reserved for war correspondents. A week or so ago our Bellesteiros was killed by an unfortunate goring. If only you had been able to admire the magnificence of his funeral cortege passing in Zaragoza! Only Victor Hugo was able to inspire a similar deification in your country. For the emotional experience of touching the coffin of the national hero, one is knocked down in the streets. Such a strong passion is overwhelming. It is hypnotic. It hardly leaves any place for really political emotions. Even in raising the famous specter of the war, the professionals will not succeed in awakening political life in Spain." Breton, p. 861.

with the Central Powers because they, too, believed in an authoritarian and hierarchical social order, whereas their enemies identified with the Entente because they were certain that in a Europe made safe for democracy, Spain would also be democratized. Animosity between the two groups was intense, reflecting the seriousness of the domestic issues that divided them. It is said that in Barcelona and other cities movie theaters at first hesitated to show newsreels of the war for fear their halls would become scenes of battle.[54]

The hopes of the pro-German elements were the first to be aroused. The rapid drive of the German armies through Belgium, the thrust into France, and the devastating blow dealt the Russians at Tannenberg created an impression of German invincibility. As the Germans seemed about to enter Paris, and as the French government withdrew to Bordeaux, the ranks of the Central Powers' supporters in Spain rapidly swelled and nearly everyone was convinced that the Allies were already defeated. "Every day," wrote Count Romanones, there were "fewer friends of the Allies, and even fewer those who had confidence in the final victory of the [Entente]."[55]

The paradox of pro-German sentiment in Spain was the almost complete lack of congruence between Spanish and German interests. Strategically, Spain (the only neutral entirely surrounded by Allied powers) was best served by continued cooperation with Britain and France in the western Mediterranean. Commercially, she was almost wholly dependent on the British navy and merchant marine for the imported coal, raw materials, and foodstuffs needed to sustain her economy, and for the export of commodities such as minerals and oranges, vital to her prosperity. With Germany Spain had virtually no trade. Nearly every consideration of present interest and future well-being pushed the nation toward the Allies, and yet the ruling groups never accepted the apparent logic of such a rapprochement. Their reasons were political and ideological rather than strategic. Above all, they sensed the division within the country and understood that intervention would be only a prelude to civil war and, perhaps, social revolution. Beyond that, they were drawn to the Central Powers by virtue of the authoritarian principles that these nations embodied and repelled by the democratic ethos of the Allies, which seemed to them incompatible with the survival of the oligarchical regime in Spain.[56]

The crucial fact was that the great majority of the Spanish people simply felt that Spain was morally and materially outside the European struggle, and they had no desire to join either side. Pacifism had become part of the national mood, and as the war became progressively more destructive Spain's neutrality was the more cherished. Interventionist proposals only infuriated the majority of workers, so that any attempt to emulate the Portuguese by sending troops to the Western Front was a political impossibility.[57] At the same time, intervention on the German side was strategically inconceivable because of the British fleet; the best the pro-German elements could hope for was neutrality, under cover of which Spain could at least be a haven for German espionage activities. Understanding that if Spain entered the war it could only be on the side of the Allies, they argued for an "absolute" neutrality that was, in effect, a pro-German policy. (Absolute neutrality, said the young Salvador de Madariaga, was the "Prussian helmet" that Spain wore "down over her eyes.")[58] Brilliantly organized and lavishly financed, pro-German propaganda in Spain was designed to convince the public that the slightest deviation from neutrality would result in sending the nation's young men into the trenches. The ruling groups were so committed to "absolute" neutrality that the policy was never seriously debated in the Cortes, and the Spanish government remained locked in a diplomatic posture increasingly in need of modification as hopes for an early German victory faded.

The main bastions of pro-German sentiment in Spain were the Court, the Army, the Church, and what may be termed the nationalist intelligentsia. King Alfonso at first seemed to lean toward the Allied side; and though he was careful to keep his views to himself, he was said to have remarked during the early days of the war, "Only the *canaille* and I are francophiles."[59] But the March Revolution and the increasingly republican coloration of the Allied cause soon turned him in the other direction, and he was more and more suspected of covert support for Germany. María Cristina, the Austrian-born Queen Mother, was of course wholly committed to the cause of the Central Powers; and since Alfonso could not or would not restrain her, she set the tone for the whole Court.[60]

The Army, for the most part, was also pro-German. The admiration that Spanish officers felt for German military prowess dated from the Franco-Prussian War and exerted an influence almost apart from the ideological issues of the European conflict. Yet, like the German militarists whom they eulogized, the officers were also attracted by the vision of a social order in which state, nation, and army would be fused in disciplined solidarity.*

The most formidable defender of the Central Powers in Spain was the Catholic Church. From the lowliest parish priest to the highest clerical ranks, the clergy were nearly all hostile to the Allied cause. All Church-affiliated newspapers, such as *El Debate* and *El Universo*, launched incessant attacks against "impious" France and "perfidious" England. Such an attitude was not without its paradoxes, ignoring as it did the German despoliation of Catholic Belgium, the burning of the famed Catholic library of Louvain, the staunch Protestantism of the Prussian nobility, and the fact that France and Italy were, after all, great Catholic nations. But the clergy, like the ruling politicians, were deterred from taking a pro-Allied stance by the intensity

* Salvador de Madariaga no doubt exaggerated a little when he wrote: "At the present moment, the ideas prevailing among the Spanish officers would strike Hindenburg and Ludendorff as somewhat militaristic." "Spain's home war," p. 381.

of the domestic struggle. The victory of the Allies had to be opposed because it would strengthen liberal and anticlerical tendencies within Spain; that of the Central Powers had to be supported because it would revitalize the principles of authority, discipline, and devoutness in a threatened society. The blows struck by German armies on the battlefields of Europe were viewed as blows against the enemy within. The German attack on France was the will of God and the German Emperor the instrument of His divine purpose. Indeed, the Spanish clergy were convinced that the Kaiser, though conforming outwardly to the Protestant faith, was really a secret son of the Church. They confidently expected that after Germany's victory he would not only return temporal power to the Pope but would bestow upon Spain Gibraltar, Portugal, and French Morocco.[61]

The views of the Church harmonized with the broader current of pro-German sentiment that pervaded Spanish life in this period, drawing its strength from the bitterness accumulated over three centuries of frustration and failure in contests with the French and the English. The strongest weapon of the pro-German propagandists was the argument from history, the recital of the many occasions when these powers had either contributed to or profited from Spanish decadence. History, pride, national and religious feeling—all sealed the sensibilities of Spaniards toward the Western democracies. Although the illiterate and apolitical two-thirds of the country might look upon the conflict with vacant impartiality, the more informed, literate, and nationalistic elements could only harbor hostile feelings toward Britain and France and were instinctively drawn to the enemies of those powers, whoever they might be. These Spaniards felt an affinity with the Austrians for historic and dynastic reasons, and with the newly formed German Empire because they knew almost nothing about it and because it had never harmed them. The fires of anti-Allied feeling were mainly fueled by antipathy to England, which was popularly regarded as the cause of most of Spain's misfortunes. Above all, British possession of Gibraltar was an unpardonable injury. Pro-German orators were capable, on occasion, of speaking of "poor France," but for England they had no pity. They were convinced that the British, in addition to dominating Spain economically, were contemptuous of Spanish abilities, and they found this difficult to forgive.[62]

Although most of the intelligentsia favored the Allied powers, a number of distinguished figures supported the German cause, some as authentic admirers of German civilization and others merely as enemies of France or Britain. For some, the war offered an opportunity to condemn France as an "immoral" society whose cultural elite had habitually disdained Spanish efforts in all areas of endeavor. Among the pro-German intellectuals were such men as Rodríguez Marín, the Director of the National Library; Emilio Cotarelo y Mori, Secretary of the Royal Academy; Francisco de Carracido,

Director of the Cisneres Institute of Madrid; and the novelists Pío Baroja and Jacinto Benevente. The utterances of these men reveal that concern for the regeneration of Spain was not a monopoly of the Left. Many of them shared the Left's despair over Spanish reality, but they sought its transformation not by means of French or English liberalism, but through an infusion of German discipline and organization.*

Pro-Allied Sentiment

Since the masses were indifferent, and the ruling classes hostile to the Allied powers, the guardians of pro-Allied sentiment in Spain were mainly the members of the left-bourgeois parties and the Socialists—that is to say, the democratic intelligentsia, though support for the Allies also came from the regionalists, and even from segments of the Liberal Party. The position of the Allied supporters was a morally difficult one, requiring the ability to ignore patriotic and nationalistic appeals against Spain's ancient enemies, who also happened to be the defenders of liberal and democratic values. The friends of Britain and France had to struggle not only against a predominantly pro-German public opinion but, one suspects, against some of their own deeper feelings as well. The emotional energy that this demanded was generated in the course of the severe domestic struggle they waged against the conservative-clerical-military forces. The pro-Allied position was thus much more than mere sentimentality for the democratic nations, having its roots in the enduring conflict between progressive and conservative Spain. The sharpness of this conflict inevitably pushed each side toward a more intransigent support of one set of belligerents or the other. The separation between foreign and domestic spheres became blurred, and the failure of the democratic intelligentsia to support the Allies to the limit would have seemed to them little less than capitulation to their internal enemies. The Allies had to be defended, even exalted, and the war had to be given transcendent meaning. The insistence of the majority of Spaniards on absolute neutrality had to be denounced as immoral, since it alienated Spain from the nations upholding freedom in the world.[63]

The pro-Allied Spaniards were the "Westernizers" of a backward and insular society—men stirred by Western liberal ideals that they wished to see transform Spanish life. Even those who had been educated in Germany re-

* Griffith, pp. 364–65. The ideas of the pro-German intellectuals are dealt with in Lantier, "L'attitude des intellectuels espagnols." Lantier (p. 42) quotes Pío Baroja: "I believe that if any country can definitively crush the Catholic Church, it is Germany. Only Germany can banish forever the old Jehovah with his gang of hook-nosed prophets and their descendants, the squalid monks and the pedant priests. If there is a country that can do away with the old rhetoric, with the old Spanish traditionalism, dirty and coarse, with the Latin and Semitic scab, it is Germany. If there is a country that can substitute science, order, and technology for the myths of religion or democracy, and for the force of Christian charity, it is Germany." See also Lantier, "Quelques points de vue espagnols," p. 18.

mained under the spell of France and the great Revolution of 1789, to whose ideals they were even more attached than their French counterparts, since they, after all, still lived under an *ancien régime*. What they wanted—what all the men of the Left, including the Socialists, wanted in 1914—was that Spain should have its 1789, or, more precisely, its 1793. What they would get, of course, would more nearly resemble 1848.[64]

The great majority of the Spanish intellectuals became supporters of the Allies. Among them may be mentioned the historian Rafael Altamira, the philosopher Miguel de Unamuno, the journalist Ortega y Gasset, and the writers Benito Pérez Galdós, Blasco Ibañez, Emilia Pardo Bazán, Felipe Trigo, Alvaro Alcalá Galiano, and Hermógenes Cenamor. Most of these figures signed a manifesto, "Words from some Spaniards," that appeared in 1917. In this they proclaimed their support for the Allies and their hope that an Allied victory would end war in human affairs, so that over a regenerated world peace, justice, and reason would prevail.[65]

The Socialists and the War

There was reason to believe, in August 1914, that the Spanish Socialist Party would adopt an orthodox antiwar posture. The PSOE had a reputation for being doctrinaire and leftist, and its adherents regarded themselves as solidly pacifistic. Spain was not a belligerent and was not threatened with invasion. There seemed to be no need to sacrifice Socialist principles to "defensist" policies or to treat the war as anything more than the clash of two equally sinister imperialisms. The Party's initial response, indeed, echoed the antiwar resolutions of the Second International. On August 2, the National Committee issued a statement against the war, impartially condemning all belligerents and urging strict Spanish neutrality.[66] But as German armies poured into Belgium and France, pacifist sentiment within the Party's ranks evaporated with startling rapidity. The majority of Socialists, forced to confront their own democratic premises, discovered that they could not view the possible collapse of France and Britain with doctrinaire detachment. Almost overnight they abandoned the pacifist internationalism that had so recently led them to condemn Spain's Moroccan adventure and moved toward an overtly pro-Allied position. This retreat from dogma was the result, above all, of the dramatic upsurge of pro-German sentiment among the conservative forces, which put almost irresistible pressure on the Socialists to move in the opposite direction and embrace the Allied cause.[67] The few militants who could resist this dialectic were not so much revolutionary firebrands as especially dogmatic and plebeian centrists, such as Manuel Cordero or Andrés

---

On Spain's response to the war, see also Santiago Roldán López, "La consolidación de la vía nacionalista del capitalismo español durante la I Guerra Mundial," *Anales de Economía* 11 (July–Sept. 1971), pp. 17–91.

Saborit. The newly recruited bourgeois intellectuals, on the other hand, went over almost en masse to the side of the Allies, Núñez de Arenas being nearly the only exception. On August 30 Iglesias announced that although the Socialists continued to favor neutrality, they did so only for expedient reasons, and that if Spain were less vulnerable, the Party would favor intervention on the side of the Allies.[68]

Neither Iglesias nor any other Socialist leader attempted a systematic apologia for the Party's drift from prewar orthodoxy, probably because its causes were in fact more visceral than intellectual. Nevertheless, the Republican-Socialist Alliance had reflected a growing commitment to a specific form of government—the bourgeois-democratic republic—and was bound to undermine the dogma that all capitalist powers were alike and to draw the Socialists toward the Western democracies. In the face of the threat that Maura had posed to democratic freedoms in Spain, Iglesias had not hesitated to join hands with the Republicans; it was to be expected that he would now give his faithful support to those who defended democratic liberties in a European context.

As the Kaiser's armies advanced, the Socialists adopted an increasingly anti-German tone. Among the belligerents, only the Germans and the Austrians were labeled as imperialists, and hopes for their early defeat were frequently expressed. *El Socialista* made every effort to place the Allies in a favorable light, even to the point of construing their military reverses as evidence of the purity of their prewar intentions. The voting of war credits by the German Socialists evoked expressions both of shame and of self-righteousness among the Pablistas, who had always acknowledged the Germans as their teachers. The similar action of the French Socialists was not mentioned.[69] The fervor of the Socialist commitment to the Allied cause grew with each passing month of the war. Not only did no initiative for peace emerge from the PSOE, but the peace initiatives of other European Socialists were opposed. The Spanish party refused, for example, to participate in the Copenhagen Congress of neutral Socialists held in January 1915.[70] All through this year Iglesias elaborated the antipacifist position, warning against a premature peace that would not extirpate the "gangrene" of German imperialism and establish the clear supremacy of the democratic nations.[71]

Most Spanish Socialists—even many members of the prewar opposition—followed Iglesias in his support of the Allied war effort. The few who did not, the minoritarians, were a mixed and incohesive group in which three currents were visible. One was composed of men who were otherwise loyal Pablistas but who would not surrender their prewar pacifist dogmas. This group centered around Andrés Saborit and the journal *Acción Socialista*, which became an outlet for antiwar writings that *El Socialista* would not print.[72] A second group of dissidents contained the remnants of the prewar "Revisionist" opposition of the New School and was led by García Cortés and Núñez de Arenas, both of whom moved with alacrity from Revisionism to Zimmerwaldism. García Cortés edited the journal *España Nueva*, which also became an outlet for pacifist pronouncements, as did the journal *Justicia Social* of Reus. The third element in the antiwar minority included the Young Socialists of Madrid, among whom figured Ramón Lamoneda, José López y López, Ramón Merino Gracia, and, again, Núñez de Arenas. In August 1914 Lamoneda composed a vigorous antiwar manifesto; and a year later the Young Socialists of the capital were the only group in Spain to send their adherence (though no delegate) to the Zimmerwald Conference. Although the Madrid Young Socialists maintained their pacifist position throughout the war, pro-Allied sentiment steadily eroded the pacifist convictions of the Young Socialists in the provinces; and in the 1915 Zaragoza conference of the Federation of Young Socialists (FJS) they voted down a pro-Zimmerwald resolution introduced by Lamoneda and Núñez de Arenas. Thus in Spain alone the Socialist antiwar minority grew smaller rather than larger as the war progressed—clear testimony to the severity and polarizing effect of the domestic social struggle.[73]

The links between the Spanish minoritarians and the antiwar elements north of the Pyrenees were somewhat tenuous. No Spaniards attended the Zimmerwald Conference; and the impact of that movement (although Saborit printed its manifesto in *Acción Socialista*) was rather limited in Spain.[74] Of course, the minoritarians read French newspapers and, like their European counterparts, shunned all discussion of the immediate causes of the war (which might make Germany seem primarily responsible), preferring to dwell upon its remoter origins, its economic causes, and the mutual guilt of all capitalist powers. But such reflections were rigorously excluded from *El Socialista*, and the majority of Spanish Socialists continued to be wholly involved in the fate of the democracies and the course of the military struggle. The French Socialist "Gabier," resident in Madrid, complained that the leaders of the PSOE knew only the "defensist" line of *L'Humanité*.[75]

Thus Spanish Socialists roughly mirrored the division that appeared among the Socialists of the belligerent nations between a patriotic majority and a pacifist minority, which were linked, despite their disagreement over the war, by common democratic assumptions. But the presence of the third element in the European spectrum—namely, the revolutionary ultra-Left, whose leader was Lenin—was more difficult to detect within the Spanish party. Most Spanish Socialists, whether majoritarian or minoritarian, were at heart democratic and deterministic, regarding the revolution as an event far in the future, to be imposed by the mass of the people. Few of the minoritarians accepted, or perhaps even knew of, Lenin's "Left-Zimmerwald" position that the war should be ended not merely by restoring the status quo ante but by means of social revolution. There were a few incipient ultra-leftists among the Madrid Young Socialists; but the most authentic revolutionary Left was to be found among those Anarchosyndicalists of the CNT who, though slow to learn of Lenin's views, went beyond mere pacifism and instinctively favored ending the war by a popular revolution.

Socialist majoritarians and minoritarians had their first major confrontation at the Tenth Congress of the PSOE, held in Madrid, October 24–31, 1915. The main resolution of this gathering, drawn up by the aging Dr. Jaime Vera and cosponsored by Julián Besteiro, eloquently endorsed the pro-Allied position, as well as the continuing need for domestic cooperation with the more progressive elements of the bourgeoisie. The "failure" of militant Socialism was attributed to "the sterility of its policy of isolation" and to an excess of "romantic pacifism." Against the policy of Socialist isolation, the resolution asserted: "We advocate the policy of penetration and struggle in the bourgeois world, in which we should act decisively in order to influence minds and ... events, in order to take advantage of bourgeois skills, and, in particular, to establish every kind of communication with all the progressive elements; for every progressive action works in our favor."[76]

Regarding Spain's policy toward the war, the Vera resolution, despite its passionate commitment to the Allied cause, reasserted the party's conviction that neutrality was necessary, since the masses would neither comprehend nor support the need for intervention. The minoritarians, however, were not satisfied with a mere reaffirmation of the need for neutrality, and sought to have prewar pacifist orthodoxy unconditionally proclaimed. Their chief spokesman was Dr. José Verdes Montenegro, a dogmatic provincial schoolteacher, who told the congress that he was "astonished" by the National Committee's prowar utterances and disturbed by its attempt to distinguish between the imperialisms of the contending powers. Militarism and "Kaiserism," he said, had nothing to do with the war, which had been produced simply by "bourgeois expansion." Therefore, he said, "I accuse the bourgeoisie, not singling out any one part of it, since all bear responsibility for this collective crime. I do not believe that the triumph of Germany will mean the oppression of the world, or that of France its liberation. The world will continue in its course."[77]

Verdes's pacifism drew a reply from the formidable Julián Besteiro, professor of philosophy at the University of Madrid, author of a doctoral thesis on "Voluntarism and intellectualism in contemporary philosophy," and a convert from the Radical Party—a man whose abilities had led to an unusually rapid rise in the Socialist Party. Besteiro, who now sat on the national committees of both the PSOE and the UGT, was already emerging as the most articulate exponent of Pablismo and was beginning to be perceived as a possible heir to Iglesias. He was a man of unassailable character, with a powerful if somewhat unoriginal intellect, who, perhaps partly from a residence in Germany, had absorbed a thoroughly social-democratic approach to

Socialism. Despite his education, his humanistic temper (he was a product of the liberal Institute of Free Education), and his exposure to other political movements, he found the sectarian and doctrinaire atmosphere of the PSOE peculiarly congenial. Accepted at once into the inner circle, he was never tempted to employ his exceptional talents against the dogmas or traditions of the Party. There were, perhaps, two Besteiros: one was a radical republican, hostile to the monarchy and willing, as he would prove in August 1917, to move vigorously against it; the other was a cautious, sectarian Socialist, wedded to a deterministic Marxism whose final goal, the classless society, lay very far in the future. Besteiro was, in fact, a Spanish Menshevik, decent and democratic, convinced that the next step for Spain could only be a bourgeois republic, which, though the Socialists would chastely refuse all positions of power, would be the unavoidable gateway to Socialism.[78] Yet in the debate with Verdes Montenegro he adopted a curiously voluntarist tone.

Besteiro sought, in effect, to reconcile Marx and Clemenceau. He conceded to Verdes that the war stemmed from the concentration of international capital, and that both sides were imperialistic. But he insisted that upon the economic foundation of German imperialism had risen a "Pan-German ideology" that made it the most aggressive and dangerous of its species. To discover which nation had started the war, he said, one had only to refer—as Verdes had not been willing to do—to prewar diplomatic history, where German guilt was clearly revealed. Verdes's assertion, moreover, that the world would continue on the road to Socialism no matter which side emerged victorious impressed Besteiro not as Marxism but as a kind of "Moslem fatalism" that could only lead to disaster. By acting in the present, Socialists could in fact modify the future and avoid making themselves "propitiatory victims" of historical inevitability. But this would require struggle in the international arena against "reaction," which was centered in Germany.[79]

Besteiro easily carried the day, and the Congress passed the pro-Allied Vera resolution with only a few of the modifications suggested by the minoritarians. The final clause of this document seemed to echo the views of Entente statesmen in its denigration of a negotiated peace that might leave the "German menace" hanging over future generations. The resolution was approved 4,090 to 1,218, which suggests that the antiwar minority embraced at most about 25 percent of the party. The PSOE was small at this time; and of its 14,332 members, only some 6,000 were represented at the Tenth Congress.[80]

One of the most curious aspects of the Tenth Congress was the delegates' absorption with the ideological implications of the war and their relative unconcern about its economic impact on Spain. This would change. Since early 1915 rising prices and rising unemployment had produced disturbances in scattered regions, and the government's inaction ensured that worse times were coming. By mid-1916, the increasingly irate mood of the workers would be a major Socialist concern.[81]

The Anarchosyndicalists and the War

The contrast between Socialist and Anarchosyndicalist responses to the war was striking. Whereas the Socialists followed the conflict with complete absorption, convinced that the future of Western civilization hinged on an Allied victory, most Cenetistas regarded the war with doctrinaire cynicism, professing to see only an equality of war guilt among the belligerents. Finding no justice in the existing social order of Europe, they insisted that it was of no concern to the workers which side won. They demanded Spain's absolute neutrality in the war, and would continue to do so despite the complaints of the Republicans and the Socialists, the provocations of German submarines, and the embarrassment of sharing a position with the most reactionary elements in the country. When they discovered that a number of their old idols in the international Anarchist movement—men such as Kropotkin, Malato, and Grave—had issued a "Manifesto of the Sixteen" declaring support for the Allied cause, they angrily repudiated them.[82]

The only dissenters from this antiwar orthodoxy were some Anarchosyndicalist militants in Galicia and Asturias led by Ricardo Mella and Eleuterio Quintanilla, who had been favorably influenced by the Manifesto of the Sixteen. This group published *Acción Libertaria* in Vigo, later bringing it to Gijón under the name *El Libertario*. They were supported in their efforts on behalf of the Allies by the Zaragoza Anarchist journal *Cultura y Acción*, whose staff included José Chueca, and by *El Porvenir del Obrero* of Mahón. These "minoritarians" were heatedly denounced by the majority of Catalonian Anarchosyndicalists, and the violent antiwar polemics of *Tierra y Libertad* and *Solidaridad Obrera* easily prevailed within the CNT. Indeed, the trend among the Cenetistas reversed that of the Socialists, so that the number of antiwar converts increased as the war progressed. Most Syndicalists—even those working overtime to supply war goods to France—remained hostile or at least indifferent toward both sets of belligerents throughout the war, a mood almost certainly reinforced by the pro-Allied declarations of both the Radicals and the Socialists. Conflicts between Cenetistas and Radicals were especially violent; demonstrations and denunciations were common, and on one occasion even gunshots were exchanged over the neutrality issue.[83]

Late in 1914 the Ateneo Sindicalista of El Ferrol proposed that an international antiwar congress be held in that city. The Catalonian Anarchists and Anarchosyndicalists eagerly took up the idea and resolved to send delegations. The plan was prominently featured in the pages of *Solidaridad Obrera* and *Tierra y Libertad*, and numerous propaganda meetings were held to explain to the workers the imperialist nature of the war and the purpose of the congress. It was in these meetings that the young Anarchist militant Angel Pestaña, who had only arrived in Barcelona in August 1914, achieved his first prominence in the Syndicalist movement. In the end, the congress (scheduled for May 1, 1915) was never convened, since no sooner had the delegates arrived than the Dato government, obsessively anxious to avoid offending any of the warring powers, declared it dissolved. The Cenetistas nevertheless managed to hold a clandestine conference at which they began to plan the reorganization of the CNT, which had been in disarray since the repression of 1911.[84]

The Anarchosyndicalists regarded themselves as the only sincere neutralists in Spain, since, as they well knew, both the Left and the Right would have carried the country into the war on one side or the other had circumstances permitted. They remained loyal, then, to the doctrine of the primacy of the class struggle; and they revealed little trace of sentimentality for either set of belligerents, insisting that there were no institutions north of the Pyrenees worth saving. Such an attitude inevitably led to the accusation that the CNT was "Germanophile," a charge lent weight by rumors (which proved to be not unfounded) that German Embassy money was finding its way into the hands of some Cenetista journalists.[85] It was also observed that Cenetista strikes sometimes had the effect of slowing shipments of war goods to the Allies.[86] The Cenetistas were angered by the charge that they were pro-German and defended themselves vigorously, standing their ground against the rising tide of Aliadofilismo and Germanofilismo in Spain.[87] José Negre summed up the views of most Syndicalists when he said, "Let Germany win, let France win, it is all the same to the workers, who will continue to be exploited and tyrannized just as before the war, and probably more than before."[88]

The question, however, was whether Spain could in fact preserve her neutrality or even the stability of her regime in the face of the economic and political pressures generated by the war—pressures that in 1916–17 would inevitably be translated into agitation on behalf of some sort of Spanish intervention, as well as into revolutionary rhetoric designed to speed that intervention. Neutrality was proving as perilous as it was profitable.

CHAPTER TWO

The Ordeal of Neutrality

Spain's declaration of neutrality in 1914 enabled her to avoid the trials of a military involvement and may be credited with preserving the monarchy of Alfonso XIII from premature collapse. But even the carefully observed non-involvement of the Dato and Romanones governments could not provide a barrier against the intrusive economic consequences of the war. The Spanish people had to cope with many of the privations experienced by the warring nations, but without the spirit of unity that a common military danger might have aroused and without the economic controls the belligerent governments used to protect their populations. Thus even as the war stimulated some sectors of the Spanish economy, bringing opportunity and enrichment to a few, it also steadily pushed up the cost of living and the rate of unemployment, helping to impoverish the many. By sharpening class conflict and further polarizing an already divided society, it generated a growing feeling of resentment and frustration that would help turn Spanish workers against the regime in August 1917. This radicalization of the labor movement, along with the inertia and ineptitude of the ruling parties, would finally compel Socialist and Anarchosyndicalist leaders to think about joint action in defense of the workers' living standards—a move that some on both sides hoped would culminate in the fusion of the UGT and CNT. At the same time, this first step toward cooperation would be impeded not only by the clash of doctrine and temperament but also by differing perspectives on the war. The tension between Socialist Aliadofilismo and Cenetista neutralism would be one more obstacle to unified action.

The Economic Consequences of the War

Any analysis of the economic impact of the war in Spain is hindered by a lack of monographic studies and by the scarcity and frequent unreliability of statistical data, especially data relating to the labor movement.[1] But the central issue emerges clearly enough: how much importance should one give economic as opposed to political or ideological factors in explaining the urban revolutionary movement of the summer of 1917 (see Chapter 3) and the rural upheavals of 1918–20 (see Chapter 5)? Were these movements chiefly a result of rising living costs and growing unemployment in an otherwise booming economy, or did they stem more from the deepening political crisis in the Peninsula, and perhaps even from the example of the March and November Revolutions in Russia? This study is mainly concerned with the political history of the Spanish Left, but some effort must be made to assess the impact of the economic forces unleashed in Spain by the European conflict and to relate these forces to other causal factors.

It is essential to recognize, first, that the economic consequences of the war were extremely uneven: some regions and social groups prospered while others suffered, and boom conditions and recession often existed side by side or followed one another in quick succession. The validity of Vicens Vives's contention that the war generally favored the urban-industrial zones over the agrarian[2] is suggested by the fact that the value of industrial exports expanded more rapidly than that of any other economic category, rising from 251.31 million pesetas in 1913 to 608.89 million in 1915; by contrast, the value of food exports actually declined in the same period, though it would rise thereafter. Similarly, the prices of manufactured goods consistently rose more rapidly than those of agricultural items throughout the war, reflecting, again, the greater prosperity prevailing in the industrial sphere.[3]

The relative prosperity of the urban areas, conjoined with the depressed condition of many rural areas, disturbed the "equilibrium" between the rural and urban zones and set in motion an accelerated current of migration to the cities, which, though its precise dimensions remain uncertain, was substantial. Thus, between January 1914 and January 1919 Madrid grew by 76,268 (12 percent), Barcelona by 61,979 (10 percent), and Bilbao by 9,722 (10 percent).[4] If it is recalled that the general rate of population increase in this five-year period was less than 1 percent per annum, it becomes clear that more than half of the urban growth during the war resulted from rural migration.[5] The upsurge of this migration first became noticeable in 1915 and reached its peak in 1916–17. The flow of the "new workers" into Catalonia was perhaps most conspicuous and was especially heavy from Murcia as well as from Alicante, Valencia, and Castellón. A curious side effect of this influx of peasant-proletarians was a sudden rise in the number of industrial accidents, attributable, so the factory inspectors believed, to the migrants' lack of general culture.[6]

Rural emigrants also made their way in substantial numbers to Madrid, Valencia, Bilbao, and to the mining and industrial zones of Asturias; and there can be little question that the ranks of the industrial proletariat expanded significantly during the war. But the widely quoted estimate of F. G. Bruguera that the proletariat grew in this period by 60 percent seems untenable. It is true that the growth in certain categories of industrial labor between 1910 and 1918 (the period used by Bruguera) was rather impressive: the number of miners rose from 90,000 to 133,000, that of metalworkers from 61,000 to 200,000, that of textile workers from 125,000 to 213,000, and that of transportation workers from 155,000 to 212,000.[7] These figures would not be inconsistent with Bruguera's claim, save for the fact that we do not know how much of the increase came as a result of the boom years of 1912–13 and how much thereafter. A more modest growth figure emerges from data released by the National Federation of Spanish Miners in 1923, which suggest that the number of miners (of all types) in Spain increased by about 20 percent from 1914 to 1918—an increase that probably approximated that of factory workers as well.[8]

In this connection it must be reiterated that the apparent prosperity of the war years represented something less than complete utilization of Spanish productive forces or full employment of the labor force. This reality has been obscured by the wartime rise in prices, which caused the *value* of Spanish exports to increase steadily even as the total tonnage declined. When the latter figures (in thousands of metric tons) are examined, Spain's wartime "boom" seems less impressive:[9]

Year	Imports	Exports
1913	5,785	14,871
1914	5,349	11,136
1915	3,820	9,264
1916	4,141	10,906
1917	2,278	9,319
1918	1,413	7,464

It is clear, then, that the source of Spain's "prosperity" during the war lay not in an increase in the volume of exports, which actually declined relative to the peak year of 1913, but rather in two things: first, the inflation of prices, which carried the monetary value of the country's total exports from 0.87 billion pesetas in 1914 to a high of 1.36 billion in 1916; second, the sharp decrease in imports, whose monetary value fell from 1.31 billion in 1913 to only 734 million in 1917 and 576 million in 1918.[10] The decrease in imports resulted from the severance of commerical contacts with the Central Powers and Russia, as well as from the determination of the Allies (especially after the start of 1917) to keep for their own war needs the manufactured articles, raw materials, and foodstuffs previously exported to the Peninsula.[11]

The drop in imports, together with the rising value of exports, meant that Spain, a poor nation that had always had a deficit in her foreign-trade balance, almost overnight began to experience a positive balance of payments and a sudden flow of gold across her frontiers (figures in pesetas times 100 million):[12]

Year	Exports	Imports	Balance
1914	8.6777	10.2197	−1.5420
1915	12.4824	9.7032	+2.7792
1916	13.6155	9.1297	+4.4857
1917	13.1131	7.3382	+5.7749

Whereas on July 10, 1914, Spain had less than 343 million pesetas in gold in the Bank of Spain, by December 31, 1917, she possessed a metallic reserve equal to 2,053,664,836 pesetas and (with a guarantee of 95.53 percent in specie for bills in circulation) was contemplating going on the gold standard. However, as in the Siglo de Oro, the influx of gold was accompanied by the growing impoverishment of the Spanish people. The forced reduction of imports, though it caused gold to flow into the national coffers, could only mean severe scarcities of food and manufactured goods, rising prices, and increasing austerity for urban and rural workers. Spain, as a French observer noted, appeared more and more like a miser starving in the midst of useless treasure.[13]

Before analyzing the nature and extent of the hardships experienced by the mass of workers, it would be well to say something about the fortunate minority—and it was only a minority—that benefited from the war boom. By 1915 the most conspicuous, though not the most important, result of the war for Spain was the prosperity that came to certain sectors of the middle and upper-middle classes, especially in Catalonia and the Basque Provinces. Not only was the internal market now entirely in the hands of Spanish producers, but there was added to it the heavy demand of the Allied powers for weapons, uniforms, textiles, leather goods, food, and raw materials. Spaniards would cheerfully have produced for both sides, and limited quantities of goods undoubtedly found their way into German hands. But the overwhelming proportion of Spanish war production went to France and England. Profits were very high, with the greatest gains going to the Vizcayan iron and steel manufacturers, the Catalan textile and light metals manufacturers, the cattle, grain, and olive growers, the shippers, and the mining interests. Substantial profits were reaped, above all, by speculators who facilitated the exportation of virtually anything required by the Allied war machine, without concern for the consumption needs or welfare of the Spanish people. Foodstuffs, raw materials, and all kinds of scarce consumer items were freely sold abroad without effective regulation or restraint by the government until the early part of 1918.[14]

Nor did it prove politically possible, at any time during the war, to impose a tax on surplus profits, the revenues from which could have been used to alleviate popular distress. The agrarian interests of the Center and South, whose views were expressed by the Castilian centralizer Santiago Alba, sought to impose such a tax exclusively on Catalan and Basque manufacturers, whose high profits were, indeed, notorious. This was blocked in the Cortes by the Catalan leader Francisco Cambó, who called attention to the also very substantial profits of the landed classes.[15] The result was a deadlock, and untaxed profits continued to pour into the country, aggravating the already extreme maldistribution of income. Some spectacular fortunes were made, and there appeared in these years, in contrast to the rather staid, God-fearing bourgeoisie of the prewar period, a *nouveau bourgeoisie* that was profiteering, speculative, and not averse to high living. More selfish and reactionary than their predecessors, according to Vicens Vives, they would be one of the causes of the intensified labor conflicts of the postwar period. This class, like its counterparts elsewhere, revealed an inevitable discrepancy between its cultural level and the economic heights to which it had so rapidly risen. Its members drove large motor cars, dressed lavishly, paraded gilded women, patronized the cocktail lounges that were then appearing in Spain, and in general made themselves odious to a hard-pressed and puritanical proletariat. Their high profits went for everything except extensive investment in new plants and modernized equipment. Although production increased strikingly in some industries, the overall technical competence of Spanish manufacturers remained depressingly inadequate, and, aside from an accelerated trend toward concentration, there was little sign of the industrial transformation that the war should have produced.[16]

The high profits and vulgar affluence of the new bourgeoisie tended to obscure the fact that large sectors of the Spanish people were adversely affected by the war, being subjected to a relentless belt-tightening that lacked even the consolations of patriotic sacrifice. Several factors converged to worsen the workers' situation. For one thing, the outbreak of war sharply reduced the great current of migration that had flowed to the New World in the early years of the century and had acted as a safety valve for pressures threatening the stability of the Restoration system. Whereas 194,443 people had departed in 1912, emigration dropped to 66,596 in 1914 and 50,359 in 1915.[17] The surplus rural population that had once made its way overseas now had to stay where it was, migrate to Spain's own industrial centers, or go to France. At the same time, the first news of the war led many Spaniards who were already working abroad to seek sanctuary in the Peninsula, joining the competition for work in the relatively few industrial centers. Although the tide of migration to France would soon begin to rise again, especially after mid-1915, this temporary reflux added to the pressures that bore on Spanish workers. Also detrimental was the ever more acute lack of shipping, which crippled various industries and caused an especially serious crisis in the fruit-growing regions of the Levantine Provinces, thus motivating still more thousands of peasants to make the march to the city. All these factors added their weight to the substantial prewar flow of rural-urban migration already described, and the result was an accumulation of population in the cities that the uneven industrial expansion stimulated by the war could absorb only in part.[18]

The immediate impact of the war on Spanish industry was hardly favorable, and the last months of 1914 saw a decrease in production, a sharp drop in exports (which fell nearly 20 percent), and growing unemployment. The situation was most critical in Barcelona. Ninety-eight percent of the city's cotton and woolen thread production, for example, had gone to the now inaccessible Russian market. Textile mills reduced the work week by two days and eliminated night work, the dye industry was temporarily paralyzed, and other industries also fell into depression.[19] Yet recovery from this initial crisis came rather quickly. The cotton textile industry, which employed 95,000 workers and predominated among Catalonian enterprises, regained its vigor and began to produce diligently for the Allied war machine—even though it was plagued by recurring shortages of cotton (owing to the uncertainties of maritime transport) and by periodic shutdowns that produced some chronic unemployment even in this "booming" industry. The Barcelona light metals industry—producing everything from howitzers to aircraft engines—also benefited greatly and underwent expansion, even though it, too, was hindered by shortages of raw materials that kept it from growing as it might have. Shipping difficulties forced some industries to shut down altogether, thus requiring many Catalan workers to emigrate to France in order to utilize their skills; but at the same time new industries were established, and the old industries, in general, considerably increased their labor force.[20]

The industries of Madrid appear to have benefited less and suffered more from the war than was the case in Barcelona, doubtless because both construction and transport, which formed the backbone of the capital's industrial order, were thrown into a prolonged crisis, as was the printing trade, by war-related shortages.[21] The Basque Provinces, with their heavy industry, shipbuilding, and mining, probably fared best of all. A somewhat euphoric observer noted in 1918:

> Bilbao is today one of the most flourishing cities in Spain, and I will even say in Europe. One sees life and exuberance wherever one looks. Businessmen stride about in bustling preoccupation. Trucks and automobiles are constantly racing through the streets.... The people are all at their posts—some at their desks, some beside their forges, but all contributing their part to these gigantic labors.... How beautiful is the spectacle of an active people![22]

In Asturias there was soon evident a rise in mining and in light metal manufacture. But conditions in the mining towns, which filled up with peasant migrants from Castile, León, Aragon, and elsewhere, were deteriorating. A visitor to the town of Mieres in 1918 described it as "without doubt the dirtiest, most unhygienic, and most uninhabitable in Europe," and observed that the lack of housing forced thousands of people to sleep in the arroyos and to pay as exorbitantly for water as in the deserts of the Rif.[23]

The rising cost of living produced increasingly insistent wage demands on the part of the workers, and these were, in general, agreed to by employers, who did not wish to see the flow of profits interrupted.* Few figures are available, but it is estimated that the wages of Catalonian workers had risen 20 to 50 percent by 1918, with the greatest increases going to the skilled workers.[24] The exceptionally well-organized Asturian miners were able to win increases of about 50 percent, but here, as elsewhere, wage raises were never quite able to catch up with rising prices.[25] At the same time, wage boosts necessarily led to increased labor costs for employers and thereby made their own contribution to the inflationary spiral. The granting of higher wages, it may be noted, worked no great hardship on the larger industrial firms, which were working to meet foreign demand, but it did handicap medium-sized and small firms operating on narrower margins.[26]

The impact of the war on the peasants and landless laborers in the countryside is difficult to generalize about, since there were great regional variations. On the whole, after an initial decline, the years 1915-17 were fairly good. In the latifundio provinces, for example, the demand of the warring nations for food resulted in much new acreage being brought into production, with a consequent rise in employment and in wages.[27] The peak of agricultural production and prosperity came in 1916; by mid-1917 both were on a descending curve. Thus the export value of foodstuffs, which (in millions of pesetas)[28] reached 402 in 1915 and 533 in 1916, declined to 532 in 1917 and to 333 in 1918.[29]

Several factors contributed to the gradual contraction of agricultural production: the growing shortage of shipping, largely due to stepped-up submarine warfare; the lack of adequate supplies of fertilizer, much of which came from abroad; the British decision early in 1917 to reduce imports to a minimum; and the inadequacy of the Spanish rail system. Hardest hit were the Levantine provinces, where the lack of shipping frequently caused oranges and other commodities to pile up on the docks. Thus Spain exported 456 million kilos of oranges in 1915, 383 million in 1916, and only 216 million in 1917, with the result that unemployment and hunger became increasingly acute in the citrus-growing regions, forcing the peasants in ever-growing numbers to make their way to industrial Catalonia and—on an even larger

---

* In assessing the amount of domestic discontent, it is worth noting that the number of strikes and strikers remained below the level of the peak prewar year until 1918. See Balcells, p. 181.

scale—to France in search of factory work.[30] In the 27 months from January 1916 to March 1918, it is estimated that 219,801 Spanish emigrants—about 70 percent of them from Valencia, Alicante, Castellón, Murcia, and Almería— reached France.[31] In most of Andalusia (excluding Almería), however, the situation remained fairly stable through the end of 1917, and an observer for the Institute of Social Reforms reported virtually no emigration from Cordoba and Huelva provinces, this being apparently true of western Andalusia generally.[32]

The Conservative government of Eduardo Dato gave way on December 9, 1915, to the Liberal government of Count Romanones without producing discernible changes in official policies or practices. Neutrality continued to be carefully observed, despite the Count's inner reservations; and at the same time the economic position of the workers continued to deteriorate. The new ministry was committed to resolving the problem of living costs, but increasingly grave divisions within the ruling party prevented coherent and concerted action. Without doubt, the great political failure of 1916 was the inability of the regime to create a protective buffer between Spain's economic system and those of the nations at war. Although as early as 1915 the government established Juntas de Subsistencias to regulate prices, this proved a useless gesture, and prices continued to rise under Romanones as they had under Dato. Nor were any effective efforts made to prevent the exportation of food, raw materials, or manufactured items vital to Spanish living standards. A poor harvest in 1915, along with wartime restrictions on the importation of grain (much of which had formerly come from Russia), raised the cost of bread to new heights and produced a mood of exasperation, especially among urban workers, which, if not precisely revolutionary, would lead large numbers of them to support the antiregime movement of the summer of 1917.[33]

The price of some necessities of life rose even more rapidly than the general price level. Between August 1914 and January 1918 the following increases took place: wheat 72 percent; corn 80 percent; barley 83 percent; rice 98 percent; chick-peas 70 percent; and potatoes 90 percent.[34] While more than a billion pesetas in gold were locked up in the vaults of the Bank of Spain, and while politicians and industrialists rejoiced over Spain's "prosperity," there were widespread hunger and unemployment, as well as recurring bread riots in various cities. Such disturbances began as early as 1915, often caused by the breakdown of the rail system and even by the deliberate withholding of foodstuffs by local municipalities, and they increased in number during 1916. Before the end of the war authorities in nearly all the larger cities were compelled, from time to time, to distribute bread and even money to starving, angry mobs.[35]

Nevertheless, one hesitates to place a wholly economic interpretation on the revolutionary general-strike movement in Spain in the summer of 1917. Certainly it lacked the element of mass spontaneity so often associated with hunger-induced upheavals and must be described, on the whole, as a movement planned at the top rather than ignited from below. The greatest spontaneity, as we shall see, was displayed by the workers of Barcelona, where wages had better kept up with prices than almost anywhere else in Spain. Available statistics indicate that the general price rise by March 1917 was substantial but not, in fact, catastrophic:[36]

Period	Price Index (1913 = 100)
September 1914	106.9
March 1915	107.7
September 1915	113.8
March 1916	117.6
September 1916	120.3
March 1917	123.6
September 1917	136.1
March 1918	145.4

It is true that the most rapid rise in prices (12.5 points) came during the period April–September 1917; but the revolutionary movement in August of that year was planned as early as the autumn of 1916 and was agreed upon in March 1917, before the really sharp price rise occurred. It is worth noting, too, that the price rise was even higher in the rural towns, reaching by March 1918 the figure of 149.3, or nearly four points more than in the larger cities;[37] yet the country districts, especially in Andalusia, were remarkably somnolent during the August movement, a non-response that can only raise doubts about any conception of the August strike as a kind of spontaneous reaction against rising prices and economic deprivation.

It is true that the fairly moderate rise of 16.7 points from September 1914 to March 1917 came at the end of a much longer period of rising prices in Spain.[38] Still, Spain did not suffer inflation to the same degree as other European nations, whether belligerent or neutral. Using 1914 as 100, the price levels in various countries by October 1917 were: Spain 141, Germany 209, France 184, Britain 204, Netherlands 188, Norway 261, and Sweden 181.[39] In this connection, however, one must remember that the Spanish people (who spent, on the average, three-quarters of their wages for food) lived closer to the subsistence level than most other Europeans, and that even relatively modest price rises could produce considerable hardship.

Nevertheless, the fact remains that the most acute distress of the Spanish working class was experienced not before but after the August 1917 general strike. The winter of 1917–18 (to get ahead of our narrative somewhat) was the worst of the war. The coal supply for Madrid was greatly reduced, so that electrical power had to be shut off from 9:00 P.M. to 6:00 A.M. and the streetcars forced to run at half speed. The inadequacy of rail transport impeded the normal flow of agricultural produce and also of Asturian coal. The result was the maximization of hunger and cold in the cities, an increase in assaults and robberies in the streets, and a rise in infant mortality.[40] The ranks of the beggars of Madrid—estimated by *El Sol* to number about 28,000—were swelled, and from the long lines of women queuing up to obtain food there were frequent cries of "Down with the profiteers and hoarders!"[41]

But this very great increase in mass privation produced no revolutionary outburst in the cities, where it was most acute. Indeed, the next surge of mass rebellion would come in the countryside and for reasons (as Chapter 5 will seek to show) that were less economic than ideological, being connected with the news of the Bolshevik Revolution. This is by no means to deny the importance of economic factors in the upheavals in Spain during the period 1917–20; but it would seem that these factors were decisive only in conjunction with political and ideological influences, which were of primary importance in determining the timing and scope of the disturbances. It is to a discussion of this political and ideological context that the next several chapters are devoted.

The Pact of Zaragoza

All through 1915 there had been sporadic strikes against the high cost of living; and in 1916 strike activity increased and became more organized. In January a construction workers' strike in Barcelona was turned into a general strike; in February there was a general strike in Valencia; and in March the Guardia Civil killed one worker and wounded five in a crowd demonstrating in the streets of Logroño. Some of the strongest protests against the government's inaction came from Asturian workers, among whom radical sentiment grew more rapidly than in the capital. Thus Isidoro Acevedo and Manuel Llaneza, the Asturian delegates to the 1916 UGT Congress in Madrid (May 12–13), brought with them a bold proposal that may have gone beyond their own wishes. Their resolution called for the launching of a national general strike, in conjunction with the CNT, in order to force the government to take action against both inflation and rising unemployment. Perhaps to the surprise of the Asturians, this challenge was taken up by Julián Besteiro, who had become the leading figure in the Congress because of the illness of Pablo Iglesias.[42]

The general strike was regarded by many Socialists as an "Anarchist" weapon that should be used sparingly. But Besteiro himself had once advocated such a measure against the Moroccan War, and he was prepared to adopt the same procedure against the economic crisis. Besides, membership in the UGT had been dropping disturbingly since 1913, when it had totaled

147,729, and during the course of 1916 it would fall to around 110,000.[43] Something had to be done, and Besteiro had no intention of letting himself be outflanked on the left if he could help it. He would accept even the idea of cooperation with the Anarchosyndicalists, although this tactic was resisted by conservative UGT leaders like Vicente Barrio.

The resolution that finally emerged from the Congress called for a careful escalation of pressure on the government. First, the UGT would demand once more that the government lower transportation rates, initiate public works, regulate internal trade in order to meet the consumption needs of all Spaniards, suppress excessive business and industrial privileges, and terminate unproductive expenditures, especially those for the war in Morocco. Second, a propaganda campaign on behalf of these measures would be launched in order to bring the largest possible number of workers into the struggle. Third, a series of public meetings and demonstrations would be held on the same day all over Spain. Fourth, the UGT National Committee would begin to gather information about the state of mind of workers in various cities and regions so that, along with the regional representatives, it could decide within the space of three months on the desirability of launching a one-day general strike as a warning to the government. Finally, after this strike and provided the government failed to take action, the Committee would again call a meeting of regional representatives to decide on further action.[44]

One notes in this plan the characteristic procedures of Spanish Socialism— the deliberation, the careful planning, the cautious advance toward specified objectives. But how well the Socialist temper would combine with that of the more volatile Cenetistas in a common struggle remained to be seen. Coincidentally with the UGT Congress in Madrid, the CNT held a meeting in Valencia. This assembly, attended by 70 delegates representing 700 organizations, was also concerned with organizing a campaign against rising living costs and on behalf of amnesty for political prisoners. The possibility of co-operation with the UGT was raised by Angel Lacort of the Zaragoza Labor Federation and was seconded by Salvador Seguí. A delegate was dispatched to Madrid to inform the Ugetistas of the CNT's desire for a united front. The Valencia Assembly also, for the first time, expressed the concern for concentrating and simplifying the unions of the CNT that two and a half years later would lead to the creation of the powerful Sindicatos Unicos. Finally, the Cenetistas formed a permanent committee to lead the campaign against the rising cost of living. This was headed by Seguí and included Francisco Miranda, Secretary of the CNT National Committee (then based in El Ferrol), and Angel Pestaña, representing the Catalonian Regional Confederation (based in Barcelona).[45]

Under the economic pressures generated by the war, the two major labor movements of the Peninsula now sought to overcome profound philosophical and temperamental differences and achieve a rapprochement. The UGT was the larger organization at this time, with about 100,000 members. The CNT still had only some 15,000 adherents and would not commence to grow rapidly or solidify its organizational base until 1918. Within the CNT, Seguí and the Catalan moderates were most interested in the UGT alliance, whereas the Anarchists dragged their heels. When the issue was debated in the Ateneo Sindicalista, Anarchist speakers were willing to accept a limited union of the two labor bodies within Catalonia but ruled out absolutely any question of fusion. Indeed, all speakers stressed the dangers of cooperation with the UGT as long as the leaders of the Socialist Party had any influence in that organization.[46]

Nevertheless, discussions with a view to joint action of the two federations began in May 1916 and climaxed with a meeting in Zaragoza in mid-July. The UGT was represented by Besteiro, Largo Caballero, and the reluctant Vicente Barrio; the CNT sent Seguí, Pestaña, and Lacort, with the last presiding. On July 17 the Pact of Zaragoza was signed, formally allying the two organizations. A manifesto was issued proclaiming the agreement of the UGT and the CNT to work together to force the government to take action on the question of living costs and suggesting a general strike as the chief means of exerting pressure. This Pact, marking the first time that Socialists and Anarchosyndicalists had ever agreed to cooperate, caused a sensation in Spain. Workers of all persuasions were elated, while the privileged classes experienced dismay and even panic. The Romanones government, taken by surprise, apparently expected an immediate assault on the established order and acted accordingly: constitutional guarantees were suspended; hundreds of trade-unionists were briefly jailed; and the arrest of all the signers of the Pact was ordered. At about this time the increasingly powerful Railworkers' Union of the North waged and, to the surprise of most, won a strike for union recognition against the Compañía del Norte, in which effort they were aided by the Asturian miners. The sudden capitulation of the Compañía (as well as of the government) was not only a stunning victory for the railworkers but also helped to maximize the impact of the Zaragoza agreement.[47]

Under the terms of the new accord joint meetings were held in various cities. The gathering in the Salon of St. John in Barcelona was typical, with speakers reiterating demands that the government return food prices to the level of 1911–13, that a public works program be launched, and that all labor prisoners be granted amnesty. The propaganda campaign now moved into high gear, and meetings were held in most of the industrial centers of Spain to protest the government's inertia. Finally, on November 26, delegates of the UGT and the CNT—Besteiro, Largo Caballero, Barrio, Seguí, and Pestaña—met again in Zaragoza and signed an agreement to launch (in mid-December) a general strike, which, at the insistence of the Socialists, was to be limited to 24 hours. The Romanones government, unable to control the economic crisis, began to view the labor movement with mounting apprehension.[48]

The Liberal ministers were not kept uninformed. As early as June 8, the National Committee of the UGT, led by Besteiro, had visited Count Romanones to inform him in detail about what the workers wanted and what steps they planned if his government failed to take action. The demands centered on the lowering of prices, the solution of the employment crisis, a broad amnesty, and an immediate end to the Moroccan War. Assurances were given by Romanones; but, as before, no action was forthcoming, and on November 20 labor delegates visited the Prime Minister again to announce that unless the government took immediate, positive steps to curb the economic impact of the war, the 24-hour strike would be carried out. Once more promises were made, and once more concrete actions failed to materialize.[49]

Consequently, on December 18, 1916, the first successful national general strike in the history of the country was carried out, with the total number of strikers exceeding the combined membership of the two participating labor confederations. The strike was especially complete in Madrid, the life of the city being virtually brought to a standstill. This peaceful strike was intended as a warning to the government of more formidable actions yet to come; and on the same day of the strike the National Committee of the UGT, again led by Besteiro, visited Ruiz Jiménez, Minister of the Interior, to repeat Labor's demands. Again the Socialist leaders were turned away with soft words and vague promises, and the government continued its policy of "suicidal inhibition."[50]

Vistas of Peace

Nineteen sixteen was the last year of relative serenity for the monarchical regime in Spain. Although the economic situation steadily worsened for the majority of the population, the political situation held fairly stable. The workers were under increasing pressure, but they continued to seek remedies within the system and to contemplate chiefly economic actions. Among the potentially rebellious left-bourgeois parties, always less concerned with purely economic problems, there was growing resentment over the nation's continued aloofness from the Allied cause; yet they remained for the most part sullenly reconciled to the neutrality policy. German submarine warfare, though a serious problem, had not yet become critical, and the neutralist mood of the masses was, in any case, discouragingly evident. At the same time, the leftists derived comfort from their impression that King Alfonso was at heart pro-French and would eventually encourage a closer relationship between Spain and the Allied powers.[51]

For those who crossed the Pyrenees from war-darkened Europe, Spain was an oasis of light, another world. Visitors were almost unnerved by the blaze of light that poured from the luminous boulevards of Madrid and the glittering *ramblas* of Barcelona. They were fascinated by the insouciance of the crowds who strolled the streets day and night, oblivious to the unheard thunder of guns far to the north. Victor Serge, the wandering Russo-Belgian Anarchist, arriving in Barcelona from France in the fall of 1916, rejoiced to find beyond the Pyrenees "vistas of peace and abundance ... no soldiers on leave counting up the hours ... no frenzy for life on the eve of death." There were instead the quiet villages of Catalonia, with their tree-lined squares and tranquil air. Above all, there was Barcelona, "making merry, with its *ramblas* illuminated at night and luxuriously sunlit by day, full of birds and women." Here, too, "The cornucopia of war was gushing away ... the factories were working full blast, and the companies were positively coining gold. Zest for life ... was shining at you from the faces and shop windows, oozing at you from the banking-houses, smacking you on the back. Everything was going mad."[52] Even Madrid, more grave and sedate, made an unforgettable impression. The French journalist Jean Breton, fresh from the war zone, could not help being "startled ..., fascinated, relieved, and shocked all at once" by the glare of lights, by the majestic nonchalance of the madrileños, and by the numbers of young men on the streets. "I breathe more freely," he wrote, "but even so I feel my heart constrict, and I ... repeat mechanically to myself, 'How far this is from the war.' "[53]

To Leon Trotsky, unexpectedly thrown out of France late in 1916 for his antiwar activities as editor of *Nashe Slovo*, Spain was another planet. He might have expected, as he later wrote, to be exiled to Holland, Sweden, or Switzerland; but to be thrust unceremoniously across the Spanish frontier was like a "comic dream." "I had not the slightest intention of making a trip to Spain at the end of 1916. Still less had I conceived of studying the interior of the Model Prison in Madrid."[54] As his train rolled south from Hendaye, he wrote in his diary: "We move toward the interior of the Iberian Peninsula. This is not France, but something more Southern, more primitive, more provincial, rougher.... Sandy plains, hills covered with sickly brush and feeble shrubs. Grey dawn. Stone houses without adornment; a sad country.... But why was I here?"[55] The Spaniards on the train, wrapped in their capes, looked remote and unapproachable; in reality, they were "indefatigable talkers." Trotsky was impressed by the great number of "problematical existences" that he observed in Madrid. The intense poverty, the masses of paupers in the train station, and the general lack of sanitation reminded him of Bucharest or Belgrade. It occurred to him that Spain was similar to Rumania, "or, better said, Rumania is a Spain without a past." The lights of Madrid "simply dazzled" him; but in spite of its electricity and its banks, the Spanish capital seemed a provincial city. "Movement without purpose," he jotted in his notebook. "Absence of industry. An abundance of hypocritical devotion.... Much coffee is drunk, but little absinthe. Men remain seated and speak like people who have much time to dispose of.... Time has no value for the Spaniard."[56]

For the restless Trotsky, time had much value, and he spent his days studying art in the Prado and his evenings in his hotel room translating the daily paper with the aid of a dictionary. He encountered the French Socialist Gabier and was told that the Spanish Socialist Party was "totally under the influence of French social patriotism." He wished to visit Daniel Anguiano, then Secretary of the PSOE, but learned that the latter was in jail for 15 days for having ridiculed Catholic doctrine. Trotsky commented: "Fifteen days: a mere bagatelle. In other times, in this same Spain, Anguiano would simply have been burned in an *auto-da-fé*. It remains for the skeptics to deny, in the face of this, the benefits of democratic progress."[57]

Since the French authorities had thoughtfully sent a wire to the Madrid police, identifying Trotsky as a "dangerous Anarchist," he was not long at liberty. During seven hours in a Madrid police station he had an opportunity to observe the Spanish police in action, "or, to put it more exactly, in inaction." Though noting that their cultural level did not match that of their French counterparts, he observed that they were not, as a rule, rude to their clientele, but instead displayed a certain "Southern affability." He decided that Spaniards in general were "not inclined to ferocity; that is, they do not force themselves, for professional reasons, to be fierce." During his interrogation he was politely asked whether he had been at Zimmerwald—a name no doubt supplied by the French police—and what views he had presented there. His answers did not satisfy his interviewer, and he was courteously informed that the ideas he held were "too advanced" for Spain, and that his presence on Spanish territory could not be tolerated.

It was ordered that Trotsky be "secretly" escorted to the Model Prison to await deportation. The police agent entrusted with this task presented himself in a state of inebriation, and a large crowd gathered around the police car while the agent tearfully told Trotsky of his great love for the people of Russia. "In all this," recalled Trotsky, "there was something extremely Russian." At the Model Prison he was instructed to remove his hat, but refused, sensibly replying, "It is not a church." On the whole, he found more courtesy here than he had encountered in the jails of Russia. He was intrigued to discover that there were three classes of cells in the Model Prison, but concluded that there was logic in this. "Why," he asked pedantically, "should there be equality in the prison of a society based on inequality and divided into three classes: the possessors, the disinherited, and the intermediate?" He encountered the prison chaplain who expressed sympathy with his pacifism and said to him consolingly, "paciencia, paciencia." He discovered that nearly all Spanish policemen were pro-German, and recorded the remarks of one of them:

Our francophiles? They are that for money. You can believe me. They all get *pasta* from England and France. Naturally, for a Spaniard it is difficult to be an anglophile. . . . But francophile? Why not, if they pay well? England supports Portugal against us and does not want a strong Spain. Gibraltar! Gibraltar! Nor is France on our side. France has its eyes on Catalonia. If Germany wins, Gibraltar will be ours. If France wins, we will see Barcelona taken from us. I am a germanophile for ideas. Romanones is a francophile for money.[58]

Meanwhile, the Republican deputy Roberto Castrovido, arriving at the prison to visit his friend Torralba Beci, heard from the jailors that there was an "extraordinary Russian" incarcerated there who, despite the language barrier, could not hide his remarkable talents and whom the jailors had come to regard as a "superior being." Castrovido befriended Trotsky and later made a speech on his behalf in the Cortes, protesting the treatment he had received. A controversy began in the newspapers in which the political leftists attacked the behavior of the police but at the same time, as supporters of the Allies, condemned Trotsky's "pacifism." The Right sympathized with his "Germanophilism" but feared his "Anarchism." "In this confusion," recalled Trotsky, "nobody could understand anything."[59]

Trotsky was freed shortly but was ordered to proceed to Cadiz, where he would be placed on a ship. Daniel Anguiano, who escorted him to the Madrid train station, would never forget the Russian leader's "sharp and cold silhouette, his sharply lined features, which reflected an extraordinary energy."[60] Less than a year later Trotsky would be one of the rulers of Russia. Within three and a half years he and Anguiano would meet once more following the Second Comintern Congress in Moscow.

Trotsky spent six weeks in Cadiz under police surveillance. Refusing, as always, to waste time, he read Spanish history in the decaying municipal library and practiced conjugating Spanish verbs. On a park bench he chatted with a 22-year-old Spaniard who spoke of his country "in tones of complete despair."

We shall disappear from the face of the earth. Spain has remained behind in everything. We are in a state of complete decadence. We once dominated the world; now we are a third-rate nation. There is no industry. Horrible ignorance. Our students do not learn. Nobody does anything. If the city councils have some money, they spend it on the bull rings but not on the seaports and the schools. . . . From this situation only the republic can save us, and this will come only with war. War would be the salvation of Spain; it would save us from annihilation. But we are not prepared for war. We don't want to cover ourselves with shame. That is why we are lost! . . . We cherish the belief that after the war there must be great changes.[61]

In January 1917 Trotsky sailed for New York. A short time later he wrote back to a Spanish acquaintance that because of the "violence" of the Spanish character and the severity of the agrarian problem, he considered Spain, next to Russia, the country most likely to experience a revolution.[62] This feeling was shared by an increasing number of Spanish workers, especially by those in the Anarchosyndicalist camp. The editors of *Solidaridad Obrera*, recognizing, like Trotsky, that the war had turned Europe into a kind of revolutionary powder magazine, foresaw that 1917 would be a year of social upheaval. They detected signs that the European peoples were no longer passive and resigned, and they were sure that revolution was on the march in Germany and Russia. They sensed that the Russian people were about to rise up in "rebellious dignity" against their oppressors; and their prayer was: "Long live peace via revolution! How the murderers of the people and the enemies of liberty and humanity will pay for their sins! ...Oh just and saving revolution, do not delay!"[63]

The Russian Revolution in Spain

The premonitions of *Solidaridad Obrera* were soon confirmed. On March 8 a revolutionary movement broke out in war-weary Petrograd and quickly spread to other Russian cities. What began with bread riots, demonstrations, and an ill-timed factory lockout ended in revolutionary violence and the desertion of a substantial portion of the garrison to the side of the insurgent workers. Tsar Nicholas, who to the end understood nothing, abdicated on March 15, and nominal power was transferred to the Provisional Government created by the Duma and representing chiefly the bourgeoisie. This government, lacking a solid social class to rest on, remained suspended in a void. Real authority lay with the mass-based Petrograd Soviet, which, however, refused to participate in the exercise of power. Because of this anomalous situation, and because of the Provisional Government's unwise decision to continue Russia's active participation in the war, the last chance for democratic government in Russia was lost and a tempting power vacuum created.[64]

By the early spring of 1917, less than two months after Trotsky's departure from Cadiz, the political stability of the Spanish monarchy was also beginning to break down, and Spain, too, was drifting into revolution. The genesis of the revolutionary mood that swept over the men of the Left in the spring and summer of 1917 was complex; but the underlying cause, as in Russia, was unquestionably the war. It was wartime inflation that triggered the rebelliousness of the workers and, in some measure, of the military. It was the war that generated the feeling of ideological resentment, which, brought to the boiling point by the German declaration of unrestricted submarine warfare, turned all political leftists, whether Reformists, Republicans, Radicals, or Socialists, actively against the monarchy. It was wartime prosperity that in large measure prompted a resurgence of Catalan nationalism and a new aggressiveness among the Catalan bourgeoisie. It was the war, finally, that produced the Russian Revolution, whose impact on the revolutionary movement in Spain, though not decisive, was not negligible and, indeed, requires clarification.

García Venero has described the question of the impact of the March Revolution in Spain as a "scientific problem," which perhaps suggests the elusiveness of the matter.[65] In the long run, the Revolution, though a product of the war, would acquire a life of its own and become a force for change independent of the great conflict. But in Spain, in the spring of 1917, its effect was still subordinated to that of the war: that is, it was felt more at the top of Spanish society, among the politically aware pro-Allied elements most preoccupied with the military struggle, than at the bottom, among the apolitical masses who were, on the whole, indifferent to the war's outcome.

The attitude of the urban and rural workers toward the March Revolution is, of course, difficult to ascertain, but it seems to have been fairly well reflected in the Anarchist and Anarchosyndicalist press. Thus, for example, the encouragement that the editors of *Tierra y Libertad* drew from the March events was tempered by caution and by disappointment that the Revolution was "political" and "bourgeois." They pronounced it a "formidable" movement that would perhaps inspire revolution in the rest of Europe and bring the war to an end; but even while congratulating the Russian workers, the journal urged them not to waste their time with "constitutional, politico-democratic-bourgeois illusions."[66] Within a few days the Cenetistas' fears were borne out when they learned that the Russian bourgeoisie had for the time being contained the revolutionary wave and formed the Provisional Government. They concluded that Tsarist tyranny had merely given way to the tyranny of "capitalist democracy" and to a "Maurist" revolution from above. Worst of all, the new rulers of Russia supported the war: having seen that the Tsarist system was faltering in its prosecution of the military struggle, they had overthrown it merely in order to tell the people to continue dying in the trenches. Nevertheless, the Anarchosyndicalists were sure that the Russian people, having revealed the revolutionary forces within themselves, would soon carry out a revolution of far greater magnitude—provided only that they did not fall victim to the "parliamentary virus."[67]

This suggests, at least, that the impact of the March Revolution on the Spanish working class should not be exaggerated. Victor Serge, it is true, wrote: "Even the workers on the shop floor beside me, who were no militants, instinctively understood the Petrograd days, since their imagination transposed those events to Madrid and Barcelona."[68] Similarly, the young journalist Salvador de Madariaga asserted that "the splendid news of the Russian Revolution" was spreading over Spain "like wildfire," and he called attention to "the hopes raised by the ... Revolution in many a Spanish heart."[69] There was some truth to these claims, and it seems certain that the Revolution, along with the overthrow of King Constantine of Greece, created a climate of optimism and impending upheaval that played a part in mobilizing Spanish workers in the spring and summer of 1917. But it should be stressed that this influence was diffuse and hardly ideological. The March Revolution inspired hope, but nothing like the mass exaltation that the Bolshevik Revolution in November would arouse.[70]

One suspects, then, that the March Revolution exerted its influence primarily on the bourgeois leftists like Madariaga rather than on the workers. As partisans of the Entente the leftists inevitably viewed the Revolution somewhat myopically, strictly in the context of the war. For them, the emergence of a democratic Russia meant that the "one stain" on the Allied escutcheon had been removed and that the war had at last and unequivocally assumed its true meaning as an ideological struggle.[71] They immediately felt freer—and this was the crucial thing—to advance toward what was then called an "interventionist" position, which to them really meant no more than a foreign policy of unconcealed pro-Allied benevolence. When they finally comprehended that the King did not in fact share their own ideological perception of the war and had no intention of encouraging a diplomatic move toward the Allies, their revolutionary and republican feelings rapidly revived. The main consequence of the March Revolution in Spain was thus the somewhat indirect stimulus it gave to the antimonarchical feelings of the political leftists; it still remained for the war to provide the deeper motive force—both economic and ideological—behind the Spanish revolutionary movement of 1917.[72]

The Socialist response to the March Revolution was even more restrained than that of the Anarchosyndicalists. The party newspaper gave good day-to-day coverage of Russian events, but Pablo Iglesias (recovering from a gallbladder operation) and his lieutenants almost completely abstained from editorial comment. Thus the expanded May Day issue of El Socialista, less than two months after the fall of the Tsar, did not even mention the Russian Revolution, and Besteiro devoted his long column to certain problems of Madrid's municipal government. The essentially revolutionary manifesto written by Besteiro at the end of March, in which an impending general strike was announced, likewise made no reference to the situation in Russia.[73]

The silence of the Socialists stemmed, of course, from their profound absorption with the war, which, as Andrés Saborit said, was "the one terrible reality that superimposes itself on everything . . . and diminishes every other fact."[74] The Spanish Socialists were in the grip of what George Kennan, in another context, has called an "unbalanced preoccupation" with the struggle against Germany. Their state of mind was similar to that of the peoples of Britain and France, of whom Kennan has written:

> The Western democracies had by this time convinced themselves, as embattled democracies have a tendency to do, that the entire future of civilization depended on the outcome of the military struggle. . . . The contest comes to be viewed as having a final, apocalyptic quality. If we lose, all is lost. . . . There will be nothing to be salvaged. If we win, then everything will be possible . . . the forces of good will sweep forward unimpeded.[75]

Thus in May 1917 *El Socialista* commented that peace would be welcome "if it means the annihilation of the powers of imperialism and oppression that smother our sister peoples of Germany and Austria and threaten to smother the whole world!" But it would be "calamitous for us, calamitous for Humanity" if the Central Powers should conquer, or if the peace should be "only an armistice" leading to even more devastating conflicts in the future. Therefore, said *El Socialista*, "We are in spirit fighting beside the nations that defend themselves from aggression, that proclaim ... the liberty of the oppressed peoples, that carry within themselves the germ of redemptive revolutions."[76]

Given this intense commitment to the Allies, the Socialists' silence on the March Revolution was not to be wondered at. As "revolutionary" Socialists, they could scarcely go so far as to condemn it; but since it cast doubt on Russia's ability to continue the war at the side of her allies, they were unable to generate enthusiasm for it. Their state of mind was thus the reverse of that of the Anarchosyndicalists, who displayed an equally unbalanced preoccupation with the approaching social revolution. For the Cenetistas all the issues of the war and the fate of democracy had been subordinated to the revolutionary apocalypse, which, as *Solidaridad Obrera* remarked, would "end all wars and all tyrannies, political as well as economic."[77]

The Continuing Campaign Against Inflation

Meanwhile, all efforts to jar the Romanones government into effective action against the still-rising cost of living had ended in failure and frustration. The one-day strike in December 1916 had produced no tangible results, and the pressures of inflation and unemployment were bringing the working-class mood close to the boiling point. When Romanones suddenly closed the Cortes on February 27, this seemed to the workers the last straw. On March 5, 1917, representatives of the UGT and CNT assembled, this time in Madrid, to implement the warnings they had already issued and to plan a movement of even greater scope. Labor leaders from all over Spain gathered in the Casa del Pueblo in an atmosphere of anger and incipient rebellion. The leading Socialists present were Besteiro and Largo Caballero, now exercising the power that was slowly slipping from the hands of the ailing and more conservative Iglesias, who was not present. The Cenetistas were represented by Seguí, Lacort of Zaragoza, and the fast-rising Pestaña, who was experiencing his first close contact with the Madrid Socialists. The discussions were carried on in an unusually fraternal atmosphere, and out of them came a manifesto (written mainly by Besteiro) that called for a general strike within three months' time—an action that because it was to be of unlimited duration would necessarily acquire political and revolutionary overtones. It was clear that Labor's efforts were shifting from the economic and the ameliorative to the political plane, and that the question of the regime had now been posed. Having finally despaired of obtaining relief from the existing system, the workers were contemplating its replacement.[78]

After the signing of the manifesto a somewhat boisterous public meeting was held in the theater of the Casa del Pueblo, in which the speakers outdid one another in fiery pronouncements. The disapproving right-wing Socialist, Oscar Pérez Solís, recalled that the speeches were so full of ardor and the propositions brought forward so "terrible" that they constituted a virtual ultimatum to the government. This, as it turned out, was also the view taken by Count Romanones who (as Tsarist Russia trembled on the brink of revolution) was disposed to see "subversion galloping through the most aristocratic streets of the Palace district."[79] Even as the meeting dissolved, its manifesto was declared to be seditious; and its originators, along with hundreds of other militants, were arrested before the day was out. Constitutional guarantees were suspended throughout the country. Seguí, Pestaña, and Lacort were able to get as far as Zaragoza before being picked up by the police and taken back to Madrid, where they were imprisoned for a few days in the Moncloa prison. Because of the extreme austerity with which the Cenetista leaders necessarily had to travel, Pestaña found himself penniless after his release and had to borrow his train fare back to Barcelona.[80]

Since the UGT and CNT had agreed to launch a general strike of unlimited duration—that is, one evidently intended to bring about a fundamental change of regime—the problem was to coordinate the revolutionary efforts of a labor movement that was still small, ill-organized, and divided. Energy had to be conserved for the grand effort, and premature outbursts avoided. Surprisingly, the first unscheduled and spontaneous outburst occurred not among the mercurial Anarchosyndicalists but among the Socialists of Valladolid, who decided on March 8, 1917, to launch a general strike protesting the arrest of the labor leaders a few days before. The long-time leader of Valladolid Socialism, Remigio Cabello, was in flight from Romanones's police, and the leader in charge was Pérez Solís. Because the Madrid meeting of Socialists and Cenetistas had itself threatened strike action if any of its members were arrested, the idea arose in Valladolid of doing what the workers had threatened to do. A general strike was declared in the somewhat naïve expectation that it would be spontaneously seconded all over Spain. Had Cabello been present, he might well have prevented this démarche; but Pérez Solís decided to go along with the rank and file. The city of Valladolid was paralyzed. All businesses were closed and since the police could not control the violent demonstrations that broke out, army troops had to be sent in. After two or three days the Valladolid workers discovered that nowhere else in Spain had their action been seconded, and they brought it to an end. Although the idea had probably not been his, blame for the failure fell on the head of Pérez Solís, and he was, for a time, in disgrace. Largo Caballero would later place some of the blame for the failure of the August general strike on the premature movement in Valladolid, which, he believed, exhausted energies that would better have been saved until August.[81]

This abortive effort notwithstanding, the revolutionary wave was rising all over Spain, and nowhere more rapidly than in Catalonia. The Cenetistas now exhausted the treasuries of their unions in order to buy pistols and make bombs, and a "fever of activity" spread through the ranks of the CNT. But the problem was that the fever rose so much more rapidly among the Anarchosyndicalists of Catalonia than among the Socialists in Madrid.[82] Never was the temperamental incompatibility of the two movements more evident. The Cenetistas obviously envisioned an Anarchist insurrection in which the workers, with the aid of bombs and pistols, would tumble the regime in a day or two of street fighting, and in reality their thought hardly extended beyond the confines of Catalonia. The Socialists, by contrast, in their sober and excessively deliberate way, were planning a massive, solidly organized strike movement in the whole of Spain, and one able to meet the full counterblow of a regime fighting for its life. Whereas most Cenetistas were thinking of a purely labor action, a general strike waged by the masses in which the whole political structure and the politicians of both the Right and the Left would be swept aside, the Socialists, as the principal planners of the impending movement, were looking beyond purely trade-union efforts and conducting negotiations with the left-bourgeois parties. They had no illusions that a Socialist revolution was then possible in Spain and wanted only to replace the oligarchical regime of landowners and bureaucrats with the rule of the more enlightened bourgeoisie; their goal was not a Syndicalist utopia but a bourgeois republic. Beyond this, the Socialists seemed more aware than the Anarchosyndicalists that at least a portion of the Army had to be won over, and this they were trying to do.[83]

The pace of Socialist preparation, then, was very deliberate, and the CNT leadership was under increasing pressure from its followers to move quickly. The leaders were conscious of the rising élan of the Syndicalist workers and did not wish to see the wave of popular emotion reach its crest and break before the revolutionary movement was launched. This conflict between Catalonian spontaneity and Castilian deliberation created mounting tension between the two movements; and it would twice force the UGT to send representatives to Barcelona in order to preserve relations and to prevent a premature outburst by the Cenetistas.

The Campaign Against Neutrality

Simultaneously with Labor's campaign against inflation there began to take shape among the leftist parties, including many pro-Allied Socialists, an equally vigorous campaign against absolute neutrality. This, too, would have revolutionary implications. Perhaps as early as the summer of 1916, there had begun to mature among the democratic intelligentsia the conviction that Spain should move closer to the Allied powers and, without sending troops into the trenches, assume a posture of either limited cobelligerency or overtly benevolent neutrality. At the very least this movement sought a rupture of diplomatic relations with Germany to protest unrestricted submarine warfare. In the deeper sense the "interventionist" campaign, which was vociferously opposed by the Anarchosyndicalists, was motivated by fear that Spain was drifting toward complete isolation from the liberal, democratic, and progressive forces of the modern world. The desire to join with those forces was very intense among political leftists and was strengthened, as we have seen, by the overthrow of the Tsarist regime in Russia.

More immediately, the interventionist movement was fueled by an essentially patriotic resentment of German attacks on Spanish ships, and especially by the passivity of the Spanish government in response to numerous sinkings. The German submarine campaign was at its height in the early months of 1917, and its ravages had a serious impact on many of Spain's industries. Perhaps the most notable casualty was the orange trade of Valencia, which was thrown into depression because exporters could not procure enough shipping. Not surprisingly, the Valencia region became a center of antineutralist agitation, as well as a source of increased peasant migration to the industrial centers of Catalonia. But in spite of everything the Romanones government continued to insist upon Spain's absolute neutrality; and it consistently refused to associate itself with the peace initiatives of President Wilson, fearing that the concept of a "peace without victors," could only arouse the antagonism of both groups of belligerents.[84]

The attitude of the Socialist Party toward neutrality was changing in this period, and there was less talk about the need for strict aloofness from the struggle. The German declaration of unrestricted submarine warfare on February 1, 1917, was a great shock; and it was at about this time that the followers of Pablo Iglesias began to realize that absolute neutrality was in fact a pro-German policy. In March, shortly after the Russian Revolution, the Party issued a manifesto urging the government to take stronger action against the individuals and organizations within Spain who were in various ways aiding the German submarine blockade. The ministers were urged to take "all effective measures necessary to guarantee the normality of Spanish economic life." To leave no doubt about their seriousness, the Socialists declared that if opposition arose to the government's attempts to suppress pro-German espionage, "The Socialist Party will lead the struggle against whatever elements ... oppose difficulties to the work of legitimate national defense." A further stimulus to intervention resulted when the United States entered the war on April 2, followed by several of the Latin American republics. By the end of the month Iglesias—perhaps following the lead of Melquíades Alvarez—was urging upon his party the desirability of Spain's severing diplomatic relations with Germany, though he reminded his followers that Spain's unpreparedness must preclude an actual declaration of war.[85]

The interventionist mood was brought to fever pitch by the April 9 sinking of the Spanish ship *San Fulgencio*, which was bound from Newcastle to Barcelona with 2,000 tons of coal. There was special anger over this sinking, since the destruction of the ship clearly damaged Spain rather than the Allies. In the face of public wrath, pro-Germans began to fear that the episode would impel the government to abandon its neutrality; and, indeed, Romanones now seems to have decided that the time had come for Spain to consider modifying her policy. He proposed to send a stern note to the German government, as a prelude to severing diplomatic relations. But the majority in the Cortes, reflecting the consensus of the Restoration parties, refused to support the strong wording Romanones desired, and the Count now professed to believe that he had no alternative but to give up his office. His resignation on April 19 touched off not merely a political but a constitutional crisis; and it came as a great shock to the interventionists, many of whom had earlier criticized him for not showing more sympathy for the Allied cause. The hasty reaffirmation of absolute neutrality by the incoming government of Luis García Prieto angered them still more.[86]

The Left's disillusionment with King Alfonso reached a peak at this time, and republican sentiment continued to grow rapidly. As in other European countries, the republican movement in Spain had been declining for some time before the war, reaching its lowest point by about 1914. There were many parties and many leaders, but there was little dynamism, coherence, or vision. However, the war's increasingly ideological coloration helped reawaken the republican movement in the Peninsula, enlarging its ranks and infusing it with a new and aggressive spirit. By the spring of 1917 the republican current was gaining, especially as a result of the growing conviction that the King was himself pro-German. During the early years of the war the Left had been beguiled by Alfonso's apparent sympathy for the Entente and had accepted a truce with the monarchy in the expectation of an eventual move toward a pro-Allied foreign policy. But the *San Fulgencio* sinking had forced the King to show his hand, requiring him to make known his opposition to the strong Romanones note. This "betrayal," which coincided with a provocative speech by Antonio Maura advocating diehard neutrality, gave new impetus to the republican movement.[87]

The pro-Allied forces (many of whom had not been openly antimonarchical) now acquired a revolutionary and actively republican spirit and prepared to add their efforts to those of the workers. In late April elements of the Reformist party, led by Melquíades Alvarez, having asked in vain for a severance of diplomatic relations, once more took their stand against the monarchy and began to make overtures to the groups that lay to the left of them. Reformists,

Republicans, Radicals, and Socialists—united, for all their differences, by their frustrated fervor for the Allies—began to achieve a rapprochement. Aliado-filismo thus became one of the currents rapidly converging toward the revolutionary summer that lay ahead.[88]

The Meeting in the Plaza de Toros

The climax of the campaign against absolute neutrality came on May 27, when all the leftist parties gathered in the Plaza de Toros in Madrid to demand the severance of diplomatic relations with Germany. Organized by the journal *España* as a response to Maura's speech of April 29 and designed to coincide with the King's birthday, this meeting was essentially a gathering of the radical intelligentsia—republican politicians, intellectuals, professors, journalists, doctors, and some Socialists. It was a bravura performance by a small band of the enlightened who imagined that they could drag the great mass of Spaniards, who were either pro-German or indifferent, along in their wake. As the westernizers of a moribund nation they were demanding of that "other" Spain, which was both more numerous and more inert, that it drop the shield of absolute neutrality and join the cause of the democratic nations at least in spirit, thereby opening Spain to the progressive currents of the West. What they wanted was not Spanish military participation but rather a "moral intervention" in which Spain would somehow associate herself with the Allies.[89]

Although the March Revolution contributed something to the exaltation of the leftists, it must be reiterated that it was the war, viewed through a haze of liberal and democratic dogma, that preoccupied them almost obsessively.[90] More concerned with its ideological implications than with its economic consequences, they saw the war as a "revolution" that was certain to bring liberalizing changes to all nations, not excluding Spain, when the Allies emerged victorious. The ordeal of the leftists was that their country, by mindlessly clinging to absolute neutrality, had refused to align itself with the only nations that could provide an example for the regeneration of Spanish life. The virtual ultimatum that they delivered from the speakers' platform in the Plaza de Toros was that the monarch either had to place Spain, at least morally, on the side of the democracies or risk losing his throne. Many Socialist intellectuals, it must be said, fully shared this conviction. Perhaps more democratic than Marxist, leaders such as Besteiro, Ovejero, Fabra Ribas, and Araquistáin were at times difficult to distinguish from the republican intelligentsia.

Under the flags and banners of all the left-bourgeois parties some 25,000 people assembled. Alvaro de Albornoz began the proceedings by acknowledging that the meeting was intended to express the solidarity of the Spanish leftists with the Allied nations, among whom he cited Serbia, France, Italy, and Russia (she of the "splendid destiny" who had "marked the road that Spain must follow"), but not Britain. The Socialist Party, reluctant to participate officially in a meeting of bourgeois parties, was represented unofficially by Professor Andrés Ovejero, a one-time republican, who emphasized that he was taking part only as an individual. Nevertheless, it was clear that through him the Socialists were giving their approval to an "interventionist" and even revolutionary meeting. Although he insisted that the Socialists were neutralists and pacifists, Ovejero dwelt in rather unpacifistic fashion on the indignities that Germany's submarine warfare had inflicted on Spaniards. Above all, he was sure that the war had given rise to a "revolutionary ferment" which was, in fact, its principal meaning; the parties of the Left had come to the meeting, he said, precisely because they understood the revolutionary significance of the war. And, he added, "We come to say to the other elements of the Left: Now or never!"[91]

All the speakers who followed Ovejero were convinced that the conflict between the Allies and the Central Powers was only a European version of the latent civil war in Spain, a larger and fiercer manifestation of the continuing struggle between progressive and reactionary forces. The Republican deputy Roberto Castrovido, who had befriended Trotsky in the Model Prison a few months earlier, said that the purpose of the meeting was not to sound a "war trumpet" or carry the Spanish masses into the slaughter; but neither would it call for "peace without victors." Its purpose was to support the victory of "democracy, justice, and peace," and to ensure the defeat of "reaction, imperialism, militarism, clericalism." "The war is a revolution," he said, "and here we must make one of our own." "There is a civil war in Spain," said Menéndez Pallares, "in which all leftists must rise up against . . . reaction. Neutrality or intervention are nothing more than the themes of one [domestic] force or the other." Melquíades Alvarez, leader of the Reformists, appealed to "republicans and democrats" to have hope, since it was clear that the Russian Revolution and the prophetic words of Wilson had strengthened democratic forces everywhere in the world. The war was "the struggle of two civilizations: the West . . . of Greco-Latin origin, and the oriental." He urged Spain to sever relations with Germany in order that France and Italy (he, too, did not mention Britain) would know that Spanish democracy was at their side. The Radical leader Alejandro Lerroux qualified his earlier bellicosity by saying that what he wanted for Spain was not necessarily intervention but was by no means "the neutrality of quietism."[92]

The philosopher and sometime Socialist Miguel de Unamuno best expressed the central preoccupation of the Left when he said, speaking as much to the King as to the assembled multitude: "It depends on the King whether or not many of us who are not republicans must declare ourselves as such. I, who still have a slender faith in the monarchy . . . will cease to believe in it if it insists on neutrality at all costs. The King can be useful; but he is not indispensable, much less irreplaceable." Unamuno concluded by saying that because of all the evils of Spanish life, it was "necessary to shake the people, arousing them, making them feel the terrors of the war. . . . If the monarchy does not wish to make the revolution, we of the Left will have to make it ourselves, by refusing to be separatists from . . . humanity," by refusing to labor alone "under the weight of all the traditional obstacles."[93]

Though not officially participating in the gathering in the Plaza de Toros, the Socialist majoritarians shared virtually all the sentiments expressed there, and joined in what was, in effect, an ultimatum to the King. There were thus at least two forces impelling the Socialist Party down the revolutionary path in the spring of 1917. One of these was the economic hardship that the war imposed on the workers. The other, and this has never been stressed sufficiently, was the Party's close, emotional involvement in the war, which was always viewed as an ideological contest of transcendent importance. This involvement was, in turn, a reflection of the Party's commitment to democratic Socialism and, one may say, to republicanism. How far the resurgent republicanism of the time had won over the Socialists was revealed in the judgments rendered by *El Socialista* on the Madrid meeting. When the Reformist leader Melquíades Alvarez suggested that forms of government were transitory and lacking in fundamental importance, he was sharply rebuked for not taking an unequivocally republican stand: "One who thinks thus," said the Socialist journal, "cannot represent the revolutionary spirit of the country." One had to be "unconditionally" for either the Republic or the Monarchy. The existing regime was incompatible with the welfare of the people, and those who believed in it or expected anything from it were going against the people.[94]

The Socialist Minoritarians

The rising interventionist mood of the PSOE did not silence the Party's antiwar minority. This was revealed late in May, when the majoritarians of the Madrid Socialist Group, led by Besteiro and Dr. Jaime Vera, proposed a resolution, directed to the next Party Congress, that called on the Spanish government to sever diplomatic relations with Germany. This proposal, first made by Iglesias in April, reflected the growing strength of pro-Allied sentiment in the face of stepped-up German submarine warfare and the resignation of Romanones. The resolution was immediately attacked by the man who was emerging as the principal spokesman of the antiwar elements: Mariano García Cortés. This militant was a portly, mustachioed lawyer of about 35 who never seemed to practice law but devoted his time to journalism (he was editor of *España Nueva*), to his duties as a Madrid city councillor, and to Socialist Party politics. Originally from Andalusia, he had been active in the Madrid Socialist Group for several years before the war, almost always in opposition to the Party oligarchy. His failure to penetrate the Party's inner circle was due to the aura of calculation and contentiousness that hung about him, as well as to persistent but never verified rumors of corruption in his municipal activities. He was capable without being brilliant and was something of an authority on urban problems; yet he failed to inspire confidence. His radicalism seemed not to be rooted in revolutionary idealism or passion.[95]

The debate on the Besteiro-Vera resolution flowed through the by now wellworn channel of pro-Allied and antiwar debate. García Cortés mobilized the familiar pacifist arguments, reemphasizing the common war guilt of all the capitalist powers. He also opposed the resolution, he said, because he was convinced that the severance of diplomatic relations would inevitably lead Spain into war with the Central Powers. At the same time, he observed that the Stockholm Peace Conference had received very little attention in Spain, and urged Socialist participation in it as a way of implementing the antiwar resolution adopted at the 1907 Stuttgart Congress of the International.[96]

García Cortés's most vigorous opponent in this debate was the excitable, chain-smoking Eduardo Torralba Beci, a tall, thin, somewhat disheveled figure, a bourgeois journalist, whose intense idealism invariably prevailed over both self-interest and intellectual consistency. A few years later Torralba would be leagued with García Cortés in the founding of the Spanish Communist Party; but at this moment he was the most fervent of Allied partisans, and his remarks clearly revealed how much the Socialist majoritarians continued to be caught up in the ideological issues of the war. Wraithlike and stooped, his clothes covered, as always, by a fine film of cigarette ash, Torralba argued insistently against the pacifist position. He was opposed to going to Stockholm, he said, because "while there are parties led by men who, like Scheidemann, obey the Kaiser, honorable Socialists cannot extend their hand." He fully agreed with the Belgian Vandervelde that the best way to display a desire for peace was "to put all our forces into the defeat of Germany." For Torralba, as for most Spanish Socialists, the war in Europe was only a vaster projection of the social struggle in Spain. He could no longer support the idea of absolute neutrality because the reactionary elements in the Peninsula had appropriated that concept for themselves and were, he thought, greatly strengthened by it. The abandonment of neutrality was thus linked in his mind with saving Spain from the pro-German elements: even a war with Germany would be preferable to letting the country fall entirely under their domination.[97]

Other members of the Madrid Group debated the majority's proposal to sever diplomatic relations and the minority's demand that the Party go to Stockholm. In the end, it was clear that the majoritarians did not, in fact, have a majority—not, at least, with respect to what many regarded as an extreme proposal. Besteiro and Vera then prepared a compromise resolution, reiterating that the Socialist Party held the German Empire "directly responsible" for the war, and that the crimes committed by it could not go unpunished. Neutrality, it was asserted, was "the most powerful aid that the German bel-

ligerents have found within the Spanish nation." Because the Spanish government did not suppress German espionage, it revealed itself to Europe as a
"submissive and resigned ... accomplice of the Kaiser." But having uttered
these forceful words, the Party backed away from urging a break in diplomatic relations, concluding somewhat weakly that Spanish Socialists, "withdrawn by the principles of our Party from all governmental action," did not
have to determine the exact moment to break relations with Imperial Germany. As a further concession to minority views, the resolution acknowledged
that even after the German collapse, it would still be necessary to defeat imperialism and capitalism in all nations. It was also decided to send two delegates to the Stockholm Conference: Besteiro would represent the majority,
and Verdes Montenegro, who would have the right to speak but not to vote,
would represent the minority. (In the end, the Conference was canceled, and
the delegates never left Spain.) [98]

The essential unity of majoritarians and minoritarians within the PSOE,
despite their continuous wrangling, was revealed by their mutual commitment
to the speedy restoration of the old International and to the need for purging
the "faithless" Socialists within it. No one yet spoke of the Second International as being irrevocably ruined, and no voices were raised on behalf of
revolution as opposed to immediate peace. The Spanish minoritarians were
nearly all pacifists and democrats, not proto-Bolsheviks. As for the majoritarians, their steady loyalty to the Entente cause was remarkable, especially
in contrast with the increasing alienation of French Socialists and English
Laborites from their national war efforts. In Spain, the pro-Allied Socialists
would be fortified in their convictions by the overwhelming presence of the
pro-German majority in the country, and their ranks would hold firm until the
Armistice. [99]

The Cenetistas and Intervention

By contrast, the Cenetistas viewed the interventionist campaign with genuine alarm, fearing that an attempt to move Spain closer to the Allies, especially
if it required an open break with Germany, would involve the country in war
and send Spanish workers into the trenches. They resented the fact that to the
already heavy burden of rising living costs had now been added the gnawing
fear that Spain would become embroiled in the fighting. Manuel Andreu
expressed these twin anxieties:

> The working class suffers a terrible burden in the rising cost of living, in the rising
> cost of all necessities. Those who live by daily wages are exhausted; they can do
> no more; they have consumed their reserves, drained their credit, and lost all hope
> for a viable solution. And while hunger ravages all Spain, anxiety tortures the
> spirit because of the daily growing danger that we will see ourselves dragged by
> the merciless ones, by the purveyors of human flesh, into the European slaughter-
> house. [100]

The Cenetistas were adamant in their opposition to possible intervention: "Whether one ship or a hundred ships be sunk," said *Solidaridad Obrera*, "we do not want war." Those who wished to fight were sarcastically informed of the ease with which they might cross the frontier and join the combat, the editors promising to "admire" their sacrifice even as they lamented "how sterile and stupid" it would be. To the Syndicalists, it seemed far more sensible to use one's weapons against "more immediate enemies." They were not dazzled, they said, by the claims of patriotism or by "other trifles" of this sort. "With respect to the *patria* ... we workers have no reason to defend it. The *patria* carries us to war by force. The *patria* kills us with hunger, forcing us to emigrate. The *patria* shoots us when we ask for bread. The *patria* crushes us when we cannot pay the rent."[101]

The interventionist and anti-interventionist campaigns reached their climax in May. By this time the Anarchosyndicalists were convinced that the war could only be brought to an end by means of revolution, and they were beginning to fear that the fighting might go on indefinitely unless European workers came to their senses and imposed such a solution. The Cenetistas' "Left-Zimmerwald" perspective was most evident, perhaps, in their response to the proposed Stockholm Conference, which aroused their enthusiasm chiefly because they placed a revolutionary rather than a pacifist interpretation on it. They saw the Conference not as something intended to lead to a peace without victors, but as a means of opening the floodgates of the European revolution. For the first time, reference was made to the Leninist position at Zimmerwald; and the proposed Conference was described as a "continuation of the Russian Revolution ... the first channel opened for the conquest of all the peoples of Europe."[102]

Apparently unaware that the Bolsheviks were opposed to the Stockholm proposal, *Solidaridad Obrera* urged that the CNT send a delegation. More and more, convinced of the imminence of a Spanish revolution, the Cenetistas were filled with an apocalyptic sense that all of Europe was on the eve of momentous changes. They confessed to "a great desire to submerge ourselves in the work of the Russian Revolution, to make [the revolution] here in Spain, destroying those Spaniards of the sort that the Russian people have already extirpated from their midst." The Cenetistas also discerned that a new, revolutionary International was emerging from the war, and they wanted to be identified with it. "We do not know the attitude of the UGT," they said, "but the CNT is for revolutionary internationalism." In the end, however, no Anarchosyndicalist delegation was ever appointed to go to Stockholm, and the whole question was soon submerged by the revolutionary process that began in Spain in June, with the insubordination of the Military Juntas.[103]

In fact, the Cenetistas knew quite a lot about the attitude of the UGT, and what they knew they did not like. They were aware that the Socialists continued to support the Second International, and that a majority of them were ardently pro-Allied and "interventionist." Although the issue would seem to have been extraneous to the purposes of the UGT-CNT alliance, many Cenetistas felt a sense of outrage over the Socialists' desire to depart from absolute neutrality, and they professed to believe that this desire endangered the Pact of Zaragoza. They reproached the UGT leaders, recalling in somewhat martyred tones the sacrifices they had made in terms both of their doctrines and of their feelings in joining an alliance with the Socialists. The Cenetistas were especially irritated by a circular that the PSOE had recently sent to the constituent unions of the UGT, inquiring whether or not they favored some sort of Spanish intervention in the war. This was regarded as a violation of the Pact of Zaragoza, and the Committee of the CNT's Catalonian Regional Confederation (CRT) decided to send a delegate, José Borobio, to Madrid to talk the matter over with the UGT leaders. The resulting session was highly unpleasant for all concerned. Borobio lectured the Ugetistas on the necessity of refraining from pro-Allied activities and devoting their time to preparations for the approaching general strike; and he warned that failure to heed his advice might break the alliance between the two organizations.[104]

The Socialist leaders endured Borobio's lecture with mounting irritation, and responded angrily. Besteiro accused the Cenetistas of having waged a "Germanophile campaign"; and he reminded Borobio that there was no way for the UGT to prevent its members from expressing themselves as they wished, even if they chose to support the Entente. The UGT, he said, would shape its policy toward the war by consulting the views of the trade-union organizations that composed it, without reference to the Pact of Zaragoza. Largo Caballero, who was far from being ardently pro-Allied, added, with ill-concealed annoyance, that since the Pact was with the CNT rather than with the CRT, the matter should have been brought up, if at all, by the former organization. He further observed that the whole thing could have been handled best by mail, and that the Ugetistas could not help resenting the unnecessary sending of an emissary.* The affair, then, left a bad taste on both sides, and did little to strengthen labor solidarity on the eve of the approaching general strike.[105]

Disillusioned though they might be with their Socialist allies, the Cenetistas' revolutionary spirit continued to grow vigorously as May turned into June. The insubordination of the Military Juntas in the latter month encouraged them to declare openly their determination not to experience "the shame of still having a king by the time the armistice is signed."[106] This did not mean that they necessarily supported the establishment of a republic. It is true that some Syndicalist leaders did: Seguí, and apparently Pestaña, saw the republic

---

* One must admit that the Borobio mission had an air of provocation about it. The Anarchist elements in the CRT were ambivalent about that Pact in any case, and some would certainly have sabotaged it if they could.

as a logical first step toward their long-range goals. But the majority of Anarchosyndicalist militants were much less certain of the value of bourgeois-democratic institutions, and their support for them was highly conditional: "The Republic? Do we fight for the Republic? The people will say so, and we cannot and will not do anything but follow the people wherever they wish to go."[107] Later, *Solidaridad Obrera* would admit that if the monarchy had fallen in 1917 and a republic been set up in its place, "It would have been welcomed, but only in the certainty that on the following day we would be its ... adversaries."[108] In general, the Anarchosyndicalists regarded a democratic republic as little more than a stepping-stone to be quickly trod under foot as the proletariat moved on toward *comunismo libertario*, the apolitical and egalitarian Anarchist society of the future.

CHAPTER THREE

The Spanish Revolution of 1917

For belligerents and neutrals alike, 1917 was the hardest year of the war. The warring nations, already shaken by the profitless bloodletting of the previous year's offensives, lost all hope for an early end to the fighting as the peace initiatives of the winter of 1916–17 foundered on the rocks of obduracy and bad faith. The war went on with undiminished violence and with unaltered tactical conceptions. After the Somme and Verdun, it might have been supposed that the inability of frontal assaults to crack fortified entrenchments had been demonstrated. But in the spring of the new year the technique of straightforward thrusts was again revived, and on an even larger scale than before. The bloody and abortive Nivelle Offensive of April, which came close to wrecking the French Army, was followed by the equally vast and useless slaughter of General Haig's four-month campaign in Flanders, the latter producing gains so slight that small-scale maps could not detect them. Nor were horizons less clouded elsewhere. The Russians, having tasted ephemeral victory and calamitous defeat in 1916, approached final exhaustion. The Germans, who had all but knocked their giant opponent out of the war, were confronted by America's entry, by a tightening blockade, and by the gradual containment of the submarine offensive on which so many hopes had rested. The Habsburg monarchy, reeling with fatigue, was kept in the war only by massive injections of German aid. The Italians, seemingly on the verge of victory after two years of fighting on the Isonzo, would be plunged into disaster at Caporetto in October.

The failure to halt the conflict by the close of 1916 implied nothing less than the end of the old Europe. The new year of 1917 would be the watershed of the war and, one may say, of the twentieth century—an axial year, a violent corridor of compressed time through which Europeans would move irrevocably away from the world of 1914. By early spring it was apparent that the war, whatever its origins or original objectives, had become essentially a revolutionary force. Waged for thirty months with a minimum of strategic or tactical vision but with an ever-expanding commitment of resources, the struggle had begun to generate almost intolerable pressures within the warring nations. These pressures overwhelmed the Russian monarchy in March; and they triggered a submerged revolutionary movement that ran like a seismic disturbance through much of the rest of Europe during the course of 1917. There were military mutinies in France, sharply increased strike activity in Britain, bread strikes, a naval mutiny, and the formation of workers' councils in Germany, food riots in Austria-Hungary, and violent antiwar demonstrations in the cities of northern Italy.

The neutral nations, economically linked to the belligerent powers, could not escape the general crisis, Spain least of all.[1] The war, easily penetrating the fragile shell of Spanish neutrality, aggravated most of the nation's problems and evoked the major politico-social upheaval that had long been latent. Whereas Russia collapsed in revolution because she was the most ill-constituted of the belligerents, Spain nearly met the same fate in the summer of 1917 because she was the least viable of the neutrals. If a Spanish military contribution to the war had been attempted, on whatever scale, it seems almost certain that the Bourbon monarchy would have suffered a final erosion of support and joined the Romanov dynasty in its fall.[2]

The disturbances in Spain during the summer of 1917 naturally lacked the tragic grandeur and far-reaching impact of the Russian Revolution. But however deficient in high drama, they nonetheless constituted an authentic revolutionary experience that marked the effective end of the Canovite system after more than four decades.[3] Like the Russian Revolution, the Spanish revolt was a product of long-term "structural" stresses in a backward, mostly agrarian society and was precipitated by a politico-economic crisis resulting from the war. But unlike the upheaval in Russia, the Spanish movement was almost wholly urban, not being supported by an agrarian uprising with which it might have interacted. Whereas in Russia there had been a convergence of the main revolutionary forces (urban, agrarian, and military), in Spain these forces showed a striking lack of coordination. The discontent of the officer corps, which in any case had not yet penetrated the lower ranks, was partially appeased in June, some weeks before the Catalan-led bourgeoisie made their bid for power in a July meeting of the Assembly of Parliamentarians. The middle classes, in turn, fearful of the rising spontaneity of the masses, drew back from the subsequent revolutionary strike waged by the Socialist and Anarchosyndicalist workers in August. And the workers, defeated, lapsed into apathy well before the Southern peasants were roused to the quasi-revolutionary outbreaks that began in the summer of 1918. Thus Spain revealed most of the revolutionary forces that produced the Russian Revolution, including minority nationalism and an increasingly rebellious intelligentsia; but these forces, by failing to converge, spent themselves in a series of separate and ineffectual blows that weakened but did not destroy the monarchical edifice.[4]

The Military Revolt

The first phase of the revolutionary cycle of 1917 was initiated by the Army—more specifically, by the officer corps—from motives that were neither revolutionary nor even authentically regenerationist but, for the most part, narrowly professional. As with the nobiliary reaction that touched off the French Revolution of 1789, it would be a pardonable exaggeration to say that for Spain, in 1917, the counterrevolution preceded the revolution. Like the *noblesse* of the Old Regime, Spanish officers in this period were more concerned with status and income than with political democracy, social equality, or national revitalization. The roots of the Army's insubordination reached well back into the nineteenth century, when, as a result of incessant civil war and the weakness of Spanish institutional life, the military had been forced to become the political arbiter of the country. This resulted in a thoroughly politicized Army, and even though the Canovite system had attempted to reassert the primacy of civilian authority, many officers could not forget the dominant role they had once played.[5]

After the catastrophe of 1898, however, the Spanish people, with rare unanimity, resolved that their country should renounce, along with its colonies, any larger role in world affairs and should shun military involvements. Like Spain herself the Spanish Army thereby lost its raison d'être, along with its vision of the future tasks and goals on behalf of which it might have organized and disciplined itself. Spaniards, on the whole, preferred not to think about the Army, just as they preferred not to think about the importunate demands of the emerging proletariat. Indeed, though set apart from the workers by barriers of class and caste, the officer corps in the early twentieth century shared with the labor movement a similar sense of rejection and isolation within Spanish society.

The result of this was a kind of psychological secession, by which the officers turned themselves into a subculture nourished, like that of the Socialists and the Syndicalists, on a relatively closed and simple set of assumptions centering around its own preeminent role in national life. Toward all other social groups—politicians, intellectuals, regional bourgeoisie, workers, and peasants—the officers felt chiefly hostility and suspicion, conjoined with a vague sense of superiority. Not unlike the Syndicalists, they succumbed to an egoism that encouraged them to dismiss or minimize the claims of other groups and to assume their right, or even duty, to impose themselves on the nation. Bitter because of the Army's decline, and increasingly conscious of their own unpopularity, many officers might have been tempted to echo a phrase from the *Internationale*, saying, We have been nothing; we shall be all. This angry and somewhat paternalistic mentality, forged in the difficult years after 1898 and hardened by the fighting in Morocco, was accentuated by stresses resulting from the war.[6]

The war necessarily drew renewed attention to the unreadiness of the Army, making more evident than ever the regime's failure to maintain an acceptable level of military training and equipment. From 1914 to 1916 there were extensive debates in the Cortes regarding Army modernization, but, as with so many Peninsular problems, little effective action was taken. The Spanish Army, viewing from the sidelines the extraordinary evolution of military technology on the Western Front, remained one of the most backward forces in Europe. Although military expenses frequently consumed 25 percent of the total budget, and in some years more than 50 percent, it was the astonishing superabundance of officers (the ratio was about one officer to seven enlisted men, the highest in Europe) that took the lion's share of military expenditures. Thus 60 percent of the military budget went for officers' salaries, 30 percent for the troops, and 10 percent for equipment.[7] Nevertheless, most officers were ill-paid, and, as Stanley Payne has observed, they remained exceptionally bureaucratic in outlook, being less concerned with the chronic disorganization of the Army than with their own inadequate incomes and slow promotions.[8]

The inflation caused by the war, which was especially rapid early in 1917 because of the intensified German submarine campaign, hurt the military caste at least as much as it did the workers. It may have hurt them more, since the workers could join unions, threaten strikes, and win raises, even though these might not keep up with the steeply ascending cost of living. Moreover, the officer corps had traditionally been a path of advancement for the provincial lower-middle classes, and the task of maintaining a measure of gentility on subaltern's wages, always difficult, was now much greater. It is not surprising that a threadbare and demoralized officer corps should have envied the victories that the organized workers, especially in Catalonia and the North, were winning over employers whose intransigence was softened by high profits.

As a result of the workers' example, something of the Syndicalist mentality was absorbed by the officers, and before long one would hear satirical references to their Juntas de Defensa as the "sindicato único del gremio de la espada."[9] This is not to say, of course, that the officers viewed the workers sympathetically. Though as a rule they held no strong socioeconomic views, they were generally hostile to the labor movement, of whose realities they had little comprehension. Their animus arose partly from their historic role as the defenders of the Canovite system against plebeian turbulence and partly from their commitment to a highly centralist, if somewhat nebulous, conception of patriotism —centered largely on loyalty to the monarch—that led them to view all class and regionalist appeals in a sinister light.[10]

The officer corps, then, was not happy in the spring of 1917. Its discontent had perhaps three basic sources: the inability of the regime to sustain a viable military establishment; the impact of war-induced inflation; and a growing system of favoritism, centered around the king, under which the granting of rewards, decorations, and promotions became less and less fair, equity being defined by the disaffected officers always in somewhat bureaucratic terms. It was this last issue, particularly, that finally drove them to a frenzy of organizational activity and precipitated the crisis in crown-military relations.

The immediate background to the military crisis of 1917 was the steady encroachment of the king upon constitutional restraints designed to prevent excessive royal influence over the Army. Almost from the beginning of his reign, Alfonso had sought to secure his position by making the officer corps personally loyal to himself. The Minister of War, constitutionally required to countersign all royal decrees dealing with the military, increasingly became less a check upon the king than an instrument of the royal will. And in January 1914 a royal order of dubious constitutionality openly authorized selected officers—those enjoying the special favor the king—to communicate directly with the monarch without the inconvenience of going through the Cabinet.[11]

Until about the end of 1915, however, promotions and awards were generally handled on the basis of seniority. This harmonized with the officers' conception of their rank as a "permanent bureaucratic status, unrelated to merit, ability, service, activity, or competition."[12] But when the Liberals came to power in December 1915 established procedures began to break down: the king interfered in personal matters with increasing frequency; and two *camarillas*, the King's Military Household and a group centering around the Minister of War, gained decisive influence, arrogating to themselves the distribution of preferments. There arose a system of favoritism that benefited basically two groups: the Africanistas, that is, young officers who, through combat merits earned in often hazardous service in Morocco, hoped to accelerate their progress up the Army's bureaucratic pyramid; and selected officers, mostly generals, who had won the favor of the palace clique and the political oligarchs. Discontent was greatest among the home garrison officers of the infantry and cavalry arms. The engineers and the artillery were less disturbed because they had long avoided political favoritism through a strict system of promotion by senority, the *escala cerrada*.

Infantry and cavalry officers, then, felt increasingly neglected and mistreated Their anger was directed against the merit system, the Africanistas, the palace clique, the political generals, and the parliamentary politicians. What they wanted was more pay, more equality, more respect, and more reliance on seniority. They sought their remedies first in the formation of organizations of the trade-union or mutual-protection type known as the Juntas de Defensa and second in a demand for the escala cerrada. Somewhat lower in their priorities was the problem of the Army's military prowess and technical efficiency. The literature of the movement reveals the desire for strict adherence to seniority to be the leitmotiv, and it is difficult to escape the conclusion that the military crisis of 1917 was essentially a revolt of the bureaucrats.[13]

This is not to say that the officers' movement was entirely devoid of higher goals. Although the Juntas were never antimonarchical, despite the illusions of the Left, they recognized to some degree that the root of their problems was the reigning oligarchy. A few officers, at least, understood that the basic military reforms they desired were impossible of achievement within a regime so riddled with nepotism and favoritism. Purely professional concerns thus led toward an interest in political and social reforms and in national renovation; but since this interest was not rooted in any definite ideas or any profound understanding of the national crisis, it did not prove very durable.[14]

It has often been said that the controversy over seniority threatened the solidarity of the Army, but it would appear to have had the opposite effect. The discontent produced by royal favoritism seems to have unified the great bulk of the officers, from colonels down to lieutenants, who were neither Africanistas nor the recipients of favors from the king, against the generals and a relative handful of officers who had committed their careers to the hazards of Moroccan service. This is borne out by the fact that when the disgruntled officers began to form Juntas late in 1916, they were able to organize rapidly in garrisons all over Spain, with the exception of two locations: Madrid and Morocco. The Juntas crystallized very quickly between November 1916 and April 1917, but not until May was a Junta finally organized in the Madrid garrison.[15]

The first impulse toward the formation of the Juntas came from the Barcelona garrison, which, located in a center of regionalist agitation and indiscipline, liked to regard itself as a champion of national unity and civic order.[16] The growth of the movement was speeded by the resentment of young officers toward an antimilitary campaign then going on in the Catalan press. The organizing committee in Catalonia was headed by the liberal Col. Benito Márquez, and the earliest Juntas were those of Barcelona, Lérida, Tarragona, and Gerona. Generals were excluded; and since decisions of the Juntas were taken by majority vote, the opinions of lieutenants and captains tended to predominate.[17] The initial and basic objective was the adoption of the escala cerrada by the Infantry.

The rapid formation of the Juntas did not take the government by surprise. Count Romanones received numerous reports on their progress but delayed taking effective measures against them. King Alfonso also knew of them and, after an initial hesitation, had decided to welcome them, encouraging some of his generals to do likewise; he perhaps imagined that the Juntas could be kept subordinate to himself as one more extraconstitutional means of royal influence over the Army. Although half-hearted attempts to dissolve the Juntas were made between January and May under the Romanones and García Prieto ministries, they continued to grow in power, to the point that the government no longer had the means to control them even if it had the will. It was only now that the king, realizing he could not command the Juntas, decided that really vigorous measures had to be used against them. On May 26 the Minister of War, General Aguilera, acting with the advice and consent of the king but not, it would seem, with that of the Cabinet as a whole, ordered the arrest and court-martial of the twelve leaders of the Barcelona Junta. These officers, having assumed leadership of the movement throughout the Peninsula, had refused to sign a declaration dissolving all Juntas. From the standpoint of constitutional law the arrests were doubtless a proper step; but tactically they came too late, since the Juntas were now thoroughly organized and conscious of their power. Aguilera's action succeeded only in precipitating a countercoup by the military.[18]

The situation was now extremely tense, and there is little doubt that the country was on the verge of a military insurrection. Demonstrations of support for the Barcelona Junta came from garrisons all over Spain, and the García Prieto government was soon aware that it lacked the necessary forces to enable it to prevail. Demoralized by their own evident weakness, the ministers immediately offered limited concessions and were able to keep the crisis from escalating. The court-martial proceedings against the imprisoned officers were suspended, and the Captain General of Barcelona, General Alfau, who had carried out the arrests and who now refused to reverse himself, was recalled. General Marina, a popular, fair-minded officer brought in to replace Alfau, was immediately presented with an ultimatum from the Barcelona Junta (which had been quickly reconstituted by other officers of the garrison) demanding politely but forcefully the release of the arrested officers and official recognition of the Juntas. While Marina was debating what to do about this, and reflecting on the fact that none of the other military forces were prepared to back him in a showdown with the infantry, King Alfonso intervened once more. On June 10, taking the matter out of the hands of all his advisers and acting with questionable legality, he simply ordered the freeing of the arrested officers. The García Prieto ministry, hopelessly at odds with the Army and now, in effect, repudiated by the monarch, resigned on June 11. Its passing marked the beginning of the end of the Restoration regime as an autonomously functioning system of parties and the effective subordination of civil government to military fiat.

The colonels of the Junta Superior, who now assumed a position of virtual hegemony over Spanish life, were more obscure than distinguished; but they had the power, if not actually to govern Spain, to decide who would or would not do so. During the next six months the Army, as the arbiter of Spanish politics, would compel legalization of the Juntas, depose two cabinets, quash a revolutionary general strike, obtain a War Minister of its own choice (La Cierva), and order the closing of the Cortes. The greatest disappointment of the otherwise victorious Juntas was that the Conservative leader Antonio Maura, with whom they vaguely associated the idea of a purifying and disciplining revolution from above, would not accept power from their hands.[19]

Although the Juntas' coup could not be construed as a genuinely revolutionary action, since few officers were interested in sweeping reforms, their defiance of the state nevertheless served as the catalyst of a more authentic movement. It brought into focus all the deeper discontents with the Restoration system that had been growing for years and had been sharpened as a result of the dislocations produced by the war. Socialists, Cenetistas, Republicans, Radicals, Reformists, and Regionalists were all galvanized into action by the audacity of the Juntas; or, more accurately, their already rising movement of revolutionary protest suddenly gained new momentum as a result of the military revolt. Although the Army's amour propre—its insistence upon a privileged position and its obsession with Morocco—had for some time estranged it from the progressive forces in Spain, the men of the political Left were, on the whole, delighted with the Army's resistance to the king. Their revolutionary aspirations, already brought close to the surface by the economic crisis and by thwarted pro-Allied sentiment, were stimulated even more. A curious illusion of oneness with the officers possessed many leftists. On the basis of a few phrases about "renovation" in the Juntas' manifestos of June 1 and June 25, they were led to believe that they could work together with the Army in order to displace the monarchy and to regenerate the country politically and economically.[20]

When King Alfonso, failing to discern the political springtime that had unexpectedly blossomed with the fall of García Prieto, appointed not a regenerating figure but the tired and politically somewhat destitute Eduardo Dato to head the new government, the opposition's cup of discontent overflowed. The enemies of the Restoration system—workers, left-bourgeoisie, and regionalists—began to unite against this stubborn reaffirmation of the Turno, hoping, or even expecting, that the Army would be with them either actively or passively. Early in June a Republican-Socialist-Reformist alliance, to which the Cenetistas loosely adhered, began to solidify, and for a while it seemed that the Catalan Regionalists might also be counted on. However, the Dato government came into power prepared to save the monarchy by immediate and substantial concessions to the Juntas. These concessions, the foremost of which was the prompt approval (June 12) of the seniority-oriented *reglamento* drawn up by the officers, dissipated whatever real revolutionary sentiment the Juntas may have had and ensured that the Army would now become the defender rather than the nemesis of the regime. In view of the crucial role that the military has played in most modern revolutions, one may say that the optimum period for revolution in Spain in 1917 was perhaps the ten days from the issuance of the Juntas' ultimatum on June 1 to the resignation of the García Prieto government on June 11—ten days that shook, if not the world, the Spanish Peninsula and saw the disaffection of the military at its height. With the advent of Dato and the Conservatives, the regime's moment of greatest vulnerability had passed.[21]

The Bourgeois Revolution

In Russia, before the March Revolution, the bourgeois moderates in the Duma attempted to save the country by reforming the structure of the state and focusing power in the Duma. The Miliukovs and Maklakovs, however, failed in their efforts to liberalize and stabilize the regime, and the tide of popular revolution, which they had hoped to stem, swept over them. In Spain in 1917 the same role was played by the Catalan bourgeoisie, whose Miliukov was the brilliant leader Francisco Cambó.[22] The Catalan industrial class had been greatly strengthened by the war boom, which had enhanced the economic position of industry relative to agriculture in several parts of the Peninsula. Supported by the Basque and Asturian industrialists, the Catalan middle classes felt increasingly self-confident and willing to challenge the long uncontested political control of the landed interests, with the result that throughout 1916 relations between the Lliga Regionalista (the party of the conservative Catalan bourgeoisie) and the two monarchical parties had steadily deteriorated.[23]

The Regionalists did not fail to sense the peril inherent in the popular revolution that threatened the Peninsula, but they were more conscious of the promise it held out for a restructuring of the Spanish state. Their situation was paradoxical: like the bourgeois rebels of 1848, they were on the one hand a revolutionary class with certain advanced views struggling against a landed oligarchy and on the other hand a conservative class vis-à-vis the industrial proletariat. All things considered, and in the Spanish context, they played a progressive role. Their fervent desire, as Cambó said, was to "de-Africanize" Spain and make it a part of European society. They did not wish to abolish the monarchy but to democratize and decentralize it. They were regionalists who wished to transcend regional boundaries. Cambó's great goal was to convert the Lliga into the nucleus of a broad political coalition that would attract as much popular support as possible and would also combine the industrial and mercantile bourgeoisie of all Spain in a struggle against the landed and financial oligarchy centered in Madrid and Andalusia. In this way he hoped to revitalize the whole country from Catalonia—that is, to submerge the Catalan problem in the wider problem of Spain and to achieve particularist goals through the rise of a federative "Great Spain."[24]

Thus the Catalan capitalists saw their opportunity in the rising wave of revolutionary feeling and in the crisis created by the Military Juntas. They resolved to try to ride the gathering social storm, to take charge of the revolutionary situation into which the country was sliding, and to lead all the classes and regions of Spain in an attempt to wrest power from the oligarchy. Cambó, as Aunós Pérez has said, was going to try the boldest and riskiest of all political maneuvers: though essentially a conservative spirit, "He intended ... to unite all the revolutionary forces of the country in a compact body in order to launch them as a kind of battering ram against the decayed fortress of the *turnante* parties."[25]

Cambó and the Regionalists made it clear that the revolutionary path was not their first choice, that they preferred to reconstruct the country legally, through the meeting of a constituent Cortes; and they joined in urging the government to reopen the Cortes that Romanones had suspended on February 27. Nevertheless, the military crisis of June 1 was immediately perceived by Cambó as a moment of historic importance—chiefly because the monarchy had for the first time lost its military bulwark—and he was resolved to take advantage of it. On June 15 the Lliga issued a manifesto, from the dying hand of the Catalanist leader Prat de la Riba, that set forth the basic autonomist objectives of the bourgeois revolution. Not long after this Cambó traveled to Madrid, where he again urged the opening of the Cortes and visited a number of political figures, including Pablo Iglesias, whose cooperation he asked and to whom he offered a seat in the proposed provisional government.[26]

On July 5 a Lliga-inspired meeting was held in the Ayuntamiento of Barcelona, attended by virtually all of Catalonia's deputies and senators, and representing nearly all political parties. The June 25 manifesto of the Juntas was circulated, and Cambó charitably described the Junta uprising as an "explosion of patriotism" that could and should lead to the regeneration of Spain. As its main order of business, this gathering again asserted the need for Catalonian autonomy and for a federative reorganization of the Spanish state. Most crucial was the demand for an immediate meeting of the Cortes, which would function as a constituent assembly in drafting a new political order. It was resolved, finally, that if this point were not at once conceded, the Lliga would summon an extraordinary—and presumably constituent—assembly, to be held in Barcelona on July 19. Cambó's speech here suggested the delicacy of the Lliga's situation, caught as it was between the obduracy of the government and the radicalism of the leftists. Just as, before the meeting, he had warned of the "danger" of prolonging the existing situation in Spain, so now he stressed the urgent need "to channel the desires of the nation before irreparable consequences supervene."[27] It was evident that he wished to prevent a social revolution by making a political revolution, since, as he said, "the most conservative thing in the circumstances was to be a revolutionary."[28]

Prime Minister Dato, whose party would be a minority in the Cortes and who feared public interrogation about his and the king's concessions to the Juntas, was not in the least tempted to reconvene the parliament, whether as a constituent body or otherwise, since he was certain that this would only trigger the revolutionary movement he feared. He therefore rejected the demands of the Lliga and denounced the proposed extraordinary assembly, saying that if it were held it would constitute a "truly seditious act" punishable by law.[29] The Catalans sarcastically responded by telegram, saying that such zeal in the defense of the constitutional prerogative ill became those who had turned the whole of Spanish political life into a "fiction."[30] They went ahead with their plans.

Dato, in turn, immediately suspended constitutional guarantees and imposed a strict censorship. The Regionalists' demands, coming so soon after the military coup, created an atmosphere charged with tension and revolutionary expectation. The days between July 5 and July 19 were filled with clandestine meetings and manifestos, with rumors and exhortations, and, from the government side, with threats, remonstrances, and the wholesale confiscation of newspapers. What had been a dialogue between the Lliga and the regime now became a diatribe. In the conservative press accusations were spread that the Catalonian movement was, in fact, "separatist," or that at the very least its goals were the establishment of a pro-Allied federal republic and Spain's intervention in the war.[31] The only leftist criticism came from the Cenetistas, who, unreconciled to their class enemies and indifferent to nationalist appeals, said that the July 5 resolutions were merely an "anchor" to which the Catalan bourgeoisie wished to cling in order to halt the approaching "avalanche" of the popular revolution.[32]

That Cambó feared the possibility of a violent popular revolution cannot be doubted. When it became clear that the Dato government would not accede to the demand for a constituent Cortes, and that the July 19 meeting would be held, the Lliga distributed a circular urging the Catalan people to avoid all public demonstrations, to stay at work in their shops and factories, to avoid gathering in the streets, and "not to proffer *gritos* or *vivas* of any kind."[33] Even more revelatory of the cautious, legalistic mood of Cambó and his colleagues was a confidential message that the Lliga sent to all its supporters who held municipal offices in Catalonia, advising them how to deal with possible popular reactions to the anticipated arrest of the Parliamentarians. They were told that, above all, the indignation of the people should not take violent forms, and that if a clearly revolutionary situation arose, they should work to preserve order, aided by "the persons of greatest authority" in the region. Most important, they should be on guard against "outsiders" who might come into the province wishing to foment a revolt.[34]

The government showed not the least passivity in the face of the challenge leveled by the Lliga and its allies. On July 19, Barcelona resembled an occupied city, with security police and Guardia swarming everywhere. The Ayuntamiento, in the Plaza of San Jaime, was surrounded, and all other probable meeting halls were under close surveillance. But the Parliamentarians had also made their preparations. The delegates gathered at a certain hour in a predetermined place unknown to the authorities, where they divided into groups, entered taxis, and began to cruise randomly through the city, with the confused police, who had picked up the scent, attempting to follow them in cars. Just as it seemed that the bourgeois revolution would be dispersed amid the traffic of Barcelona, the one person in each group who knew where the Assembly was to meet ordered his cab driver to proceed to the Restaurante del Parque. Here the delegates, innocently enough, had lunch, after which they walked quickly to the nearby Palacio de la Ciudadela, which was the headquarters of the Executive Committee of the Exposition of Electrical Industries and was not guarded by the police. When all were gathered—by about 5:15 P.M.—the president of the Assembly, Don Raimundo de Abadál, broke the expectant silence and declared, "The Assembly is constituted." This produced a great ovation from the delegates, with the non-Catalans shouting "Visca Cataluña!" and the Catalans crying "Visca España!" The tone of the meeting, conducted of course in Castilian, would deliberately be very *españolista*.[35]

Some 68 deputies and senators from all parts of Spain were present, of whom 46 were Catalans; this was approximately one-tenth of the membership of the suspended Cortes. One of the disappointments of the occasion was the refusal, despite urging by Cambó, of Maura or any of his followers to attend the Assembly, which was thereby given a leftist coloration (because of the presence of the Republicans and Socialists) not entirely pleasing to the Lliga. The Regionalists had earlier hoped that the June crisis would be resolved by naming Maura rather than Dato as Prime Minister. Indeed the extreme efforts made by Cambó to prevent any revolutionary incidents in connection with the Assembly had been designed to win the approval not only of the Army but of Maura as well.[36]

A previously formed committee of notables[37] had already prepared a list of resolutions, and these were quickly passed by the delegates, who expected to be interrupted at almost any moment. The government was denounced as an obstacle to fundamental reform, and the Assembly affirmed the absolute necessity of settling the new organization of the state by means of a new and constituent Cortes. It was further resolved that the Cortes could not be convened by the Turnante parties, who would inevitably "adulterate" the suffrage, but only by a government that truly represented the "sovereign will of the country." With respect to the uprising of the Juntas, the Assembly asserted the necessity that the action of the officers lead to a "profound renovation" of the nation's life, lest it otherwise lose in the eyes of the nation the character of a patriotic initiative and become no more than "a sterile act of indiscipline."

The military crisis, then, had to be given a political solution.[38] Finally, the Assembly formed three commissions: one to deal with constitutional reform; one to deal with national defense, education, and justice; and one (headed by Pablo Iglesias) to deal with social and economic problems. These groups were to prepare reports that would be considered at a future meeting of the Assembly.

As the members of the commissions were being chosen, police began surrounding the building, under orders to disperse the Assembly. The police chief of the city, Bravo Portilla, followed by a colonel and several men of the Guardia, entered respectfully holding their tricorn hats in their hands. There followed a series of exchanges so decorous and restrained, so marked by gravity and noble declamation, that the whole affair seemed like a gathering of stage Romans in some neoclassic drama. President Abadál conveyed to Bravo Portilla the essentially revolutionary tenor of the gathering by calmly asserting that the members of the Assembly, "as the embodiment of the Legislative Power, could neither heed nor submit to the orders of any other power." The serenity, firmness, and moderation with which these words were uttered, says Pabón, "paralyzed" the agents of the government, who withdrew in confusion as the work of the Assembly continued.[39]

The civil governor of Barcelona, Leopoldo Matos, now entered the chamber determinedly, only to be courteously informed that he would be regarded as another delegate and given a chair next to the presidential table—provided he would agree to talk "man to man" without reliance on coercive force. The disconcerted governor gradually let his voice drop to a conversational tone and quietly urged the Parliamentarians to disband, to which Abadál again serenely responded that the Assembly was resolved to yield to nothing less than "brute force." Politely acknowledging Matos's great personal merits, he informed him that the Assembly nevertheless recognized no higher authority than its own and therefore could not comply with his orders. At this point Abadál began to read the resolutions of the Assembly, imperturbably ignoring the governor's efforts to declare the meeting dissolved. In the end, Matos brought some 70 Guardia into the room and, placing his hand lightly on the shoulder of each deputy, in order to symbolize "brute force," arrested all the assembled Parliamentarians one by one; they obediently filed out, only to be released from custody outside the building.[40]

The restraint of the whole performance reflected—and was only made possible by—the desire of the Dato government not to create a violent scene but to pass the affair off as of little consequence. This coincided with the desire of the Parliamentarians, manifested in their determinedly calm demeanor, to keep talking as long as they could, since they realized that every minute the Assembly survived added to its importance. In the end, by managing to meet at all and to pass its resolutions, however hurriedly, the Assembly would seem to have gotten the better of the bargain. However, by preventing violence, the government had astutely avoided striking the spark that in a highly charged atmosphere might have touched off a revolutionary outburst. As it was, news of what had happened spread rapidly through the city, and the Parliamentarians were greeted with great popular acclaim wherever they presented themselves.[41]

Aside from a strike launched in Valencia, the most demonstrative support for the Assembly came, ironically, from the "apolitical" Cenetistas of Barcelona, who were by this time bursting for action of any kind. As Victor Serge said, the National Committee of the CNT "did not ask itself any fundamental questions. It entered the battle without knowing its ultimate perspective or assessing the consequences of its action." Of course, it could scarcely do otherwise, since it was "the expression of an expanding power which could not remain inactive." The idea of seizing Barcelona was seriously discussed by the Anarchosyndicalists, but in the end they expended their energies in sporadic demonstrations and street violence, which accomplished little but the letting off of steam. "We were beaten," wrote Serge somewhat dramatically, "in a day of sunshine and shouting, of impetuous crowds and chases in the streets, while the cautious black hats charged lazily and pursued us without enthusiasm."[42]

Before their dispersal the Parliamentarians had not failed to schedule another meeting of the Assembly, to be held in Oviedo on August 16. By that date, however, the moderate and legalistic initiative of Cambó and the Lliga would be overtaken and left behind by the revolutionary effort of the Socialists and their allies, who launched a general strike on August 13. Thus the Assembly effort, which had sought to unite a broad spectrum of progressive forces extending from Mauristas to Socialists, had in effect failed. It is difficult to avoid the conclusion, moreover, that the failure hinged on the "defection" of Maura, whose reluctance to participate, after a career spent in eulogizing the idea of a conservative "revolution from above," will perhaps never be entirely explicable. Where he would ever have found a more legal or moderate revolution than that led by Cambó was not clear. The abstention of the Mauristas seriously weakened Cambó's claim that the Lliga was at the head of a "national" movement, even as it strengthened the threatened regime's contention that the Assembly represented only a factious minority of Regionalists and leftists.

Perhaps even more crucial was the fact that only Maura could have served as a bridge between the Assembly and the Junta officers, who greatly admired him. Vital as it was for the Juntas to raise their self-centered protest to a higher political plane by means of the Assembly, this was almost impossible for them when that body was canted so far to the Left. The political discernment of the officers was never remarkable, and to them the Assembly was nothing more than an alliance of Regionalists, Republicans, and Socialists, all of whom aimed at "separation."[43] Nevertheless, in the period after July 19 there seemed to be a continuing possibility that the Juntas and the Assembly might yet effect a rapprochement on the basis of their common desire for a renovating, constituent Cortes. What was no doubt essential, as Pabón has said, was that a situation of order be preserved, which would encourage the officers to move against the government rather than on behalf of it. Cambó, of course, knew of the general strike being planned by the Left, but he hoped that it would not be carried out.[44]

Liberal historians have tended to see the prospects of the Assembly as favorable and have supposed that with a certain amount of luck the monarchical regime might have been both preserved and reformed. They have believed that the parliamentary system, by being enabled to function honestly, could have come to represent the "sovereign will" of the Spanish people—or at least of the nation's vital forces—thereby laying the foundation for a progressive modernization of Spain under the stabilizing aegis of the monarchy. In this way, so the argument runs, the dictatorship of Primo de Rivera, the abdication of the king, the Second Republic, and the Civil War might all have been avoided. Thus Salvador de Madariaga speaks of the "grave but hopeful crisis of 1917, which went by without leaving behind beneficial results of any importance."

> This movement might have been the true salvation of Spain and, in particular, of the monarchical system, had the crown been more convinced of the advantages of a parliamentary form of government and had the hotheads of the labor movement been less convinced of the advantages of revolution. As it happened, the moderate but bold and statesmanlike action of the Parliamentary Assembly fell flat under a combined attack coming from the extremists of the Right and of the Left.[45]

What might have issued from the Assembly, had it not been followed 25 days later by a revolutionary general strike, is impossible to say. Perhaps the Mauristas and then the Juntas would have been drawn into it, in which case the regime would necessarily have been transformed. On the other hand, Maura's antipathy to any "opening to the Left," along with the officers' almost unreasoning suspicion regarding the "separatist" ambitions of the Regionalists, seem, in retrospect, nearly insuperable barriers to the renovating coalition that Cambó envisioned. Leaving this issue necessarily unresolved, we must turn to an examination of the circumstances under which the third revolutionary movement of 1917 was launched—by the "hotheads," as Madariaga calls them, of the labor movement.

The Revolution of the Left

The third and most extreme phase of the Spanish revolutionary movement of 1917 took the form of a general strike intended to usher in a bourgeois-democratic republic. The principal leadership in this was supplied by the Socialists, whose long-standing sense of economic and ideological grievance against the regime had coalesced in early spring with the outraged Aliadofilismo of the Reformists, Republicans, and Radicals. Thus behind the revolutionary purpose of the strike were a variety of motives: acute economic discontent, due to rising inflation and unemployment; anger over the refusal of the monarchy to effect a rapprochement with the Allied Powers, or even to protest the torpedoing of Spanish vessels by German U-boats; democratic desire for a political transformation that would enable Spain to confront the postwar world with dignity; the deepening conviction of labor leaders that only a republic would give the labor movement the free environment needed for its growth; and, finally, an opportunistic recognition that the regime, because of the military uprising, was extremely vulnerable.

The Socialists, in effect, chose to help the Spanish middle classes make the democratic revolution that the latter were too weak to make by themselves, recognizing that the labor movement would greatly benefit thereby. Some Socialist majoritarians (Besteiro, Fabra Ribas, and Torralba Beci would be typical) seem to have shared the republican and pro-Allied motives of the democratic intelligentsia, whereas the minoritarians (one thinks of Largo Caballero, Andrés Saborit, and Isidoro Acevedo) were less susceptible to "Wilsonian" issues and motivated more by the domestic economic failures of the regime. A mixture of motives was also evident among the Catalonian Syndicalists; whereas the "pure" Syndicalists, led by Seguí and Pestaña, accepted the goal of a democratic republic as a necessary transitional step toward a Syndicalist society, the more extreme Anarchosyndicalists hoped, as always, for some vaster transformation; neither group of Cenetistas, of course, was motivated by any concern for the Allied democracies, and both wished to preserve an absolute neutrality.

The general strike of August 1917 would be, above all, a political strike with concrete objectives: the departure of the king, the creation of a provisional government, and the summoning of a constituent Cortes to preside over the restructuring of the national life. The Socialists would agree to participate in the proposed provisional government, but only marginally, in a supervisorial capacity. Consoled by a Marxian vision of inevitable historical stages, they would be resigned to the fact that for some while the preeminent role must be played by the capitalist bourgeoisie, who had to construct the economic edifice that the workers would someday inherit. As the prime movers of the republican movement in 1917 the Socialists would be in a difficult situation, having to try to embolden their Republican allies on their Right even as they sought to restrain the impetuosity of the Anarchosyndicalists on their Left. In the end, the orchestration of forces that they desired would prove impossible to achieve, and the Dato government would succeed in triggering the movement before it was fully prepared.

The origins of the August Movement went back to the Pact of Zaragoza in July 1916, when Ugetistas and Cenetistas had allied themselves for the first time, and to the 24-hour general strike jointly conducted by the UGT and CNT in December of that same year, which had left the impression that much larger efforts would be forthcoming if steps were not taken to resolve the economic crisis. More recently there had been the joint UGT-CNT meeting in the Casa del Pueblo in March, which had issued a manifesto threatening a general strike of unlimited duration within three months unless remedial economic action was taken. Whether this strike, tentatively scheduled for June, would ever in fact have been launched, given the proverbial caution of the Socialists, is an open question.[46] As it turned out, the stream of labor unrest was suddenly merged with the current of general political protest unleashed by the resignation of Romanones in April and the mutiny of the Juntas in May and June. The result of this would be to make explicit in the workers' protest what had only been implicit in Besteiro's March manifesto: the republican and revolutionary goals of the movement.

Nearly all the leftists applauded the revolt of the officers. Melquíades Alvarez, whose views seem to have closely paralleled those of his personal friend Iglesias, viewed the mutiny magnanimously, calling it "the beginning of a national renovation." Speaking, one may say, for nearly all leftists, he added:

> We no longer favor, then, palliatives or timid efforts at reform. If Spain wishes to be saved, it is necessary that the revolution follow its course, and that the Army join with the people in order to build a new regime, which shall be founded on respect for the sovereign will of the nation and shall have as its only ideal the regeneration and progress of the country.[47]

On the whole, Alvarez seems to have imagined that the revolutionary movement, relying on a general strike, could be peaceful. The response of the Radical chieftain Alejandro Lerroux was less measured: he and his followers greeted the defection of the Army with rude rejoicing and offered to send 800 men to free the Junta officers imprisoned in Montjuich.[48] The Socialists showed more restraint. On June 8 the Madrid Socialist Group discussed the situation and, though not going so far as to praise the Juntas, acknowledged that "all that had happened" was attributable to the arbitrariness of the regime. At the same time, they branded the concessions of the government "shameful and unworthy," and firmly opposed the possibility that the civil power might be impaired by the military, and that Maura might be brought in as the savior of the regime and the instrument of reaction.[49]

A few days later Iglesias—who, as usual, was quite ill—spoke in more positive terms about the Juntas. He was gratified that the officers had demonstrated by their actions that they had no love for the monarchical regime, and he noted the parallels between the Juntas' critique of the system and that made by the "progressive elements." If the action of the Juntas could be coordinated with that of all other enemies of the reigning oligarchies, thought Iglesias, the "suppression" of the existing regime could be achieved.[50] But in contrast to this relative optimism, a meeting of Socialist minoritarians presided over by García Cortés assailed the actions of the Juntas in rather violent terms and expressed fears of a military dictatorship. Still, some leftist speakers suggested that the organizing activities of the officers should be imitated by the proletariat, which should encourage the forming of juntas by privates and noncoms.[51]

The general strike, which had been on the agenda for a year and had become more urgent since March, now entered on a phase of serious political preparation. Only a few days after the Juntas delivered their ultimatum to the García Prieto government, representatives of the UGT met with Melquiades Alvarez —who acted as a mediator between the Socialists and the Republicans—in order to create a revolutionary coalition including Socialists and leftists of various shades. By the terms of an agreement signed on June 5, this coalition agreed to work for the establishment of a provisional government, presumably to be headed by Alvarez, whose purpose would be to convene a constituent assembly. The expectation of the Socialists and their allies was that this action would lead to a bourgeois-democratic republic. It was further agreed that if the Army tried to establish a military dictatorship, the general strike would be declared immediately, even though its preparation might not be complete.[52]

The Cenetistas did not sign this pact and were not formally a part of the coalition. In addition to the ideological barriers involved, their old enmity for Lerroux would seem to have prevented any closer rapprochement. Nor was it clear that all Cenetistas accepted the idea of a democratic republic even as a transitional step. Nevertheless, they did collaborate unofficially with the Revolutionary Committee, which was composed of Iglesias (for whom Besteiro substituted), Alvarez, and Lerroux. The Socialists, too, disliked the presence of Lerroux, whom they had denounced on numerous occasions and had excluded from the Republican-Socialist Alliance; but since the death of Nicolás Salmerón, Lerroux had been the Republican leader with the greatest following, and an alliance with him was felt to be unavoidable.*

On June 16, only a few days after the formation of the Dato government—

---

* Among the Cenetistas who worked with the Committee were Seguí, Pestaña, Eusebio Carbó, Eleuterio Quintanilla, and Manuel Buenacasa. It was Buenacasa who traveled to Madrid in June to discuss the strike with the Executive Committee of the UGT. Greeted by Largo Caballero with unexpected cordiality, he was introduced to Iglesias and informed that the UGT had just voted its support for a general strike. Among the Socialists who collaborated most closely with the Committee were Andrés Saborit, Largo Caballero, Indalecio Prieto, Remigio Cabello, Daniel Anguiano, Manuel Cordero, Manuel Llaneza, and Teodomiro Menéndez. The most prominent Republican collaborator was the Catalan deputy Marcelino Domingo. See Saborit, *Julián Besteiro,* pp. 132ff; García Venero, *Historia de las internacionales,* II, 154.

which was badly received by the Left and seems to have spurred revolutionary preparations—the parliamentary groups of the Reformists, Republicans, and Socialists met in Madrid to confirm the agreement that had been reached earlier in the month. Here it was "agreed definitively," as Morato says, to overthrow the political regime because of its "incompatibility with democracy and the impossibility of using it to correct the ever deeper evils from which the country suffered."[53] In mid-July the National Committees of the PSOE and the UGT met and came to two important decisions: it was agreed that Iglesias should attend the upcoming second meeting of the Assembly of Parliamentarians, and, after a lengthy debate, that the question of Socialist participation in a possible provisional government should be decided in the affirmative, with Iglesias accepting a post as minister without portfolio. All members of the PSOE and UGT committees voted in favor of this except Besteiro and Virginia González.[54]

At this point, the movement of the Catalonian Regionalists momentarily overshadowed the rising republican effort, as the Assembly of Parliamentarians held its brief session on July 19. Since many leftists were in attendance, the Revolutionary Committee of the Republicans and Socialists was pushed into the background, and aside from the strike in Valencia and the Cenetista demonstration in Barcelona, no mass labor effort on behalf of the Assembly was carried out. This was, of course, as Cambó had wished it to be; but the Socialist intellectual Luis Araquistáin deplored the fact that no general strike had been launched, calling this the "missed psychological moment" that allowed the government to move from a defensive to an offensive strategy.[55]

That the general strike was not declared resulted simply from the fact that the Socialist leaders had not yet completed their very systematic preparations. With their customary concern for the wider picture, they knew that the allies labor needed for the final struggle were not ready: the left-bourgeois parties were still hanging back, anxious to rebel but uncertain that the time was right; and the support of the Army, which the Socialists considered essential, had not been secured.[56] By contrast, the Cenetistas, especially the more fervent Anarchists among them, were reluctant to grasp the importance of having allies in the struggle. The uprising of the Juntas and the insubordination of the Parliamentarians had greatly stimulated their revolutionary impatience and made them eager to accelerate the launching of the general strike. Iglesias discovered this when, arriving in Barcelona for the meeting of the Assembly, he found himself besieged by the aroused leaders of the CNT, among them Valero, Seguí, Pestaña, and Francisco Miranda.

The interview was less than cordial. Iglesias, Pestaña wrote, "listened to us with a peevish, disagreeable air, which, to tell the truth, bothered us." The old Socialist leader expressed surprise (or perhaps skepticism) at the rapidity with which Cenetista preparations were advancing and simply said that the UGT could not work in that way, and that the Anarchosyndicalists would therefore have to temper their activities. Pestaña reports him as saying, "You, the manual workers, see it thus, but we, the intellectuals, see it in a different way." In the end, the Cenetista leaders, who were being sorely pressed by their febrile followers to begin the revolutionary strike, withdrew, "somewhat in despair" over the fact that the Socialists were determined to continue their (to Cenetista eyes) painfully slow preparations.[57] Indeed, it was not only the Catalonian workers who were impatient. Dolores Ibarruri has described how some of the Vizcayan miners were busily making bombs in this period and impatiently awaiting an initiative from Madrid: "The political temperature was rising. We went without sleep, waiting for the call to action at any moment. Time passed, and there was a risk that our revolutionary ardor would subside. The workers were impatient and began to whisper about the leadership, which had hinted at such momentous events to come."[58]

Iglesias was able to secure from the Barcelona Syndicalists a pledge to wait only four days more before unilaterally launching a revolutionary strike in Catalonia alone. Largo Caballero, to counter this "crazy proposal," then decided to visit Barcelona and talk personally with the Cenetista leaders. When he joined them at a secret night meeting at Valvidriera, in the mountains outside the city, a somewhat violent discussion ensued among the pine trees, during which the angry Anarchosyndicalists waved pistols, fired shots in the air, and vented upon Largo their frustration with the sluggish pace of Socialist planning. Nevertheless, the stolid UGT chieftain was able to convince them of the need for a more coordinated strike effort, and to dissuade them, for the time being, from acting prematurely. Some Cenetistas complained about the growing liaison between the PSOE and the left-bourgeois parties, to which Largo replied that this link was not only vital but had been forged with the approval of both Seguí and Pestaña—a fact confirmed, perhaps with some embarrassment, by the two militants themselves. It is worth noting that the Valvidriera meeting, originally called to launch an independent strike, was presided over by the Anarchist militant Francisco Miranda, then secretary of the CNT National Committee, rather than by Seguí or Pestaña, who were less impatient with the pace of Ugetista preparations and more aware of the need for careful planning. The meeting ended in unfraternal coldness, with the militants walking down the mountainside in twos and threes, while Seguí and Pestaña accompanied Largo and sought, without much success, to placate him for the harsh treatment he had received.[59]

Something of the Cenetistas' state of mind was revealed in a manifesto that their National Committee released in mid-July. In contrast to the limited objectives of the UGT, the demands of this document were numerous, sweeping, and in places less than lucid. Although the Cenetistas supported the overthrow of the monarchy, it was uncertain whether or in what degree they would accept a republic as its successor; thus they agreed to the calling of a constituent assembly but insisted on the right of the sindicatos to veto its decisions. The manifesto offered ameliorative proposals: the seven-hour day, the English Week, a minimum wage, the suppression of piecework, and the abolition of work for children under fourteen. But there were more utopian demands as well: the dissolution of the standing army and its replacement by militia; the abolition of diplomacy; a federation of Europe; the declaration of wars only after a plebiscite and with the proviso that the fighting be done only by those who voted affirmatively; the abolition of tariffs; the abolition of the Senate; the separation of church and state; the dissolution of convents and the closure of churches for an unspecified length of time; a divorce law; municipal and regional autonomy; nationalization of the soil and subsoil, as well as of labor and social security; the establishment of free and compulsory rationalist schools; the prohibition of all spectacles that "corrupt or brutalize" the people, such as bullfights; and the establishment of basic civil liberties. Finally, the manifesto demanded, for the present, the maintenance of absolute neutrality—to be combined with efforts to foment revolution in all the belligerent countries. This manifesto, which was described as "neither a minimum nor a maximum program," appeared to be, like so many Cenetista expressions in this period, a somewhat rudely drafted and uneven compromise between the Anarchist and the more purely Syndicalist tendencies within the CNT.[60]

The Valencia Strike

Simultaneously with the July meeting of the Assembly of Parliamentarians there had broken out in Valencia a premature strike movement that was to have a fatal effect on the fortunes of the impending general strike and on the whole revolutionary movement of 1917. Presumably intended to demonstrate support for the Assembly, the strike (which was joined by the railworkers, without the approval of their unions) expired in a void, with two unfortunate consequences: it left the Valencian workers psychologically depleted and unable to participate effectively in the general strike less than a month later; and it led to a dispute over the discharge of a number of railworkers, whose union retaliated by declaring a national strike of railworkers to start on August 10. This action forced the hand of the UGT leaders, who felt compelled for reasons of solidarity to push up the date of the general strike to August 13, some time before their preparations were completed.

The genesis of the Valencia strike has remained obscure. The impatient Cenetistas, however, cannot be blamed for it, since the Republicans led by Félix Azzati, dominated the labor movement in Valencia at this time. Largo Caballero attributed the outbreak to the Republican deputy Marcelino Domingo, who traveled through the city and convinced the workers that the Assembly needed their support in the form of a strike. It has also been suggested that the strike was begun by two labor figures, Azzati and Ramón Cordoncillo, who were acting as *agents provocateurs* for the Dato government, which understandably preferred to fight one sector of the labor movement at a time.[61]

The Valencia strike ran its course by July 23, and the situation returned to normal in the province. But the Compañía del Norte de Valencia, still angry over the fact that a strike the previous year had compelled them to recognize the Railworkers' Union, now chose to take reprisals, dismissing 35 of the strikers. This stirred up great resentment among the Valencia workers, and the matter was referred to Madrid where a railworkers' commission was already negotiating with the head offices of the Compañía on matters relating to the earlier strike. The railworkers now declared that unless the dismissed employees were rehired, they would call a strike on August 10. This, of course, dismayed the leaders of the UGT, who were still in the midst of planning the revolutionary general strike. Extremely anxious to have the rail stoppage postponed, they brought much pressure to bear on the Railworkers' Union. The railworkers themselves, beginning to realize the inadvisability of their strike, made substantial last-minute concessions, and in the end they demanded only an "explanation" of the firings. On August 8, bowing still further to UGT pressure, they even agreed to postpone the strike. But on the same day the Compañía, as if determined not to let the conflict die out, declared that it would not undertake any discussion of the dismissals, since these were a matter of its "internal rules."

This intransigent attitude was upheld, if not actually inspired, by the Dato government, which refused to intervene. The Minister of Development, the Viscount de Eza, had at first been disposed to place the authority of the government on the side of conciliation and settlement; now, under pressure from Dato and from the Interior Minister, he reversed himself and let the situation slide toward conflict. Consequently, by a one-vote majority, the committee of the Railworkers' Union reaffirmed its decision to call the strike on the tenth, hoping somewhat ingenuously that the Compañía and the government would eventually back down, as they had a year earlier. But the government actually wanted this strike, which promised to precipitate the threatening general strike while its preparations were still incomplete. As the journal *La Tribuna* said, "The workers have fled from the strike and the government has thrown them into it."[62]

In pursuing this policy the government only obeyed the law of self-preservation; and complaints about its duplicity would seem to fall beside the mark, since it was faced with a revolutionary strike whose announced objective was to bring down the monarchical regime. The oligarchs of the Turnante parties in this period may have lost the capacity to govern—indeed, they had never governed creatively—but they seem not to have lost the belief in their right to rule. Perhaps this, in the final analysis, was why the Spanish Republic did not arrive in 1917. Without minimizing the ineptitude of the monarchical parties in most areas, it is difficult to suppress a certain admiration for the cunning and decisiveness with which the Dato government met the revolutionary threat. There was no failure of nerve, and by provoking the strike prematurely the government was able to introduce an element of confusion into it from which it never recovered. At the same time Dato and his Interior Minister, Sánchez Guerra, skillfully drove wedges of mutual suspicion between the Catalonian bourgeoisie and the leftist parties, and also between the Army and the people. In effect, they played the various rebellious groups off against each other and used one crisis, that of labor, to help dampen another, that of the insubordinate officer corps. It is not surprising that a grateful king later awarded the Cross of Charles III to Sánchez Guerra for the role he played in defeating the August Strike.[63]

The August Strike Movement

The men of the Socialist strike committee—Besteiro and Saborit for the PSOE and Largo Caballero and Anguiano for the UGT—made every effort to halt the tide of events. They knew that neither the workers nor the bourgeois leftists were ready, and that to call the strike at this time would probably lead to disaster. But they also understood that the railworkers were resolved to go ahead in the face of the challenge thrown down by the Compañía, and they feared that withholding the support of the UGT would have serious consequences. They were certain that the rail strike, whether officially supported or not, would touch off spontaneous partial strikes all over the country, and these would effectively dissipate the energies needed for the general strike. As Besteiro later acknowledged, the strike committee also feared that a rash of uncontrolled partial strikes might produce "enormous" casualties among workers who clashed with the authorities, for which the Socialists, he thought, would have to bear the responsibility. The result of all this, assuming that the UGT withheld its support, would be absolutely nil; and the disgruntled workers, it was feared, would carry away the feeling that the Socialist leaders were not competent to lead.[64] The Socialists, then, faced a dilemma not dissimilar to that confronted by Lenin and the Bolsheviks a few weeks earlier in Petrograd, during the July Days: the problem of how to ride with a spontaneous but premature surge of the proletariat without being carried to destruction by it.

As soon as the Railworkers' Union reaffirmed its strike date of August 10, the national committees of the PSOE and UGT met to decide on a course of action. Iglesias, who had been ill since his return from the July meeting of the Assembly, sent word from his sickbed that he supported the general strike, but only as a matter of solidarity with the railworkers, since he opposed giving it a political or revolutionary objective. In this he was unanimously overruled;

and the directors of the two Socialist organizations, committing, in effect, the tactical error that Lenin had avoided, decided to begin the general strike on August 13. Thus the summer of 1917 marked the effective eclipse of Pablo Iglesias as the real—as opposed to the symbolic—leader of the Socialist movement. His health had in fact been deteriorating for some time, and he had not been closely involved in the plans or activities of the Party since June 1916, though his advice continued to be carefully weighed. The two foremost leaders in 1917 were thus Besteiro and Largo Caballero, both temperamentally moderate men who were momentarily possessed by a revolutionary optimism that would not prove to be characteristic of either. Their rationale for the pacifistic revolt they were planning seemed to be that the regime was in fact tottering, and that a bourgeois-democratic republic would provide a far more favorable milieu for the expansion of the incipient labor movement than that offered by the monarchy of Alfonso XIII.[65]

The mood of the Socialist leaders was more grim than exalted. When Melquíades Alvarez heard that the railworkers had decided to strike, he hurried from his Oviedo headquarters to Madrid and, after several days of searching, finally located the Socialist strike committee in their hiding place, whereupon he tried to dissuade them from the impending action. They glumly told him that they recognized the unreadiness of the movement and its poor chance of success; but they were convinced that they had no choice but to follow the lead of the railworkers, and rather than break with them they would prefer that all went down to a common ruin. After hearing this uncomforting declaration, Alvarez, somewhat demoralized, returned to Asturias on the last train before the strike began. The only solace he could derive from the situation was that the left-bourgeois parties had not signed the strike manifesto and could perhaps avoid the fate that seemed to await the Socialists. As for the men of the strike committee, the one hope to which they continued to cling was the possibility that the Army might still be a revolutionary force and would either support or condone the strike, thereby rescuing it from disaster.[66]

The strike manifesto, drawn up by Besteiro on August 12 and signed by all the members of the strike committee, was not a radical document but seemed more like a restatement of the demands raised earlier by the Assembly of Parliamentarians. It called for a political rather than a social revolution: there was no question of economic demands on the propertied classes, and the theme of social change was not stressed; in effect, the workers were limiting their objectives to helping the liberal bourgeoisie seize power. The main departure from the position of the Assembly lay in the fact that the Socialist manifesto called for the overthrow of the monarchy. Yet at the same time the workers were urged to avoid violence and to display only fraternal feelings toward the soldiers who might confront them.[67]

The signal for the start of the strike was the publication, in *El Socialista* and in the Republican daily *El País*, of articles that were signed by Besteiro and contained the secret code phrase "cosas veredes." Things began to go wrong almost immediately. The newspapers that carried the code words, the strike manifesto, and some necessary instructions failed in many cases to reach their destinations, the government having thoughtfully sequestered the editions at the Central Post Office. Thus there was difficulty in getting the word to labor groups in many parts of the Peninsula. On August 15 the police discovered, probably through an informer, the hiding place of the strike committee, which was located, appropriately enough, at 13 Calle del Desengaño. The government's statement to the press suggested that the committee members had been discovered hiding under beds and in earthen jars; in fact, they had just sat down to dinner, and, beyond requesting that they be permitted to finish their meal, they offered no resistance.[68]

The next blow, probably not unanticipated, was the defection of the Catalan Regionalists. Frightened by the rising labor movement, the Lliga hastily announced that neither it nor the Assembly of Parliamentarians would take part in the strike. Indeed, throughout the course of the August Movement there was no contact between the Socialists and the bourgeois Regionalists, save for a nervous message from Cambó pleading that assaults on factories or property would be counterproductive.[69] The illusion of Army support, too, was shattered when the officers of the Juntas led their units against the workers without the least hesitation and even with considerable vigor. The workers pathetically cheered the soldiers, as they had been instructed to do, but were met with charges, bullets, and a display of force that went far beyond the demands of the situation. Next, the Republican allies of the Socialists, already alarmed by the precipitancy of the strike, were further demoralized by its disastrous unfolding. With the exception of a few leaders, such as Marcelino Domingo, they failed to support the workers' efforts vigorously. The crowning blow, however, was the fact that the strike, though it grew out of a rail dispute, was not supported by even a majority of the country's railworkers. Those on the Madrid-Zaragoza-Alicante and Madrid-Cáceres-Portugal lines continued work as usual; and Ramón Cordoncillo, head of the Southern Railworkers' Union, refused to lead his workers into the movement, alleging that his union's policy was not to support "political" strikes. Finally, the government spread rumors that Pablo Iglesias had died.[70]

Even so, the strike spread over large areas of Spain. The major centers of disturbance were Madrid, Barcelona, Valencia, Vizcaya, and Asturias, and there were also major stoppages in Huelva, Galicia, Zaragoza, Burgos, Vitoria, Sabadell, and Tarrasa. A notable exception was Andalusia, where, aside from the Río Tinto mines, both urban workers and peasants remained dormant. The Anarchosyndicalists of the region refused their cooperation on the grounds that the strike was political.[71]

In Madrid, the strike got off to a faltering start. Only the bricklayers, bakers, and printers joined it, and at no time did it prove possible to cut off either the water supply or the electrical power of the city. All construction work was halted, and some print shops were closed; but the great daily papers of Madrid continued to publish throughout the strike, since the government had had the foresight to send soldiers and workers from government print shops to replace the striking printers. The only newspapers not published were *El País, El Socialista, España Nueva,* and *El Mundo.*[72]

On the second day, disorientation set in when it was learned that the strike committee had been arrested, and the substitute committee proved unable to step into the breach, not seeming to know what to do. The masses, as Isidoro Acevedo later wrote, were "ready for anything," but they lacked leadership, as well as the weapons that might have enabled them to stand against the essentially punitive actions of the military. Despite the Socialists' advance instructions to make the strike peaceful, some violent disorders broke out in various parts of the city. Many of these were caused by the determination of the Dato government that the trams should continue to run and the equally great determination of the Ugetistas that they should not. One of the most lamentable occurrences of the whole strike took place in the Model Prison, when the inmates responded to the turmoil outside by staging a violent demonstration. Feeling unequal to the task of quelling a near riot, the prison authorities called in troops, and these turned out to be nervous, inexperienced peasant soldiers, who began firing through the bars of the prison galleries, leaving eight dead and thirteen wounded. Still more serious was the use of machine guns against unarmed strikers in the working-class Cuatro Caminos district. Even before the end of the week the strike was defeated in Madrid, having been effectively quelled by the soldiers, who also went around hammering with gun butts on store fronts until the owners opened for business. Thousands of workers stayed in the streets for several more days, displaying dogged loyalty to the cause, but by August 18 the strike was extinguished.[73]

In Barcelona, the CNT ran its strike in virtual independence from the UGT in Madrid. The Revolutionary Committee, entirely distinct from that in the capital, included Seguí, Miranda, Tomás Herreros, José Viadiu, and several others. In contrast to the Ugetistas, who had sought to keep the strike peaceful, the Cenetistas from the start thought in terms of a violent, revolutionary effort.[74] However, Captain General Milans del Bosch had made thorough preparations, and there were reportedly no fewer than 12,000 troops concentrated in the city. A state of war was proclaimed on the thirteenth, machine guns were emplaced at strategic points, and troops were sent on continuous patrols through the streets.

As in Madrid, the strikers at once tried to stop the trams from running; and since the motormen, non-Cenetista workers loyal to the monarchist deputy

Faronda, were guarded by soldiers, shooting broke out. Here, too, the military acted very aggressively, and on the second day of the strike, the Cenetistas began to retaliate. Barricades were set up, and some sharp engagements were fought. The main centers of disturbance in Barcelona were the Plaza de Cataluña, the Ramblas, the University, and the districts of Gracia and Las Atarazanas. There were also some very violent outbreaks in the industrial towns of Gerona and Sabadell, with ten persons being killed in the latter place.

A regrettable aspect of the fighting was the tendency of some Cenetistas to fire at patrolling soldiers from windows and rooftops, using pocket revolvers and frequently shooting from ridiculously long distances. This infuriated the troops, who sometimes responded by firing indiscriminately in all directions. Not a few wounded soldiers were later found to have been struck by Mauser bullets, which were fired only by the troops themselves. The Captain General ordered that window blinds in the city be kept raised at all times; but the sniping continued, and in some cases artillery pieces were turned against apartment buildings in reprisal. For five days most factories, businesses, and shops were closed, and the streets swarmed with soldiers who strictly controlled the movement of all civilians. There were indications, however, that the troops employed in Barcelona were not entirely pliant tools of their officers. Sometimes, when ordered to fire on workers, they persisted in firing into the air; and squads escorting prisoners to jail would sometimes release them when out of sight of superiors.[75]

One of the most active of the Cenetista strike leaders in Barcelona was Angel Pestaña. "I am neither a brave man nor a coward," he later wrote, "and I am unable to attack anyone. . . . But [the strike] was a revolutionary movement of the people, and I, who had proposed and defended the idea that they should make one, was duty-bound to go into the streets and honor my words." Pestaña was delegated by the Barcelona strike committee to act as liaison with the various groups that had joined the movement. He held discussions with Dr. Juliá of the Separatists, with Colonel Macía of the Catalanists, and with the Republican Marcelino Domingo.[76]

One group with which Pestaña certainly did not have contact was the Lliga Regionalista and its adjunct the Assembly of Parliamentarians, whose members kept entirely aloof from the workers' struggle. When, very early in the strike, the rumor circulated that the Lliga had given its support, Cambó and his lieutenants hastily proclaimed to the newspapers that they were in no way responsible for the strike. When the government accused the Lliga of complicity, Assembly spokesman Abadál replied that this assertion was "so absurd that in other times we should not have taken the trouble to answer it." Clearly, Cambó was vitally concerned to dispel the incipient myth that the Lliga had first provoked the strike and then abandoned it.[77]

Gradually, the soldiers of Milans del Bosch leveled the barricades in Barcelona and reduced the various centers of resistance. By the eighteenth, as in Madrid, the strike was over. Some members of the Cenetista strike committee, including Seguí, were arrested, but Pestaña escaped to a small town in Aragon, where he hid for a month before returning to Barcelona. When he finally returned, he was startled to learn that he was not being sought by the police—for the reason that one of the bodies found in the streets had been identified as himself.[78]

In Vizcaya the strike, waged with unusual intensity, was led by Indalecio Prieto in Bilbao and the manufacturing zone and by Facundo Perezagua in the mining regions. By the end of the first day the life of Bilbao had been brought to a virtual standstill, with some 100,000 workers going out on strike. The city's newspapers were not published, and trains and streetcars did not run. Virtually every market, restaurant, and bar was closed, and food was extremely scarce. In contrast to Barcelona, the strike in Bilbao, at least for the first three days, was entirely peaceful. According to Prieto, "Not a single shot was fired against the police, not one, on the part of the people ... not a single soldier was badly treated, no one was injured, and there was no act of aggression against the armed forces." This impression of total peacefulness is confirmed by other observers. However, the derailment of a train, though perhaps an accident, was blamed on the strikers, and public opinion began to turn against them. On the sixteenth there were bloody clashes between strikers and soldiers. Fearing that the local Regiment de Garellano (which had been garrisoned in Bilbao for many years and contained many Basques and some Socialists) might not be reliable, the government brought in Leonese troops, who are said to have displayed no qualms about firing into crowds of Basque workers.[79]

The strike lasted longest in Asturias, where it was led by Isidoro Acevedo in the capital city of Oviedo and by Manuel Llaneza in the mining zone. Cooperation was also extended by Melquíades Alvarez of the Reformists and by some Republicans. The workers of the entire province responded enthusiastically to the strike call. The mines and factories were all abandoned, including the arms factories of Oviedo, whose workers had been producing at top speed for the Allies. Even many peasants in the region seconded the movement. The core of the Asturian strike forces was the 14,000-man Miners' Union, headed by Llaneza; its members were highly motivated, strongly organized, and took the revolutionary objectives of the strike very seriously.[80]

Here, as everywhere else, the government displayed great vigor and decision. The strike leaders were given little chance to guide the movement, but were pursued from refuge to refuge until captured. Llaneza and his lieutenants Menéndez and Martín were hunted down and finally arrested at the country villa of Melquíades Alvarez. Acevedo and his lieutenants, however, remained at liberty, keeping in touch with Alvarez and awaiting orders from

Madrid, which of course never came. The government's control of newspapers, telephone, and telegraph was so complete that the various regions of the Peninsula were entirely isolated from one another, with the result that the strikers in one city knew nothing of how the strike was faring elsewhere. When the Asturian workers finally learned that the movement had been snuffed out in all other parts of Spain, and that the Socialist strike committee had been arrested, they were somewhat daunted; but they nevertheless decided to continue their movement on the basis of solidarity with the still-striking railworkers of the Compañía del Norte. Their hope was that if the Asturian coal mines remained closed, the government, unable to import coal because of the war, would face so great a fuel crisis that it would compel the Compañía to come to terms. The Asturian workers, already famous for their toughness and discipline, had been earning exceptionally high wages because of the war boom and thus had sufficient resources to keep the strike going three weeks longer than in any other region. The first break in the united front of the strike forces in Asturias, according to Acevedo, came from the Anarchists of Gijón, who requested that the Movement be terminated. By this time the railworkers, who had been the original cause of the premature strike, were also beginning to grow weary; and so, early in the fifth week, the strike came to an end.[81]

The general strike, of course, hit many other areas. Miguel de Unamuno gives a vivid description of events in Salamanca, where the movement was "completely peaceful." The provincial governor came out on the morning of the thirteenth, with an honorary escort, to try to prevent the closing of businesses in the Plaza Mayor. To a shopkeeper who said he had closed his shop not for fear of violence but because it pleased him, the governor replied that he would be considered a "suspect." Considerable effort was expended to make the people believe that the strike had been provoked by "French and English money" in order to break the neutrality policy and take Spain into the war. Thus a French consular agent was arrested and taken ostentatiously to jail in broad daylight, so that none could fail to see, and so that all would deduce French complicity in the strike. Civil employees were sent into the streets, says Unamuno, to spread sensational rumors designed to demoralize the strikers. Conscientious bourgeois gentlemen presented themselves to the authorities as honorary police, saying that they wished to prevent Spain from being dragged into the war. In order to persuade the soldiers to fire on the workers should the occasion arise, they were asked: "Which would you prefer, to fire here against the rebels or to get killed in the trenches?"[82]

Whereas in Spain the general strike was interpreted by conservatives as an antineutralist act plotted by pro-Allied elements and even paid for by French and English gold, the Allies themselves interpreted it as a pro-German scheme to disrupt Spanish war production. This incomprehension was a source of despair to many Socialists. "There is, doubtless, an immanent historical justice," wrote Luis Araquistáin, "which will give victory to the Allied nations in spite of the dullness and mental limitations of many of their political representatives." And he reminded those representatives that "the men who in Spain had defended the Allied cause from the beginning of the war, with a tenacity, a spontaneity, an energy, and a disinterestedness perhaps equaled but not surpassed in any other country" were not "the instruments of German stratagems."[83]

The Impact of the August Strike

After their arrest the members of the Socialist strike committee—Besteiro, Largo Caballero, Anguiano, and Saborit—were taken by truck from the Calle del Desengaño to a military prison in the La Latina district. Here they were forced to disrobe, issued prison garb, and subjected to verbal abuse. They were kept incommunicado for about one month, under the surveillance of guards who, for the first few days, had orders to shoot into the cell in response to any suspicious movement. Besteiro noted the extreme simplicity and ingenuous fear of the officers and soldiers guarding him, who seemed to view the Socialist leaders as terrifying, malevolent figures. The Ministry of War, perhaps instigated by Sánchez Guerra, was pleased to convey to the prisoners' families hints that they had been or momentarily were to be shot, though in fact this was never contemplated.[84]

On September 29 a military council, meeting in the San Francisco Barracks at Madrid, tried the case of the Socialist leaders, who were able, as it turned out, to obtain good legal representation. Besteiro emerged as the spokesman of the group and made an eloquent defense before the tribunal, saying that the Socialists had "aspired to have the general strike constitute a kind of plebiscite, which by its uniformity, scope, and high humanitarian and cultural attributes would achieve effective moral force." He admitted, however, that the strike actually carried out "was not the one we would have desired but that which was imposed by the government."[85] The sentence, handed down on October 4, was life imprisonment for Besteiro, Largo Caballero, Anguiano, and Saborit, with lesser penalties (up to eight years) for lesser collaborators. Virginia González, whom the government, either from gallantry or expediency, chose not to regard as a collaborator, was freed unconditionally. The publisher Luis Torrent, a member of the Socialist National Committee who had printed the strike manifestos and instructions, was sentenced to eight years. And one of the defending lawyers, Captain Julio Mangada, offered such a spirited defense of the Socialist leaders that he was arrested by his military superiors and given 15 days confinement.[86]

After sentencing, the Socialist leaders were moved to the Model Prison; but since it was feared that they might become objects of popular adulation in Madrid, they were transferred in chains to the military prison at Cartagena, where their isolation would be virtually complete. As their train neared its destination, and the prisoners caught sight of the city of Cartagena and of the sea beyond, they spontaneously rose to their feet and sang the *Internationale*, which, it is said, greatly affected their guards. At the station there was no crowd, since the local population had been intimidated. "Only one pale young man, almost tearful, taking off his hat, saluted us repeatedly and ostentatiously, without daring—it would not have been allowed—to give us his hand."[87]

The condemned Socialists were now dressed in prison uniforms, their heads were shaved, and their beards and moustaches were clipped off. A local photographer was permitted to take a picture of the distinguished jailbirds, now so strangely shorn, and the Madrid journal *ABC*, with inspired miscalculation, printed it on page one, perhaps imagining that it would provide a salutary warning to the people. Instead, the picture had enormous impact, touching off a wave of pro-prisoner sentiment that grew stronger with each passing day and would ultimately carry the four men from their cell in Cartagena to the opposition benches in the Cortes.[88]

Although it was no doubt true that the harsh suppression of the August Strike produced bitterness and despair among Spanish workers, along with a feeling of having been betrayed by the elements (mostly republican) who had done so much to create a revolutionary atmosphere, the actual impact of the August events on the trade-union structure of the UGT and the CNT was not excessive. The Cenetistas, in any case, had only recently begun their organizational work in the Peninsula and thus suffered no great setback; nor did the Ugetistas, who had more to lose, experience a serious disruption of their organizations. Indeed, the left-Socialist journal *Nuestra Palabra*, founded on the first anniversary of the Strike, boasted that the Strike "did not at all affect the admirable composition of the UGT."[89] It is true that in the year following the Strike the membership of the UGT declined by about 10,000 members, leaving it at 89,601 in mid-1918.[90] But since the membership had been declining steadily since 1913, it is clear that the drop cannot be attributed entirely to the August defeat; much of it must simply have reflected the continuing inroads of inflation and unemployment on the ability of Ugetista rank and file to pay their dues. As for the Anarchosyndicalists, they recovered quickly. A new (and clandestine) National Committee was formed in the aftermath of the August Strike, and the CNT greatly increased its organizational efforts. These would culminate in the formation of the Andalusian Regional Confederation early in 1918, and in the Congress of Sans of the Catalonian Regional Confederation a few months later, in which—partly as a result of the August failure—the tactic of industrial unionism would be adopted.[91]

There was much criticism of the August Strike within the Socialist ranks. Right-wing militants, such as Indalecio Prieto and Oscar Pérez Solís, had viewed the effort skeptically from the beginning, feeling that the "republican fetishism" was both unwise and premature. And Pérez Solís later deprecated the strike as a *revolución de opereta* and as *el fiasco más terrible.*[92] But even those who accepted the essential validity of the movement and its goals were highly critical of the way it was carried out. Manuel Llaneza called attention to the basic contradiction: the strike was clearly intended as a revolutionary effort, yet it adopted strictly pacifistic methods. Llaneza, not a very revolutionary Socialist, nonetheless complained bitterly that the strike committees had not acquired the weapons necessary to give the workers some chance of success.[93]

The strike leaders defended themselves, saying that because the strike had unavoidably been called prematurely there had been no time to arm the workers. And Besteiro told the deputies in the Cortes that he would indeed have supplied weapons to the workers if he had had the opportunity, carefully adding that he would only have given them pistols, and these solely to the more dependable nuclei of trade-union militants.[94] Still, it is questionable that the Socialist leaders would have armed the workers even if the opportunity had presented itself; for the truth was that they were, without exception, a most pacifistic group of men, with scarcely any *blanquisme* in their makeup.* Moreover, during the spring and summer of 1917 they accepted the conventional wisdom, as reiterated by figures like Unamuno and Melquíades Alvarez, that the Spanish state was in such disarray and so bereft of public support that power would be theirs for the taking. The government, they felt, could be seized *cruzando de brazos*—merely by the workers laying down their tools and withholding their services.[95] Ortega y Gasset criticized this facile optimism:

In 1917 . . . the workers and the men who then wanted a republic attempted a *revolucioncita*. The military impertinence of July had made them believe that this was the moment. The moment for what? For battle? No; on the contrary. The moment for taking possession of the government, which seemed to be lying

---

* "Besteiro was one of the most pacific men I have known in my life. His true *afición* was the study of philosophy. As a professor of logic in the University of Madrid, he published an interesting pamphlet on "The possibility of *a priori* synthetic judgments" that revealed to many youths of my time the secret of the philosophy of Kant. In a better-run country, Besteiro would have been a great professor of metaphysics; in Spain he had to occupy himself with politics, like everybody else. He became a Marxist, perhaps as a result of his studies of Hegel. . . . But he never intended to make a violent revolution. He hated violence instinctively. Although he believed himself liberated from Catholic prejudices, he awaited the advent of Socialism as a kind of manna from heaven, as a dialectical fruit of the economic evolution of capitalism, which would supervene necessarily and unavoidably, without his or his party's having to fire a single shot." Balbontín, p. 138.

upside down in a ditch like a *res nullius*. This looked easy, and the Socialists and Republicans did not want to bother about asking anyone to help them. There was no calling on the rest of the nation with fervent and deeply liberal words. They took it for granted that almost the entire world wanted the same thing that they did, and they proceeded "to raise a shout" in only three or four neighborhoods of as many other towns.[96]

In the end, one must say that Dato's spoiling action, by precipitating the strike prematurely, succeeded even beyond his expectations. For it not only saved the regime during the turbulent summer of 1917 but also, by casting a pall on the revolutionary optimism of the Socialist leaders, ensured that in the immediate postwar period—when the regime, discredited by the Allied victory, was more vulnerable than it had been in 1917—no revolutionary assault would be launched. There is reason to believe that if the August Strike had not been attempted and defeated, the unbroken revolutionary confidence and stored-up energy of the Left would almost certainly have burst out in a revolutionary effort during the post-Armistice period, probably early in 1919. And at that time many converging factors would have favored revolutionary aims: a rapidly expanding labor movement, filled with combative spirit; urban and agrarian upheaval; regionalist ferment; and, to fan the flames of internal unrest, the winds of Wilsonian idealism that swept over Europe at the time of the Armistice. It is difficult to believe that an effort like that of August, better prepared and launched in the post-Armistice context, would not have ended the monarchy and brought the Republic eleven years early. That such a revolutionary attempt was not in fact made in 1918–19 would seem to reflect in large measure the sobering impact of the August Strike on the men who had been its guiding spirits—Besteiro and Largo Caballero—as well as on the majority of lesser Ugetista leaders.[97]

But the August Strike, for all its disappointments, proved less disastrous than it had at first seemed to be. The labor unions, as we have seen, remained intact and in a position to grow rapidly after mid-1918; and the PSOE, after the April 1918 elections, came out of the affair with its parliamentary contingent increased from one to six deputies and with the sympathy of much of the nation. The editors of *El Sol* might well ask, less than two years later: "What was resolved by the repression of Dato and Sánchez Guerra in 1917? Are we not convinced that since that time, and as a result of the repression, the labor organizations have strengthened and perfected themselves, the elements of the extreme Left accentuated their radicalism ... and [that] there has been aroused the desire for a tremendous revenge?"[98]

Would Spain have joined the war on the side of the Allies if a republic had been established in 1917? In the aftermath of their defeat, the Socialists and their Republican allies understandably played down this aspect of the movement, tending to stress the economic sources of their discontent. But the passionate Aliadofilismo of the Socialist majoritarians and the left-bourgeois parties was too evident in the years 1914–17, particularly on the eve of the uprising of the Juntas, to permit one to imagine that Spain's foreign policy would not have been significantly altered if a republican regime had been installed. Some writers have not hesitated to assert what pro-German Spaniards asserted at the time—namely, that a victory by the Left would have brought Spain fully into the war.[99] This, however, seems unlikely. Despite the pro-Allied vehemence of the leftists, contemporary evidence suggests that nearly all of them drew back from actual as opposed to "moral" intervention in the war; and it is not likely that a victorious Spanish Republic would have gone much beyond the severance of diplomatic relations with Germany, combined with attempts to crack down on German agents in the Peninsula and halt such abuses as the secret refueling of U-boats off the Spanish coast. In sum, there would have been no declaration of war on Germany, but there would certainly have been an effort to convert Spanish neutrality from a pro-German to a pro-Allied posture.[100]

The Fall of the Dato Government

It will be well to turn now to the broader political repercussions of the August Strike—specifically, to its impact on the Canovite system. The government of Prime Minister Dato did not long survive its triumph over the workers' movement. If the cabinet had hoped to sail serenely on a tide of postrevolutionary reaction and popular approbation, it was disappointed. No sooner had the echo of applause died away than there began a furious campaign of opposition from all sides. By early September it was clear that the Dato regime had in fact suffered a serious loss of prestige and power, a loss in which the crown and the Turnante parties shared. As long as constitutional guarantees remained suspended, the hostility of nearly all sectors of opinion toward the government remained somewhat muffled; but when the Constitution was restored on October 7, that hostility blazed forth. The most potent opposition came from the Juntas and from the Lliga, who, in effect, wished to shoulder aside the hollow, insubstantial parties of the Turno and govern the country in their own right. Other vital forces would also emerge in the period that lay ahead. The chief politico-constitutional result of the August Movement, then, was that it brought to an end, and made it impossible to resume, the Canovite system of oligarchical parties isolated from the life of the country. At the same time, it marked the beginning of an effort to govern Spain by means of an authentic parliamentary system responding to authentic forces.[101]

The malaise of the Dato cabinet and the need to construct a ministry not based on the Turno made September and October of 1917 months of intense political confusion—a crisis perhaps not wholly dissimilar to that afflicting the Russian Provisional Government at the same time. In Russia, too, one saw a discredited regime without popular support seeking to sustain itself against more spontaneous and real forces pushing up from below. In Spain, as in Russia, confusion and uncertainty at the top were matched by continuing unrest and disaffection in the lower levels of society. In contrast to Kerensky's Russia, however, Spain's revolution from below had been contained for the moment. The urban effort had expended itself, and the always latent rural upheaval had not yet been ignited. The vital difference between the Spanish and Russian regimes, and the thing that saved the Spanish monarchy, was the fact that the vacuum of political power was effectively filled by the military Juntas, which remained united and resolute in their ascendancy. Many troubled hours lay ahead for the monarchy which, with the strike of postal and telegraph employees in February and March of 1918, would reach perhaps its moment of maximum crisis. But the Army, having lost whatever antimonarchical feeling it may have nourished earlier, would ensure Alfonso's continued presence on the throne, at the same time guaranteeing that his dependence on his officers would be greater than ever before.[102]

For Prime Minister Dato, however, the Army had increasingly little regard. After briefly exulting over the vigorous repression they had meted out to the workers, the officers quickly realized that their zeal had backfired and that they had lost the support of public opinion. They discerned that Dato had used them for his own purposes and in the process had cleverly driven a wedge between the Army and the people. Army spokesmen now began to criticize the government for permitting and even encouraging the August outbreak. The officers' ire toward the Dato regime grew day by day, as did their political activity, which was increasingly directed at the liquidation of the Turnante system. The Juntas virtually turned themselves into a political party, going so far as to contemplate putting up their own candidates for election. Above all, they placed heavy pressure on the king to get rid of Dato, the man who had saved his throne.[103]

The other assertive political force in the post-August period was the Lliga Regionalista, which had been shaken by the proletarian turmoil of the general strike and now feared the possibility of popular revolution much more than it had in July. Thus Unamuno would talk of the "terrified Spanish bourgeoisie" and its growing desire for *orden*.[104] The Lliga now sought, therefore, to complete its detachment from the leftists and, moving to the Right, began to agitate for a government of concentration. Since the August Strike had discredited the Assembly of Parliamentarians in the minds of many, Cambó, convinced that the Assembly was the only means by which a thoroughgoing revolutionary upheaval could be avoided, now undertook a speaking tour to rebuild public support for the goals of the Assembly movement. He made further efforts to win Maura over to his cause, and at the same time spoke harshly of the Dato government and its policy of divide and conquer.[105]

The Juntas, meanwhile, continued to demand Dato's departure and, with true constitutional *gaucherie*, went so far as to communicate their desires directly to the king on October 23. This, in turn, left Alfonso no alternative but to withdraw his confidence from the Prime Minister, which forced Dato's resignation on October 27.[106] With the fall of Dato there succumbed not just a ministry but the whole system of artifically rotating parties, which had been the political motor of the Restoration system. But if the Turnante parties were no logner able to govern, neither did there yet exist a system of authentic parties that could. From October 27 to November 3 feverish efforts were made to construct a government that could take control of the drifting Spanish state. Sánchez de Toca, García Prieto, and Maura all failed in efforts to form a new ministry. And the mere knowledge that Maura had been called on for this task angered both workers and republicans, touching off demonstrations all over Spain, and renewing the cries of "Maura no!" Political tension was at its height, and there was a widespread feeling that the monarchy was running out of options and that its dissolution could not be far off.[107]

In the meantime, on October 30, the second meeting of the Assembly took place in the Ateneo in Madrid. But whatever hope there was for a rapprochement between Regionalists, left-bourgeoisie, and Socialists vanished when, in the midst of the meeting, Cambó received a call from the king to come to the palace and help in the formation of a government (García Prieto's second attempt) that would save the monarchy. Cambó went, and the creation of the new government was assured. The Catalan leader professed to be satisfied with García Prieto's rather limited guarantees, and he encouraged two of his political allies—Sr. Ventosa of the Lliga and Sr. Rodés of the Esquerra Party—to accept positions in the new cabinet. But to the Socialists and the bourgeois leftists, this ministry could not possibly be satisfactory, for two main reasons: first, García Prieto refused to promise the summoning of a constituent Cortes, or even to concede that the existing Cortes should act constituently; second, the new cabinet would include Juan de la Cierva, a "man of 1909," a champion of the Juntas, and above all one who symbolized the old, unregenerate politics of the Turno. La Cierva, in fact, was to be the dominant figure in the cabinet, and would have as his purpose the pacifying of the Juntas and the bringing of them back into a proper constitutional relationship with the monarchy.[108]

For Cambó, it was Hobson's choice. He knew, though unwilling to admit it, that the new government represented a repudiation or at least a nonrecognition of the Assembly's aims; yet he greatly feared that if García Prieto failed to form his government, the last hope for the preservation of the monarchy would be lost, and the country would succumb to the proletarian revolution whose coming had been heralded by the August Strike. Cambó had no doubt that it was in his power to throw the country into chaos by withholding his assent to the García Prieto government, yet he refused to do so. Thus, just as the bourgeois revolution, embodied in the Assembly, seemed on the verge of success as a result of the monarchy's deepening political bankruptcy, its leader chose not to deliver the coup de grace but to make peace with the king and, to a degree, with the Turnante parties. This, of course, was not accomplished without a split in the ranks of the Assembly and the alienation of the men of the Left, who, as they evoked memories of 1848, deplored the "betrayal" of Cambó. It should be noted, however, that the new Minister of the Interior was the Viscount Matamala, a politically neutral figure whose presence in the cabinet reflected the new government's intention to hold, for the first time, honest elections without interference from Madrid—a commitment that would be honored in February 1918.[109]

The new government, confirmed on November 3, was a government of "concentration"—the first that the monarchy had known—composed of members of all the major parties with the exception of the Conservative Datistas. Thus was brought to a close the crisis that had begun with the ultimatum of the Juntas on June 1 and had deepened with the Assembly of Parliamentarians in July and the general strike in August. The political system of the Restoration had been abandoned, but the monarchy had been preserved, and the social revolution—that Iberian *Pugachevshchina* that the propertied classes increasingly feared—had been averted for the time being.

Not so fortunate was the Provisional Government in Russia, which was also fighting for its life in this same period. Its fall on November 8 would signify, however briefly, the victory of the same authentic if somewhat anarchic forces that in Spain had been successfully checked by the resolution of the ministerial crisis. The fall of Kerensky and the rise of Lenin would usher in a new type of "soviet" regime in Russia, which would soon begin to make a strong appeal to the messianic and egalitarian aspirations of working classes everywhere. In Spain, that appeal would become apparent almost immediately and would introduce another and by no means minor source of unrest into Spanish national life in a period in which the old stability of the Turno had broken down and a new and more democratic stability had yet to be found.

CHAPTER FOUR

The Bolshevik Revolution in Spain, 1917-1918

On November 7, 1917, armed forces of the Bolshevik Party in Petrograd staged a successful assault on the Provisional Government headed by Alexander Kerensky, driving it from power and transferring nominal control of Russia to the All-Russian Congress of Soviets and actual power to Lenin and his followers. The relative ease with which the Bolshevik seizure was accomplished reflected the fact that state power in Russia, after eight months of freedom and turmoil, had almost entirely evaporated. Lenin's small but willful sect carried out its coup d'état in a virtual power vacuum, seeking to superimpose itself on the anarchic spontaneity of the popular revolution that had broken out the previous March. Moving rapidly to placate the mass pressures that had helped bring them to power, the Bolsheviks issued an appeal for an immediate end to the war on the basis of a peace without annexations or indemnities, and at the same time they promulgated a decree abolishing the property rights of all landlords and granting the land, which was nationalized, to the peasants on the basis of individual utilization. Eight months later they nationalized the majority of large-scale industries, many factories having already been expropriated by the workers.

Inevitably, these dramatic actions created the impression that in Russia there had been established, for the first time in history, a workers' society of unexampled justice and equality. It also came to be widely believed that this society had dispensed with all the age-old instrumentalities of coercion and domination, so that nearly perfect freedom prevailed. Needless to say, Russian reality was considerably more complicated than this, and it was not long before a new structure of authority and, indeed, a new despotism emerged from the chaos of the Revolution. But even though they lacked reliable information about Russian events, millions of European workers, exhausted by the war and disillusioned by the peace, were prepared to embrace the Revolution as a redemptive event and as the embodiment of all their desires for a better world. Unwilling to live without hope, they illuminated the Revolution's shadowy form with their own dreams and aspirations.[1]

The first news of the Bolshevik triumph found both sides of the Spanish labor movement still in disarray after the August repressions. In an effort to regroup their forces, Socialists and Syndicalists were intensely preoccupied with the amnesty campaign that had been launched on behalf of those imprisoned during the summer. This campaign, which reached its climax in November and December, produced hundreds of meetings, thousands of speeches, and a remarkable upwelling of public sentiment on behalf of labor.[2] On November 11, the first elections since the August Strike were held, on the municipal level. Maurists, Republicans, and Socialists all did well in Madrid, and the large number of votes cast for the former members of the Socialist strike committee was an early intimation of the unexpected popularity they had achieved.[3] The amnesty campaign was the occasion for still another quarrel between the Cenetistas, who urged another general strike to force the government to grant amnesty, and the Socialists, who thought this inappropriate and were certain that the new García Prieto government would in any case have no choice but to concede the amnesty that was desired. The difference of opinion led to a rupture of discussions that had been under way with a view to the possible unification of the two labor organizations.[4]

The August debacle and the capitulation of Cambó left a residue of bitterness in the workers' organizations, especially among the Cenetistas. Under the urging of Seguí and Pestaña they had temporarily muted their hostility to bourgeois governmental forms on the eve of the August Movement, and many of them now regretted their lapse from orthodoxy. In the aftermath of their defeat, and under the impression of the not-always-intrepid behavior of the republican leaders in August, the Cenetistas found their antirepublican and apolitical instincts strongly reinforced. The defection of the Lliga, said *Solidaridad Obrera*, had been the final "betrayal" by the bourgeois and republican elements, who, in joining their support to the monarchy and forgetting the republic, had abandoned both the people and the memory of the August Movement. The Syndicalist Gonzalvi wrote that the unexpected solution to the ministerial crisis fell "like a bomb" among the workers. "Abstention from the polls," he said, "is the proper response to this sort of thing."[5]

When some of the bourgeois leftists, in their pro-Allied newspapers, criticized the Bolshevik Revolution as pro-German, the Anarchist journal *Tierra y Libertad* lashed out at them in barely printable language:

> Some of these scoundrels of the pen have the temerity to call themselves "ultra-revolutionaries." Ultra-scoundrels! You demonstrated your revolutionism foully last August, hiding yourselves in the waterclosets of your houses, from whence some of you wet your pens in the basin of your filth and wrote your excremental lies and insults against the revolutionaries of Spain, just as you now write them against the revolutionaries of Russia.[6]

Moving from scatology to pathos, the editors of *Tierra y Libertad* asked how there could be anywhere a truly rebellious man "who does not feel his heart beat with enthusiasm upon reading the news from Petrograd, who does not consider the Russian revolutionaries as his brothers in ideas and in revolution?" They were gladdened by the fact that Kerensky, a "dictator in a Phrygian cap," had been pulled down by the Revolution, and they expressed the hope that all the other tyrants of the earth—"monarchical, republican, and capitalist"—would be similarly destroyed. To the Spanish republicans, they addressed these uncharitable words:

> You, the cheating republicans hereabouts ... you are miserable and degenerate pygmies before the grandeur of the Russian maximalists whom you insult in so cowardly a way.... You do not represent any sane or generous idea. Your bourgeois republic, which you are incapable of establishing because of cowardice, does not represent even the least progress over the monarchy of Alfonso XIII.[7]

The Cenetistas thus turned still more decisively against the idea of a democratic republic, which, in the spirit of pre-August unity, they had half accepted as a transitional step toward the stateless and egalitarian society they desired. Unlike the Socialists, whose faith in parliamentary politics was revived by the unexpected electoral gains of the post-August period, the men of the CNT were more convinced than ever that the workers would have to seek their salvation in the repudiation of all political power. Even power that was organized provisionally and revolutionarily would be as "dangerous" for the proletariat as all previous governments had been.[8] The Bolshevik Revolution, intruding into the Peninsula at this moment of renewed disillusionment with bourgeois political forms, at first struck the Cenetistas as being precisely the total repudiation of political and governmental institutions that they had advocated. Mistaking the Russian "maximalists" for Anarchists, they were initially unaware of the dictatorial role of the Bolshevik Party. For a brief but beautiful moment, the Bolshevik Revolution appeared to them as a confirmation of the vision of revolutionary spontaneity that had been the ideal of virtually all Spanish revolutionaries since the nineteenth century.[9]

Thus the Cenetistas retained an essentially Anarchist conception of the revolutionary process, emphasizing its social rather than its political aspects. They envisioned a spontaneous, self-consummating revolution of the masses, which, though it might be violent, would require a minimum of organization or dictatorial guidance. In contrast to the Socialists, they clung to the appealing fiction that the crucial thing was the destruction of the old order, and they believed that the new order of freedom, equality, and cooperative association could be expected to emerge more or less spontaneously, since it was, after all, natural. That there might have to be a political revolution prior to or in the midst of the social revolution was a view the Cenetistas were reluctant to accept. The state, they felt, should not be captured but destroyed, its place being taken by local, self-governing communes, as the purer Anarchists believed, or by federated unions, as the Syndicalists supposed. They retained, then, a somewhat unreflective faith in the value of sporadic and audacious blows struck by "determined minorities" in order to galvanize the masses into action. In their obsession with revolutionary spontaneity, the Cenetistas sought to impose on the Spanish labor movement the essentially pseudorevolutionary tactics of the isolated uprising, the "pure" general strike dissociated from any broader political movement, and the terrorist *atentado*. These measures, mainly symbolic, were designed not only to enhance the consciousness of the masses but to trigger that popular upheaval from which so much was expected.[10]

As for the Anarchists *qua* Anarchists, there prevailed among them elitist assumptions, a feeling of ideological superiority, and a conviction that the Anarchist groups would have to constitute the *deus ex machina* of any popular revolution. Yet it was characteristic of these elements that they had not forged the organizational weapon—a centralized and disciplined party—that alone could have made their influence decisive over the flux of the revolutionary process. They remained divided into many small groups, which clustered around and sought to influence the larger mass of the CNT even as they jealously guarded their own independence and spontaneity.[11]

Whether mainly Anarchist or Syndicalist in outlook, then, the Cenetistas, in the autumn of 1917, remained committed to revolutionary spontaneity and instinctively wary of the Blanquist-Leninist idea that a resolute and ideologically girded minority should seize political power and endeavor to carry out a social revolution from above. The idea of a transitional "dictatorship of the proletariat," so often denounced by Bakunin, still seemed to most of them a heretical conception, harmonizing neither with their inherited creed nor with their temperament.[12] Thus the encounter between Russian Bolshevism and Spanish Anarchosyndicalism in the years 1917–23 would form another chapter in the old quarrel between the principles of "consciousness" and "spontaneity," which had absorbed and divided both Russian Narodniki and Social Democrats in earlier decades and which was now shifted to an international arena. This was essentially the quarrel between those who, in the manner of a Tkachev or Lenin, viewed the revolutionary process mainly from above, as a problem in elite guidance, and those who, like Anarchists generally, were temperamentally disposed to view the process from below, as a problem in mass upheaval. Leninism, though at first its essential nature was far from clear, would soon reveal itself as the maximal assertion of "consciousness," or organizational elitism, among modern revolutionary movements, whereas Spanish Anarchosyndicalism would emerge as the supreme exaltation of mass "spontaneity."[13]

In the presence of the Bolshevik achievement in Russia and the revolutionary ambience in Spain, the Anarchosyndicalists would for the first time be required to rethink their conception of the revolutionary process. They would be genuinely stirred by the Bolshevik accomplishment and challenged by the idea of an "organized" revolution for which (as they soon realized) Bolshevism stood. The encounter wtih Leninist ideas would result in a painful dilemma: how could the Cenetistas reconcile the Anarchist ethos of spontaneity, apoliticism, localism, and (at least in theory) noncoercion with the authoritarian demands of really serious revolutionary action? The question, in the autumn of 1917, was the degree to which the Anarchosyndicalists would be willing or able to modify old convictions and instincts in the direction of Bolshevism, with its more modern, organizational, and power-centered outlook. What was at stake, in the final analysis, was the potential strength and viability of the Communist movement in Spain, in the creation of which the Anarchosyndicalists would necessarily have to play an important part. This would not be the first time that Anarchists had confronted the ends/means dilemma; but the recent Bolshevik example carried with it the compelling weight of pragmatic success, and the result was a crisis of Anarchist belief.[14]

Anarchists Assess the Bolshevik Revolution

By far the most affirmative and immediate Spanish response to the Bolshevik Revolution came from the "pure" Anarchists of *Tierra y Libertad*. From the first days of the Bolshevik seizure of power this journal was filled with jubilant speculation about the Russian upheaval. What had been somewhat qualified enthusiasm for the March Revolution, which was viewed as "bourgeois," now came close to millenarian rapture. The mood of defeat produced by the disastrous summer was dissipated, and the Barcelona Anarchists were suddenly convinced that mankind stood on the brink of an Anarchist apocalypse. A regime of capitalism, war, and infamy seemed to be sliding into the abyss. "It is the crisis of an entire social order," said *Tierra y Libertad*. "A world of tyranny and slavery ... is collapsing. ... The world is being swept by the revitalizing breath of the advancing social revolution!"[15]

With their vision obscured by distance and desire, the men of *Tierra y Libertad* felt certain that the Bolshevik Revolution was an Anarchist event. On November 7 they confidently wrote that in Russia, "Anarchist ideas ... have triumphed"; and a week later they declared approvingly that in Petrograd the decision had been taken to eliminate the army and to liquidate "authority." In late November the journal referred to the Bolshevik leaders as "'those who have put into practice the principles of justice and equality of Anarchist Communism"; and still later the Bolshevik regime was described as being "guided by the Anarchist spirit of the maximalists."[16] Lenin's decision to turn the land over, in effect, to the peasants made the greatest impression on the Barcelona militants. "Of the three capital evils," said *Tierra y*

Libertad, "property, the state, and religion, the worst is property." Therefore, the Revolution, by returning the land to the peasants, had acted with "such strict justice" that this alone fully justified it, since the result had been to create for the first time a society based on true social equality.[17] Bolshevik efforts to terminate the war were also warmly applauded, especially since they were linked to the possibility of social revolution in the belligerent nations.[18] Finally, the form of the emerging Bolshevik social order, which appeared to place power in the hundreds of soviets that had mushroomed all over Russia, was extremely appealing to the Barcelona Anarchists, since the Soviets were everything that Spanish Bakuninists had themselves yearned for, being spontaneous, local, popular, nonbureaucratic, and, in theory, all powerful within their own spheres. Inevitably, they reminded the Cenetistas of the autonomous "communes" that had always been the *summum bonum* of Bakuninist thought.[19]

But the Anarchist will to believe, powerful though it was, was soon challenged by the more sober suspicion that the regime of Anarchy could not be built in a day, and that the new social order in Russia was not in fact Anarchist. It was conceded by the editors of *Tierra y Libertad* that Anarchism as the negation of the state in all its forms could not be established in an isolated country surrounded by warlike bourgeois states. Beyond that they asserted, reverting to the abstract-ethical level of Anarchist consciousness, "We are the first to proclaim that our ideals of love, justice, and liberty will never be imposed by the violence of a revolution, or even by light moral coercion... [but only by] the increasing elevation of the human spirit toward Goodness, Truth, and Liberty."[20]

The Barcelona Anarchists thus revealed a fundamental ambivalence toward the Revolution. In the weeks and months following the Bolshevik seizure of power they fluctuated between the millenarian belief that it had established "Anarchy" in Russia and a doctrinaire skepticism that such a society could ever be established by violence and coercion. The confusion of their responses reflected the always inherent contradiction between Anarchist ideals—which were entirely humane, pacifistic, and anti-authoritarian—and the ruthlessness that revolutionary action demanded.[21] The October Revolution posed with fresh urgency the old question of how Anarchist belief in the absolute sovereignty of the individual and in the rejection of all coercion and all forms of political power could be reconciled with the need, which Russian events seemed to make evident, for proletarian violence and dictatorship. The Committee of the Anarchist Federation of Catalonia recognized the dilemma when it declared:

> We Anarchists share a highly humane principle, by virtue of which, as men, we do not hate anyone. We proclaim the sacred right to liberty and to life... and we are enemies to all violence because violence is not an expression of right [or of]

justice.... Why, then, are we Anarchists revolutionaries? ... It seems on the surface that there exists a certain conflict ... between our ideological principles ... and our revolutionary action.[22]

Some Anarchist militants confronted the problem of libertarian coercion with little hesitation. One of them wrote candidly in *Tierra y Libertad* that the establishment of Anarchism would, after all, require a "revolutionary period of many years," during which the Anarchists would have to place themselves in authority in order to assure the triumph of the revolution. This was necessary because revolution was the equivalent of war, and all war necessitated "leaders and authority." It was thus "very logical" to see the Russian "Anarchists" acting as *jefes* of the Revolution and assuming dictatorial authority. The Russian Revolution, according to this militant, was not yet an Anarchist society, but it offered the "direct means" by which to achieve one. All the Anarchists of the world would have to do as the Russian "maximalists" had done: they would have to "destroy authoritatively ... the present edifice based upon privilege and injustice in order to begin constructing the great city of happiness, Anarchy."[23]

More tortuously, the Committee of the Anarchist Federation of Catalonia sought to reconcile theory with practice and to discover a rationale for revolutionary violence by reflecting upon the fact that social injustice was, after all, embodied in institutions. If, they said, Anarchist actions resulted in the liquidation of the men who represented those institutions,

> we are the first to lament it from the humane point of view, because we do not wish to destroy the individual, who to us ... is respected and sacred, even though he be a despot. We try to destroy institutions, but when the men who represent them, obdurate in their power, judge themselves the main part of those institutions, they lose their human character and become mechanical agents causing supreme pain to all. Then it is just, and even noble, to abolish them.[24]

The contradiction inherent in Anarchist inhumanity was explained, then, on the basis that men were destroyed only incidentally and insofar as they were identified with unjust institutions. In this way, thought the Committee, one might resolve the "apparent conflict between our philosophic principles ... and our revolutionary enthusiasms."[25]

Thus, under the spell of the Bolshevik Revolution, Spanish Anarchists began to think, as never before, about the uses of authority and the rationales of violence. The idea of the dictatorship of the proletariat began to enjoy a surprising vogue among them, and there was a growing acceptance of the Leninist proposition that revolutions had to be organized, that not everything could be left to the workings of spontaneity. Of course, the early attraction of the concept of the proletarian dictatorship was closely related to the lack of precise information about its operation in Russia. For many Cenetistas it meant little more than "firm revolutionary action" in order to facilitate the liquidation of the capitalists, in contrast to the parliamentary and legalistic methods of the reformists and Socialists.[26] That the Russian dictatorship involved the coercion of classes other than the nobles and the bourgeoisie, and that it had a political party at its core, was not perceived in the early months of the Revolution.

In the immediate aftermath of the Revolution the isolation of Russia helped to foster an image of the Bolsheviks that was most attractive to the frustrated revolutionists of the CNT. Lenin's quasi-Anarchist pamphlet *State and revolution* had a special impact. At a time when the Anarchosyndicalists were beginning to reflect on the virtues of "consciousness" in the revolutionary struggle, this work made it appear that the Bolsheviks had discovered the value of "spontaneity." Lenin's pamphlet, as Joaquín Maurín said, was the "doctrinal bridge" that linked Bolshevism with Anarchism and Syndicalism.[27] The Spanish Anarchosyndicalists found it difficult to disagree with Lenin's basic thesis: the bourgeois state, rather than being gradually infiltrated and taken over by the workers, as the Socialists anticipated, had to be smashed completely. In its place would be erected, according to Lenin, not a true state but a sort of half-state or transitional state.[28] The Cenetistas, of course, were opposed to any state at all; but they were attracted by Lenin's essentially Anarchist phraseology, his emphasis on the value of "armed masses," and his failure to mention the dictatorial role to be played by the revolutionary party. They noted the Russian leader's conviction about the absurdity of linking the words "freedom" and "state"; and they applauded his affirmation that "while the state exists there is no freedom ... when there is freedom, there will be no state."[29]

State and revolution was, in fact, an aberration in the long line of Leninist tracts; and its expression of revolutionary ultra-leftism and idealism was far from characteristic of Lenin's outlook, which was marked instead by suspicion, and even fear, of mass spontaneity, and by an obsession with the Party as a revolutionary vanguard.[30] Yet, though Lenin's quasi-Anarchist mood scarcely survived the year in which the pamphlet was written, it helped to convert many European Anarchists, not least in Spain, to passionate, if illusionary, support of the Bolshevik regime.[31]

The Syndicalists and the Bolshevik Revolution

Not until November 11 did the Syndicalist journal *Solidaridad Obrera* comment on the Bolshevik seizure of power. It then endorsed the new regime in Russia; but the millenarian tone of *Tierra y Libertad* was lacking, and it was clear that the enthusiasm of the Syndicalist editors did not burn as brightly as that of their Anarchist comrades. They acknowledged that the Bolsheviks had shown "the road to follow," but at the same time they lamented that the coup d'état might prolong the war. "Do you understand ... our indecision?" they asked. "Do you understand the bitterness we feel at our inability to form a concrete judgment of the Revolution?"[32] By January 1918 *Solidaridad Obrera* had come to feel that the Revolution might make the possibility of peace more rather than less likely; but its editors still maintained a cautious tone. "There will surely come a day when we will understand with certainty what is happening in Russia"; but not until then could one speak "on the basis of clear proofs ... and, without fear of errors, extend to Spain the ... lessons that this great movement gives us." Without "concrete information" it was "excessively adventurous, and very conducive to lamentable errors," to speak about a movement whose outlines were still so unclear.[33] In remarkably prudential tones the editors of *Solidaridad Obrera* stressed that their sympathies were always with those who revolted against injustice, but nothing more. "We are at the side of the Russian revolutionaries because they have risen against [the same forces] that oppress us here in Spain; but we do not have a source of certain information."[34]

Six months later, *Solidaridad Obrera* was still lamenting that the news from Russia was "every day more confused and contradictory"—so incoherent that it was difficult to form judgments. Though admitting that the Revolution would greatly influence the development of the European peoples, the Syndicalist journal, more fearful of dictatorship than the Anarchists, remarked somewhat cryptically that when speaking of the "forms and characteristics of the Revolution in its executive phase" it was necessary to be circumspect, "because we do not like exaggerations or truculence in matters of such gravity and importance."[35]

The restraint of *Solidaridad Obrera*, which contrasted sharply with the growing enthusiasm of most Cenetistas, may be explained in several ways. In part it reflected the caution of the practical, organization-minded men who tended to dominate the unions and committees of the Catalonian Regional Confederation; and in part it was due to the personal influence of Angel Pestaña, the editor of the journal, who, despite his Bakuninist background, had been moving gradually away from Anarchist insurrectionalism. But mainly it would seem to have been a reflection of the rising conflict between Anarchists and Syndicalists within the CNT. It was among the "pure" Anarchists and Anarchosyndicalists that the most extreme revolutionary optimism found expression at this time, whereas the "pure" Syndicalists, like their UGT counterparts, were increasingly conscious of the unreadiness of the workers and of how much would be lost by the kind of bold, precipitate action that the Bolshevik coup seemed to sanction. Thus the Syndicalists, almost unconsciously, muted their response to the Revolution, knowing instinctively that its effect would be to strengthen Anarchist extremism and place the seal of approval on excessively adventurous tactics.

Of course, not all the contributors to *Solidaridad Obrera* were so restrained. One of the most enthusiastic pro-Bolsheviks was Manuel Buenacasa, soon to become secretary of the CNT National Committee, who represented the intransigent Anarchosyndicalist current. His remarks reveal the idealized and mythic shape that distance and isolation gave to the Bolshevik Revolution at this time. The Russian soviets, he declared, were very similar to the Anarchosyndicalist labor federations in Spain; and those who controlled them were the "maximalists, Anarchists, [and] pacifists who follow Lenin and Maxim Gorky." In commenting upon the fact that Lenin had been made "president" of the Soviet government, he was careful to place a question mark after the word "government"—apparently in the hope that it would turn out to be, somehow, not a government.[36] Very soon, nevertheless, he became one of the most ardent Cenetista converts to the idea of the dictatorship of the proletariat.

Another Anarchosyndicalist writer, who signed himself "C. Desmoulins," expressed the feelings of many Cenetistas when he declared it entirely fitting that Spanish workers should study the new order of things in Russia and view "with a certain envy and admiration those who have discovered how to transform and liberate that country in a manner so rapid, complete, and definitive." He observed that the Bolshevik Revolution found Spain in "the last stage of iniquity and slavery." However, "In spite of this inexplicable apathy, this strange stupor of the Spaniards, hungry, oppressed, and resigned, one hope illuminates us on seeing the change carried out in Russia.... Why cannot the same thing happen here? A simple act produced [the Revolution] in Russia; a cause equally simple could produce it in our country."[37]

The Socialists and the Bolshevik Revolution

The Madrid Socialists, still engrossed in the military effort of the Allied Powers, were considerably less enthusiastic than the Cenetistas in their response to Russian events. Although one biographer claims that Pablo Iglesias greeted the Revolution "with jubilation,"[38] it would be nearer the truth to say that he and his lieutenants were filled with gloom. They virtually refused editorial comment for many months and left little doubt that they viewed the Revolution as the herald of a separate peace and therefore as highly inopportune. In a rare pronouncement a few days after the Bolshevik takeover, *El Socialista* said: "The news from Russia fills us with bitterness. We sincerely believe ... that the immediate mission of that great country was to put all of her strength into the enterprise of crushing German imperialism."[39]

The first truly laudatory reference to the Bolshevik Revolution did not appear in *El Socialista* until March 1918, not long after the signing of the Brest-Litovsk Peace Treaty; and it came, significantly, from a member of the recently created Socialist Students' Group (a group that would later help to found the Spanish Communist Party). Manuel Cardenal, a young university student, responded with messianic fervor to the new Bolshevik regime, viewing it as the embodiment of Christian and Tolstoyan ideals: "The shade of the aged Tolstoy appears before us, venerable and austere, and with him Kropotkin, Gorki, etc.... In the minds of all of them was that divine essence of love and peace that is today the Russian Revolution." The teachings of Jesus had been ignored for twenty centuries:

> But the divine teaching was not lost. Tolstoy recovered it. Trotsky puts it into practice today.... To the unjust force of German imperialism, the Russians, as Trotsky has proclaimed, are going to resist only with *brazos cruzados*. The Russians do not wish to return evil for evil.... In 1918 hatred and war were conquered with love. Against German bayonets the Russian revolutionaries placed their generous hearts. And hearts are stronger than bayonets! Across blood-drenched Europe, I salute you ... oh noble Russian revolutionaries![40]

But the majority of Socialists continued to be absorbed with matters other than the social revolution—chiefly with the fate of the embattled Allied democracies and with the opportunities of the domestic political scene. It appeared that because of the government's decision to hold "sincere" elections there might be extensive Socialist electoral gains in the offing. In the general elections of February 24, 1918, the PSOE, in electoral alliance with the Republicans and Reformists, won its first important success since the initial victory of Iglesias in 1910. Six Socialist deputies, including the four former members of the 1917 strike committee, were elected to the Cortes, along with 144 municipal councillors in 58 *ayuntamientos*. The deputies were Iglesias and Besteiro (Madrid), Largo Caballero (Barcelona), Daniel Anguiano (Valencia), Saborit (Oviedo), and Indalecio Prieto (Bilbao). In Madrid the Socialist vote exceeded that of the most popular candidate of the Republicans, who, in general, also lost ground in the nation as a whole.* The "glorious felons"—the former strike committee—were now released from Cartagena Prison, and their return to Madrid assumed the character of a triumphal procession. In all the stations along the route their train was, as Saborit has written, "assaulted by the multitude, delirious with enthusiasm, heaping upon us flowers and Vivas!" At Atocha Station in Madrid the demonstration acquired spectacular proportions, even as Besteiro modestly implored the crowd not to cheer the committee but to work instead for Socialist ideals.[41]

By and large, however, the elections of 1918 were disappointing to the progressive elements. The central government had indeed refrained from intervening, but the forces of inertia, habit, and local *caciquismo* had succeeded in delivering the lion's share of the vote to the traditional parties. As a result

---

* This was perhaps the first election in the history of the Restoration regime in which a government actually ran the risk of being defeated. Cuadrado, II, 799–816.

of fraudulent practices, large expenditures, and gerrymandered constituencies, the relatively honest vote of the cities was "drowned in a sea of blind peasant votes."[42] In particular, the success of the Catalan Regionalists was less than had been hoped for, casting doubt on their ability to push through their scheme of constitutional reform. However, the election also reinforced the impression that the traditional parties of the Turno were breaking up—Conservatives and Liberals were each split three ways—and that the fragmented pattern of seat distribution in the Cortes would make it extremely difficult to construct a cabinet able to govern. Although the Liberal factions were the major winners, no single faction had a majority; and since García Prieto and Romanones could not cooperate, the combination that would command a majority in the Cortes was not immediately evident. As a solution to the impasse, and as a way of avoiding either dictatorship or anarchy, there arose an idea that the war had imposed on various other European powers. On March 21, under considerable pressure from King Alfonso, a "national" government was formed, headed by Maura and containing the leaders of all parliamentary groups except the Socialists, who, in addition to their hatred of Maura, continued to fear the contaminating influence of the bourgeois parties.[43]

The Socialist leaders were nevertheless greatly encouraged by an election victory in which the Sisyphean labors of so many years had begun to pay off; and despite their opposition to ministerial participation they were more than ever committed to electoral tactics. The Syndicalist vote for Largo Caballero in Barcelona, even though the voting here and in other Anarchist areas was marked by considerable abstentionism, encouraged them in the hope that the Catalan masses might ultimately accept Socialist leadership.[44] Consequently, the appeal of a "catastrophic" social revolution, whether in Russia or in Spain, was not very great. Iglesias's May Day speech, which made no mention of the Russian Revolution, was so moderate that *El Sol* was delighted, saying that the Socialist Party was at last losing its "sectarian prejudices, its rancorous spirit, and its indomitable aloofness from the governance of the state." The Madrid journal was convinced that the PSOE was "hourly more disposed to act in a positive way in constructing the *patria futura*."[45]

One militant who contributed much to the growing impression of reasonableness emanating from the PSOE was the Catalan Socialist Antonio Fabra Ribas, political advisor to Largo Caballero and a frequent spokesman for the Party in this period. Fabra, who had worked for a time on the staff of *L'Humanité* in Paris and was a friend of Albert Thomas, was a prototypical partisan of the Allied cause who saw the war simply as a conflict between "imperialism" and "democracy."[46] He viewed England, for example, with unusual sentimentality, not as a bastion of imperialism but as "the land of the Magna Charta, the cradle of liberty and of parliamentarianism." At times Fabra came close to urging Spanish intervention in the war; and he became, as well, a devout Wilsonian who wished to see the American president's ideas adopted as the "immediate program" of the Socialist Party.[47]

Fabra Ribas had a serene faith in the inevitable triumph of Socialism. As one who felt possessed of insight into the historical process, he viewed with approval the rise of the liberal bourgeoisie in Spain and reminded his audiences that the Catalan middle class had an important role to play in Spain's reconstruction. He deplored the Catalans' emphasis on nationality, seeing them chiefly as an economic class; but he recognized their historical necessity and modernizing function and urged the widest possible autonomy for Catalonia and for all regions. Very much committed to the "two-stage" conception of revolution, he stressed that the working class should not consider itself completely dissociated from the class that exploited it, but should rather prepare ultimately to receive from that class its "inheritance." Socialists, without losing their identity, should cooperate with the liberal bourgeoisie in order to destroy their common enemy, the oligarchy, and should be grateful that the bourgeoisie had released energies and created wealth. For Socialism, said Fabra, wished to socialize not poverty but production, and needed a prosperous Spain in order to carry out its designs. Socialists should not forget their historical mission, but the bourgeoisie should be allowed to "furnish" the house that the Socialists would one day occupy. About the Russian Revolution Fabra had virtually nothing to say.[48]

"Nuestra Palabra" and the Minoritarian Critique

The great concern of the Socialist majoritarians with immediate political issues had caused even so intense a supporter of the Allied cause as Torralba Beci to complain, in April 1918, that the PSOE was absorbed with domestic problems and indifferent to events "two steps beyond our frontiers." "Transcendental" social events like the Russian Revolution, he said, were being almost completely ignored.[49] This was not true of the minoritarians, who had been immediately aroused by the Bolshevik Revolution but were not permitted to express their feelings in the pages of El Socialista, from which, as opponents of the war, they were mostly excluded. In August 1918, displeased with the Party's prowar policy and coolness toward the Russian Revolution, Mariano García Cortés and Ramón Lamoneda took the lead in founding a new minoritarian journal called Nuestra Palabra after Trotsky's Paris newspaper Nashe Slovo. That this organ began publication on the first anniversary of the 1917 general strike was not coincidental but was intended to call attention to the need for a revival of revolutionary Socialism. The defeated movement of the previous summer had acquired a mystique for the Nuestra Palabra militants that they wished to utilize in order to bring the Party back to the presumably pure Socialism of the prewar period. The small, amorphous left wing of the PSOE took a major step toward cohesion and greater influence as it sought to carry out, from a revolutionary perspective, a systematic critique of Pablismo.[50]

The pages of *Nuestra Palabra* revealed two blurred but discernible tendencies: left-centrist and ultra-leftist. The left-centrists were mostly members of the prewar opposition and considered themselves disciples of Jean Longuet in France. Their leftist credentials went back to their resistance to the Republican-Socialist Alliance of 1910 and to the Party's pro-Allied policy in 1914. Like Longuet, they were basically pacifists whose revolutionary impulse, though more vigorous than that of the majoritarians, was perhaps more intellectual than visceral. In this group were to be found Mariano García Cortés, Ramón Lamoneda, Virginia González, Manuel Cordero, José Verdes Montenegro, César González, Juan José Morato, Luis Mancebo, and José Calleja of Asturias; Cordero and Verdes Montenegro, though among the founders of *Nuestra Palabra*, were shortly to drop out. Two other antiwar left-centrists who were conspicuous by their absence were Andrés Saborit and Gómez de Fabian. The incipient ultra-Left was represented by the Young Socialists Ramón Merino Gracia, Rito Esteban, Jaime Aparicio, and Emeterio Chicharro, and by an older Party regular from Alicante, Rafael Millá.[51]

The differences between the two groups would not become significant until the early months of 1920, and for the moment all these militants were united by their hostility to the prowar enthusiasm of the majoritarian Socialists, by their nostalgia for the August Strike, and by their great admiration for the Bolshevik Revolution. They were the first Spanish Socialists to insist on the profundity of the social revolution unfolding in Russia and to assert that this movement, rather than the war, was the crucial event of the era. "One of the greatest surprises we Spanish Socialists are going to receive when the war ends," wrote César González, "is the revolution that is being carried out by the Russian workers." The Russians were involved in "an intensively Socialist labor, the most grandiose revolution in the history of humanity." And if their republic survived, it would be the first "tangible demonstration that our ideas and theories are not mere utopias." Nevertheless, complained González, most Spanish Socialists scarcely noticed this great movement, and some even viewed it with "coolness" and "animadversion."[52] That the majoritarians should neglect the Bolshevik Revolution and its peace initiative in favor of the "stupid polemic" between pro-Allied and pro-German partisans was a source of despair. "It seems," wrote Lamoneda wearily, "as if the very special conception of war traced out by Socialist doctrines had never existed, as if Marx and his advocates within the International, in arguing that conflicts between nations are phenomena dependent on the capitalist structure of society, had propounded an absurdity."[53] When, inevitably, the majoritarians accused the *Nuestra Palabra* adherents of *germanofilismo*, the latter replied that their position on the war was pacifist but "not neutralist" and was, in fact, identical with that of Jean Longuet. They did not feel, they said, the least sympathy for the pro-German elements in Spain, whom they regarded as apostles of "reactionism and barbarism."[54]

In contrast to most of the new journals that appeared during 1918–19 in response to the Bolshevik Revolution, the tone of *Nuestra Palabra* was, on the whole, sober and responsible. Its contributors wished to combat the trend toward bourgeois democratism in the PSOE, but they were prepared, as González said, to move with great circumspection and with toleration for a diversity of opinion within Spanish Socialism. They wished to create "a lively journal, full of vigor, which does not wish to be separated from the Socialist trunk, since this would lead to its death, but, rather, aspires to be an organ aiding [Socialism] to breathe, to grow, and to develop." In a manner curiously similar to that of the right-wing Socialist Oscar Pérez Solís, whose critique of the PSOE was then being serialized in *El Sol* (see pp. 203ff), the left-centrists conceived their task as an assault on a rigid Pablista orthodoxy and an oligarchical party structure. Thus during 1918, as the war moved toward its end, the revolutionary-reformist dogmas of Pablismo were under attack by "outsiders" of both the Right and the Left.[55]

There was as yet only minimal information about the Bolshevik Revolution, but *Nuestra Palabra* dimly discerned the emerging outlines of a collectivist society. The minoritarians were especially stirred by the "Syndicalist" aspects of the Soviet order: Russia, it seemed, had become a "workers' state," the factories and mines, as they learned from radio broadcasts, being entirely directed by councils of workers to which "administrators and engineers" were subordinated. This meant that unions no longer had to defend the interests of the workers against employers, and that all energies could be used to increase the productivity of labor.[56]

But the minoritarians' attitude toward the Revolution, though somewhat reverential, did not degenerate into mysticism or idolatry. There remained an element of restraint and even a willingness to acknowledge that the Bolsheviks, too, had made mistakes.[57] In particular, Bolshevik ideas about the splitting of the International were initially resisted. The revolution in Germany was hailed with great enthusiasm, and *Nuestra Palabra*, wishfully imagining that it was the minoritarian Socialists who had assumed power there, acknowledged that the Germans, for obvious reasons, would be better able than the Russians to carry out an authentic Socialist revolution.[58]

Above all, the militants of *Nuestra Palabra* resisted the idea that the Bolsheviks represented some new form of Socialism. They did not differentiate between the Right and Left factions at Zimmerwald and identified the Bolsheviks with such minoritarian Socialists as Paul Louis, MacDonald, Kautsky, and Bernstein, believing that the Russian leaders had done "no more than apply, in the exceptional circumstances of Russia, the extremist formulas adopted [at Zimmerwald]."

Bolshevism, as a doctrine, does not exist. What the Bolsheviks are doing is simply implanting the Socialist program from [their position in] the government; their doctrine is, therefore, a Socialist one. If we Socialists in Spain were to go around calling ourselves Bolsheviks, we would be no less ridiculous than those [conservatives] who are fighting against "Spanish Bolshevism." What is Bolshevism? ... [It is simply] Socialism in the hour of truth.[59]

Thus the men of *Nuestra Palabra* followed the lead of the French minoritarians in eulogizing the Bolsheviks while refusing to concede them a monopoly of Socialist ideology.

Minoritarian praise for the Bolshevik Revolution blended into a general, if restrained, critique of the PSOE and its policies. No hint of schismatic sentiment appeared in *Nuestra Palabra*; indeed, the new journal pledged itself to proceed with "great respect" and "fraternal spirit" toward those Socialists who differed with it.[60] Nonetheless, many of the themes developed were subversive of Pablismo: hostility to the war, viewed as a purely economic conflict; indifference to the cause of the Allies; skepticism of President Wilson; contempt for the League of Nations; glorification of the August Movement and criticism of its leadership; advocacy of a purified International; desire for a rejuvenated Spanish Socialism; resentment of the Party hierarchy; and opposition to the Republican-Socialist Alliance, conjoined with a feeling of real hostility for the left-bourgeoisie.

Feelings on this last point ran strong. The minoritarians regarded the Alliance as the Party's first fall from grace and as the root of many subsequent evils. José Calleja complained that it had been prolonged even after the threat from Maura had passed and despite the "betrayal" of the Republicans in the summer of 1917. In spite of everything, the Alliance survived, and the Socialist Party continued to walk "arm in arm with the Reformists and Republicans, holding meetings of leftists, making leftist campaigns, while precious time is lost, which, if dedicated to [Socialism] would very quickly place us in a position to make the revolution of the people and for the people." For such a revolution, a "purely Socialist" and "purely labor" effort would be needed.[61]

Underlying all specific grievances was the feeling that the PSOE had drifted away from the "purest essentials" of its prewar pacifism and internationalism, losing its revolutionary dynamism in the process. The old urge to revolt had been lost, it was believed, in the swamps of bourgeois reformism. Not unlike the militants of the CNT, the *Nuestra Palabra* minoritarians had their antibourgeois sensibilities revitalized by the experience of the August Strike and by events in Russia; and they began to move away from the Pablista notion that in a backward country a lengthy bourgeois phase would have to precede the proletarian revolution. Lamoneda declared this two-stage idea to be an "ideological distraction" that only encouraged a continuing alliance with the Republicans and an avoidance of genuine class struggle.[62] Similarly, the Asturian Calleja charged that the Spanish bourgeoisie, like the Russian, was incapable of carrying on the revolutionary struggle that would give the people "more bread, more justice, and more liberty." In Spain, he said, only the working classes and the common people were revolutionary; and since the whole burden of the impending revolution would fall on them, why should they seize power only to turn it over to the bourgeoisie? The proper thing was to imitate the Russians by forming soviets and establishing the dictatorship of the proletariat.[63]

The *Nuestra Palabra* militants made no frontal attack on Iglesias, who, as the incarnation of the Party, was virtually above direct criticism. At most they hinted that the Iglesias of 1918 was not the revolutionary Iglesias of 1898.[64] But much criticism was leveled against what the minoritarians regarded as an excessive tendency toward conformity and obedience within the Party. Some comrades, they said, regarded with great suspicion all those who did not adhere to an authorized viewpoint, even though that viewpoint might be "perfectly erroneous." Indeed, many anti-German Socialists seemed "enamored of the least worthy characteristic of the Teutons: blind discipline."[65] Thus, although they never ceased to stress the need for Party solidarity, the *Nuestra Palabra* militants accused the Party leadership of rigidity and asserted the right of dissent and of Socialist self-criticism.

One area where the leaders of the PSOE and UGT were especially vulnerable to criticism was their handling of the August Strike. Right-wing Socialists like Pérez Solís or Indalecio Prieto might denigrate the whole episode as a *huelga ciega*;[66] but for the minoritarians the mystique of the 1917 movement was closely linked to the *politique* they wished to pursue against the Pablista oligarchy. The strike's failure provided a convenient weapon with which to attack the Socialist leaders and, at the same time, enhance the left-centrists' revolutionary self-image. At the Fourteenth Congress of the prestigious Printers' Federation, meeting in Zaragoza in September, Lamoneda and two other "outsiders"—the elderly, sanctified, but increasingly ignored Antonio García Quejido and the Asturian patriarch Isidoro Acevedo—joined to denounce the inadequate preparation of the August Strike and the "folly" of having attempted it without weapons. "We must declare, filled with bitterness, that the movement ... led to an abortion of the revolution, because revolutions, unfortunately, are not made *cruzando de brazos*." Above all, said Lamoneda, the next revolutionary effort had to be prepared with extreme care and carried out without the cooperation of the republican parties.[67]

Little is known about the collective existence of the *Nuestra Palabra* group in 1918-19. None of the militants involved left any memoirs or apologiae, and the historian, restricted to the polemical pages of their weekly journal, can know only what they wrote and little of what they felt or did. The group in 1918 was very small, beginning with seven members and rising to seventy by the end of November.[68] Thus Lamoneda referred to himself as a soldier in ranks that were "more than modest"; and García Cortés acknowledged that there were, in fact, proportionally fewer minoritarians in the PSOE than in any of the other European Socialist parties.[69] It cannot be said, moreover, that these militants, most of whom may be described as plebeian doctrinaires, possessed great ideological depth or originality. Their articles, written in a vigorous but pedestrian style, frequently reflected a gleaning of the French radical press. Nor can it be assumed that their motives were entirely unmixed. In the cases of Lamoneda and García Cortés, especially, an element of opportunism can be sensed—a recognition on their part that the attractive images of the August Movement, of "pure" revolutionary Marxism, and, increasingly, of a successful Bolshevik Revolution could be wielded to the embarrassment of the entrenched "insiders" of Spanish Socialism. Nevertheless, the *Nuestra Palabra* partisans must be regarded as the core group of the six pro-Bolshevik Socialist factions that came to the fore in 1918–19,* mainly because the continuity of their leftism stretched back so far, to their prewar rejection of the Republican-Socialist Alliance, and also because they were based in Madrid and were able to publish the chief minoritarian journal in Spain for more than eighteen months (until March 1920). The men of *Nuestra Palabra* organized many pro-Bolshevik meetings in the Red Autumn of 1918, and they would be gratified to see a growing number of pro-Allied Socialists coming over to their more revolutionary creed during the disillusioning days of peace. From the ranks of their group would come most of the leaders who spawned the two Communist parties that appeared in Spain in 1920 and 1921. It would not be an exaggeration to say that *Nuestra Palabra* was the cradle of Spanish Communism.

The End of the War

From the middle of 1918 there were signs that the Spanish labor movement was beginning to revive from the low point of the previous summer; and that nonstop inflation, rising unemployment, and the less tangible but perhaps no less powerful force of the Russian Revolution were once again pushing the country toward an acute social crisis. Since early spring the braceros, small peasants, and workers of Andalusia, largely in response to the news of the Russian land seizures, had been organizing sindicatos at a phenomenal rate, as well as engaging in strikes, demonstrations, and quasi-revolutionary clashes with the authorities. The urban labor movement, having reached its nadir early in 1918, began to grow rapidly after midyear—this being especially true

---

* These six factions, from which Spanish Communism would eventually emerge, were: (1) the *Nuestra Palabra* group; (2) the New School; (3) the Young Socialists; (4) the Socialist Students' Group; (5) the Asturian and Vizcayan anti-*aliadófilos*; (6) the repentant Madrid *aliadófilos*, who would move to the Left after the Armistice.

of the Anarchosyndicalists, who after June were committed to the tactic of industrial unionism. It was in this period that the Sindicato Unico began to acquire an all-conquering mystique, and workers, especially in Catalonia, Levante, and Andalusia, began to pour into the new unions as into the Promised Land. The CNT unions grew at a substantially more rapid rate than those of the UGT, partly because of their overtly more revolutionary temper, which matched the popular mood, and partly, it would appear, because the Anarchosyndicalists had embraced the Bolshevik Revolution with so much greater frankness and fervor than the Socialists. The strike activity of urban workers, too, rose substantially after the middle of the year.

The war, of course, still held Spain in an iron grip, and the continued torpedoing of Allied and Spanish vessels contributed to a punishing rise in the cost of living and to increased unemployment.[70] An almost desperate situation developed in Murcia during July and August, when the price of food rose to new heights and there were violent bread riots and even assaults on public buildings. The tide of emigration from this afflicted province and its neighbors became a virtual exodus, with large numbers of the migrants making their way to Barcelona and other Catalonian industrial cities. In July the city of Barcelona—responding somewhat tardily to a peasant influx that had gone on since 1915—opened a "hotel" for immigrants and transients largely to cope with the flood of Murcianos. Migrants and their families were to be given shelter while looking for jobs; but if they found no work within three days, they were to be invited to leave the city.[71] Other areas were also affected by the war-induced labor crisis. One correspondent in Salamanca reported that in the space of a few days nearly 1,000 emigrants had left the province, many of whom were quoted as saying that they had found it impossible to live on five reales per day. The migration of Spanish workers abroad acquired new volume, and by November 1918 it was estimated that a total of 600,000 Spanish workers labored in other countries.[72] To hardships imposed by the war there was added a disaster of nature: the worldwide influenza epidemic had reached Spain in the spring and was spreading over the whole Peninsula by early autumn; in one day in Barcelona there were 297 deaths from the disease.[73]

Amid the rising tide of social disorder in Spain, the partisans of Bolshevism felt a growing concern about the survival of the Revolution in Russia. The Civil War, which had begun in the spring of 1918, along with the mounting scale of foreign intervention, caused a certain amount of despair in leftist circles. The Socialist minoritarian César González wrote: "Everything seems to indicate that the maximalist state is nearing its end [and] is inevitably condemned to perish." This was a great tragedy, he said, since for the minoritarians the class struggle was "a thousand times more interesting" than the struggle between the imperialist powers. The Spanish Left, having seen its principles vindicated by the Bolsheviks, felt in this dark moment "morally obliged to proclaim our absolute and complete solidarity with those comrades, who may perhaps pay with their lives for this profoundly Socialist gesture."[74] Manuel Buenacasa, the most internationally minded of the Cenetistas, wrote some extremely bitter articles in *Solidaridad Obrera*, denouncing the Allied interventionists and their Spanish supporters as those who "in the holy name of progress and liberty have conspired to strangle the power and government of the Russian people." Buenacasa warned that although the "maximalist forces" might be in retreat, the world was nevertheless on the eve of "the social war."[75]

Allied intervention in Russia put the majoritarian Socialists in an awkward situation, since their loyalty to the Allies was now patently in conflict with loyalty to the first "workers' state." "Will the prowar Socialists," asked José Calleja, "continue proclaiming the excellent progressivist ideas of the Allies?" If they had hitherto done so in good faith, was it not now "time to confess their error and ready themselves to imitate ... the Russian Bolsheviks?"[76] But, of course, the disciples of Iglesias had no intention of recanting at this point, as the war entered its terminal stages; and they simply maintained a discreet editorial silence on the intervention question. In late August *El Socialista* spoke enthusiastically about American participation in the war, reminding its readers that America did not fight for egoistic or sordid reasons but for "the liberty and civilization of the whole world."[77] And in the Madrid Socialist Group, the pro-Allied majority inserted into a resolution a phrase lamenting that the Russian Revolution had had the effect of lengthening the European conflict.[78]

Less concerned with the Revolution than with the war, Spanish Aliadófilos and Germanófilos watched in fascination the vast ebb and flow of battle on the Western Front. In April 1918 *El Sol* was certain that the road to Paris lay open for the German armies.[79] But with the failure of the German spring offensive the tide changed swiftly: from mid-July on, the resurging Allied armies began to gather impressive momentum; and by September, with the piercing of the Hindenburg line, Spanish observers were certain they were seeing the beginning of the end.[80] The rapidly rising wave of Spanish social unrest in the latter half of 1918 thus had as its backdrop the faltering revolution in Russia and the onward drive of Allied forces against crumbling German defenses.

The collapse of the Central Powers coincided almost exactly with the political exhaustion of the national government formed less than eight months earlier. Having accomplished little renovative work, and perhaps sensing the end of an era, the Maura ministry submitted its resignation on November 6. The formation of a new (and short-lived) government by García Prieto based on the old parties and the old politicos produced exasperation and bitterness among the political leftists, who, expecting that the coming of peace would facilitate the transformation of Spain, knew that this would only be possible if power were in the hands of new men and new parties. The attempt to revive the old system, in the face of the triumph of the democracies, jeopardized the hopes upon which their ardent pro-Allied sentiment had been based and threatened the dream of Spanish regeneration that had made the war endurable. Thus *El Sol* burst out:

> We say to all Spaniards capable of reflection and energy: This cannot be! It must not be! We are resolved not to tolerate Spain's entering the time of peace without possessing a strong public organization, a respectable and respected government, [and] political groups composed of clear heads and executive temperaments, free of fetishisms for the old, quick to cut out decayed institutions, ossified structures, prejudices.[81]

But in the end, after the fall of García Prieto, a new Liberal ministry was formed (December 6) by the old oligarch Count Romanones. This was a choice largely dictated by the necessity for Spain, even at this late hour, to make a serious approach to the Allied powers. King Alfonso was anxious to abandon the ever-deepening isolation into which the country was falling, and, not averse to presuming on the good will of the victors, he hoped that Spain might obtain a seat at the peace conference, or at least some voice in the negotiations. One of Romanones's first actions as premier would be to take a train to Paris, where he would seek out Woodrow Wilson and try to obtain assurances regarding Morocco and Catalonia, to which it was feared Wilsonian principles might be precipitously applied.[82]

The sudden signing of the Armistice found large segments of Spanish opinion stunned and unprepared. Oscar Pérez Solís wrote that despite the crash of empires and thrones and the advent of a crisis not equaled, he thought, since the fall of the Roman Empire, the Spanish masses were like some country rustic who "with an imbecilic air contemplates an exotic spectacle." The "immense majority" of the nation, he said, showed a very shallow comprehension of what transpired before their eyes: "Just as earlier, when astonished by German military successes, it had not occurred to them to say more than 'Qué tíos!', now they do no more than exclaim 'Qué cosas suceden!' "[83] The pro-German elements, of course, were dismayed by the sudden German collapse. As they recognized in the last months of the war that they had backed the wrong protagonists, their ardor for the Central Powers rapidly cooled, and they lapsed into baffled silence. Journals such as *La Nación* and *La Iberia*, which had been subsidized by the German Embassy, quickly folded.[84] All the conservative forces in Spain suffered a serious loss of face as the result of the Allied victory, and the prestige of Socialists and republicans correspondingly rose to new heights. Amid the confusion and disarray of the Germanófilos, the men of the Left experienced a revival of republican euphoria and began

to speak out with remarkable and even seditious boldness. There was a growing feeling that the final hour of the Spanish monarchy had arrived, and that
it could and should be swept aside along with the German Empire to which,
during the war, it had lent its secret sympathy. As early as July, Besteiro had
revived the republican theme. In a speech commemorating Bastille Day, he
reminded his audience that the war was a "revolutionary" force, which, he
hoped, would lead to the disappearance of "the most powerful cause of all the
national misfortunes," that is, of the monarchy.[85] By October the Republican
leader Marcelino Domingo, emboldened by the increasing discomfiture of
the forces of order, openly spoke with great harshness about the Army and
urged Republicans and Socialists to take power. Spain had to become a republic,
he assured his listeners, so that she might belong to the new League of Nations
soon to be formed.[86] On November 5 the Radical leader Alejandro Lerroux
made a revolutionary speech in the Casa del Pueblo in Barcelona, confiding
to his audience that the republic was "very near," and that he himself was
"very close" to power in Spain.[87] In a meeting in Zaragoza in mid-November
both Largo Caballero and Angel Lacort called for the overthrow of the regime
and the establishment of a democratic republic.[88] Finally, following a mid-
December speech by Cambó in the Cortes, Besteiro astonished the chamber
by punctuating the sudden withdrawal of the Catalan deputies with loud
shouts of "Viva Cataluña!" and "Viva la República!" He was joined by Saborit, who cried out repeatedly "Viva la Revolución!" There ensued, it was
said, an "indescribable tumult" of shouts, cheers, and protests, amid which
Count Romanones tried in vain to speak.[89]

Nevertheless, although they obviously appreciated the stimulus that the victory of the Entente gave to the republican cause, and although they frequently
employed revolutionary rhetoric, the Socialist and Republican leaders in this
period, in the end, conveyed no concrete plans and made no overt move against
the monarchy. Thus the memory of the abortive August Movement, along
with the unexpected boost it had given to Socialist parliamentary ambitions,
may have helped preserve the Bourbon monarchy through a post-Armistice
period inherently more threatening to it than the turbulence of 1917.

Still, the majoritarian Socialists greeted the end of the war in an aggressive
and optimistic mood. As between the two towering figures of the postwar
world, Wilson and Lenin, they put their faith in the American President,
whom they now admired for the "profoundly pacifist" spirit he embodied.[90]
In their eyes, as the Anarchists of *Tierra y Libertad* sarcastically observed,
Wilson had become a virtual Socialist.[91] The League of Nations proposal made
a deep impression and helped many Socialist militants assuage whatever concern they may have felt regarding the Party's intense prowar policy. "Wilson
is a poet!" exclaimed Araquistáin in a tone of gratitude; and Francisco Núñez
Tomás, one of Iglesias's most devoted lieutenants, pronounced Wilson's

League and peace proposals an "enormous triumph" for democracy.[92] The conviction of most majoritarians was that the world, and Spain, had entered upon a new stage: "This hour of peace," they affirmed, "opens a new era in history, the era of Socialist democracy, [which will] see the reconciliation of all nations and the advent of a new era of justice, peace, and labor."[93]

But within the majoritarian ranks, long-suppressed doubts rose almost immediately to the surface. A small but growing group of militants, all strongly pro-Allied, found their Socialist consciences suddenly reawakening after the long interregnum of the war. Now that German imperialism had been vanquished, these men began to succumb to long-resisted radicalizing forces, the chief of which was the lure of the Russian Revolution. In a meeting held in the Casa del Pueblo early in November, Evaristo Gil observed that he had supported the Allies from the start of the war because he believed that an Allied victory would make possible the revival of Spain. "But today," he said, "when victory is certain, I cease to be an Aliadófilo in order to become purely a Socialist."[94] The desire to return to a more virile Socialism also animated Torralba Beci, the most sensitive leader of the Socialist Party, who began moving leftward immediately after the Armistice, and who would soon become one of the most intense partisans of Bolshevism. What disturbed Torralba was the Allied decision to punish a transformed and democratized Germany and to intervene in revolutionary Russia. "Today," he said bitterly, "we are closer to Socialist Germany, Austria, and Russia ... than we ever were to the French Republic, to democratic England, and to constitutional Belgium. Above all else we are Socialists." And for real Socialists, he insisted, the arrival of peace could only mean the beginning of class war.[95]

This was precisely the view of the Socialist minoritarians and of the Catalonian Anarchosyndicalists, who, though perhaps feeling a secret admiration for President Wilson, chose to apply the canons of leftist orthodoxy to the question of the peace as they had to the war. For them, the League of Nations was only a capitalist cabal, and the Wilsonian vision was but the "dream of the liberal bourgeoisie." The peace, they were certain, would be a "bourgeois peace, hateful and cynical."[96] To those who urged a republican solution in Spain, the Cenetistas retorted that the Spanish people, absorbed with "that great, burning reality," Russia, knew perfectly well that republics had come to their historical end.[97] Also interesting were the signs of a growing rapport between pro-Bolshevik Anarchosyndicalists and those Socialists who had become partisans of Lenin—a tendency, however incipient, that at least hinted at the possibility of creating a unified revolutionary Left in Spain, at last bridging the gulf of mutual suspicion and animosity that divided Spanish workers.[98]

Among the *Nuestra Palabra* minoritarians the end of the war produced further radicalization and new assertions that the monarchy, which they were certain was toppling, would be replaced not by a sterile republic but by a regime committed to "social transformation." Hostility toward the left-bourgeoisie, which the Socialist minoritarians shared with the Cenetistas, began to surface with increasing insistency during the post-Armistice period. The minoritarians contemptuously observed Republican banquets celebrating the Allied victory, and whatever lingering appeal a bourgeois-democratic republic may have held for them rapidly faded. This mood was especially pronounced among the Young Socialists, who now began to regret their former enthusiasm for the Entente and to move to the Left, surrendering to Bolshevism and sending assurances of support to the *Nuestra Palabra* group from all parts of Spain. Cándido Val spoke for the Madrid Young Socialists: "We desire that there should be made in Spain an essentially Socialist revolution, exclusively of the people and for the people. We are against all the bourgeoisie, red or blue.... A bourgeois republic does not satisfy our aspirations."[99]

The Russian Revolution Rediscovered

Against the majoritarian Socialists' dream of a Wilsonian republic, then, there emerged an increasingly influential counterview: the Leninist conception of an immediate social revolution that would overleap the stage of a bourgeois-democratic republic and enter at once into the struggle for a classless, workers' society. The inspiration for this vision, of course, came from the Russian Revolution, which had broken out in a preindustrial, peasant society that (as a growing number of Spaniards recognized) was not unlike Spain herself. Spanish interest in the Revolution began to pick up almost immediately after the Armistice. Already in the South, according to Díaz del Moral, a "Russian fever" was rapidly spreading among the peasants and braceros.[100] In cities all over Spain there were scores, perhaps hundreds, of "pro-Bolshevik" meetings and demonstrations from autumn 1918 through 1919. Typical was a rally held in the Casa del Pueblo in Madrid on November 10. Emeterio Chicharro, Cándido Val, Evaristo Gil, García Cortés, and Virginia González all spoke, with Gil observing that Spain was now where Russia had been the previous March and likening the recently formed Romanones government to that of Kerensky.[101] Even more emotional was the *ágape bolcheviquista* staged by the Young Socialist leader Ramón Merino Gracia and by the *Nuestra Palabra* group on January 17, 1919. The most solemn homage was paid to the "magnificent labor" of the Russian Bolsheviks; and, at the end, all joined in singing the *Internationale*.[102]

Everything conspired to fan the blaze of pro-Bolshevik enthusiasm. The rise in the cost of living continued, undeterred by the Armistice, and, as *Solidaridad Obrera* said, "to the great surprise of us all."[103] The most immediate and serious economic consequences of the Armistice appear to have been felt in the Basque and the Asturian industrial and mining areas, perhaps most among the Asturian coal miners, who rapidly gravitated toward Bolshevism.[104] According to the anti-Bolshevik labor leader Baratech Alfaro, the Russian Revolution inspired "a prodigious current of emulation, which reached with rolling force even the countries most distant from the original center." In Spain, he said, the workers were fired by the example—"or more exactly, by the fantastic descriptions"—coming from Russia, and threw themselves "unrestrainedly into a crazy procession toward the beckoning illusion of utopia."[105]

The "rediscovery" of the Bolsheviks after so long a preoccupation with the war indeed produced an upwelling of emotion within the Spanish labor movement and an intensified feeling of identity with the struggle in Russia. Many militants revealed an almost pathetic desire to unite in spirit with the redemptive Bolshevik masses. Thus Torralba Beci affirmed that when the revolutionary moment finally came, the Spaniard would eagerly open his door, exclaiming: "Enter, Bolsheviks! Search my home, probe all my affairs, hear the story of my life. You will not find here more than a life of labor, of sacrifice, of struggle with injustice." Then, said Torralba, "the Bolsheviks would embrace him, would carry him along with them, would call him brother."[106] The mysticism of the Madrid Students' Group was no less stirred, and they directed an open letter to the student organizations of Russia, reminding them that the great Tolstoy himself had once affirmed the brotherhood and common redemptive mission of the Russian and Spanish peoples; and they declared, "No other people has understood so deeply as ours the agony and the glory of the Russian Revolution." Only the Spanish people had been able "to comprehend intuitively, from the first moment, the immensity of your creation [and to call themselves] *bolcheviques*."[107]

A rash of "Bolshevik" journals now appeared in various parts of Spain, most of them emanating from Anarchist or Anarchosyndicalist quarters. One of the earliest was *El Maximalista* of Barcelona, which first appeared on November 2, 1918, and which adhered to an extreme Anarchosyndicalist position —antirepublican, anti-Socialist, antiparliamentarian, antiwar, and even anti-European.* The editors described their weekly journal, not inaccurately, as a "hoja de subversión social y espiritual." They were, above all, violent partisans of the Russian Revolution, proclaiming that it was necessary to do "everything possible to establish maximalism in Spain." Once the Revolution

* "Europe!... We have already talked at length with the Europeanizers, with those who do nothing more than say that we are not sufficiently European, as if to be European, in the sense they give to the word, were a necessity and an indispensable honor. No, we will not say such a thing [because we do not wish] to speak foolishness.... Spain has perhaps gained much by remaining apart from the European current that has... produced the greatest crime in history. No, we are not Europeans; here [in Spain the only Europeans] are the shipowners and merchants who have sent shoes and uniforms to clothe the French and English corpses." *El Maximimalista*, 2.xi.18.

came to the Peninsula, they hoped that the first measure taken to "sanitize" and purify the atmosphere would be to "deport or shoot all those who directly or indirectly have intervened in politics." This meant that Spain would no longer have "one monarchist, one republican, or one Socialist."[108]

Hostility toward the Socialists was especially pronounced. The editors of *El Maximalista* were conscious of the phenomenal growth of the Syndicalist unions in Catalonia and other parts of Spain, and of the fact that they were outstripping the UGT, from whose ranks they were attracting many of the younger and more activist workers. The journal pointed out exultantly that at the end of 1918 the CNT had no less than 107,096 members (mostly in Catalonia), more than the UGT had in all of Spain.[109] One finds here early signs of a Cenetista hubris that would grow steadily through 1919 and pose a severe barrier to cooperation between the two major Spanish labor movements. But it was perhaps the rapidly culminating war that remained the major concern of *El Maximalista*. The editors considered themselves staunch pacifists; yet they asked, in more or less Leninist terms, whether it might not be preferable that the war continue, so that the other belligerent peoples could imitate the Russians by seeking "peace through revolution."[110]

On December 3 advertisements appeared in Barcelona for a journal to be called *El Bolchevista*, which was to be the "defender" of the Russian Revolution. Sponsored by a militant body calling itself the Grupos los Rebeldes, the new journal was intended for Syndicalists and for "flexible" Anarchists.[111] On December 19 there appeared in Madrid the journal *El Soviet*, edited by Miguel Pascual and dedicated to "intellectuals, workers, and soldiers." This paper was essentially Anarchist in outlook, and its pages portrayed Soviet Russia as a sort of Anarchist utopia—a paradise, perhaps, for intellectuals.

> To the dawning in the East one also owes the proof that the principle of authority, upon which the order of the people is based, is false. . . . For the Russians of today there is no more authority than that of intellectual capacities, without the use or the abuse of force. . . . In factories and workshops, in mines, in the *campo*, etc., there have been formed juntas of capable workers, of the most intelligent; and production has been organized collectively. The engineer, the architect, the professor share with the manual worker the first fruits of a condition of liberty that has turned the Russia of cossack and landlord into the Russia of labor and equality.[112]

According to Augusto Lagunas Alemany, "the holy Communism of Kropotkin and Tolstoy" had been converted into "the norm and the program" of the Russian Bolsheviks. The Soviets, he said, had "leapt over" old republican concepts and "mediocre Socialist theory" in order to make a spiritual revolution, out of which had come a "very human" regime based on the freeing of the land, equality of rights and duties, laws derived from natural principles, and rational pedagogy. In an article entitled "Idearium Bolcheviki," the editors of *El Soviet* portrayed the new society as one characterized by the "disintegration and bankruptcy" of the state, which had been replaced by soviets from which "the bourgeoisie and the plutocrats" were excluded. The existence of a workers' dictatorship was acknowledged, but it was pointed out that this was exercised only against the capitalists. The army, navy, magistrates, clergy, and police were all said to have been "totally dissolved." Finally, the new soviet regime was said to have established free love.[113]

The Red Scare

By the autumn of 1918 it was evident that Spain was sliding into a revolutionary or prerevolutionary situation. And this crisis, which by March 1919 would lead some of the major conservative journals to demand a dictatorship to save the country from Bolshevism, possessed something that the crisis of August 1917 had lacked: both an urban and a rural dimension. In the South the peasants, almost entirely apathetic during most of the war, had inexplicably begun to move against their landlords, commencing in early spring. In the grip of a mysterious ferment they formed combative new unions, waged numerous strikes, rioted, burned crops, demanded repartition of the land, and invoked the specter of the Russian Revolution. In Catalonia the Syndicalist movement, growing with astonishing rapidity since the middle of the year, was an unknown quantity, laden with menace for the Catalan bourgeoisie. The origins, objectives, organization, and tactics of the proliferating Sindicatos Unicos were shrouded in obscurity. All that was known was that the movement, led by implacable men of unknown antecedents, was expanding rapidly, achieving an unprecedented organizational cohesion, and preparing to strike against the bourgeois order. There were even rumors—largely unfounded, as it turned out—that the Syndicalist-Bolshevist movement (the two phenomena were usually equated) was beginning to penetrate the lower ranks of the Army, so that the Catalonian garrisons were in danger of being "Bolshevized."[114]

The privileged classes persisted in believing that the rising wave of strikes and the spreading urban and rural violence had chiefly external causes. The Conservative Manuel Burgos y Mazo expressed the conviction of many middle-class Spaniards, saying: "From the first moment, I saw that the social and revolutionary propaganda was...inspired by foreign elements; that there had been established a direct influence and an intense solidarity between other countries and our own." Foreigners in Spain, especially Russians and Germans, had formed "revolutionary centers" for the "constant diffusion of Syndicalism and Anarchism."[115]

More than a few thoughtful Spaniards were disturbed by the apparent similarities between their own increasingly restless country and pre-1917 Russia.

Ortega y Gasset identified the Russians and the Spaniards as "the two *pueblo* races of Europe," which, though located at opposite ends of the "European diagonal," were both characterized by an alarming contrast between the spontaneity and vigor of their masses and the diminutiveness and incapacity of their ruling elites.[116] "Anything is possible in Spain," he gloomily remarked. "One day the proletarian blast will blow, and we shall be swept from end to end as the Sirocco sweeps the desert dunes."[117] "What would happen," asked another middle-class liberal, "if the lower depths of society succeeded in breaking the bonds that contain their desires for material satisfaction?" The example of Russia, he advised, "should not be ignored by any Spaniard, since here in Spain one has in aggravated form all the factors that provoked the Russian anarchy."[118] The Republican Marcelino Domingo, in a widely quoted remark, called Spain "the Russia of the West,"[119] and the French journalist François Denjean affirmed that Bolshevik propaganda was "bound to have a profound impact among a people who in so many ways resemble the people of Russia."[120] Nor were bourgeois anxieties eased by the exultant tone of the labor press:

> The Socialist revolution that stirs the whole world and, in glorious fashion, governs in Russia, is also coming to Spain. Our proletariat, which is not so torpid or irresolute as our politicians imagine, begins to stretch its limbs.... The affair of August 1917 was a small anticipation. That which approaches is more serious. Tremble, rogues! The hour of justice arrives![121]

The conservative classes, in fact, dreaded the possible effects of Russian conspiracies in an atmosphere so charged (as they believed) with revolutionary potential. When, in January 1919, a rumor circulated that a boat had arrived in Barcelona with Lenin on board, it was widely credited and caused a veritable panic in some circles.[122] At about this same time the Center for Nobiliary Action issued a plea urging the Spanish nobility to endeavor to meet the impending revolutionary movement with greater dignity than that displayed by their Russian counterparts.[123] Numerous books and pamphlets began to appear, calling attention, either in alarm or in anticipation, to Spain's peculiar resemblance to tsarist Russia.[124] In a mood verging on panic, the authorities began making indiscriminate arrests of both Spaniards and foreigners suspected of being "Bolshevik agents." Russians living in Spain—of whom there seem to have been a surprising number—immediately fell under suspicion, and arrests and expulsions began. Two boatloads of Russian emigres sailed from Barcelona in January 1919, bound for their homeland and accompanied by forty Spanish marines.[125]

Many such expulsions would follow during 1919, as the conviction grew that Russians were somehow responsible for the escalation of Syndicalist activity in Spain. Among those arrested was a Russian national named Weisbein, who, from the Model Prison in Madrid, wrote the newspapers to protest his arrest, asserting, "I am a Russian citizen and have committed no crime." The humorist writer for *El Sol*, Julio Camba, commented:

A Russian citizen who has committed no crime!... The contradiction at once strikes the eye. It is as if one should say "a murderer who has killed no one," or "a thief who did not rob anybody." Does Sr. Waisbein [sic] think it a small crime to be Russian? Russia is a country that is too cold, too distant, and too complicated, and it has always inspired deep suspicions in our police. In Madrid, Sr. Waisbein, it is too difficult being Catalan or Gallegan [to imagine] that one might be permitted to be Russian. If you wish to live tranquilly among us, make yourself from Vallecas or Getafe and forthwith renounce all Muscovite pretensions.... I do not know in which article of our penal code Russian citizenship is condemned, and therefore I cannot give the number to Sr. Waisbein. What is certain, nevertheless, is that insofar as the Spanish police suspect that someone might be Russian, they search for and arrest him. If I have not been in Russia, it is because I have not wished, upon returning, to be locked up forever in the Model Prison. There is no way to be Russian in Spain, Sr. Waisbein.... Take my advice: forget your language and adopt the citizenship of Cuatro Caminos, which, since the fall of Germany, is the most distant country from which one may hail and still be tolerated in Madrid.[126]

The Socialists of the New School held a meeting in the Casa del Pueblo to protest the expulsion of the Russians. Núñez de Arenas, Manuel Pedroso, Indalecio Prieto, and the republicans Madariaga and Castrovido all spoke out against the government's actions and in favor of the Soviet Republic. The result, said *Nuestra Palabra* on January 25, was an "exaltation" of the Russian Revolutionaries and "a true Bolshevik meeting." Such manifestations, of course, only deepened the anxiety of the ministers.

Socialist Rapprochement

The upsurge of sympathy for the Russian Bolsheviks was general among the leftist forces in Spain after the Armistice, most of all in the Socialist camp. Even pro-Allied, Wilsonian Socialists such as Julián Besteiro or Indalecio Prieto finally found kind words to say about the Revolution; and it seemed that at last there was some possibility of rapprochement between the Right and Left of the Socialist Party. At least a few of the antiwar Socialists were not immune to the general euphoria and were prepared to concede that the Allied victory was not such a bad thing and would perhaps aid the cause of Socialism.[127] The Aliadófilos, for their part, found increasing merit in the Bolsheviks and were willing to acknowledge that the Revolution had not fatally impaired the Allied war effort.[128] Leaders such as Besteiro, Largo Caballero, and Prieto participated in at least some of the pro-Bolshevik meetings, invoked the names of the martyred Luxemburg and Liebknecht, and occasionally interjected vivas for Soviet Russia.[129] True, the majoritarians were still committed to a bourgeois-democratic republic rather than to a social revolution *a la russe*; but their renewed militancy at least brought them somewhat closer in mood to the left wing of the Party.

This is not to say that the quarrels generated by the war entirely dissipated with the Armistice; but the majoritarian-minoritarian division within the ranks of the Socialists seems to have become, for a time, blurred and uncertain. This was evident in the UGT congress of October 3–10, 1918. When it was proposed that efforts be made to unify the UGT and the CNT, most delegates, whether of the Right or the Left, were able to concur. The Left, perhaps, showed more desire for a fusion with the Anarchosyndicalists, but it was noteworthy that Besteiro joined with such antiwar leaders as Acevedo, Virginia González, and Saborit in support of a resolution designed to open up discussion with the Cenetistas on this matter. The conservative trade-union leader Vicente Barrio, by contrast, attacked the unification proposal vigorously.[130] The resolution finally adopted stated that the UGT wished to resume at once the friendly relations with the CNT that had existed just before the August Strike, and it empowered the UGT National Committee to make every effort toward uniting "as soon as possible" all the labor forces of Spain in "one single national organization."[131]

The congress, the first to be held since the revolutionary summer of 1917, also debated the conduct of the August strike committee. The Vizcayan antiwar leader Facundo Perezagua made a leftist critique of the strike's management, saying that it should not have been attempted without weapons and should not have had as its purpose merely the bringing to power of a Lerroux or a Melquiades Alvarez. In ritual phrases, he castigated the Republicans once more for their "treason." More conservative critiques came from Manuel Llaneza, Remigio Cabello, and Prieto, the last asserting that the strike had not been glorious, but only a failure.* Largo Caballero made a lengthy defense of the strike committee's actions but admitted that the strike had indeed been gravely and unavoidably premature.[132]

On the whole, the majority-minority confrontation in the congress was kept within bounds, and much of the delegates' anger over the events of August was deflected from the strike committee to Ramón Cordoncillo, the head of the Southern Railworkers' Federation, who had refused to lead his men into the strike and was not able to explain his conduct satisfactorily. He was the

---

* "On behalf of 45 workers who were fired in Valencia [there was] a strike that resulted in thousands of workers being fired. It is necessary to refrain from waging strikes for reasons of dignity; we must not wage them when the enemy wishes, nor with a *plazo legal* so that the enemy may prepare and concentrate forces in the places of greatest revolutionary sensibility. The best weapon is surprise." Prieto also asked: "Why did we second the striking workers? If they couldn't be convinced [not to strike], they should have gone on alone." *Nuestra Palabra*, 12.x.18.

target of much verbal abuse in the congress—which seemed determined to blame the failure of the strike largely on him—and he was later expelled from the UGT. In the end, the delegates overwhelmingly approved the strike committee's conduct.[133] That Largo Caballero's image had not been tarnished is revealed by the fact that in this assembly he was elected General Secretary of the UGT, a post that he would hold for twenty years.[134]

Though it sent a message congratulating the Soviet Republic on the first anniversary of the Revolution, the congress nevertheless passed without difficulty a resolution of continued adherence to the conservative International Workers' Association, or Amsterdam International. With some prescience, Largo was even able to push through a resolution excluding the whole question of international affiliation from the next three congresses of the UGT, that is, for the next six years—though, in fact, it would again become an issue at the 1920 congress.[135]

The delegates, perhaps feeling ideologically challenged by the Russian Revolution and by the recent Syndicalist Congress of Sans, adopted—for the first time in the UGT's 30-year history—a set of fundamental principles designed to reaffirm the essential features of Pablismo in its syndicalist guise. The central declaration of this not very revolutionary document read as follows:

> The [UGT] is above all an institution of producers, organized by groups related by trades and liberal professions, [which] in order to maintain firm unity respects the widest freedom of thought and tactics in its components, so long as these are within the revolutionary orientation of the class struggle and tend to work toward the complete emancipation of the working class, [which will] someday assume control of production, transport, and the distribution and interchange of social wealth.[136]

The majoritarian-minoritarian division was somewhat more discernible in the Eleventh Congress of the Socialist Party, held from November 24 to December 3. But even here the war's end seemed to soften and mute factional disputes.[137] Some of the more extreme minoritarians, represented by Rafael Millá and by Eduardo Ugarte of the Young Socialists, brought forward a condemnatory motion against the National Committee for having conducted a too passionately pro-Allied campaign in El Socialista and for having treated the Russian Revolution with less understanding than it merited; but this move did not arouse the congress unduly and was easily voted down, 51 to 5.[138]

Reflecting the intense republican ferment touched off by the defeat of the Central Powers, Fabra Ribas now raised the question of possible Socialist ministerial collaboration in a revolutionary or renovational regime. His motion urged a positive response by the Party to "the possibility or the necessity of participation in power, even within a monarchical regime, when it is a matter of carrying out elections for a constituent Cortes, elections in which it will be necessary to safeguard ... the integrity of the suffrage." Besteiro led the opposition to this measure, revealing himself, as in the summer of 1917, strongly against Socialist ministerial collaboration. More faithful to Guesdist convictions than Fabra Ribas, he seems to have feared that Socialist ministers would, inevitably, be morally discredited by efforts to exercise power in a bourgeois ministry. Besteiro felt that the initial stages of any attempt—whether by a republic or by a regenerating monarchy—to put an end to the innumerable vices of the existing system would necessarily be chaotic and "imperfect," and that this would almost certainly "break the moral force" of those who first took over the reins of power. Not unlike those Russian Mensheviks who, perhaps more from diffidence than from doctrine, preferred to let the bourgeoisie keep command through the unexpectedly stormy seas of the Revolution, Besteiro feared the upheaval and confusion of a revolutionary regime and doubted that the Socialists had sufficient "technical capacity" for the task. Concerned, above all, with the moral purity and integrity of the Party, he was resolved that the "shadows" and "stains" that were bound to fall on a new, renovating republic should not fall on the Socialists. Someday, he said, the Socialists might share in power, but in Spain that day was still distant. The majority of the National Committee, whose spokesman on this issue was Saborit, disagreed with Besteiro; but when the matter was put to a vote the Fabra Ribas resolution was narrowly defeated, 6,278 to 6,157.[139]

But more important in the Eleventh Congress than political issues were social questions. There was a strong feeling, not limited to the minoritarians, that the Party, absorbed by the drama of the war and caught up in the August Movement and in the ensuing political struggle, had been losing its social orientation and concern with concrete social problems. This conviction blended with a general recognition that the Party's minimum program had been, in large measure, left behind by the passage of time. Since 1912, in fact, there had been efforts to formulate a more modern set of programmatic principles, which had failed chiefly because of preoccupation with the war. Challenged by the new era that seemed to be opening up as a result of the Armistice, the Party now took the opportunity to adopt a new minimum program.[140]

There was special concern about the Party's apparent indifference to the agrarian question.[141] This could be no secondary matter in a country still overwhelmingly rural and in a period when acute agrarian unrest, stirred by peasant land seizures in Russia, was beginning to trouble the southern provinces. Despite the PSOE's relative indifference to the land question over the years, it had nevertheless acquired a surprisingly large contingent of members in the South; the largest single group of Socialist adherents (more than 5,000), in fact, came from Andalusia.[142] However, since the 1915 Congress the Party had lost about 8 percent of its Andalusian membership,[143] and there was general concern over its failure to win the support of the peasants, who at that very moment were being drawn in increasing numbers into the rapidly expanding Anarchosyndicalist movement.

Since before the war there had been efforts to formulate a program designed to attract braceros and small farmers, but until this moment little had been done. Now, with the aid of Socialist-affiliated agrarian organizations, such a program was worked out and was presented to the Congress by the indefatigable Fabra Ribas. As a minimum proposal it provided for parcellation—that is, for individual peasant proprietorship rather than for collectivization. A pious proviso was added stating that individual ownership should not involve exploiting the labor of others and recommending—without demanding—collectivization as the best mode of agriculture; but all in all, the proposal was clearly a victory of reality (some 90 percent of the peasants desired individual tenure) over Socialist orthodoxy.[144] This of course drew the fire of the Party's leading Marxist purist, the dogmatic theoretician Verdes Montenegro, who found the agrarian proposal essentially "conservative." More radical than Lenin himself in this regard, Verdes objected to the Party's continued toleration of the small proprietor and spoke of the obstacles this would place in the way of scientific, mechanized farming. A spirited debate between Verdes and Fabra Ribas ensued; but, in the end, with the unanimous support of the peasant delegates, the new program was approved, 32 to 2.[145]

In connection with the passage of the new agrarian program, many delegates urged that an intensive propaganda campaign be launched throughout Spain, and in two areas especially: the agrarian South and Catalonia. There was a general feeling that the Party had to capitalize on the popularity it had won by its martyrdom in the August Strike, and that if a more aggressive proselytizing activity were not carried out, the Socialists would soon be overwhelmed by the rising tide of Syndicalism. The Congress agreed to expand Socialist propaganda activities greatly, and early 1919 would see, in fact, a Socialist counteroffensive that scored some successes, especially in Andalusia.[146]

It was also proposed that the Republican-Socialist Alliance be dissolved; but there was as yet little unanimity among the minoritarians on this point since both Núñez de Arenas and Acevedo still favored the Republican connection, and the initiative was easily voted down.[147] Another issue tending to produce a majoritarian-minoritarian division was the nationalities problem. The majority, urged on by Besteiro, wanted to acknowledge the reality of national feeling, including that of the Spanish regions, whereas leftists such as Verdes Montenegro and, less dogmatically, Núñez de Arenas sought to recall the Party to the Communist Manifesto's insistence that the workers had no fatherland. The underlying question here was the degree of support that the Party should give to the bourgeois Catalan Regionalists, who, in the Wilsonian aftermath of the war, were experiencing a powerful revival. In the end, the Congress agreed that the various nationalities of the Peninsula should be fully recognized—to the degree they desired—but that the affirmation of nationality should not lead to a diminution of human liberties.[148]

All in all, the spirit of factionalism seemed less evident in this congress than in the recent past; and this was especially true with respect to the matter of the International. All delegates were agreed on the need to revive the Second International and on the choice of the Party's representative—Julián Besteiro—to the first postwar congress of the International, then scheduled to be held in Berne early in 1919. There was also unanimity on the delegate's instructions: he was to support the Russian Socialists' proposal for an investigative commission to examine conditions in the Soviet Republic, and also to urge the advisability of postponing discussion of Socialist responsibilities in the war, in order to ensure harmony within the International. With respect to the Bolshevik regime, all the PSOE delegates now felt able to join in a motion hailing the Russian Revolution as "the triumph of the revolutionary spirit of the proletariat," and in a resolution protesting all intervention in the Soviet Republic. With equal alacrity most delegates joined in supporting the League of Nations proposed by President Wilson. The congress concluded with a declaration of republican faith, unanimously approved, which asserted that no fundamental reform could be expected under the monarchy.[149]

After the Congress the minoritarians expressed general satisfaction with what had been accomplished, and despite their earlier critique of oligarchical tendencies they were comforted by the fact that the PSOE, whatever its "rightist" shortcomings, was the only party in Spain with "truly democratic practices." César González expressed the views of most minoritarians when he said that he hoped the approaching organizational conference of the Second International would succeed in harmonizing the different tendencies to be represented in it, carrying to a "happy conclusion the work of conciliation that today is more than ever necessary." At the same time González did not hesitate to criticize the Russian Bolsheviks, whose impending demise he had so recently lamented, for having broached the idea of a new International from which large numbers of Socialists would be excluded. The "Russian extremists," he said, "though filled with doctrine, nevertheless do not seem to possess a great political sense."[150]

By and large, then, ideological differences between Socialist majoritarians and minoritarians in the post-Armistice period did not seem insurmountable, and the Party was more united at this moment than for some time past. This newfound solidarity was encouraged not only by the ending of the war and its divisive issues but also by a growing feeling, shared by nearly all Socialists, that Spain was at last on the move, that the political and social ice-jam of the Restoration system was breaking up, and that great changes were in the offing. Inspired by hope, the Socialists experienced a brief era of good feeling, which would last only until about the middle of 1919.

CHAPTER FIVE

Andalusia and the Trienio Bolchevista, 1918-1920

The rising optimism of Spanish workers stemmed in some measure from the wave of quasi-revolutionary agitation that moved across southern Spain—especially Andalusia, Levante, and Extremadura—in 1918–20. The strikes, riotings, demonstrations, crop burnings, and exaltations of this period, known as the Trienio Bolchevista, led many, especially among the Cenetistas, to dream of mounting a broad, urban-rural revolutionary offensive against the regime. The perennial Bakuninist theme—that urban revolutionaries had to arouse and enlist the peasant masses in order to win success—was once more revived, and efforts were made to carry the Syndicalist message into the countryside. There was, in fact, a mutually stimulating interaction between rural Andalusia and urban Catalonia in these years. The peasants and small proprietors of the latifundio regions were the first to be aroused from lethargy by the news of the Bolshevik Revolution; and when their enthusiasm invaded industrial Catalonia, the Syndicalists were inspired to strenuous organizational and propagandistic efforts, which in turn reinforced the rebellious temper of the countryside.[1]

The Andalusian peasantry had of course experienced "exaltations" before—nearly every ten years, in fact, in a cycle that with mysterious regularity stretched back into the nineteenth century, when the disentailment of Church and municipal lands had disrupted traditional tenures.[2] The last upheaval, influenced by the myth of the general strike, had reached its climax in 1903–4, leaving the peasants thereafter in a condition of indifference and hopelessness. Early in 1914 the Andalusian labor movement had once more begun to revive. Organizational activity had been resumed, Anarchist groups and sindicatos had started to multiply, not rapidly but steadily, and all the precursory symptoms of another great period of agrarian agitation could be sensed. This movement was aborted, however, by the coming of the war, and by early 1917 the number of groups and the level of activity had once more greatly declined. Neither the March Revolution in Russia nor the August Strike Movement in Spain could rouse the southern peasants, largely because of the better pay and nearly full employment that the wartime demand for foodstuffs made possible.[3]

Strike activity in Andalusia was at a low ebb: in 1915 there had been only three strikes; in 1916, one; and in 1917, six.[4] Although the Syndicalist movement in Catalonia had been slowly gathering strength since 1914, this had as yet had little impact in the South. The new Anarchosyndicalism, with its more organizational and ameliorative message, seemed to lack the appeal that the "pure" Anarchist apostles had exerted in the agitations at the turn of the century. Promises of mere material improvement did not effectively capture the imagination of the Andalusian workers, who were responsive only to more millenarian appeals.[5]

This apathy began to dissipate in the early spring of 1918, to be replaced by a rising wave of organizational activity, strikes, confrontations, and meetings. Hundreds of Anarchist militants, whose enthusiasm was always the key to a revival of activity in Andalusia, once more felt their hopes rekindled; and with newfound energy these *obreros conscientes* began the struggle to create workers' societies and to expand their membership. The first of the new unions appeared in the early spring, and by autumn the organizational activity of the peasants was gaining momentum rapidly: in Córdoba province alone, between the summer of 1918 and the summer of 1919, more than a hundred new sindicatos were created. As a consequence, the number of strikes also soared, and the social peace of the region was at an end.

It would be possible to attribute this new cycle of agitation to the delayed impact of wartime price rises.[6] But, though the surge of prices doubtless exerted an influence, the millenarian enthusiasm that permeated the Trienio Bolchevista suggests that it was primarily the product not of deepening misery but of rising expectations. The Anarchist workers' rebellious mood had never, in fact, really been extinguished, and they had impatiently "watched the horizon, awaiting each day the rosy-fingered dawn that would put an end to social injustices." The March Revolution in Russia had not stirred them because they saw in the rise of the Provisional Government not a social but merely a political transformation. The August Strike had also failed to inspire, since it, too, was regarded as a political movement. But the Bolshevik Revolution, coming virtually at the nadir of peasant faith, provided the new social myth that had historically been needed to trigger upheavals in the countryside. To produce the new agitation of 1918, said Diaz del Moral, there was required only an "evocative word"; and that word proved to be "Russia."[7]

The shell of peasant apathy in Andalusia, then, was broken mainly by an impulse from the outside, by news of the Russian land seizures that had been encouraged and sanctioned by the new Bolshevik regime. The fascination that the November Revolution exerted in the south of Spain was thus closely related to the ever-present hunger for land in the latifundio provinces, and to the popular conviction that there must someday be a redivision of the soil, which, as all knew, belonged only to those who worked it.* Although the southern peasants had remained indifferent to the issues of the war, they seemed instinctively to grasp the agrarian nature and importance of the Russian Revolution. For them, the Bolshevik victory had a single but very vivid meaning, being essentially the spectacle of an oppressed peasantry breaking its chains, sweeping aside its landlords, and seizing the land that belonged to it. To all other aspects of the Revolution they were largely indifferent.

This vision of Russian events began to penetrate the consciousness of southern peasants and braceros late in 1917. But it remained underground—"fermenting," as Díaz del Moral said, in the mass of the *campesinos*—while the political life of the middle classes, the conflict of parties and programs, continued to dominate the surface of Andalusian life, unconnected with and oblivious of what was stirring in the depths. As always, the democratic-political revolution of the republicans and Socialists ran on one level and the social revolution of the masses on another.[8] The scholarly Bernaldo de Quirós, of the Institute of Social Reforms, was astonished by the speed with which news of the peasant land seizures traveled from the Russian steppes to the fields of Andalusia. It appeared, he said, as though there were "secret and intimate affinities...of still inexplicable origin, between the serfs of the most distant extremities of...Europe."[9] Yet there was, in fact, nothing mysterious about the rapid spread of the Russian news among even the submerged masses of Andalusia: the word was carried almost entirely by the labor press and by agitators of various ideological hues.

After November 1917 the hitherto somewhat somnolent pages of *Tierra y Libertad, Solidaridad Obrera, La Voz del Campesino, La Voz del Cantero,* and other journals were filled with inflammatory praise for the new Bolshevik regime, which, they proclaimed, was giving peace to the Russian nation, bread to the workers, and land to the peasants. The high rate of illiteracy among the southern peasants was not an insurmountable barrier to the spreading of this message. The fact that the braceros and many of the small peasants of Andalusia were not distributed evenly over the land but were, for much of the year, concentrated in pueblos containing from 8,000 to 25,000 inhabitants facilitated exposure to the written as well as to the spoken word.[10] Even in the fields and in the labor barracks of the great estates, the literate few read and reread newspaper accounts of the far-off revolutionary events. The southern provinces were inundated with Anarchosyndicalist literature, and a news-

---

* "The land exists for the common well-being of men, and all have an equal right to possess it. It has been created for the fruitful activity of the workers who produce, even though the slothful rich unlawfully keep the products of their labor. All property acquired by the labor of others is illegitimate. Only that is legitimate which is obtained by personal, direct, and useful labor." Quoted in IRS, *Información sobre el problema agrario,* p. 6.

paper was the "most appreciated gift" that could be made to a farm worker. "Always the same spectacle was observed: a worker reading and others listening with great attention."[11] In scenes that were suffused with an almost religious feeling, the braceros gathered around their campfires or oil lamps night after night to hear—and sometimes to repeat, almost as a sort of litany—the words that conveyed to them a vision of the distant revolution.[12]

Also effective was the prophetic zeal of scores and even hundreds of Anarchist and Anarchosyndicalist preachers (as well as a few Socialists), who carried the Russian news all over the region, ceaselessly propagandizing the mass of the workers. The first on the scene, in the spring of 1918, were the native Andalusian Anarchists. Like the *prophetae* of earlier millenarian movements, they were simple, ill-educated men—visionaries of great personal purity and often of extraordinary eloquence. The impact of their words on the untutored braceros and peasants was very great; and it was they, nearly as much as the newspapers, who encouraged the mood of millenarian expectancy. Perhaps the most famous of these Anarchist preachers was Salvador Cordón, who, under the burden of his mission, changed his name to Kordoniev. From March 1918 to February 1919 this orator put forth a remarkable effort on behalf of the Bolshevik Revolution and its redemptive message of land reform. Cordón spoke on hundreds of occasions, wrote dozens of articles and pamphlets, and carried on controversies with the Republicans and Socialists. Always defending the most extreme measures, he aroused the workers to such a degree that his meetings frequently ended in riots. As an ardent believer in the coming victory of "Bolshevism" in Spain, he surpassed all other agitators.[13]

The Russian news excited much of southern Spain from Extremadura to Levante but especially that portion of Andalusia lying south of the Guadalquivir. Within this area the most enthusiastic response was observed in Córdoba province, which became the central focus of the agrarian agitations of the Trienio Bolchevista. The reason for this primacy would seem to have been related to the fact that land in the province was broken into numerous small parcels, juxtaposed to large estates. Indeed, many of the great estates, or sections of them, were leased out in small plots to peasants who spent part of their time as petty proprietors and part as workers on the latifundia. Many villages were filled with these small but hardly prosperous proprietors and contained relatively few of those peasants who lived exclusively by wages. The proportion of workers in Córdoba province who possessed at least some land—whether owned or leased—was "enormous," according to Díaz del Moral, and the energy with which the Cordoban peasantry conducted the struggles of the Trienio probably had to do with this fact.[14] In towns where small peasant proprietors were predominant, the agitations were carried on with vigor and tenacity; in towns inhabited largely by landless laborers with no means of subsistence beyond their wages, the movements of 1918–20 were short-lived and lacking in intensity.[15] That some measure of well-being be-yond the subsistence level was needed for rebellious activity was demonstrated by the fact that everywhere it was the small cultivator rather than the bra-cero or town worker who assumed leadership of the organizational and agi-tational efforts of the period.

This fact of small proprietorship, aside from occasionally raising some awkward questions about who was or was not a *patrono*, also may help to explain the decided bias of the peasants toward individual ownership of the land, despite the fact that both Anarchosyndicalists and Socialists advocated some sort of collectivization as the ultimate and ideal solution to the agrarian problem. Earlier attempts to propagandize against individual ownership had met strong resistance, especially in Córdoba province. And during the Trienio Bolchevista both Anarchosyndicalists and Socialists temporized with their own principles and avoided strong stands in favor of collectivization. Indeed, the Cenetistas did not actually adopt a collectivist program formally until 1923; and Brenan estimates that about 90 percent of the peasants continued to prefer parcellation of the land.[16]

The waves of agitation spread outward, and revolutionary enthusiasm was stimulated by still other "great events" in the world. The fall of the German and Austrian monarchies at the end of 1918 led many peasants and workers to wonder how, if these states had fallen, such a fragile thing as the Spanish monarchy could long survive them. Soon, said Díaz del Moral, it was no longer simply the *obreros conscientes* who were agitators. As apathy and the habits of submission were replaced by rising hope, there emerged "hundreds and thousands" of enthusiastic apostles of Bolshevism, both in the pueblos and on the estates. "In the street, in the tavern, workers propagandized inces-santly, at all hours. It was impossible to resist; the avalanche dragged every-one along."[17] An extremely militant mood—a veritable "Russian fever"—swept over great numbers of peasants, so that Russia became an obsession about which many of them could not stop talking.

> All conversation turned inevitably toward the Russian theme. If one spoke of sowing, there arose at once the question: What is sown in Russia? Does it rain much? How much can a *fanega* of land produce? If one spoke of the tempera-ture, they would at once interrupt: In Russia is it warm or cold? And for what reason? Which way does Russia lie? Is it very far?[18]

Through much of the commentary of this period there ran a kind of mil-lenarian excitement. Typical was the exhortation in *La Voz del Campesino*: "Prepare yourselves, workers of Spain, for the fact that at any moment the clarion of justice may sound! Oppressed and desperate people, the hour has arrived to demand accounting from our enemies for all the crimes they have committed against *el pueblo productor*." A militant in the town of Adamuz wrote that "great changes in all the states of the world are expected [and] the working class must prepare for the great commotion, which, effacing all vestige of slavery, will open to all mankind the broad fields of a happy existence."[19] Above all, the news of the Russian land seizures aroused the sense of a new dispensation. By the autumn of 1918, wrote Bernaldo de Quirós, there had penetrated the consciousness of many Andalusian peasants

> the conviction of what they called "the new law," decreed they knew not by whom, when, or where, but of which they spoke publicly, with all ingenuousness, even in front of the *señores*. And [they did this] with tranquil joy, since, by virtue of it, they, the last representatives of so many disinherited generations turned to dust in the earth, after having fertilized it with their labor and their pain, their tears, and even their blood, were seeing at last the hour of the *inversión de posiciones*, of a redistribution of the good things of life.[20]

The desire for land and the expectation of receiving it—all of it and not just part of it—were constantly voiced in this period and provide an important key to understanding the agrarian disturbances in the latifundio regions. All the congresses of agricultural workers formulated the demand for land, and most manifestos and pamphlets spoke of it. The French observer, Costedoat-Lamarque, encountered peasants in various pueblos who gravely informed him that the king had actually signed a decree providing for the repartition of the land but that the local caciques were thwarting its implementation.[21] Everyone who was close to the situation recognized that only a division of the great estates would satisfy the peasants. A proprietor in Puente Genil remarked somewhat sourly: "The field hand is presently winning what he wants [in wages]; nevertheless, he is not satisfied: his desires [*concupiscencias*] are being stimulated by the Anarchist preachings he hears, and he is waiting for the hecatomb, for the revolution...that will transform everything and convert him into a *señor*."[22] A typical peasant manifesto of this era was "The Russian Revolution: The land to those who work it."

> The land is ours because we have watered it with our sweat. Let us take possession of it and defend it to the death. It is no longer a time for requests or demands. It is the time to "seize." A little courage, and we will gain possession of what belongs to us. Peasants, let us follow our Russian brothers and quickly begin the era of social justice that we desire so much.[23]

Thus the agrarian disturbances in Andalusia may well have been due less to rising prices than to rising hopes. It is of course true that prices had risen steadily since 1914, and with special rapidity after the spring of 1917.[24] But the wages of the braceros had also risen, by about 300 percent, and several sources suggest that the workers were appreciably better off in the autumn of 1918 than they had been at the outset of the war.[25] Thus Ortega y Gasset wrote in *El Sol* early in 1919 that the agrarian problem could not be reduced to "the politics of bread and wages." The problem, he said, was not essentially economic; it was "juridical," in the sense that the peasants' movement challenged the very foundation of the social order in the region, that is, the latifundio system. "Within a few months," wrote Ortega, "there may rise up [in Andalusia] perhaps a hundred thousand men brandishing peaceful pitchforks with warlike frenzy. Well, then, these hostile men will not demand bread, they will demand *tierra*."[26]

Syndicalists versus Socialists

The Trienio Bolchevista was marked by conflict not only between workers and employers but also between Syndicalist and Socialist proselytizers. Andalusia has usually been regarded as the domain of the Anarchists and the Anarchosyndicalists, yet the Socialists had a significant clientele there, with Andalusians in fact forming the largest single group (5,454 members) within the PSOE. During the war the Socialist leadership, caught up in pro-Entente excitement, had neglected social questions in general and the agrarian problem in particular. The approach of the Armistice, along with the outbreak of the Andalusian disturbances, had reawakened the Party's concern regarding the land question; and the matter had been debated in the 1918 Socialist Congress (see Chapter 4), where it had been resolved that the Party, on the basis of a modified agrarian plank, would step up its propagandistic and recruiting efforts in Andalusia.

Though gaining new adherents, the Socialists were essentially on the defensive here, as they were everywhere else in the Peninsula during the course of 1919, trying, as *El Sol* said, to "contain" the Syndicalist advance.[27] A determined Socialist effort was launched in Andalusia beginning late in 1918; and in order to match the rhetoric of the Cenetistas, a more radical tone entered into Socialist propaganda. As this campaign gained in intensity early in 1919, relations between Socialists and Syndicalists in Andalusia became strained; the antipolitical bias of the Syndicalists was often very fervent, and the electoral interests of the Socialists sometimes generated extreme hostility. That not all Andalusian workers shared the Cenetista aversion to politics, however, was revealed in the elections of June 1, 1919, in which the Socialist Party received the largest percentage of its votes precisely from Andalusian voters.[28] Socialist trade-union membership in Andalusia also grew substantially, though not so dramatically as that of the CNT. Between October 1918 and July 1919 a total of 44,755 workers entered the unions of the UGT, bringing its total membership to 134,356. Of these, 31,500 were agricultural workers and 28,900 were from the Andalusian region.*

* The membership of the Andalusian Regional Confederation of the CNT, by contrast, reached 100,854 by December 1919; *Memoria del congreso de 1919*, p. 14. The figure of 31,500 UGT agricultural workers (in all of Spain) compared favorably with the Anarchosyndicalist membership of the Spanish Federation of Agricultural Workers, which totaled 25,092 in February 1919; *El Sol*, 10.ii.19.

As the Socialist Party, or at least numerous elements within it, turned left-ward during 1919, and as popular enthusiasm for the Russian Revolution grew, Socialist proselytizers began to draw as heavily upon the Bolshevik myth as did the Cenetistas. Like the Anarchosyndicalists, the Socialists fo-cused their efforts on the pro-Bolshevik masses of Córdoba province. Among the outstanding Socialist agitators in this region were Juan Palomino Olaya, Gabriel Morón, Francisco Azorín, and Juan Morán, all of whom were active as early as the first part of 1918. As elsewhere in Spain, Socialist printed pro-paganda was scarce. Whereas copies of *Tierra y Libertad* and the pamphlets of Anarchists such as Sánchez Guerra or Salvador Cordón were sold by the thousands, only a few hundred copies of *El Socialista* were bought in the whole of Córdoba province. Socialist efforts in this region culminated in an assembly held in the city of Córdoba, April 17–19, which was attended by Largo Caballero and brought together both peasants and miners, as well as Syndicalists and Socialists. A provincial federation of agrarian workers was created, with 24 sections and 14,751 members, and this body immediately en-tered the UGT.[29]

With respect to the contest between Syndicalists and Socialists during the Trienio, a few generalizations may be made. The ideological constancy of the Andalusian workers and peasants should not be exaggerated; they were, in fact, highly changeable, and at meetings often gave equally vigorous applause to successive speakers of diametrically opposed viewpoints. They could easily be led, by those whom they trusted, down the path either of extremism or of moderation, of antipolitical or of political tactics. Whether a pueblo or a workers' society was Syndicalist, Socialist, or "neutral" in this period often seemed to depend more on the leaders than on the rank and file.[30] Although the Syndicalists clearly won the proselytizing battle in 1919—in Córdoba province they had about 60 peasant associations to perhaps 25 for the Socialists—the overall "drift" during the whole of the Trienio appears to have been from Syndicalism toward Socialism.[31] Speaking only of the Cordoban region, Syn-dicalist strength (centered in the town of Castro del Río) was greatest in the populous flatlands and much weaker in the Sierra Morena; the Socialists, by contrast, were stronger in the mountainous townships of the Sierra and cor-respondingly weaker in the flatlands. Both Socialists and Syndicalists com-peted vigorously for the allegiance of the Sierran miners (e.g., in Peñarroya), with the Socialists having the greater success. On the whole, however, the Sierra regions did not play nearly the role in the agitations of the Trienio that the flatlands did.[32]

In addition to the contest between Socialists and Anarchosyndicalists, there also broke out in this period a struggle between Syndicalists and Anarchists within the Andalusian Regional Confederation of the CNT. This was largely a generational conflict stemming from the influx of younger militants into the movement. The newcomers were not always well versed in the Anarchist doctrines that had been so popular in Andalusia around the turn of the century, and in any event they regarded Syndicalism as the wave of the future. These youthful contingents, usually more urban in their outlook, clashed with the older Anarchist militants, whose thought was rooted in the countryside and in the past. The result was a schism within the ranks of the Andalusian Cenetistas and the expulsion from the Andalusian Regional Confederation of the most prominent of all the survivors from the heroic age of Andalusian Anarchism: Sánchez Rosa.[33]

The Quasi-Revolution

The actual course of the agrarian upheavals in Andalusia during 1918–21 may be briefly charted. The "great Anarchosyndicalist exaltation," more intense than all previous disturbances, got under way in May and June of 1918 with successful strikes that gave the first strong stimulus to the forthcoming organizational frenzy. After a slight lull during July and August, while the great majority of workers were busy with the grain harvest, the movement regained momentum again in the fall as the number of unemployed workers grew. The agitation was then given a new and extremist impulse by the fiery Syndicalist congress held in Castro del Río—the true storm center of the Trienio—on October 25–27. Here a minimum program was agreed upon and a combined attack organized. Only a week later there broke out the first of the Trienio's great general strike movements, this one involving 34 Cordoban towns and achieving an unprecedented degree of coordination. The dominant classes of the region were greatly surprised and fearful in the face of this vigorous peasant effort; and in all parts of Spain, as the European war was ending, there was increasing anxiety about the situation in the South.[34]

The height of the agrarian disturbances came between the autumn of 1918 and the summer of 1919. In March 1919 there took place a second major and well-coordinated general strike, which united virtually all the Cordoban towns. In this province—indeed, all over Andalusia, as well as in Extremadura—isolated groups of peasants began to invade the fields. In some cases they "expropriated" the landowners and began dividing up their estates; in other instances they burned crops in the fields and, less often, destroyed houses. During the summer large tracts of ripening grain were burned, and olive groves, orchards, and vineyards were also destroyed. Observers noted numerous fires burning in the fields. The American author John Dos Passos wrote, "Here, as everywhere else, Russia has been the beacon flare," with the result that since 1918 "an extraordinary tenseness" had come over the lives of the Andalusian masses. Perhaps mistaking the true psychology of the peasants, Dos Passos wrote that arson had become "the last resort of despair." At night, he said, "The standing grain burns mysteriously, or the house of an absentee landlord, and from the parched hills where gnarled almond trees grow, groups of half-starved men watch the flames with grim exultation."[35]

There were increasingly violent clashes between the Guardia and the workers of the newly formed and toughly disciplined sindicatos—episodes of "virtual warfare," as Costedoat-Lamarque called them, in which the women were often especially aggressive. In perhaps a hundred Andalusian towns, wrote Manuel Buenacasa, "true experiments in the collective expropriation of capitalist wealth" took place. And in such substantial towns as Aguilar and Montilla, as well as in many smaller ones, "Bolshevik-type" republics were proclaimed. In Cadiz province workers rioted to enforce their demand that all agricultural machinery be withdrawn from use.[36] The movement reached its most intense phase in May 1919 with the unleashing of the third of the great Cordoban general strikes, one that many workers felt certain would be "the last," ushering in the new era of social justice. This was largely a Syndicalist effort, from which the Socialists were somewhat detached. The peasants were at the highest pitch of enthusiasm, and everyone, both peasant and landowner, was anticipating a revolutionary outbreak in June, to be followed by an attempt at a "black repartition" analogous to that carried out in Russia.[37]

At this point, and for the first time, the civil authorities in Córdoba province departed from the policy of marked restraint, and even sympathy, that they had so far displayed. Hitherto, for example, the provincial governor had limited himself to maintaining public order, and had even, on occasion, extended his good offices on behalf of the workers against their employers. But now—with the cooperation of the Maura government, which sent General Emilio Barrera south with some 20,000 troops—army units occupied many of the pueblos, while the workers' centers were closed and their juntas arrested. These measures broke the growing momentum of the movement without extinguishing it. In particular, there were extensive crop burnings throughout the summer of 1919. The agrarian agitations resumed in the autumn, but with some diminution of force as the less resolute and less doctrinaire workers began to withdraw from the unions. The movement, even though declining, would be subject to far more severe treatment by the authorities during 1920, in the course of which it would finally expend itself, leaving the southern peasantry once more unorganized and apathetic.[38]

It should not be imagined that the quasi-revolutionary disturbances of this period were limited to Andalusia. Peasant unrest also spread through the provinces of Valencia, Alicante, Zaragoza, Murcia, and Extremadura. In the last region the same demands for a redistribution of land were voiced, and there were many crop burnings, as well as the occasional destruction of *fincas*, which forced some landowners to flee to the larger towns.[39] In Valencia province the Syndicalist enthusiasm, largely under the leadership of Eusebio Carbó and his journal *La Guerra Social*, also spread rapidly, both in the towns and among the workers in the vast rice fields. Here, as in Andalusia, the Syndicalists made great efforts not only to organize the peasants and workers but also to engender in them a revolutionary spirit. That they succeeded to some degree is indicated by the week-long strike in Valencia in the spring of 1919 (known as the *huelga de saqueo* because the workers emptied the stores of foodstuffs), during which the strikers renamed various streets and plazas "Lenin," "Soviets," and "Revolución de Octubre."[40]

The Syndicalist message was also spread in Aragon, where the CRT once more undertook to send speakers and organizers. The Anarchosyndicalist Santolaria and other Catalan militants organized the local federation of workers' societies in Zaragoza. Angel Pestaña, Evelio Boal, and Simón Piera also came to the aid of the Aragonese workers, and lent themselves to a campaign of Syndicalist subversion among the troops of the Zaragoza garrison, thus planting the seeds for an abortive uprising in the Carmen Barracks in January 1920. Even the terrorist attack, which had not been known yet in Zaragoza, made its appearance as an import from Catalonia.[41] While Syndicalism was coming under increasing official pressure in Barcelona, Syndicalist proselytizing continued to meet with considerable success in other, principally southern, regions of Spain. At the end of 1920 Salvador Seguí would report the following figures for CNT membership: Aragon, 60,000; Andalusia, 160,000; Levante, 180,000; Galicia, 55,000.[42]

Castile, despite the efforts of the Cenetistas, was not significantly penetrated by Syndicalism in this period, although there were increasingly frequent collisions between Socialists and Syndicalists in the Madrid workers' centers toward the end of 1919.[43] Here, too, a quasi-revolutionary atmosphere prevailed during at least part of 1919. Beginning in February there were widespread bread riots in Madrid, during which some two hundred food stores were looted. An American correspondent, noting the "actual physical hunger" around him, wrote that "present-day Spain has much in common with prerevolutionary Russia"; and he reported an almost universal feeling that the revolution was imminent.[44]

This subjective impression aside, the central and northern regions of Spain, where the labor movement was dominated by the Socialists, presented, on the whole, a quieter picture during 1919 than the regions to the south and east. The Socialist Party was content to pursue electoral politics, enlarge its ranks and those of the UGT, step up its propaganda efforts, and attempt to contain the Syndicalist offensive. When Maura once again assumed the premiership, in April, the PSOE convened a national plenum in Madrid (May 10), whose task was to decide whether, in the face of this dreaded consummation, the Party should withdraw from electoral participation—presumably to prepare the revolution—or whether it should continue parliamentary activity and electoral alliances. With only a few dissenting votes, it was decided not only to continue the electoral liaison with the Republicans but to extend it to include the Reformists.[45] Thus the Socialists participated in the next national elections, which were held, under rather corrupt circumstances, on June 1, 1919. In this contest, the Party retained, without adding to, the six seats gained the previous year.[46]

In the Cortes, Besteiro joined with such other "leftist" leaders as Romanones, García Prieto, Alba, Lerroux, Alvarez, and Alcalá Zamora to protest the government's electoral methods and to plan obstructionist strategy. The general impression of Socialist capacity and constructiveness continued to grow. Shortly after the election Cambó, commenting on the moribund condition of the Republicans, observed, "If the number of Republican deputies in the Cortes were converted into an equal number of Socialist deputies, the aspect of the Spanish Parliament would change absolutely, and there would be manifest in the Cortes what is a reality in Spanish life: that there are only two vital affirmations, that of the workers and that of the autonomists." All other parties, said Cambó, represented only the "immense death zone of Spanish politics."[47]

Despite the rapid expansion of the UGT unions, then, the sobered Socialist leaders planned no repetition of the general strike of 1917 but were content to carry on the slow war of electoral attrition that Pablo Iglesias had launched decades earlier; and this despite the risk they ran of being left behind by the rank-and-file Socialists, who, under the spell of the Russian Revolution, were being increasingly radicalized. The essentially conservative tone of postwar Socialist trade-union activity had been revealed early in 1919, when the UGT leaders had gained an interview with the then prime minister, Count Romanones, in order to present to him a very practical and unrhetorical set of proposals: legal recognition of labor unions, the eight-hour day, a minimum wage tied to the cost of living, guarantees for the right of association, accident insurance, weekly rest, labor contracts, retirement benefits for workers, social security for maternity and illness, and social security against lockouts.[48] There were no paeans to the Russian Bolsheviks and no revolutionary threats. The mood of the Ugetista leaders, determined yet very sober, contrasted with the increasingly exalted attitudes that prevailed in the even more rapidly expanding ranks of the Catalonian Syndicalists, into whose hands the revolutionary initiative now fell.

This "abdication" of revolutionary leadership by the Socialists, who were the ones perhaps best equipped to give overall direction to any movement against the monarchy, condemned the Cenetistas to a leadership role they were not really suited to play. Inspired by the Bolshevik Revolution and by the quasi-revolutionary agitations in the South, many Anarchosyndicalists would be tempted to try to go too far too fast. Always beguiled by the notion that a single spark might ignite the revolutionary blaze, the extreme

Anarchosyndicalist leaders would be more concerned with converting strikes into uprisings than with the hard organizing and unifying labors that alone could have made the CNT a viable revolutionary instrument. The CNT would reach the very height of its power in 1919, but it would gravely understimate its enemies and overplay its hand.

CHAPTER SIX

The Apogee of Anarchosyndicalism

The Conditions of Conflict

The victory of the Allied powers did not bring the dawn of progress that many Spaniards had confidently predicted. Instead, the Armistice signaled the beginning of an era of crisis that would surpass in intensity even the revolutionary year of 1917. No fewer than four basic conflicts were interwoven in the life of postwar Spain: one political, involving the struggle of the Left against oligarchy and caciquismo; one regionalist, involving the struggle of the Catalan bourgeoisie for autonomy; one agrarian, flowing out of the revived enthusiasm of the Southern peasants about the prospect of land redistribution; and one industrial, stemming from the renewed optimism and aggressiveness of the urban working class.

It was the last of these, industrial conflict, that most preoccupied the country. The wave of excitement that swept over the Spanish proletariat after the war was especially intense among the workers of Catalonia. Linked to the resurgence of the whole European working class, this renewed vitality had about it something elemental and even inexplicable. As elsewhere in Europe, masses of workers were seized by a combative enthusiasm that led them into labor unions in unprecedented numbers and sustained them through a more vigorous phase of strike activity than had previously been recorded in Spain. And it was not mere economic distress that moved them: like the peasants of Andalusia, the Catalonian workers were aroused more by hope than by despair. It was true, certainly, that the economy began to contract almost as soon as the Armistice was signed, but this decline proceeded relatively slowly; prosperity slackened but did not immediately vanish. The high level of exports was essentially maintained through 1919 and into 1920 owing to the continued demand of the European economies, which had not completed their adjustment to peace. Some depression in the Catalan textile industry could be observed as early as February 1919, and there continued to be much hunger and unemployment. But in general the economic situation during the first two postwar years remained favorable enough to permit a remarkable increase in the number of organized workers, as well as industrial conflict on a large scale. When economic collapse finally came, at the end of 1920, the collapse of the workers' offensive would accompany it.[1]

Thus it was perhaps more the psychology of the period than its economics that explained the depth of the postwar crisis. During the war years tensions and expectations had accumulated, and it was almost inevitable that with the sudden cessation of the conflict the pent-up emotions of the workers would find release. Despite their seeming indifference to the issues of the war, they, too, had acquired a hopeful and even somewhat millenarian attitude, assuming that the end of the great struggle would necessarily bring great and beneficial transformations. This feeling was strongly reinforced by the example of the Bolshevik Revolution, which had begun to capture the imagination of the workers even before the Armistice was signed. More than any other one factor, the Revolution was responsible for the feeling of hope—vague yet compelling—that pervaded the Catalonian masses in this era, convincing them that the advent of the workers' society of equality and justice was no longer a dream but a possibility.[2]

Other factors combined to produce an explosive situation in Catalonia. The labor force of the region had expanded greatly during the war, swelled by large numbers of peasants displaced from the war-afflicted regions—chiefly from Valencia, Murcia, and Almería, but also from Aragon and elsewhere. The proportion of peasant-proletarians in Catalonian industrial cities appears to have reached a peak around the time of the Armistice. These migrants contributed a volatile element that could not fail to strengthen the hand of the more extreme Anarchosyndicalists even as it impeded the organizing and disciplining labors of the moderates. The impact of this mass of angry and illiterate provincials on the development of the Catalonian Regional Confederation (Confederación Regional del Trabajo, CRT) has been difficult to document; but all sources agree that they were more susceptible to extremist appeals than other groups, and that Anarchist proselytizers successfully converted them from blacklegs to *obreros conscientes*.* In fact, no one controlled the "new workers" very well, and this is one reason why the CRT in the postwar period frequently gave the impression of a movement barely under control and eager to go beyond the more sober aspirations of the moderate Syndicalist leaders. It should be noted, too, that the majority of the Anarchist militants—as opposed to the "pure" Syndicalists—were themselves from out-

---

* The Anarchist Ricardo Sanz wrote: "Those workers...who arrived in Barcelona by the hundreds...were at first very badly received because of their conduct as strikebreakers and cheap laborers; [but] when they had lived for a time in the city...working and associating with their fellow workers, they were easily converted, being transformed very quickly into *obreros conscientes* and authentic revolutionaries. They carried within themselves, these ex-peasants, the seeds of hatred and rebellion, which had accumulated in the dry lands, where the conscience of the cacique [and of the overseers] was even more arid than the virgin soil of the region." R. Sanz, p. 20.

side Catalonia, and that a large percentage of the *pistoleros* of this era seem to have been recruited from the ranks of the so-called Murcianos.[3]

Also conducive to labor conflict on a grand scale was the changed attitude of Catalan employers, who, foreseeing an era of economic retrenchment, lost the willingness to grant wage demands that they had revealed during the boom years of the war. When the rising expectations of the workers, who were now more numerous and more formidably organized than ever before, collided with this new intransigence, the stage was set for intense industrial and social conflict. The years 1919–20, though only relatively less prosperous than 1918, would prove to be considerably more turbulent, and Catalonia would seem on several occasions to be on the brink of revolution.[4] The abdication of the Socialists in this era left the revolutionary initiative in the hands of the CNT, which, with its Anarchosyndicalist ideology, was perhaps as close to the temper of the Spanish masses as any organized movement could have been. Indeed, Cenetista leaders were increasingly aware after mid-1918 that their organization was riding an impressive wave of popular revolutionary discontent. The belief arose that it would be possible to join the two component parts of this wave, urban and rural, into a unified movement able to topple the regime.

Although this chapter will not fail to deal with the *révolution manquée* of 1919, it will be more concerned with the failure of the organizational objectives of the moderate Syndicalists. For the most promising possibility at this time was not, after all, that of an egalitarian social revolution ushering in a Proudhonian paradise, but rather the chance that the moderates, led by an energetic and talented organizer like Salvador Seguí, might create out of the postwar ferment a greatly expanded, disciplined, and potent labor organization able to make the weight of the workers felt in Spanish life.[5] This dream would dissolve, not because it was inherently unrealistic but because—and this may be taken as the thesis of the present chapter—the leaders of the CNT, swamped by the new workers, were fatally divided between moderates and extremists. Defeat and disaster flowed in no small measure from the competition between those who wanted to complete the organizational task before essaying revolution and those who, inspired by the Bolshevik example, impatiently sought to begin the revolution at once. Thus in the course of 1919 victories would be thrown away and opportunities wasted as the already febrile masses were urged on to impossible objectives by the extreme Anarchosyndicalists. The moderate Syndicalists, caught between the zealotry in their own ranks, the extremism of the masses, and the obduracy or incomprehension of the authorities, would go down to defeat.

Nevertheless, during 1919 the CNT reached the apogee of its postwar power and influence. "Such was the power and combativeness of the Confederation," wrote Buenacasa, "that our movement absorbed all the interest of the political and social life of Spain....One did not speak of anything but the Confederation, its struggles, its men. The men of the other doctrines and parties were eclipsed into nothing." Indeed, the CNT grew at a remarkable rate during this year, rising in Catalonia alone from 107,096 members late in 1918 to 345,000 by the end of 1919, and in the Peninsula as a whole to about 700,000. Syndicalism was now penetrating regions, such as Asturias and Vizcaya, that had always been considered safely Socialist.[6]

Industrial Unionism: The Sindicato Unico

Much of the new power and appeal of the CNT stemmed from its adoption, in the summer of 1918, of industrial unionism in the form of the Sindicato Unico. This tactical advance was but one aspect of a new phase of organizational effort motivated in large part by the fiasco of the August Strike. Before 1918 the CNT had not been very significant numerically, and its unions were almost all organized along craft lines, without regional organization or cohesion. Outside Catalonia, where the CRT provided an intermediate level, adherence to the CNT came through isolated sindicatos; and since there were perhaps 350 of these, it was hard for the National Committee to maintain communication and coordination. But as a result of the August defeat, the Andalusian disturbances, and the growing numerical strength of the unions, there came a new organizational thrust. In the spring of 1918, for the first time, the National Committee began to make regular contacts with the disparate member organizations outside Catalonia, and efforts to create regional entities were undertaken. At the Congress of Seville, under the guidance of Catalonian Syndicalists, the Andalusian Regional Confederation was organized, with more unions but fewer members than the CRT. The CNT now had two vigorous nuclei: Andalusia and Catalonia. Some 30,000 Andalusian workers were represented at Seville, and it was confidently agreed that "in case the revolution breaks out in Spain, [the Andalusian Regional Confederation] ought to take charge of it in order to give it its true character." The journal *Acción Solidaria*, organ of the new confederation, was launched and began intensive Syndicalist propaganda efforts.[7]

The next major organizational advance came at a congress of the CRT held in the Barcelona district of Sans from June 28 to July 1. Present were 164 delegates representing 198 organizations and 73,860 members. This was an extremely businesslike gathering, dominated by the moderate Syndicalists. Little or no Anarchist rhetoric was heard, and there were only infrequent references to the Russian Revolution, the discussion centering almost entirely on organizational questions.[8]

The Congress of Sans represented the culmination of a centralizing process that had been going on since 1915, when, in response to the growing concentration of Catalonian industry, the first industrial union had been formed in

Barcelona. The August debacle speeded industrial unionization by convincing a majority of militants, including many Anarchists, that particularist scruples had to be overcome and a more potent organizational weapon forged. The crucial decision of the Congress, then, was to jettison craft organization as the basis for the CRT and to adopt compulsory industrial unionism. It was agreed to construct industrial unions—that is, Sindicatos Unicos—in each major branch of production, and to make all existing craft unions simply sections of these. Thus, for example, the metals industry of Barcelona would be organized as a single sindicato with subordinate sections for welders, braziers, machinists, and so on. Each sindicato would be headed by a *junta general* composed of representatives from all its sections; and when this body approved a strike proposed by any one section, all sections would be obliged to render assistance, either by joining the strike or by giving monetary aid. The sindicatos, as the basic units, would be grouped into local federations, and these, in turn, into regional federations, which would form the CNT. The Sindicatos Unicos, then, represented a great advance in centralization within industry, and were a potent new force that would drive Catalan capitalists toward correspondingly larger entities of their own, thus encouraging an escalation of industrial conflict. But the degree of centralization, though impressive, should perhaps not be exaggerated, since the workers in any factory, through their factory delegates, still had the right to deal directly with their employers and, if they chose, to begin a strike independently.[9]

In most respects the decisions of the Congress of Sans were moderate, having a Syndicalist rather than an Anarchist tone. The delegates, as Manuel Buenacasa disapprovingly noted, "did not endorse a frank declaration of libertarian principles." Thus, for example, the resolution on "direct action" was not everything that the more militant Anarchists would have wished: its essence was that in conflicts between capital and labor the unions were obligated to utilize direct action as the "preferred means," but only "so long as circumstances of true *force majeur* ... do not demand the use of different formulas." To many of the more doctrinaire Anarchosyndicalists, this hedging formulation seemed, at best, to give mere lip service to the ideal of direct, unmediated, and unpoliticized relations between worker and capitalist proclaimed by Cenetista ideology. As not infrequently happened in this era, it was the essentially Anarchist militants who were found lecturing the "pure" Syndicalists on the need for strict adherence to Syndicalist principles. Buenacasa thought the contradictory wording was intended as a sop to the few Socialists in attendance at Sans; and this may have been the case, for it is true that the Seguí-led Syndicalists had shown interest in resuming the ties with the UGT that had been ruptured by the August defeat.[10]

The Congress, somewhat indirectly, reaffirmed the apoliticism of the CRT by excluding professional politicians from holding offices within the sindicatos and by forbidding nonlabor groups from intervening directly in the activities of the unions. The sindicatos, moreover, were not to have their headquarters in any political center.[11] Another resolution that seemed nicely balanced between Syndicalist "possibilism" and Anarchosyndicalist orthodoxy was that pertaining to the basic goal of Cenetista activity, whether revolutionary or ameliorative. It was resolved that the unions should seek all the benefits they thought "pertinent" in order to counterbalance the economic power of the capitalist world; but at the same time they should be "essentially concerned" to prepare their members for the abolition of wages, which were identified as "the basis of the disorder and injustice of bourgeois society." More clearly Anarchist was a resolution in favor of establishing "rationalist" schools.[12]

The new Committee of the CRT, chosen at Sans, was made up mainly of moderate Syndicalists: Salvador Seguí, Salvador Quemades, Camilio Piñon, Salvador Ferrer, and Juan Pey. Angel Pestaña was continued as editor of *Solidaridad Obrera*. The two principal leaders of the CRT were, of course, the ebullient Catalan Seguí and the dour Leonese Pestaña. Though not personally close, these two militants complemented each other well: Seguí was a more charismatic speaker, whereas Pestaña was a superior journalist; Seguí was almost completely undoctrinaire, never having been an Anarchist, whereas Pestaña retained traces of his Anarchist past despite the essential moderation of his activities. Neither of these leaders shared in the emotional intoxication with the Bolshevik Revolution that swept through the ranks of the CNT in these years, and both were pragmatic realists at heart.

The Anarchist Orientation of the CNT

The new Committee of the CRT contrasted both ideologically and temperamentally with the new (provisional) National Committee of the CNT, selected three months later, in September, which Buenacasa, who headed it, later described as "an Anarchist group." This new Committee, which sought from September 1918 to December 1919 to keep the CNT on a "straight, libertarian, and federalist orientation," was composed of Buenacasa as acting general secretary, Evelio Boal as first secretary, Andrés Miguel as treasurer, Vicente Gil, and José Ripóll. Buenacasa and Boal were the Committee's dominant figures, and they and their companions succeeded in launching an organizational drive of considerable scope and vigor. Coopting five other militants from the Barcelona Local Federation of Trade Unions, the National Committee divided the various regions of Spain between its members, each one undertaking a heavy labor of correspondence and organization—all of which had to be done in longhand, since the CNT possessed, as yet, no typewriters or paid secretariat. In addition to the Andalusia-Extremadura region, Buenacasa also took charge of international relations with European and American organizations of libertarian tendency.[13]

Buenacasa, born in Zaragoza province in 1886, had originally studied for the priesthood, attending a Franciscan seminary near Seville for five years;[14] but by 1905 his religious faith had waned, causing him to leave the school and return to Zaragoza, where he was employed as a carpenter. Influenced by the Anarchist savant Vicente Carmona, Buenacasa absorbed the libertarian creed and became very active in trade-union work. As editor of the Zaragoza Anarchist organ *Cultura y Acción*, he showed a modest talent for journalism. Married in 1911, he had to flee with his bride across the French frontier to escape the repression that followed the assassination of Canalejas. He revealed himself as a bright, alert, highly sectarian young militant with a self-confessed passion to meet famous people. He traveled to London in 1912, where he met Enrique Malatesta. In 1914 arriving for the first time in Barcelona, he immediately sought an interview with the patriarch of Spanish Anarchosyndicalism, Anselmo Lorenzo. And in 1916 he conversed with Lenin and Zinoviev in Lausanne. Among Spanish Anarchosyndicalists Buenacasa had one of the widest acquaintances with the European labor movement and its personalities. Few militants were more dazzled than he by the Bolshevik Revolution, and he was clearly thinking of himself when he wrote, some years later: "For many of us, for a majority, the Russian Bolshevik was a demigod.... The splendor of the Russian conflagration blinded us.... Who in Spain, being an Anarchist, disdained to call himself likewise a Bolshevik?"[15]

Evelio Boal, who was about the same age as Buenacasa, was a native of Valladolid. Apprenticed as a printer, he had decided to dedicate himself to the theater and, though small, wizened, and tubercular, with an unusually dour personality, had undertaken to become a comic actor. After a few years, claiming to have abandoned a "brilliant" career on the stage, he returned to the printing trade and to journalism, writing numerous articles for *Tierra y Libertad* under the name of "Chispazos." Boal, a heavy drinker, was sufficiently indiscreet at times that his companions on the National Committee ordered him never to go into bars without them. At first, and perhaps understandably, Boal had not inspired confidence in many of the Syndicalist leaders, but his superior intelligence and organizational ability soon gained him a reputation as a *científico*. His talent, along with his obvious dedication and surprising capacity for hard work despite his fail physique, made him one of the three or four most esteemed and influential leaders of the CNT in the postwar era.[16]

In the half-acknowledged contest between Anarchists and Syndicalists within the Confederation, the two main committees—the Catalonian Regional and the National—represented the two polarities of Anarchosyndicalist ideology. The CRT Committee was in reality the more powerful of the two, since two-thirds of all Cenetistas were under its sway and other regional federations were still in the process of formation. As we have seen, it represented an essentially urban and Syndicalist mentality, and was closely geared to the

immediate needs of the working masses. It also had a more consecutive existence in this period and was able to pursue its own policies in essential independence of the National Committee.[17] The National Committee itself did
not, in fact, give any direct representation to the various regions of Spain,
since the statutes of the CNT required that it be staffed by militants resident
in the particular city where it happened to be located. At this time, therefore,
it was entirely filled with men who represented the nine major Sindicatos
Unicos of Barcelona. In fact, there gravitated to the National Committee militants of a more Anarchist stripe, who seem to have represented rather faithfully the sectarian fervor of the provincial Anarchists. Floating, as it did,
above the day-to-day operational concerns of the Sindicatos, the National
Committee tended to take a more elevated and ideological view, concerning
itself with the long-range goals of the movement. Between the Regional Committee, which inclined toward moderation and "economism" in practice, and
the National Committee, which retained its revolutionary and utopian spirit,
the tension was almost constant.*

There were three other influential foci within the peculiarly loose and informal Cenetista power structure: the Barcelona Local Federation, headed by
José Molins; the Catalonian Federation of Anarchist Groups, which exerted,
as might be expected, a rather nominal control over the entities composing
it; and the editorial offices of *Solidaridad Obrera*, presided over by Angel
Pestaña. The last, Pestaña has suggested, may have been the major locus of
influence within the CNT at this time. Referring to his editorial office as
the "Holy See of the committees of the Confederation" and the "center of
all activities," he boasted: "I alone transacted more business in a day with
reference to the organization than the three committees... transacted in a
whole week." Insofar as this was true, it was largely caused by the Cenetista
aversion to paid officers. Since all members of the three committees had to
work full time to support themselves, they were not able to receive workers
or transact business until nine or ten o'clock at night—a time when most
workers were either in bed or in the cafes. By contrast, the offices of *Solidaridad Obrera* were open most of the time, and the militants tended to gravitate
there, seeking information and asking questions. That Pestaña, who until
1922 never sat on any of the CNT or CRT committees, was nevertheless for
several years the number two man in the Confederation, second only to the
incomparable Seguí, would seem to verify the importance of the editorial
office as a seat of power.[18]

* Regarding this division, Nettlau says that "[The National Committee] was not able
to stand up to the Regional Federation and its powerful leaders, who really had the
fullest autonomy; or, to put it differently, while the men of the [National] Committee
were highly concerned with the cause of Anarchism, the members of the Regional Committee, who led the immediate struggle and whose [lives] were at stake, were primarily
concerned with the question of power and with those tactical considerations that seemed
advisable at the time." Nettlau MS, p. 251.

The rapid expansion of the CNT and its adoption of the new "mass" unions lent urgency to the question of whether its Anarchist orientation could be maintained. In the latter part of 1918 a national Anarchist congress was held in Barcelona in order to deal with this problem. Among the notables present were Eusebio Carbó (Levante), Eleuterio Quintanilla (Asturias), Tomás Herreros (Catalonia), Sánchez Rosa (Andalusia), and Galo Díez (Vizcaya). Discussion centered on the Anarchist involvement in trade unions, and the consensus of the congress was that the challenge presented by the growth and restructuring of the sindicatos should be squarely met. Rather than remain aloof in doctrinal purity, Anarchists should join the unions, take an active part in their governing juntas, and attempt to infuse them with Anarchist ideology.[19]

Whether a libertarian consciousness could in fact be transmitted to the masses was a crucial question. Some regarded Anarchism as an inherently elite doctrine and saw an unavoidable contradiction between Anarchist orthodoxy and mass membership. These "pure" Anarchists preferred a smaller CNT that could retain its ideological integrity; they also favored small craft unions, which they could dominate ideologically, and feared that the huge new Sindicatos Unicos, with their masses of *inconscientes* would prove difficult to permeate with Anarchist ideas.[20] The Anarchosyndicalists and "pure" Syndicalists, however, welcomed the influx of doctrinally indigent masses. They counted on using them as a weapon against the bourgeois order and would worry later about giving them an Anarchist consciousness. In the winter of 1918–19 even many of the stricter Anarchists were hopeful that organizational and educational activity within the sindicatos could win the masses to a comprehension of libertarian ideals. Buenacasa, doubtless with some exaggeration, later expressed great satisfaction with the Anarchist campaign launched at this congress, saying that the results "could not have been more flattering," and that within a few months the unions of the CNT were "perfectly infused with the Anarchist spirit."[21]

Syndicalism and Catalanism

The "pure" Anarchists were not the only ones concerned about the rapid growth of the sindicatos. The ministers who governed in Madrid greatly feared the use to which this new force might be put during the era of social instability created by the Armistice. There were, in fact, two movements in the postwar period that by virtue of their aggressive demands and their sway over large masses genuinely alarmed the government and monopolized its attention: Syndicalism and Catalanism. These were, no doubt, essentially antithetical movements—the one exalting class and the other nationality—but the sudden vogue they attained was in both cases largely due to the *fin de guerre* atmosphere in Europe and in Spain, in which for a brief moment all things seemed possible. Both movements felt the force of the ideological winds blowing over Europe in the aftermath of the war, the Syndicalists being no less inspired by Leninist deeds than the Catalanists by Wilsonian promises.*

Since Catalonia had been the most pro-Allied region in Spain, it is understandable that Catalan nationalists were greatly stimulated by the Allied victory and by the war's Wilsonian denouement. Nowhere in Spain, and perhaps nowhere in Europe, did the grand illusion of a peace based on the principles of democracy and self-determination achieve more resonance than in Catalonia, whose citizens felt that their right to national identity had been confirmed by the Allied victory. The campaign for autonomy that had foundered with the Assembly of Parliamentarians in 1917 was revived, and the most aggressive stand within this movement was taken by the Catalan leftists, who hoped to channel the nationalist enthusiasm of the masses into a republican revolutionary movement. A newly founded Republican Federation, headed by Lerroux, Giner de los Ríos, Castrovido, Domingo, and Marraco, demanded complete autonomy for Catalonia and issued a manifesto saying, "We want power. Spaniards, join us in demanding it and, when the time comes, in seizing it."[22] The Madrid ministers, and especially the king, were prepared to make concessions, and the immediate issue was whether a home-rule statute would be drawn up exclusively by Catalans or by an extraparliamentary commission composed of Catalan and non-Catalan notables. The Catalan leftists were intransigently opposed to the second procedure, and in this they were joined by the Socialists, who in this period gave their support to the cause of Catalan autonomy—a policy validated a few weeks earlier at the November Congress of the PSOE. There was, nevertheless, an element of passivity in the Socialist demeanor at this time, which contrasted with the revolutionary initiative they had displayed in the spring and summer of 1917.[23]

The extremism of the leftists placed Cambó once more in the eternal dilemma of the *haut bourgeois*—caught between the reaction of Castilian centralizers, who would deny all autonomist aspirations, and the revolutionary impetuosity of the Catalan leftists, who sought to move toward a vaguely "social" republic in which, as Cambó recognized, the interests of the bourgeoisie would suffer. That Cambó was willing to revive the autonomy campaign owed partly to his bitterness over the failure of the national government, but also to a conviction, which he shared with the king, that the best antidote to the European-wide revolutionary turmoil and to the rise of "Red Syndicalism" in Catalonia was the cultivation of a sane and moderate Catalan nationalism in a context of regional autonomy. On November 14, 1918, Cambó

---

* One may say that the Leninist mystique proved to have greater durability in Catalonia than that of Wilsonism, which was soon overwhelmed by the rising tide of proletarian unrest and middle-class anxiety. Wilson's popularity in Catalonia, says Francés (p. 433), "dissolved like a cube of sugar."

had an interview with King Alfonso in which both men voiced concern over the revolutionary ferment in Europe and in Spain. They discussed the threat of the Syndicalist movement, as well as the current rumors that subversion was beginning to reach the rank and file of the Army in Catalonia. Alfonso confided to Cambó his fear that the end of the war might well mean the resumption of the revolutionary movement that had been aborted in 1917. The concern of both men was focused, of course, on Catalonia, where all the currents of postwar discontent seemed to converge. Cambó told the king that it was essential to revive the Catalanist ideology in order that its essentially unifying and constructive influence might overcome, and provide a channel for, the social and political discontents created by the war and the Armistice. Alfonso seemed to be convinced of the wisdom of this course, and, remarking that autonomy "no longer frightened anybody," he urged Cambó to go to Barcelona and launch a campaign on its behalf.[24]

Meanwhile, autonomist ferment had already begun. As early as November 10 there were demonstrations in the Plaza de Cataluña in Barcelona, and Catalan flags were carried down the Ramblas by impassioned crowds singing the national hymn *Els Segadors*. In Madrid there were counterdemonstrations, in which cries of "Death to Catalonia!" were heard. In the capital the king was reviled for his supposed sympathy to the Catalan cause, and in Catalonia, for his insufficient sympathy.[25] When the music-hall star María Focella was so injudicious as to sing in a Barcelona theater a song ending in the words "Long live Spain," she was driven from the stage, and a wave of rioting was set off in which there were several deaths. Catalan students demonstrated violently in the streets, demanding among other things that their professors give lectures only in the Catalan tongue.[26]

But despite the gravity of the home-rule crisis, the king and his ministers seemed to grasp the essential conservatism of the Catalan movement. As the king's interview with Cambó suggested, they were less disturbed by regionalism, whose men and motives they understood fairly well, than by Syndicalism, which they scarcely understood at all. The great capital of Barcelona, as the Syndicalist stronghold, was increasingly regarded with anxiety and suspicion—in Burgos y Mazo's words, as "an ever-smoldering bonfire of proletarian sedition" capable of showering the sparks of Syndicalist rebellion across the length and breadth of Spain.[27]

The Syndicalist Propaganda Campaign

Such impressions were strengthened when, on December 22, the Catalan Syndicalists began an extensive propaganda effort in the already troubled provinces of the South. In the course of this campaign, which was actually organized by the Committee of the CRT with Seguí taking the lead, the Cenetistas sent out some of their most effective speakers and organizers: Seguí, Pestaña, Molins, Buenacasa, Mira, and numerous others. These militants concentrated their efforts in Andalusia and Levante, where their objective was to convert and organize the town workers while at the same time making efforts to penetrate the countryside and reach the small peasants and braceros.[28] The first propaganda meeting, held in Valencia on Christmas Day 1918, coincided with the Sixth Congress of the Federation of Agricultural Workers (FNAE). Here Buenacasa and Mira spoke to good effect, and the Congress decided that it should take its 99 sections and 25,092 members (of whom more than 15,000 were Cordoban peasants) into the CNT *en bloc*. The visiting Syndicalists found that references to the Bolshevik Revolution evoked a warm response from the delegates, who themselves made numerous demonstrations of sympathy on behalf of the blockaded and embattled Soviets.[29]

Nearly thirty more propaganda meetings were held in the next two or three weeks, in such cities as Alicante, Jerez, and Córdoba, and in Seville, where a branch of *Solidaridad Obrera* was established. The speakers also traveled to the rural areas, where they found the peasants receptive to discussions of the Russian land seizures and of the need for soil repartition in the latifundio regions.[30] Syndicalist proselytizers received the cooperation of various Anarchist groups in the South, who nevertheless made clear their acceptance of Syndicalism as a "method of struggle" rather than as an ultimate goal. Though soon interrupted, the Syndicalist tour would be proclaimed a success by virtue of the encouragement it gave to the formation of new sindicatos and the stimulus it was said to have imparted to the rising tide of peasant disturbances, which, according to *El Sol*, seemed to have gained in vigor immediately thereafter.[31]

The ministers in Madrid were dismayed by the Syndicalist specter that had loomed up so suddenly. The journalist Manuel Aznar expressed their concern when he described the CNT as a "disquieting enigma," a "gigantic question mark" on the Spanish horizon. "Who can say," he asked, "what will come out of those syndical organizations, which are now being born and which appear already bursting with a formidable power?"[32] This anxiety was compounded by the Syndicalist linkup with the rebellious Andalusians, as well as by the persistent rumors that Syndicalist propaganda was being carried on by "certain elements" in the barracks.[33] The ministers refused, moreover, to draw comfort from the fact that the Syndicalists were taking no part in the continuing and often violent demonstrations of the Catalan nationalists and, indeed, had declared their lack of interest in the "bourgeois" autonomy movement.[34]

The Catalanists themselves recognized that the "most formidable Catalan reality" at that moment was not the autonomist but the Syndicalist movement;[35] and Ortega y Gasset would soon be describing Syndicalism as "the sole organized force in Spain."[36] The picture drawn by the journalist Aznar was of a vast, organized, implacable, and mysterious force methodically planning a revolutionary overthrow of the existing society:

> Never ... have the workers felt so certain of their strength and of their victory. Haste does not consume them, nor does eagerness to arrive at a victory [make them precipitate]; they weigh and measure their forces with serenity, ... and they prepare, as a major power studies its great battles, a plan of general uprising, coordinated and connected in its multiformity, a proletarian rebellion against the social order.[37]

By January 16 the nerves of Count Romanones and his ministers could bear no more. Constitutional guarantees were now suspended, and scores of Cenetista leaders were arrested, many of them still in the midst of their propaganda work in the South. Among those jailed were Seguí, Buenacasa, Herreros, and Negre. But if Romanones thought that this would prevent the long-awaited Syndicalist blow he was mistaken; and he may even have hastened its coming.[38]

The La Canadiense Strike

While Catalan nationalists, in the Cortes and in the streets, were pressing the need for home rule in Catalonia, the Syndicalists were planning an action intended to decide, in effect, who would rule at home. The first major test of strength of the newly expanded and reorganized CRT began on February 5, with a strike against Ebro Power and Irrigation, a Canadian-British enterprise popularly known as La Canadiense. This firm supplied electric power from the Ebro river to the homes and factories of Barcelona, and was therefore the key to the whole industrial complex. The strike, along with the ensuing conflicts, ensured that the autonomist movement would be relegated to the background for some time as the national problem was suddenly overtaken by the social question.[39]

The choice of La Canadiense for the first great labor confrontation of the postwar period was not fortuitous. Although there was an authentic labor dispute in progress there, the decision to strike a company so vital to the region's industry had as its wider purpose the winning from Catalonian employers of full recognition for the Confederation, along with the acknowledgment of labor's right to conduct its affairs in a free atmosphere. The second objective may be regarded as essentially political, in that it would enable the CNT's rapid growth to continue and assure the organization's position as one of the most powerful forces in the life of Catalonia and of Spain. This, one must feel, was the principal stake in the La Canadiense strike.[40] In the event, Cenetista resoluteness combined with the stubbornness of management to produce a 44-day strike so intense and complete that the city of Barcelona was virtually paralyzed, a strike never since equaled in magnitude in Spain. Most important, the action was the first major test of the new organizational weapon, the Sindicato Unico—specifically the Sindicato Unico of Water, Gas, and Electrical Workers, whose successful organization would make it possible to bring into the strike not only the La Canadiense workers but those from the other power companies in the area as well.

The strike had its origins in January, when the company—responding, it would appear, to the end of the war boom—sought to reduce the wages of certain categories of workers. When some of those affected turned to the Sindicato Unico early in February, eight of them were fired. Three days later, on February 5, all the workers of the affected section declared a work stoppage—in effect a plant occupation—and sent a delegation to the civil governor, González Rothwos, urging his intervention in a dispute that had now come to center on the right of unionization. The request was in vain; and after the expulsion by the police of 140 workers from the resisting section of the La Canadiense plant, the strike expanded until it included the employees of all the electric companies in the area. Some 600 streetcars were idled, paralyzing public transportation in Barcelona province and plunging the city into a darkness that Pestaña likened to "the end of the world." When the textile workers joined the strike shortly thereafter, some 70 percent of all the factories in the Barcelona industrial region were shut down.[41]

Much of the strike's organizational work was shared by the Sindicatos Unicos of Construction, Woodworking, and Metallurgy, all under the guiding spirit and organizing genius of Salvador Seguí, despite the fact that he was in prison at the time. The role of the civil governor seems not to have been a constructive one. When the head of La Canadiense, Mr. Peter Lawton, at first proved to be disposed to conciliation, he was quickly pushed into an intransigent posture by González Rothwos.[42] Count Romanones was more inclined to moderation; but even he saw the necessity of ordering troops to take over the power plants in order to restore light to Barcelona, which he did on February 21. Now the remaining employees of the Barcelona waterworks joined in the strike, which became complete with respect to electricity, gas, and water. When the companies sought to publish an ultimatum threatening the workers with dismissal unless they returned to work, the Printers' Union imposed a "red censorship" on all Barcelona newspapers, delaying its appearance for several days.[43]

The next move was made by the Captain General of Catalonia, Milans del Bosch, who proceeded to conscript into the Army all the employees of the electric, gas, and water services between the ages of 21 and 31. Canalejas had successfully used this tactic to thwart a large rail strike in 1912, but it proved less effective on this occasion: most of the workers drafted simply did not appear, and those who did refused to carry out their duties.* As a result of this mass resistance, nearly 3,000 workers were interned in Montjuich Prison, and a state of war was proclaimed in Barcelona province.[44] Despite these measures, the Romanones government was every day more concerned to reach an agreement with the Sindicatos. Indeed, there was very little else it could do. The resort to conscription had failed, and the equipment and cables of the power companies were, despite the military takeover, approaching breakdown and possible destruction. In Andalusia, the agrarian disturbances were becoming serious, and in Madrid there were recurrent bread riots and lootings. At the same time, the Socialists were threatening to bring the UGT into a solidarity strike with the CNT, an action that could have spread the conflict throughout Spain.

Romanones was a realist, and he bowed to circumstances: González Rothwos was suddenly removed as civil governor, and the Catalan engineer Carlos Montañés, who also happened to be an officer in La Canadiense, was appointed in his place. Chief of Police Martorell was replaced by the more liberal Gerardo Doval. Most crucial, perhaps, was Romanones's decision to send his personal secretary José Morote to Barcelona to contact the parties involved. Morote succeeded in arranging talks between management and the strike committee, and the two eventually signed a strike settlement on March 17. The terms can only be described as a capitulation by the employers and something close to total victory for the workers: all imprisoned workers were to be freed, except a few who were subject to trial; all strikers were to be rehired without penalties of any kind; general wage raises were granted; the eight-hour day was conceded; and the workers were to be paid for the time they had been on strike.[45]

The victory of the Sindicatos was complete. What remained was to win the agreement of the Barcelona workers to the terms of the settlement. Since they, too, were approaching the limits of endurance, this should not have been difficult. However, the mood of the extreme Anarchosyndicalist militants was increasingly exalted, and their hold over the workers very great. Recent events—the triumph of the Bolsheviks, the agitations in Andalusia, the riots in Madrid, and now the sudden capitulation of the Barcelona employers—had stimulated the belief that the revolution was not far off. Not interested merely in consolidating the gains of the La Canadiense strike, these activists succumbed to hubris and demanded a continuation of the strike until the capitalist enemy was completely vanquished and the millenium achieved. Until this moment the Anarchist groups had been kept under control by the superb organization

---

* Pestaña later claimed that the workers were left completely free to decide whether or not to report for work; but it is difficult not to believe, with Fernández Almagro (p. 352), that the extraordinary pressures placed on the men by union leaders stiffened their resistance.

and discipline generated by the La Canadiense strike. Now, in the moment of victory, they threatened to get out of hand, appealing to the already inflamed Barcelona workers and apparently hoping to touch off the proletarian upheaval for which they longed. In a relatively small meeting held in the Teatro del Bosque on March 19, the intransigents were in fact able to persuade some workers to reject the bases of the settlement; Seguí and the other strike leaders therefore decided to call another and much larger meeting for the following day.[46]

The climactic moment came on March 20, when some 25,000 Barcelona workers met in the Plaza de Toros de las Arenas. Here they were addressed by the heads of the various sindicatos who, led by Salvador Seguí, urged acceptance of the terms of the settlement and a return to work, so that the great victory could be consolidated. From the stands, however, a militant minority of *exaltés* severely heckled the speakers and exhorted the workers to continue the strike. Since these were armed and aggressive men, mostly members of the Anarchist action groups, they perhaps exerted something more than mere moral pressure.[47] The first few speakers were easily shouted down, and it began to look as though the meeting would be a debacle for the moderates. But the leader whose influence had, above all others, to be overcome was Seguí, the man of the hour, who was nearly at the summit of his success as a labor leader, with victory almost in his grasp.

Salvador Seguí

Salvador Seguí was born into a peasant family in the pueblo of Tornabous, near Urgell, on December 23, 1890.[48] When he was two years old his parents migrated to Barcelona, which was then in a phase of expansion, drawing large numbers of workers from the countryside. The only son of indulgent parents, Seguí grew up in an industrial suburb of the Catalan capital as an exceptionally willful and even rebellious youth, intractable where formal education was concerned. At the age of ten he chose to take a job and was apprenticed to a housepainter; but he had gone to work mainly in order to be free of parental constraints, and what he really sought was not work but freedom and a life of adventure in the streets of Barcelona. He proved to be a restless apprentice and an indifferent housepainter, going from one master to another and working no more than was absolutely essential. For several years he ran free in the streets with other undisciplined adolescents, absorbing instruction from the life of the city. But though he verged on delinquency, there were intellectual overtones to his life. He was an obsessive reader, frequenting the library of the painters' union, the Biblioteca Arus, and even the library of the University. He read Nietzsche in this period, and for a brief time *Thus spake Zarathustra* was his Bible. He and some other turbulent youths founded a group called Los Hijos sin Nombre, which passed the time drinking in a disreputable tavern in the Calle del Arco de Teatro and formulating irreverent critiques of the existing order of the world.[49]

Later, Seguí was the central figure of the Círculo Español, an informal debating society that met in the old Café del Paralelo and included intellectuals, Bohemians, Anarchists, Socialists, writers, and transients, all gathering in an atmosphere of camaraderie and free-flowing conversation. Everything was discussed: politics, art, speeches in the Cortes, books, philosophy, astronomy, social problems. The only criteria for membership were wit and a certain lack of social respectability. The habitués of the Circle belonged essentially to a subculture whose members divided their time, as Viadiu says, between the *cárcel* and the *calle*. There were a number of radical foreigners who attended, some of them deserters from the French army. And, always, the plainclothes police sat a few tables away, with ears cocked and brains dazed by discussions of Nietzsche, Kant, Bakunin, Stirner, Proudhon, or Marx.[50]

Though a mediocre housepainter and a willful apprentice, Seguí very early took an interest in trade-union affairs, discovering his métier as an agitator and organizer. He first spoke in public at the age of twelve, and at fifteen he was effectively haranguing crowds on street corners and serving as a member of the junta of his union. He emerged as a remarkably self-confident figure, aggressive and frequently involved in affrays of various kinds. By the time he was eighteen he was entering regularly into debates and polemics within the syndical organization, often rising up at meetings to challenge the speakers and to deliver extemporaneous orations. On one occasion he challenged José Negre, one of the founders of the Syndicalist movement, earning at this time the sobriquet "Sugar Boy" (El Noi del Sucre).[51] Around 1906–7 he carried on violent controversies with the Lerrouxist Radicals, who sought to discredit him by accusing him of complicity with the terrorist Juan Rull. Unable to get the public retraction he demanded, the volatile Seguí, with a few friends, invaded a Radical meeting in the Teatro Condal. When he was refused permission to speak, the gathering quickly became a melee, at the height of which a Radical militant was shot dead. Although Seguí denied responsibility for this, he spent nine months in jail. As for the terrorist Rull, Seguí later, though without great enthusiasm, testified against him in court.[52]

Seguí, now nineteen, took some part in the events of the Tragic Week, having to flee the city thereafter and work for a time in Gualba. He attended the congress of the Bellas Artes in 1911; and in 1914 he was a delegate to the abortive antiwar congress in El Ferrol, whose holding he had opposed. In January 1915 he was named president of the Barcelona Federation of Construction Workers, and subsequently took the lead in organizing a score of new sections and turning the Federation into a potent and unified organization—the base of his power within the CRT.[53]

Despite his stormy adolescence, Seguí matured as an attractive and integrated personality. He was physically large, powerful, good-natured, and occasionally hot-tempered. Possessed, as Victor Serge observed, of "an ordinary degree of ugliness," Seguí was at the same time endowed with a compelling charm that even his enemies found difficult to resist. Few who met him escaped the impression of boundless energy, spiritual health, and greatness that he exuded. Though a widely read autodidact, who occasionally disconcerted his proletarian audiences with references to Greek literature or Chaldean history, Seguí was only an average writer.[54] He conquered instead with the spoken word, and was acclaimed as perhaps the greatest crowd orator in Spain. Whether in an amphitheater or in a committee room, Seguí's emotional, vibrant tones and rising inflection electrified his audiences, and there were few who could override his powerful elocution or halt the torrential flow of words.[55]

The irony of Seguí's career lies in the fact that despite the nihilism of his youthful views and the demagogic skills that he commanded as an adult, he emerged as a profoundly moderate leader. His unusually quick and clear intelligence was wholly disinclined to whatever was theoretical or extreme, his temper was urbane and secular, and he was mainly absorbed in practical problems of organization and tactics. He had, in fact, never been an Anarchist; and if he occasionally quoted Nietzsche or Bakunin, it was more from conceit than from conviction.[56] Yet Seguí had a vision of his own: that of a vast, harmonious, organized, disciplined, and invincibly powerful Syndicalist movement, which would encompass all the workers of Spain and one day be able to take charge of the country, substituting itself for the defunct state power of the bourgeoisie. In this sense he was perhaps, as Raymond Carr has said, "strategically" a revolutionary, one who comprehended that such a task was the labor of years and even decades.[57] His clash with the Anarchists came chiefly over their desire to use the organization prematurely in their struggle for an immediate revolution. Whether the right moment would ever have come for Seguí—whether he would have been able, in the end, to stake his hard-won organization on a revolutionary gamble—is, of course, impossible to say with certainty. He often remarked that he wished to become the Lagardelle or Griffuelhes of the Spanish labor movement; but one can wonder whether, if he had lived longer, he would not have emulated Léon Jouhaux—or Largo Caballero—instead.[58]

No doubt Seguí's commitment to revolution was sincere. Certainly his rhetoric had a revolutionary tonality that was persuasive to masses of Catalonian Cenetistas who would never have accepted the leadership of an overt or self-confessed reformist. Yet he was no less convinced than the Socialist leaders of the UGT, with whom his enemies sometimes compared him, that the revolution in Spain lay far in the future, after a lengthy period of preparation.[59] Like the Ugetistas, he recognized that the labor movement was still in its infancy, and for the present he was concerned with fostering the power, organization, and material well-being of the Syndicalist masses. In doing so, his strong sense of tactical realism dictated the need for accommodation and alliance with other groups and forces in Spain. Of all the Cenetista leaders, none was more prepared than he to contemplate an "opening to the right."[60]

The revolutionary ferment of the period 1918–20 aroused in Seguí an ambivalent response. He was gratified by the momentum the labor movement was acquiring, but he could not escape the feeling that Spanish workers were not ready to take over the reins of society. He wondered, in the words of his biographer Viadiu, whether it was wise to "produce the disintegration of the enemy prematurely . . . without having in one's hands the . . . means to guarantee that the overthrow would have the lasting character" necessary. The contradiction between the growing revolutionary fervor of the Spanish masses and their lack of technical and cultural preparation was Seguí's "torture"; and it was, of course, the principal reason behind his lack of enthusiasm for the Bolshevik Revolution, whose contagious example he feared. Thus he incurred the hostility of the Anarchist action groups and would continually be confronted by "a gale of insults and defamations capable of paralyzing anyone who did not have a will of steel and solid, deeply rooted convictions." While seeking to guide the inconstant Catalonian masses and withstand the extremists, Seguí would often experience moments of bitterness.[61]

In the Plaza de Toros meeting, Seguí and the other leaders confronted a turbulent assemblage of workers who were not themselves certain of what they wanted and who were being incited by the Anarchists of the action groups to prolong the strike. The Anarchists justified their intransigence by the fact that not all the arrested workers had been freed; but in reality they seem to have been hoping for some kind of "final" victory over the bourgeoisie. From the platform Francisco Gironés, Simón Piera, Paulino Díez, and Francisco Miranda all spoke, amid constant interruptions and threats from the audience, urging the workers to accept the settlement and return to their jobs. The Anarchist Miranda, who as a rule was no moderate, was especially harassed when it became clear that he, too, was urging a return to work. The issue was entirely in doubt when Seguí stood up to speak, and the majority of the assembled workers appeared to be in a more bellicose mood than ever— noisy, excited, and barely under control.

Talking in Catalan, as he nearly always did, Seguí reasoned, argued, chided, and even swore at his restless audience for more than an hour before he was able to subdue and dominate them. With characteristic audacity, he told them they had only two choices: to return to work and await the promised release of the prisoners, or to march with him immediately to Montjuich and release them by force, which would of course have meant, as Seguí pointed out, the beginning of the revolution. In the face of this somewhat stark posing of the alternatives, the workers fell into sobered silence. Seguí then proposed an immediate return to work, giving the authorities three days in which to set free all prisoners; if this condition were not met, an immediate general strike would be declared. He shouted, "Is it agreed, then, to return to work?" And after the slightest hesitation, the answer came back like rolling thunder: a loud, unanimous "Yes!" The meeting was over and, for the moment, the La Canadiense victory was saved.[62]

The General Strike

The Barcelona workers had won an impressive victory and seemed about to consolidate it. Yet almost immediately, partly because of their own immoderate desires and partly under pressure from the Anarchist action groups, they proceeded to throw it away. When the Captain General of Catalonia refused to release the prisoners still in custody, apparently on the advice of the Military Junta, the moderate Syndicalist leaders were disposed to give the matter more time and to reach some sort of compromise. But the recalcitrance of the Army and of the local authorities (though not of Romanones himself) was the opportunity the action groups had been waiting for. Exerting every kind of pressure, and in some cases overriding by threat of force both the leaders and the rank and file of the unions, they were able to throw the CNT into a general strike on March 24, even as the regularly constituted strike committee was still negotiating with the authorities.*

This was, as Buenacasa later admitted, the "greatest tactical error" that the CNT could have committed.[63] Immediately on the heels of the previous strike, the workers had to begin a new period of economic hardship, police repression, and clandestine operation, during which the morale and cohesion of the Cenetistas would be seriously eroded and the way opened for a revival of Anarchist terrorism. The general strike by no means produced the immediate collapse of the CNT, whose sindicatos continued to grow with great rapidity; but it began a gradual displacement of moderate, established union leaders by extremist elements and paved the way for the domination of the unions by the Anarchist action groups.[64] Looking back, the Syndicalist leaders would later recognize that the massive solidarity and discipline of the La Canadiense strike had been a tour de force—almost an aberration—that could not be maintained against all the forces of spontaneity, indiscipline, and extremism within the Confederation.[65]

Just three days, then, after the settlement of the La Canadiense strike a

---

* Guillén Salaya writes (p. 24): "The 'groups,' the 'special delegates,' overrode the leaders, and, with the force of their pistols, decreed again the general strike. From this moment the will of the members in the sindicatos counted for nothing. The thousands of workers organized 'democratically' in the Sindicatos Unicos had neither voice nor vote. They obeyed for good or ill the dictatorial orders of the 'special delegates.' "

new, and general, strike was proclaimed, this being, as Baratech Alfaro says, the "last challenge" of the militant Anarchosyndicalists to the state. By noon on March 24, as the result of a remarkably coordinated effort by the action groups, the strike in Barcelona was total. Factories, shops, stores, businesses, offices, dockyards, and even banks were closed. "The triumph of the *grupos*," writes Baratech, "was grandiose, epic. Never in the annals of the labor struggle had there been anything like it." The workers did not in all cases comprehend why a new strike had been called so soon after the first one; but such was their discipline that they responded by instinct, hoping the leaders would before long apprise them of the reasons. In the end, however, the general strike would create resentment among many workers, since its purpose was unclear, its calling irregular, and its results disastrous. Almost overnight, the workers would lose everything gained in the La Canadiense strike.[66]

As before, electric power in Barcelona was cut off by the strikers, and public transportation was paralyzed. But this time the authorities responded with vigor and decisiveness. Martial law was immediately declared, and troops were brought into the city, where, apparently expecting a revolutionary outburst, they deployed machine guns, cannon, and cavalry units. Even more effective, perhaps, was the activity of the Somatén, an ancient rural militia force now operating in the city and staffed by about 8,000 bourgeois volunteers who patrolled the streets 24 hours a day. With the cooperation of the Army, the Somatén compelled stores and businesses to remain open and also arranged a system of provisioning that kept the city going despite all Cenetista efforts. At the same time, they carried out a systematic intimidation on the streets of all who gave the appearance of being workers. The volunteers, Army, and Police all took part in the arrest of union leaders, who were rounded up in large numbers, the greatest stroke being the arrest of all 200 members of the Cenetista general strike committee. On April 2 all unions were closed down, their records impounded, the collection of dues forbidden, and the trial of many labor leaders ordered.[67] Simultaneously, a Royal Decree established the eight-hour day, to go into effect after October 1; Spain thus became the first country in the world in which this limit was established by law. The decree doubtless achieved some of its intended purpose, which was to encourage workers to return to the factories. Although the strike went on, during its second week it began to wane, as some factories, part of the streetcar system, and most businesses and stores were able to resume operation. Workers in growing numbers broke discipline and returned to their jobs; the most stubborn resistance was shown by the metallurgical and construction workers, who did not resume work until late in the third week. By April 14, the general strike was at an end.[68]

The consequences of this impetuous and ill-advised action were uniformly bad for Catalonian Syndicalism. For one thing, it compelled the Employers'

Federation of Barcelona to undertake a reorganization (August 9) that not only gave it greater potency but also threw power into the hands of the most extreme employers—those whom Pérez Solís would call "bolchevistes de orden."[69] The industrial situation was polarizing, and the moderates on both sides were being pushed from the stage. The Catalan capitalists began to contemplate resorting to their most drastic weapon: the lockout. They also began firing militant workers from their factories in substantial numbers, at the same time circulating extensive blacklists.[70] Action had brought reaction, and the employers had conceived their own fierce vision of the class struggle. Their intransigence would startle even the Conservative Minister of the Interior Burgos y Mazo, who assumed office in July. Though noting the "growing frenzy" of the proletariat, he was even more dismayed by the "hard, unjust, provocative, and disruptive egoism" of the majority of capitalists. He had no doubt that the "shortsightedness" of the business class contributed greatly to the strength of the radical movement in Spain: "Is there a better incubator of Anarchism and Syndicalism than they provide?"[71]

The end of the general strike coincided with the resignation and somewhat hasty return to Madrid of Governor Montañés and Police Chief Doval, who were, in effect, forced out of Barcelona by the combined will of the Employers' Federation and the Military Juntas (whose spokesman was Milans del Bosch). This unexpected alliance between the Army and the Catalan bourgeoisie was directly related to the Syndicalist threat and reflected the bourgeoisie's reassessment of where its principal interests lay. The ouster of Montañés and Doval, in turn, caused the resignation of Count Romanones, on April 15, and brought into the open a fundamental divergence of opinion regarding the best method for handling the Sindicatos Unicos and the suddenly proliferating hordes of organized workers. The Romanones-Montañés policy, despite its apparent toughness, was actually predicated on the unavoidable coexistence of both unions and employers and the desirability of eventually normalizing relations between them. By contrast, the Army-employer plan was predicated on a virtual war of extermination designed to liquidate the unions in their formative stages.[72] Many employers, fearing that the relative prosperity of 1919 would not last, did not want to have to confront the Sindicatos during the harder days ahead. The La Canadiense strike had warned them of the CNT's potential power, and they preferred to give battle now rather than later. Many capitalists sincerely felt, as Peirats says, that it was a matter of life or death to eliminate the powerful labor confederation before it became still more potent.[73]

This tough policy would prevail during the spring and summer of 1919. For the result of Romanones's resignation was the return to power of Antonio Maura, whose short-lived government (April to July) proved willing to sanction a continuation of martial law in Barcelona, as well as harsh measures against the peasants in Andalusia (see Chapter 5). Thus the policy of anti-Syndicalist repression was continued for four months after the end of the ill-fated general strike, and the most energetic measures were used in an effort to suppress every sign of Syndicalist activity.[74]

Repression: May to August, 1919

Successive Spanish governments in this era did not follow a consistent policy toward the Syndicalist movement. Instead, they alternated between phases of severe and unintelligent repression, which, by failing to distinguish between moderate and extremist elements, actually favored the growth of Anarchist intransigence, and phases of conciliation that never lasted long enough to demonstrate the value of moderate tactics. Thus to the complex syndrome of social, economic, and psychological factors nourishing the Anarchosyndicalist phenomenon in Catalonia was added the impact of state policy, which, with its periodic mania for closing down the sindicatos and jailing their leaders, virtually handed the workers over to those best equipped to operate clandestinely and most disposed to meet violence with violence: the Anarchists of the action groups.

Between May and August the unions of Catalonia lived under the martial law imposed by Milans del Bosch. Their existence was not recognized, their leaders were imprisoned or forced to flee, and their activities—especially the all-important collection of dues—were strictly forbidden. During this period, according to Balcells, no less than 43,000 Cenetista militants were imprisoned.[75] Nevertheless, the unions survived underground, and even flourished. Because of the discipline and organization they had achieved prior to the general strike, they were able to weather with some ease this first of the three major blows that would be leveled against them in the period from 1919 to 1922.* The workers and their leaders remained remarkably confident and full of fight. New, secret governing bodies were created, and a small army of union delegates—now operating within rather than outside the factories—collected tens of thousands of pesetas every month.[76]

But during this same period there began a major shift of power and influence within the CRT. Up to this time the regional committees and the juntas of the unions had been dominated by relatively more experienced and more moderate militants. These men, personified by Salvador Seguí, paid a certain amount of lip service to Anarchist principles and revolutionary objectives, but they were increasingly pragmatic in their thinking, focusing more on means than on ends and concerned above all with material and organizational gains.

---

* The three major phases of repression were: (1) under Milans del Bosch, May to August, 1919; (2) under Count Salvatierra, January to May, 1920; (3) under Martínez Anido, November 1920 to October 1922.

It seems evident that on the eve of the repression of 1919 something like a Syndicalist bureaucracy was in the process of formation—despite all the obstacles placed in the way of bureaucratization by Cenetista attitudes and traditions, and especially by the lack of paid officials in the sindicatos and committees. The ever-perceptive Díaz del Moral hints at the beginnings of this transformation:

> The great triumphs achieved by means of organization and collective actions; the spread of the Syndicalist press, which, though still directed in large measure by libertarians, cultivated mainly union themes; the habits of discipline with which *convivencia* in workers' organizations and the heat of battles infused the members; the structuring of the new unions in Sindicatos Unicos, which subordinated individual activity and that of the sections ... to collective ends, restricting the liberty so sedulously defended by Anarchism: [all] were slowly modifying the convictions of the leadership groups, who, without being aware of it, unconsciously moved toward pure Syndicalism, radically opposed, at bottom, to fundamental Anarchist principles.[77]

This progression from Anarchist spontaneity and amateurism to Syndicalist bureaucracy and professionalism was, under normal conditions, the almost inevitable path of a mass labor organization—even of one rooted in the Catalonian milieu—and it had already been traced out north of the Pyrenees, by the French CGT. But under the heavy-handed repression of 1919, the historical process was, in effect, reversed. Increasingly, the regular leaders—those incipient bureaucrats—were being jailed or forced into exile, and the "new men" of the Anarchist action groups were gaining control of the clandestine juntas and committees of the CRT. As a result of the police persecution, the Dutch newspaper *Nieuwe Rotterdamsche Courant* observed, "Men of moderate and sane views are abandoning the leadership of the unions, which thereupon falls into the hands of the young, the champions of extremist views."[78]

Anarchists Versus Syndicalists

Repressive state policies thus impinged on the continuing struggle between Anarchists and Syndicalists within the CNT, tipping the balance in favor of the former. This contest had begun with the founding of the organization and had occasionally produced some sharp polemics. After about 1915 the differences between the two factions grew greater but were muted in their expression because of the pressures of the labor struggle. Max Nettlau, an Austrian savant and a "pure" Anarchist, refers to this relative truce as a "misleading and frequently dishonest solidarity" that was not broken until the Manifesto of the Thirty in 1931.[79] As early as 1916, the Anarchist Mas-Gomeri, writing in *Tierra y Libertad*, had declared the "beginning of hypertrophy" in Syndicalist ideals because of the "purely practical or commercial" nature of the Syndicalism of the time. He and the Syndicalist Manuel Andreu carried on a polemic that ultimately ended in blows in a Barcelona cafe: Andreu had given a talk entitled "Syndicalism is sufficient unto itself" and had said that Anarchism, which he described as "literary lyricism," was no longer needed in Spain.[80] In 1917 there was a sharp dispute between the editors of *Tierra y Libertad* and the Syndicalist José Negre—the first general secretary of the CRT—who complained in *Solidaridad Obrera* that certain Anarchists who were "confessed anti-Syndicalists" and who refused to accept office in the committees of the sindicatos nevertheless desired to be "the arbiters of Syndicalism," dictating orientations, tactics and beliefs. And, said Negre, "if attention is not paid to them, they quit ... they sabotage the organization, and they declare ... the failure of Syndicalism."[81]

One of the most frequent sources of theoretical dispute was the question of the trade unions' future role in a postrevolutionary society. Whereas the Syndicalists, succumbing to the mystique of the sindicato, reverently regarded that organ as the combat unit of the present and the producing and governing unit of the future, the Anarchists, having fallen under the spell of the "free commune," of course thought otherwise. In an exchange in the spring of 1917, the Anarchist Neno Vasco said that if the sindicato tried to be "single and closed, the exclusive proprietor of the means of production," then Syndicalism would be no more than a "medieval neocorporatism, which will produce a new form of servitude." Or, "If there are envisioned," he said, "a central regulating commission for production and a permanent syndical bureaucracy, the end result will be a social-democratic state, with a new division of classes." By contrast, the Anarchist ideal was that the society of the future would have a "multiplicity of groups"—groups for production, groups for intellectual, aesthetic, and moral needs, and "the free commune for local interests."[82] On the tactical level, the Anarchists' most constant criticism, especially from 1916 onward, was that the Syndicalist leaders exercised their power too conservatively and let "revolutionary opportunities" slip by. The Syndicalists were accused of being overly fascinated by the economic opportunities of the moment while ignoring the "hard-fought spiritual and moral initiative" that had been won by more than fifty years of Anarchist struggle.[83]

These early disputes had no important practical consequences; but they revealed the dual nature of the CNT and presaged a more serious clash between Anarchists and Syndicalists in 1919–20, as the organization grew to vast proportions and as the stakes of the struggle became greater. This clash could probably not have been avoided, since it was rooted in the conflict that inevitably arises between the ideal and the real—between, in this case, Anarchist aspirations and Syndicalist imperatives. The Anarchist mentality was bound to be more or less dissatisfied with a mass Syndicalist movement that necessarily tended to develop its own goals, its own governing personnel, and its own set of vested interests. The root issue was whether the CNT was to be an end in itself or merely the instrument of some higher purpose, namely, that of the always-impending Anarchist revolution. What complicated the controversy was that Anarchism in Spain, as everywhere else, suffered from a split personality. There were two essentially antithetical sides to Anarchist consciousness, frequently combined in the same person: that of the saintly savant or "pure" Anarchist, and that of the revolutionary putschist willing to resort to nonlibertarian and terrorist methods. So it was that in this period the Seguí-led Syndicalists were criticized from two rather different perspectives, both authentically Anarchist.[84]

The purest Anarchists, associated with *Tierra y Libertad*, had been immediately stirred by the news of the Bolshevik triumph; but they were soon dismayed by the statist and authoritarian trends within Russia, even as they were angered by the materialism and willingness to accept favors from the state displayed by the new masses of the CNT. They could not reconcile themselves to the workers' absorption in the struggle for "small gains" or to their lack of understanding of Anarchist principles. In fact, these purists were too pure for this world and had never really accepted the trade-union tactic. For them, Anarchism was something ethereal and beautiful, and they were extremely reluctant to see it sullied by being applied in the sweaty world of Syndicalism. Increasingly in late 1919 they were to be heard denouncing the throngs of materialistic, ideologically untutored, and anonymous workers who were being swept into the unions by the Cenetista organizational campaign and under the spell of the Bolshevik Revolution. Their doctrinaire protests against both Syndicalism and Bolshevism would become increasingly shrill in 1920.

But the "pure" Anarchists, in gradual decline since the turn of the century, were neither very numerous nor very influential in this period, and the main opposition to what may be termed Seguismo* came from more ruthless and activist militants who can best be described as extreme Anarchosyndicalists. Their quarrel with Seguí was not based on the mass characteristics of modern Syndicalism, which they accepted, but on the reluctance of the "pure" Syndicalist leaders to use the massive trade-union organization more aggressively— one may say, more recklessly—in pursuit of the Anarchist revolution, which they always believed to be very near. They resented the placing of bread-and-butter issues ahead of opportunities to strike a blow at the bourgeois order, whose toughness and durability they consistently underestimated. Above all, perhaps, they differed with the Seguistas in their greater willingness to use authoritarian measures. In some part of their consciousness there doubtless subsisted a libertarian commitment to the sacredness of the individual, to

---

* Neither this term nor the use of "Seguistas" to denote the Seguí-led Syndicalists had any currency at the time, and I use them simply for convenience.

nonviolence, and to noncoercion; but on the more visceral level of revolutionary *praxis* they were irrestistibly drawn to violent and dictatorial tactics. Unconsciously, but completely, they accepted the belief that the revolutionary end justified the means, and this was why they, among all the Cenetistas, were most drawn to the Russian Bolsheviks and to the idea of the dictatorship of the proletriat.[85]

The Anarchosyndicalist tendency was similarly divided in this period between a group of somewhat older, doctrinally competent, and established militants who, unlike the Seguistas, had not lost their Anarchist orientation, and the newer, younger, and more violent men who came into the CNT and the action groups in the later stages of the war or in the postwar period. To the first group belonged such prewar militants as Buenacasa, Boal, Carbó, Galo Díez, and the like; to the second belonged the Durrutis, Ascasos, Olivers, Sanzes, Escartíns, and Casanellas, who would dominate the terrorist underworld of postwar Barcelona.[86]

The youthful newcomers to the Anarchosyndicalist movement were not always well versed in Anarchist doctrine. The better ones among them were provincial zealots in whom a latent millenarian fervor had been aroused by a whole series of transcendent and unsettling events: the war, the Russian Revolution, the Armistice, the upheavals in postwar Europe, and the peasant agitations in Andalusia. Psychologically they were perhaps men of the seventeenth century who, on the basis of an often remarkably meager Anarchist theology, were consumed by the vision of a world made pure again by the redemption or elimination of all those elements—labeled "bourgeois"—who were not fitted to live in it. They were also marginal men who had drifted away from the agrarian regions and into the industrial world of Catalonia without finding roots. Filled with bucolic aversion to the regimentation, authoritarianism, and class divisions of factory society, they had difficulty accepting the right to existence of the capitalist class and the value of partial or ameliorative struggles for material benefits within the industrial context.

Among the less admirable of the newcomers even the pretension of Anarchist ideology was absent, and there prevailed perhaps only one idea, namely, that regular work was drudgery and exploitation and was to be avoided insofar as possible. These men, the truly marginal, quasi-criminal elements, were neither precisely regular workers nor hardened criminals but vacillated between the two existences, working one day and carrying out some act of petty criminality the next. Clearly, many of them found in their sometimes ill-assimilated Anarchist slogans a rationale for the release of antisocial and even homicidal impulses.

Manuel Buenacasa, who appears to have cooperated with them at the time, later referred to these elements as "the newcomers, those without ideas ... the ambitious ones, the hotheads ... the roving youths [who] saw their hour approaching." The leaders of the CNT, he said, found themselves "enveloped in the dirty vortex and unable to struggle against the gigantic wave of bullies and spongers who dominated in that ambience." It was under these circumstances, as Buenacasa acknowledges, that the assassination of employers and others began "on a large scale," with the Confederation unable to find the means of preventing it. Violence became a veritable system; yet, of the thousand *atentados* carried out, recalled Buenacasa, "very few could qualify as revolutionary deeds."[87]

Angel Pestaña also complained about the marginal elements entering the CNT during the great "avalanche" that inundated the organization from the last half of 1918 on, too many of whom belonged to "that special class of men who live on the indefinite frontier between labor and common crime."* These youths, as Pestaña observed, adopted a superficial and verbal Anarchism that was much influenced by the old Anarchist admiration for the terrorist assault, or *atentado personal*.[88] He also perceived that the young demi-Anarchists of the action groups had been "inflamed" by the Bolshevik Revolution, which, by virtue of the romantic haze through which they viewed it, seemed to them somehow a vindication of the whole tradition of Anarchist violence. Thus the Revolution, thought Pestaña, had helped create the "necessary ambience" for terrorist activity in Spain—a hypothesis partially confirmed by the terrorist Ricardo Sanz, who acknowledged that the Anarchist youths of the action groups "burned with desire for the definitive triumph of the Russian Revolution."[89]

The Birth of Terrorism

The use of terror had a long history in the Spanish Anarchist movement. Rarely eulogized on a theoretical level, it was frequently condoned in practice and reflected the dark side of Anarchist consciousness, clearly at variance with the elevated ethical content of libertarian doctrine. As a recent study has emphasized, the use of terror by Catalonian Anarchists served several purposes.[90] "Strategic" terrorism, such as the attempted assassinations of King Alfonso in 1905 and 1906, was designed to trigger a revolutionary movement. But terrorism also had a tactical function, as in the struggles between Anarchists and republicans for influence over the workers or in the efforts of the

---

* They were, said Pestaña, of a type that was "neither worker nor habitual delinquent ... [who] one day or one season is working but another day or season quits work; and since they have no resources, they must live any way they can." They were the ones who "one day catch hold of a wretch and exploit her and the next day go to the shop and appear to be good and worthy workers. In the depths of their consciousness exists only one preoccupation: to satisfy their sensual desire to live at whatever cost, be it crime, robbery, the exploitation of women, or whatever. This part of the people is more numerous than one might think, above all in populations whose life is industrial." Pestaña, *Lo que aprendí*, p. 177.

Anarchists to disrupt election contests. Terrorist bombings—usually with no casualties—were, above all, a symptom of the disorientation and tactical bankruptcy of the declining "pure" Anarchist movement after about 1903. There may even have been an element of ideological *machismo* in many of the seemingly purposeless bombings of the prewar period, and the Anarchist groups, which J. Romero Maura aptly likens to delinquent gangs endeavoring to strengthen subcultural solidarity, sometimes used bombs simply to demonstrate their superior purity to themselves and to other groups. Before the war, terrorism was always an issue between Anarchists and Syndicalists, with the latter disparaging it because it threatened to bring reprisals detrimental to the free atmosphere necessary for the proper functioning and growth of the sindicatos. Even so, Syndicalist leaders never seemed able to raise compelling theoretical arguments against the use of terror and usually gave aid and comfort to the terrorists themselves.[91]

Anarchist terrorism underwent still another mutation during and after the war, as it became intimately involved in the syndical struggle of the workers against their employers. During the last years of the war, young militants from various Anarchist organizations began to form themselves into the more compact entities known as "action groups," of which there were perhaps two or three in 1916 and many more later. These groups began to carry out assassinations of employers who refused to make wage concessions that their employees demanded and that were, no doubt, usually justified in view of the high profits being made. This rather drastic approach to labor relations was apparently begun by a few leaders of the Textile Union. Farré Moregó indicates August 3, 1916, as the date when the *atentados sociales*, which had occasionally taken place earlier on a spontaneous basis, began to acquire the character of a "system" adopted by the action groups.[92] As a labor tactic the atentado gained the support of still other trade-union leaders who felt that the absolute intransigence of the employers—which was coupled with a habit of precipitately yielding, when threatened with violence, what they would not yield from equity or reason—justified the use of assassination.[93]

Thus the terrorist tactic—a Spanish version, perhaps, of the "rationalization of weakness"—had its origin in the mundane desire for material benefits rather than in revolutionary aspiration as such. The irony is that at the very time this unorthodox and ultimately self-destructive tactic was being sanctioned, the Cenetistas were in the process of creating an unprecedentedly strong labor organization, which, as the La Canadiense strike demonstrated, could have won by the normal methods of strike and peaceful coercion most of what the workers wanted. At the very moment that the CRT was emerging as a potent, modern, disciplined, and organized movement, there was being grafted onto it a parasitical terrorist apparatus—a kind of Anarchist Mafia—that would play no small part in carrying the Syndicalist organization to disaster.[94] Yet, the trade-union leaders helped bring the terrorist plague down on their own heads, since it was they, after all, rather than the young Anarchist pistoleros, who originally singled out the employers who were to be killed and who paid the wages of the youthful assassins who did their bidding. As for the mass of workers, they viewed the assassination of employers with placid indifference, believing that every *patrono* dead was one class enemy less.[95]

At first the motives of the young terrorists were visionary and altruistic. They were in the grip, as Pestaña writes, of a "mystical and apocalyptic idealism."[96] While aiding the sindicatos they apparently also felt that—with pistols and bombs—they were bringing the revolution closer. Thus the Anarchist "propaganda of the deed" was translated into an industrial context. The atentado became a Spanish vulgarization of the Sorelian idea of "direct action" that in France and Italy had always implied collective rather than individual action—strikes, boycotts, even sabotage, but not the murder of individuals.[97]

The ill-fated general strike of March may also have contributed to the upsurge of terrorism within the ranks of the CRT, for the dismissals of union activists carried out by the employers, along with the rigorous use of the blacklist, left dozens of militants absolutely unable to find employment. The result was that they swelled the membership of the *grupos de delegados especiales*—that is, of the action groups—and were employed to bring certain pressures to bear on the mass of workers. The "delegates" were each given a pistol and a weekly salary of 70 pesetas, and were sent around to the factories to encourage remittances from the numerous workers who, in the aftermath of the general strike debacle, had ceased paying their dues. From this moment, says Baratech Alfaro, these ex-workers were increasingly drawn toward the vices and pleasures of terrorism and lost their interest in regular work.[98]

As the Anarchist action groups continued to swell with new recruits, the terrorist system quickly underwent, as Pestaña says, a "denaturalization."[99] Many of the newcomers proved to be drawn from the proletarian *bas fond*, and were little more than ideological desperados who quickly came to prefer the exciting life and relatively high pay of the gunman to the prosaic and ill-paid drudgery of the factory worker. Thus the action groups were soon composed of a mixture of *exaltés* and opportunists, with the latter apparently displacing the former as time went by. The supremacy of means over ends was again demonstrated as assassination began to emerge as an end in itself, becoming, as Buenacasa says, a "system" and even an "industry" that employed scores of hired gunmen.[100] Ultimately, this industry would carry out attacks against hundreds of employers, overseers, and strikebreakers in the years 1917–22.[101] It would also acquire an iron grip on the sindicatos, which would not really be broken until the coming of Primo de Rivera's dictatorship.

By mid-1919 the action groups were collecting heavy, compulsory levies from the workers, most of which went to pay the salaries of the gunmen, with the balance being spent on propaganda, strike funds, and ministering to prisoners. The gunmen "commercialized" themselves, says Pestaña, and killed at so much a head, scaling their fees according to the rank of the intended victim.[102] One of the earliest of the atentados illustrated the abuses to which the system could give rise. In 1916 the employer Barret was killed by pistoleros of the action groups on the orders of Eduardo Ferrer, president of the Metalworkers' Union. This was presumably done because Barret was considered strongly antilabor and was influential in the employers' organization. It later turned out that Ferrer was in the employ of the then police chief Bravo Portillo, who had been paid German money to eliminate Barret, whose factory was working day and night turning out howitzers for the Allies.[103]

The actual locus of power within the CRT in this period, as between Anarchists and Syndicalists, is difficult to establish with precision. A secret, almost unacknowledged civil war went on within the sindicatos and the committees, in which control alternated between the Anarchist groups and the moderate Syndicalist leaders, who, when out of jail, formed the CRT committees and competed with the more doctrinaire Anarchosyndicalists.[104] The membership of the Regional Confederation is best visualized as having three layers. At the top was a relatively small group of moderates who followed the lead of men such as Seguí, Pestaña, Molins, Quemades, Peiró, and Piera. In the middle, following the lead of the Anarchist groups, was a larger body of extreme Anarchosyndicalist militants, many of whom were *arrivistes* recently risen to influence in the organization by virtue of the mass jailing of the regular militants. At the bottom was the great mass of Cenetistas, who alternated between materialism and messianism, reform and rebellion, apathy and excitement—who were equally capable, that is, of being led toward revolution or toward a moderate Syndicalism focused on small gains.[105]

At the heart of the Anarchist-Syndicalist struggle was precisely the problem of how to utilize the hordes of workers who had poured into the Sindicatos Unicos since the middle of 1918. Were they to be led toward immediate revolution, as the Anarchosyndicalists wished, or were they to be led, as Seguí seemed to be trying to lead them, toward integration with and acceptance of the bourgeois order? During periods of repression the extreme Anarchosyndicalists tended to dominate the clandestine committees and sindicatos of the CRT, whereas during phases of official relaxation, as the organization was able to rise once more to the surface of Catalonian life, the "pure" Syndicalists were able to regain control. When left to make a free choice, the mass of workers generally seemed more disposed to follow Seguí in his heresies and "possibilism" than the dogmatic Anarchists in their austere indifference to material considerations. However, the workers were often very volatile, uncompromising, and hard to control, being easily led toward extreme tactics.

The inability of the moderate Syndicalists in these years to suppress the terrorist tendency within their organization was a sobering fact. Among those who spoke out earliest against the atentados was Salvador Seguí, whereas Angel Pestaña, though not a proponent of the tactic, was closely associated with many of the terrorists and for some time condoned without exactly approving their actions.[106] Pestaña's behavior, which was emulated by numbers of militants, no doubt arose partly out of fear of the violent propensities of the men of the action groups; but it may have owed more to a strong feeling of solidarity with all Cenetistas, even with those who were, in fact, leading the organization down dark and dangerous paths. There was an extreme reluctance to do anything that might land a comrade in the clutches of bourgeois justice. In his memoirs, Pestaña leaves little doubt that although the terrorists were not precisely consubstantial with the syndical organization, they were known, sheltered, and employed by it; and he speaks of a "collective complicity." "Bound by our love for the organization," he writes, "not only would we not denounce [the atentados], but if necessary we would go out into the street to defend the organization when it was attacked." Still, he admits, it was a "terrible dilemma" to have either to remain silent, and thus be an accomplice, or to talk and thereby become an informer.[107]

The resort of the Anarchosyndicalists to terrorist methods was not long in producing a counterterror on the part of the employers. That the cause-and-effect relationship ran this way has been conceded by both Buenacasa and Pestaña, who admit that the *pistolerismo* of the employers came only as a response to the atentados of the action groups.* The nucleus of the counterterror apparatus was a band formed in 1918 by the German espionage agent and adventurer "Baron" de Koening, and one of its leading members was a certain Bravo Portillo, who had only recently been displaced as chief of police in Barcelona owing to the disclosure of his pro-German espionage activities by Pestaña in *Solidaridad Obrera*. Bravo Portillo was of great usefulness to Captain General Milans del Bosch and to the employers because of his knowledge of Syndicalist circles, gained over many years of service with the police, and his contacts with numerous informers within the CRT. The de Koening band was reported to receive no less than 50,000 pesetas per month from the

---

* Buenacasa, p. 68; Pestaña, *Lo que aprendí*, p. 176. To this testimony may be added the opinion of Governor Julio Amado, who, though deploring the intransigence of the employers, acknowledged that they had been sorely provoked by Cenetista terrorism (Madrid, *Ocho meses*, pp. 32–34). For a far less candid statement by Pestaña, see his *El terrorismo*, p. 15: "We are revolutionaries, yes....But we are not criminals who ambush or assassins who hide in the shadows! To confuse [the revolutionary with the criminal], as our governors and politicians do, is to give proof of extreme ignorance. To demand vigorous measures against the sindicatos on the supposition that they are the ones who practice terrorism...is infantile."

Employers' Federation. With this money they hired gunmen and began a campaign of retaliative assassination against the Cenetistas, which by 1923 had caused hundreds of deaths. The first and most spectacular exploit of the band was the murder of the president of the Textile Workers' Union, Pablo Sabater ("El Toro"), on July 19, 1919. This action, by virtue of the *lex talionis* that prevailed, soon resulted in the shooting of Bravo Portillo on September 15 of the same year, and that of his accomplice Eduardo Ferrer shortly thereafter.[108]

Attempted Reconciliation: August-December

By July it was clear that the martial law imposed in March by Milans del Bosch had succeeded neither in liquidating the sindicatos nor in abating the Cenetista menace. Despite the most massive arrests, the unions carried on their activities and maintained an impressive rate of expansion. Cambó and the Regionalists themselves recognized the bankruptcy of this policy. Comprehending that the unions could not be suppressed by force, they urged a change of course, and in this they were joined by a growing number of politicians in Madrid. On July 20, the Maura government, having lost its parliamentary majority, fell from power and was replaced by a Conservative government headed by the Datista leader Sánchez de Toca, who was committed to a policy of reconciliation and pacification in Catalonia and in Andalusia.[109]

The new Minister of the Interior, Manuel Burgos y Mazo, shared the view that the social unrest in Spain, whatever its domestic sources, was part of a "sinister design," a general European conspiracy with lines of influence that ran as far as Berlin and Moscow. He was obsessed by the activities of "foreign agents" in Spain and was certain that foreigners—especially Russians—were "pullulating" in Andalusia and Catalonia, "carrying out active Bolshevik or Anarchist propaganda." He sent word to the governors of all provinces to be alert for the presence of such individuals, with the result that foreigners continued to be arrested in considerable numbers. With some pride, Burgos y Mazo wrote: "And not a few hundred of these did I expel from the country."[110]

Despite his state of near panic, Burgos y Mazo nevertheless appointed a perceptive and intelligent individual to the post of civil governor in Barcelona. This was Julio Amado, editor of *La Correspondencia de España* and a man of unusual independence of mind. Amado arrived in Barcelona in mid-July to find the Syndicalist organization "absolutely in the power of the ... terrorist elements." Militants such as Seguí and Pestaña, he reported, were "not leading" the organization but were either in jail or in flight. Yet, he observed, "The sindicatos, operating secretly, were more powerful than ever" and had continued collecting their members' dues with "perfect regularity."[111]

Immediately after stepping off the train, Amado made a speech indicating that he had come as an impartial emissary of the Madrid government, and that he intended to keep his door open to "all social classes." Within 72 hours of this gesture of amity he received a message from Salvador Seguí indicating that if the governor were indeed prepared to be impartial, the Syndicalists wished to initiate talks with him. Not long after, Amado received Seguí in his office, and within ten days of his arrival in the city he had succeeded in bringing representatives of the workers and the employers together and getting the dialogue between them resumed. Both sides accepted the provisional formula that Amado suggested: the state of war would be lifted; the sindicatos would be legalized; all strikes and lockouts, by virtue of which some 70,000 workers were without employment, would be terminated, and there would be an immediate return to work; finally, all disputes and claims between workers and employers would simply be left pending, to be resolved by a Mixed Commission composed of equal numbers of employers and workers and presided over by the mayor of Barcelona.[112]

Seguí and his colleagues readily accepted the Mixed Commission, but the task of convincing the more doctrinaire Anarchosyndicalists to participate in this body was extremely difficult. Learning that some 400 leading militants were imprisoned in the Barcelona jail, Amado sent his deputy, Francisco Mira, to talk with them. Mira told the workers that he bore an "olive branch" from the governor, who was prepared to free them and restore the sindicatos to legal existence if they would agree to support the Commission in its efforts to resolve the vast number of labor conflicts in Barcelona. After a certain amount of soul-searching the prisoners finally voted, early in September, to accept the governor's offer, although militants like Manuel Buenacasa were most reluctant to become involved in such a "governmental" project, which, by its (supposedly temporary) departure from "direct action," violated the canons of Anarchosyndicalist orthodoxy. Before long, many of the militants would regret their acquiescence, and the Mixed Commission would become a *cause célèbre* in the struggle between Anarchists and Syndicalists within the CRT. Nevertheless, as the result of this decision a general amnesty was declared, and the great majority of workers were able to return to work on September 9.[113]

Although Amado's pacification restored a surface tranquility to the life of Barcelona, it did not subdue the underground conflict between Anarchists and Syndicalists within the sindicatos, which gained in intensity.[114] Amado's "olive branch" and the whole march toward "governmentalism" and rapprochement with the employers was repugnant to the more genuinely revolutionary Cenetistas, with their harsh, sectarian temper. Their mood now was one of anger and frustration, stemming from the fact that because of the legalization of the sindicatos and the restoration of constitutional guarantees the moderate Syndicalists were regaining their positions within the organization and leading the workers down the road of conciliation. It seemed intolerable to the extremists that the "pure" Syndicalists, instead of taking the enormous increase in the numerical strength of the sindicatos as the signal for an immediate assault on the capitalist citadel, should be timorously absorbed in compromises and commissions.[115]

In their efforts to compel the moderate leaders to follow a more revolutionary course, the Anarchosyndicalists did not shrink from threats of extermination. As early as January 1919 police informers had reported that Seguí's life was being threatened by the Anarchist groups because of his reluctance to place the CRT on a more revolutionary course.[116] And especially after the launching of Amado's reconciliation policy, as control of the sindicatos began to slip from the grasp of the extremists, relations between Anarchosyndicalists and "pure" Syndicalists deteriorated rapidly. Precisely because the Seguistas were so successful in drawing the great mass of the workers into accommodating tactics, it was observed that within the workers' centers in Barcelona "passions were seething and battles constantly breaking out." On at least one occasion Governor Amado felt it necessary to station contingents of Guardia near the union halls to prevent what promised to be bloody clashes between the Cenetista factions. There were numerous fist fights and brawls in and near the workers' centers, and gunshots were occasionally heard. During Amado's governorship there were several attempted atentados against Seguí and Pestaña, though whether these were in warning or in earnest is impossible to say.[117]

Syndicalist Proselytizing: Seguí and Pestaña in Madrid

The moderate Syndicalists could not, of course, afford to forswear revolutionary goals explicitly; but their appraisal of the balance of social forces was more sober than that of the Anarchists. The revolution they sought was one located further in the future, after the workers had raised their cultural level and created an irresistibly powerful organization that would unite workers in every part of the country. To the fostering of that vision of syndical power they now devoted themselves, hoping to spread the gospel of the Sindicato Unico all over Spain. In late September and early October, as the CRT, once more functioning legally, was nearing the peak of its numerical strength in Catalonia, and as Syndicalism was becoming the rage in workers' centers everywhere, Seguí and Pestaña launched themselves on a propaganda campaign outside Catalonia, focusing especially on the national capital.*

* This interlude, from early September to mid-November, marked the real apex of the CNT's fortunes in the postwar period, coming as it did after the defeat of Milans del Bosch, the granting of amnesty, and the death of Bravo Portillo (September 15) on the one hand and before the failure of the Mixed Commisison and the launching of the lockouts (November 15) on the other. The Madrid journal *España* said (16.x.19): "The moment could not have been more favorable. After victories in Barcelona won by dint of organization and fiber, both of steel ... the expectation had to be great. How have these men defeated the powerful employers' organization, the powerful military organization, and an iron-handed government like that of Maura and La Cierva? How did they win, with what force, by what means, and with what ultimate aim?"

The two Syndicalist leaders—perhaps not ungrateful to leave the internecine turmoil in Barcelona—arrived in Madrid like conquering heroes. The
victory in the La Canadiense strike, the proliferation and power of the Sindicatos Unicos, the successful defiance of Milans del Bosch's martial law—these
things had been followed by the Madrid workers with intense interest, and
large crowds appeared wherever the two men spoke. The journal *España*
was led to recall other, similar arrivals. "Involuntarily," its editors thought
of Cambó and his Regionalist colleagues "when, at critical moments, they
arrived in the capital of Spain to the roll of the presses, long telegraphed messages, and extensive commentary." It was difficult to deny to the Catalans
"this political aptitude for creating an atmosphere of curiosity on the one hand
and for taking advantage of the psychological circumstances of the moment
on the other." Speaking of Pestaña (who seemed to make a greater impact
than Seguí on the Madrileños), *España* said:

> Beneath his words, fluent and familiar, reserved in manner, and behind his fig-
> ure, lean and awkward, repeating the great tribunal gestures, the figure of a
> man consumed by exterior forces and by interior passion, there could be di-
> vined, in the depths of Barcelona, a great social power, full of immense youthful
> energy, and of vast and clear ambitions.... [Both men] have had on us an
> effect contrary to that of Cambó. Behind Cambó we always saw, in Catalonia,
> a force inferior to the image that his words gave us.... Behind the Syndicalists
> we have seemed to see a force greater and more fearsome for the regime in
> power than the image mirrored in their speeches.[118]

There was speculation that Seguí and Pestaña had come to Madrid to seek
a liaison with the Socialists, but if this was in fact an objective it was pursued
very secretly. Rather, the two leaders appeared to be on a serious proselytizing
mission; and the displeasure and uneasiness of the Socialist leaders in the face
of this challenge were evident. The Socialists, still committed to the old craft
unionism and more disposed than ever to gradualism and electoral tactics,
were on the defensive. Chastened by the August debacle and reluctant to embrace Bolshevism or utilize a more revolutionary rhetoric, the UGT leaders
had watched the rising Syndicalist tide with some anxiety, knowing that many
younger workers were deserting to the CNT.[119]

Pestaña, speaking in the Casa del Pueblo while Socialist leaders glumly
listened, explained to the Madrid workers the evolution of Catalonian Syndicalism and urged them to recognize that although the craft unions had been
adequate in their day, syndical organization, like everything else, had to evolve
and rise to the exigencies of the times. He patiently explained the structure
and functioning of the Sindicatos Unicos and the nature of Syndicalist "direct
action"; and with respect to the latter, he endeavored to demonstrate that the
CRT's participation in the Mixed Commission was completely justified. While
carefully refraining from suggesting that the Sindicato Unico was necessarily

the "absolute truth" or the "last word" in labor organization, he nevertheless persuasively argued for the adoption of this form.*

Seguí, his Catalan accent discernible, also spoke on behalf of the Sindicato Unico, but two themes distinguished his discourse from that of Pestaña. First, seeming to echo the quarrels he had been having with the more doctrinaire Anarchists in Catalonia, he asserted for the Sindicatos a hegemony that went beyond that implied by Pestaña. Seguí was at some pains to declare that the Sindicato Unico took precedence not merely over the Socialist craft unions but over the Anarchist groups as well. Apparently as concerned to throw down a challenge to his Anarchist rivals as to win over the Socialists, he asked, "Are the Anarchist groups, despite the very good intentions they show, the ones who can safeguard the complicated [productive] organization and assure to the [postrevolutionary] community ... everything necessary for life?" His answer to this was negative, and he suggested that the Anarchist position involved little more than moral aspiration and "letting off steam." In a phrase that would reverberate in Cenetista circles for some time to come, he affirmed that "neither the Socialist Party nor the Anarchist groups can guarantee, after the social transformation, that consumption and production shall be completely normalized." The only force that could make such a guarantee was "precisely Syndicalism."[120]

The other theme that distinguished Seguí's Madrid speeches had to do with the relative nearness of the revolution. Whereas Pestaña, both in public and in private, was somewhat sanguine on this question, Seguí sounded not unlike some of his Ugetista counterparts as he frankly told his audience that Spanish workers were not ready for the responsibilities of power:

> What would happen right now, comrades and friends, if the revolution, triumphant all over Europe ... should come knocking on our door? You answer for me. We are not prepared. We have no organization. We would ... have to say to the bourgeoisie: "No, we do not wish to accept that responsibility; wait a minute; wait for us to orient ourselves; we do not know what to do."[121]

In place of the Anarchists' revolutionary immediacy, then, Seguí preached a doctrine of salvation through organization. Reiterating that Spanish workers were not sufficiently organized, he stressed that much more preparation was needed before a revolutionary overthrow could be contemplated. This was the case because "all ideas, absolutely all, triumph only when there is capacity and organization." Struggle and sacrifice alone, said Seguí, would achieve very little without organization; and he emphasized yet again the inability of Spanish workers to make a revolution while at the same time guaranteeing

---

* Pestaña and Seguí, p. 7. El Socialista noted (4.x.19): "In speaking as he did yesterday, Angel Pestaña, a former Anarchist, appears to have rid himself of the old individualist ideas."

that the transfer of power would be made "with the greatest normality possible."[122]

This brought Seguí to the question of the Russian Revolution. For perhaps the first time, he made clear publicly that his enthusiasm for that event was very much under control and was strongly influenced by his perception of Spanish realities. The Spanish proletariat was not ready for revolution, he said, and the workers of Hungary, Russia, and Germany had shown by their recent actions that they were equally unprepared to put into practice "Socialism in the economy and liberty in politics." In Russia, owing to a "lack of technical preparation" and to harassment by the international bourgeoisie, industry and labor had not developed in a "normal" manner, and the "heroic" Russian workers, in spite of "gigantic efforts," had not been able to consolidate their new state. Seguí hastened to add that the Spanish Syndicalists' attitude toward the Russian Revolution went well beyond the limits of mere sympathy and in fact made them "allies" prepared to defend the Revolution at all costs. Nevertheless, he warned, this position did not require a complete acceptance of Russian methods: without wishing in the least to censure the Bolsheviks, he had to affirm that the revolution in Spain "must be something very different." Seguí was willing to recognize—perhaps somewhat theoretically—the necessity for a proletarian dictatorship, but he emphasized that control must be vested not in a political party but only in the sindicatos. Finally, in a calculated but incongruous reversion to the Anarchist theme, Seguí concluded his speech in the Casa del Pueblo by saying: "We are, in the end, Communists; but our Communism is distinguished somewhat from that of the Russian comrades. They follow Marx; and we, today as before the Russian Revolution, continue to believe that reason was on the side of Bakunin."[123]

This gesture aside, little in Seguí's well-publicized speech can have pleased the extreme Anarchosyndicalists, whether in Madrid or in Catalonia. In effect, he had warned against insurrectionalism, placing the revolution in a remote future; he had minimized the role that the Anarchists would play in the approaching social transformation, identifying the Sindicato Unico as the only guarantor of the postrevolutionary social order; and he had, however cautiously, denigrated the Russian Revolution.

The Anarchist counterattack against all this was launched two weeks later from the pages of the Madrid journal *Espartaco* which had recently been founded, with the aid of Catalonian Anarchists, for the specific purpose of combating the "pure" Syndicalist trend identified with Seguí. The central theme of *Espartaco*'s critique was precisely the crucial importance of the Anarchist groups in the postrevolutionary society. Syndicalism, insisted the new journal, could only be a means to revolution and could never constitute a genuine aspiration or ideal for the community:

Syndicalism, friend Seguí, is a force lacking in idealism, and cannot be taken as more than a weapon of combat. It is a means of struggle in a capitalist society, never a goal for man's aspirations. When this bourgeois and unequal society disappears, the sindicato will either be transformed totally or will cease to exist, since without inequality men will not have to employ that weapon against anyone.[124]

The Syndicalists, said the Andalusian Anarchist Diego Alonso, simply had to understand that when the overthrow of bourgeois society had taken place the usefulness of the sindicato would end, and it would necessarily give way to "Anarchist groups of production and exchange." This was essential, he thought, because a Syndicalist society would be "as defective and tyrannical for the individual as the present society."[125]

Of the two Catalan leaders, Pestaña evidently enjoyed the greater popular success in Madrid. This was partly, no doubt, because his Leonese accent was more pleasing to the Madrileños than Seguí's Catalanized diction. But beyond that, it was he who better expressed the revolutionary mood of the rank-and-file workers. In his speeches he revealed a revolutionary optimism that Seguí did not share, and in private talks in Madrid cafes he hinted that if the CNT kept up its rate of organizational growth, the revolution would probably come during the summer of 1920. He urged the Madrid workers to step up the fight against the Socialist leadership and to prepare, by means of partial strikes and constant agitation, for the "final battle."[126]

The Lockout of November 1919

Seguí and Pestaña returned to Barcelona in mid-October to find a surface calm still prevailing. The great majority of workers within the CRT remained under the control of the moderate Syndicalists, and during September and October there were no atentados and no serious clashes with the authorities or the employers. On September 10, as a sign of rapprochement, the junta of the Barcelona Institute of Social Reforms was reconstituted, now being composed of five employers and five workers. And on October 20 the Second Congress of the Employers' Federation was held in Barcelona without the workers' carrying out any act of violence or protest against it.[127]

In late October the sessions of the Mixed Commission began, with Seguí heading up the CRT delegation. The first phase of negotiations lasted only three days but achieved a surprising amount of progress before breaking up over the question of the manner in which work would be resumed. The employers demanded that the strike be suspended 48 hours before the lockouts were ended, whereas the workers wished to see strike and lockouts terminated simultaneously. After three days, Governor Amado succeeded in getting the Commission together again, and, despite the heat generated, it was clear that the discussions were being conducted by the moderates on both sides and could be successful. This is suggested by an incident related by Amado. Before the Mixed Commission began its sessions, one of the employers said to the governor, half jokingly: "You will not accomplish anything until you exile Seguí one hundred leagues from here." After the interruption of the talks, the same man said to Amado: "When the Commission is reorganized, try to get Seguí, because that fellow is worth something and we can come to an understanding with him."[128]

Thus the Mixed Commission continued its labors, still with remarkable accord, through the remainder of October and into early November.[129] On November 2, in the midst of the discussions, Seguí and José Molins, Secretary of the Local Federation of Trade Unions in Barcelona, gave their signatures on behalf of the CRT to the text of the Royal Decree that had been enacted to establish the Commission on October 11. The last clause of this decree was of special importance and would be a source of irritation to the more febrile Cenetistas: delegates from a particular factory could no longer declare strikes unilaterally but would instead be required to get the consent of the whole Sindicato. By November 12 the efforts of the Mixed Commission were brought to a successful conclusion; and on that date the representatives signed a kind of provisional labor-relations statute, which was expected to become law as soon as possible. This document, signed for the CRT by Seguí, José Duc, Simón Piera, Saturnino Meca, and Manuel Moyano, gave the Mixed Commission the following powers: to hear and resolve labor disputes in any industry or trade; to fix minimum wages for each locality and each industry; to advise the government on carrying out all social legislation; to minimize conflicts during conversion to the eight-hour day; and to propose to the government such legislation as it considered appropriate. In addition, it was agreed that all work should be resumed on November 14, and that all strikes and lockouts would be suspended until the Mixed Commission could resolve them. Finally, it was decided that all strikes would be considered resolved where the employers had accepted raises of more than 50 percent of what the workers had asked.

This agreement was a triumph for Seguí; and it offered the possibility of a return of industrial peace in Barcelona, which would have allowed the Catalonian labor movement to become not merely a powerful but a constructive force in Spanish life. In view of the actual sequel to this detente—that is, the collapse of the Mixed Commission, the revival of massive strikes and lockouts, and a reversion to terrorism—one must ask whether the responsibility for the failure of the scheme lay primarily with the employers or with the workers.

Some employers were willing to talk with the Syndicalists and to enter into the activities of the Mixed Commission; but the violent struggles since the end of the war, the Cenetista reliance on terror, and the slow contraction of the economy had radicalized most of them and driven them toward extremism. Like every other social group in Spain, the Catalonian employers suf-

fered from an egoism that made it difficult for them to concede legitimacy
or the right of collective existence to their social opponents. As early as October 20, at the Second Congress of the Employers' Federation, a secret decision had been taken against reconciliation and in favor of continued industrial warfare. In fact, the Congress resolved to break the workers' organization
altogether, and proposed to do this by means of a massive lockout that would
involve the shutting down of all industry, first in Catalonia and then in the
rest of Spain. By this decision, says Balcells, the industrial bourgeoisie of
Catalonia accepted the leadership of its "most combative and intransigent
elements." As early as November 3, some employers declared a brief preliminary lockout, even though the Syndicalist delegates had signed the Royal
Decree of October 11 only the day before.[180]

But the real coup de grace to industrial peace in Catalonia came on November 14, the day that all workers, whether on strike or locked out, were expected to return to their jobs. Almost all workers did, in fact, accept the settlement and return to work; but upon entering the gates of some of the largest
firms in Barcelona, they discovered that the employers had posted guards to
turn away all who were recognized as Syndicalist leaders or factory delegates.
Thus, in spite of the agreements that had been signed, and in disregard of
the long step toward "governmentalism" and away from "direct action" taken
by Seguí and the other moderates, the employers elected to wage a war of
liquidation against the Syndicalist organization. Although real concessions
had been made by the Cenetistas, their opponents were determined to pursue
the "global" tactics—lumping together moderate and extremist labor leaders—
that Governor Amado had warned them against.[131]

The predictable result of this attempted purge of the Syndicalist infrastructure was an angry outburst in the workers' centers, which placed the initiative
once more in the hands of the extreme Anarchosyndicalists. An immediate
renewal of all strikes was ordered; and a delegation of between 15 and 20
Syndicalists stormed down to the headquarters of the Mixed Commission and
wrathfully announced the withdrawal of all workers from that body, thus
helping to destroy what many of them had never completely accepted. It was
technically true, then, that the workers broke up the Mixed Commission,
which was never to be reestablished; but the real cause of its destruction, as
Governor Amado said, was "exclusively ... the conduct of the employers of
Barcelona."[132]

Now the employers launched the counteroffensive they had been contemplating for some time. On November 25, claiming that some workers had
not returned to their jobs, they began the largest and most crippling lockout
of the postwar period, which would idle 200,000 workers and would not end
until January 26, 1920, ten weeks later. All Catalonian industries were affected,
with the exception of public services and food industries, and a severe discipline was imposed on all employers who dared try to keep their businesses

open. The employers' counterterror (namely the de Koening Band), which had been restrained during the tenure of Governor Amado, was again unleashed when Amado left the city on December 10. The mood of the employers was, in general, exalted and combative, and Amado did not exaggerate when he described them as "stubborn men, of profoundly retrograde opinions ... who wished to smash the Syndicalist organization and remold it to their desire and caprice."[133] Burgos y Mazo agreed with Amado on this point:

> The employers and other leading elements in Barcelona are mainly to blame for the horrible social state that exists there today.... What I had to listen to in ... the Ministry! The patience I needed to resist firmly ... the flood of impertinences, inconsideration, disrespect, threats, seditious actions, and *groserías* unleashed against me!... There did I listen day after day to adherents of law and order who would not obey the decrees of the government.[134]

The employers considered Conservatives like Burgos y Mazo and Amado rather too "left," and they wanted the Madrid government to proclaim the conciliation policy a failure and join in a total crackdown on the sindicatos. By this time, the Conservative leader Eduardo Dato had in fact concluded, perhaps prematurely, that the pacification policy was indeed bankrupt.[135] And under pressure from him the Conservative Sánchez de Toca government submitted its resignation—giving as its reason, however, not the situation in Barcelona but the decision of the Minister of War, General Tovar, to support the Military Juntas against the cabinet in a relatively minor dispute. The transitional "government of concentration" of Allendesalazar now came to power, appointing as the new civil governor of Barcelona José Maestre Laborde, Count Salvatierra, who was thoroughly committed to taking a hard line with the Syndicalist movement. The rhythmic but futile alternation between reconciliation and repression in Catalonia continued.

A "Lost" Revolutionary Opportunity

There were many Cenetistas who did not mourn the passing of the Mixed Commission and who hoped that the consequent heightening of social tensions would lead to a revolutionary crisis. They had from the first deplored the Commission as a negation of all that they believed in, and were, in fact, gratified by its demise. Manuel Buenacasa revealed the bitterness that many Anarchosyndicalists felt toward this body, and he denied—incorrectly, it would seem—that it had been accepted by the majority of workers in Barcelona. "The decisions of so unpopular a tribunal," he said, "outraged the workers and caused dissension between the representatives and the represented." He scornfully recalled "those ... newspaper photographs in which our representatives appeared sitting at their ease in comfortable armchairs beside their mortal enemies."[136]

For the extreme Anarchosyndicalists, the only alternative to the Mixed

Commission was a resumption of the social war. To this end, the Anarchist-dominated National Committee of the CNT, now led by Evelio Boal as Acting General Secretary, proposed that the lockout be ignored, and that the workers instead occupy the factories—thus, it was hoped, touching off the Spanish Revolution. The Committee felt certain that there were not enough troops in the country to evict 200,000 workers from their factories, and that any attempt to do so would only unleash what they all desired, a general upheaval. After surveying the revolutionary resources available to the CNT, the National Committee concluded that an uprising in Barcelona would be strongly supported by the workers in other regions of Spain; above all, they viewed the Andalusian workers as most prepared for the great "expropriating enterprise."[137]

Salvador Seguí and his colleagues in the committees of the CRT viewed the matter otherwise and refused to accept the challenge thrown down by the employers, preferring to wait out the lockout rather than to try to contest it by illegally entering and occupying the factories. Their feeling was that a revolutionary effort requiring the coordination of all the labor forces in the country, both urban and rural, was still demonstrably beyond the capacity of the CNT and would only fail, probably with dire results. Yet it was also true that mere passive resistance to the lockout would deprive the workers of wages and food and the sindicatos of money and manpower over an extended period, which would also, in the end, mean ruin. The fiery Buenacasa would look back upon this decision and lament the "beautiful revolutionary opportunity" that had been lost—the best, he thought, of the postwar period.[138] And the disgruntled doctrinaires of *Espartaco* would speculate that the Syndicalists' failure to take up the challenge of the employers was due not merely to fear but to a growing amour propre on the part of some Catalan leaders:

> Syndicalism, now guided and influenced by men who have thrown Anarchist principles overboard, who let themselves be called *señores* and *dones*, [who] confer and make agreements in government offices and ministries, who travel about in automobiles and ... sleeping cars ... is rapidly evolving in the European or North American manner, which permits its leaders to become official personages.[139]

Whatever the wisdom of the decision not to contest the lockout, the fact remained that after ten weeks the CRT would find itself seriously weakened and in the beginning stages of a demoralization that would grow progressively worse during the following year. But before we turn to this development, it will be necessary to take account of the founding of the Communist International early in 1919, and to examine the manner in which both Socialists and Anarchosyndicalists responded to its appeals and to the ideological challenge that it so insistently posed.

CHAPTER SEVEN

Spanish Labor and the Comintern, 1919

Until January 1919 the Bolshevik Revolution was little more than a beacon on the horizon of the Spanish labor movement, a resplendent but remote phenomenon that might be admired from afar but with which communication was hardly to be thought of. Then, on January 24 the first direct contact with the Revolution was made in the form of a radiogram broadcast by the Russian Communist Party, which, isolated and surrounded by its enemies, was trying to spread abroad the revolutionary message. This communiqué invited some 39 labor organizations around the world to send delegates to the founding congress of a new revolutionary International, the time and place of which were not specified. The terse, apocalyptic phraseology of the appeal—written by the same Trotsky who only two years before had inhabited the Model Prison in Madrid—contained strong overtones of revolutionary spontaneity and imminency, reflecting the early confidence of the Bolshevik leaders that the Revolution, if it were not snuffed out by the intervention of the capitalist powers, would spread rapidly across all frontiers through a chain reaction of the European masses.[1]

With its optimistic and ultra-Left emphasis on the nearness of the approaching upheaval, the primary role to be played by the spontaneous "mass actions" of the proletariat, and the uselessness of parliamentary tactics, the Moscow radiogram must have been as disturbing to the Socialist majoritarians as it was gratifying to the Anarchosyndicalists, whose insurgent mood it perfectly matched. Ironically, the message made no reference to the CNT—the true torchbearer of pro-Bolshevik enthusiasm in Spain—whose rise from obscurity had been, admittedly, very recent. The Russians mentioned only "the Left elements in the Spanish Socialist Party," a vague formula that hinted at less than detailed knowledge of the Spanish labor movement.

But even the left-centrists within the PSOE found the schismatic implications of the radiogram too strong for their taste and could not bring themselves to publish it in *Nuestra Palabra*; for the appeal, however satisfying in its revolutionary tone, threatened the almost mystical commitment of Spanish Socialists to party unity by suggesting not merely an "unsparing criticism and exposure" of conservative party leaders but an actual "splitting off" of revolutionary elements. For this reason, and perhaps because the announcement, mysteriously, was not repeated, the left-centrists expressed no desire to attend the projected congress, but remained committed to the rejuvenation of the Second International and to attendance at the forthcoming Berne Conference. As for the Cenetistas, who had witnessed the jailing of most of their top leaders on January 16 and were just entering the phase of intense conflict associated with the La Canadiense strike, they were too preoccupied to respond to the Moscow appeal, let alone contemplate sending a delegation. Thus, except among the Madrid Young Socialists, whose favorable response was instantaneous, the Moscow radiogram provoked little overt reaction from either side of the Spanish labor movement, which, like nearly all other Western movements, knew nothing of the First Comintern Congress until it was over.[2]

The Berne Conference

The Spanish Socialists' interest was focused entirely on the conference that assembled in Berne early in February 1919 to work out the principles for reconstructing the Socialist International.[3] The war had splintered the Second International, and, after four years of conflict, the member parties were sharply divided by unfraternal animosities and mutual suspicions. All parties had been invited to come to Berne, including such prodigal sons as the German and Austrian majoritarians and not excluding the intransigent Russian Bolsheviks. The majority of delegates, led by figures like Renaudel, Huysmans, Vandervelde, Henderson, and Thomas, were right-wing Socialists who had supported their wartime governments to the limit and who shared a conviction that Socialism and parliamentary democracy were inextricably linked. They were committed to evolutionary tactics and to the collaboration of classes, refusing to concede that violent revolution or class war were necessary in order for the workers to achieve their goals. Not surprisingly, the Bolsheviks refused to attend, denouncing the old Socialist organization as the "yellow strike-breaking International," the International of social patriots and counterrevolutionaries.[4] Nevertheless, there were present many left-wing Socialists, most notably the French minoritarians (by then a majority within the French Socialist Party) led by Jean Longuet, to whose moderate leftism the Spanish minoritarians also paid homage at that time. The far Left had an extremely scarce representation, and the French Socialist Fernand Loriot was perhaps its only spokesman. The single Spanish delegate was the centrist Julián Besteiro.*

The most dramatic moments of the Conference, held against the backdrop

---

* However, an international trade-union conference was held at Berne simultaneously with the Socialist meeting, and Largo Caballero was sent to represent the UGT. Renaudel, pp. 108–18.

of peacemaking in Paris and a gathering civil war in Russia, were the confrontations between the French and the German majoritarians, in which the French insisted that the future of the International would be compromised from the start unless the question of war responsibilities was thrashed out and judgment rendered. Albert Thomas and Pierre Renaudel, especially, sought to turn the Conference into a tribunal before which the German and Austrian Socialists would be forced to confess their sins. Rather violent accusations were also hurled against the German majoritarians by their fellow nationals Kurt Eisner and Karl Kautsky, and by the Austrian Friedrich Adler. The French left-wing Socialists observed that although the German Socialists had clearly been dragged along by the chauvinist tide, they could hardly be judged by the French majoritarians, who had themselves made common cause with "Allied imperialism." In the end this issue was settled by a resolution that vaguely asserted the responsibility of the "old system" in Germany and left the final determination of war guilt to a future congress.[5]

The other major concern of the men at Berne was the attitude the International should adopt toward the Bolshevik Revolution and the principle of the dictatorship of the proletariat. The views of the right-wing majority on this question were set forth in a resolution backed by Hjalmar Branting of Sweden, the presiding officer. In essence, the Branting Resolution asserted that the social organization of postwar Europe had to be based on the democratic principles of freedom of speech, press, and association, as well as on universal suffrage, and that the arbitrary expropriation of industries by a small fraction of workers could not be tolerated.[6] One might have supposed that this resolution, which easily passed, would correspond closely to the views of the Spanish majoritarians, who had supported the Allied democracies with at least as much devotion as the Renaudels, Thomases, and Hendersons. Indeed, the Aliadofilismo of the PSOE had been based precisely on the conviction that democracy was essential to the survival and ultimate triumph of Socialism; and the majoritarian leaders had also made it clear that they did not favor the establishment of a proletarian dictatorship in Spain, believing that Spanish workers were unprepared for such a responsibility. Nevertheless, the Spanish delegate, Besteiro, now unhesitatingly sided with the left wing of the Berne Conference, casting his vote against the Branting Resolution with the comment that it would be "prejudicial" to the Russian Revolution and would anticipate the decisions of the to-be-resurrected International.

On the crucial matter of whether the Conference should or should not condemn the principal tactics of the Russian Bolsheviks, the Spanish vote went to the unsuccessful Adler-Longuet Resolution, which opposed an unduly exclusive International and sought to avoid both the Right sectarianism of the "social patriots" and the Left sectarianism of the Bolsheviks. Refusing to pass a "premature" judgment on Bolshevik political methods, this moderate Left proposal expressed the desire for "free entry into the International for the Socialist and revolutionary parties of all countries conscious of their class interests."[7]

Significantly, the Berne Conference aroused little or no conflict within the Spanish Socialist Party. The *Nuestra Palabra* minoritarians strongly agreed with Longuet in believing that the Renaudels and Thomases had "no moral authority" to indict the German Socialists for their presumed misdeeds; but they nevertheless approved of the Conference's success in bringing together Socialist elements that had been "enormously far apart, and without whose agreement it was impossible to reconstitute the International."[8] Like minoritarians elsewhere, the Spanish leftists were thinking not of forming a new International but of rebuilding the old; and even as they moved toward the Comintern during the summer of 1919 they would be resolved to carry the whole PSOE with them.

The Party's unity at this moment—evident in its nearly unanimous support for the defeated Adler-Longuet Resolution—reflected not only the continuing moderation of the Left but also the leftward drift of the majority after the Armistice. It revealed as well the distinctive ideological configuration of the PSOE within the spectrum of European Socialist parties. The Moscow radiogram had called attention to the pattern fairly typical in Western Europe at this time: a large Right, labeled by Moscow the "avowed social chauvinists"; a smaller "Center," which was said to be "amorphous" and "always vacillating"; and a very small "Left-revolutionary wing."[9] The Spanish party did not correspond precisely to this schema: though "national," "patriotic," and pro-Allied, it was also "Left," intransigent, sectarian, and committed to a revolutionary overthrow of the bourgeois order at some point in the indefinite future. The PSOE had a peculiar profile: the far Right and the far Left remained extremely small, whereas the Center bulged conspicuously. This Center may be visualized as two adjacent peaks. The Right Center loomed larger in the Wilsonian aftermath of the war but shrank rapidly after about July 1919; the Left Center, enlarged by spreading disillusionment with the peace and by a mounting fervor for the Bolshevik Revolution, grew rapidly in this period and soon became the majority faction within the Party.

Early in 1919, as we have seen, there appeared to be some basis for a renewed solidarity between left-centrists and right-centrists. This was chiefly because the issue of the war had retreated, whereas the issue of international affiliation —specifically, that of the Third International—had not yet decisively intruded. The basic centrism of the majoritarians and minoritarians came to the fore: all were agreed on the need for doctrinal intransigence, for the maintenance of revolutionary objectives, and for sectarian aloofness from ministerial collaboration. At the same time, there was general agreement that the Party should continue its electoral and parliamentary participation and increase its proselytizing among the peasantry. Where right- and left-centrists disagreed was over the wisdom of continuing the Republican-Socialist Alliance and over the suitability of the bourgeois-democratic republic as an intermediate goal, the left-centrists demanding, somewhat abstractly, a social rather than a merely political revolution. But apart from a certain exaltation engendered by the Bolshevik Revolution, the leftists differed from the majority chiefly in their greater verbal commitment to a revolutionary transformation and were not prepared, for example, to forego the pleasures of parliamentary activity or to go into the streets in the near future in order to speed the coming of the revolution. Beyond this, they were burdened by their commitment to party unity— a commitment that would be placed under increasing strain as the revival of the Second International met with one delay after another and as Moscow exerted steadily greater attraction during the disillusioning spring and summer of 1919.

The Founding of the Communist International

During most of 1918 Lenin and his lieutenants were too preoccupied with consolidating the Revolution in Russia to give much thought to organizing its unfolding abroad. But late in 1918 and early in 1919 several converging factors convinced them of the need to institutionalize their commitment to world revolution in a new international organization. No doubt central to their calculations was the wave of quasi-revolutionary unrest that enveloped so much of Europe in the post-Armistice period; but they were also motivated by the collapse of their last hopes for a diplomatic rapprochement with the Allied powers, by the timely founding of the German Communist Party in December 1918, and by the efforts (in their view perverse and sinister) of conservative and moderate Western Socialists to resuscitate the Second International. For these reasons the Bolshevik leaders, with almost no warning beyond the January radio broadcast, abruptly convened the founding congress of the Third International, which began its sessions in Moscow on March 2. As a small, irregular assembly engineered and dominated by the Russians, this was little more than a rump parliament of pro-Bolshevik Socialists, very few of whom were legitimate representatives of national parties. What was missing, as the lone German delegate remarked, was the whole of Western Europe.[10]

Nevertheless, the Bolshevik purpose was served by this gathering. The task of the new International it established was to cleanse the world labor movement of opportunistic and nationalistic elements while mobilizing all genuinely rebellious workers behind the cause of revolution. The Third International, as Hulse has said, was not originally intended to be a control organization; the Bolsheviks did not yet envision the centralized structure they would later give it. Rather, its objective was essentially propagandistic. Its founding was an effort to break through the isolation imposed on the Russian Bolsheviks and to set forth certain basic principles and tactics around which revolutionary proletarian parties could rally.[11]

The ideology revealed in the manifestos and theses of the new organization was essentially libertarian, suggesting that Europe had entered a phase of spontaneous upheaval, and that the social revolution was, as Grigorii Zinoviev told the congress, "a question of the immediate future." Comintern pronouncements evoked the vision of an immediately impending revolution that would destroy all oppressive political and social structures. The need to "smash" bourgeois institutions was again and again proclaimed, and emphasis was placed on the value of "mass action" and of "direct clashes" with the old order, as well as on the need to base the emerging proletarian order on such "mass organizations" as revolutionary trade unions and soviets. There was much criticism, though no explicit repudiation, of bourgeois parliamentarianism, which was declared to be lying "in bloody ruins." An authoritarian undertone was present, as in some of Trotsky's writings on economic organization, but little or no mention was made through most of 1919 of the role of the Communist Party or of the need for political as opposed to economic centralization.[12]

The great distance between Spain and the blockaded Bolsheviks ensured that the documents of the First Congress of the Communist International would be slow to penetrate the labor centers of the Peninsula. Neither Socialists nor Anarchosyndicalists had a really clear conception of the nature of Bolshevism; but on the whole, the creation of the Comintern and the propagation of its revolutionary, libertarian, and antiparliamentary ideology posed a greater challenge to the followers of Pablo Iglesias than to the Cenetistas, since these actions called into question the patient, parliamentary tactics that formed the heart of Pablismo. It was not surprising that the Socialists responded more slowly to the lure of the new International, or that the Cenetistas, seeing in the Bolsheviks fellow ultra-leftists—or so they believed—mostly favored immediate entry into the Comintern. But in fact, the Third International would have a divisive effect on both sides of the Spanish labor movement, appealing strongly to the authentically revolutionary types and creating doubt and resistance among the reform-minded, who were to be found in both organizations. Revolutionary rhetoric would be put to the test and "false consciousness" challenged. Indeed, the Comintern question illuminated the operative ideological divisions on both sides of the postwar labor movement as few other issues did. What was at stake, in the final analysis, was the possible emergence of a unified, pro-Comintern revolutionary working-class movement embracing the whole of the Peninsula and ending the old animosities between Marxists and Bakuninists. In general terms, one may say that the emergence of such a Bolshevik party in Spain would have required the Socialists to become more revolutionary and the Anarchosyndicalists less spontaneous, while both would have had to accept international discipline (though this was only implicit in 1919).[13]

The Right Center and the Comintern

The several ideological tendencies within the Socialist Party, never sharply defined, were in flux during the course of 1919, and it will be convenient to survey the reactions of each to the issues raised by the Bolshevik triumph in Russia and the birth of the Third International. Since the Right Center of Iglesias, Besteiro, and Largo Caballero was the majority position during the first half of 1919, as well as the focus of Party orthodoxy and the target of critiques from both left-wing and right-wing Socialists, it will be well to begin with that group.

Although the term "right-centrist" has frequently been used to characterize the Socialist majoritarians, it is worth noting that they did not regard themselves as rightists or moderates within the Socialist world. There were, in fact, relatively few self-confessed reformists or right-wing Socialists in the PSOE, and Revisionism had generally received a cold welcome within the Party. Militants like Iglesias, Besteiro, García Quejido, Fabra Ribas, and Núñez Tomás retained a radical self-image despite their "defensist" position during the war, their continued support for the electoral alliance with the Republicans, and their parliamentary gradualism. They measured themselves not against the hitherto almost nonexistent Socialist left wing but against the inertia and conservatism of the ruling classes and against the shallow political panaceas of the Republicans. They felt like revolutionaries within their moribund society; and if they were not prepared to begin the social revolution at once, this, as they frequently made clear, was only because the working class was inadequate in numbers and in consciousness to take the reins of society. They therefore insisted that there had first to be a bourgeois-democratic revolution to create the conditions for proletarian ascendency.

The right-centrists had played a leading part in the revolutionary movement of 1917, trying to assist the anemic Spanish bourgeoisie to make the revolution it was too weak to carry out unaided. And they still believed, despite the August debacle, that they wanted a republican revolution, though, admittedly, they were more cautious than they had been in 1917 and were also held back by the growing conservatism of the trade-union leaders. The behavior of their representatives in the Cortes of 1918–19, especially that of Besteiro, Largo Caballero, and Saborit, was rather bellicose and not very much like that of men trying to assimilate themselves to the bourgeois system; they were regarded by the deputies of the Turnante parties as dangerous revolutionaries.[14]

No doubt it was a question of the perspective from which the right-centrists were viewed. They themselves, whatever their practice, wished to feel that their doctrine was a "radical" and "pure" expression of the Marxist commitment to class struggle and proletarian revolution. Thus, though they acted, in the words of Raymond Aron, as though Bernstein were correct, they continued to think and to talk as though Kautsky were in possession of the truth. This meant walking an ideological tightrope. The right-centrists collaborated (a term they did not like to use) in municipal, provincial, and national legislatures, in electoral coalitions with the left-bourgeoisie, and in the Institute of Social Reforms; but on numerous occasions they utilized a rather intransigent vocabulary, and, above all, they drew back with dread from the ultimate collaboration, that of participation in bourgeois ministries. Residues of Guesdism helped to explain this restraint, but the right-centrists also seemed to recognize that a determination to remain aloof from ministerial power, connoting as it did self-denial and moral superiority, was one of the few tangible things separating them from the left-bourgeois parties. In this connection the restraint of Besteiro, who was eminently *ministrable*, has to be admired—and should be compared with the behavior of the Millerands, Briands, and Vivianis who found a Socialist future without ministerial position too bleak to be endured.[15]

Although the centrist synthesis of "revolutionary-reformism"—a combination of verbal radicalism and reformist praxis—might not withstand the most searching theoretical analyses, it must nevertheless be viewed as eminently functional in the Spanish context, for it reflected the majoritarians' instinctive understanding of their Party's situation in a country still so unready for Socialism. They sensed, without clearly articulating it, that in the incipient phase of capitalism and in the peculiarly repressive-permissive Spanish political environment, the Socialist movement could only survive and be held together by an artful combination of doctrinal extremism, reformist practice, and a certain detachment from the temptations of power at the highest level.*

Thus Besteiro had been careful to preserve and even to accentuate the sectarian tone of Pablismo in the face of continuing speculation, especially after the 1918 elections, that the Party was at last losing its narrow, cultlike character and would soon be participating in a Spanish ministry. The rapid growth of the PSOE and its unions since the second half of 1918, along with its more numerous deputies and its enhanced stature as a supporter of the victorious

---

* Joseph Schumpeter, in his discussion of the German Socialists, reported a similar attitude: "But they realized that in the given situation there was not much for the party to do except to criticize and to keep the banner flying. Any sacrifice of revolutionary principle would have been perfectly gratuitous. It would have only disorganized their following without giving to the proletariat much more than it got in any case.... Such small additional successes as might have been attained hardly warranted the party risk. Thus serious, patriotic and law-abiding men continued to repeat the irresponsible slogans of revolution and treason ... blissfully conscious of the fact that there was little likelihood of their having to act upon them." *Capitalism, socialism, and democracy*, p. 345.

Allies, had suggested to many that Spanish Socialism was coming of age; and there were those who felt that in the near future the Socialists would begin to play the decisive role to which Ortega y Gasset had summoned them amidst the drift and disorder of national life. Ortega, heartened by the moderation of the Party's 1918 May Day Manifesto, had singled out the Socialists and Regionalists as the only uncorrupted elements in national politics, urging them to participate in the governing of the country.[16] But to all such suggestions Besteiro—now the movement's chief spokesman—replied that any collaboration with the governments of the monarchy, in the existing political climate, could only imperil the purity of the Party. Even if the monarchy should be swept away and replaced by a republic, he said, he would still believe that "the mission of the Socialist Party would be that of remaining at its post and limiting its activity to a mere surveillance (*fiscalización*)." He justified this position on the basis of the Party's weakness and the "diffuse" quality of its membership in many parts of the country.[17]

What Besteiro did not say but seems intuitively to have recognized was that ideological intransigence and moral aloofness were essential in a basically hostile and corrupt political environment. If the PSOE were not to go the way of the republican parties, losing first its credit and then its clientele, it would have to tread a difficult path between the overt reformism that it could not embrace and the genuine revolutionism that would transform its democratic nature and in all probability lead it to disaster. The need to be concerned with the confidence of the rank and file was perhaps especially compelling in Spain, where, as Indalecio Prieto said, the Socialist masses had "an exquisite regard" for the independence and purity of their leaders.[18]

If aloofness from ministerial power and efforts to preserve an image of austere integrity constituted one pillar of Pablismo in this period, respect for the "two-stage" concept of the revolution was another. Again, the limits of the Pablista revolutionary impulse were best revealed in the post-Armistice period by the statements of Besteiro. His mood during the last months of the war and right after the Armistice had been one of renewed belligerence and revolutionary expectation. In common with most republican and Socialist leaders he had seemed to view the prospect of the monarchy's fall with revived interest, seeing this as a logical accompaniment of the Allied victory. Adopting a more radical rhetoric, he had participated in a number of virtually revolutionary meetings and had spoken of the impending "disaster" of the regime. "It is now or never," he said to one of his audiences in this period.[19] And yet, in contrast to his boldness in 1917, Besteiro made no revolutionary plans. The moment could not, perhaps, have been more propitious; but the Socialist leader held back, and it is difficult to be certain about his reasons.

Possibly Besteiro had been cowed by the ordeal of 1917, as his detractors charged; perhaps he was beguiled by the electoral prospects opening up before the Party; and almost certainly he was deterred by the resistance of the trade-union leaders (men like Manuel Llaneza, José María Suárez, Trifón Gómez, and Vicente Barrio), who, because of their concern for the organizational structure of the UGT, were opposed to a renewal of the adventure begun in August 1917. Like the German August Bebel in 1906, Besteiro may have been forced to comprehend the reality of the power relationship between a relatively small party and a substantial trade-union movement. In all probability, the union leaders had made it clear that the tail would not wag the dog. Certainly, both Besteiro and Largo Caballero, in the period after August 1917, acted like men who had lost their mandate to lead the masses of the UGT into revolutionary ventures. Besteiro nevertheless remained committed in principle to the necessity of a bourgeois-democratic revolution in Spain, even as he firmly rejected the idea, then gaining currency within the Party, that the workers should march directly to the social revolution.[20]

Besteiro made it clear that he did not oppose the dictatorship of the proletariat—in Russia. Unlike the German centrist Karl Kautsky, who had condemned any Socialist coup in an economically backward country,[21] he saw the proletarian dictatorship as an "ineluctable necessity" in Russia; and he was inclined to believe that the Russian Bolsheviks, faced with the choice (as he believed) between a "Socialist dictatorship" and anarchy, had done well in facing up to the situation. But Besteiro differed from the Bolsheviks and from the growing Left within his own party in his conviction that Bolshevik methods would only lead to disaster when applied in the Western nations, among which he clearly included Spain. Spanish workers, unlike their Russian counterparts, were not, in his view, ready for a proletarian dictatorship. His Menshevist bias remained: while the left wing was increasingly talking of the need to skip over the bourgeois-democratic republic and move directly to a Socialist society, Besteiro and most of his colleagues on the National Committee of the PSOE would cling to the belief that the only conceivable next step for Spain, as in August 1917, was a bourgeois republic in which the Socialists would remain aloof from ministerial participation, serving merely as overseers and censors of the new regime.[22]

Underlying this conviction, and constituting a unifying bond between rightists and left-centrists, was a skepticism regarding the revolutionary capacity of the Spanish workers, coupled, it would seem, with an unspoken optimism about what the Party might accomplish electorally in the postwar era. The majoritarians could not bring themselves to believe that social revolution was as yet a realistic possibility in Spain. Andrés Saborit was especially frank on this point in a speech in the Casa del Pueblo in September. The proletarian dictatorship was justified in Russia, he said, because of the "highly abnormal" conditions prevailing there and because of the need to prevent the overthrow of the Revolution—once it had occurred—by the forces of bourgeois reaction. But Saborit lacked confidence in the sophistication of the Spanish masses. "We are dreaming," he said, "if we think of establishing the Soviet regime here when, unfortunately, we can see how many proletarians still live under the tutelage of religion, and how, in the countryside, [there are] legions of *mozos* who wear the military uniform and reveal their lack of class consciousness by firing on their own comrades if so ordered."[23]

Spain, then, was not ready for social revolution because of the *inconsciencia* of her masses; and the mounting campaign on behalf of the Soviets and the Comintern was unfortunate, thought Saborit, because it divided the ranks of Socialism at precisely the moment when they most needed cohesion and discipline. In another speech, to the Young Socialists two months later, Saborit said: "Let's speak less of Russia and [instead] make sure that in Spain there are every day more readers of our press and more members in our party."[24] As for the Second International, there was an increasing tendency during 1919 for the right-centrists, reflecting their own modest drift to the Left, to admit, as did Saborit, the necessity to "cleanse the failure and betrayal" into which many leaders of that organization had fallen. But that task, it was felt, was best carried out by the International itself, into which, said Saborit, "we can infuse a new wisdom."[25]

The Right-Wing Critique of Oscar Pérez Solís

To the right of the Pablista revolutionary-reformists there were, early in 1919, a small number of scattered individuals who shunned the revolutionary "false consciousness" and rhetorical formulas of the right-centrists and promoted a kind of Spanish Revisionism or reformism, which was unrevolutionary, undoctrinaire, and even covertly monarchical. A number of Socialist trade-union leaders fell into this category, along with political leaders such as Indalecio Prieto, Remigio Cabello, and Oscar Pérez Solís. Of these, it was the last who, in the autumn of 1918, offered perhaps the most penetrating critique to which the centrist ambiguities of Pablismo had been subjected.

Intellectually speaking, Pérez Solís was virtually alone on the far Right of the Party, which was probably as he wished it. The special circumstances of Spanish Socialism—its marginal and ever-threatened position in Spanish political life—had placed a premium on a radical, unifying creed and thereby inhibited the emergence of a genuine and numerous right wing, which could only be the product of growth, success, and security.[26] True, the intellectuals and habitués of the New School had flirted with Revisionism in the prewar years, chiefly, it would seem, as a ploy against the party oligarchy. And as late as the autumn of 1918, a few months before they came out for Bolshevism, the same men were pleased to describe their group as the counterpart of the British Fabian Society.[27] But genuine right-wing or revisionist Socialists were quite rare in Spain. Pérez Solís was perhaps the most authentic and, until his sudden about-face in 1921, the most consistent and articulate spokesman for reformism in the PSOE. Because of the pivotal role this militant played in the years 1919–21—moving from right-wing Socialism to Bolshevism—his career and ideas shed an unusual amount of light on the nature of Pablismo. Since he was also the only Socialist leader who left behind a more or less revealing autobiography, the reader will perhaps indulge my somewhat extensive treatment of this most interesting and most controversial of all Spanish Socialists in this epoch.*

Pérez Solís, a very complex individual, came to Socialism after more than a decade in the Artillery Corps (1898–1909). As early as 1906, having risen to the rank of captain in this elite service and with a promising career ahead of him, he decided that he had, in fact, no true vocation to the military, but was more deeply interested in social questions and, above all, in the life of the working class. Increasingly he became conscious of a desire to make contact with the anonymous and uncorrupted masses, to understand the conditions of their existence, and to try to lead them to a better life. Having lost the religious faith of his childhood, he had begun, as he himself later recognized, to seek God in the people. Unmarried, romantic, emotional, and increasingly alienated from the petit bourgeois Spain from which he had emerged, he briefly immersed himself in a sentimental and platonic Anarchism. This owed largely to the influence of a strangely eloquent Andalusian peasant conscript, with whom Solís formed perhaps the deepest personal attachment of his life. Accompanied by his young Anarchist friend and dressed in ragged proletarian attire, he frequented the cafes and gathering places of the workers incognito, eager for contact with the virile social class to whom he was sure the future belonged.[28]

After the accidental death of his friend, around 1907, Pérez Solís rapidly moved away from Anarchism and began to read Marxist literature with great avidity, quickly branching out into philosophy, political economy, sociology, and related subjects. The more rigorous and scientific quality of Marxism impressed him favorably; and he would later come to be known as a "man of doctrine" within the Socialist Party, a feat, as he himself admitted, that was not supremely difficult.[29] Late in 1909, Solís made his first contact with the Socialist movement, in the somnolent garrison town of Valladolid, where his family then lived. His great literary abilities and his energy quickly became

---

* Pérez Solís, as will become apparent, was not, strictly speaking, a Revisionist, and he makes no references to Bernstein in any of his writings. A closer parallel would perhaps be with the reformist German Social Democratic leader Georg von Vollmar, who, like Pérez Solís, had been an army officer and had formed his Socialist ideas in a largely agrarian region, South Germany, just as Pérez Solís's Socialism was shaped by rural Valladolid. The two men had in common the belief that Socialists should moderate their opposition to the government, emphasize practical reforms, and come to terms with national sentiment. See Russell, pp. 133–34; Schorske, pp. 81–83. The extremely able Indalecio Prieto held, in this period, views very similar to those of Pérez Solís, except that he supported the Republican-Socialist Alliance and in addition failed to articulate his convictions with the clarity and completeness that Pérez Solís achieved.

apparent, and before long he was made editor of the Valladolid Socialist organ *Adelante*, which he ran even as he performed his military duties. Soon Pérez Solís joined with the older leader Remigio Cabello and another labor leader to form a triumvirate that governed the Party in that province.[30] In 1913 he resigned his army commission to devote himself full-time to the Socialist cause.

Increasingly torn between his desire to be an apostle to the masses and a growing careerist ambition to make his way to the Cortes and become, in effect, the democratic cacique of Valladolid, Pérez Solís nonetheless emerged as an effective, popular leader of the urban and rural workers of the province. He was an unusually vigorous speaker, capable of both considerable warmth and sharp-edged satire—an attractive and formidable figure to the Valladolid proletariat. Yet there was always a residue of aristocratic disdain in him, a consciousness of the *hidalguía* he had inherited from his mother; and through-out his public career he would occasionally be heard expressing contempt for the masses whom he loved and could so successfully sway but whose "vulgarity" and inconstancy repelled him.[31] Nevertheless, given his intellectual gifts and his polemical talent, there was every reason for Pérez Solís to rise to the top of the Socialist Party; for despite its proletarian and even anti-intellectual bias, the Party embraced a growing number of intellectuals in the period after the Tragic Week and raised several of them (Julián Besteiro and Fernando de los Ríos were outstanding examples) to the highest prominence. The tragedy of Solís, if such it was, stemmed less from intellectualism than from geography and character.

Pérez Solís's greatest mistake, given his ever-rising ambitions, came at the very beginning of his labors as a Socialist, when he chose to launch his career in the sluggish backwater of Valladolid. Not only were his strenuous efforts to organize, uplift, and regenerate the retarded masses of the area doomed to failure, but his provincial location meant that he would encounter the Madrid Socialist leadership less as a hierarchy to be scaled than as an enemy to be resisted. Having entered the Party in a romantic and doctrinaire "Left" mood, Pérez Solís first clashed with the Madrid leaders over the issue of the Republican-Socialist Alliance, which he opposed for ideological reasons but also from his life-long empirical conviction that the republican parties were hopelessly corrupted. However, after a few years in the "petit bourgeois ambience" of Valladolid, he began to move, almost insensibly, to the Right. Now the Madrid leadership began to draw his fire from another part of the compass altogether, as he chided them for their verbal intransigence and doctrinaire addiction to the formulas of class struggle and antimonarchism! The Socialist leaders may be forgiven for concluding that Solís—who may merely have suffered, like Mussolini, from oversensitivity to his milieu—was unreliable and even eccentric.[32]

Pérez Solís's move to the right wing of Spanish Socialism was understandable, given the Valladolid environment and the concrete problems that the Socialists confronted there. The chief of these were the drowsy pace of economic life and the lack of industry, so characteristic of Castile as a whole, which precluded a vigorous proletariat and bourgeoisie as well as clear-cut class conflict between them. Thus Pérez Solís, along with Cabello, adopted a primarily political strategy, focusing on the need to break the power of caciquismo—personified in Valladolid province by the Duke of Alba. This did not altogether please the Madrid Socialists, since it sometimes brought the Valladolid leaders into conflict with republican elements with which the Party had electoral alliances. Pérez Solís later wrote that it was the petty struggles of Valladolid, having nothing to do with the "high problems" of Socialism, that had undermined the early inflexibility of his leftist and orthodox convictions. The situation there, he observed, was not really suited to the maintenance of a purely Socialist movement, but was "more adequate for the development of a semi-Socialist democratic movement, which was just what we Socialists headed up."[33] He also blamed the war, which, with its exaltation of nationalist feelings everywhere, had pushed the whole Spanish Party to the Right, and himself most of all, so that he became "one of the most notorious rightists" in it. Had he not been exiled from Valladolid late in 1919, for lese majesty against the Duke of Alba, he might well have ended up, he later wrote, as a "left-wing monarchist."[34]

Character also played a part in Pérez Solís's estrangement from the Party oligarchy. There was much of the iconoclast in him, along with considerable originality of thought and an often great vivacity of expression. These qualities made him unwilling or unable to cover nonrevolutionary practice with the verbal formulas and revolutionary incantations that came so naturally to other leaders. He confessed to having an overdeveloped critical instinct and seems to have enjoyed too much the role of dissenter, truth-teller, and myth-destroyer. One of his most cherished self-images was that of the embattled heretic, surrounded by Philistines and courageously exposing conventional wisdom. Except when communing with large, adoring audiences of workers, he was never happier than when declaiming unpopular truths in front of some outraged gathering of Party members. In the broadest sense, the dilemma of Pérez Solís was that his social thought was too advanced for the republican parties, where temperamentally he perhaps belonged; yet, at the same time, he lacked the gravity, the stability, and the willingness to conform that might have facilitated his acceptance by the Socialist oligarchy. In contrast to the other Socialist leaders, he was unconventional and irreverent, and his mounting ambition was perhaps too apparent.

Thus Pérez Solís did not share in the republicanism toward which the Socialist Party was increasingly drawn after 1909, but remained convinced that the monarchy could be made useful to Socialism. After the debacle of the premature Valladolid strike in April 1917 he was censured, and for a time he withdrew from the Party. He even attempted briefly to set up a rival Socialist Party "of more intellectual substance" and of a more "conservative spirit" than the existing one, to which end he published two issues of a journal called *El Pueblo*.[35] Partly because of this temporary rupture with the Party, Pérez Solís gave only half-hearted support to the August Strike Movement, which failed to capture his imagination.[36] His interest, up to the end of 1919, focused almost exclusively on trying to arouse the urban and rural workers and petty proprietors of Valladolid and its hinterland, in order to break the power of the local caciques and, it would seem, send himself as a deputy to the Cortes. That he might have become "one cacique more" crossed his mind—just as it occurred to Unamuno, who suspected that Pérez Solís would become the leader of a "caciquismo from below."[37]

Despite the disesteem of the Madrid Socialist leaders, the career of Pérez Solís was beginning to show much promise by the spring of 1918. As a devout reader of the regenerationist Macias Picavea he favored both national renovation and regionalism; and his warm support for the Catalanist movement came to the attention of Francisco Cambó, who, on behalf of the Lliga Regionalista, was trying to arouse and unite progressive forces everywhere in Spain by popularizing regionalism and by urging the democratizing of the oligarchical system of government. As a talented man of the Left who could inspire the masses but was at the same time unsectarian, moderate, and monarchical, Pérez Solís was a natural candidate for the broad, national movement Cambó was seeking to call into being. He visited Cambó in Barcelona early in 1918, and an informal alliance grew up between the two men, with the Catalan leader urging Solís—unnecessarily, it would seem—to run for the Cortes.[38]

Meanwhile, Solís had gradually been winning a certain amount of national attention. As early as January 1915, the deputy Rodrigo Soriano had called him to the attention of the Cortes as "a man of demonstrated intelligence and . . . of an exquisite moderation and admirable propriety in his methods."[39] Endowed with a fine journalistic talent, Solís began publishing articles in *España* in 1917, for the first time reaching a national audience. But the "takeoff" point in his career appeared to have been reached when Ortega y Gasset, also impatient with republican rhetoric, began in the early autumn of 1918 to print in *El Sol* a series of corrosive antirepublican articles written by Solís.[40]

Throughout 1918–19, Pérez Solís seemed destined for a successful and perhaps brilliant career in national politics. He spoke often, and always with good effect, at political gatherings, Party assemblies, and on at least one occasion in the Madrid Atheneum. But his attention was focused almost exclusively on Spain's domestic problems, and especially on the problem of caciquismo, in the destruction of which he saw a key to the regeneration of Spain and, no doubt, to the advancement of his own political ambitions. International events—the war, the peacemaking, the Russian Revolution, and the problems of the Socialist International—did not absorb his interest. He was a partisan of the Allies during the war, but without the passionate intensity of many of his fellow Socialists.[41]

Pérez Solís's critique of the Socialist Party was less immoderate than his assault on the parties of the republican Left, but it was nevertheless one of the strongest indictments ever brought against Pablismo. The trouble, he felt, went back to 1909, when the Socialist Party had begun to fall under the spell of two ideas: republicanism and revolution. Even after the threat to political liberties associated with Maura and the Tragic Week had subsided, the Socialists had clung to their electoral alliance with the Republicans and had become, in effect, "one more republican party." The best energies of the Party were now spent in talking about the horrors of Maurismo and in pursuing the phantasm of an unrealizable republic. It was painful, wrote Solís, "to see the foremost men of Spanish Socialism running here and there with revolutionary prescriptions and sounding the republican bell, slaves of the politics of tumult, obsessed with the idea of ending the Monarchy but incapable of bringing in a better regime."[42] The republic, he felt, was unattainable because neither the military, nor the middle classes, nor the masses desired it. A revolution in Spain could only lead to chaos and counterrevolution, for there was no "solidly organized middle-class political force" to take over the authority that might be wrested from the deposed regime. Beyond that, he had no confidence whatever in the revolutionary will and capacity of the Spanish masses. The people, he thought, were so "inert," so paralyzed with ignorance, that they could provide no support for a republican government; hence the men of the Left would end by governing as badly as the men of the Right.[43]

The trouble with the republicanizing trend, thought Solís, was that it had led the Socialists into the same pseudo-revolutionary *palabrería,* the same "sterile vociferations," as the republicans; and it could well end by losing the masses to the Anarchosyndicalists. At the same time, the Socialists, while chasing the will-o'-the-wisp of the republic, had seriously diluted the social substance of their creed, and had forsaken the hard labor on behalf of concrete social reforms, especially agrarian reform, that alone could lead to the revival of Spain. It was a "crass error" to imagine that any people could prosper as the result of purely political and formal changes. The important thing in Spain was to create a "robust economic life," which was "the indispensable condition of all national regeneration." Not only must the monopoly of the landlords be broken, but all impediments to the "full flowering of industrial capital" must be swept away. Therein, said Pérez Solís, would lie the true revolution. But who among the Socialists, let alone the republicans, talked about such things as rural credit, rent reform, court reform, the latifundia, irrigation, fertilizers, and, above all, economic freedom, "the *sine qua non* for all other freedoms?"[44]

As between a republic that might leave intact the juridical bases of landed property in Spain and a monarchy that would revolutionize them, Solís left no doubt that he would support the monarchy. Although he had no more faith in the traditional monarchical parties of the Turno—those "mutual-aid societies for public exploitation"—than he had in the parties of the Left, he had not yet lost his faith in the monarchy itself as the possible instigator of a revolution from above. Such a revolution was the only kind in which he, as a declared enemy of revolutions from below, had any faith. He felt that "the modern mission of kings is to put themselves at the head of their peoples, leading them to democratic conquests."[45] Besides, there were still men associated with the Monarchy who were "susceptible of instruction." What Solís therefore wanted was a "national" party such as Joaquín Costa had once urged, one that would embody the best people and "revolutionize" the bases of Spanish life. Among these people he included some Mauristas, some of those who followed Count Romanones, the "totality" of those led by Melquíades Alvarez, and the "men of action" of Catalan nationalism.[46]

Clearly, Pérez Solís also hoped that the Socialists would be included in such a "national" government. But this, as he saw, would require a transformed Socialism. "I dare to say," he observed, "that Socialism should be profoundly patriotic and nationalist." Rather than reflecting the aspirations of a single social group, it should aspire "to reconcile in the bosom of democracy all the classes of the national society." Like Ortega y Gasset, with whom he shared various perspectives, Pérez Solís wanted the Socialist Party to surrender its cultlike character, and to do this not in order to enter into dubious revolutionary or electoral ventures with the republicans but in order to join in a "national" government of regeneration from above. He chided the Socialists for their horror of ministerial collaboration. Did they think they were not "collaborating," he asked, when they entered municipal, provincial, and national legislative bodies, or when they worked so closely with the Institute of Social Reforms?[47]

Above all, Pérez Solís wanted the Socialists to temper their ideological inflexibility, their insistence on orthodoxy among the membership, and their tendency to reduce Socialism to "rigid doctrinal formulas for the use of the faithful, who worship the creed without understanding it." For him, Socialism was "a distant land toward which, by different routes and different marching tunes, many men proceed. . . . Everything converges at the end of the journey; but who dares to impose the same course upon all?" One was a Socialist when one could say aloud: "I believe that the present society is unjust; I believe that its division into classes is iniquitous; I believe that society must construct itself upon the collective ownership of the means of production." Beyond this profession of faith it was possible "to deny all and to discuss all"; and

Solís made a plea for the "glorious mania of thought" and for more liberty of opinion within the Party. He also criticized the PSOE—though always with a measure of restraint—for its oligarchical tendencies, which, he thought, ill became it as a leader in the struggle against oligarchy and caciquismo in Spain.[48]

It is not surprising that the Russian Revolution failed to inspire Pérez Solís, since he was, at heart, distrustful of the masses and committed to an elitist solution to Spain's problems. In this he did not in fact differ greatly from the Socialist leadership, whose reserve about the Revolution probably matched his own. But, characteristically, he felt it necessary to express himself too forthrightly. He asserted publicly and often that the Revolution was premature, and that when the "floodwaters" receded the Russian masses would be found incompetent to assume the governing function. Nor was he at all tempted to extrapolate from Russia to Spain: there was even less possibility of a successful Spanish revolution, he said, since, in contrast to the Russian situation, the Spanish Army remained entirely obedient to the regime. As an ex-officer, he was sure that a few properly placed machine guns would suffice to disperse any and all rebellious workers. "Therefore," he said, in obvious censure of the leaders of the August Strike, "it will not be I, miserly with the people's blood, who encourages the workers...to cruel and sterile sacrifices."[49] Not surprisingly, Pérez Solís remained, at the same time, one of the few unconditional defenders of the Second International within the Socialist Party.

Growth of the Left Wing

Pérez Solís was the exception to the rule within the ranks of Spanish Socialism, for the great majority of militants were falling increasingly under the spell of the Russian Revolution and beginning to drift leftward with the quickening radical current even before the Armistice was signed. In part this movement was merely the reestablishment of the natural equilibrium in a party that had always been one of the "Left" parties of the Second International until the displacement caused by the war. Thus the general leftward shift affected men as temperamentally moderate as Besteiro, Prieto, and Largo Caballero, who now revived their Guesdist intransigence. But in addition to this normal readjustment there also blossomed a new radicalism, which for the first time carried substantial elements of the PSOE beyond the confines of the "revolutionary-reformism" of Pablo Iglesias and toward the more genuine—as well as more perilous—revolutionism of the Russian Bolsheviks. Whereas a Pérez Solís, from the far Right, would urge the Party to change its theory to coincide with its reformist practice, the men of this "New Left" would wish to see Socialist practice brought into harmony with revolutionary theory.

The consolidation of the Socialist left wing had come late in Spain, and not until August 1918, with the founding of *Nuestra Palabra*, had it achieved much cohesion. Its leadership in the postwar period continued to be largely in the hands of Mariano García Cortés, Ramón Lamoneda, César R. González, Virginia González, and the increasingly radical Manuel Núñez de Arenas of the New School. This group would undergo further radicalization in the course of 1919, moving from the pacifist centrism of Jean Longuet to an acceptance of Bolshevism; but its progress along this path is far from well documented, and the internal history of the Left Socialists in this period remains very obscure.[50] What is clear is that as antiwar minoritarians, unburdened by sentimental ties to the Entente powers, they were able to respond immediately to the Bolshevik Revolution. In contrast to the majority, they began to reflect on the similarities rather than the differences between the Spanish and Russian situations, believing that in Spain as in Russia the increasingly vigorous proletariat might well be able to play the revolutionary role denied to the impotent bourgeoisie. Inspired by events in Russia they began to talk of the possibility that Spain could leap over the "bourgeois" stage and move immediately into a Socialist revolution.[51]

Mariano García Cortés was the central figure on the Socialist Left at this time, combining in a curious way the mentality of a municipal councillor with a dispassionate revolutionary extremism. His election to the presidency of the prestigious Madrid Socialist Group in early 1919 displaced Besteiro from that office and marked the shift of both the Group and the Party to the Left. During the war the voices of the minoritarians in the Madrid Group had generally been lost in a chorus of Aliadofilismo. But early in 1919 the Group became the scene of a power struggle between the moderate, pro-Allied elements and a revivified Left. The election that carried García Cortés to the presidency also resulted in a new committee of the Madrid Socialists, with all but two members representing the left wing of the Party and with César González as Secretary. There now appeared the first signs of a widening rift between the Madrid Group and the National Committee of the PSOE, which continued to be dominated by Iglesias, Besteiro, Largo Caballero, Saborit, and other right-centrists.[52]

Through the spring and early summer of 1919 the conflict was muted by the fact that despite all ideological and personal differences, both the Right and Left generally agreed on the need to revive and refurbish the Second International and on the importance of incorporating the Bolsheviks within it. Even the Bolsheviks' radio summons to form a new International, received in January, had evoked a very cautious response from the *Nuestra Palabra* militants. As left-centrists they remained committed to the concept of a broadly unified, albeit moderately purged, International. And even before this commitment to international unity came their commitment to the unity of the

PSOE. They made it clear that their caution with respect to the new International was largely due to their having "no desire to provoke schisms" within the Socialist movement, and this was a position to which they would tenaciously cling.[53] Even after they recognized the need for a new International, around the middle of 1919, they would hold steadfastly to the ideal of Socialist unity and exert every effort to take a united party into the Comintern.

García Cortés seized every opportunity to radicalize the Party in the early months of 1919. Under the auspices of the *Nuestra Palabra* group a very large number of "pro-Bolshevik" meetings were held, at which the new Russian leaders were praised and defended with great warmth before increasingly large and enthusiastic audiences. Among the most regular participants in these meetings, which were usually held in the Casa del Pueblo, were García Cortés, Lamoneda, Evaristo Gil, Virginia González, and Ramón Merino Gracia. Along with these, militants such as Núñez de Arenas and Andrés Ovejero often spoke for the New School, as Manuel Cardenal and José Antonio Balbontín did for the Young Socialists. Republicans such as Roberto Castrovido and Alvaro de Albornoz also expressed their enthusiasm for the Bolshevik Revolution. Meetings—some of them sponsored by the New School—were held to commemorate the deaths of Rosa Luxemburg and Karl Liebknecht, to protest the expulsion of Russian nationals resident in Spain, to memorialize the Paris Commune, to protest Allied intervention in Russia, to celebrate the anniversary of the Bolshevik Revolution, and to condemn possible Spanish participation in the Allied blockade.[54] Perhaps the most impressive pro-Bolshevik demonstration of this period was staged by the Madrid Socialist Group on May Day 1919. A sizeable procession marched from the Plaza de Isabel II to the Plaza de la Independencia, where, with red flags streaming from the rostrum, various orators paid homage to the Russian Revolution, while the assembled throng responded with repeated cries of "Viva Rusia! Viva Rusia!" After the meeting, a large group of demonstrators marched to the French Embassy, which they assaulted with stones in order to protest the Allied intervention in Russia.[55]

The New School

The second element within the expanding left wing of the PSOE was the New School, which embraced many of the middle-class intellectuals who had made their way into the Party since about 1909, among them Manuel Núñez de Arenas, Andrés Ovejero, Eduardo Torralba Beci, Manuel Pedroso, Julio Alvarez del Vayo, Luis Araquistáin, and Leopoldo Alas. The state of mind of these men in the early part of 1919 would have to be described as complex. Before the war some had dabbled in Revisionism; during the war they had given themselves, with the exception of Núñez de Arenas, heart and soul to the cause of the Allies; and as late as November 1918 they viewed the New School as the Spanish counterpart of the British Fabian Society, "fully democratic and leftist."[56] They had drunk deep of Wilsonian idealism, and all of them, accustomed to regarding the war as a "revolution," had come to expect that the end of the fighting would signal the beginning of the regeneration not merely of war-torn Europe but of moribund Spain. Yet almost as soon as the Armistice was signed, and even before the peace terms were revealed, they began to fear that their idealism had been misplaced and misused. While still under the spell of Wilson the intellectuals of the New School began to succumb to the promise of Lenin and the Bolshevik Revolution. On January 19, 1919, in a meeting held to protest the expulsion of the Russian nationals from Spain, Núñez de Arenas "officially" announced for the first time that the New School, formerly a citadel of Revisionism and Allied sympathies, had now become an ardent supporter of the Bolshevik Revolution. At the same meeting Leopoldo Alas struck a note that would often be sounded by the Left, urging his listeners to discount stories of Bolshevik violence and to remember, in any case, that violence was inseparable from revolution.[57]

The views of the journalist Manuel Pedroso were perhaps typical. For a time he embraced both Wilson and Lenin: Wilson because he proposed a democratic society of free nations; Lenin because he stood for the principle of socialization within those nations and, ultimately, for the disappearance of the state apparatus. Pedroso was aware that revolutions were not made with "white gloves and madrigals." He knew that the Bolsheviks had used terror and that a good many "inadaptables" and dissenters had been shot out of hand; but he regarded all of this as necessitated by the Russian struggle against counterrevolution. All was justified, in the end, by the fact that Bolshevism stood for a historic break with older, outworn conceptions of sovereignty, including the "fictitious concept" of popular sovereignty. For Pedroso, Bolshevism in the post-Armistice period was an almost anarchistic attempt to "dissolve power among all of the governed and thereby to avoid forever the tyranny of power."[58]

The best minds among Spanish intellectuals, men such as Unamuno, Ortega y Gasset, Altamira y Crevea, or Pérez de Ayala, were not even momentarily seduced by Bolshevism;* but some sectors of the younger or less established

---

* Unamuno perceived that Spaniards who greeted the Bolshevik Revolution as an "Anarchist" phenomenon were in the grip of a delusion, and he made the point that dictatorship and Anarchism were "two mutually exclusive concepts." As for Lenin, Unamuno wrote: "Lenin is like a prophet of Israel, and what he preaches is a new religion. Materialistic, if you like—we do not think that is what it is—but a religion. Atheistic, undoubtedly, but a religion. And a religion that will end up in a type of Buddhism. An Asiatic religion in any case, engendering a Lamaism like that of Tibet. . . . As Christianity in order to triumph . . . had to ally with paganism and with gentile Hellenic philosophy, thus will Bolshevism have to ally with bourgeois economic philosophy." *El Liberal* (Madrid), 3.vii.20; quoted in *Almanaque de Tierra y Libertad*, p. 198. Besteiro had also derided the Socialists—"Bolcheviques de ocasión," he called them—who imagined that Bolshevism had anything to do with Anarchism or the weakening of state power. *El Socialista*, 1.v.19. For Ortega y Gassett's criticism of Marxism, see *Invertebrate Spain*, pp. 172–78.

intelligentsia experienced a certain radicalization under the impact of the Russian Revolution and the disappointments of a peace from which too much had been expected. Manuel Pedroso and Julio Alvarez del Vayo symbolized the turn to the Left of a number of idealistic, semi-Socialist intellectuals who, in the face of a disillusioning postwar world and a still stagnant Spain, would move from Wilsonianism to Leninism. Indeed, these two not only reflected but influenced that evolution. Having served as correspondents in wartime Germany, both men had considerable knowledge of the European Socialist movement, and especially of German Social Democracy. Both had been acquainted with Rosa Luxemburg, and they were convinced that the German majoritarians had betrayed the German revolution and conspired in the murder of Luxemburg and Liebknecht. In an emotion-filled meeting on the evening of January 25, 1919, Pedroso contrasted the Socialism of Schiedemann and Ebert, which he called "Kaiserism without the Kaiser," with the Socialism of the two German martyrs, who had desired to make a "profound and universal revolution"—which, he said, was the only kind of revolution Spaniards could be interested in. He urged Spanish Socialists to emulate the example of the German Spartacists.[59]

One of the most emphatic defenders of Bolshevism in this period was a militant who was not closely associated with either the *Nuestra Palabra* group or the New School but who sat on the National Committee of the Socialist Party and had been the personal secretary of Pablo Iglesias. This was Daniel Anguiano, Secretary of the National Federation of Railworkers, whose almost saintly integrity and devotion to the cause outweighed, in the minds of most Socialists, his relatively modest intellectual attainments. Anguiano was a good and simple man who took the revolutionary protestations of Pablismo seriously enough to be deeply inspired by the Bolshevik Revolution, which he seems to have regarded as an essentially "syndicalist" phenomenon. In a speech on February 10, he went well beyond the cautious radicalism of the other Socialist leaders and advocated the subversion of "those proletarian elements who dispose of the elements of force" in Spain—that is to say, the rank and file of the army. He was sure that Spain was on the eve of a revolutionary transformation, and, evoking a favorite theme of the Socialist Left, he called for close cooperation between Socialists and the Anarchosyndicalists of Catalonia and Andalusia. And, though he still spoke of the need for a "bourgeois republic," he seems to have regarded this as a very ephemeral stage on the road to the impending social revolution. In Anguiano, Spanish Bolshevism would soon find one of its most sincere and least self-serving recruits.[60]

End of the Wilsonian Dream

The mood of the Socialist rank and file became more radical with each passing month of 1919, as inflation, unemployment, and food shortages took their toll of the workers' morale and well-being. Nevertheless, it was not until June or July that support for the Second International began to erode seriously, and significant numbers of Socialists began switching their allegiance to the Third International. The abandonment of the old organization was related to the increasingly revolutionary mood of the workers, but also to the sharp disappointment with which the pro-Allied elements received the terms of the Versailles Treaty. A large majority of Spanish Socialists had supported the Allied cause with a perhaps too-intense idealism. By permitting exorbitant hopes to grow up regarding the transformations that peace would bring, Iglesias and his lieutenants had made Pablismo a hostage to the fortunes of the postwar world, since the disillusionment was bound to be great.

The pain of blighted illusions was sharpest among those Socialist intellectuals and militants who had insisted for four years that an Allied victory would end war as a factor in human affairs and redeem the world for democracy and Socialism. The harsh terms of the Versailles settlement cast grave doubt on these hopes and were, indeed, a severe disappointment. As Torralba Beci wrote in *El Socialista*, the same idealism that had put the Spanish militants so ardently on the side of the Allies during the war now compelled them to recognize that the peace of Versailles was not "the peace of the peoples, the peace of right and reconciliation" that had been promised. Rather, it was an iniquitous and dangerous peace, a capitalist and imperialist settlement that opened up a "terrifying vision" of new wars.[61]

In the aftermath of Versailles Torralba Beci became convinced for the first time that the Communist International could and should conquer its rival, and that the moment had come to separate revolutionary from evolutionary tendencies within Socialism. In this he reflected the views of other "Wilsonian" intellectuals such as Núñez de Arenas, Ovejero, Araquistáin, Morato, and Pedroso. Ovejero, who had been almost lyrical in his defense of Wilsonian ideals, now remarked bitterly that the League of Nations had become merely a second Holy Alliance, for the defense not of thrones but of capital. The Second International, he thought, had been "buried in the trenches," and it was time to proclaim the Third.[62] Rives Moyano, remembering his own wartime support for the Entente powers, observed that in view of the ruin of Wilson's Fourteen Points, the time had come for Socialists to cleanse themselves of the "bourgeois infection" by becoming Bolsheviks.[63]

Significantly, it was men such as these—the disenchanted intellectuals and passionate ex-Aliadófilos—rather than the more consistently leftist (and plebeian) wartime minoritarians, who became, in July and August, the earliest Spanish converts to the Third International.* This organization, with its

* *El Sol* observed (21.vii.19) that "In Madrid [those who support the Third International] will not be those militants who have most stood out for their propaganda in favor of Bolshevism, but some of those who were the most extreme *aliadófilos* during the war."

apocalyptic creed, seems to have offered itself almost as a means of expiation, a way out of the spiritual cul-de-sac into which their romantic support of the Allies had led them. Several factors converged to strengthen its appeal: the difficulties encountered by the Second International in reorganizing, which led many Socialists to view it as all but moribund; the grave disappointment of the peace terms, signed on June 28; and Trotsky's dramatic call for another congress of the new International.[64] Thus July saw a sudden upsurge of support for the Comintern among Spanish Socialists; and by the end of the month the Committee of the Madrid Socialist Group agreed to call a special meeting precisely to consider possible entry into the new International.[65]

The struggle within the Madrid Group now intensified as the right-centrist leadership of the Party, personified by Besteiro and Largo Caballero, confronted the rapidly expanding Left. When the two leaders returned from the founding congress of the International Association of Workers in Amsterdam in July, they were confronted with a whole series of resolutions clearly hostile to the National Committee and its basic policies—resolutions regarded by Besteiro as constituting little less than a "censure" of the national organization. The more important of these called for the ending of any further political collaboration with the left-bourgeois parties, protested the postponement of the upcoming Party Congress by the National Committee, demanded the revelation of all political offices held by Party members, and urged the preparation of a new revolutionary movement like that of 1917 but without the "foolishness" of the August Strike. However, the Madrid Group did not yet take a firm stand on whether or not the Party should adhere to the Third International.[66]

The National Committee, understandably fearful of the extremist mood beginning to sweep through the Party's ranks, had indeed sought to delay the convening of a congress. To counter this strategy Torralba Beci proposed to the Madrid Group the holding of a plebiscite within the Party on the question of adherence to Moscow. Torralba had now swung entirely over to the view that the "bourgeois republic" had to be jettisoned and that Spanish Socialists had to go directly to the social revolution. He was convinced that the European war had been equivalent to the passing of "five generations": the Revolution of 1789, which he had once awaited for Spain, had already triumphed, he decided, "with all its egoisms, its cruelties, and its crimes of class." Europe was now squarely in an era of bourgeois imperialism that made it impossible to carry out the Wilsonian program and urgently required the entry of Socialists into the Communist International.[67]

Socialists Debate the Third International

The question of Spanish Socialist adherence to the Comintern was now unavoidably posed, and would be the all-consuming preoccupation of the Party for the next two years. No less than three extraordinary congresses would be devoted to the issue between 1919 and 1921, each of them more violent and more embittered than the last. There swept through the Socialists' ranks in this period, as one anti-Bolshevik militant observed, a "wind of madness" that fanned the controversy to white-hot intensity, producing unseemly outbursts, destroying old friendships, and threatening the very life of the Party. The upsurge of pro-Bolshevik emotion within the hitherto tranquil and disciplined Party was a kind of ideological gale, whose rising force narrowly missed carrying the Party into the Comintern in 1919, did carry it in during the following year, but by 1921 had ebbed sufficiently to leave the decimated Party once more outside the sphere of Moscow and stranded somewhere between the Second and Third Internationals. The Socialist debate on Bolshevism began in the middle of 1919 amid a mounting national tumult and rising revolutionary expectations; it would end in the middle of 1921 during one of the most severe official repressions to occur in Western Europe.[68]

During the summer of 1919 the pages of *El Socialista* were thrown open to discussion of the question of international affiliation, and the rank and file were encouraged to make known their views. The debate never reached great heights of doctrine or eloquence, but it showed that a substantial majority of the Party were gravitating toward Moscow. And the Madrid Socialist Group, continuing its own radical evolution, finally voted on September 2, by an overwhelming majority, in favor of the Party's adherence to the Comintern.[69]

The increasingly leftist temper of the Party was disturbing to the ex-majoritarians—as they must now be called—and especially to Pablo Iglesias. The Spanish Socialist Party had belonged to the Second International since the latter's founding, and many of the Party's veterans viewed "with profound feeling" the crumbling of the illusions with which they had enveloped that organization. Iglesias's attitude on the international question is not well documented because of his chronic illness, the infrequency of his writings in this period, and his apparent desire to maintain a low profile with respect to a highly charged issue. It is clear that he and his lieutenants would have much preferred salvaging the Second International if this had been in any way possible; but it is also evident that they had decided against trying to meet the powerful gusts of pro-Bolshevik enthusiasm head on. *El Socialista* was now given over almost exclusively to eulogies of Soviet Russia and praises of the new International.[70]

However, the prospect of a plebiscite disturbed Iglesias and forced him to break his silence. In an article in the Party journal he said that although he did not wish to comment on the "substance" of the proposal, he had to object to the use of a plebiscite, since it was fundamental to the Party's modus operandi that all important decisions be taken in Party congresses in order to facilitate the widest possible debate of the issues. A plebiscite, moreover, would run the serious risk of dividing the Socialist forces. The idea of a plebiscite was, in the end, dropped; but Torralba Beci's proposal nevertheless achieved what was probably its desired effect: within a few days the National Committee agreed to convene an extraordinary Party Congress in December.[71]

Shortly after this, in late October, the Asturian Socialists held a special congress in Oviedo, whose strident debates indicated that Asturian enthusiasm for the Bolshevik Revolution may have surpassed that of all other Socialist regions. The inexorable contraction of coal and other production since the Armistice had bred in the miners and metalworkers of this area an increasingly radical frame of mind, and had encouraged salvational hopes regarding Russian Bolshevism. At the Congress young militants like José Cuesta and José Calleja, reflecting the "Left" mood of the Asturian workers, supported a resolution favoring the immediate adherence of the PSOE to the Comintern. Only with difficulty was the leader of Asturian Socialism, Isidoro Acevedo, able to hold off the leftist thrust and guide through the Congress a more moderate resolution looking toward the "reconstruction" of the Second International, albeit on the basis of an acceptance "in principle" of the ideology of the Communist International. The resolution provided that if the results of the upcoming Geneva Conference proved unsatisfactory by reason of "fundamental discrepancies" with the spirit of the Comintern, the PSOE would then give its allegiance to Moscow. With its willingness to wait a few months in order to let the Second International demonstrate a revolutionary character before abandoning it, the Asturian resolution was almost precisely that which the Party Congress would adopt two months later in Madrid.[72]

Meanwhile, on September 5 the Madrid Socialist Group, moving ever more rapidly toward the Left, voted (272 to 97) in favor of the Party's dissolving the Republican-Socialist Alliance and severing all relations with the left-bourgeois parties, this being regarded as a logical prelude to Socialist adherence to the Comintern. Largo Caballero spoke out against the severance of electoral alliances and, in a heated exchange, had the ill grace to remind Torralba Beci of the time, not too distant, when that militant had himself been a fervent supporter of the alliance with the Republicans, to which Torralba could only reply that conditions had changed a great deal since the Armistice. Largo Caballero was also anxious to deny the allegation that there were reformists and revolutionaries—a Right and a Left—within the Party: "Here," he said, "we are all Socialists." But the trade-union official Santiago Pérez was more candid when he simply said: "We are not prepared for revolution,"[73] a remark suggesting, again, that even though the Ugetista masses may have been drunk with the wine of Bolshevism, their leaders had been permanently sobered by the outcome of the August Movement.[74]

The Emergence of the Ultra-Left

This revolutionary pessimism was not shared, to say the least, by the third element within the expanding left wing of the Spanish Socialist Party, that is, by the Young Socialists (Federación de Juventudes Socialistas, FJS). This organization had originated after the turn of the century among the youths of the Socialist Circle of Bilbao, who had formed the first group, under the guidance of the young writer Tomás Meabe. The Young Socialists were officially constituted at the time of the Fifth Congress of the PSOE in 1905, and held their first congress in 1906, during which the constitution for the FJS was drawn up. There were then some 20 sections and 1,116 members, about one-third of them in Bilbao.[75] The organization was intended primarily to serve the Party as an auxiliary, especially during elections, and also to instill a Socialist culture in the youth of Spain through lectures, assemblies, and excursions.

Over the years the FJS devoted its energies largely to the campaign against militarism and the Moroccan involvement; but during the war a majority of members, especially those outside Madrid, were swept along by the pro-Allied current.[76] The ranks of the FJS expanded rapidly in the postwar period, to perhaps 7,000 members by 1920; and in some areas, such as Asturias, it would claim a numerical strength perhaps three times greater than that of the Party itself.[77] Its members were mostly skilled manual workers, and included relatively few students or white-collar workers. Like the Socialist Party, the FJS prided itself on its *obrerista* character. The "shock detachments" of the Young Socialists, as a Soviet scholar has termed them, were the young metalworkers and miners of the Basque Provinces and Asturias, along with the woodworkers, tobacco workers, and printers of Madrid.[78]

The Young Socialists had long been used in street confrontations and in some of the more violent aspects of electoral campaigning, and they were, as Pérez Solís observed, more or less addicted to the "cult of force."[79] It was said of the especially vigorous Asturian members that they were "soldiers by necessity, rebels by instinct, blind in the struggle, and ready at all times to go to the sacrifice, disputing among themselves, like true heroes, the place of greatest danger in the . . . battle."[80] Never noted for doctrinal sophistication, the Young Socialists were more remarkable for their idealism and passionate state of mind. They knew, as *Nuestra Palabra* observed, "how to die on the altar of an ideal that they only vaguely discerned, with a smile on their lips and with the defiant gesture of . . . martyrs."[81]

The proclivity of the Young Socialists for violent activism reflected, no doubt, the natural nihilism of the young, as well as the contagious example of the revolutionary Syndicalists in Catalonia.[82] But it also had its roots in the special sensitivity of Spanish youth to the backwardness and disorganization of the national life. The consciousness of Spain's "decadence" lay most heavily on the young people of the country, and it was probably not by chance that the name of the FJS newspaper was *Renovación*, whose pages spoke so frequently of the need for national resurrection. It was characteristic that an officer of the Juventud, López Baeza, should speak (at the 1918 Cartagena Congress) of the monarchical regime as being "incompatible with the salvation of the country," and that he should emphasize the existence of "renovating desires that when they triumph will create . . . a country free and modern . . . the arbiter of its own destiny."[83] The Young Socialists had been deeply disappointed by the failure of the 1917 revolutionary strike, and they—more than any other group in the Party save the *Nuestra Palabra* faction—continued to cultivate the myth of the August Movement, in the hope that that effort would be repeated.[84] They had held their congress in Cartagena precisely to express solidarity with the August Strike leaders imprisoned there, whose number even included the president of the FJS, Andrés Saborit.

Socialist youths were clearly in search of some regenerating idea, and it is not surprising that Bolshevism, displacing Pablismo, won converts so rapidly among the younger militants. Of all the components of Spanish Socialism, it was the Juventud that responded most impetuously to events in Russia, and for many Young Socialists the quest for national renovation quickly became fused with the cause and fortunes of the Russian Bolsheviks. Thus the early months of 1919 saw a rapid radicalization of the youth movement and a steadily growing number of adherences by Young Socialists all over Spain to the pro-Bolshevik *Nuestra Palabra* group. It was likewise the Young Socialists who proclaimed the earliest adherence by any Spanish labor group to the Third International. On the very day that the Bolshevik radiogram arrived in Spain the Committee of the Madrid Young Socialists, receiving the news only minutes before a scheduled meeting of the whole membership, unhesitatingly decided to propose to them that the Madrid Group adhere to the projected new International. A short time later this resolve was accepted by the general meeting, unanimously and "without discussion." Thus was made manifest the ideological cleavage that for some time had been growing between the Party and the increasingly radical Madrid Young Socialists, who from that moment became the embryo of the first Communist Party in Spain.[85]

Another, and much smaller, pro-Bolshevik youth organization was the Socialist Students' Group (Grupo de Estudiantes Socialistas, GES), which was founded in Madrid shortly before the August Strike.[86] The middle-class university students who formed the core of the group frequently gathered in the liberal confines of the Atheneum, to hold discussions and to utilize the splendid library housed there; they were also given space in the Casa del Pueblo. A representative member was the young law student José Antonio Balbontín, who was the group's president during the period 1918–19. Balbontín, a magistrate's son, was a fiery pro-Allied liberal who had quarreled so bitterly with his Germanophile professors that he was forced to give up his ambition to become himself a professor of law. His pious father had hoped that this brilliant son would become "el más grande poeta moderna de la fe cristiana"; but Balbontín had read too many antireligious books in the library of the Atheneum and had lost his faith, lapsing, as he said, into "metaphysical melancholy," without, however, losing his essentially religious nature. Chronically torn between the opposing world views of Nietzsche and Tolstoy—that is, attracted by violence but also repelled by it—Balbontín, like most of his companions, was no Marxist but inclined, rather, to philosophical idealism and, on the level of ideology, to the "sublime" Anarchism of Kropotkin. The *Conquest of bread* was the "catachism" of the Students' Group, he said, and was appreciated because in it "there palpitated a fervent and humane Christianism."[87]

The ranks of the Socialist Students were enlarged by an influx of middle-class youths who had been stirred by the spectacle of the August Strike and interested for the first time in the struggles of a proletarian class of whose existence they had hitherto scarcely been conscious.[88] The group's manifestos gave expression to a kind of Spanish *narodnichestvo*, a romantic desire on the part of privileged youths to establish contact with the Spanish masses, to uplift and educate them, and to bring them the redemptive message of Socialism. The young radicals confessed that they were "ashamed to belong to a society so vilely constituted as the one . . . in which we live," and they felt it would be a "diminution of our dignity as men if we did not join our efforts to those of the proletarians in the struggle that will redeem the world."[89] They were sure that bourgeois society was everywhere on the brink of a transformation that would usher in "the reign of justice, in which there will be neither oppressed nor oppressors." They readily admitted that they were few in numbers amid the "amorphous" and indifferent mass of university students, but stressed that they were *conscientes* and that their motives were pure. They were pleased to note that they brought "no class interest" to Socialism but were, instead, "apostles."[90] In April 1918 a GES manifesto modestly proclaimed that in times "when Justice is a myth, Law a farce, and the Good a historical memory, all those of us who . . . possess souls sufficiently developed and in a state of complete purity, by virtue of being educated in [the universitites]" were obliged "to join in singing a vibrant hymn to life in this landscape of death, [and] to preach and establish among men the religion of love and labor as the only source of regeneration."[91]

To implement their elitist pretensions and vaguely Tolstoyan philosophy the Socialist Students also prepared a specific program: the bringing of courses in practical subjects to the workers, who at the same time would be assisted in developing "Socialist souls"; lectures in the Casa del Pueblo by professors from the University; the publishing of Socialist tracts; the arranging of propaganda excursions in order to create workers' organizations in the pueblos; and proselytizing wherever possible.[92]

Despite their idealistic philosophy—a melange of Nietzsche, Kropotkin, and Tolstoy—when the Bolshevik Revolution broke out, wrote Balbontín, "All the Socialist Students of our group became, like Lenin, inflexible Marxists."

> The first Communists recruited in Spain by the Revolution . . . were the students of our group. We became Communists at the very moment Lenin succeeded in taking over the Kremlin. We saw in that dazzling event the dawn of a new, redeemed humanity, the real beginning of human history, as Marx had predicted. The Communist Manifesto of Marx and Engels was then converted into a true and unassailable Bible.[93]

The latent fanaticism of the students was kindled by the Revolution, and they were overcome by the urge to proclaim its message to the proletarian masses. They were persuaded, recalled Balbontín, that solely with the "fascination" of their eloquence they would be able, in a very short space of time, to arouse to revolt all the workers of Spain and of the entire world. They were absolutely convinced that they would see the triumph of the Spanish revolution while still in the flower of their youth.[94]

Animated by this vision, the Socialist Students expended their small treasury in order to make propaganda trips to the pueblos around Madrid and to hire halls where a few Socialist workers and peasants, with their wives and children, came to listen in polite incomprehension to orations on Bolshevism delivered by privileged youths from the capital.* The students' impact on their listeners was less than overwhelming. The febrile workers and peasants of the South were already beginning to stir under the news from Russia, but the stolid plebes of Castile were largely unmoved—a fact of which the young proselytizers were oblivious.

> We did not take notice, then, of the absolute coolness of the ambience, nor did we know how to interpret the full meaning of the profound silence—which seemed to us meditative—of those youthful listeners, workers and peasants, who were more likely to tumble down the sun than to rise in rebellion. We were so intoxicated by our own illusion that the weak, courteous applause at the end of the meeting was sufficient to reaffirm us in our certainty that the Spanish social revolution was rapidly advancing.[95]

---

* "There attended the meeting [in Segovia] the good Socialists of the old city, whose aspect was so idyllic that they looked like shepherds of the pre-Roman age. In the first row there were seated some mothers, who were nursing their babies with disturbing familiarity. As I loudly announced the next revolution, one of the babies burst out crying, and the mother sweetly pleaded with me not to talk so loudly, so as not to frighten the child." Balbontín, p. 144.

It was clear that the Bolshevik Revolution appealed to the essentially religious mentality of the students. "What displeased me most," wrote Balbontín, "in my first readings of Marx was precisely that desire of his to materialize, to reduce to technical formulas and to economic ciphers, what was [Marxism's] most intimate essence—an ethical and, to a certain degree, a religious truth." That essentially Christian truth, so far as the Socialist Students were concerned, was the core belief—which, they felt, stood even though all the rest of Marx's doctrines might fall—that "it is not just that a minority of idlers should live in abundance while the great mass of the workers die in misery."[96] Communism, then, became for youths like Balbontín "a magnificent substitution for the lost Christian faith"; and Marx became "a kind of Biblical prophet who announces the great catastrophe, with formulas more technical than those of Isaiah." Lenin was "something like the Christ of the Evangel, who returned to earth for the second time, armed with the power of the proletarian masses, in order to redeem all the slaves of the world."[97] Confronted by the Bolshevik victory, Balbontín felt like St. Teresa, expecting not to live in the "heaven of the Revolution" but, rather, to die for its triumph. He confided this poem to his diary:

> *Salve*, divine emanation of Russia,
> Which rejuvenates the earth with its breath!
> *Salve*, light beam of the triumphant People!
> I want to fly in the light of your reign!
> Oh, Kingdom of Gold of which Christ dreamed!...
> ("The humble shall be first").
> Kingdom of all lonely souls!
> Source of all mystical dreams!
> I want to die in your glorious radiance...
> I have seen God in the Soul of the People![98]

Although Marxism appealed to the Socialist Students as a secular religion of love, there were, nevertheless, a few stirrings of the terrorist impulse among them. A transplanted Argentine student named Lillo had "a macabre plan to pulverize Spanish society, leaving not one stone in place"; and a certain Ubieta, who collected books about Anarchist terrorists, had dreams of being the "executive arm" of some great *atentado*. The most impetuous (and "most amusing") of all the Socialist Students was Eduardo Ugarte, who one day brought a package of dynamite into the Students' office in the Casa del Pueblo, remarking that he intended to blow up the Conservative minister Rodríguez San Pedro, who had recently helped crush a strike. Ugarte had learned that the minister heard mass every day in the Church of San Luis in the Calle de la Montera, and he planned to put the bomb, with a timing device, under the prayer desk. Balbontín was opposed to the idea; and when Ugarte could not find anyone to arm the weapon for him, he finally threw it into the river. It was shortly after this that he decided to make a trip to Russia in order to fight in the Red Army.[99]

The exact relationship between the Socialist Students' Group and the Young Socialists remains obscure. The Students appear to have viewed themselves as a kind of intellectual politburo of the Madrid Juventud; but the latter movement had its own leaders and worker-intellectuals, and felt no urgent need for tutelage. Nevertheless, there was at least a limited overlapping of the two organizations. Among those who figured in both groups were Ramón Merino Gracia, Eduardo Ugarte, and Manuel Cardenal, all members-to-be of the first Communist Party in Spain. Members of the GES who were not at the same time members of the Young Socialists but who would help found the Partido Comunista Español early in 1920 included Juan Andrade and Gabriel León Trilla. Altogether, about 45 out of the 120 Socialist Students were to give their allegiance to the new party. In October 1919 the young *narodniki* of the GES, presided over by Eduardo Ugarte and declaring that they wished to be the "extremists" of Spanish Socialism, gave their adherence to the Third International.[100]

The Question of Labor Unity

The rapid growth of both sides of the labor movement in 1918–19 and the rise of revolutionary expectations in the post-Armistice period inevitably raised the question of unifying all the proletarian forces in Spain. The left-Socialists displayed the greatest interest in this subject, whereas the right-centrists and especially the right wing revealed somewhat less enthusiasm about the possibilities and benefits of unification. The leftists viewed Socialist-Syndicalist rapprochement not merely as a logical corollary of their adherence to the Comintern, but as the *sine qua non* of the social revolution in Spain. The great mass of the workers on both sides, they knew, favored it; the authorities greatly feared it; and the Bolshevik theses strongly implied its desirability. Within the Socialist Party the left-centrists took the initiative in urging that overtures be made to the Cenetistas and that obstacles to unity be cleared away. Indeed, some of their hostility to the Republican-Socialist Alliance stemmed directly from their knowledge that it was repugnant to the men of the CNT.[101]

Behind much of the fusionist sentiment within the PSOE and UGT was the unvoiced assumption of many Socialists that their superior doctrinal competence would enable them to take the leadership of the Syndicalist masses. During the autumn of 1918 they had watched the soaring growth of Catalonian Syndicalism less in apprehension than in awe and anticipation, and had wondered aloud where the allegiance of the hordes of newly organized workers would ultimately lie. Knowing little about the Anarchist infrastructure of the Sindicatos Unicos, they had allowed themselves to hope that those masses might, in the end, be won for Socialism. The popularity that the Socialist strike committee had gained in Barcelona, and the fact that the workers of that city had gone to the polls for Largo Caballero in large numbers in the 1918 election, led a growing number of Socialists to believe that in the future the Catalonian working class would turn to the Casa del Pueblo in Madrid for guidance. At the very least, the direction of this burgeoning force was felt to be uncertain: Would the Catalonian workers maintain an autonomous organization? Would they go with the republican Left? Would they ally with the Catalan Regionalists? No one could say for sure. Fernando de los Ríos, writing late in 1918, had been optimistic that the "new proletarians" of Catalonia would turn to the Socialists and to political action, but Oscar Pérez Solís was less certain of this.[102] There were, as well, persistent rumors that despite the bellicose apoliticism of many Cenetista militants, some of the more moderate leaders—Seguí was most often named in this connection—were interested in electoral participation.[103]

It seemed, then, to many Socialists that the distance between themselves and the Cenetistas was narrowing. They had observed the La Canadiense strike with complete absorption, and were impressed by the Syndicalists' discipline and determination. In response to the apparent trend of the Catalan workers toward economism or possibilism, there was increasing talk in Socialist circles about the "convergence" of the UGT and the CNT. In a speech early in September the Young Socialist López Baeza took note of the march toward "governmentalism"—via the Mixed Commission—by the men of the Catalonian Regional Confederation. He observed that in addition to meeting with representatives of the state the Cenetistas were beginning to make use of strike funds and of "partial" strikes, in contrast to their earlier obsession with the general strike. There were no longer, Baeza decided, any "fundamental differences" between Socialists and Syndicalists; and if the leaders of the two movements did not find the way to unity, the masses, he thought, would probably impose it themselves.[104]

By the late summer of 1919 serious efforts were again being made by the UGT National Committee—responding to pressure from the leftists—to reach an understanding with the CNT that might lead "as soon as possible to the fusion of all the labor forces of Spain in one single national organization." The Catalan Socialist Durán was instructed to commence negotiations with the Cenetista leaders in Barcelona; but on this, as on so many issues, the CNT councils proved to be divided. Angel Pestaña and, especially, Salvador Seguí were favorably disposed to unification and even planned to present or support fusion resolutions at the approaching national congress. However, the fusion question was not within the jurisdiction of the Committee of the CRT, and the Anarchosyndicalists of the National Committee—Buenacasa and Boal primarily—viewed the Socialist overtures with a skepticism that verged on contempt. Made arrogant by the great growth of the CNT, they envisioned the rapid spread of Anarchosyndicalism over the entire Peninsula and the absorption of the Ugetista forces in the not too distant future. Thus when Durán tried to make contact with them, he was rebuffed and his request for an audience was denied.

In a subsequent letter to Largo Caballero the Cenetista leaders tried, somewhat lamely, to justify their unwillingness even to negotiate on the grounds that only a congress of the CNT could approve union with another organization. While claiming to be for unity "in principle," they refused, as we have seen, to agree to any kind of conference or preliminary discussions. The paradox here was that the militants who thus rejected the fusion efforts so strongly supported by the pro-Bolshevik Socialists were themselves the most ardent defenders, within the CNT, of the Bolshevik Revolution. Whereas within the Socialist ranks a special concern for labor unity went hand in hand with support for the Comintern, within the CNT these two objectives were split apart; and the "pure" Syndicalists, though not much aroused by the Bolshevik myth, were the strongest supporters of labor unity and of cooperation with the UGT.[105]

Anarchists, Syndicalists, and the Comintern

Disagreement over the fusion issue was only a surface manifestation of the deeper struggle within the CNT over the organization's fundamental objectives. Much of the fascination that the Bolshevik Revolution held for the intransigent Anarchosyndicalists stemmed from the fact that its influence seemed to be all on the side of revolutionary and extremist tactics. Despite the fact that their worship of spontaneity was perhaps less harmonious with Bolshevism than was the "pure" Syndicalists' absorption with the organizational weapon, it was almost inevitable, in view of the hopes that the quasi-revolutionary situation in Spain had aroused, that the Anarchist-oriented Syndicalists would embrace Bolshevism and identify with it. It was also inevitable that they would seek to use it, consciously or otherwise, against their moderate Syndicalist rivals. The deeper issue here was that of revolution versus reform: the Anarchosyndicalists favored the Bolsheviks and were eager to join the new, revolutionary Communist International because they were themselves revolutionaries; the Syndicalists were cooler toward Moscow largely because the reverse was true.[106]

The Anarchosyndicalists' quite genuine commitment to a Spanish revolution explained their continuing support of the Russian Bolsheviks, despite numerous intimations from 1919 onward that Soviet Russia might not be an Anarchist utopia. Whereas the admiration of the "pure" Anarchists for the Revolution had rested largely on myth and misunderstanding, and began to erode during the year following the Armistice, the enthusiasm of the Anarchosyndicalist majority within the CNT, though hardly free of illusions, rested on the more solid foundation of genuine revolutionary affinity and would prove more durable, lasting until about mid-1921.

The ideological impact of the Bolshevik Revolution on the Anarchosyndicalists was substantial. Among these militants, less doctrinaire and more tough-minded than the "pure" Anarchists, the prestige of the Russian Bolsheviks successfully called into question even the central Cenetista myth of revolutionary spontaneity and evoked a latent Jacobinism. Over a period of nearly three years they would show a more realistic concern with the problems of revolutionary power and organization than they had ever revealed before. They did not cease, however, to be Anarchists in their basic temper, and they were careful to keep one foot in the Anarchist groups even as they threw themselves into trade-union activity and wrote eulogies to Bolshevism. They entered the sindicatos not as meliorists or with the idea that the trade-union organization should become an end in itself, but rather with an almost evangelical determination to bend the unions to Anarchist purposes. Unlike the "pure" Anarchists, however, they were not primarily concerned with doctrinal or ethical questions, and they revealed at all times a more authentically revolutionary temper.

Where the "pure" Anarchists were, in practice, made cautious by their concern for principles and the "pure" Syndicalists by their concern for organizational structure, the Anarchosyndicalists tended to be insurrectional, adventurous, impatient, and ready to practice or at least condone violence. Unlike the "pure" Anarchists they were not willing to wait for propaganda to transform the lagging consciousness of the masses before trying to make the revolution. They were prepared to believe that the good society might, in fact, grow out of the barrel of a gun, and they did not draw back even from giving their support to the terrorism of the "action groups," as well as to a variety of other quasi-revolutionary tactics. At the same time, they were willing, with the tactical pragmatism of real revolutionaries, to take the lessons of the Russian Revolution to heart and make ideological concessions to Bolshevism as they understood it. They continued through 1919–20 to talk with surprising frankness about the need for revolutionary organization and a transitional dictatorship.[107]

There would seem to be little question—though this is of course difficult to document—that within the CNT the Bolshevik Revolution became a ploy in the extremists' struggle with the moderate Syndicalists. Inevitably, there was an attempt to capitalize on the Russian mystique in order to embarrass and discredit the "pure" Syndicalist leaders. Because of the hold it had over the mass of Spanish workers, the Revolution offered itself as a tempting and powerful instrument that might be utilized to force the moderates out of the rut of reformist tactics and to impel the CRT and CNT down the revolutionary road. The somewhat hasty adherence of the CNT to the Comintern, which would be voted at the 1919 Congress in the face of much evidence of "authoritarian" tendencies in the Soviet Republic, certainly had this as one of its purposes. The Bolshevik myth, which by implication put the seal of approval on extremist tactics, could in this way be used—or so it was hoped—to radicalize or silence the faint-hearted and the reformist.

The more moderate Syndicalists were placed, in fact, in an awkward situation. Their response to the Revolution, as we have seen, had been less warm than that of the Anarchosyndicalists. Their praise for it was not lacking in sincerity but was evidently restrained by their want of a genuinely revolutionary spirit, which in turn reflected their sober conviction that Spanish workers were unready to maintain production or guide society in the event of a successful revolution. Militants such as Salvador Seguí, Salvador Quemades, Angel Pestaña, Juan Peiró, José Viadiu, Simón Piera, and José Molins were, because of their concern for the organization, the more or less unconscious harbingers of an evolution toward reformism and accommodation that had already overtaken most French Syndicalists. In their own minds, no doubt, these men were revolutionary realists who knew that the revolution could not come until the workers had expanded their ranks and strengthened their organizational capacity. For this reason they had pioneered the Sindicatos Unicos and had constantly urged the need for more organization and discipline, as well as the need for salaried officials, strike funds, and the like. But it is difficult to resist the feeling that for these leaders, most of whom were native Catalans, revolutionary commitment had at some point given way to the desire for coexistence and for organizational growth as an end in itself.

Thus the moderates' response to the Bolshevik Revolution had a restrained and ritualistic quality. They did not fail to sense the desire of the Anarchosyndicalists to use the Bolshevik triumph as a rationale for rebellion, and they feared precisely this too-rash emulation of the Russian example by a labor movement that was not yet ready. But although they were not reluctant to point out—as Seguí did in his October speech—the flaws they detected in the Soviet regime, they were careful never to cease to praise the Revolution in principle, since the enthusiasm of the Spanish masses for the Bolsheviks continued to run very high and precluded any unfriendly criticism.

The depth of this popular enthusiasm, it should be noted, would be clearly reflected in two dramatic labor congresses, one Socialist and the other Syndicalist, held in December 1919, whose major task would be to decide for or against adherence to the new Communist International and to the Bolshevik conception of revolutionary struggle. To an analysis of these two congresses, and of the unsuccessful struggle for labor unity that went on within them, we must now turn.

CHAPTER EIGHT

Debate on the Comintern: Two Congresses

The climax to the first phase of the debates on the Bolshevik Revolution and the Communist International came on December 10, 1919, when the Socialists and the Anarchosyndicalists convened national congresses, both groups meeting in Madrid but fortunately at locations about a mile apart, in the Casa del Pueblo and the Teatro de la Comedia, respectively. The moods of the two assemblies presented evident contrasts. The Socialists had been holding congresses regularly, and their expansion during 1918–19 had been impressive without resulting in an inundation. Despite the ever more radical temper of the Terceristas within their ranks, their sessions, on the whole, were marked by discipline and decorum; only a few outbursts marred the dignity with which they customarily conducted their affairs. The Party leadership, not sharing the left-centrists' enthusiasm for the Russian Bolsheviks, was able in this congress to retain control and to head off, by means of concessions, the adherence to Moscow probably desired by a majority of the delegates. Right-centrists and left-centrists found themselves still sufficiently close together to obviate thoughts of schism or revolt.

The mood of the Party was one of tempered optimism. The PSOE and the UGT had grown greatly since the end of the war, but the ranks of the Anarchosyndicalists had expanded even more rapidly, and the Socialists were well aware of the threat that the Cenetistas posed to Socialist efforts in all parts of the Peninsula. The CNT, which better expressed the increasingly radical mood of the Spanish masses at this time, had soared to a claimed membership of about 700,000, while the UGT had risen to about 200,000 and the PSOE from 15,588 to 42,113.[1] Thus the Socialists were at once gratified by their gains yet concerned about the scope of the Anarchosyndicalist challenge; and they were greatly irritated that the Cenetista congress should be held in the very capital of the Socialist movement, seeing this as a deliberate provocation.

The Syndicalist congress in the Teatro de la Comedia was a more turbulent affair. As the first national gathering of the Confederation since 1911, it was filled with a mass of exalted delegates little known to one another and still less accustomed to parliamentary procedures. Yet all seemed certain that their surging movement was the vanguard of an impending revolution in Spain. In contrast to the Socialist congress, this assembly was largely under the control of the extremists, that is, the militant Anarchosyndicalists; and it ended by committing the CNT (after a much briefer debate than the Socialists had engaged in) to immediate adherence to the Communist International. This move, of course, reflected less the Cenetistas' conversion to Leninism than their readiness for revolution and their desire to embarrass both the moderate Syndicalists in their own midst and the cautious Socialists gravely debating a short distance away in the Casa del Pueblo.

The Socialist Party Congress of 1919

The National Committee of the Socialist Party, still dominated in late 1919 by the loyal followers of Pablo Iglesias, had viewed with displeasure the campaign launched by Torralba Beci in favor of a plebiscite on the international question. Its members—who no longer reflected majority sentiment—were far from enthusiastic about holding a party congress in the overheated, pro-Bolshevik atmosphere that then prevailed; but the idea of a plebiscite, which would almost certainly have carried the Party into the Comintern, held even less charm. Forced to choose between the lesser of two evils, they had elected to summon an extraordinary congress of the Party for December 10–15. The chief task of this assembly would be to resolve the problem of divided international loyalties—to decide, that is, between renewed adherence to the Second International, with its somewhat tarnished mystique, and allegiance to the new, unsullied International of Moscow, which shone in the reflected light of the Russian Revolution.

The opening session made it clear that the right-centrists were still completely committed to parliamentary gradualism, despite their occasional lapses into revolutionary rhetoric. Besteiro, in a conciliatory address clearly intended to placate the Left, spoke in praise of the October Revolution, conceding that whatever deficiencies the Bolshevik regime might have were mainly due to the chaos it had inherited. He professed to believe that the principles governing the conduct of the Bolsheviks were "exactly the same principles that should infuse the activities of all the militants of the International"; and he was even willing to affirm that the dictatorship of the proletariat was "indispensable" for the triumph of Socialism. But having gone this far, Besteiro proceeded to qualify his remarks. It should not be imagined, he said, that the dictatorship of the proletariat had to take the same form in all countries. On the contrary, this form had to vary according to the degree of development and the industrial level in each country. In the end, therefore, the Spanish Socialist Party had to condemn "the servile imitation of the procedures employed in one certain nation" as an error that would lead to the most egregious failures. Thus

Besteiro appeared to be urging—for Spain if not for Russia—the Kautskian view that the aim of the Socialist revolution had to be the establishment of parliamentary democracy, and that the "dictatorship of the proletariat" could simply be a powerful parliament dominated by the workers.[2]

Besteiro also declared that the best way to defend the Russian Revolution and ensure the triumph of Socialism everywhere was to refrain from weakening the existing International and, instead, to strengthen it in every possible way. Therefore, the PSOE should continue its adherence to the Second International, which, he believed, was "the most powerful Socialist organization in existence today." Obviously thinking of the ranging power of the British Navy, he also reiterated that there could be no revolution, in Spain or elsewhere in Western Europe, until the workers of Great Britain had seized power there—a view that Marx himself had upheld. In conclusion, Besteiro revealed what was plainly a growing faith in the possibilities of parliamentary action by urging the delegates to recognize that as long as a Spanish parliament existed, it should be utilized in order to carry on "a labor of penetration, criticism, and the diffusion of our ideas."[3]

In contrast to the restrained equivocations of the right-centrists, some of the overtly right-wing delegates spoke out with provocative frankness against the proletarian dictatorship and the Comintern, touching off occasional disturbances among both delegates and visitors. In a caustic speech punctuated by shouts and protests from an angry gallery, Indalecio Prieto, the boss of Vizcayan Socialism, left no doubt about his hostility to the Left, his dislike of radical intellectuals, and his provincial's scorn for Madrid. The whole matter of the Comintern offended his intensely practical and reformist mentality, and was, he thought, nothing but a tissue of "verbiage and intellectualisms." Referring to a pro-Comintern speech made earlier by the scholarly Madrid professor Andrés Ovejero, Prieto impatiently described its content as "all Byzantinism and literary dilettantism in the Madrid style." It was precisely in Madrid, he believed, where the ambience was entirely suited to "radical vehemencies" and where there were so many partisans of the Third International, that the revolutionary spirit was most *blando*. At this point a commotion broke out in the gallery. When order was restored, Prieto concluded, saying it was simply "inexplicable" that the pro-Comintern Socialists would not realize the danger of bringing before the congress something that was, after all, only a "social experiment," an untried new order that all Socialists supported but whose success still lay in the future. He, too, supported the Russian Revolution, he said, but he could not accept the idea that the ideology of Lenin and Trotsky should take precedence over all other Socialist doctrine.[4]

Even more wounding to the sensibilities of the pro-Comintern Left was the speech of Oscar Pérez Solís, who continued to be the Party's most skeptical voice where the Russian Revolution was concerned. The Revolution, he complained, was "spiritually obstructing" the deliberations of the congress. The Russian Bolsheviks were, after all, not so much Socialists as nationalists, and the possibility of a definitive triumph of Socialism in Russia lay in the distant future, after certain necessary and fundamental conditions had materialized. The Russian Revolution, said Solís, was not the product of such necessary conditions, which could only emerge in the fullness of time. Rather, it was an aberration, the result of discontent, hunger, and mass restlessness—a "gesture of rage" against Tsarist tyranny.[5]

Though not a partisan of republics, Pérez Solís believed that between the fall of the defeated Tsarist regime in Russia and the ultimate triumph of the proletariat there had to be an "intermediate organization," the democratic republic, which was necessary in order to prepare the workers to govern. After all, he asked, "Are the workers capable of controlling production by themselves?" To this no doubt rhetorical question his increasingly restless and angry audience spontaneously roared "Yes!"—to which Pérez Solís, not in the least intimidated, shouted back a defiant "No!," and the chamber again dissolved in disorder. When the uproar had quieted, the unchastened speaker proceeded to read certain passages from Engels indicating that writer's disbelief that a political revolution could consolidate an economic revolution. Therefore, said Solís, amid another rising chorus of groans and protests, "It is not yet possible to realize a social revolution in Spain, since the working class has not yet reached a cultural level that permits it effectively to replace the capitalist class." He thus remained unconditionally faithful to the old International. "I am of the Second International," he said; "I belong to the Second International, and I will see that my Party continues in it."[6] Probably none of those present in the Casa del Pueblo on that December evening could have imagined that within little more than a year Pérez Solís would become a convert to Bolshevism and a founder of the Spanish Communist Party.

The views of the left-centrists, set forth in a statement prepared by García Cortés, Verdes Montenegro, and Núñez de Arenas, had obviously been greatly radicalized since the Berne Conference in February, when their hope had been for unity and forgiveness within the Second International. Now these militants bitterly denounced the old International, condemning its nationalist fragmentation during the war, its failure to purge the prowar Socialists afterwards, and its fall into class collaboration by supporting the "unworthy farce" of the League of Nations. They denied that the postwar International had any spiritual link whatever with the pre-1914 organization, whose memory they revered: for it had divorced itself from the Communist Manifesto and was now "absolutely" without Socialist content; its leaders, moreover, refused to comprehend that mankind had entered upon the "definitive phase" of the Socialist revolution, in which the working class would seize power and impose its *salvadora dictadura*.[7]

In place of the old, cynical, and corrupted International, said the left-centrists, there had arisen the Third International, "born in Moscow in the heat of the Socialist revolution, full of idealism and of hopes," and based on the principles of the Communist Manifesto. It was imperative that Spanish Socialists adhere to the new International; and, as the Terceristas acknowledged, this action would require the adoption of its ideology. That ideology imposed two main obligations: resolute efforts to unite all Spanish proletarians on the basis of class struggle and the dictatorship of the proletariat; and work within all types of labor organizations in order to persuade them that their continuing fight for partial economic gains must be joined with "incessant" action against the bourgeoisie, in a revolutionary manner whenever circumstances permitted. The left-centrists, inveterately electoral, did not fail to observe that the parliamentary struggle was both permissible and necessary, but they warned against the "illusion" that the final victory of the proletariat could be won at the polls. Nor did they imagine that parliamentarianism could be the model of the approaching Socialist regime, which would instead be based on "committees" of workers who would take charge of production.[8]

The ideological battle lines of the Right, the Right Center, and the Left Center were now drawn, and it remained for various pro-Comintern delegates to advance to the rostrum and plead for the immediate adherence of the Party to the Moscow International. The secretary of the National Committee, the unpretentious Daniel Anguiano, ingenuously informed the delegates that if it were true, as Besteiro had remarked, that the principles of the Russian Bolsheviks corresponded exactly to the principles of Socialism, then adherence to the Third International was indeed imperative, so that Spain could experience the "maximum penetration" of revolutionary Socialist ideas. Allegiance to Moscow, Anguiano believed, would help mold the thoughts of Spanish workers, revealing to them the uselessness of reform and the need for a forceful seizure of power even as it encouraged the necessary spirit of sacrifice. The austere provincial schoolmaster Verdes Montenegro, in his turn, likened the Communist International to the Protestant Reformation, which had struggled so nobly on behalf of the "pure principles" that the Catholic Church had adulterated. The Spanish Socialists, said Verdes, had to decide their international affiliation by following not the road of practicality but the road of principles and ideas. Next, Andrés Ovejero, perhaps forgetting his own passionate support for the Allied cause during the war, rhetorically asked the congress how it would be possible for the Socialist Party to stay in an international containing men who had voted war credits, strengthened monarchies, and formed "Holy Alliances." The Second International, said the learned professor, drawing on a cliché of the time, was *un cadáver insepulto* in which there would remain only those Socialists who wished "to govern beside the bourgeoisie."[9]

Perhaps the most effective plea for adherence to the Third International was made by Mariano García Cortés. If the Spanish Socialists believed, he said, that the conquest of political power was only a distant prospect, something for future generations to achieve, then they should adhere to the policy of Pérez Solís. But if they believed that the present generation would be the one to make the revolution—and García Cortés clearly sensed that most of the delegates wished to believe this—then a more radical policy was imperative. He was willing to admit that revolutions could not be "decreed," since they were the product of circumstances that were impossible to foresee; yet he could not help feeling that Spain, similar to Russia in so many ways, would soon make her own revolution, and in a manner very similar to that of the Russians themselves.[10]

There is reason to believe that if the delegates had been asked to make a clear choice between the position of Besteiro and that of García Cortés, their radical mood would have led them to support the latter, and they would have voted the Party into the Comintern by a substantial majority. But both sides felt a profound concern for party unity and a strong disposition to avoid an either/or choice through some compromise measure. The seeds of this compromise would be found in the text of an essentially conservative resolution submitted to the congress by Pérez Solís and Fabra Ribas:

> The Extraordinary Congress of the Spanish Socialist Party declares:
> That as there is only one proletariat, there cannot and should not be more than one International.
> That the imperative duty of all Socialists is to work for the unification, nationally and internationally, of all forces hostile to the regime of capitalism and in favor of socializing the means of production, distribution, and exchange;
> And it agrees:
> First, that the [PSOE] should continue its adherence to the Second International;
> Second, that a delegation should be sent to the next International Congress of Geneva with the mission of requesting (a) that the proper sanctions be applied to those individuals and to those [national] sections whose conduct has not been in harmony with what is demanded by Socialist principles; and (b) that there be adopted the measures necessary to achieve the fusing in one single organization of the sections presently affiliated to the Second and Third Internationals.[11]

Thus the resolution clearly favored unequivocal adherence to the Second International but at the same time made concessions to the leftists by vaguely recognizing the need for some purging of the old International and some effort to unify the two existing organizations. The conciliation of the Left was carried further, and the road to compromise opened up, by the Asturian delegate Isidoro Acevedo, who was critical of the Second International but looked not so much toward Moscow as toward a revolutionary unification of the

whole international proletariat. Thus he proposed to the congress, as an amendment to the Solís-Fabra resolution, essentially the same measure he had a few
weeks earlier pushed through the congress of the Asturian Socialists. This
proposal urged that the Socialist Party

> continue membership in the Second International until the meeting of the next
> international congress, at which our delegation will bring forward ... resolutions
> looking toward a union with all the Socialist parties of the world; and if this
> should not be possible, because of fundamental discrepancies with the Third In-
> ternational that the partisans of the Second International wish to maintain, [we
> will] enter ... the Third International upon the termination of said congress.[12]

At the approaching Geneva Congress of the Second International (scheduled
for January 1920), then, the Spanish Socialists would be committed to actively
supporting the unification of all proletarian forces in one organization; and if
this effort was thwarted by the too-stubborn resistance of conservative Socialists, they would leave the Second International and enter the Third.

Thus, as the result of a behind-the-scenes agreement, the question of the
Party's international allegiance was presented to the delegates in the form of
a single unified resolution, and a straight vote for immediate adherence to the
Comintern was never taken. The fact that the Solís-Fabra-Acevedo resolution
was approved by the rather narrow margin of 14,010 to 12,497 votes suggests
that in a clear contest between the Second and Third Internationals, the latter
would easily have carried the day. An unknown but certainly substantial proportion of the favorable votes were plainly cast by men who preferred the
Comintern to the Berne International but who placed party unity above all
else. Few of the negative votes, by contrast, can have connoted support for the
Second International, since the partisans of that body knew the resolution was
almost certainly the best they could do in the prevailing climate of opinion.
Thus it was evident that the decision to remain with the old International was
highly provisional, accompanied by so many reservations that ultimate adherence of the PSOE to Moscow had to be regarded as very probable.[13]

The leftward drift of the Party was further revealed at this congress by the
success of the left-centrists in finally securing the dissolution of the electoral
alliance that had linked the Socialist Party to the republican parties since 1910
and to which, indeed, the Socialists largely owed the fact that they now had
six deputies in the Cortes. Since its inception the Republican-Socialist Alliance
had grated on the centrist consciences of many militants, who knew that it
was vital to the electoral prospects and political potency of the Party but could
not deny, at the same time, that it was a form of collaboration with the bourgeoisie. Some militants, such as Virginia González, had been consistently
against the Alliance from the start, but a larger number had viewed the matter
more ambivalently: they knew that the liaison was difficult to square with

intransigent assertions about the class struggle; but they were by no means unwilling to hold political office themselves and, if possible, gain entry to the Cortes, these ambitions being more difficult to realize without the alliance.

Nevertheless, during 1919 the left-centrists had become aware that the link with the Republicans not only violated the canons of Bolshevism but, by irritating the Cenetistas, also stood in the way of the unification of all revolutionary forces in the Peninsula. After strenuous debate, and over strong opposition from such right-centrist and right-wing leaders as Besteiro, Largo Caballero, and Indalecio Prieto, the decision was taken (14,435 to 10,040) to dissolve the alliance, which just eight months earlier, in response to Maura's return to power, had been nearly unanimously reaffirmed by a national plenum of the Party. Of course, the Party by no means gave up its electoral activities; but these would now be carried on in purity and isolation and would presumably have a more "revolutionary" purpose.[14]

Mention must be made, finally, of the first "revolt" of the ultra-Left within the Socialist ranks. This occurred at the Fifth Congress of the Federation of Young Socialists, which met on December 14–18, immediately following the Party congress. The Juventud were greatly displeased by the failure of the PSOE to adhere to Moscow, and pro-Bolshevik feeling was very intense. The Asturian delegates Questa and Loreda proposed, therefore, that the Federation give its immediate adherence to the Comintern, regardless of the position taken by the Party. Manuel Núñez de Arenas, although a Tercerista himself, argued against this, suggesting that the Young Socialists might agree "in principle" to enter the Third International but that they should postpone their final entry until after the Geneva Congress. The Party and the Juventud, he thought, ought to enter the Moscow organization simultaneously. In the end, however, a majority of delegates voted in favor of unconditional adherence to the Comintern.[15]

Another step toward a possible schism between the youth movement and the Party resulted from the Federation's selection of a new National Committee dominated by pro-Comintern elements associated with the Madrid section. Since the Armistice, the Madrid Young Socialists had been moving to the Left even more rapidly than the other sections. Traditionally, the Madrid group had been outweighed by the provincial sections and had usually formed an avant-garde opposition within the FJS;[16] but now, with the help of the increasingly extremist Basque and Asturian sections, the struggle for power was resolved by choosing a Committee made up entirely of members of the Madrid Juventud, among them a number of militants who would later split with the PSOE and form the first Communist Party in Spain.* The man who would be the catalyst of the Madrid Young Socialists' secession from the PSOE was

* Ramón Merino Gracia, Manuel Ugarte, Manuel Cardenal, Pedro Illescas, Luis Portela, Tiburicio Pico, Rito Esteban, and some others.

at this moment still in the mid-Atlantic, aboard a ship bound for Spain, and would arrive in Madrid about ten days after the close of the FJS Congress. This was Michael Borodin, who would be the first Comintern agent in Spain.[17]

The Congress of the Comedia

The Madrid Congress of the CNT, held a few blocks away in the Teatro de la Comedia, was convened at a time when the Cenetistas had attained the height of their self-confidence and power; it represented the culmination of eighteen months of riotous organizational growth and spreading Syndicalist enthusiasm. The massive lockout launched by the employers in mid-November, following the collapse of the Mixed Commission, had not yet had its full impact on the sindicatos, and few Cenetistas realized that their movement had already reached its apogee and was about to begin a gradual descent into impotence. The mood of the majority of delegates was one of bellicose optimism and revolutionary anticipation. They were completely dazzled by the rapid expansion and proliferation of the Sindicatos Unicos during 1919, and by the seemingly invincible power these represented—a power sufficient, it seemed to them, to enable the CNT to take control of the country.[18]

But mixed with the euphoria of the Anarchosyndicalists was some bitterness toward the moderate Syndicalists for their restraining influence over the Catalonian Regional Confederation and for their deviations from Anarchosyndicalist orthodoxy during the course of 1919. There was special resentment that the moderates had been willing to respond to the conciliatory overtures of the Sánchez de Toca government and enter into a dialogue with the bourgeois enemy. And resentment had turned into anger when the Seguí-led Syndicalists refused to accept the challenge of the lockouts by invading the factories of Catalonia and raising the banner of revolution. The suspicion crystallized that the "pure" Syndicalists were trying to lead the newly enrolled masses not toward revolution and libertarian Communism but toward "governmentalism" and adjustment within the capitalist framework.[19] Thus the period immediately before the convening of the congress probably marked the low point in the popularity of Seguí and Pestaña among the more militant Anarchosyndicalists.[20]

It was against this backdrop of thwarted revolutionary aspiration and outraged Anarchist orthodoxy that the Congress of the Comedia held its sessions. The moderate Syndicalists, who were well aware of the crisis the lockouts were beginning to produce in the ranks of Catalonian Syndicalism, thought the timing of the congress less than propitious and had asked the organizational committee (Buenacasa, Moises López, and Mauro Bajatierra) for a postponement; but this body had been planning for the meeting since April, and its members, resentful of the Catalan moderates in any case, were in no mood for delay. Aroused and even angered, the Anarchosyndicalists viewed the national congress as, in no small degree, a summoning of the libertarian forces of the Peninsula to join in a counteroffensive against the economist heresies of the CRT. It would be for them an instrument of ideological revenge and—to use Buenacasa's term—of revolutionary "rectification." The Cenetista adherence to the Comintern, approved by acclamation at the end of the congress, was almost certainly an expression of this general intent to undermine and discredit the moderates and would have behind it, therefore, both conviction and calculation.[21]

Enthusiasm for the Bolshevik Revolution ran very high and was a recurrent theme in the Congress of the Comedia. A sympathetic Republican journalist, Angel Samblancat, described the gathering as a "Congress of Soviets," and Buenacasa later acknowledged that "the immense majority of us considered ourselves true Bolsheviks."[22] The shortage of reliable information from Russia meant that none of the delegates had precise knowledge of the new Soviet system; but as would-be revolutionaries in Spain, they could not but feel an emulative admiration for those who had destroyed bourgeois power in Russia. As Buenacasa said, the Cenetistas saw in Bolshevism "the revolution we dreamed of."[23]

The opening of the congress, as Buenacasa cheerfully admitted, caused a "sensation." Some hundred thousand manifestos had been distributed to announce the event, and the Teatro de la Comedia was filled to capacity by a vast and heterogeneous public. There were 437 delegates present, many dressed in colorful regional costumes and all chattering excitedly. From the Northern Region came such distinguished Cenetistas as Bernardo Pascual, Juan Fernández, Galo Díez, and Juan Ortega. In the Andalusian delegation could be seen the notables Juan Guerrero, Sebastián Oliva, José Chacón, Antonio Jurado, Juan S. Carrión, Roque García, and the indefatigable Salvador Cordón— ("Kordoniev"). The Levantine delegation included the brilliant and fiery polemicist Eusebio Carbó, as well as Juan Rueda, Diego Parra, José Miró, Emilio Molina, and the incipient Communist-Syndicalist Hilario Arlandis. The Catalan delegation was, of course, the largest of all, with 128 delegates, and included such names as Salvador Seguí, Angel Pestaña, José Canela, Saturnino Meca, Simón Piera, Juan Peiró, Pedro Rico, Emilio Mira, and—as a recent fugitive from the Socialist Party—Andrés Nin, who would soon become the leader of the Communist-Syndicalist tendency. Nin, not yet well known, would play virtually no role in this congress, yet within a year and a half he would be General Secretary of the clandestine National Committee of the CNT. The Aragonese delegation included—besides Buenacasa—Zenon Canudo, Ramón Acín, Antonio Domingo, and Francisco Calleja. The moderate Syndicalist delegation from Asturias was made up of Eleuterio Quintanilla, José María Martínez, Avelino González, Aquilino Moral, and another Communist-Syndicalist-to-be, Jesús Ibáñez.[24]

The Catalonian delegation, according to Buenacasa, gave the impression of "greatest strength," but Andalusia had the delegation of "Anarchism *par excellence*." The delegations of Galicia and the North were also "excellently oriented"—that is, very Anarchist in outlook—though the moderate Asturian delegation would of course have to be excluded from this judgment. The Levantine and Aragonese delegations were divided on most questions and, along with the temporizing Castilian delegation, were not quite satisfactory from a libertarian standpoint.

The numerical strengths of the delegations were: Catalonia, 128; Andalusia and Extremadura, 73; Levante, 71; Aragon, 30; Galicia, 28; Vizcaya, Santander, Rioja, and Navarre, 24; the two Castiles, 55; Asturias, León, and Palencia, 19; the National Committee, 8; and the CGT of Portugal, 1.[25] These delegations represented a membership divided regionally as follows:[26]

Andalusia	109,854
Aragon	24,098
Balearic and Canary Islands	3,891
Catalonia	433,746
Levante	136,354
North	30,418
Central	26,740
TOTAL	765,101

When one subtracts the number of workers who were represented in the Congress but who were not then affiliated (*no federados*) with the CNT, this figure declines to 699,369, which was probably rather close to the actual strength of the CNT at this moment.

The sessions began on the morning of December 10, amid the expectant clamor of hundreds of delegates, observers, journalists, and stenographers. The frail figure of Evelio Boal, the first of several chairmen the Congress would have, rose to quiet the tumult and launch the meeting:

> People of Madrid! Workers of Spain! After eight years of silence imposed by the reactionary classes, the Confederation has succeeded in organizing this great meeting. The Confederal Committee takes advantage of this solemn moment to greet the workers of Madrid, to welcome the representatives of the other workers of Spain, and to give proof, above all, of our fraternal sympathy to the victims of the capitalist and authoritarian terror who languish in the prisons of the world.[27]

So commenced the Second Congress of the CNT, a gathering that would know many moments of exaltation, excitement, and confusion. Although the delegates' enthusiasm for the Bolshevik Revolution was very strong, it is important to note that it would always rest on a firm substratum of Anarchist conviction. Unlike the French Syndicalist Congress of Amiens, with which it may be compared, the Madrid Congress was certainly as much Anarchist as Syndicalist in spirit. The majority of delegates, in contrast to their French counterparts of 1906, evinced no desire to be freed from sectarian influences.[28] Indeed, to the irritation of many of the "pure" Syndicalists, the congress would for the first time officially commit the CNT to libertarian Communism—that is, to Anarchism—as the ultimate goal of its endeavors. That the congress was dominated by the extreme Anarchosyndicalist elements would be revealed in several ways: by its denunciation of the Mixed Commission, by its hostility to national industrial federations, by its rejection of efforts to promote the fusion of the CNT and the UGT, and, ironically, by its adherence to the Communist International. The debates held on the last two of these issues most clearly revealed the currents then competing within Spanish Anarchosyndicalism, and the balance of this chapter will be concerned with them.

The Fusion Question

Discussion of the fusion issue was launched by Evelio Boal, who informed the delegates of the UGT unification initiatives and the exchange of letters between the two organizations, and who stated that the National Committee of the CNT had properly refused to enter into discussions on unity because of its lack of a mandate from a national congress. Boal insisted that the CNT's responses had been "amicable" throughout and could be regarded as favoring an eventual agreement.[29]

The most forceful and cogent support for labor unification came from the Asturian delegates, whose unions had already achieved a substantial degree of unity with the Socialist sindicatos of their region and who had good reason to know that the UGT could not be conjured out of existence. The moderate Asturian Syndicalist José María Martínez of Gijón offered a particularly strong defense of unification, reminding the delegates that the UGT was not, after all, an ephemeral organization. Some Cenetistas, he said,

> imagined ... that the CNT, safeguarding the purity of its Syndicalist principles, should continue ahead in its work of absorption, so that the UGT would disappear after a while. I don't believe this. Whether you like it or not, the UGT has a strong, organized core that cannot be absorbed by the CNT, however long the struggle lasts. And to understand this is difficult if you live in Catalonia or in certain other capitals of Spain. It is necessary to go to the provinces in order to understand that there are organizations committed to the UGT that will never leave it, whatever tactics the CNT uses.

Martínez warned that although the CNT was, at that moment, very strong and numerically superior to the UGT, there was "no guarantee that tomorrow things might not be different and the UGT be judging us by the same criterion that we use here."[30]

The members of the outgoing (but still incumbent) National Committee, seated together at a table near the presiding officer, followed the Martínez speech with increasing impatience. And eventually one of them—probably Buenacasa—abandoned all pretense of neutrality and stood up to speak against fusion efforts, laying stress on the ideological differences between the two organizations and the dangers of sacrificing principles to achieve unity.[31] Other delegates immediately chimed in with attacks on the notion that there should be "politicals" within the CNT. The Madrid Anarchist Mauro Bajatierra somewhat irascibly asserted that the Ugetista leaders did not really want unity but were only trying to give the masses that impression. The Andalusian delegate Paulino Díez argued that although fusion was necessary, it was also imperative to sustain a "completely revolutionary organization," not one with "an essentially political character." He reminded the delegates that the CNT, after all, was going forward to the creation of a Communist society, and that it was therefore necessary to "extirpate all political tendencies" and to focus on "the most rapid possible attainment of *comunismo libertario*." Díez made a remarkably frank, even blunt, summation of the Anarchist orientation of the CNT:

> The principles and ideas that infuse the organization in Catalonia are well known, and these are none other than the principles of Anarchism. The basic principle of the organization is Anarchist. We must say that the individual [member] aspires to a completely Anarchist ambience and that the conscious minorities, who forcefully carry along the masses by means of their convictions and by their decisions, show themselves to be partisans of [Anarchism].

In concluding, Díez returned to the antipolitical theme, noting that both manual and technical laborers could be recognized as "workers" but not "he who has a political profession, since he has not calloused his hands or engaged in mental work to augment production."[32]

The speaker who followed Díez was Jesús Ibáñez, an Asturian delegate representing the construction workers of Mieres. His words merit attention less for their influence on his audience—which appears to have been mostly negative—than because they revealed the rather wide variety of views expressed in the Congress of the Comedia. Ibáñez, an ordinary working man who seems to have had some exposure to French revolutionary Syndicalist ideas, would later become a founder of the Communist-Syndicalist tendency in the CNT. He now found himself speaking to an unfriendly audience and felt impelled to lecture the delegates, telling them that the greatly augmented CNT membership did not give them the right to "feel superior" or to think they could impose a tactic that had to be accepted even by workers who did not share the theories of the CNT. With an unsectarian tolerance of other labor creeds that would be the hallmark of Communist-Syndicalism—and which was irritating to most of his listeners—Ibáñez urged the Cenetistas to give the Socialists their due, since they also looked forward to the establishment of "Communism." He went further, suggesting to the ever more restless delegates that the "political feelings" of the Socialists had to be respected, since they, like the Cenetistas, were authentic representatives of a particular sector of the proletariat. The fusion of the Spanish working class, he said, could only be achieved on the basis of respect for the ideologies of both sides.[33]

At this point the Asturian was interrupted by the volatile Eusebio Carbó, who objected to a reference that Ibáñez had made to the "leaders" of the CNT. Breaking into the speech, Carbó delivered an angry monologue on the fact that there were "no leaders" (directores) in the CNT; nor anyone who tried to "play games" with the proletariat, he added. Ibáñez immediately apologized to the prestigious Valencian but doggedly insisted, amid rising sounds of displeasure in the hall, on the importance of approaching the Socialists with "courteous procedures." His final words were drowned out by a swelling chorus of groans and angry mutterings.[34]

All of this was too much for the Levantine Anarchist Leonardo Buendía, who rose with barely suppressed anger to say to Ibáñez, "I wish you would deal with great caution with this matter of [Anarchy], so sacrosanct for me, and examine your conscience before you speak that word, since Anarchy means the perfection of humanity." Buendía reported that the sentiment of his own sindicato was totally opposed to unification with those who engaged in political activity, or even with their followers, with whom the Cenetistas could not have "the least relationship" until the UGT leaders were cast aside.[35]

In an apparent effort to crystallize the debate, Angel Pestaña now introduced a resolution calling for the creation of a new, all-encompassing national labor organization, to be called the Confederación General del Trabajo. The essence of Pestaña's proposal was that positions in the new organization were to be absolutely closed to anyone holding political office on any level. Rather unrealistically, the UGT was asked to respond, "if possible," within 72 hours, presumably so that the Congress of the Comedia—which would still be in session—could take steps to consummate the movement toward unity. Pestaña's position, as he elaborated it later in the congress, contained two essentials: absolute autonomy for the sindicatos against all centralizing tendencies; and, again, an absolute ban on union officers' holding political offices, although mere membership in a political party would be acceptable.[36]

A more conciliatory and realistic proposal for unity was brought forward by the Asturian delegation, led by Eleuterio Quintanilla. This resolution also recognized that a single national organization was an "imperious necessity" and should be independent of all political parties. But it did not explicitly insist on the incompatibility of union office and political office, thereby, in effect, acknowledging the right of the many elective officials among the UGT leaders to remain at the head of their organization—a proviso clearly intended to facilitate rather than frustrate unification. Quintanilla also called for the holding of an extraordinary national congress of all organizations belonging to the two federations to work out the conditions of unification—conditions to which the present congress would agree in advance to submit.[37]

Salvador Seguí, ever the pragmatist and much in favor of unification, suggested that this resolution was not incompatible with that proposed by Pestaña, and that the two should be synthesized. Quintanilla respectfully disagreed, saying that Pestaña's resolution would impose a previous condition on the Socialists, making the contract between the CNT and the UGT an unequal one. He urged again a "noble and generous submission" to the decisions of a congress "superior to us all."[38] Pestaña, who seemed to be caught between his recognition of the need for unification and a desire not to offend his more Anarchist followers by being too reasonable, returned to the rostrum to talk about the dangers of making a pact with "elements that we know beforehand do not represent the spirit of the workers."[39] Quintanilla rejoined the discussion to argue volubly but not always with complete clarity that the holding of political office by union leaders would perhaps be an advantage rather than a disadvantage, since as political representatives they would have not merely their political constituency but also the force of organized labor behind them. But he quickly turned from this not very Syndicalist argument, concluding that in any case the Cenetista contact would not be with the "political" Socialist leaders but with the "Socialist masses." He also expressed confidence that since the Cenetistas outnumbered the Socialists by "800,000" to 200,000, the principles of the larger entity would surely prevail within the united organization.[40]

Quintanilla went on to speak at some length, and with great earnestness, about the experiences of the Asturian Syndicalists and their success over the years in cooperating with the Socialists—a cooperation, he said, that had given "repeated proofs of the efficacy of the policy of attraction, of approximation, of concord." And he reminded his listeners that it had been the individualist Anarchists, with their scorn for syndical activity, who had earlier permitted the Socialists to capture most of the Asturian working class. Above all, Quintanilla's address revealed a lack of sectarian feeling. He spoke approvingly of the competition of labor tendencies in Asturias and of the resulting "richness" of ideological manifestations. During the competitive cooperation of Syndicalists and Socialists in such centers as La Felguera and Gijón, he said, "never did the elements that dominated use their strength . . . to attempt a policy of absorption. . . . We tried to incorporate our ideas into the hearts and minds of the masses . . . but we did not view with rancorous and sectarian suspicions the progress of the opposite tendency . . . and never, never— understand this well—[did we try] the policy of absorption that I observe trying to establish itself here." Instead, in Gijón, there had been a "fusion" of the local labor forces, and this, said Quintanilla, had ended conflict between Syndicalists and Socialists without the former being in the least politicized by the latter.[41]

Simón Piera, the powerful president of the Construction Workers' Union of Barcelona and an ally of Salvador Seguí, took this opportunity to speak out against an earlier suggestion that the congress should make a clear and concrete declaration of Anarchist principles. Foreseeing the obstacles this would set in the path of labor unification, he suggested that such a step would mean doing what the Ugetistas had done: accepting political guidance. Echoing the Charter of Amiens, Piera affirmed that in the unified national labor organization of the future there should not be represented "any political tendency, however radical it may be"; for Syndicalism had only one mission, that of solving economic problems, and it should deal "only with the workers."[42] Piera, who was highly respected, was able to make this assertion without creating a storm, but when the Catalan delegate José Arbós defended essentially the same thesis—namely, that both Socialists and Anarchists were "political"—there were angry outcries from his listeners.[43]

Eusebio Carbó rose again to deliver a somewhat belligerent speech in which he opposed any unification that would compromise the "fundamental principles" of the CNT. He recalled with bitterness the fact that he had attended the 1916 UGT congress, had tried to talk, and had been denied the floor. He reminded the delegates that in those days, when the Cenetistas had numbered only 50,000, the Socialists had scorned them and called their movement a "phantasm." "Now that we are strong," he said, "the UGT congress urges fusion." Carbó concluded, amid sounds of approval from the delegates, by asserting that there should be no fusion congress that did not conform to the "postulates" of the CNT, an organization whose chief glory, he said, was that it was the inheritor of the First International. Nevertheless, once his hostility to the Socialists had been vented, Carbó seemed disposed to support unification as envisioned by the Pestaña resolution.[44]

One of the more moving speeches against labor unification was delivered by the Andalusian delegate Manuel Chacón, who said that his delegation was unanimously opposed to the fusion idea. (When the presiding officer questioned this assertion, the Andalusians, to a man, rose to their feet and shouted their support of the speaker.[45]) Chacón made an emotional appeal on behalf of the purity of the Anarchist ideal, which, he said, was "something more elevated" than had been implied by many of the speakers. It was something "as delicate and fragile as crystal," and should not be carelessly treated by the delegates. Turning to the issue at hand, the Andalusian reiterated his "complete opposition" to both the Pestaña and Quintanilla resolutions. There could be, he said, no agreement with those who pursued the goal of "a regime where men have to govern men." For real freedom, after all, meant "absolute liberty" in one's actions; and wherever men had to "order and obey" there could be no liberty. Nor could Chacón imagine that there were workers anywhere who had actually resigned themselves "to being governed by anyone or being under the discipline of anyone." It was difficult, finally, for him to see how, in the present congress, "where there are men who feel the most noble and grand ideal that the human mind has conceived, which is the Anarchist ideal," there were also men who could deal "casually" with the workers' aspirations. Chacón concluded, amid signs of warm support and approval from the delegates, by asserting that he had expressed the views not merely of the Andalusian delegation but of a majority of the congress, in which appraisal he was probably correct.[46]

From a very different perspective, Mariano Serra of the Zaragoza labor organization reminded the congress that the workers of Zaragoza had not yet been absorbed by either of the two main Peninsular labor movements, and that their support went to the Pestaña resolution and the idea of a single national organization. But Serra objected to the imposition of a deadline on the Socialists, and he warned that the workers of his region, who wished to do justice to both the CNT and the UGT, would not fail to discern which of the two was throwing obstacles in the way of unity. The best thing, he thought, would be a "dissolution" of the two contrary labor movements and the achievement of a genuine fusion: that is, the creation of a single national organization governed by "new men." For this reason, said Serra, the Zaragoza workers also supported the Quintanilla resolution.[47]

The session of December 12 ended without the fusion issue having been brought to a vote. That night, Pestaña and Quintanilla met at a gathering of the Catalonian delegation, discussed their respective resolutions, and recognized the wisdom of combining them in one unified fusion motion. This decision, which was opposed by a minority of the delegation, was a major concession to moderation on the part of Pestaña; yet he failed, presumably because of illness, to appear in the congress the following day or to exert much leadership of the pro-fusion forces, whose efforts were marked by a lack of coordination.[48]

Meanwhile, a third resolution had been formulated by Enrique Valero of the Barcelona Construction Union. This proposal, couched in unconciliatory and even arrogant terms, more fully expressed the mood of the majority of delegates than either of the other two resolutions. In what was nothing less than a parliamentary coup by the National Committee, this resolution was suddenly introduced to the congress by Manuel Buenacasa on the morning of December 13, at a moment when the delegates had obviously grown weary of the fusion debate and were beginning to call for a vote. The meaning and possible consequences of the Valero resolution were never debated by the congress, and its ready acceptance by the majority revealed the prevailing desire of the self-confident Cenetistas to wage war on the Socialists rather than to ally with them in a common struggle:

> Considering that the tactics and ideological stand of the CNT and of the UGT are diametrically opposed, and that they are completely defined and are therefore known to everyone, the sindicatos who subscribe understand that the two organizations ought to undertake not fusion but the absorption of the elements that make up the UGT. First, because the Confederation represents a number of members three times greater; and second, the tactics followed by the Confederation being known by all, as was said, and representatives of the UGT having been invited to this Congress, by not attending it they have demonstrated that they are not in agreement with the said tactics, and it would be useless to hold another Congress, since they have not convinced us to adopt their methods of struggle.
>
> In addition, those who [make this proposal] entreat that the Congress publish a manifesto directed to all the workers of Spain and conceding them a period of three months for their entry into the Confederation, declaring yellow those who do not do it.[49]

Clearly, this proposal, which was prepared in haste and crudely drafted, rejected any conception of a negotiated unification and could only be regarded as an ultimatum to the Socialists to join the CNT within three months or be read out of the labor movement.

After reading the resolution to the congress, Buenacasa, speaking for the nine members of the outgoing National Committee, declared their support for the Valero resolution and uttered this warning to the moderates:

> Not only as direct representatives of the nine great sindicatos of Barcelona but as simple individual union members, they inform the Congress, without [intending] coercion of any kind, that if the new Committee that replaces us does not follow the practices of libertarian and antipolitical action supported by us, up until today, we shall struggle within our own sindicatos to make impossible all union or fusion that is not established on the bases and practices aforementioned.[50]

This statement was immediately seconded by the Andalusian delegates and helped make clear, if any doubt remained, the determination of the extreme Anarchosyndicalists not to lose control of the organization as the result of fusion with the Socialists and to keep it on a libertarian course at all costs.

The Valero proposal, so suddenly interjected, threw the congress into confusion, and the Anarchist forces moved quickly to put the matter to a vote. When the astonished Quintanilla tried to get the floor, he was ignored by the presiding officer, and a member of the National Committee, Evelio Boal, was recognized instead. With the evident purpose of putting pressure on the moderates, Boal proposed that since the majority obviously favored the Valero resolution, only those who were opposed should stand and vote, identifying themselves and indicating the number of members they represented. On this basis the voting now took place, resulting in 169,125 votes for the Asturian resolution, 323,955 for the Valero resolution, and 10,192 abstentions.[51]

This action, a classic manifestation of hubris, would soon be regretted by most Syndicalists, for the CNT began to decline almost immediately after the congress under the heavy blows of the lockout and the repressive measures of the new civil governor of Barcelona, Count Salvatierra. And within a few months Salvador Seguí would be making strenuous efforts on behalf of a UGT-CNT alliance, in order to save the Cenetistas from the ferocity of this anti-union offensive. A measure so ill-advised as the Valero resolution reflected, one must think, not merely the traditional animosity between the two labor movements but also the immaturity and puerile overconfidence of the "new proletarians" who had flowed into the CNT in such vast numbers since mid-1918. Given these two circumstances, unification efforts at this time, however rooted in the self-interest of both federations, were inevitably doomed to disappointment. The attainment of any kind of meaningful "fusion" would have required, realistically, either the curbing of Cenetista volatility and apoliticism or the displacement of the exceedingly sober "political" leaders of the UGT; neither course was a practical possibility at this time.

The Debate on the Comintern

The other great debate of the Congress of the Comedia dealt with the question of the CNT's adherence to the Communist International and made it clear that only a handful of Cenetistas had yet undergone the attitudinal transformation on which an authentic conversion to Bolshevism depended. There were large numbers of pro-Bolshevik enthusiasts in the congress but remarkably few Bolsheviks. The paradox—as it would later seem—of this gathering was that those who were most adamant in supporting adherence to the Comintern were also the most confirmed Anarchists.

Among the few who both understood and accepted the Bolshevik approach to revolution was the Valencian Hilario Arlandis, later to be a leader of the Communist-Syndicalist faction. Arlandis, a carpenter and an ex-Anarchist, was the most outspoken proponent of Bolshevism in the congress, evoking an almost Leninist vision of how the revolution had to be made in Spain. His willingness to talk in terms of a centralized and disciplined proletarian dictatorship went far beyond that of most Cenetistas, who were only slowly moving in this direction. Confronting—like Ibáñez before him—a none too friendly and sometimes unruly audience, Arlandis tried, with only moderate success, to win the delegates over not to the Bolshevik Revolution, which they already embraced, but to support of the actual principles advocated by the leaders of that revolution.

Lacking the personal force and prestige of a Pierre Monatte or an Alfred

Rosmer, Arlandis sought to convince the Anarchist elements that the progress of capitalism and technology had made obsolete the notion of "spontaneous production" by small Anarchist groups, to which so many of them still clung. He insisted that such groups could not maintain production after the revolution and would therefore fail. Recalling that the Bolsheviks, because of the discipline they had imposed upon labor, production, and distribution, had been criticized as "centralizers," he boldly asserted: "I say that [centralization] is absolutely necessary, and that we cannot work in any other manner." But in this context such a remark was excessively blunt, even provocative, and few of the delegates could accept it. Arlandis, who held in his hand a copy of the theses of the First Comintern Congress, was moving too directly against what was still the dominant myth of the Confederation, namely, the benign efficacy of spontaneity and decentralization. He concluded by urging immediate and unconditional adherence to the Comintern.[52]

The several other theses on the Comintern put forward at the Congress of the Comedia expressed a variety of viewpoints, ranging from advocacy of unconditional adherence to that body to criticism and rejection of it for being too authoritarian and centralist. One proposed resolution approvingly asserted that the Bolshevik Revolution "embodies, in principle, the ideal of revolutionary Syndicalism" and "has abolished the privileges of class and caste, giving power to the proletariat [and] establishing the temporary proletarian dictatorship in order to assure the conquest of the Revolution." But another proposal, though recognizing that the Comintern had adopted "revolutionary methods of struggle," asserted that the goals it pursued were "fundamentally opposed to the anti-authoritarian and decentralist ideal" of the CNT.*

In fact, there was no shortage of adverse comment regarding certain phases of the Russian Revolution. Despite the overwhelming support that the Revolution itself enjoyed in the congress, there were a number of delegates—nearly all from the ranks of the moderate Syndicalists—who were aware of some of the negative and nonlibertarian features of the Soviet regime. The most prominent of these persons was Salvador Seguí, who reiterated the themes he had advanced in his October speeches in Madrid. Seguí continued to view the Revolution with remarkable detachment. He reminded the delegates that the incapacity of the Russian workers for the task of maintaining production had led

---

* *Memoria del congreso*, p. 342. There was also a lengthy debate on how far the CNT should go in trying to help the Soviets against the blockade of the capitalist powers, which it then seemed that Spain might join. A Valencian delegate observed that in the Congress militants had spoken "boastfully about the extremely powerful organization of the CNT," and he urged that the organization not draw back in any way from giving aid to the Bolsheviks, even to the point of sabotaging goods that might be exported for use against the Russian comrades. But, in the end, the congress recognized that the declaration of a general strike or the use of sabotage on behalf of the Bolsheviks would be "self-defeating" since it would give the government an excuse for repressive measures. *Ibid.*, pp. 341, 354.

to the establishment of a Bolshevik "tyranny," and that the masses had really gained nothing from the upheaval. Where tsarist officials had once plundered the peasants of the fruits of their labor, Soviet soldiers now did the same.

Implicit in Seguí's remarks, as in his earlier speeches, was the assumption that the Spanish revolution was still a very distant prospect. Like the Socialist Julián Besteiro, he felt that there could be no successful upheaval in Spain until British workers had made their revolution. And to attempt the revolution before Spanish workers had raised their technical and cultural level would only lead to a "disaster" like that in Russia. Nevertheless, Seguí also urged giving conditional adherence to the Comintern, and he concluded a speech permeated by revolutionary pessimism with an incongruous but ringing appeal to the workers to rise, at some unspecified future time, in "holy revolt." Despite its almost entirely unrevolutionary tenor, Seguí's speech was well received and testified to this cautious but charismatic leader's undiminished ability to arouse an audience of Spanish workers.[53]

The most impassioned critique of the Bolshevik Revolution came from Eleuterio Quintanilla. In eloquent and even prophetic tones, the Asturian asserted that although the Revolution might be a kind of "luminous dawn" that would show humanity the way to redemption, it nevertheless did not embody the principles of the CNT. What disturbed him was that the events in Russia, though unquestionably constituting a social revolution, did not have the popular, spontaneous character that was the ideal of Spanish revolutionary Syndicalism. He called attention to the fact that the Bolshevik Revolution had been carried out by a political party, and observed that it was therefore a revolution of the Marxist or "classic" type, which the men of the Bakuninist International had fought from the beginning and which the Cenetistas considered "authoritarian, centralist, and castrating." The true revolution, admonished Quintanilla, had to be a popular revolution in which the masses participated through their sindicatos.[54]

While acknowledging that dictatorship and violence were in conflict with the pacifist ideals of the Confederation, Quintanilla did not deny their necessity. No successful revolution, he said, could be made entirely through persuasion, and at some point it would have to use "the decisive argument of force." But he made one important stipulation: the revolution had to be consolidated not by a government, "however revolutionary it might be," but rather by the "central representation" of the syndical organizations of each country; in this way the revolution would be a popular one in which the "armed people" would play the major role. Therefore, said Quintanilla, the Spanish Confederation should avoid the Russian example, and, though giving their sincere support to the Revolution, the Cenetistas should by no means adhere to the Comintern. That International, he insisted, was not a Syndicalist entity but rather "a specifically political organization, profoundly political, essentially political." Quintanilla concluded with a plea for the revolutionary purity of the CNT:

> I, as an Anarchist, working in the groups of [Anarchist] persuasion, where one can operate without bearing the collective representation of the organized working class, would not find it inconvenient to sustain, in principle, adherence to the Third International. But as a union worker, as a member of the great *falange* of the Confederation, I have to speak here for the integrity of our personality, for the clarity of our principles. We cannot, we should not, be in the Third International. The Confederation must keep itself apart from all contact, from all concurrence ... with any political party.

Only by such aloofness from all political organizations, said Quintanilla, could the CNT continue to affirm the integrity of its collective personality against the bourgeois parties and the Socialists.[55]

Even though his critique of the Revolution had remarkably little impact on the exuberant mass of pro-Bolshevik delegates, Quintanilla was nevertheless expressing the underlying views of the great majority of Cenetistas about the nature of the revolutionary process. He had skillfully evoked the vision of a spontaneous and popular revolution that was so congenial to the temper of Spanish workers, and which, having been reinforced by a thousand Anarchist tracts, would prove to be one of the great obstacles to Bolshevik proselytizing within the CNT. But the restless Cenetistas were not, in these final hours of the congress, prepared to take much interest in doctrinal expositions. In contrast to the prudent and sober Socialists debating the same issue in another part of the city, they were prepared to give their approval to the Bolshevik Revolution and to the Comintern largely on the basis of emotion and impulse. No small part of their eagerness to adhere to the Comintern stemmed from their animosity toward their Socialist rivals, who, as they were pleased to believe, had "calumniated" the Russian Revolution. They wanted to show, by means of their adherence, which group in Spain had the greater revolutionary vigor. Typical was the exclamation of Carbó:

> I recall another sympathetic note with respect to the Russian movement. It is something that surges spontaneously in my veins, that has roused me many times. ... It is one of those things that has told me most clearly that the Russian movement has great worth, even though we lack documents with which to judge it exactly. It is having seen the Spanish Socialists, for the space of three years, cover it with ignominy, shame, and discredit.[56]

In the same vein, Manuel Buenacasa, earlier in the congress, had said: "Since the Socialists have not done it, we who are not Socialists must be unanimously agreed to aid the Russian Revolution, but with deeds rather than with words."[57]

What emerged most clearly from the debates on the Comintern was the divided consciousness of the Cenetistas, who approached the Bolshevik Revolution both as libertarians deploring all violence, coercion, and state power and as revolutionaries inescapably concerned with the uses both of violence and of power. In contrast to most French Syndicalists in this era, a majority of Cenetista leaders continued to think of themselves as both Anarchists and Syndicalists, and phrases such as "we Anarchists," or "to us, the Anarchists," recurred many times in the debates of this Syndicalist congress, suggesting the ambivalence under which they labored.

Nowhere was this ambivalence, this painful reappraisal of Anarchist verities, more evident than in an address by Carbó. The Russian Revolution, he said, "is the most transcendental fact that the history of the world records . . . the grandest attempt at liberation that men have ever carried out, leaving far behind the historical events that preceded it." But had not the congress noted, he asked, "how, as a result of *el hecho ruso*, one speaks with disconcerting naturalness of the transfer of powers, of the dictatorship of the proletariat?" And was it not true that this "violates, infringes, and poisons the libertarian essence of our doctrines?" For in speaking of the dictatorship of the proletariat, said Carbó, "one is speaking of the state; and the state for us is the historic conservator of privilege; it is the political reason for our slavery; it is something that fundamentally negates the very essence of the human personality." Did this mean that the Anarchosyndicalists were the enemies of the dictatorship? "From the point of view of principles," replied Carbó, "yes; but from the point of view of urgent, unavoidable reality, no." Having thus appeased his Anarchist conscience, he proceeded to utter an odd hymn of praise to the proletarian dictatorship: "We justify the dictatorship; we admire the dictatorship; we desire that the dictatorship should come. . . . We admire it, we justify it, and we love it. . . . We sing of it and we love it, [since it must serve] to establish the reign of justice in the world. . . . We therefore admire and love the dictatorship of the proletariat."[58]

Despite this flight into hyperbole—significant in that it came from one of the more doctrinaire Anarchists in the CNT—the fact is that the Cenetistas approached the Communist International, as Peirats has said, in something less than a mood of unconditional surrender.[59] The resolution of adherence formulated by the National Committee first declared the Spanish Confederation to be "a firm defender of the principles sustained by Bakunin, which infused the First International." Second, it declared that the CNT "adheres, provisionally, to the Third International, because of the revolutionary character that governs it." This adherence, however, was to be only until such time as there could be organized—and held in Spain—"the international congress that must establish the principles [that ought] to govern the true International of workers."[60] In fact, the resolution was a compromise between the Anarchosyndicalist militants who wanted an unconditional adherence and the moderate Syndicalist militants who wanted no adherence at all. In this form the motion to join the Comintern was passed by acclamation, with almost unanimous approval and marked enthusiasm. But as though to make certain that this step should not be construed as an ideological change of course, a group of delegates immediately proposed another resolution declaring that the final goal of the CNT was "libertarian Communism," that is, Anarchism. This, too, was quickly approved by boisterous acclamation, to the irritation of the "pure" Syndicalists, who of course wanted the Confederation to remain wholly Syndicalist and aloof from all sectarian ideologies.[61]

In the aftermath of the Congress of the Comedia three men were chosen to carry the adherence of the CNT to Moscow: Angel Pestaña, Salvador Quemades, and Eusebio Carbó, of whom only the first would be able to complete the journey. Before discussing the Pestaña mission, however, it will be necessary to survey the impact of the Comintern issue on the Socialist side of the labor movement in the early months of 1920, and to examine the circumstances under which the first Communist Party made its appearance in Spain.

CHAPTER NINE

The Birth of Spanish Communism

The Borodin Mission

The two congresses of December 1919 left little doubt about the intensity of Spanish labor interest in the Bolshevik Revolution; but it cannot be said that the leaders of the Communist International revealed a reciprocal concern for Spain or took special note of the Cenetista adherence to their cause. Lenin and his followers were aware of the anomaly involved in their own seizure of power—in the name of the proletariat—in an industrially immature and mostly peasant nation. In terms of Marxist theory, there was no way in which their coup d'etat could be justified in isolation from a general upheaval; and the formation of the Comintern in the spring of 1919 was intended to encourage the spread of the Revolution to the rest of Europe and the world. But although the Russian Bolsheviks presented themselves as the solicitous midwives of universal revolution, they were, in fact, primarily absorbed with Germany and, beyond that, with France, England, Italy, Czechoslovakia, and a number of other countries, not excluding the colonial and semicolonial lands of the East. Spain, which was both Western and underdeveloped, capitalist and semi-colonial, seems to have engaged the interest of the Moscow strategists very little; and there was no labor movement anywhere about which they were less informed. This was hardly surprising, for Spain's chronic isolation had made her mysterious to observers far less removed than the Russians. And although middle-class Spaniards might uneasily suspect that Spain was the "Russia of the West," it was not in search of their own backward image, after all, that the Bolsheviks had turned westward: they sought the salvation of their revolution not in retarded nations but in advanced and industrialized countries where proletarian forces were strongest.[1]

Apart from Trotsky, therefore, none of the Comintern leaders appear to have had much interest in a Spanish revolution. Dmitrii Manuilsky would later report that for Moscow in this period "a small strike in Germany had more importance than all that happened in Spain"; and the Spanish delegate to the 1920 Comintern Congress would remark, after his first conversations with Zinoviev, that the Russian leader was "almost totally ignorant" of Spanish affairs, having "only a few vague memories with the name Barcelona attached to them."[2] Lenin's writings in this period, too, may be perused in vain for references to Spain, which seems to have been as much on the periphery of his concern as Iceland or Andorra.

In December 1919 there was some optimism in Comintern circles that the Peninsula might be on the eve of a great upheaval. The journal *Communist International* hopefully observed that "the spark of a revolutionary blaze" had begun to flare among the Spanish working classes, and that nothing appeared likely to halt "such an impetuously unfolding movement, which ... must lead to a proletarian revolution."[3] But by April 1920 the feeling was that the continued lack of cohesion of the Spanish proletariat might delay the revolutionary movement "quite a long time," and that the clock of Spanish history had only reached 1905.[4] This discounting of revolutionary possibilities in Spain was general among the Moscow leaders. Fascinated by what E. H. Carr has called the "parallelism of revolutions," the Bolsheviks persisted in discovering parallels with their Revolution in countries where they were lacking (as in Germany) and often failed to discern them in lands where they were perhaps more apparent.[5]

It was appropriate, then, that the first Comintern agent came to Spain somewhat accidentally, and that he did not stay long. This was Michael Borodin—later to be famous as an apostle to the Chinese—who did not arrive in Madrid until January 1920. Borodin, born to the name Gruzenberg in Vitebsk in 1884, had been taken to the United States as a young boy but had returned to Russia around the turn of the century to engage in revolutionary work, first with the Jewish Bund and later, after 1903, in the Bolshevik Party. After carrying on Party activity in Riga for a time, he returned to the United States, where in 1908 he organized and directed a progressive business school. In 1918 Borodin was back in Moscow once more, and, after attending the First Congress of the Comintern, was sent on a mission to Mexico. There his task was, first, to convince the Carranza government to recognize the Soviet Republic and accept himself as Ambassador, and, second (this being contingent on the first), to finance and organize the Communist Revolution in Latin America.[6]

The Mexican mission was terminated because Carranza responded unfavorably to Borodin's overtures—and because the Russian, through a complicated mishap, lost his means of financing revolutionary activity in the New World. Thus Borodin sailed from Veracruz late in 1919, together with the Indian Communist M. N. Roy and a young Mexican-American leftist who went under the name "Ramírez." He had not originally had any intention of visiting Spain, and had no special knowledge of the country beyond a casual recollection that the labor movement there was chronically divided between Socialists and Anarchists. Nor did Borodin have any particular interest in Spain, which he viewed only as a stopping-off place on his way back to Europe from the unsuccessful Mexican venture. He was apparently ordered to see, without spending too much time, what he could do there, since no emissary of the Comintern had yet established contact with the Spanish Left. His instructions were very general, as indeed they had to be, given the Comintern's slight knowledge of Spain.[7]

Borodin, Ramírez, and Roy landed at La Coruña during the last days of 1919 and, without pausing in that Anarchist stronghold, entrained at once for the capital. Along the way they purchased whatever Madrid newspapers were available, Ramírez reading them to Borodin, who knew no Spanish. Among the labor publications they looked for signs of sympathy with the Russian Revolution and for hints of factional unrest within the Socialist ranks. Once in Madrid, Ramírez served as Borodin's contact man and, ironically, made his first approach to the scholarly Menshevik Fernando de los Ríos, whom he encountered at the Ateneo. It was de los Ríos who introduced Ramírez to the leading Madrid left-centrist, Mariano García Cortés. From this encounter flowed a series of meetings in Borodin's hotel room attended by a small group of leftists: García Cortés, César González, Virginia González, Manuel Núñez de Arenas, José López y López, Ramón Lamoneda, Daniel Anguiano, Ramón Merino Gracia, and a few others. Borodin also talked with Angel Pestaña at about this time, but the meeting appears to have been inconclusive. In fact, Borodin made no effort to establish contact with the CNT or to proselytize among the Anarchosyndicalists, for whom he is reported to have felt "great scorn." Nor did he have any greater esteem for the right-centrist leaders of the Socialist Party, whose revolutionary spirit he entirely discounted and with whom he chose not to confer.[8]

Borodin made an extraordinary impression on the Madrid leftists, who were awed not least by his appearance. With his shaggy black mane of hair, penetrating eyes, and spadelike beard, he seemed the very incarnation of the Revolution. Despite the barrier of language, the Spaniards sensed the force of intellect and the extensive culture possessed by the deep-voiced Russian; nor were they immune to his very great personal charm. At the same time, they found him to be an excessively subtle and secretive personality, a man given to frequent whispers and to furtive glances over the shoulder.[9]

Certainly, Borodin pursued an ambiguous policy toward the Spanish Socialists, though the source of this may have resided less in his somewhat Byzantine personality than in the ambivalent international strategy adopted by the Russian Bolsheviks in 1919–20. For in this era the Moscow leaders were concentrating their hostility on the centrists of European Socialism, choosing to regard them as the supreme enemy and launching against them attacks more violent than those mounted against the parties of the Right. Yet the Bolsheviks also wished to secure the adherence of those Socialist parties that had not participated in the Berne Conference, or at least had not voted for the anti-Bolshevik Branting Resolution. This might take time, however, and there was an immediate need for Communist parties in the West. Thus the March 1919 Comintern Congress had been followed by a dual effort on the part of the Bolsheviks: on the one hand, they wanted to obtain the majority support of friendly Socialist parties, hoping to win the masses of European workers for the Comintern; but on the other hand, they wanted, for tactical and prestige purposes, to form at once Communist parties, however small, in those countries where they had not yet appeared.[10]

This dualism may explain the contradictory impression that Borodin made on the Spanish left-Socialists. He gave some leaders, such as García Cortés, Anguiano, and Núñez de Arenas, the distinct impression that he wished them to continue working within the Party in order to engineer its adherence to Moscow; and Núñez de Arenas would later assert categorically that Borodin had not asked for a schism.[11] Other militants, mostly among the Young Socialists, were equally convinced that the Comintern agent wanted them to work for a split in the Party.[12] Insofar as Borodin did exert pressure in this direction, he found the majority of Spanish leftists firmly, even passionately, opposed to schismatic efforts and determined to take a united party into the Communist International. They were certain, as they later explained to the Comintern agent Graziadei, that they could render greater service to Moscow by working within the PSOE to convert a majority to their position—something they had every expectation of doing, despite the failure of their efforts in the December congress.[13] On the whole, Borodin seems to have remained skeptical of the left-centrists and doubtful of their revolutionary capacity. He would later be quoted as saying of them that "nothing can be expected from that *camarilla*, who are *izquierdistas de palabra* and very bad in action."[14]

Unable to achieve (or unwilling to push for) an agreement to split the PSOE, Borodin suggested what must have seemed the next best thing: the establishment of a new, pro-Bolshevik daily newspaper, to be financed by money from the Comintern. This seemed to win more agreement; but when it came to implementation, most of the leftists drew back, perhaps sensing the schismatic implications of such a step. Only Merino Gracia of the Madrid Young Socialists proved willing to support a proposal of this kind. By this time Borodin was in close touch with the Juventud—who, it will be recalled, had voted adherence to the Comintern only two weeks earlier—and he appears to have decided that if there were to be a Communist split from the Party, it would have to be accomplished by the younger elements. Disappointed by what he regarded as a lack of revolutionary fervor among the Spanish Socialists, and no doubt anxious for some larger arena of activity, Borodin departed from Spain in mid-January, after a sojourn of only two weeks. However, he left behind his secretary, Ramírez, with instructions to work among the Juventud for the schism that Moscow desired.[15]

The Formation of the Spanish Communist Party

The Young Socialists of Madrid were a fertile field for the schismatic efforts of Ramírez, who stayed on for another three or four months, meeting nearly every day with various members of the Left in the Café Nueva Montaña on the Calle Fuencarral. Here, over coffee cups and wine glasses, he helped bring the young extremists of Spanish Socialism to the logical culmination of the drift to the Left that they had experienced since the end of the war.[16] The turning point, perhaps, was the decision to postpone until July 31 the Geneva Conference of the Second International, at which efforts were to be made to find a basis for uniting all Socialist parties, including the Russian Bolsheviks, into one revolutionary International. Still angry over their party's failure to adhere to Moscow at its December congress, and increasingly distrustful of the Socialist leaders, the Madrid Juventud decided that the moment had come to form a Communist Party. Their criticism of the Party leadership, increasingly strident since December, now passed beyond the limits of what could be construed as loyal opposition. *Renovación* flatly asserted that there was "a revolutionary political outlook that Besteiro, Largo Caballero, and Prieto will never develop," since those leaders had been educated and accustomed by too many years in democratic Socialism to the "minimum program of small gains, achieved, little by little, after an exhausting collaboration with bourgeois ministers." Consequently, it was said, neither the ideology nor the temperament of these moderates could provide the workers with an "energetic, negative, and revolutionary" activity designed not to collaborate with the bourgeoisie but to finish it off.[17]

The Young Socialists revealed a fierce and hitherto unsuspected antiparliamentary spirit, probably stimulated by Comintern pronouncements since early 1919. They were equally critical of such pro-Comintern leaders as García Cortés and Núñez de Arenas, whom they accused of having succumbed to the same democratic virus as the right-centrists. They charged these older militants with favoring a "timid democratism" whose fatal flaw was that it would lead the workers to imagine there might be "anything useful in the legislative labor of a bourgeois parliament." Against this tendency, the Young Socialists urged an aggressive policy of "revolutionary attack."[18]

By the end of February the Madrid-dominated National Committee of the FJS, after some urging by Ramírez and after having been promised Comintern money for their journal, came to a bold and secret decision to try to transform the Federation into a Spanish Communist Party. This was to be accomplished by nothing less than a coup d'etat, an intra-party *pronunciamiento*. The strategy adopted was that of a sudden declaration by the National Committee rather than the more democratic and problematical method of encouraging preliminary debate and calling a constituent assembly of all sections. The date selected for the formation of the new party was April 15, and letters were sent out to all FJS local committees directing them to convoke assemblies of their members on that date, and to make known to them at that time, but not before, an "important decision" taken by the National Committee. This was, of course, the decision to found the Partido Comunista Español (PCE). Thus the plan for the coup was to be kept secret until the last moment, effectively precluding extended debate or counterpreparations. Only in this way, it was felt, could the deeply rooted instinct of party unity be thwarted.[19]

On the appointed date, meetings of all FJS sections were held, the formation of the PCE was proclaimed, and the founding manifesto was read. This document was a faithful echo of the theses of the Communist International, proclaiming that capitalist society was undergoing its "final decomposition," and that the goal of the workers had to be the dictatorship of the proletariat and the regime of soviets. The manifesto also reflected the antiparliamentary animus so evident in earlier Comintern statements, asserting that the parliamentary and municipal activity of the Spanish Socialist Party had been indistinguishable from that of the left-bourgeois elements, and that the new Communist Party would, by contrast, reject every minimum program and have as its only goal the social revolution. The new social order would be founded precisely "on the ruins of the parliamentary regime and of bourgeois democracy."[20] (Almost incongruously, the manifesto also contained an explicit recognition of the continuing need for parliamentary participation—an addendum that reflected not the true feelings of most PCE militants but rather their desire to avoid an influx of Anarchist or quasi-Anarchist elements into the new party.[21]) Finally, the young men of the PCE made no apology for the schism. Seemingly without guilt as a result of their assault on the primal father, Pablo Iglesias, they declared the fetish of unity to be, under the existing circumstances, "reactionary" and self-defeating. "Let the division come," they said; "we only regret the time we have lost."[22]

The Madrid section of the FJS held its meeting in the salon of the Casa del Pueblo. In the presence of about 100 militants, the sealed envelope was opened and the startling declaration read. The ensuing debate was turbulent and marked by numerous "incidents." Ramón Merino Gracia, Eduardo Ugarte, and Tiburicio Pico argued for schism and the formation of the new party. The opposition was led by César González, who quickly perceived that his forces were being confronted with a fait accompli and would be outvoted. Not without bitterness, he acknowledged that there were now two workers' parties in Spain—a fact that he doubted would benefit the proletarian cause— and without waiting for the vote he withdrew from the salon, taking perhaps 25 percent of those present with him, among them Evaristo Gil and Vicente

Calaza. The majority of the Madrid section then approved by acclamation the decision of the National Committee to turn the FJS into the Spanish Communist Party, and the schism was consummated. "We came to the meeting as Socialists," rejoiced Ricardo Marín ("Alejandro González"); "we left as Communists."[23]

The response from the provinces, however, was less than uniformly favorable to the coup of the National Committee. Some sections voted to go along with the proposed metamorphosis and become sections of the PCE; but many others did not. When the tumult had subsided, perhaps less than 1,000 militants out of the 5,000–7,000 members had adhered to the new party; and the real heart of the PCE would be perhaps no more than 50 or 60 febrile youths in Madrid. The most serious blow to the viability of the PCE was the failure to enlist the powerful and radical Asturian section. This almost certainly resulted from the efforts of Andrés Saborit, who had been president of the FJS for several years, having only recently retired after reaching his thirty-sixth birthday, and who, as the Socialist deputy from Oviedo, maintained close connections with the Young Socialists of Asturias. In Vizcaya, too, the majority of the Juventud, though fervently pro-Comintern, chose to stay within the Socialist Party, at least for the time being. Another disappointment was the "treason" of José López y López, president of the National Committee, who refused to go down the path of schism with his comrades. Thus the only real strength of the PCE was in Madrid, and the leaders of the coup were forced to recognize that they had acted prematurely, having been at the head of the Juventud for only a few weeks before attempting to convert it into the PCE. One result of their precipitancy was that the FJS—with the assistance of Fabra Ribas, among others—was almost immediately able to reconstitute itself with about the same total membership as before.[24]

No longer welcome in the Casa del Pueblo, the young secessionists of the PCE took as their headquarters a cellar in a building on the Calle General Alvarez del Castro, with two windows at street level and a few chairs and tables more or less forcibly removed from the Socialist center. Here they began their energetic labors on behalf of the revolution in Spain, immediately revealing various symptoms of the "disorder" of left-wing Communism against which Lenin was even then rallying the Comintern. Founded about ten days later than the German KAPD, which it generically resembled, the PCE would be until June 1921 the only Communist party in the Iberian Peninsula. The journal *Renovación* was now converted into *El Comunista*.[25]

On the whole the founders of the PCE were an able group of young men, hardly any of them over the age of 25. The majority of the rank and file were workers, and considerable emphasis was placed on the Party's proletarian character. But, in fact, a disproportionate number of the leaders were middle-class intellectuals. The general secretary of the new party was Ramón Merino

Gracia, a slight, bespectacled school teacher about 26 years of age, who, with his dark beard and nervous mannerisms, conveyed an impression of intensity, asceticism, and humorlessness. Something of a pioneer in progressive methods of education, he had written a textbook on mathematics and was filled with zeal for the intellectual uplifting of the masses. He was a bachelor who was rarely seen in the company of women; and after the death of his mother, to whom he was deeply attached, he had withdrawn from political activity for about a year. His return to political life came in 1918 and was prompted by news of the Russian Revolution, to which he dedicated his *ágape bolchevista* early in 1919. Although intelligent, skilled as a polemical writer, and adequate as a speaker, Merino Gracia lacked the oratorical gifts and personal magnetism that might have made him a great leader. He had, moreover, a pedagogical manner that did not always sit well with his younger colleagues; and, though he was certainly on the far Left in his views, he lacked some of the impetuousness and "ultra" tendencies that so distinguished the other members of the PCE.[26]

Juan Andrade, as editor of *El Comunista* and the PCE's most outstanding journalist, was in many ways the leading figure within the new party. Though not a university student, he was a talented young intellectual who had belonged to the Socialist Students' Group (but not to the Juventud) and had moved in the ideological ambience of the Madrid Atheneum. Until 1918 he had been a member of the Young Radicals of Lerroux, and had helped edit *Los Barbáricos*. He was, in fact, the Robespierre of the PCE, filled with revolutionary ardor and ultra-Left idealism, austere, eloquent, and angry. Highly sectarian and committed to a revolutionary vision of great purity, Andrade was perhaps the most uncompromising and intransigent of all the young militants. He was entirely prepared to be a martyr to his cause, and would be in prison nearly a dozen times during the 1920's. The Comintern agent Antonio Graziadei found him possessed of "a fine intelligence and a genuine Communist culture," but thought him excessively "opinionated."[27] He greatly impressed his colleagues with his ruthlessness in debate and "boundless pride," but also with the rectitude and unselfishness of his character.[28]

Andrade himself perceived the underlying turbulence in his nature, and admitted that "everything associated with violence and struggle attracts me greatly."[29] Above all, he was ultra-Left, belonging to that exalted minority within European Communism in the early 1920's who regarded Lenin and the Bolsheviks as opportunists insufficiently pure in their revolutionary idealism. Lenin's *"Left-wing" Communism: An infantile disorder* inspired his wrath, and he did not hesitate to call it "abominable."[30] Andrade lived with two pious, middle-class maiden aunts, and combined his career as a revolutionary with a job as a minor functionary of the state he was endeavoring to overthrow. Occasionally conscious of needs less exalted than the making of the revolution, he once wistfully inquired of a correspondent in Holland whether there were not a Dutch *compañera* who might come to Spain, since "I would enjoy talking with women who are not like the Spaniards, that is, very beautiful but very ignorant."[31] With his "hard, cruel pencil" Andrade kept *El Comunista* up to high journalistic standards and was convinced that "his" journal was superior to anything of its kind in Europe.[32]

Eduardo Ugarte was from an upper-middle-class family. His father, a well-known liberal lawyer, was a professor in the Instituto de Segunda Enseñanza in Madrid; and the younger Ugarte studied simultaneously in the School of Law and the School of Philosophy and Literature at the University of Madrid. He was a member of the Young Socialists but had also joined the Socialist Students' Group at the time of its founding. He was highly intelligent, mentally agile, and multilingual, but lacking in *mesure*. No one in the ranks of Spanish Socialism responded to the Russian Revolution with more messianic fervor than Ugarte, and early in 1919 he conceived the idea of making a pilgrimage to Russia in order to fight in the ranks of the Red Army. Borrowing eight thousand pesetas from his father for the journey he got as far as Stettin, where he was arrested and imprisoned by the authorities. He was freed through the intervention of the Spanish Consul and returned to Spain via Berlin, where he seems to have had some contact with the Left opposition within the KPD. He arrived back in Madrid in time to become a member of the National Committee of the Federation of Young Socialists and to help engineer the formation of the PCE.[33]

Antonio Buendía, like Andrade, was one of the young intellectuals associated with the Madrid Atheneum. Born in Andalusia of a modest family, he was nevertheless able to pursue studies at the University of Madrid. Here he joined the Socialist Students' Group and participated in the founding of the PCE. His command of languages made him useful as a translator on the staff of *El Comunista*, and perhaps also led to his being sent on a mission to the Italian Socialists, which was only marginally successful.[34]

Ricardo Marín ("Alejandro González") was the son of a railroad worker, but was himself not really of the working class, being rather a Bohemian or déclassé who always lived a nocturnal and somewhat irregular existence. As a would-be poet and journalist he had emigrated to Cuba, where he worked on newspapers until expelled from that island early in 1918. Returning to Spain, he joined the PSOE and worked on the staff of *El Socialista*. He was a founding member of the PCE and performed valuable services during 1921 on the editorial staff of *El Comunista*, to which he contributed articles signed "Charivari."[35]

Gabriel León Trilla was born in Valladolid, the son of an army colonel. He was a student of philosophy and literature at the University of Madrid and belonged to the Socialist Party and the Students' Group, though not to the Young Socialists. He joined the PCE at the time of its formation and contributed articles and translations to *El Comunista*. In 1921, after the disaster of Annual, he was drafted into the army and sent to Morocco, from whence he ultimately deserted to France, not returning to Spain for several years.[36]

Luis Portela, born in Madrid, was, at the age of 19, one of the youngest of the PCE leaders. A printer by profession, he was highly intelligent, idealistic, and energetic. Despite his youth, he was a member of the National Committee of the FJS and of the Committee of the PCE from the time of its founding. Like his colleagues, he adhered to an exalted ultra-Left creed and would for several years play a prominent role in the fight against parliamentarianism within the Communist movement.[37]

Emeterio Chicharro was a carpenter who had joined the Young Socialists before the war. In July 1917 he had agitated among the soldiers being sent to Barcelona to suppress the Assembly of Parliamentarians. For this he had been forced to flee to Portugal, where he remained until about May 1918, when the amnesty extended by the Maura government enabled him to return to Madrid. He then became actively involved in the leadership of the Woodworkers' Union, entered the National Committee of the FJS, and eventually became a founding member of the PCE.[38]

Among the other more or less prominent members of the PCE were: Vicente Arroyo and Gonzalo Sanz of the Madrid Woodworkers' Union; José Illescas of the Metalworkers' Union; Joaquín Ramos of the Dependiente de Comercios; Rito Esteban, the proprietor of a small tailor shop; and Rafael Millá, a 40-year-old printer from Alicante who was the only regular older member of the PSOE to cast his lot with the PCE.[39]

Ultra-Leftism

The young militants were self-consciously on the ultra-Left of the European Socialist movement, and their heroes were figures such as S. J. Rutgers, Henrietta Roland-Holst, Anton Pannekoek, Amadeo Bordiga, the leaders of the German KAPD, and the Vienna Communists. They were thus the Spanish manifestation of the "infantile disorder" that began to plague the Comintern early in 1920 as the Moscow leaders themselves turned away from advocacy of ultra-leftist ideas toward a more rigid imposition of the tactical norms presumably validated by Russian experience. The Russian Bolsheviks now began to denigrate "putschism," terrorism, and an excessive reliance on spontaneity, at the same time emphasizing the need for parliamentary participation and work within existing trade unions. At bottom, this shift in policy reflected a growing, if only half-acknowledged, skepticism about the imminence of a European revolution—a skepticism that the ultra-leftists did not yet share, least of all in Spain.

The ultra-leftism of the PCE was essentially indigenous in origin, reflecting the young militants' own passionate state of mind, as well as certain realities of the Spanish situation, in which the widespread penetration of Anarchosyndicalist attitudes had made parliamentary activity anathema to broad sections of the urban and rural proletariat. At the same time the youths of the PCE were in close touch with the Amsterdam Bureau of the Comintern, which during its brief career (February–May 1920) had sought to encourage antiparliamentary attitudes among the Socialists of Western Europe, including Spain.[40] The principal link between the Amsterdam Bureau and the Spanish Communist Party was Juan Andrade's correspondence with Rutgers and G. J. Geers in Holland. From the Dutch militants the PCE received advice, encouragement, and a stream of articles by writers such as A. Pannekoek, H. Roland-Holst, and H. Gorter, which were translated and reprinted in *El Comunista*. The Spanish Communists also regularly received copies of *Die Rote Fahne* and the Vienna journal *Kommunismus*. They were likewise in correspondence with Van Overstraeten of the Belgian ultra-Left, and with Amadeo Bordiga in Italy.[41]

The core of the ultra-Left ideology shared by most PCE militants was opposition to parliamentary tactics. This position was adhered to with something less than the apolitical fanaticism that the Anarchists displayed, but with more than the merely pragmatic and dispassionate recognition of Spanish realities that some of the young Communists claimed for it. The attitude of the PCE was no doubt closer to the tactical abstentionism of Bordiga than to the millenarian negation of the Cenetistas; but it was nevertheless an emotionally rooted conviction and not a mere tactical expedient. It was, moreover, in conflict with Lenin's belief that Communists must always participate in bourgeois parliaments, if only "negatively," in order to bring revolutionary propaganda to the workers who still placed their faith in such institutions. Since the proportion of workers who had such faith was probably lower in Spain than in almost any other European country, the antiparliamentarianism of the PCE cannot be dismissed as mere left-wing extremism with no basis in reality.*

In purely formal terms, the stand of the PCE on the parliamentary issue

---

* Lenin's attack on the antiparliamentary thesis, launched in April 1920, was directed chiefly at the German Left-Communists and insisted, in effect, that the Bolshevik experience in Russia provided a model sufficient to guide the other European parties. Having in mind mainly the West European situation, in which the great mass of the people accepted parliamentarianism either actively or passively, Lenin's point was that, just as the Bolsheviks had entered the Russian Duma, so must Western Communists enter bourgeois parliaments in order to *reach* the many workers still beguiled by such institutions. The Communists, he said, "must tell [the masses] the bitter truth." They "must call their bourgeois-democratic and parliamentary prejudices—prejudices." But in Spain, as the Left-Communists of the PCE were well aware, the masses had long known "the bitter truth," and their animus against parliaments and politicians was, indeed, one of the major sources of Anarchosyndicalism in the Peninsula. It is the measure of Lenin's ignorance of Spanish conditions that he did not grasp this fact, and that he, along with the other Comintern leaders, continued to insist on the uniform application of a tactic that could only be counterproductive for Spanish Communists. See Lenin, *"Left-wing" Communism: An infantile disorder*, pp. 39–48.

was in accord with the Leninist position. Thus the new Party's theses asserted that in the "preparatory periods" of the social revolution Spanish Communists would use all modes of action necessary to prepare the masses for the decisive phase, including "participation in elections, in parliament, in municipal governments, and in [provincial assemblies]."[42] Yet in practice the antiparliamentary bias of militants like Andrade, Ugarte, and Portela went beyond Leninist pragmatism and came close to being an absolute that was often passionately upheld. Andrade openly admitted to the Dutch Communist Geers that he and his colleagues were simply not in accord with the principles of their own party in this matter, and that they felt completely at liberty to pursue a different policy.[43] In pragmatic terms, certainly, the young Communists had their eyes focused on the masses who revolved in the orbit of the CNT and who could never be won over, they believed, by a movement advocating electoralism.

The antiparliamentary tactic was warmly argued by Luis Portela who, in various articles, stressed the apolitical nature of the Spanish masses and urged the PCE not to try to swim against this powerful current but to rely instead on syndical action, factory councils, and soviets.[44] Emeterio Chicharro also took this position, saying that he thought parliamentary action ineffective everywhere, but especially in countries like Spain, "where the great mass of the people feel an aversion" to it. Chicharro also expressed the traditional fears of the Left that Communist deputies would go the way of all parliamentary flesh, ending up as reformists like the German Social Democrats. The place of the PCE, he insisted, should always be "in the street, in contact with the working masses."[45] By contrast, the general secretary of the Party, Merino Gracia, disappointed his more extreme colleagues by returning from Moscow early in 1921 as a supporter of the orthodox Leninist position, which sought to impose parliamentary tactics in all countries regardless of local conditions. He had become convinced of the value of an "international revolutionary discipline" that transcended any ideological variations; and, reaffirming the PCE's own theses, he asserted that the party had to tread the narrow path between "Socialist parliamentarianism" on the one hand and "Syndicalist apoliticism" on the other.[46]

The dissolution of the Amsterdam Bureau early in May was a blow to the anti-electoralism of the PCE youths and an embarrassment to them in their struggle with the left-centrists of the Socialist Party, who had denounced the April schism as premature. The Amsterdam Bureau had strongly supported the PCE in its split from the Socialist Party, and had gone so far as to disavow the FJS when it succeeded in reconstituting itself after the Communists' break. The young Communists themselves, not in the least intimidated by the Bureau's demise, continued to assert their solidarity with the Dutch leaders—Rutgers, D. Wijnkoop, Roland-Holst, and the rest—who, they felt, represented the "true revolutionary Communism."[47] When Lenin's pamphlet on "left-wing" Communism came to their attention, the young militants were "extraordinarily indignant" and made it clear that they would continue to remain on the Left of the European Communist movement. Andrade was deterred from attacking Lenin in *El Comunista* only by the fact that the PCE was desperately in need of money, for which it was at that moment negotiating with the Comintern.[48]

A somewhat Sorelian theme that ran through many of the pronouncements of the PCE and related (whether as cause or effect is difficult to say) to the antipathy toward parliamentary activity was hostility toward Socialist intellectuals. Andrade was especially exercised about this question. On the eve of the national elections of December 1920, he wrote a caustic analysis of the unfortunate "adoration of the intellectuals" in which Socialist workers indulged for want of proper class consciousness. He deplored the deference that workers accorded to intellectuals who happened to command two languages—one of them no doubt learned in "foreign cabarets"—and the "stupid mania" that the rank-and-file Socialists revealed in giving the highest party offices to "bourgeois intellectuals disguised as Socialists." It was intolerable that these men, filled with "ancient bourgeois ideology," should exercise such influence and constitute the major obstacle to revolutionary advance, making the Socialist Party a class party only in appearance. Most distressing of all was the "candidate fever" that had seized the Socialist intellectuals, causing young militants —Andrade named Ramón Lamoneda and José López y López—to forsake the hard and true revolutionary path of the PCE for the possibility of a seat in the Cortes. Andrade's prescription was a harsh one: "Every proletarian who has a really intransigent class spirit not only must be suspicious of the intellectual who militates at his side but must cast him out of the ranks, as if he were the bacillus of an infectious disease: reformism."[49]

On the question of trade-union activity, however, the PCE was not ultra-Left but followed the example of the Russian Bolsheviks rather than that of the German KAPD. Convinced that the rank and file of Spanish trade unionists were revolutionary even if their leaders were not, the Spanish Communists felt that the unions of the Peninsula, whether affiliated with the UGT or with the CNT, were worth fighting for. Unlike the "Left opposition" in Germany, they threw themselves energetically into efforts to win control of the committees of the sindicatos and showed a strong determination not to remain isolated and without roots in the working masses.[50] Their long-range objective was to infiltrate both of the major Spanish labor confederations and achieve the unification of all Spanish workers on the revolutionary basis of allegiance to the Communist International. On the very day they proclaimed the formation of the PCE the young militants also published a plea to the unions of the CNT, in which they asserted the need for labor unity and expressed doubt that the syndical forces of Spain would ever unite under the "opportunistic and antirevolutionary" Socialist Party. The Cenetistas were encouraged to contribute to the formation of the PCE, and it was emphasized that the Party's goals conformed absolutely to those of the Russian Bolsheviks.[51]

During the rest of 1920 the young Communists, despite their limited numbers and resources, made great efforts to penetrate the trade unions of the Madrid area. In this they encountered the violent hostility of the Ugetista leaders, especially when they tried to sell *El Comunista* in the Casa del Pueblo, and harsh words, as well as blows, were exchanged on more than one occasion. Nevertheless, they appear to have won a certain amount of sympathy among the workers, especially the younger ones. They gained considerable influence, perhaps actual control, over the metalworkers' and woodworkers' unions; and they attended the UGT Congress in July 1920 in order to agitate for labor unity and for workers' councils. In the late summer of the year the PCE exerted some influence over the strike of the Madrid metalworkers by virtue of the fact that José Illescas—a founding member of the PCE—was secretary of the strike committee, of which three out of four members were claimed as Communists.[52] "Delegates" from the PCE were also sent to such cities as Barcelona, Zaragoza, and Valencia, where they made efforts to form Communist groups and to penetrate the unions of the CNT. Excited by the revolutionary ferment in Andalusia, the Communists also wanted to conduct active work among the braceros and small peasants of that region, but they lacked the funds and the personnel needed to proselytize so far from Madrid. Occasional propaganda sorties in such places as Córdoba and Seville were nevertheless carried out.[53]

The PCE youths were as critical of the leaders of the CNT as they had been of the men who headed the UGT. Militants like Salvador Seguí or Salvador Quemades, they said, were guilty of "the most shameful opportunism" and of a "betrayal of the principles of revolutionary Syndicalism." They accused these moderate Syndicalist leaders of "barefaced deviations toward a policy of collaboration" with the bourgeois republicans, and denounced them as reformists no better than Largo Caballero or Besteiro. Seguí, who had frequently insisted that Spain was not ready for revolution, was described as purveying a "Social Democratic ideology," and Quemades was characterized as a "bourgeois laborite." The leaders of the PCE noted signs of disaffection among the Cenetista masses, and they conjectured that the hegemony of the "pure" Syndicalists within the CNT would not long endure.[54] For the rank-and-file Cenetistas, the PCE revealed a genuine admiration, based on the greater class consciousness that they displayed and on the fact that far more than the Ugetistas they avoided collaboration and reformism.[55] It was also noted with approval that a "majority" of the Cenetistas had come to accept the need for a transitional dictatorship; and hopes were expressed that they would move from seeing this as a syndical dictatorship to accepting the dictatorship of a party, that is, of the PCE acting in the name of the proletariat.[56]

The PCE emerged as a classic example of ultra-leftism, incorrigibly sectarian and idealistic. The few dozen *muchachos* who constituted the core of the Party were bound together in the mystical communion that only idealistic and embattled young men can know, welded to one another by youth, ideology, and a common struggle. Andrade wrote: "The persecution I suffer is truly horrible. But none of this matters because my Party comrades are worth a million. You can't imagine the enthusiasm that exists in all of them and creates such solidarity."[57] The sense of mission was affirmed by *El Comunista*: "We are a party born for revolution; there burns in us the sacred flame of youth and idealism, and we have a clear and serene vision of our historical duty."[58]

Intense sectarianism was reflected in the Communists' jealous love for their party and for their "dear" journal *El Comunista*, as well as in the pain many of them felt at the possibility of being forced to fuse with the numerically greater but ideologically flaccid centrists of the PSOE—a prospect that would be opened up by the adherence of the Socialist Party to the Comintern in the June Congress of 1920. Such a fusion, they thought, would be "monstrous and enormously prejudicial" at a time when the vital need was to avoid *confusionismos* and *centrismos* and to achieve "dogmatic clarity" as well as "revolutionary intransigence."[59] A good deal of ink was spilled regarding the virtues of a small party and the value of elitist purity, and some bitterness was expressed regarding the left-centrists' decision to continue working within the PSOE in the hope of bringing the whole Party into the Comintern. The animosity that the young Communists felt for these "hypocrites," as they repeatedly called them, was very great, so that much of their energy was consumed in polemical attacks on other pro-Comintern Socialists. With unquestioning sectarian pride they viewed themselves as the only true disciples of Bolshevism in the whole of the Iberian Peninsula.[60]

Also in keeping with the ultra-Left psychology of the PCE was a tendency to yield to the temptations of direct action and of the insurrectional mystique. For example, the Anarchist uprising in the Carmen Barracks in Zaragoza, which occurred three months before the founding of the PCE, had caught the imagination of the young Communists-to-be, and two of them, Portela and Illescas, had gone to jail briefly for urging that the Madrid Socialist Group pass resolutions in support of the mutiny.[61] As a group the young men of the PCE tended to be tough and aggressive; and they were not unwilling to invade the meetings of their opponents, hurling epithets, throwing punches, and disrupting parliamentary procedures. The source of much of this aggressiveness lay in their conviction (at least in 1920–21) that Spain was on the brink of upheaval and that the revolution was imminent, as well as in a voluntarist feeling that history had to be given a push. They had founded their party, as Andrade acknowledged, not to fight a patient battle over a period of many years but in the confident expectation of guiding an approaching revolutionary struggle of massive proportions.[62]

The Socialists and the Comintern

The febrile youths who formed the PCE were not the only ones within the Socialist Party to be disappointed by the decision to postpone the holding of the Geneva Conference from January until July. The delay also further radicalized the more numerous left-centrists and led them to doubt that the Second International would ever succeed in reorganizing itself. They now regretted their willingness to compromise in the December congress and felt that the new delay "absolutely nullified" the hedging resolution voted there. On January 10, they published a manifesto announcing the start of their campaign for the immediate adherence of the PSOE to the Third International. This was necessary, they said, in order to avoid the "grave risk" that the Spanish Socialists might remain indefinitely "confounded" with the reformist and pseudo-Socialist elements—something that would, they feared, drive the workers to desert the Socialist ranks en masse. The left-centrists were also sure that the Second Comintern Congress would meet in the spring, before the Geneva Conference, and they felt it indispensable that the Spanish Socialists be represented there. Various international conferences were being scheduled in this period—by the Swiss Socialists, by the German Independents, and by others—but the manifesto of the left-centrists emphasized that the only "viable" International was that of Moscow.[63]

The Asturian Socialists were especially indignant over the delay of the Geneva Conference, and within two weeks the Committee of the Asturian Federation, unanimously and without discussion, passed a resolution urging the immediate entry of the PSOE into the Third International.[64] This was communicated to the Executive Committee in Madrid, which agreed to hold a plenum on February 21 to discuss the new situation. Very loath to relinquish their ties with the Second International, the oligarchs of the Committee—Iglesias, Besteiro, Tomás, Saborit, and the rest—decided at this meeting to make one last effort to salvage the old affiliation. They voted to send Besteiro and Anguiano to the Rotterdam Conference of the Action Committee of the Second International, scheduled for March 1920. The two delegates were instructed to work for the reorganization of the International in such a way as to "incorporate the spirit" of the Third International, thereby unifying all the labor forces of the world.[65]

But the Rotterdam Conference accomplished little or nothing, and the Spanish participation in it was something of a fiasco. The two delegates were arrested when they reached the Dutch frontier, and Anguiano was found to be carrying a letter from the Committee of the FJS—written in English by Ramírez and intended for the ill-fated Amsterdam Bureau of the Comintern. The burden of this message was a plea for money in order to carry out Communist propaganda in Spain and to publish a periodical. This alone was sufficiently embarrassing to the old-line Socialists, since it appeared to the world as though the PSOE was begging abroad for money to make the revolution in Spain. Besteiro himself asked, "What has become of the immaculate morality of the Spanish Socialist Party?"[66] In the end, Anguiano was held futilely at the frontier, while Besteiro was allowed to proceed to the conference; and when the two finally returned to Madrid, Anguiano was in disgrace and had to retire, at least temporarily, as secretary of the National Committee.[67]

It was at this point, after the failure of the Rotterdam Conference, that the struggle between right-centrists and left-centrists within the Socialist Party for the first time assumed a threatening character, raising at last the serious prospect of schism. Rotterdam had been the last card of the Party leaders, and they were left stunned and uncertain of their course, lapsing into a silence that the leftists regarded as sinister. The truth was that leaders such as Besteiro, Largo Caballero, and de los Ríos had given up their hopes for the Second International but could not bring themselves to go into the Third, which they felt to be excessively dominated by Moscow. In a mood of resignation and foreboding, they now conceded what the left-centrists had demanded: another extraordinary congress to consider the international question, this to be held in June.[68]

Meanwhile, the formation of the PCE on April 15 antagonized the left-centrists within the PSOE nearly as much as it did those to the Right, and it prompted the calling of a general assembly of the Madrid Socialist Group on April 24. In this meeting Merino Gracia, the Secretary of the PCE, was required to defend himself against charges of having "calumniated" a comrade —namely, Largo Caballero—in the March 17 issue of *Renovación*. The assembly was called at the urging of Largo, who resented being accused of an unrevolutionary outlook and who of course deplored the founding of the PCE and the soliciting of aid from foreign Communists. Since the left-centrists had a majority in the Madrid Group—García Cortés was president—it is clear that many of the Terceristas also supported punitive measures against the PCE. The debate centered largely around the nature of the Borodin mission in Spain, of which Merino Gracia gave an account flattering to the Young Socialists; in the end, he was expelled from the Party.[69]

Despite the chastisement administered to Merino Gracia and to the PCE, there was no diminution of pro-Bolshevik enthusiasm within the Socialist ranks. The Party was growing rapidly in this period: whereas it had numbered only 15,588 at the beginning of 1919, by the spring of 1920 it had grown to about 53,000.* The unions of the UGT had also grown at an impressive rate, and the mood of most Socialists early in 1920 was one of revolutionary optimism and deepening doctrinal intransigence. There was a widespread desire to recapture the spirit of the pristine Socialism of the Communist Manifesto, to separate the Party from contact with the bourgeois parties of the Left, and to expunge evolutionary and reformist tendencies. The postponement of the Geneva Conference only swelled a tide that was already running strongly toward Moscow.[70]

In theory, the Party had three options in dealing with the international issue. As Manuel Pumarega said, the question was whether it would adhere to the Segunda, Tercera, or Reconstructura.[71] The first of these was scarcely a realistic possibility, since the Second International had by now become a preserve of the British and German majoritarians, who were unabashedly reformist and unwilling to make even verbal concessions to the idea of an imminent revolution or to the dictatorship of the proletariat.[72] The Spanish Party—small, embattled, and increasingly radical—provided little soil for the rooting of overtly reformist doctrines and no clientele to support the few leaders who still looked toward Geneva. Hardly any voices were raised on behalf of the Second International in the spring of 1920, and, in fact, the chorus of denunciation grew louder every day. The left-centrists composed a lengthy indictment of the old International: its partisans had not prevented war in 1914; they had voted for war credits; they had let themselves be dragged along by the wave of patriotic nationalism; they had participated in wartime governments; and at the Berne Conference they had supported the bourgeois League of Nations while criticizing the Russian Revolution and the proletarian dictatorship.[73] The Second International, said the Terceristas, had begun to die in 1914 and was now only a "cadaver" that did not merit the disputes that were threatening the unity of the Party. "If the Party remains stamped with the spirit of the Second International," warned Iván Tarfé, "within a few years, like republicanism, it will be dead."[74]

Another option available to the Party was the *via media* that was beginning to open up between the Second and Third Internationals. With the decision of the Strasbourg Congress of the French Socialist Party in February 1919 to leave the Second International without at the same time entering the Third, a "centrist" or "reconstructionist" position was affirmed, to which other parties might rally—as did the Austrian and Swiss parties, as well as the British Independent Labor Party. Essentially these groups sought a middle ground between the right-wing majority of the international labor movement, which insisted on pursuing exclusively evolutionary tactics and democratic trade

---

* It is worth noting that 33,000 of these had not paid their dues and thus had no representation at the 1920 Party Congress. *El Socialista,* 14.vii.20.

unionism, and the left-wing minority encompassed by the Comintern, which was revolutionary but at the same time excessively sectarian and Moscow-oriented. The desire of the Reconstructionists, as Borkenau has said, was to create an International in which the Russians would be "members but not masters."[75] This option, like that of the Second International, had almost no support within Spanish Socialist ranks at this time. Certainly, the left-centrists were opposed to it. Lamoneda and Núñez de Arenas asserted that the Reconstructionist position was a "confused, vacillating" point of view with no raison d'être. "Reconstruct what?" they asked. "Can one unite and harmonize the German majoritarians and the Russian Communists?" Even the right-centrists seemed to lack enthusiasm for the middle way, and perhaps the only outspoken partisan of this tactic was Fabra Ribas.[76]

The last option was the Third International, whose mystique reached, in the revolutionary spring of 1920, perhaps its moment of maximum attraction for the Spanish Socialists. Excited by the Russian Revolution and by the upheavals both in Europe and in Spain, and at the same time frustrated by the inertia of traditional forces, they were seeking some magic key to unloose the social revolution in Spain. They felt certain they had found it in the Moscow International. They were convinced, as a skeptic put it, that a "simple adherence" to the new instrumentality would endow them with "a miraculous power." "The Third International," said one enthusiastic militant, "carries within it a new Socialist vision.... It implies, necessarily, an intensification of revolutionary action and a recrudescence of the war against the bourgeoisie, which will take on a character of extreme violence."[77]

Against such expectations, the men of the National Committee, finding themselves increasingly in the minority on the international question, could fight only a delaying action. They did not dare meet the pro-Bolshevik storm head on, but hoped rather to deflect it or see it spend its force. Though preferring to remain within the Second International, the Besteiros, Largo Caballeros, and Saborits of the Party elected neither to defend vigorously the Geneva International nor to attack intemperately the Comintern. They had decided, as Saborit later wrote, largely to abstain from taking part in the debate, "giving *paso libre* to those who represented, apparently, the will of the majority of the Party."[78] Thus the defense of the old international affiliation would be left to the right-wing minority—to men such as Oscar Pérez Solís and Indalecio Prieto.

In the face of the pro-Comintern current, the right-centrists merely urged caution: they called attention to the unwisdom of making such an important decision on a "sentimental and confused" basis, suggesting that adherence to the distant Moscow International might leave the Spanish Party dangerously isolated within the European labor movement.[79] At bottom, both they and their antagonists within the Party understood that the decision to adhere to the

Third International would inevitably mean new tactics, and that new tactics would require new leaders. Manuel Pedroso caught the poignancy of the moment when he wrote, on the eve of the 1920 Congress:

> To the men who until now have guided the Party, this great rumbling of the Third International sounds like danger. They love their creation—the work that they invested years in creating, which, once grown strong, escapes from their hands.... The [Party] is of the greatest value to them, by reason of paternity; but the Russian Revolution is an explosion of history, the overflowing of consciousness, which breaks its integument. Aspiration always defeats reality. The man who embodies promise always defeats the man who has already done his work. Therefore, in this struggle between two tendencies of Spanish Socialism, the Party will emerge with the impetus of rejuvenation—with greater vitality, because it has to travel a new path and create for itself, along with new organs, a new reality.[80]

The possibility of Party disruption oppressed the minds of both factions as the Congress approached. Pablo Iglesias, the creator and as yet unimpugnable symbol of the Party, was too old and ill to think of attending; but he understood the divisive power of the forces unleashed by the Bolshevik Revolution and sensed the impending destruction of his life's labor. On the eve of the Congress he composed one of his infrequent articles for *El Socialista*, in which, with pathetic earnestness, he appealed to the Socialists' instinct for unity and urged that delegates be sent to both the Geneva and the Reconstructionist Congresses but not to Moscow. Pérez Solís, writing in the same issue, gloomily predicted the approaching "decomposition" of the Party.[81]

The left-centrists, by contrast, were more sanguine. Though pledged to Moscow and committed to infusing the Party with a more revolutionary spirit, they were nevertheless deeply concerned with unity. Few, if any, of them had accepted the need for purges or exclusions from the Party. Moscow's promulgation of the Twenty-one Conditions lay more than a month in the future, and most Terceristas agreed with Andrés Ovejero that the Comintern would make allowance for the "specific peculiarities of each country in the revolutionary process." They were certain that the Moscow leaders would not try to impose "immutable rules" on the adhering parties.[82]

The 1920 Socialist Party Congress

In fact, the 1920 Congress proved to be something of an anticlimax. Less than a handful of delegates were prepared to make a fight for either the Second or the Reconstructionist International, and the only real issue was whether to go to Moscow with or without conditions. Among the three or four who were willing to raise their voices on behalf of the old International was the brilliant and not always predictable Pérez Solís. Solís had recently been exiled from his long-time base in Valladolid for having libeled the Duke of Alba, the cacique of that region. He was at this moment seeking to create a new place for himself within the ranks of the Vizcayan labor movement headed by Indalecio Prieto, who had brought him to Bilbao to edit the Party journal, thinking him a kindred conservative Socialist.[83] Partly owing to the impact of the superheated Vizcayan environment on his impressionable nature, Pérez Solís would before long begin an evolution toward the far Left of the Party. But the spiritual travail through which he was passing had not yet affected his reformist ideology, and he continued to serve as a pillar of the Right in the 1920 Congress.

He refused, as he said, to let himself be carried along by "that sentimental movement" on behalf of the Russian Revolution. The day before the session began he had complained in *El Socialista* that "the god of success has a multitude of adorers," and that the Revolution in Russia had created a "dangerous illusion"—dangerous because the conditions that had produced it did not exist in other countries. For those in the West who expected a similar revolution within a brief span of time, he said, "the disenchantment will be terrible." He did not believe that adherence to Moscow would transform the spirit of the Spanish masses, which, he thought, would continue to be characterized by "pusillanimity."[84]

Thus, standing before a Congress in which the great majority professed to believe in the possibility of a social revolution in the near future and wished adherence to the Comintern, Solís admitted, with characteristic irony, that he had come to speak "in the name of something archaic: in the name of the Second International." Yet his remarks were more in the nature of an attack on the Russian Bolsheviks. To the irritation of the Terceristas, he hammered at what he believed to be a lack of congruence between the Revolution and the Communist International, insisting that the Bolsheviks were no more the "whole" of the Russian Revolution than the Jacobins had been of the French Revolution. It was also an error, said Solís, to imagine that adherence to the Comintern would mean an immediate upheaval in Spain, for "revolutions are not willed." In Russia the fall of the regime had come only after the country had reached a state of complete decomposition; and Spain, Solís submitted, was not yet in such a condition. "I know the realities of my country," he said, "and in spite of all the revolutionary verbiage, I do not believe in the revolutionary capacity of the Spanish people."[85]

One of the major objections that Pérez Solís had made to the Terceristas—and repeated on this occasion—was that they were merely verbal revolutionaries who did not accept the logic of their own violent rhetoric. Now, in concluding his far from popular speech, he delivered a curiously prophetic obiter dictum. Whereas he had earlier identified himself simply as a "lowly Menshevik," he now admitted: "There struggle in me the sentimental, romantic man and the man of scholarship ... of *cerebro*. If I were to let myself be carried along by sentiment, I would run toward those who proclaim the Third International, but with one condition: maximum violence." Solís acknowledged that by temperament he was an "extremist," and that if he were to accept the Third International, he would (presumably in contrast to many of the Terceristas) accept it "with all its consequences, without parliamentarianism, without collaboration of any sort, without *reclamaciones* to the ministers." For the Comintern, he said, rebuking the left-centrists, "is action, it is revolution. To enter into it is to go *to* the revolution, *by* the revolution, and *for* the revolution."[86]

In spite of the inflammatory conservatism of Pérez Solís, the 1920 Congress did not center around an ideological collision between the partisans of the Second and Third Internationals. When the vote was taken on the option of remaining in the old International, less than half a dozen hands were raised; thus the contest was simply between two different ways of adhering to the new Moscow organization. The resolution of the left-centrists, brought forward by García Cortés, Daniel Anguiano, Luis Mancebo, and Eduardo Vicente, called for immediate withdrawal from the Second and "unconditional entry" into the Third International. Among the tactics deemed appropriate for such a move were "uncompromising" class struggle, the unification of all Spanish workers, the proletarian dictatorship, and the system of workers' councils.[87]

The resolution of the right-centrists bore the names of the Asturians Isidoro Acevedo and José María Suárez and of the deputy from Granada, Fernando de los Ríos. It took note of the "understandable" but excessive influence of the Bolsheviks on the doctrines of the Third International and observed that this had led to a "doctrinal exclusiveness" and "dogmatism" that were prejudicial to the unification of all Socialist forces. It nevertheless called for adherence to the Comintern, but with a set of conditions that would both astonish and amuse the Moscow leaders: (1) The Socialist party would maintain its autonomy in all tactical questions, since tactics had to be conditioned by the situation of each moment and by the psychology of each people. (2) The PSOE would retain the right to revise in its congresses the doctrines of the Third International. (3) The PSOE would represent within the Comintern the ideal of the unification of all Socialist forces desiring to coexist under the same ideals, and would oppose all unjustified excommunications and dogmatisms, thereby aligning itself with the French Socialist Party and the German USPD; it would attend with this unifying purpose all congresses that might be held.[88]

The right-centrist resolution was thus a peculiar compromise between the Tercerista and Reconstructionist positions. Just as the year before the Party had gone to Berne in a spirit of unity with the Russians, so this year it would go to Moscow with the goal of reconciling all the European revolutionary Socialist parties.

Fernando de los Ríos, a grave and mellifluous orator and an authority on the agrarian problem, was a recent convert from the Republican Party and a man of brilliant, if somewhat professorial, intellect—an admirer of Albert Thomas, whom he resembled in appearance. He was known to be rather less than a revolutionary firebrand, and his support for the conditional entry of the PSOE into the Comintern was clearly motivated more by dire necessity and tactical shrewdness than by any inherent enthusiasm he felt. Indeed, with his lofty and immaculate presence, his well-trimmed beard, his sartorial conservatism, and his moderate, decent Socialism, he would become for the Russian Bolsheviks, after his confrontation with them in Moscow late in 1920, the incarnation of all they found wrong with Spanish Socialism. De los Ríos defended his resolution somewhat gloomily, noting that the failure of the Second International to carry out its duty in 1914 had made it necessary for the Spanish Socialists to withdraw from it; and once one had withdrawn from the Second, he regretfully noted, one could only go to the Third International, since despite its "nebulous character" it was the only nucleus with "sufficient attraction." But in its attractiveness, he thought, there was also a weakness: it would encourage the unfortunate propensity of the Spanish people to wish for a messiah to do for them what they could not do for themselves. Their "excessive confidence" in it might well be a source of failure.[89]

The unconditional Terceristas, led by García Cortés, Núñez de Arenas, Lamoneda, and Anguiano, immediately launched an all-out assault on the conditions demanded by the right-centrists. García Cortés, in an eloquent and ironic speech, asserted that with respect to the first condition the Moscow leaders had already recognized that different tactics were required in each country. As for the second condition, to accept it, he thought, would be to assert the doctrinal superiority of the PSOE and to set it up as the censor of all other parties. García Cortés thought this "a little bit grotesque" in view of the extremely limited number of comrades within the Spanish Party who possessed any deep knowledge of Marxist doctrines.[90]

Antonio Fabra Ribas, virtually alone, rose to defend the Reconstructionist position. He was followed by Besteiro, who delivered a bitter, dispirited speech, suffused with skepticism: he doubted the Terceristas' goal of trying to unify all the workers of Spain; he doubted that the soviets were a panacea; he doubted that the much maligned Second International had been, in fact, reformist; and he was gravely concerned that the extremists were "compromising the moral concept of the Party"—a reference, no doubt, to the Rotterdam episode. Largo Caballero made an equally inconclusive address, and it was clear that the leaders of the now badly shrunken right-centrist faction were seeking only to weather the storm of *izquierdismo* until better days arrived. The helm of the Congress was in the grasp of the leftists.[91]

This is not to suggest that all of the leftists present were satisfied with the proceedings. Up in the galleries, the belligerent young ultra-leftists of the

PCE—Andrade, Buendía, Illescas, Ugarte, Portela, and others—were present in force and were looking for an opportunity to disrupt the sessions. Discovering the Russian émigré and Menshevik journalist N. Tasin seated in the chamber, they began to bawl out protests, denouncing him as a "traitor" to the Socialist cause and as a "calumniator" of the Russian Bolsheviks—a man who should not be admitted to the Casa del Pueblo. When Besteiro and Largo Caballero announced that for reasons of courtesy Tasin would not be expelled, the young militants shouted imprecations at those esteemed leaders. Now the angry Socialists—temporarily suspending the proceedings—began advancing up the aisles toward the young disrupters seated high in the gallery, not knowing who they were or precisely what cause they represented. Fabra Ribas, leading the way, encountered amid the tumult Juan Andrade, who hurled an insult at him. "Who are you?" asked the startled Fabra. Andrade replied: "I am he who insults you in *El Comunista* every two weeks, and he who insults you now to your face. Shameless one! Traitor!" And, as Andrade later recalled with pride, "I accompanied the insult with a blow." Insults were also hurled at Manuel Llaneza and Indalecio Prieto; and before they were finally ejected from the Chamber, the young Communists managed to assault Tasin, Illescas delivering a blow that knocked the distinguished Russian down. More blows were struck, and pistols were even brandished. Andrade recalled with satisfaction, and perhaps with some exaggeration, that when his group finally departed, the salon looked like "a field of battle."[92]

In spite of everything, the business of the Congress was carried on, and, as the result of efforts by both sides, a disruptive confrontation between the two major factions was avoided. After further debate, in a tense but controlled atmosphere, the two pending resolutions were fused into one, this being a step designed to safeguard what both sides held dear—the unity of the Party—while permitting the longed-for rapprochement with Moscow. The pro-Bolshevik majority in the Congress gave up the phrase "unconditional entry," substituting "immediate entry," and the conditions stipulated in the de los Ríos resolution were accepted—but with the deletion of the final phrase implying that the PSOE might attend a Reconstructionist or some other conference before going to the Second Congress of the Comintern in Moscow. The vote on this measure, taken on June 19, was 8,269 in favor, 5,016 opposed (many of whom doubtless wanted unconditional entry), and 1,615 abstaining. At the urging of the absent Pablo Iglesias, a fourth condition was added later in the sessions to the effect that the PSOE would continue to participate in municipal councils, provincial assemblies, and the Cortes. This addendum reflected the rather widespread belief in labor circles that adherence to the Comintern required a renunciation of parliamentary activity, and it clearly did not meet with the disapproval of the highly electoral left-centrists.[93]

Thus the Socialist Party cast in its lot with the Comintern in the early summer of 1920, with evident relief that the ideological crisis had been weathered and the cherished unity preserved. Yet the adherence to Moscow had been given in an ambivalent form—so ambivalent that Fabra Ribas would write in *L'Humanité* that the resolution adopted "could be considered Reconstructionist," though he admitted that the deletion of the clause dealing with the sending of delegates to other congresses placed the PSOE in "une situation spéciale."[94] The crisis, in fact, had not been resolved but only deferred. When the Party's emissaries to Moscow arrived there later in the year, they would find that in the course of the Second Comintern Congress Lenin's authoritarian spirit—amplified by some of the more extreme delegates—had been distilled in the Twenty-one Conditions, which envisioned a quite centralized and disciplined international organization that would, in fact, impose "immutable rules" on its member parties. With respect to such an organization, so unlike the little-known and half-mythic Comintern of 1919–20, there could be no consensus within the PSOE, but only insoluble discord and division.[95]

New tactics called for new leaders, and the Executive Committee that had not favored the Comintern was now replaced by one that was overwhelmingly Tercerista. The new Committee included Antonio García Quejido, Daniel Anguiano, Ramón Lamoneda, César González, Antonio López Baeza, Manuel Núñez de Arenas, Andrés Ovejero, Luis Araquistáin, Antonio Fabra Ribas, and Fernando de los Ríos. Interestingly, the Congress had also returned Besteiro and Largo Caballero to the Committee; but these two, unreconciled to membership in the Comintern and unwilling to be in a minority, resigned and were replaced by García Cortés and de los Ríos. At the same time, de los Ríos and Anguiano were chosen to carry the Party's highly conditional adherence to Moscow and to negotiate entry into the Comintern. They immediately began preparations for their long journey.[96]

The UGT and the Comintern

The Unión General de Trabajadores held its Fourteenth Congress shortly after the close of the Socialist assembly. Since it was implicit in Spanish Socialist theory, which derived from the French Guesdists and the German SPD, that the trade unions were to be subordinated to the political leadership of the Party, the popular assumption was that the UGT would go as the Party had gone—toward Moscow. The Socialist trade unions, after all, had expanded rapidly in this period, rising from 89,601 in July 1918 to 211,342 in May 1920.[97] The workers who flooded in included large contingents from Andalusia, Asturias, and Vizcaya, and these would seem to have been as much under the spell of the Russian Revolution as the many workers who entered the unions of the CNT at the same time.

But to the surprise of most, the Congress proved singularly docile and voted overwhelmingly to remain within the conservative Amsterdam International, the syndical counterpart of the Second International. It was not the decision to stay with Amsterdam that elicited surprise, however, but the onesidedness of the vote and the fact that the Terceristas proved unable to mount a vigorous campaign on behalf of the Comintern. This was typical of the experience of trade-union organizations in other Western countries in this period; and it reflected, in part, the fact that no clear alternative to the Amsterdam International had yet emerged, since the Red International of Labor Unions had not yet been proclaimed. But one would not have expected a Spanish labor organization to behave like the German Trade Union Federation. Conditions in Spain were not typical of Western Europe; and despite assertions to the contrary,[98] it is questionable that the Spanish labor movement contained substantial elements whose mentality would justify calling them a "labor aristocracy." Spain would seem to have been one of the few countries in the West in which the revolutionary spirit of the workers had not been seriously dampened by the reflection that they had something substantial to lose if a revolutionary upheaval occurred. The fear of being reduced to "Russian standards" could not be a significant deterrent to revolutionary enthusiasm in the Iberian Peninsula.

Thus the explanation for the overwhelming defeat of the Comintern at the UGT congress should be sought less in the mood of the Ugetista masses than in the anxieties of a power structure dominated by a cohort of long-term reformist leaders. This structure was buttressed both by Socialist mores, which emphasized bureaucratic continuity and authority, and by the syndical principles of Pablismo, which stressed craft as opposed to industrial unionism. Craft organization, here as everywhere else, minimized the impact of mass enthusiasms while maximizing the influence of entrenched leaders. That the leaders of the UGT were strongly positioned was largely owing to the Socialist insistence on paid and permanent officials, who comprised a syndical bureaucracy in which the Michelsian law of oligarchy had had more or less free rein for decades.[99]

Thus the challenge of the Russian Revolution again pointed up a basic difference between the two major labor organizations in the Peninsula. It revealed that the Socialists' rival, the CNT, was an anomaly, almost a contradiction in terms: a mass trade-union organization that steadfastly retained its antibureaucratic and revolutionary spirit. This was little less than a tour de force, achieved only at the price of an extremely open, hence vulnerable, organizational structure—run by amateurs, one might say—that was directly influenced by mass emotions and easily penetrated by zealous minorities. The UGT, by contrast, though its legions were equally febrile, was revealed to be under the control of a relatively permanent corps of functionaries—pragmatic and prudent men who preferred to deal with things material, immediate, and concrete and who were only embarrassed by upsurges of primordial enthusiasm. It was precisely for these reasons, of course, that the UGT had not, in this era of pro-Bolshevik excitement, grown as rapidly as its rival. Neither would it decline so precipitously when the élan of the masses began to fade.[100]

Francisco Largo Caballero

Francisco Largo Caballero, as general secretary of the UGT since 1918, had readied the organization to withstand the onslaught of the Terceristas, and was himself well prepared to fight for reformist internationalism. Born in the Chamberí district of Madrid in 1869, Largo experienced a Dickensian childhood. Like three other great figures of the labor movement—Pablo Iglesias, Indalecio Prieto, and Angel Pestaña—he lost his father at an early age, in his case as the result of a separation when he was four years old. He received the equivalent of a third-grade education in church schools before being sent out to seek employment at the age of seven; and from that time he toiled in the workshops of the capital, constructing paper boxes, binding books, and making rope. At the age of nine he found his métier as a plasterer—then considered the "aristocratic" trade within the construction industry—and revealed his precocity by becoming, at 16, a master (with two apprentices) in the trade he would actively pursue until 1905.[101]

In May 1890 Largo, then 21, was employed on a project in the Fuencarral district of Madrid when he heard for the first time about Pablo Iglesias. Fellow workers returning from a May Day celebration told him that the Socialist leader, speaking on behalf of the newly founded UGT, had urged the workers to unite in *sociedades de resistencia* in order to force the government to decree the eight-hour day. Although he himself had not even seen Iglesias, this, strange as it may seem, was Largo's Road to Damascus, and he returned home that evening filled with a consuming ambition to become a labor organizer.[102] Immediately quitting the Fuencarral project, he soon organized the Madrid Plasterers' Society; and not long afterward he joined the UGT, whose headquarters, run by García Quejido, were at that time in Barcelona. Only after four years of active work in the UGT did Largo join the Socialist Party, becoming a member of the Madrid Socialist Group. It was the trade-union movement that became the almost obsessive focus of his life; and it was not only his great ability but also his extreme attention to the performance of his syndical duties and to the minutiae of organizational life that gave him his ascendancy in the movement.[103] About the time he formed the Plasterers' Society he finally met Pablo Iglesias, whose simple words, he later recalled, were like light in the "darkness" of his mind. Iglesias again spoke of the need for organization; and in view of the pertinacity of his remarks, it seemed "incredible" to Largo that the workers should continue to permit themselves to be victims of capitalist exploitation.[104]

A plasterers' strike on behalf of the eight-hour day, organized by Largo in the fall of 1890, was the first official strike of the UGT in Madrid. It was a thorough success and validated, to his satisfaction, the superiority of Socialist methods over those of the Anarchists, who were strongly opposed to the Ugetistas' emphasis on permanent strike funds, regular dues, and trust in governmental action, as in the establishment of maximum working hours. Nor would Largo forget the hatreds generated by the struggles of those days. By a process of mutual repulsion, he felt compelled to become, as a labor leader, everything that the Anarchists were not: cautious, disciplined, organizational, dispassionate, and essentially reformist. He emerged, in fact, as the proto-typical labor bureaucrat, a man in whom hard beginnings had failed to nour-ish the more spontaneous human qualities. Austere, self-contained, sparing of words, often caustic or even morose, his vision was focused more on the foot-hills of labor aspiration than on the towering but distant ranges that some of his fellow Socialists discerned. This is to say that he was almost completely absorbed in the day-to-day struggle to win tangible benefits for one of the most impoverished working classes in Europe.[105]

If the Marxism of Iglesias was uncomplicated, that of Largo Caballero was primitive, amounting to little more than ingrained hostility toward the capital-ist class—something he had learned from experience rather than from books—and a conviction that the salvation of the working class lay in organization and political action. His "Socialism" was essentially the belief that the work-ers had to participate in the political process in order to consolidate the gains they might win in economic struggle against their employers. The achieve-ment of "small gains," he thought, would not diminish but strengthen the workers' ability in some remote future to appropriate to themselves the in-struments of production and distribution. Though quite intelligent, Largo was no intellectual and was willing to leave theory to the professors and jour-nalists, retaining as his political adviser in these years, for example, the mod-erate Menshevik Fabra Ribas. One may believe his admission that he did not read *Das Kapital* until 1931; and it may be wondered with what absorption he had read the Communist Manifesto. That he would someday become the "Lenin" of Spanish Socialism could not, in this era, have been foretold.[106]

The turning point in Largo's early career was his election to the Madrid municipal council in 1905, after which he ceased active work as a plasterer and became a full-time functionary of the UGT. By the time of the 1920 Congress he had held many other important offices: president of Mutualidad Obrera; membership on the Committee of the Institute of Social Reforms; president of the Madrid Socialist Group; membership on the 1917 August Strike com-mittee; deputy to the Cortes; and, by decision of the 1918 Congress, general secretary of the UGT. Early in 1919 he attended the labor conference at Berne as the representative of the UGT, and later that year he traveled to Amsterdam to participate in the constituent congress of the so-called Amsterdam International. Here he spoke with particular vigor against the Spanish campaign in Morocco, urging that it be brought to an end as quickly yet as honorably as possible. But his Sisyphean spirit, as we have seen, had not been uplifted by the Russian Revolution, and he seems always to have regarded this phenomenon with the dour eye of a functionary, as an intrusive and disruptive force with dubious applicability in the Spanish context.[107]

The UGT Rejects the Comintern

Largo and the other oligarchs of the PSOE-UGT, having so recently lost control of the Party to the Terceristas, were determined to cling all the more tenaciously to the trade-union movement and to keep it securely in the orbit of Amsterdam. The atmosphere of the UGT Congress, which met in late June, was less democratic and far more controlled than that of the Party gathering in the same month. The young Communists of the PCE were not far wrong when they condemned the machinations of Largo Caballero's *caciquillos* in the provinces and the "nearly perfect interlocking of the bureaucratic machine."[108] A substantial number of delegates from the outlying areas (especially Andalusia) appear to have been chosen by Largo himself, and an unusually large number of proxy votes were in the hands of the National Committee. The result was a relatively innocuous agenda, with carefully regulated sessions in which the pro-Comintern forces were helpless to affect the course of events. Only three sections in the entire federation were able to muster enough votes within their ranks to request the entry of the UGT into the Comintern, and the issue was never for a moment in doubt. The leaders were clearly determined to prevent an adherence to the Comintern at all costs; for this action would also have logically required the fusion of the UGT with the CNT on terms that could only lead to the displacement of the conservative, established heads of the Socialist organization. The PCE's few delegates, Illescas among them, deplored the "total lack" of revolutionary spirit in the Congress and struggled, unsuccessfully, to bring before it two resolutions: unification of all labor forces on a revolutionary, that is, pro-Comintern, basis; and the establishment of workers' councils.[109]

The debate on the Comintern issue centered around the question of whether or not the Spanish proletariat was ready for revolution. Against the conviction of the Terceristas that the country was in a "completely prerevolutionary" phase, the hierarchs of the UGT argued that despite appearances a genuinely revolutionary situation did not exist, and that separation from Amsterdam and adherence to Moscow would therefore be inappropriate and unwise. Perhaps the dominant figure in the Congress, apart from Largo Caballero, was the powerful boss of the Asturian miners, Manuel Llaneza.[110] Llaneza had performed well in August 1917 but had apparently lost whatever taste for revolution he had once had. He opposed going to Moscow, he said, because it would mean the renunciation of the quest for immediate economic benefits and would prevent the workers from seeking government intervention in industrial conflicts. He believed in any case that Spanish workers still lacked sufficient class consciousness to make a successful revolution and were in the grip of an egoistic preoccupation with material gains. José María Suárez, head of the UGT in Oviedo, echoed Llaneza, saying that although in terms of "sentiment" there was indeed a revolutionary ambience, in terms of *fuerza* there was not.[111] Largo Caballero, joining the debate, bolstered the anti-Comintern offensive of the leadership by stressing the large membership and great power of the Amsterdam International and suggesting the unwisdom of breaking with such a potent organization, especially in view of the fact that the Spanish labor movement was momentarily gaining greater recognition than ever before in the ranks of the International.

Most speakers at the Congress argued along similar lines, and the few voices raised on behalf of the Comintern were in vain. When the question of adherence to Moscow was put to the test, it was overwhelmingly rejected, by a vote of 110,902 to 17,919. Thus for the first time in the history of Spanish Socialism a wedge was driven between the trade unions and the Party; and the PSOE was left as a general staff cut off from the masses without whom its new, Moscow-oriented revolutionary tactics would be of little use. In order to emphasize this, Largo Caballero, in a remarkable departure from his usual taciturnity, pointedly informed a reporter for *La Voz* that the UGT would not again be drawn into a political strike like that of 1917, that is, into a strike whose purpose was to substitute a bourgeois republic for the monarchy—which was to say, in effect, that the UGT would not be available for any type of revolutionary action.[112]

Yet the Ugetista leaders did not want to seem wholly opposed to prevailing labor currents; and the Congress was careful to declare that despite the severe rebuff given to the UGT in the 1919 assembly of the CNT, further efforts should be made to unify the two major labor organizations of the Peninsula. The sincerity of this gesture was, no doubt, open to question, but it would appear to have expressed the feelings of the Ugetista rank and file, who, like the Cenetista masses, seem always to have favored the uniting of the two organizations and to have been less impressed than their leaders by ideological and other obstacles to unity.[113]

Thus in August 1920 the UGT National Committee once more wrote to the heads of the CNT to urge that a unification congress be held. This time prospects were more favorable. Whereas in the Congress of the Comedia the Cenetistas had succumbed to a hubris that blinded them to the realities of their situation, by mid-1920 they had been to some degree chastened by adversity. The Confederation at this moment had only just emerged from a period of repression and clandestine existence under the harsh governorship of Count Salvatierra; and the respite under Dato, who became prime minister in May, would be very brief. Consequently, the UGT initiative found the Anarchosyndicalist leaders in a more receptive mood than they had displayed during the whole course of 1919—receptive, in fact, to a new labor alliance not unlike the one that shook Spain in 1917.[114] Before turning to the domestic tribulations of the Catalonian Syndicalists in 1920, however, it will be necessary to follow the several delegations—Anarchosyndicalist, Socialist, and Communist—that Spanish workers sent to Moscow during the summer of this turbulent year in order to convey their support for the Russian Revolution and their desire to join the Communist International.

CHAPTER TEN

The Road to Moscow

The Spanish revolutionary Left—ardent in its support of Bolshevism but divided as always—sent three separate delegations to Moscow in the summer of 1920 to carry its adherence to the Comintern and to investigate the realities of the new Soviet order. The Anarchosyndicalists were represented by Angel Pestaña, the Communists by Ramón Merino Gracia, and the Socialists by Fernando de los Ríos and Daniel Anguiano—the last two delegations arriving too late to participate in the labors of the Second Comintern Congress, whose sessions began on July 22. Because they entered Russia at different times, the several Spanish emissaries would make only limited contact with one another. And separated as they were by barriers of ideology and organizational amour propre, the three delegations would have little more in common than the illusions they all shared regarding the libertarian and permissive character of the Communist International.

What the Spaniards would discover in Moscow was that the spirit of the Comintern had undergone a transformation since its First Congress. As a result of the revolutionary failures of 1919 in Hungary and in Germany, the earlier reliance of the Bolshevik leaders on the essential spontaneity of the revolutionary advance had yielded to a recognition that the process would be more protracted than they had supposed. Thus the early months of 1920 saw in the diplomatic sphere a phase of detente between the Soviets and the Western powers, while in the realm of revolutionary tactics the Bolsheviks were placing ever greater stress on the need for a more centralized, long-range guidance of the international revolutionary movement. This revised approach to the problem of world revolution was forcefully articulated in Lenin's *"Left-wing" Communism, an infantile disorder*, published at the end of April, and not even the optimism created by the sweep of the Red Army toward Warsaw in July would alter the authoritarian trend. For the new realism, though mainly a result of the disappointments of 1919, harmonized with the deeper impulses and Jacobin proclivities of Lenin and his colleagues and was reinforced by the renewed self-confidence they had gained from their almost miraculous victory over the forces of the counterrevolution in Russia.[1]

The Bolshevik leaders were now more convinced than ever of the applicability of the Russian revolutionary experience to all other nations, and they adopted an increasingly tutorial attitude toward the Socialist and Syndicalist movements of Europe. Lenin insisted that "Not a few but all of the fundamental and many of the secondary features of our revolution are of international significance.... At the present moment in history the situation is precisely such that the Russian model reveals to all countries something, and something very essential, of their near and inevitable future." And the essential thing revealed, he believed, was the indispensability of "absolute centralization and the strictest discipline."[2] Thus the Bolshevik leader reasserted, in effect, the importance of Party control and institutionalized dictatorship—two elements that had been muted in his 1917 pamphlet *State and revolution*. He now insisted that European Socialists and Syndicalists disabuse themselves of the notion of an essentially democratic or spontaneous revolution, to which so many of them still clung. Trotsky drove home the same point with his pamphlet *Terrorism and Communism*, in which he asserted that one who aimed at the end could not reject the means but had, rather, to accept revolution's ineluctable corollary: dictatorship and repression.[3] The distribution of Lenin's and Trotsky's authoritarian pamphlets among the delegates to the Second Congress, then, symbolized the Bolsheviks' hardening attitude toward precisely those illusions—whether democratic or decentralist—that the Spanish delegates were carrying with them to Russia.[4]

The Pestaña Mission

The Anarchosyndicalist delegation to Moscow was chosen immediately after the Congress of the Comedia in December 1919, at which, it will be recalled, the adherence of the CNT to the Comintern had been impetuously proclaimed. Not wishing the organization's adherence to be "merely platonic," the Committee of the CRT, to whom the task had been delegated, chose three prominent militants to go abroad. Since the Catalan organization was under increasingly severe pressure as a result of the lockout launched in November, the initial task of the newly appointed emissaries was to contact labor organizations in France, Italy, and elsewhere in order to induce them to join in a retaliatory boycott of Spanish exports. Only after concluding this mission were they to rendezvous in Berlin and from there proceed to Moscow. The three men chosen were Angel Pestaña, Salvador Quemades, and Eusebio Carbó, only the last of these being a fervent partisan of Bolshevism. Since Carbó was jailed in Italy and Quemades unable to advance farther than Paris, it was left to Pestaña to make the journey from Berlin to Moscow alone. Only in Berlin, moreover, did the Cenetista leader learn of the summoning of the Second Comintern Congress and obtain from the CRT in Barcelona authorization to continue on his journey as a delegate to that body.[5]

In Berlin Pestaña encountered Alfred Rosmer of the French CGT, and the two men—after participating in a stirring march down Unter den Linden to protest against Pilsudski—traveled together toward Moscow. Their route took them by train from Berlin to Stettin, from there by boat to Revel, and from Revel to Petrograd, again by train. Pestaña passed the hours, as Rosmer later recalled, talking optimistically about the revolutionary situation in Spain, which it seemed to him had never been more favorable.* As he crossed the frontier into Russia some three months after his departure from Barcelona, even Pestaña—an unemotional Leonese who had never been very ardent about the Revolution—admitted that his first sensations were "enthusiasm, admiration, and intense joy," and he confessed to a "momentary disequilibrium." But he was also sobered by the sad faces of the Russian multitudes, which reflected, he thought, the "immense martyrdom" they had suffered: "Not one smile, not one flash of joy, not the slightest manifestation of happiness.... And an impenetrable silence. It seemed as though those mouths had never spoken or smiled."⁶ Pestaña would be haunted throughout his 70-day sojourn in Russia by this silent suffering, which he encountered at every turn. Looking at endless boulevards and buildings gaudily covered with enormous banners, and at the thousands of red flags flying over the rooftops of Petrograd, his practical and puritanical mind could only reflect on the sacrifices that this revolutionary ostentation imposed on the ragged workers of the city.⁷

The Evolution of an Anarchist

Pestaña's compassion stemmed in part from the fact that he himself had risen from the ranks of the disinherited, and it would be well at this point to say something about his origins and ideological evolution. Born in the Leonese village of Santo Tomás de las Ollas in 1886, he was the only son of a rough, wife-beating construction worker. His mother fled from her husband while Pestaña was still an infant, and he was raised by his father, who in the late 1880's and 1890's traveled around the north of Spain digging railroad tunnels or working in the mines. The elder Pestaña, although a "perfect Voltairian," wanted his clever son to study for the priesthood, regarding this as a trade rather like that of miner, bricklayer, or carpenter, but more lucrative. His hope was that his son would not become the "work-burro" that he had been. However, at the age of 11 Angel went to work as a cookhouse helper in a mining camp at Cobarón, Vizcaya, where his father then worked; and he traveled with his parent in a constant search for employment:

* Rosmer recalled the layover in Revel: "The hours passed; Pestaña had found a subject of conversation that he was always happy to develop: the present situation of Spain, more favorable to the overthrow of the Alfonsine regime than it had ever been. For the first time, in effect, revolutionary unrest was not confined to Catalonia, among the workers; it was developing in parallel fashion in the agricultural regions of the South.... The peasants were in revolt, and their movement had gained sufficient breadth to make not only possible but urgent the joining of the two movements." *Moscou sous Lénine*, p. 54.

From Cobarón we returned to Castro Urdiales, from there to Sopuerta, from there to La Cena, to Galdames, to La Arboleda, and to other places in the mining region of Vizcaya. Then we went to work on the railroad from Bilbao to San Sebastián.... Then to Zarauz, where we worked the whole time in the boring of a tunnel, returning again to Bilbao, where we worked for some time, my father in the mines and I carrying buckets.[8]

It was in this period that Pestaña received the only formal education he was to have: a few months in each of several elementary schools in such places as Las Barrietas and Castro Urdiales. He would later claim a total of two years schooling in all; yet he possessed great native intelligence and a sensitivity and idealism that belied the harshness of his beginnings.[9]

When Pestaña was 14 his father died of pneumonia contracted in the mines, and he found himself alone, abandoned by his father's "friends," in the grim, anomic world of the mining zone, where the struggle for life was too hard and the mixture of provincial types too disparate to permit feelings even of human, much less proletarian, solidarity. "That was my first encounter with life," he later wrote. "Never until then did I understand human ingratitude or the hardness of feeling created by poverty."[10] He now went to work as a miner, digging coal for two pesetas per 12-hour day but never ceasing to observe the life around him:

The only thing to study in that atmosphere was the men. And they presented themselves naked... [since] their ignorance, which was extreme, prevented them from knowing how to feign.... Before my gaze... there daily filed past types worthy of the closest attention. The most common type was the *aventurero*, a mixture of violence and cruelty. A violent type. A type both violent and mean-spirited. Since those groups [of miners] were composed of motley elements, each one looking out only for himself, they practiced a ferocious individualism. In addition, the misery of their condition caused a habitual mean-mindedness toward others and toward themselves. Vizcainos, Asturianos, Aragoneses, Navarros, and Gallegos—one may say that these represented 90 percent of the mining population of the *cuenca vizcaina* of those days. Without doubt the majority were usually Gallegos.... Among the blasphemies, oaths, gross and vile phrases, and immoral exclamations—but all said without malice, with the greatest naturalness in the world, [in compensation] for the sexual continence that the lack of women imposed—I went along growing and understanding life and men, educating myself and learning.[11]

Leaving the mines, Pestaña worked for a time on the rail line that was then being extended from La Robla to Valmaseda; and from there he gravitated to the railyards of Bilbao, where he worked cleaning locomotives. He soon acquired the ambition to become a fireman, but was instead demoted for refusing to divulge to his foreman the author of a satirical picture scrawled on a wall. His motivation destroyed, he began to neglect his duties and was soon fired. In this manner, he believed, the "whole course" of his life was changed: "From that moment the incentive that I carried in me, which had made me love the locomotives, now moved me to open rebellion against the source of my misfortune."[12]

Meanwhile, the versatile Pestaña had become interested in theatrical life and was working part-time as a wardrobe assistant in the theater of Arriaga, which permitted him to attend performances, to earn 40 centimos every night, and to familiarize himself with a different world. There now followed jobs in a foundry in Deusto, on a construction project in Basurto, and as a bricklayer on various construction sites. For two months during the winter of 1903–4 he went without employment, sleeping in freight cars and going for days without food while, "hungry, half-naked, and barefoot," he sought employment in the streets of Bilbao. Yet it was in this same period that Pestaña, along with some other rootless youths, formed an "artistic group" called the Lope de Vega, which managed to obtain engagements in small-town theaters near Bilbao, during which the dour Pestaña played guitar accompaniment for flamenco singers.[13]

Pestaña's "initiation into the social question" came while he was still working in the railyards of Bilbao, as the result of reading an article in the Anarchist journal *El Obrero Moderno*, published in Murcia. His account of his conversion is worth recording:

> Since I did not understand the doctrinal and philosophical articles, my preferences were for the literary and the sentimental. Among these I found one in which the author related, with powerful emotion, [the story of] his life, broken and destroyed by his experiences in the war . . . which stirred me to the depths of my being. But emotion was changed into an inexplicable curiosity when, in the last paragraphs of the article, the author said that such evils would end, [and that there would be established] on earth the reign of love, justice, and fraternity.
>
> I had always heard it said that the Anarchists held secret meetings [in which] they cast lots in order to go and kill kings, ministers, and notables; that the bomb, the dagger, and extermination were their laws; that their purpose was the destruction of the human race by fire and assassination. Now I found myself reading something that told me the Anarchists . . . wanted equality, fraternity, and love among men. Perhaps there will be still other Anarchists, I thought. And with this hope I read and reread the article four or five times. My whole being was moved by the misfortune of that man who saw his life broken, truncated, ruined by having been in the war.[14]

Pestaña finally discovered among the railyard workers an authentic Anarchist, who introduced him to other Anarchists and supplied newspapers and pamphlets that the young Leonese read avidly. At length he became a convert to the Anarchist faith, which clearly filled a spiritual void in his existence and appealed to his idealistic nature:

My fellow worker spoke of Anarchism with such reverence, with such sentiment, with such emotion; there was in his words such love and such generosity for men and for things . . . I acquired the conviction that the ideal [of Anarchism], which elevated man so high, which made him so good, which formed him so comprehensively, was the ideal of human perfection, of absolute justice, of the reign of fraternity among men.[15]

With the security of the neophyte, who believes that he has seen in the haze of his dreams the God in whom he believes, I began to work for those ideas, which I had not examined, and was absolutely ignorant of, but in which I believed with the disinterest and sincerity with which one believes in the ideal . . . desiring not his own benefit but the general good. Little by little, I was accustoming myself to the prophetic tone with which the propagandists of Anarchism always expressed themselves. And I myself, in the first years of my activity, did the same.[16]

Meanwhile, the rootless Pestaña continued to work at an astonishing variety of jobs, one after another: as a packer in a mirror factory, as a boilermaker, as a farm laborer, and in various other capacities. His first arrest came around 1906 in the town of Sestao, as the result of his having given a speech on behalf of the eight-hour day. Carried off to jail and brutally beaten, he was left for weeks in a damp underground cell without bed or blankets. After his release he continued as a member of the peripatetic flamenco group, playing engagements in Torrelavega, Cabezón de la Sal, Llanes, Oviedo, Sama de Langreo, and Gijón. In Gijón he finally left the band, deciding that he no longer cared for "that kind of life."[17] His conversion to Anarchism was bringing out the latent puritanism in his nature—he no longer drank, for example—and expanding his social consciousness as well. Learning that he was again being sought for trial because of his Sestao speech, he now fled to France, where he spent nearly two years as an itinerant laborer. The first real trade he acquired was that of sandalmaker, learned from an Aragonese expatriate, which he practiced in the city of Bordeaux, where he also married and began to acquire some stability.

Around 1908 Pestaña moved to Algiers, gave up sandalmaking, and, as the result of a "fortuitous accident," acquired the trade of watchmaker, which enabled him to earn 45 francs per week. His interest in the Anarchist movement continued, and it was during his sojourn in Algeria that he published his first article in *Tierra y Libertad*, entitled "El comunismo entre los mormones."[18] The Tragic Week in 1909 fired his imagination and first planted in his mind the idea of someday moving to Barcelona. But it required the French mobilization in 1914, which immediately threw Pestaña out of work, to force his decision to move, in August of the same year. In Barcelona he quickly found employment as a watchmaker in the Calle de la Cera. He also immediately visited the offices of *Tierra y Libertad*, making known his arrival to his *compañeros de ideas*, and obtained an interview with the "old fighter" Anselmo Lorenzo, who had only a few months to live and could not have guessed that the solemn young Leonese would become one of the great leaders of the CNT.[19]

Pestaña paid a visit to the Centro Obrero and also joined the Ateneo Sindicalista, whose members were even then being agitated by the theme of Anarchism versus Syndicalism. His first participation in the affairs of the Barcelona labor movement was a speech on this question, in which he impressed his audience by the ease with which he talked but also by the fact that he spoke in Castilian—which led to a brief flurry of speculation that he was a labor spy. Pestaña continued to join in the debates of the Ateneo in subsequent weeks, wrote some articles for *Tierra y Libertad*, and, rather quickly, gained a certain prominence. Above all, he made himself known by his participation in meetings and lectures. What was curious, as he himself acknowledged, was that he was able to take part in labor activities, gaining prominence and considerable influence, without belonging to any sindicato or other labor organization. For by now he had established his watchmaking shop in his own home and belonged only to the Watchmakers' Guild, which was not a part of the local federation of Barcelona trade unions and which, "given its particularist character, ... remained aloof from the genuinely *obrero* milieu." Pestaña's voice and pen alone enabled him to win in a few months a place in the Barcelona labor movement that might have required years to gain in a different organizational context.[20]

Pestaña's first major role in the CNT was as a delegate to the abortive anti-war congress summoned by the Anarchosyndicalists in El Ferrol in May 1915. In the ensuing months he rendered valuable service as an organizer and agitator in the efforts then being made to unionize women workers in the textile industry. But in the latter half of 1915 he again had to flee to France, this time as the result of an intemperate article in *Tierra y Libertad*, which ran him afoul of the Law of Jurisdictions. After his return to Barcelona in 1916, he achieved his biggest step on the road to power and influence within the CNT by gaining appointment as editor of *Solidaridad Obrera*. Though never brilliant as a journalist, Pestaña was chosen because it was felt that his ability and integrity would enable him to redeem the Syndicalist organ, which had fallen into disrepute. For some time "Soli" had not been adequately financed by the Barcelona Local Federation, and its directors, in order to continue publication, had secretly decided to accept money from the German embassy in return for printing occasional pro-German articles. This explained, for example, the campaign that the journal had waged against the emigration of Spanish workers to France. The paper had even agreed to carry cabaret advertising. The result of all this was that it completely lost its popularity with the Barcelona workers, who on one occasion organized a boycott against it. Pestaña, however, proved able to rehabilitate the journal, to restore its reputation, and, through his exposé of Bravo Portillo's pro-German espionage in 1918, to clear it of any Germanophile taint.[21]

In all his activities Pestaña revealed qualities of prudence, moderation, and tact that distinguished him from the more febrile Anarchists. Indeed, the ever more responsible role that he played in the Catalonian labor movement inevitably led him away from "pure" Anarchist principles; and although he had always thought of himself primarily as an Anarchist, his close identification with the Syndicalist movement increasingly caused him to share the concern of Salvador Seguí and other moderates for short-term gains, as well as their desire to avoid rash actions that might imperil the life of the organization. Quite rapidly, though perhaps unconsciously, Pestaña made the transition from Anarchist ideologue to Syndicalist functionary. Despite his efforts to maintain contacts with the "pure" Anarchists of *Tierra y Libertad*, a rift gradually opened between him and those intransigents, so that by the summer of 1920 they regarded him as lost to the cause.[22] Even the nervous Interior Minister of 1919, Manuel Burgos y Mazo, saw in him a moderate who, in contrast to the extreme Anarchosyndicalists, wished to avoid precipitous actions, at least until the Syndicalist movement was better organized.[23]

It is hardly surprising, then, that Pestaña's response to the Bolshevik Revolution was from the beginning somewhat subdued, in sharp contrast to that of the extreme Cenetistas. He never spoke against it, but his remarks in praise of it were conspicuous mainly by their absence. Not in the Congress of Sans, in the Congress of the Comedia, or in the pages of *Solidaridad Obrera* had he uttered any paeans to the Revolution. Probably he shared Seguí's fear that the Bolshevik example might lure Spanish workers into premature rebellion. Although somewhat more of a revolutionary optimist than Seguí, Pestaña, like any "pure" Syndicalist, always stressed the need for prudence and organizational preparation and opposed putschist tactics. In the end, the revolutionary-reformist dualism that characterized so many Cenetista leaders remained; and it is this circumstance that helps to explain the peculiarity of Pestaña's behavior in Moscow, where he would appear in the guise of an intransigent Anarchist while obscuring (perhaps unconsciously) his essential moderation with ringing libertarian phrases. Especially on the question of the proletarian dictatorship he would be more adamantly doctrinaire than many of his Anarchosyndicalist colleagues in Spain, who were even then being won over to the concept. Still, the suspicion arises that his rejection of the dictatorship stemmed less from its clash with libertarian principles than from his own unacknowledged lack of an urgent and authentic revolutionary impulse.*

* This is not to suggest that Pestaña was involved in any conscious deception. Rather, he was, in my opinion, in the grip of a revolutionary "false consciousness." In Spain, where he was in touch with concrete reality, he was, in effect, a moderate Syndicalist;

The Second Comintern Congress

In Petrograd Pestaña met Zinoviev for the first time and was among the delegates accompanying the Comintern leader on a special train that carried them to Moscow on the eve of the Second Congress. It was in the course of this journey that he discerned Zinoviev's almost complete ignorance of the Spanish labor movement. Yet the atmosphere was cordial, and it was evident that the Bolsheviks were eager to win over the European Syndicalists even as they sought to wean them from their ultra-Left propensities. When one of the delegates refused a bowl of soup in the dining car, Zinoviev laughingly said, "Faut la manger; c'est la discipline!"[24]

Arriving in Moscow the delegates were driven immediately to the headquarters of the Communist International. Here Pestaña, Rosmer, and the other Syndicalists attended a special session of the Comintern Executive Committee (ECCI) held to proclaim the founding of the Red International of Labor Unions (RILU), which would operate parallel to the Comintern and in opposition to the recently resurrected and reformist Amsterdam International. This news apparently came as a surprise to Pestaña. Although an article by the Russian trade-union leader Tsyperovich urging the formation of a Syndicalist International had been read at the Congress of the Comedia, he claimed not to have heard of the proposed organization until his arrival in Russia, and he carried no instructions from the CNT regarding it. Trouble arose at once in the form of a manifesto entitled "To the Syndicalists of all nations," which had been drawn up beforehand by the man who would head the new organization, A. Lozovsky, aided by the British Syndicalist J. T. Murphy and in consultation with Lenin. This document, presented to the newly arrived Syndicalist delegates as a fait accompli, clearly implied the subordination of the world Syndicalist movement to Communist political leadership. In addition to affirming the need for the dictatorship of the proletariat, it also spoke of the necessity for a "close and indestructible alliance between the Communist parties and the trade unions."[25]

The authentic Syndicalists present at this meeting were not slow to grasp

---

in Russia, where he bore no responsibilities, he could give free rein to his principles. Certainly the *informe* that he wrote at the request of the Second Congress was convincingly Anarchist in tone. In this document Pestaña was at pains to stress the "federative" structure of the CNT and to insist that the results obtained through it had been "so satisfactory that [the Cenetistas] would not agree to give them up at any cost." With a hint of defiance, he added: "[They] have no strike funds, or mutual aid, or cooperatives. They form only a revolutionary organization of class struggle, in the heart of which the Anarchists exercise a preponderant influence, to the point that we could say they orient and direct it." Pestaña, "Rapport de la confederation nationale du travail," *Le mouvement communiste international*, pp. 188–89. Nevertheless, Pestaña's "intransigence" was more evident in Moscow than in Barcelona.

the implications of the document. The German Anarchosyndicalist Augustin Souchy was perhaps the most forthright in his opposition, attacking the concept of the proletarian dictatorship and advocating Communism "without dictatorship or dictators." Jack Tanner of the British Shop Stewards was less resistant, accepting the need for a transitional dictatorship but urging that it be in fact a dictatorship of the workers' organizations. Pestaña, though obviously dismayed by Lozovsky's manifesto, was anxious to be cooperative. He noted that the commitment of the CNT to apolitical tactics, along with its opposition to the conquest of political power, clearly separated it from the RILU manifesto. But he also acknowledged that the Congress of the Comedia had given its adherence to the Comintern; and this fact, he thought, made it incumbent upon him to accept the manifesto, since to do otherwise (he believed) would have the effect of nullifying the decision of the congress. Nevertheless, he pointed out to the members of the ECCI that everything in the manifesto relating to the proletarian dictatorship, the seizure of power, and the cooperation of Syndicalists with Communist parties would be subject to whatever reservations the CNT might impose. Pestaña urged, in fact, that the document be amended; but the pro-Bolshevik majority refused to consider this, and in the end the Spaniard placed his signature on the document, on behalf of an alleged 1,000,000 Spanish Syndicalists. His willingness to do so reflected not merely the skillful pressure applied by the Bolsheviks but the fact that he had not yet taken their measure and did not wish to begin the revolutionary collaboration—which he knew to be greatly desired by nearly all Cenetistas—with an act of obstruction.[26]

Pestaña also clashed with the Bolshevik majority of the ECCI over a paragraph in the manifesto that condemned the "treason" of the Syndicalist organizations during the war. Insisting that most of the revolutionary Syndicalist organizations of the world had opposed the war and preserved their integrity, he objected to their being condemned *en bloc* in such a way as to impugn his comrades of the resolutely antiwar CNT. With the assistance of Rosmer, he was finally able to force Radek, who was then presiding, to modify the text in this regard, though this was done only with "bad grace." In the end, when the document was published, the clause remained in its unamended form.[27]

This meeting, it must be said, gave but a foretaste of the authoritarian and centralizing pressures to which the Syndicalist representatives were to be subjected in Moscow. Indeed, the first item on the agenda of the Second Congress dealt specifically with the apolitical and decentralist policies of the European Syndicalists and made clear that although the Bolsheviks desired to have the Syndicalists as allies, they were determined to dictate the terms of the alliance. In a long and not very conciliatory address Zinoviev spoke out against the Anarchosyndicalist emphasis on the primacy of trade unions in the revolutionary struggle—a preoccupation that the Russian leader felt to be no longer in harmony with the needs of the time. He deplored the Anarchosyndicalists' fervent "worship" of the masses and their desire to substitute the masses for the party. With complete frankness he stressed the need for a proletarian dictatorship closely controlled by the Communist Party, assuring his listeners that the masses, as experience would reveal, could only gain revolutionary success when they had a powerful and centralized political leadership to show them the way and to act as a "general staff." Without such leadership, said Zinoviev, the working class was but a body without a head. Almost provocatively, he insisted that the antiparty arguments of the Syndicalists were actually a concession to "bourgeois ideology," and that in practice those arguments only gave support to the counterrevolutionary activities of the social democrats.[28] Revolutionary Syndicalism was a step forward, he said, only in comparison with "the old and decaying counterrevolutionary ideology" of the Second International; in comparison with Communism it was actually a "step backward."

In somewhat scolding tones Zinoviev condemned the Syndicalist devotion to revolutionary spontaneity and trade-union autonomy: what was needed, in place of "formless" (*bezformennie*) unions living only from day to day, was a "centralized, military, iron-disciplined party." Again and again Zinoviev insisted that revolutionary leadership had to be "organized" and "disciplined," and that "all questions" had to be under its control. Neither the spontaneous soviets nor the trade unions, he said, could be permitted to take the place of the party. To all those who thought otherwise, "We say: you are wrong. In the present situation we need a Communist, Marxist party to lead the labor unions, to infuse them with strength, to point the way, to be for them the guiding star." Zinoviev reminded the delegates, finally, that for the Russian workers the party was "sacred, something exalted, dearer than life"; and he expressed the hope that in this feeling they would be emulated by the workers of the entire world.[29]

The Syndicalist delegates listened to Zinoviev's discourse in stunned silence, comprehending for the first time the scope of the Bolshevik vision of party hegemony; and when the Russian leader finished, they rose angrily to defend the autonomy of their movement. Bolshevik-Syndicalist relations experienced their first major crisis as Zinoviev's theses provoked what was virtually a Syndicalist rebellion. The major roles in this oppositional effort were played by Tanner of the British Shop Stewards, Souchy of the German Anarchosyndicalists, and Wijnkoop of the Dutch ultra-Left. Pestaña joined his protest to that of the others, delivering an effective speech that fell in the midst of this somewhat tumultuous debate. His address appears to have been better understood by the delegates than by the overburdened translator, who recorded it only in part.* Yet it had a significant impact on the congress.

As an Anarchist, Pestaña emphasized the importance of mass spontaneity in the revolutionary struggle, making a sharp distinction between the Bolshevik coup d'état and the Russian Revolution as a great spontaneous upheaval with, so to speak, a destiny of its own. The idea that the revolutionary process in the various countries depended on the existence of a Communist Party he called a "gratuitous and pretentious" affirmation that went against history. European revolutionaries, he said, had been told to look at Russia and to find in this "beautiful spectacle" the practical confirmation of Bolshevik arguments; but when one did this, one saw nothing more than a revolution that had already been made before the Bolshevik seizure of power and a social system whose effects were not yet sufficiently clear to permit any deductions. After further protestations against the idea that a party could "make" a revolution—which had not been precisely Zinoviev's point—Pestaña traced a quite Anarchist conception of the genesis of revolutionary movements. Against the Leninist emphasis on "consciousness" and elite control of the revolutionary process, he composed a eulogy to spontaneity that was reminiscent of Bakunin, observing didactically that "revolution is the manifestation, more or less violent, of a condition of the spirit favorable to a change in the norms governing the life of a people, which, by a constant labor of several generations . . . emerges from the shadows at a given moment and destroys without pity all obstacles standing in the way of its goal."[30]

Revolution, said Pestaña, was a "natural product, which germinates after many ideas have been sown [and] after the land has been sprinkled with the blood of many martyrs." It was possible, he acknowledged, that in certain countries the workers would want to group themselves into political parties; but in Spain there was no such desire, and history, he believed, showed that "revolutions, beginning with the great French Revolution, are made without party."[31] Leon Trotsky, seated in the congress, could not forbear to call out at this point, "You forget the Jacobins!" But Pestaña only reiterated doggedly that one did not need a Communist Party either to make or to preserve the revolution, and that the conquest of political power was not essential to the emancipation of the working class. To Trotsky and the other Bolshevik leaders he said, "You did not alone make the revolution in Russia; you cooperated in its making, and you had the good fortune to attain power."[32]

The first rebuttal to the Syndicalists came from Lenin himself. He did not

* Even though Pestaña spoke in French—and thus was understood by almost all the delegates—he was poorly served by the translator/recorder (presumably Balabanova). I have pieced together the missing portions of this, his principal speech, with the aid of his own *Memoria* and Rosmer's *Moscou sous Lénine*.

reply directly to Pestaña's remarks—indeed, he ignored the Spanish question altogether—but addressed himself primarily to the British Syndicalists, going rather quickly to the heart of the problem besetting Syndicalist-Bolshevik collaboration. He noted that although most Syndicalists accepted the dictatorship of the proletariat and even acknowledged that it should be controlled by a "resolute and conscious minority," they persisted in rejecting the Communist Party. He tried to convince them that this was a mistake, and that the difference between the Bolshevik and Syndicalist positions was inconsequential. After all, he observed, "If Comrade Tanner says that he is against the Party, but that the revolutionary minority of the most resolute and conscious proletarians should lead the entire working class, then I say that there are really no differences between us." For such a minority could be nothing but what was called a party: if the leading minority were really class-conscious and able to lead the masses and solve all problems, then it actually became a party. If the Syndicalists admitted that only the conscious minority of the working class could lead the proletariat, "they should then, perforce, admit that such is exactly the essence of all our theses."[33]

Trotsky, fresh from the war zone, also rose to respond to the criticisms leveled against Zinoviev's theses. As the former editor of *Nashe Slovo*, Trotsky sought to appeal to the Syndicalist representatives as an old comrade who knew them well and appreciated the vigor of their revolutionary spirit.

> Just because I know that the Party is necessary—and I know very well the worth of the Party—and just because I see on one side Scheideman and on the other side American, Spanish, or French Syndicalists who, unlike Scheideman, not only want to struggle with the bourgeoisie but really want to tear its head off, I say: I prefer to negotiate with these Spanish, American, and French comrades in order to demonstrate to them that for the fulfillment of the historical mission with which they have been charged, the destruction of the bourgeoisie, the Party is indispensable.[34]

Echoing Lenin's appeal, Trotsky reiterated, in a "comradely way" that the Communist Party was really identical with the revolutionary Syndicalist minority that would be found within the proletarian labor unions and upon which the Syndicalists themselves had placed so much stress. Turning to the Spanish delegate, he remarked: "Comrade Pestaña says: 'I do not wish to concern myself with this question; I am a Syndicalist and I do not want to talk about politics, still less ... about the Party.' This is extremely interesting. He does not want to talk about the Communist Party so as not to insult the revolution." What had to be acknowledged, said Trotsky, was that even in a revolutionary situation someone had to make decisions. Who, he asked, would make these decisions in Spain? It would be, he thought, "the Spanish Communist Party—and I am confident that Comrade Pestaña will be one of the founders of this Party." Those Spanish Syndicalists who united on the basis of the theses of the Second Comintern Congress would form "nothing else than the Spanish Communist Party."[35]

Zinoviev himself had been nettled by Pestaña's critique of the Party Theses and rose the next day to respond personally. He sought to demonstrate that one could not wait until the advent of the revolution in order to establish the Party, as Pestaña had seemed to suggest. Though acknowledging that one could not "make" a revolution, Zinoviev urged the need for planning, preparation, and propaganda, which only the Party could fulfill. "We must tell every worker," he said, "and also every revolutionary Syndicalist who is serious about the revolution—and I know that Comrade Pestaña is one . . . who takes the revolution seriously—that [our decision must not be to] wait until the revolution comes and surprises us."[36]

But hopes for Pestaña's conversion to Bolshevism were premature, and he struggled vainly to regain the floor in order to refute his prestigious critics. The opportunity to speak was consistently denied him, and he would later remark that he had found the procedures of the Comintern Congress oppressive and autocratic in comparison with those of the CNT. In fact, as an Anarchosyndicalist, he felt more than a little isolated and ill at ease in the Moscow Congress. Many of the problems that absorbed the attention of the majority of delegates were highly political in nature, and Pestaña was restrained by both his ideology and his mandate from entering into them. Thus he abstained from voting in some of the most crucial debates of the Second Congress, such as those dealing with the conditions of admission of Socialist Parties to the Comintern, and withdrew to the periphery of the assembly.[37]

Even in his work in the trade-union commission of the Second Congress Pestaña inevitably collided with the redoubtable Karl Radek, whom he labeled perhaps not unfairly, a "rabid anti-Syndicalist."[38] Here, too, the major issue was of little immediate concern to Pestaña since it had to do with whether revolutionary Syndicalists and Communists should enter reformist unions or attempt to found new, revolutionary unions. At the same time, the issue that Pestaña himself chose to raise in the commission was not likely to arouse the enthusiasm of the Bolsheviks—namely, the need for decentralization and de-bureaucratization in the European unions. To his dismay, he discovered that the Bolsheviks did not intend to "reform," that is, to decentralize, the structure of the conservative unions, but merely to take over leadership of them. Pestaña spoke out against this and on behalf of the decentralization and spontaneity so cherished by Spanish Syndicalists. "They listened to me," he later admitted, "as one listens to the rain, and that as under a roof."[39] Before long, he decided that, given the pro-Bolshevik majority of the trade-union commission, he was wasting his time in an opposition doomed to futility; and he ceased even to contribute to the discussions of that body. When the time came to debate the commission's resolution on the floor of the congress, making it necessary to choose someone to speak in dissent, Pestaña felt that since he and Souchy represented the authentic opposition, one of them would be selected. He was "astounded" that both he and the German were "implacably excluded."[40]

The Organizational Committee of the RILU

Only in the organizational committee of the Red International of Labor Unions—which met following the close of the Second Congress—was Pestaña able to exert some part of the influence that was due the representative of nearly a million Spanish Syndicalists. The formation of this committee, chaired by Lozovsky, reflected a growing Bolshevik concern over the rapid expansion of the reformist Amsterdam International during 1919. The workers of Europe, instead of flooding into soviets in quest of the millennium, had poured instead into the existing trade unions in search of material gains. The Amsterdam International was clearly meeting with greater success in its organizational efforts than the Second International, and the Bolsheviks were, in fact, more fearful of it. They viewed it, as the American Communist Boris Reinstein said, as "an international lightning rod" designed to deflect the thunderbolts of the revolution, and they resolved to counter its pretensions as quickly as possible. This intent, coupled with the prevailing myth that the workers of the West were on the verge of revolution, led to the birth of the RILU (or Profintern)—a dramatic countermeasure designed to win the masses away from the "yellow" Amsterdam organization and make possible their control by Moscow.[41]

The revolutionary Syndicalists had for some years—since the London Congress of 1913—intended to create an authentically revolutionary trade-union international, and the idea, it will be recalled, had been revived at the Congress of the Comedia in December 1919. This authentic Syndicalist impulse to international solidarity was now drawn into the whirlpool of the Russian Revolution and would find a somewhat dubious embodiment in the Profintern. At the heart of Syndicalist-Bolshevik collaboration in this period was, above all, the problem of the relationship that this presumably "apolitical" organization would bear to the intensely political Communist International.

Certainly, the Bolsheviks had launched the idea of a revolutionary trade-union international in a manner calculated to appeal to Syndicalist sensibilities. G. Tsyperovich, the chairman of the Petrograd Council of Trade Unions, published a widely disseminated article in the autumn of 1919 in which he evoked a glowing vision: the trade unions of the world, by means of their international organization, would dominate the economic planning and production of the entire globe.[42] Such a conception could not fail to be attractive to Western Syndicalists, who, though anxious for revolutionary collaboration with the Bolsheviks, were entirely opposed to surrendering their autonomy and freedom of action and naturally looked forward to a world run by unions and not by commissars. Their earnest hope was that they could co-operate with the Bolsheviks in the revolutionary struggle on a comradely basis of equality and mutual esteem.

In retrospect, it is evident that the Bolsheviks were inherently unable to engage in the kind of free collaborative effort desired by Western Syndicalists. Just as in Lenin's dichotomized world there were but two ideologies, "Social-ist" (that is, Leninist) and "bourgeois," so there could be but two relation-ships in life: submission or opposition. A spontaneous movement like revo-lutionary Syndicalism, though it would be praised and even courted for its revolutionary spirit, could only arouse among the Bolsheviks, on a deeper level, feelings of distrust and a desire to subdue and to dominate. Indeed, the probable failure of collaborative efforts had been clearly signaled in a well-publicized statement by Zinoviev on the eve of the Second Congress, in which he cheerfully acknowledged that Soviet trade unions were becoming mere "departments of state," and that each Communist group within an industrial union was "merely a kernel of the local branch of the Communist Party ... whilst the Central Committee of the Party, by its dominating influence, con-trols the All-Russian Committee of the industrial unions."[43]

It was precisely this assumption of Communist stewardship that the Syndi-calists encountered in the organizing committee of the Profintern and that caused feelings to run high. At one point Souchy and Tanner angrily with-drew from the sessions, and Lozovsky, though he refused to yield on any substantive point, began to fear that the committee might be disrupted. He therefore made a conciliatory plea, urging that consideration of various "diffi-cult questions" be postponed until the meeting of the First Profintern Con-gress, scheduled for the following year in Moscow. Pestaña, who had re-mained in his seat, replied in a similar vein, assuring Lozovsky that he would continue to participate in the organizational labors of the Profintern and would try to see that the CNT attended the founding congress with the most numerous delegation possible. Yet he also urged the members of the com-mittee to harbor no illusions that the ideological convictions of the Spanish organization would change.[44]

A further step toward conciliation was taken when Mikhail Tomsky took over as chairman of the committee and revealed a more moderate and accom-modating spirit. Tomsky consented, for example, to a modification of the wording of the RILU convocation statement; and it was now agreed to in-vite to the first congress all organizations that "without having made any express declaration [in favor of the seizure of political power] nonetheless practice the revolutionary class struggle." On the basis of this change, Pes-taña was able to persuade Souchy and Tanner to return to the RILU planning sessions. It was at this point, as well, that Armando Borghi of the extremist Unione Sindicale Italiana reached Moscow and obtained Pestaña's aid in gaining the admittance of the USI to the forthcoming congress, overcoming the resistance of the Bolsheviks, who favored Sergio D'Aragona's more pliable Confederazione Generale de Lavoro. Shortly thereafter, the organizational committee completed its work, with some issues still pending but having maintained, despite disagreements, "a certain cordiality and harmony."[45]

Impressions of Soviet Russia

Pestaña, probably thankful to be away from terror-gripped Barcelona, spent more than a month traveling in the Soviet Union after the close of the Second Congress. Unlike many of the delegates to Comintern congresses, he was not dazzled by the hospitality and showmanship of his Bolshevik hosts. Emma Goldman found Pestaña to be "one of the clearest minds" among the Syndicalist delegates, and she has testified to the alert and critical spirit he brought to the Russian scene. Along with Alexander Berkman, Goldman confirmed for the Spaniard the rumors that had been reaching the West regarding the Bolshevik persecution of Russian Anarchists. But it is clear, in any case, that Pestaña was not very favorably impressed by what he saw in Russia, and that he continued to judge the new order from a wholly libertarian perspective.[46]

The theme that ran through Pestaña's various writings on his Russian journey was, in essence, the tragic incongruity between the libertarian spirit of the Revolution and the dictatorial spirit of the Bolshevik Party—a spirit that he chose to regard as emanating from the "Germanic," formalistic, and authoritarian character of Lenin himself. Thus Pestaña remained faithful to the Anarchist vision of a spontaneous, libertarian, and self-fulfilling revolution, and it was against this mirage-like image that he measured the Soviet achievement. Rather like the Russian Anarchists who had been criticizing the Bolshevik dictatorship since its inception, Pestaña saw the Revolution—in its "essential" nature—as a profoundly libertarian phenomenon which, if left to its own dynamic, would inevitably achieve the "socialization" of all the means of production. The Revolution, then, was not a mere chaotic breakdown of social norms that might lead anywhere or nowhere; instead it was the manifestation of a mysterious and beneficent spontaneity, which, if not interfered with, would inevitably have destroyed the old order while at the same time permitting a new and more natural order of things—namely, a Communal society—to emerge.

Pestaña thus revealed his faith in a kind of benign revolutionary teleology, insisting that the Revolution, if not "corrupted" or deflected, would necessarily move "in a definite direction," toward the maximization of freedom and equality. The tragedy of the Russian Revolution, he thought, was that the spontaneous communism of its first phase—when the people, having overthrown the Tsarist tyranny, had proclaimed "the right of everyone to everything (*de todos a todo*)—had been overthrown by the "new communism" of the Bolshevik Party. The Party rather than the people had become the owner of all property and had taken upon itself the organization of all labor; the result, he lamented, was not true communism but merely state ownership of everything and the rewarding of people not according to their needs but according to their productivity.[47]

There was tragedy, then, in the clash between the Party and the Russian people. The Russians, Pestaña decided, were "apathetic, slow in [their] behavior, and marked by an indolence inconceivable even for Latins." Lenin, who was un-Russian in his willfulness and methodicalness, had sought to impose upon this indolent nation a "methodical, regular, uniform organization" designed to ordain and foresee everything and to leave nothing to "fecund and spontaneous initiative." Lenin had sought to turn Russia into a huge factory, "a Taylor System, where all movements, gestures, and actions will be determined in advance." But his authoritarian and regimenting vision, Pestaña believed, would ultimately fail, since all theories of proletarian dictatorship and of the Bolshevization of the masses would inevitably be shattered against "the reality that no one can deny: instinct." Human instincts, Pestaña was sure, would always oppose the most tenacious resistance to statist formulas. The "real, the dynamic, and the living" would never cease to struggle against the fictitious, the static, and the moribund. "Exuberant life, in all its vigor," would always oppose itself to norms that sought to curtail or destroy it. Each people had its own character and instincts, which it was "insane" to assault violently; and the character of the Russian people, in particular, was wholly opposed to the statist, centralized, and disciplined social order that Lenin and his collaborators were trying to impose.[48]

A final conversation with Lenin, just before Pestaña's departure from Russia, did not alter the Spaniard's Anarchist conception of the revolutionary process. More of a purist in this regard than many of his Anarchosyndicalist comrades in Spain, who were gradually being converted to the idea of the proletarian dictatorship, Pestaña continued to deny the need for institutionalized authority in the midst of revolutionary upheaval. In response to Lenin's polite query whether his experience of the new Soviet order had changed his views, he replied with disarming frankness, saying that during the long journey from Barcelona to Moscow,

> One doubt assailed us continually. In the face of the unknown . . . we asked ourselves many times this question: "Are we Anarchists mistaken in the fundamental aspects of our doctrine?" And we will not deny the fear we felt as we [approached] the moment of having to join, perhaps, in the negation of those ideas defended by us with such ardor, which formed the small intellectual baggage of our life. One does not renounce without pain . . . ideas that have been dear to us.[49]

But despite such fears, said Pestaña, the fact was that everything he had observed in Russia had merely "confirmed and fortified" him in his convictions,
the chief among these being the belief that revolution, though bound to be
bloody and violent, had no need for a dictatorship, whether proletarian or
not. He concluded the interview with a final invocation of the theme of spontaneity: "Revolution is no more than the people in arms, who, tired of enduring injustices, of being deprived of their rights ... protest these things, take
up arms, and go into the street to impose by force of numbers the social organization they consider more just. In this there is violence, certainly, but there
is not dictatorship."[50] To carry out the revolution, then, there was no need to
establish a class dictatorship. In order to dispossess the bourgeoisie it was necessary only to "arm the people."[51]

Whatever ennui these earnest declarations may have inspired in Lenin has
not been recorded. In spite of their diverging viewpoints, the two men parted
amiably enough, with Lenin merely murmuring "You are wrong, Pestaña,
you are wrong." Lenin also urged the Spaniard to return for the next Comintern congress and to bring other Spaniards with him.* The Bolshevik leader
later expressed his admiration for Pestaña, perceiving him as "an intelligent
and puritan worker, blessed with a great gift of observation and critical sense,
for whom the idea of liberty was the keystone of his ideological edifice."[52]
For his part, Pestaña continued to feel for Lenin "profound sympathy and
unlimited respect."[53]

After a last visit to the home of the aged Anarchist leader Kropotkin, Pestaña departed from Russia in mid-October. He stopped first in Berlin, where
he conferred with a number of European Syndicalist leaders and helped to
plan the Syndicalist conference that would be held in the German capital in
December to work out a common policy to be followed in the approaching
Profintern Congress.[54] It was also at this time that he contacted and held
several conversations with the two Socialist delegates de los Ríos and Anguiano, who were only now making their way to Russia (see Chapter 9). On October 23 Pestaña reached Milan—then in turmoil over the factory occupations
by Socialist workers—where he planned to discuss the Congress with the
Italian Syndicalists. Despite his efforts to remain incognito, he was almost
immediately arrested by the Italian police. The documents and notes he had
carried with him from the Second Congress were confiscated, and he was held

---

* Pestaña also confided to Lenin his belief that with few exceptions the delegates to
the Second Congress had revealed a "bourgeois mentality." He had discovered, he said,
a regrettable contradiction between the speeches delivered at the Congress and the every-
day life of the delegates at their hotel, where they acted like "the most perfect bourgeois"
—complaining about the food, abusing the help, and each night putting their shoes outside
the door to be blacked by "comrade" servants. One could only laugh, Pestaña told Lenin,
at the "revolutionary" mentality of most of these men. Pestaña, *Setenta días: Lo que yo ví,*
pp. 196–97.

for two months in San Vittorio Prison. He was finally permitted to board a boat for Barcelona, but the Spanish authorities, having been alerted, were waiting for him, and he was again arrested (December 12) and thrown into the prison of Montjuich outside Barcelona.

Pestaña, known to be returning from Russia, was viewed by Spanish authorities as a dangerous person and a probable carrier of the Red Plague from the East. More than that, he arrived back in Spain not long after the appointment of Martínez Anido as Civil Governor of Catalonia and in the midst of Anido's unprecedentedly severe crackdown on all Cenetista leaders, who were being arrested and exiled by the score. The ironic consequence of Pestaña's arrest was that it kept him from making known his negative reactions to the Russian Bolsheviks, just as Martínez Anido's repression prevented the holding of a CNT congress in which the Comintern connection could be assessed and criticized in the light of new evidence. Thus the White Terror in Catalonia may have contributed to keeping the CNT in the Comintern a year and a half longer than would otherwise have been the case.[55]

The Merino Gracia Mission

The second of the Spanish delegates to arrive in Russia in the summer of 1920 was the young schoolmaster Ramón Merino Gracia, who was general secretary of the newly formed Partido Comunista Español. Merino had planned to participate in the Second Congress; but the difficulties of the journey, which brought him into Russia through Murmansk, delayed his arrival in Moscow until August 27, some time after the close of the sessions. He was nevertheless immediately invited to a meeting of the ECCI, which was attended by Zinoviev, Bukharin, Radek, and Bela Kun among others. The general situation in Spain was discussed, and Merino took this opportunity to expatiate on the shortcomings of the Spanish Socialist Party and of the left-centrist faction that had emerged during the war only to be absorbed and subverted, as it seemed to him, by the reformists. He discussed in detail the emergence of the PCE from the Federation of Young Socialists, carefully minimizing the ultra-Left tendencies of the new party and insisting that there was "not the slightest ideological or tactical divergence" between the PCE and the Russian Bolshevik Party. In response to questioning he reiterated that the PCE had not assumed a "sectarian or exclusive" character. But only Bukharin seemed to reveal at this time any special interest in the Spanish situation, inquiring about the role of the PCE in the labor unions.[56]

It was also at this meeting that Merino broached the problem then uppermost in the minds of Spanish Communists, namely, the urgent need for financial support for their journal *El Comunista*. Indeed, Merino's principal objective in visiting Moscow was to obtain the funds Michael Borodin had promised the founders of the PCE and whose nondelivery was about to cause the party journal to shut down. Upon this or some subsequent occasion it was arranged that Borodin himself would return to Madrid with money for the PCE. Following Merino's exposition, the ECCI also voted unanimously to recognize the PCE as the Spanish section of the Communist International.[57]

Immediately following his meeting with the ECCI Merino traveled to Baku, where he participated in the Congress of the Peoples of the East, a gathering rather hurriedly summoned by the Bolsheviks in order to embarrass British imperialism in Asia and to facilitate the Anglo-Russian trade negotiations then being conducted. Upon his return from Baku, Merino was granted an interview with Lenin, who, he said, did not oppose the "slightest objection" to either the principles or the tactics of the PCE and who seemed especially interested in the Spanish peasantry and in conditions of land tenure in the Iberian Peninsula. Although the Polish war had by now taken a bad turn, Lenin continued to be "profoundly optimistic" about world revolutionary prospects, insisting that capitalism was in its final agony, and that the masses were leaving social democracy for Communism in ever-growing numbers. He also warmly defended the dictatorship of the proletariat, insisting to Merino that this form had been "completely foreseen" by scientific Marxism and that the Bolsheviks had "invented nothing."[58]

After bidding Lenin farewell, Merino Gracia, at the behest of his hosts, traveled to the Southern Front, where the Red Army was confronting the troops of General Wrangel. He was greatly moved by the revolutionary spirit that he observed, as well as by the "indescribable enthusiasm" with which, as it seemed to him, the Comintern delegation was received by the Red Army troops. He was especially pleased by the fact that the Bolsheviks had organized "in our honor, great parades and military reviews."[59] Back in Moscow once more, on the eve of his return to the West, Merino encountered de los Ríos and Anguiano, with whom he had a lengthy if not wholly amicable conversation. Merino knew, of course, of the document carried by the Socialist delegates, which set forth the PSOE's conditions of adherence to the Comintern; and he would later report that this statement caused "stupefaction" among the members of the ECCI when it was presented to them in the immediate aftermath of the promulgation of Moscow's own Twenty-one Conditions.[60]

The de los Ríos–Anguiano Mission

Indeed, de los Ríos and Anguiano found themselves in an awkward situation. Having been commissioned to carry the PSOE's conditional adherence to Moscow, they discovered, a few days after reaching Berlin, that the Second Comintern Congress had itself prescribed a set of conditions for all adhering parties, which with their centralizing rigor rendered the Spanish Socialists' conditions illusory and even somewhat ludicrous. The Twenty-one Conditions left no doubt that the Russian Bolsheviks envisioned an organization rather different from the conception of the new International hitherto held by Spanish Terceristas. Instead of a confederation of autonomous national sections, in which each party would be left free to mold itself in terms of national conditions, there would be established an essentially unitary organization—centralized, disciplined, and almost entirely subordinate to Moscow. The Spanish delegates were greatly dismayed by the "manifest opposition" between Moscow's terms and the autonomy demanded by the PSOE. When they showed the Spanish resolution to Paul Levi, the leader of the German Independent Socialists, he remarked that such a document offered "not even a basis for conversation" with the Communist International. But when the Spaniards considered the possibility of returning to Madrid, he nevertheless urged them to continue on to Moscow and at least exchange views with the Russians—a course of action they decided to follow.[61]

It was also in Berlin that de los Ríos and Anguiano received a visit from Angel Pestaña on his way back to Spain. The Socialists did not at first recognize the tall, slender Cenetista leader, having seen him on only one other occasion, when he spoke in Madrid in October 1919, before Pestaña had acquired the mustache that now adorned his countenance. The Socialist delegates, joined by Jaime Alvarez del Vayo, dined on two occasions with Pestaña, who spoke amiably and at length about his experiences in Russia and left little doubt that his impressions were largely negative, especially regarding the dictatorship, the organization of the economy, and the evident suffering of the Russian people.[62]

Continuing their journey, the two Socialists traveled on by sea and rail to Petrograd, arriving on October 18. Reaching Moscow the following day, they were duly installed in the Hotel Lux and began their examination of Soviet reality. Since Zinoviev was at that moment in Germany, making his famous and successful appeal to the Halle Congress of the Independent Socialists, the Spaniards were not able to meet with the ECCI until November 2, at which time there attended, in addition to Zinoviev, Bukharin, Radek, and Clara Zetkin.[63]

The members of the ECCI must have been struck by the contrast between the two delegates. Fernando de los Ríos was the prototype of the bourgeois intellectual. Born into a wealthy and even illustrious family in Malaga province in 1879, he had earned his doctorate in law at the University of Madrid and broadened his education at the Sorbonne, the London School of Economics, and the universities of Jena, Marburg, and Berlin. Since 1911 he had been professor of political theory at the University of Granada. His published works ranged from the political thought of Plato and Jellinek to the ideas of Francisco Giner. De los Ríos had only been in the PSOE for a year and a half, having migrated from republicanism and an earlier association with Melquíades Alvarez and the Reformists. But his great ability and broad culture gave him immediate prominence within the ranks of Spanish Socialism, and he had been elected to the Cortes as a Socialist deputy in June 1919. More humanist, perhaps, than Socialist, he exuded decency, breeding, and bourgeois respectability. He was somewhat stout and addicted to the wearing of black frock coats and pin-striped trousers. He possessed, as V. S. Pritchett has remarked, "a fine black beard and a soft, educated, and persuasive voice, and a gentle enunciation."[64] His manner was unfailingly calm and professorial, his words measured, and his judgment marked by *gravitas*. All of which is to say that he was no revolutionary and that the Bolsheviks found him incredible. Two years later, at the Fourth Comintern Congress, Zinoviev would still be brooding about his encounter with the "Spanish professor."

> At that time [i.e. 1920] the reformists and half-reformists came running to us from all countries. I can still remember a Spanish professor, de los Ríos, who came to Moscow as a representative of the Spanish party.... But this professor was, after all, a professor, and was thus somewhat naive when it came to politics (amusement).... Now this professor said with almost touching naivete: "You know, comrades, I personally am a reformist, but the Spanish workers are urging that they be admitted to the Communist International, and they have sent me here in order to get them admitted."... This professor was almost a saint; he used to tell everything with complete frankness.[65]

Daniel Anguiano was a frail and unprepossessing ex-railway clerk who had begun his political life in the Federal Republican Party. Later he became head of the Railworkers' Federation, secretary to Pablo Iglesias, and a member of the Executive Committee of the UGT, as well as general secretary of the Socialist Party. Anguiano was in no sense brilliant, least of all as a speaker, but he was nevertheless greatly admired for his character (Luis Araquistáin had referred to him as a "lay saint"). Of all the pro-Comintern Socialists, Anguiano had perhaps the purest revolutionary faith, untarnished by any hint of self-serving or chronic oppositionism. He had risen high in the Party, and had even become a deputy to the Cortes in 1918—a role for which his limited speaking ability made him somewhat unsuited—without becoming an oligarch. Unlike some of the other left-centrists in the Party, he was willing to sacrifice his position and prerogatives in the hierarchy for his revolutionary beliefs. Since he spoke only Spanish, Anguiano was somewhat dependent on de los Ríos during their Russian journey; yet he was able to formulate his own, basically favorable, opinion of the Bolshevik regime.[66]

The interrogation of the Spanish delegates by the ECCI took place in two lengthy sessions, on November 2 and 22. De los Ríos began the proceedings by reading a prepared statement in which he reminded the members of the Committee that the PSOE's conditions had been formulated before those of the Comintern, and that he and Anguiano were well aware of the conflict be-tween the two documents. He then very candidly confirmed his own opposi-tion to the Twenty-one Conditions while acknowledging that Anguiano ac-cepted them. He singled out three conditions as being of particular concern to Spanish Socialists: the third, which related to the requirement of an illegal, underground organization for the Party; the twelfth, which imposed "demo-cratic centralism" on the Party; and the sixteenth, which stressed the obligatory and binding nature of decisions taken by Comintern congresses.[67]

The questioning of the Spanish delegates confirmed that the Moscow lead-ers had relatively little information on the situation in Spain. Radek asked what sort of parliamentary activity was pursued by the Socialists and was frankly told by de los Ríos that although the Republican-Socialist Alliance had been severed, the Socialist parliamentary delegation nevertheless "collabo-rated" in the Cortes, working for social legislation and seeking to modify the application of existing statutes in favor of the working class. Endeavoring to make clear the nature of Pablismo, de los Ríos insisted that the PSOE had a "revolutionary outlook" and was resolved to create an activist consciousness in the workers, which would ultimately lead them to the conquest of political power and the "transformation" of the capitalist system. But he acknowledged that most Spanish Socialists did not adhere to the "maximalist" conception, believing, rather, that the struggle for immediate benefits and legal reforms was both a necessity and a matter of principle. The majority of the PSOE, he said, were convinced that the battle for "small gains" could not be neglected, since it helped form class consciousness and, by raising living standards, also provided the material means with which the proletariat could continue the struggle.[68]

Anguiano joined in to reiterate that in the view of Pablo Iglesias there was no incongruity between reform and revolution, and that the quest for legis-lative reforms and small benefits would actually facilitate the final conquest of power. Several members of the ECCI expressed surprise that there con-tinued to coexist within the PSOE persons of very diverse views, that is, both reformists and revolutionaries. Anguiano made a somewhat diffuse attempt to explain this phenomenon, but in the end could only reiterate that those who favored unconditional adherence to Moscow were determined to gain a majority and take the PSOE, *en bloc*, into the Communist International. After a seven-hour session on November 2 the ECCI adjourned for several weeks in order to give the Spanish delegates an opportunity to familiarize themselves with the Soviet scene.[69]

When the sessions resumed on November 22, the interrogation was con-ducted chiefly by Bukharin, whom the Spaniards, impressed by his "enor-mous and persuasive dialectical power," viewed as "one of the most attractive figures of the Russian Revolution." The Bolshevik ideologue began with a lecture—from which he doubtless felt the Spaniards could profit—on the doctrinal and tactical implications of the trinity of the World Revolution, the Dictatorshop of the Proletariat, and the Regime of Soviets. He then turned to the two delegates to examine the state of their faith regarding these fundamental questions, asking each in turn if he did not feel that the social revolution was on the march and that capitalism was entering its final days. Anguiano responded in the proper spirit, agreeing that in his judgment the Russian Revolution indeed marked the beginning of the era of capitalist downfall. But de los Ríos disappointed—though he could hardly have surprised—his interlocutor by asserting his belief that neither the condition of Europe nor that of North America justified faith in the rapid progress of the world revolution.[70]

The heresy of de los Ríos went further than this. When pressed by Bukharin, he acknowledged his skepticism about the whole classical concept of catastrophic revolution to which the Bolsheviks adhered. Although he agreed that there might be some "insurrectional possibilities" in the social tensions of central Europe, his conviction was that the revolution in Germany could not and would not have a catastrophic character. If the workers took power, he said, it would be through some "methodical procedure" by which the economy would be gradually socialized and new directing bodies created in order not to disrupt production. By the same token, he said, if the workers in France, England, and Italy took control of their countries, they would only do so in such a way "as not to destroy that which they desire to encourage," namely, the power to produce goods. De los Ríos believed, in any case, that what the world confronted was not the impending collapse of capitalism but merely a crisis in its economic order. The ultimate victory of the workers, he thought, would be a far longer and more difficult process than the leaders of the Comintern imagined.[71]

Having failed—rather grandly—this preliminary examination, de los Ríos was from this point on essentially ignored by Bukharin, who directed the rest of his questions to Daniel Anguiano.[72] This comrade revealed himself to be a more apt student of Bolshevism and was able to respond affirmatively to crucial questions dealing with the Dictatorship of the Proletariat and the Regime of Soviets. He also listened attentively as Bukharin lectured him on the need to fight reformism within the PSOE and to remember always that democracy was but an "ideological residue" of the French Revolution. On this note the ECCI terminated its hearings on the Spanish Party and the session dissolved in an "ambience of mutual cordiality" that even doctrinal differences had not completely impaired.[73]

Nevertheless, the letter to the Spanish Socialist Party that the ECCI composed on December 10 and gave to the delegates to take back to Madrid was highly critical of Pablismo. With respect to the conditions carried to Moscow by de los Ríos and Anguiano, the ECCI asserted that the tenor of these provisos merely revealed the "lack of clear ideas that prevails in your party regarding the most essential questions of the international labor movement. . . . Having completely lost sight of the World Revolution, you necessarily cannot comprehend the character and meaning of the Communist International." The PSOE was accused, in effect, of confusion and a lack of revolutionary motivation; and after explaining to the Spaniards, as requested, the meaning of Conditions Three, Twelve, and Sixteen, the letter of the ECCI concluded with nothing less than an appeal over the heads of the Party's leaders, urging Spanish workers to join the Comintern and let the reformists pass into the camp of the "yellow" International.[74]

On December 10, just before their departure from Russia, de los Ríos and Anguiano were summoned to the Kremlin office of Lenin, who greeted them with "great affability" and conversed for nearly an hour. When the Bolshevik leader asked whether the Spanish Party would enter the Comintern, Anguiano replied that the Twenty-one Conditions would be very difficult for most of his comrades to accept. Lenin agreed that the Conditions were "strong," but added, perhaps somewhat pointedly, that they had been made strong precisely in order to prevent an invasion of the Third International by reformists and opportunists. De los Ríos, characteristically, asked Lenin how long he thought it would be before the dictatorship of the proletariat in Russia gave way to a regime of "full liberty" for trade unions, for the press, and for individuals. Lenin replied very frankly, saying:

> We have never spoken of liberty, but rather of the dictatorship of the proletariat, which we exercise . . . on behalf of the proletariat. Since in Russia the proletariat, properly defined, is a minority, the dictatorship is exercised by that minority and will last so long as the rest of the social elements do not submit to the economic conditions that Communism imposes. The psychology of the villages is refractory to our system; their mentality is petty-bourgeois; among them the leaders of the counterrevolution . . . have found their supporters. But the villagers have reached the conclusion that if the Bolsheviks are bad the others are unbearable.[75]

Lenin professed to be certain that the "refractory" psychology of the peasants was beginning to change, and that they were drawing nearer to the government. He acknowledged that the major difficulty of the moment was that of maintaining production so as to be able to make exchanges with the countryside. He then came to the heart of the issue that de los Ríos had raised, indicating that, in his opinion, the dictatorship would not soon be ended:

> The period of transition, of dictatorship, will be for us very long: perhaps forty or fifty years. Other countries, such as Germany and England, because of their greater industrial importance, will be able to shorten this period; but those countries, on the other hand, have problems that do not exist here, for in some of them

there has formed a working class dependent on [colonies]. Yes, yes, the problem for us is not liberty, and with respect to this we always reply: "Liberty? For what purpose?"[76]

Lenin was then asked if he did not think that concessions recently made by the Bolsheviks to foreign capital might lengthen the time of transition and perhaps even require, in the end, still another revolution to free the country from foreign economic domination. To this somewhat provocative question, Lenin responded amiably, saying that he recognized the danger, but that the concessions had been unavoidable:

> You are correct; this is going to lengthen the proletarian dictatorship and it is going to demand new struggles. But we cannot [yet] conquer foreign capitalism, which is sustained by the working masses, and we need to reconstruct ourselves economically. Russia has maintained itself for three years by means of unheard-of sacrifices, but it cannot continue suffering the present privations. And this can only be avoided either by concessions or by the outbreak of world revolution, which ... we are absolutely sure is commencing, although it develops more slowly than we should desire.[77]

Lenin concluded his conversation with the two Spaniards by eulogizing the electrification projects then under way and emphasizing their great importance for the Soviet economy. That Russia was at last entering an era of economic reconstruction was clearly a source of gratification to him: "In 1917 we awoke political enthusiasm in this country by means of our propaganda, by defining the ideas of peace and of the Soviets.... Later on we awoke in the people military enthusiasm, showing them how the bourgeois nations leagued against us. And now we are succeeding in awakening enthusiasm for economic reconstruction."[78]

Fernando de los Ríos and Daniel Anguiano returned to Spain in the last days of 1920, managing to avoid the fate that befell Angel Pestaña and reaching Madrid, in a state of near exhaustion, on December 28. Interest in their mission was at a fever pitch within the ranks of the Socialist Party, and despite the fatigue of the two envoys a meeting of the Executive Committee was immediately scheduled for the evening of the 29th. Here both men made brief reports on their trip, and the question of the Party's continued adherence to the Comintern was discussed. No decision was taken, however, other than to summon a plenum of the National Committee for January 15, 1921, at which time delegates from the various regions could express their views. De los Ríos and Anguiano were commissioned to draw up separate reports, which would be considered at that time.[79]

The January meeting of the National Committee was the moment of truth for Spanish Socialists in that the Comintern issue had now to be met squarely and the Leninist conception of the revolutionary struggle either embraced or rejected. In the face of the Twenty-one Conditions, pious enthusiasm and platonic acceptance would no longer suffice. Nor did it help matters that the two envoys disagreed so sharply in their evaluations of Soviet conditions. Anguiano's report was basically favorable to the Soviets, though containing a fundamental reservation—Bukharin had not detected this—that startled and disappointed the Terceristas. Anguiano agreed with the Bolsheviks that the war had created a revolutionary situation in Europe and opened the way for proletarian dictatorship; but to the astonishment of his listeners he denied that the dictatorship had to be embodied in a party. Not unlike the Anarchosyndicalists, he seemed to place his faith in the spontaneous solidarity and capacity for cooperation of the aroused proletarian masses. Conceding that he had had too little time to study the Soviet regime, Anguiano suggested that the dictatorship in Russia would be less cruel if power were vested not in a party but in "the masses." As for the applicability of Bolshevism in Spain, he acknowledged that the "consciousness" of the Spanish people left much to be desired; but he was also sure that Socialist adherence to the Comintern would help create the revolutionary mentality that was needed. Joining the Comintern, he insisted, did not mean trying to make the revolution "on command," nor would it involve the Party in "crazy actions"; rather, it would be the first step toward the creation of the mass consciousness that alone would make the revolution possible.[80]

Fernando de los Ríos, in his report, regretted that the Bolsheviks had not been willing to let the Socialist parties of the world observe the distinction between absolute adherence to the Russian Revolution as an event of historic significance and absolute acceptance of Bolshevik ideology and tactics, regarding which many of them had reservations. He pointedly reminded the Socialists that the conditions they had formulated in the June 1920 congress had been explicitly repudiated by Moscow. The essence of the conflict between Pablismo and Bolshevism, he thought, was the question of liberty. In the final analysis, he was opposed to adherence to the Comintern because he was opposed to dictatorship. He was willing to concede that the revolution might create a need for dictatorial methods—which were always lamentable, he believed—but he did not wish to see such methods elevated to the status of a system or principle. For the idea of liberty, he asserted, was neither "bourgeois" nor "proletarian" but "human." The democratic and libertarian ideals of the French Revolution—denigrated by Bolshevism—were universal and eternal, and all moral and political progress was in direct proportion to the degree of penetration of those ideals in the world of reality. The Second Congress of the Comintern, by enunciating the Twenty-one Conditions, had destroyed the necessary liberty of action of the European Socialist parties, turning them into "sects" and converting Socialist doctrine into an "articulated dogma." Finally, said de los Ríos, it was essential that Socialist parties have the right to continue their reformist labors, for those were vital to strengthening the revolutionary capacity of the proletariat and should only be forsaken at the precise moment when a party was actually ready to seize power.[81]

The debate on these contradictory *informes* within the National Committee was heated. It was a painful moment for some of the pro-Comintern militants. Andrés Ovejero—once a passionate Aliadófilo and now a passionate pro-Bolshevik—could not bring himself to accept the revolutionary discipline inherent in the Twenty-one Conditions. Yet the prospect of being morally dissevered from the Russian Revolution distressed him greatly. In the end, he joined with Núñez de Arenas and César González in defeating the Anguiano resolution, the last two voting negatively not because they rejected the Twenty-one Conditions but because they regarded Anguiano's views as eccentric. The Anguiano report was favored only by Anguiano, Acevedo, and García Quejido. But that of de los Ríos also went down to defeat, being supported by Azorín, Cabello, de los Ríos, Fabra Ribas, Giner, and Iglesias and opposed by all the rest. The critical letter sent to the PSOE by the Executive Committee of the Comintern was also rejected, gaining support only from Darriba, Núñez de Arenas, and César González (the last two delegates in particular emerged as the most unconditional supporters of the Comintern within the ranks of Spanish Socialism). In the face of the rejection of both the de los Ríos and Anguiano reports, the final action of the National Committee was to summon yet a third extraordinary Party Congress, scheduled for April, in order to decide once and for all on the Party's adherence to the Communist International. For the first time there was a hint of schism in the air.[82]

The Cenetistas Debate the Dictatorship

The question of the proletarian dictatorship raised equally grave issues within the ranks of the Anarchosyndicalists. During the summer of 1920, while Pestaña was in Russia, the "pure" Anarchists of *Tierra y Libertad* came out in full opposition to the Bolshevik dictatorship and to what they felt were certain Bolshevik-inspired deviations within the Syndicalist movement in Spain. Their enthusiasm for the Revolution, which had blazed so high in 1917–18 and begun to fade during 1919, was now almost completely extinguished. From various sources—perhaps mainly from the French and Italian press—they had come to grasp the harsh realities of the Russian situation. They learned of the persecution of Russian Anarchists, the suppression of the soviets, and the rise of a new bureaucratic state. It was, perhaps, this last development that most depressed them, since the hatred of all governments and all arbitrary authority constituted their reigning passion. In 1917–18, in the dawn of the Revolution, their hopes had obscured their vision and led them to believe, or half believe, that a society had at last been organized on the basis of absolute freedom, without governmental institutions or official coercion. Their disappointment when they learned the truth was very great. With bitterness they observed that in Russia all the old evils had crept back, that once again one observed

an authority that commands and, therefore, suppresses individual liberty; a bureaucracy that shoots those who do not obey and therefore stifles innovative desires; a state capitalism that militarizes labor; small rural proprietors by the thousands [who take over rather than communize the nobles' lands]; merchants who speculate with misery to ... enrich themselves and who therefore create new classes and conditions of social inequality; a new industrial bourgeoisie in the making, who, in time, will resemble that of Europe as one egg does another; and police and jails in order to better imitate the tyrannical and capitalist bourgeois society.[83]

In their disappointment the pure Anarchists were confirmed in the conviction that there was great danger in trying to make a social revolution dictatorially from above, utilizing ignorant and unready masses. One of the most persistent themes in the writings of these embittered elitists was the growing contempt they felt for the *inconscientes* masses, whether in Russia or in Spain, whose violent propensities, materialist strivings, and ignorance ineluctably formed the basis, they believed, for authoritarian regimes. They were increasingly alarmed by the enthusiasm displayed both by Spanish workers and by their Anarchosyndicalist leaders for the Bolshevik order; and their disenchantment with the course of events in Russia converged with a growing dismay over Syndicalist and "governmental" trends within the CNT. Thus the "pure" Anarchists were convinced that the Bolshevik example was the chief reason for the ease with which the Syndicalist masses were being led down the paths of terrorism (which they professed to deplore) and "materialism," abandoning the Anarchist goal of *emancipación integral*.

This view of trends within the CNT was also inevitably colored by a poignant recognition of the slow decline of "pure" Anarchism since the turn of the century. The Syndicalist tactic, far from giving Anarchism a new lease on life, had, it seemed, merely accelerated its decline. Like angry prophets of Israel, the pure Anarchists denounced the loss of the true faith and the heedlessness of the "new workers." The present era, remarked the editor of *Tierra y Libertad*, constituted

one of the most critical moments through which Anarchism has passed. Unknown to, or even reviled by, the majority—who lack sufficient mental elevation to understand it—[Anarchism] has been a little perplexed and left behind, a little outside, in the struggles that have arisen since the war, during the Russian Revolution, and in the glare of a Syndicalism ignorant of ideals, excessively coarse, and brutally authoritarian.[84]

In the same manner, the anti-Bolshevik Anarchist Francisco Jordán lamented "the propensity of all multitudes to accept as good that which achieves success." At the present time, he complained, "It has been given to us [Syndicalists] to call ourselves *bolcheviques* almost without knowing...what it is we are naming." The result was that the Cenetistas now found themselves obliged to differentiate between Syndicalism and Anarchism, whereas before these had been considered "the same thing with two different names." Under the spell of Bolshevism, said Jordán, the Syndicalists had become "almost rivals" of the Anarchists.[85]

These jeremiads signaled the retreat of the pure Anarchists into subjectivism and a kind of rarified elitism. They had once dreamed of actually realizing in the world the beautiful, anti-authoritarian ideals of Anarchism. Now they felt doubly betrayed—by the course of the Revolution in Russia, from which they had expected so much, and by the evolution of the Syndicalist movement in Spain, which they had hoped to guide along libertarian paths. Above all, the pure Anarchists were losing their faith in the people, in those "solid, barbarian elements" that Bakunin had once acclaimed. Thus the editor of *Tierra y Libertad* leveled against Spanish workers the harshest possible indictment: the masses, he said, were beginning to resemble the bourgeoisie! Excessively obedient to the commands of their Syndicalist *caudillos*, and guided by slogans rather than by Anarchist principles, the workers had succumbed to "the eulogy of [their] most ruinous passions." Ignoring Anarchist propaganda, which spoke to them of perfect justice and complete emancipation, the workers had become merely a "second part" of the bourgeoisie, sharing in the same "moral wretchedness."[86]

Thus the pure Anarchists had come to believe that a revolution made with the aid of uncultured and doctrinally unprepared masses was worse than no revolution at all. The consciousness of the workers, they insisted, had to be transformed before rather than after the awaited upheaval, or the revolution would inevitably miscarry; and the only way to transform mass consciousness, they believed, was by means of propaganda. First must come the Word. "To those," wrote José Prat, "who cry action, action, and only action, [we shout]: propaganda, propaganda, and always propaganda!" Propaganda alone could elevate the mentality of the masses and prevent the revolution from leading, as in Bolshevik Russia, merely to a perversion of libertarian ideals.[87]

This desire on the part of the pure Anarchists for consciousness not merely in the revolutionary elite but in the mass of the workers as well inevitably led them to the recognition that the revolution in Spain was still a distant prospect. Indeed, their demand for mass consciousness was little else than a demand that the revolution be indefinitely postponed. Some of these purists went so far as to suggest that the "real" revolution could never be of this world. Thus "Dionysios" (José Antonio Birlán) wrote that even if the Russian Revolution had not ended by establishing a governmental power it would still have been unsatisfactory to Spanish Anarchists. This was because

> our Anarchism will always be discontented with what surrounds us. We will aspire continually that men and things become better than they are. Anarchism will be, for us, eternally in the future. Even after living as anarchists, if this were now [possible], our ideal would not yet have been realized. [It would be] still farther on, deeper down, more within. In our *fuero íntimo* this Anarchism lives already.[88]

But this retreat into mysticism could hardly satisfy the far more numerous and activist Anarchosyndicalists within the CNT. Their revolutionary drive was too powerful and their faith in the future too great for them to acquiesce— as yet—to an indefinite postponement of the revolution. They therefore continued to accept what the pure Anarchists rejected: the essentially Leninist proposition that the revolution had to precede mass consciousness or it would never come at all. This is to say that they accepted the necessity of a proletarian dictatorship, which, after the overthrow of the bourgeoisie, would carry out the requisite social, economic and educational measures.

In response to the revolutionary pessimism of the pure Anarchists, the Anarchosyndicalist Orobón Fernández pointed out that nothing short of a revolutionary transformation of the existing regime could even make possible the "rational" (that is, Anarchist) education of the masses, which alone would enable them to live in a society of Anarchy. Even granting that it were possible to educate the masses along Anarchist lines under the present regime, he asked, "Would this not be a labor so complex and prolonged that it would retard indefinitely the overthrow of the present society?" And he added: "Would not reliance on such an educational process turn the Cenetistas into the most pacific and resigned evolutionists?" Thus Orobón accepted the dictatorship of the proletariat as a "prophylactic measure" against the counterrevolution and as a necessary condition for the "profound and intense pedagogical labor" needed to prepare the individual for a life under Anarchy. He would not, however, concede that the dictatorship should be in the hands of a party, insisting that it be under the control of the sindicatos, which he described as the "arteries" of the future society. Against the Bolshevik obsession with the revolutionary party, Orobón urged the slogan "All power to the sindicatos!"[89]

A more enthusiastic acceptance of the dictatorship of the proletariat was revealed by Manuel Buenacasa, whose utterances suggest that the idea of the "organized" revolution may have reached the peak of its popularity among the majority of Cenetistas during the summer of 1920, at about the time Pestaña was experiencing his personal disillusionment in Moscow. This is substantiated by the response of Spanish Anarchosyndicalists to the "Message to the workers of the West European countries" that Peter Kropotkin sent out from Russia in this period. Always an opponent of the October Revolution, the dying patriarch of world Anarchism bitterly observed that "Russia has shown the way in which Socialism cannot be realized"; and he deplored, among other things, the fact that the soviets had been "degraded" to a purely passive role, whereas the Bolshevik party and state were assuming an ever greater prominence.[90]

Buenacasa, certainly the most pro-Bolshevik of all the bona fide Anarcho-syndicalists, immediately sprang to the defense of Lenin and his followers with a statement that was little less than an apologia for the revolutionary state and party. Kropotkin's letter, he said, was an allegation against the Bolsheviks that would "certainly prejudice the interests of the Russian Revolution and, consequently, of the Universal Revolution." Buenacasa acknowledged that Kropotkin was correct in condemning all power as "tyranny"; but what had to be remembered, he said, was that there were some states "worse than the bad ones." The worst of all were the bourgeois states, to which the polity of the Soviets should not be compared. Of course, one could not actually defend the state, since it was clearly an organ of oppression, but it did not seem strange to Buenacasa that the party exercising the proletarian dictatorship in Russia should deny the Anarchists the right to combat "maximalism." Would Kropotkin, he asked, assuming he were in power in Russia, abandon everything to the enemy?

The letter of the old comrade, Buenacasa concluded, was filled with "abundantly unjust censures" against the "maximalists" who ordered and ruled in Russia.[91] With these words Buenacasa—now editor of *Solidaridad Obrera* in Bilbao and a major spokesman for the CNT—attained what must be regarded as the high-water mark of pro-Bolshevik enthusiasm among the Cenetistas in the postwar period. Before long the revelations of the Second Comintern Congress would be trickling into Spain, and from this time forward faith would increasingly be diluted with doubt; but for Buenacasa, in the summer of 1920, the Bolshevik legend was as yet untarnished.

The defense of the proletarian dictatorship by pro-Bolshevik militants within the CNT and the PSOE-UGT reflected their continuing revolutionary optimism during the course of 1920. There was, of course, opposition to the Comintern within both movements, but the majority of Spanish workers continued to feel great enthusiasm for the Russian Bolsheviks and to live in the expectation—or at least the hope—of a Spanish October. The critical observations of Angel Pestaña and Fernando de los Ríos regarding the Russian scene were not published until 1921, and even then do not seem to have greatly influenced the mass of Spanish workers. De los Ríos could in any case be dismissed as a "bourgeois reformist," and the views of Pestaña were not widely circulated until the early part of 1922.

Pestaña's reticence, in fact, constituted something of a mystery. It is true that he was arrested immediately upon his return from Russia and imprisoned in Montjuich. But Spanish prisons were notoriously permeable to news and information passing both ways, and if he had chosen to publicize his views early in 1921, he could certainly have done so. His delay (he did not publish a statement until November 1921) appears to have resulted from both the continued pro-Bolshevik enthusiasm of the Catalonian workers, which Pestaña was perhaps too prudent to challenge, and the desperately embattled situation of the Cenetistas vis-à-vis Martínez Anido, in which the Bolshevik myth served as a vital source of inspiration and strength. Denigration of the Bolshevik Revolution or the Russian leaders would almost certainly have worked to undermine the revolutionary impulse and combative energies of Catalonian workers in the very face of the enemy. Thus it must have seemed almost unthinkable to Pestaña, in the violent spring of 1921, that he should do anything to weaken Cenetista morale, since he knew that the Anarchosyndicalists, more than other men, lived by their myths.

In retrospect, the stubborn revolutionary confidence of the Catalonian workers, and especially of their leaders, through 1920 and into 1921 seems increasingly ill-founded and unrealistic. Even before the return of the several emissaries sent to Russia, the Spanish labor movement had reached the summit of its postwar power and was finding itself more and more on the defensive in the social struggle. This was true not only of the Socialists, who had neither grown so large nor aspired to so much as the Anarchosyndicalists, but even more of the Cenetistas, who were showing definite signs of organizational fatigue as the result of their intensifying struggle with the employers and with a newly emerged labor rival, the Sindicatos Libres. To an account of this epoch of attrition and decline in the history of the CNT we must now turn.

CHAPTER ELEVEN

The CNT in Decline

The Persistence of Terror

By most indexes 1920 was the hardest year for Spanish workers since the beginning of the war. The economy continued to contract, and the ranks of the unemployed grew steadily; yet at the same time, the curve of inflation reached its apogee, rising to the highest level ever attained in Spain before beginning to move downward once more. The ensuing deflationary process, moreover, would prove a mixed blessing, since the end of the year would find the economy sliding toward a major financial and industrial crisis. The level of strike activity in 1920 rose well above the level of the preceding year, and this was true also of the number of *atentados sociales*.[1]

Despite the steady erosion of their organizational strength in Catalonia during 1920, the Cenetistas' faith in an impending upheaval remained remarkably unshaken through much of the year; and the apprehensions of the forces of order, already heightened by news of the consolidation of Bolshevik power in Russia and by the Red Army offensive against Poland in July, were correspondingly aroused. In fact, the greatest Syndicalist threat had already passed, and 1920 would be a year of defeat and demoralization for the CNT, as the conservative forces proved able to take the offensive. Supported by the Army and by the ministers in Madrid, and aided by the workers' growing fatigue— and, to a degree, by spreading disillusionment with the Sindicatos Unicos— Catalonian employers would gain the upper hand by the end of the year, administering a decisive defeat to the Anarchosyndicalist forces.

In Barcelona, the month of January began inauspiciously. Only four days into the new year an abortive attempt was made to assassinate Salvador Seguí. Whether this was instigated (as most believed) by the employers, who generally failed to acknowledge the Catalan leader's essential moderation, or whether it was the work of Anarchist gunmen disgruntled with Seguí's refusal to confront the November-January lockout with a revolutionary factory occupation and general strike may never be known.[2] On the following day another atentado—presumably in retaliation for the attack on Seguí—seriously wounded Jaime Graupera, the president of the Employers' Federation, as he was being driven through the city in his heavily guarded car. This incident caused Captain General Milans del Bosch to close down all unions in Barcelona, to suspend publication of *Solidaridad Obrera*, and to arrest about a hundred Syndicalist leaders, most of whom, it is likely, neither knew nor approved of the plot to murder Graupera.[3]

On January 9, only a few days after the attack on Graupera, an uprising occurred among the artillerymen of the Carmen Barracks in Zaragoza. This isolated and hopeless undertaking was inspired by the Zaragoza Anarchist Angel Chueca, who, after killing the officer and sergeant of the guard, died in a futile attempt to storm the main barracks area. Seven soldiers (including their leader, a Corporal Nicolás Godoy) were summarily shot, and more executions would certainly have followed had not a spontaneous general strike broken out in the city of Zaragoza. Chueca, a strong admirer of the Russian Bolsheviks, appears to have carried out this venture on his own, without the knowledge of the Zaragoza Syndicalists and without any attempt to organize a simultaneous rising in the city. Nevertheless, an impulse of shock and fear ran through the conservative classes, and Alejandro Lerroux—himself more conservative every day—melodramatically announced that "the Soviet knocks at the door of the barracks."[4] But this attempt to foment an uprising among Spain's peasant soldiers was not repeated elsewhere; and, in fact, the rank and file of the Army, despite widespread fears, had not been significantly penetrated by either Syndicalist or "Bolshevist" notions. Mariano de Cavia of *El Sol*, in a tone almost of rueful admiration, described the impetuous Chueca as "un bolchevique de verdad." José Chueca, the dead rebel's brother, agreed with this verdict, adding that his brother had been a "mystic" for whom life had no other purpose than the making of the revolution.[5]

Disturbances now occurred among the Syndicalist-influenced workers of Gijón, which led to the closing of the unions in that city and the arrest of several score militants. On January 23 the unions of La Coruña also had to be closed. That same day Maestre Laborde, Count Salvatierra, the newly appointed civil governor of Catalonia, dissolved the Catalonian Regional Confederation and shut down a large number of workers' centers. Salvatierra, a man noted for the severity of his personality, owed both his appointment (on January 20) and the rigor of the policies he inaugurated to the new Conservative government of Allendesalazar, who had assumed power after the failure of the conciliatory efforts of Governor Julio Amado and of the Sánchez de Toca government, which had fallen the previous December. Allendesalazar, whom the newspapers dubbed "the Unknown Soldier," was, indeed, an obscure figure, and it was clear that his regime was transitional. It also became apparent that he would continue, as a "hard" Conservative, to pursue the will-o'-the-wisp of social peace in Catalonia simply by reversing his predecessor's policy. In what was becoming a type of political minuet, conciliation would once again be followed by repression; and the vacillating alternation between hard and soft policies, which had marked the course of 1919 and which so little encouraged the emergence of a moderate and constructive labor movement in Catalonia, would be continued.[6]

The closing of the Catalonian unions and the dissolving of the CRT came at a bad moment for the Cenetistas, since it was imposed during the final days of the great lockout (not fully terminated until January 26) that had kept most of the organized labor force unemployed and unpaid since the previous November. Thus the renewed disruption of the organization coincided with a phase not of rising élan but of growing weariness among the workers. The CRT, as in times past, would continue the struggle underground; but its resilience had been sapped, and during 1920 it would not be able to maintain the solidarity and combative spirit it had displayed the previous year. Even the lifting of the repression, in May, would find the organization unable to rejuvenate itself as quickly as in past eras; and the renewal of harsh measures under Martínez Anido in November would seal its fate.

For the CRT, then, the early months of 1920 marked the start of what would prove to be an irreversible decline—a reality partially obscured by the Cenetistas' own revolutionary ardor and by the fact that outside Catalonia the movement continued to grow. Manuel Buenacasa exaggerated only a little when he said that from the beginning of the lockout in November 1919 until the spring of 1922 the CRT had "scarcely any collective existence."[7] The crucial consequence of Salvatierra's renewal of repression was that it once more facilitated the displacement of the moderate leaders, who under clandestine conditions were inevitably pushed to one side in the governing of the sindicatos by the "special delegates" of the Anarchist action groups.[8] What was at stake was the tactical line to be followed by the organization. By the start of the new year the moderate Syndicalists were increasingly concerned about the danger of an imminent and severe reaction against the Cenetistas' continued reliance on terror. Some leaders, most notably Seguí, had seen this danger from the beginning, whereas others, such as Pestaña, had viewed the pistolero trend more complacently, even conceding it a kind of passive or opportunistic support. But now all the moderates—probably aware that a small but growing stream of dissatisfied workers was starting to desert to the newly formed Sindicatos Libres—were alarmed by the spreading ramifications of the terrorist tactic and resolved to try to bring it to a halt.

Toward the end of January the moderates called a secret meeting in Barcelona, with some 300 Cenetista delegates attending. This was an extremely mixed and irregular gathering, including delegates from the clandestine committees of the CRT and the CNT, from the juntas of the sindicatos, and from the action groups, as well as individual militants. Seguí and Pestaña—the latter for the first time openly—spoke with candor against the use of terror by the unions and warned of possible grave consequences. Pestaña especially criticized the bombing campaign that the Barcelona Local Federation of Sindicatos Unicos had defiantly organized to coincide with the ending of the lockout on January 26 and for which it had allocated more than 500 pesetas of the workers' money. After a lengthy discussion, a majority of those assembled agreed that the atentados and bombings should be halted at once, and that there should be a return to traditional revolutionary Syndicalist tactics.[9]

After the close of the conference, antiterrorist orders were sent out to the individual sindicatos and to the Barcelona Local Federation; but, as Pestaña later recalled, these were without the slightest effect. As if nothing had been decided, the pistoleros of the action groups continued to plan and execute their attacks with undiminished regularity. Their stubborn reliance on a tactic that could only be self-destructive for the CNT in the long run was due partly to the fact that the organization, having been forced underground, was simply no longer responsive to the wishes of its regular leaders. But it was also true, as Pestaña later said, that certain "interests" had been created among those militants who, having lost the habit of work, could not bear to return to the routine of factory life. They had found their métier in terror and wished to pursue no other. The January meeting, it may be noted, was Pestaña's last major intervention in the affairs of the CNT before his departure in March for Paris and Moscow.[10]

The fears of the moderates were not ill-founded: the employers had already launched their counterattack, and their aggressive class spirit and *élan vital* were growing daily. What the workers confronted, in reality, was a joint offensive by the Employers' Federation and the Army, who had put their lack of concurrence over the autonomy question to one side and were informally but closely linked in what one Cenetista partisan has called a *confabulación plutocrata-militar*.[11] To this alliance there also adhered the Lliga Regionalista, which, faced with the choice between furthering its nationalist aspirations and preserving its capitalist interests, gave priority to the latter. Unquestionably the enthusiasm of the Catalan bourgeoisie for autonomy had been tempered by the challenge of the Syndicalist movement, and they began to view the military presence in Catalonia with more favor.[12] The chief figure of this alliance was the military governor of Catalonia, General Severiano Martínez Anido, a tough soldier-administrator who was the real power behind Count Salvatierra's civil administration, and who, in November, would himself become civil governor. The chief of police was Colonel (later General) Miguel Arleguí, who was closely linked to Martínez Anido.

With the knowledge and approval of Martínez Anido—but not, apparently, at his instigation—there arose in the autumn of 1919 a new and competitive form of labor organization known as the Sindicatos Libres, which would become an important adjunct of the coalition forming against the Sindicatos

Unicos. These new unions, which would band together in the Corporación General del Trabajo (CGT), were not, as has so often been alleged, mere creatures of the bourgeoisie or the Army. Martínez Anido, of course, was bound to view a labor schism in Catalonia with sympathy and to await with interest the conflicts certain to result; and there is no question that the new organization, especially in its later stages, benefited from official favor and protection. But it should be emphasized that the labor discontents motivating the emergence of the Libres were authentic, and that the rebellion within the ranks of the CRT was neither artificial nor unimportant.[13]

The rise of the Sindicatos Libres was closely related to the growing influence of Anarchism within the CNT, or, more precisely, to the efforts of militant Anarchosyndicalists to divert the sindicatos from purely economic and syndical endeavors and push them toward Anarchist tactics and goals. Such efforts antagonized the by no means negligible minority of workers who were repelled by terrorist activity and anticlerical propaganda, unmoved by the vision of a republic of soviets on the Russian model, and attracted to the reformist tactics that had characterized the Catalonian labor movement of an earlier day. Thus among the precipitating causes of the schism was the resentment felt by some of the more pious, traditional, or monarchist workers regarding the enthusiasm for the Bolshevik Revolution that swept through the ranks of the CNT and especially overcame the Anarchist elements, who, in the autumn of 1919, were determined, in the name of *comunismo libertario*, to commit the CNT to the Communist International.[14]

A more fundamental cause of the schism, and one influencing a greater number of workers, was unrest over the increasingly onerous dictatorship exerted by the Anarchist pistoleros over the unions of the CRT. As authoritative a figure as Angel Pestaña testified to the rigors of that domination, admitting that vast sums of the workers' money were squandered on the gunmen of the Anarchist action groups, and that the CRT, in fact, had "lost control of itself" and thus lost its "moral credit" with the public. "The CNT," he said, "eventually fell so low in public esteem that to call oneself a Sindicalista was synonymous, ... unfortunately, with [being a] pistolero, evildoer, outlaw, and habitual delinqent."[15] Far more than any other issue, then, it was the tyranny of the pistoleros and their insatiable demands for money with which to carry on their atentados that started the exodus out of the Sindicatos Unicos and into the Sindicatos Libres.

The founders of the Libres—Ramón Sales was the most prominent—were many of them devout Catholics, belonging, it is said, to the Carlist Comunión Tradicionalista. They modeled their new organization on the Catholic free unions of Belgium and, in their statutes, drew upon Christian social doctrines. But all of this was done without reference to any confessional loyalty; and the hope of the founders, who recognized that only a small minority of the workers were religious, was that the new organization could occupy a middle ground between the Sindicatos Unicos and the Catholic trade unions, with which they did not wish to be confounded.[16]

Joining forces with elements from the Association of Cooks and Waiters, the workers led by Sales held their first meeting in the Ateneo Obrero Legitimista on October 19, 1919. About a hundred persons attended this gathering, and all of them, according to Salaya, were refugees from the Sindicatos Unicos, many of them having even been factory delegates. A constitution was approved, and the eloquent Sales was chosen as president, while José Baro became secretary. The civil governor at this time, Julio Amado, perhaps because of his sympathies for the Cenetistas and almost certainly because he foresaw added possibilities of civil strife, withheld his assent to the charter of the new organization. But the Sindicatos Libres began functioning anyway; and on December 11, only one day after the fall of the Sánchez de Toca government and of Amado, their charter was approved by the interim authority.[17]

The new organization immediately issued a manifesto appealing to all workers who were "sick of the tyranny and slavery to which we have been subjected by our so-called redeemers." The Sindicatos Libres were declared to be against the "patronal tyranny," but even more against that of the "spongers" of the Sindicatos Unicos, who were exerting "the most abject, hateful, and criminal despotism." They condemned "the bullies, the gamblers, the union rowdies—in short, all those who until now have lived at the expense of our honest work."[18] The manifesto also called for a purely trade-union organization, free of any political or religious affiliation and open to all workers, who would be united on the basis of "respect for the particular and private ideas and convictions of each individual." The appeal concluded with the cry: "Enough of tyranny! Enough of [dues payments] that are robberies!...Enough of slavery, despotism, and servitude!"[19]

In a statement published about a year later, the Libres made it clear that one of their principal motives was the desire not to belong to a revolutionary organization. They believed in the syndical struggle, they said, and would "never, never be an obstruction to the endeavors of the workers on behalf of just demands." They had no intention, they insisted, of becoming a "yellow" organization; but they firmly rejected any "revolutionary action" that seemed designed to "paralyze" industry, create starvation, and unleash the hungry masses against the "existing order of the world." To do such a thing, they believed, would in the end lead only to "a tyranny similar to that of Russia." After criticizing the Congress of the Comedia for permitting an "exiguous minority" of Anarchist delegates to commit the CNT to the dogma of libertarian Communism, the Libres suggested that the CNT, backed by "Jewish and German" bankers, was actively seeking to destroy the sources of the country's wealth and to set up Anarchist schools "without God and without law."[20]

The competition between Libres and Unicos began immediately. On December 12, 1919, while some members of the new organization were meeting in a cafe on the Calle de Tallers, several militants from the Unicos burst into the room and forced the Libres, at gunpoint, to leave the premises and march like military prisoners down the length of the Rambla, to the stupefaction of passersby. They were finally conducted to a building where a Cenetista "council of war" was meeting and where some of them were condemned to death. Only the arrival of the police, who at that point forced their way into the building, prevented what might have been a violent denouement.[21] The Libres, however, continued to flourish and were able to attract various elements away from the Cenetistas: many employees of the waterworks, 500 metalworkers from the Hispano-Suiza plants, the waiters' union, many bank employees, and some others. As early as 1920 a membership of 200,000 was claimed for all the Sindicatos Libres in Spain, but the figure for Catalonia alone is uncertain.[22]

For a brief period it seemed that despite the early clashes, the competition within the labor movement might be a peaceful one. In March 1920 a meeting in a cafe on the Calle San Andrés was attended by representatives of both the Libres (Ruperto Llado, Tomás Vives) and the Unicos. The Libres sought to explain their reasons for founding a new labor organization and asserted their intention to respect the Unicos and to cooperate with them in all economic and professional matters affecting the workers. The local representatives of the Unicos seem to have been amenable to this, though they deferred making public the terms of the agreement arrived at until the Committee of the CRT could be notified. In an attempt to formalize the understanding, Llado wrote to that body, advising its members of the founding of the new organization and saying frankly that the step had been taken because of the Libres' lack of agreement with the libertarian-Communist goal of the CNT. He reiterated that "our purpose is to act exclusively within the economic and professional sphere, in which you will find us always good comrades and faithful executors of our syndical obligations, but always with respect for the freedom of conscience and feelings of all." When a member of the Libres attempted personally to deliver this letter to the CRT Committee, however, he was given a most threatening reception and was denounced as a "traitor" to the cause of labor.[23] Less than fifteen days later, in early April, Tomás Vives, an organizer for the Libres, was shot down in the Rambla de Santa Eulalia, the first victim in what was to be a long and bloody contest between the two labor movements. The Libres had already given warning that for every one of their own killed they would exact a toll of three from the ranks of the Cenetistas.[24]

Although the Libres are usually described as an extension of the Army-bourgeois alliance, their efforts to establish themselves in Barcelona met with more than a few obstacles, lending credence to their claims of autonomy. Needing a headquarters for their union and aware that landlords would not rent to a syndical organization, they resorted to leasing the third floor of a building on the Calle de Tallers under the pretense of being a school of languages, hoping that the owners would not notice that the "students" who came and went were all shabbily dressed in the garb of workingmen. They were, nevertheless, soon raided by the police, who searched the premises and seized thousands of membership cards, pamphlets, and stamps. Count Salvatierra, by then civil governor, was suspicious of all sindicatos, whatever their coloration, and ordered the headquarters of the Libres closed down.[25]

More serious, of course, was the increasingly bitter opposition of the Cenetistas to the new organization, especially after it began to enjoy its first successes. As the Libres stepped up their propaganda and proselytizing, and made further conquests among the cooks and waiters of Barcelona (who seem to have been won over almost in their entirety) and among the rubber workers, the Cenetistas began systematically resorting to direct action against their rivals. The anti-Libres campaign began in earnest on June 7, when a metalworker named Torres was assassinated in Mataro. By this date Count Salvatierra had been replaced as governor by Carlos Bas, who was committed to a renewal of pacification and hence released from prison most of the "social prisoners" arrested by Salvatierra, including many Anarchist gunmen. These actions necessarily meant an escalation of pressure against the Libres, and the number of terrorist attacks began to mount. On July 6, one Purcet of the Cooks' Union was shot down by pistoleros of the Unicos; and on July 24 Juan Casanovas, a pro-Libres leader of the rubber workers was similarly disposed of. On October 13 Gines Mirete of the dye workers was also felled by Cenetista bullets. The Sindicatos Unicos also used nonviolent weapons against the Libres, most notably the boycott, by which they forbade their followers to work alongside members of the competing unions. But when Cenetista workers went on strike to protest the presence of Libres in the factories, their jobs were promptly taken by still other members of the new unions, and bitterness was compounded.[26]

Pacification Again: May–November 1920

Despite the rising conflict between Unicos and Libres, the period May–June in fact marked a relative hiatus in the social struggle in Barcelona and the beginning of another phase of conciliation. The first hopeful sign was the dissolution of the de Koening terrorist band, which for some while had provided employers with the gunmen needed to carry out reprisals against the Cenetistas. Recruited from a social stratum—the bas fond—not very different from that drawn upon by the Anarchist action groups, de Koening's pistoleros had gotten out of hand and had begun to initiate actions such as simulated atentados in order to enhance their importance and create a greater demand for their services. This produced a swift reaction from the employers, and in

May or June, on the orders of Interior Minister Bergamín, "Baron" de Koening was expelled from Spain and his gang largely dispersed. Their last act of terror was the murder of two Cenetista workers on May 17—an act publicly condemned by the Employers' Federation.[27] The next step toward pacification of the social scene was the dismissal (June 22) of Count Salvatierra as civil governor, for reasons apparently unrelated to the labor movement but having to do, rather, with his inept handling of the crowds that had thronged to see the visiting General Joffre on the occasion of the Fiesta of Juegos Floriales in May. Most crucial, perhaps, was the fall of the Allendesalazar government and the assumption of power by the leader of the Conservative Party, Eduardo Dato. Dato, the liquidator of the August Movement of 1917, had been preceded by two earlier Conservative premiers, one committed to pacification and the other to repression; and he appears to have decided that the time had come for a definitive resolution of the social crisis in Catalonia.

Dato first tried reconciliation. A liberal civil governor, Federico Carlos Bas, was named to replace Salvatierra and proceeded at once to free all Syndicalist prisoners and to end censorship. Bas also restored the CRT's legal right to operate openly and to reorganize its ranks. On the other hand, constitutional guarantees were not reestablished; nor did the Dato government in Madrid seem willing to place the full weight of its authority behind efforts to encourage a dialogue between workers and employers or to temper the extreme intransigence of the latter. Governor Bas, like his predecessor Amado, was struck by the employers' bellicose spirit: having been introduced to the class war by the Cenetistas, the Catalonian bourgeoisie enthusiastically embraced the concept and were obsessed, as Bas said, with the idea of "giving battle" to the workers in order to subdue them utterly.[28]

A number of other pacification measures were carried out during the early phase of Dato's new ministry. On May 8 a royal decree created a Ministry of Labor for the first time; and on June 27 a decree limiting rent increases was issued. Then, during June 27–29, King Alfonso, accompanied by his chief minister, traveled to Barcelona as a gesture of amity and was well received by the city, with neither workers nor nationalists attempting to disrupt the royal visit. Shortly thereafter Alfonso approved a measure creating a de facto regional parliament in Catalonia. The effect of all this was somewhat marred, however, by the news that Count Salvatierra, who after departing from Catalonia had become the civil governor of Valencia, had been murdered on July 30 while leaving the bullring of that city.[29]

During the relaxation in the social struggle that accompanied the first months of Dato's regime, the CRT rose once more to the surface of Catalonian life and began to reestablish the full functioning of its unions and committees. But recovery in this period was slower than in previous phases of conciliation. More and more workers proved reluctant to resume payment of their union dues and to participate in the activities of the resurrected sindicatos. This was in part the result of an inevitable decline in the labor enthusiasm that had risen to such heights in the summer and fall of 1919; and it also reflected the economic impact of the previous winter's crippling lockout. Not least, it revealed a growing resentment of the domination exercised by the Anarchist action groups over the sindicatos of the CRT. That domination, as we have seen, played an important part in the genesis and growth of the Sindicatos Libres, which increasingly became a source of attraction for those weary or disgruntled workers for whom the revolutionary vision had begun to fade. That the Libres, having fled the pistoleros of the CRT, now had to organize their own corps of gunmen in order to defend their claim to autonomy was, perhaps, ironic. The pause in the social struggle would, in any case, be very brief, as the gunmen of the Libres, reluctantly taking the place of the dissolved de Koening band, entered into violent conflict with their Anarchosyndicalist rivals.[30]

Repression Renewed

The moderate policy launched by Dato in June was not long or tenaciously pursued, and the Conservative Party was in fact divided over the wisdom of continuing it. The more liberal wing feared the results of a prolonged suspension of constitutional guarantees and felt that reestablishing them would help reconcile the workers to the government. But the right wing, led by Dato, feared that a permissive attitude toward the workers would only speed the coming of the revolutionary outburst they felt to be impending. The international scene appeared to them especially ominous. In May 1920 French Syndicalists had launched a series of spectacular general strikes in various industries with the intention of creating a total, nationwide, and essentially revolutionary general strike; and in the summer the workers of northern Italy began their dramatic factory occupations. The level of strike activity throughout Europe now rose to unprecedented heights, even as the Red Army began its headlong drive toward Warsaw. No one at the time could be certain that the Bolshevik Revolution would not soon make direct contact with the German "powder keg," thereby, it was feared, spreading revolution all over Europe. In Russia the Bolsheviks, having defeated or repelled both their internal and external enemies, were rapidly consolidating their control; and in July the Second Comintern Congress was held in an atmosphere vibrant with impending triumph. Present at that congress, as the Conservatives were well aware, was a representative of the CNT; and it was known that other Spaniards were on their way to Moscow. The adherence of the Spanish Socialist Party to the Comintern in June seemed to the overwrought Conservative leaders one more link in an ominous revolutionary trend, especially since they failed to comprehend the substantial reservations with which the Socialist commitment was given.[31]

The Liberal deputy and sometime minister Rafael Gasset captured the mood of the Conservative leaders with fidelity in a somewhat agitated book, *Rebellious humanity: The Russian Revolution; the social problem in Spain*. To think, he said,

> that [in the aftermath of war] the waters are returning to their banks, that the hurricane has been transformed into a gentle breeze, is to close one's eyes.... The inflamed Reds of Russia, the clamor of their stormy winds, the gusts of rebellion that agitate and break down the social order of the entire world, are things whose danger only the most confirmed ignorance will fail to proclaim.... The grass, then, is parched; the wind of rebellion blows continually, and every hour more violently.[32]

Gasset was disturbed by the emulative spirit aroused among European—and Spanish—workers by the Russian Revolution, and he warned that "World Syndicalism" had its "gaze fixed and its ear cocked" to everything that happened in Bolshevik Russia. Like the Conservative ministers, he regarded Bolshevism and Syndicalism simply as two manifestations of the same phenomenon; and it seemed to him that the trend toward Bolshevik ideas among the Spanish proletariat was very powerful, as was revealed when "a man of learning and intellect like Besteiro sees fit not to protest [the Socialist Party's] adherence to the Third International."[33] In the last analysis, the mood of semihysteria shared by Gasset and the Conservatives reflected an awareness of Spain's retarded condition and of her unusual vulnerability to the "gusts of rebellion" sweeping over Europe. The uprising in the Carmen Barracks, though an isolated incident, was viewed as a grave portent, though the most serious threat was still thought to lie in the Andalusian peasantry.

Of course, Rafael Gasset was more progressive than the Datistas in his approach to the problem. As a long-time champion of agrarian reform and irrigation projects, he spoke more frankly about the moral and material backwardness of the Peninsula, and about the "African existence" lived by millions of Spaniards. These realities, he felt, set Spain apart from the rest of Western Europe, placing her in the more backward category of injustice-ridden nations prone to revolution—a category, as he observed, to which Russia herself had belonged before the upheaval of 1917.[34]

Whereas Gasset concluded from such reflections that rapid and far-reaching reform was vital, Dato and his colleagues deduced the need for repression. They were genuinely alarmed by the vast expansion of the Anarchosyndicalist movement in the years 1918–20 and had difficulty distinguishing between strikes with essentially material objectives and those with revolutionary intent. This was especially true with respect to the great miners' strike in Peñarroya, which began in April and involved some 15,000 workers, and in the case of the strike at Río Tinto (June–October), which threatened to lead to a general strike of solidarity in all of Andalusia. These movements were, in fact, remote from the revolutionary scene in Barcelona and stemmed from essentially local and material causes; but they helped convince Dato that his policy of conciliation had failed and that sterner measures were called for.[35]

Amid the growing social turbulence of Spain, Dato thought he saw the familiar storm clouds of revolution on the horizon. With a feeling of déjà vu he imagined that it would be 1917 all over again, and he was prepared, as in August of that tumultuous year, to spare no effort to prevent an assault on the throne. Just as he had then capitulated to the Juntas de Defensa in order to guarantee to the regime the support of the Army, so he would now yield to the pleas of the employers and make General Martínez Anido civil governor of Barcelona, granting him the widest possible powers and countenancing even the use of the Ley de Fugas. Dato was far from sharing all the views of the military or the bourgeoisie; but he was clearly prepared to go to great lengths in maintaining a united front with these elements in order to save a regime that he viewed as gravely threatened.[36]

Not wanting to precipitate the revolution that he feared, Dato did not launch his repressive policy immediately but reverted to it by gradual stages. One of his first steps (probably a response to the murder of Count Salvatierra in July) was to suspend on August 7 the use of juries for crimes involving bloodshed— a reasonable measure, since juries dealing with accused terrorists had been uniformly intimidated in the past. Further justification for the suspension was no doubt derived from a terrorist act carried out on August 12, when a bomb was thrown into a crowded Barcelona music hall—the Pompeia—frequented mostly by workers, leaving three dead and many wounded. The turning point between conciliation and renewed repression came on September 1, when the liberal Francisco Bergamín was replaced in the Ministry of the Interior by the hard-liner Count Gabino Bugallal. It was now evident that the regime—closely supported by the Employers' Federation, the Army, and the Lliga Regionalista, all of whom had long pressed for Bergamín's dismissal—was girding itself to solve the Syndicalist question once and for all, and by force.[37]

The government's reversion to a coercive policy necessarily drove Cenetistas and Ugetistas once more toward a reluctant rapprochement. A step in this direction had already been taken by the delegates to the UGT Congress in July, when they voted in favor of making another overture to their Anarchosyndicalist rivals on behalf of labor unity. In compliance with this mandate the Committee of the UGT sent a letter (August 13) to the CNT urging the desirability of fusing the two organizations. The Cenetista reply (August 26) was skeptical in tone, asserting that the Ugetista leaders only wished to give the appearance of favoring labor unity without actually doing so. It was also noted that in its last congress the UGT had decided to continue in the Amsterdam International, even though it was known that the CNT had adhered to Moscow; this fact, said the Cenetistas, made it "almost useless" to attempt a unification. Nevertheless, the CNT leaders were prepared to name a committee of three to meet with a similar group from the UGT in order to arrange a national unification congress of the two organizations.

The Cenetistas insisted, however, that the voting of the special committee not only should not be subject to appeal to the parent organizations but should be decided according to the number of adherents each side represented—which was tantamount, as Tuñón de Lara has said, to asking the Ugetistas for an unconditional surrender.[38] The CNT letter further demanded that the UGT bar from the committee anyone holding a seat in the Cortes or in a provincial or local legislative body, as well as anyone holding an office that involved "collaboration" with the capitalist regime. To a suggestion by the UGT that the committee attempt to draft a new set of regulations acceptable to both organizations, the Cenetistas replied in a bored tone that such an endeavor did not interest them greatly, since it would be a useless and "purely bureaucratic" procedure. Committed, as always, to spontaneity, the Anarchosyndicalists remarked: "We do not believe in establishing fixed criteria of action, since no one can know where the circumstances . . . may carry us."[39] What was striking, then, was the lack of urgency displayed by the National Committee of the CNT, which seemed indifferent to whether or not labor unity was achieved.

But with the sudden dismissal of Bergamín, which was announced a few days after the Cenetista reply, the attitude of the CNT leaders underwent a transformation. The "pure" Syndicalists, who in any case had always favored unification efforts, now gained the initiative. The signs of an impending effort by the government to resolve the social question by *force majeure* convinced Seguí that a renewal of the alliance with the UGT was imperative. Persuasive as always, he was able to convince Evelio Boal, who headed the National Committee, that Dato's change of course required an immediate and realistic approach to the Socialists. On September 3 Seguí, Boal, and Quemades took the train to Madrid and, in a meeting with Largo Caballero and other Ugetista leaders, signed a pact allying (though not actually merging) the CNT and the UGT.

As soon as the agreement was signed, the new allies issued a manifesto complaining about the extreme pressure that the Employers' Federation was exerting on the Madrid government and deploring the fact that first Sánchez de Toca and now Bergamín had been forced to leave their posts as a result of bourgeois machinations. With some confidence, it was affirmed that the disunity of the labor movement, which had permitted such things to happen, would be brought to an end by the UGT-CNT alliance. An urgent demand was also made for the restoration of constitutional guarantees, even as the assembled labor leaders acknowledged that such a request might seem "paradoxical" coming from the "declared enemies of bourgeois society."[40] Not mentioned in the manifesto, but almost certainly contemplated by the Socialists, was the possibility that the pact might form the basis for a Socialist-Anarcho-syndicalist coalition in the national elections, which were then only a few months away. Indomitably electoral, the Socialist leaders had never lost the hope that the Catalonian masses could be drawn into political life on the side of the Party's candidates.[41]

The UGT-CNT pact, like that of 1916, came as a great shock to public opinion, appearing as a resurrection of the alliance that had thrown the country into turmoil in 1917. Prime Minister Dato saw it as a confirmation of the revolutionary intentions he already ascribed to the labor movement, and he resolved to adhere all the more firmly to his repressive course. That his attitude was not entirely without justification is revealed by the tone of some of the labor meetings held to celebrate the new alliance. At a rally in Barcelona on October 5, attended by Besteiro and by Martínez Gil, the fiery pro-Bolshevik journalist Andrés Nin, a rapidly rising figure within the ranks of the CNT, said: "We have made an alliance not because we want a period of peace, but rather because we want war, [because] we want class struggle." Nin, as the leader of the emerging Communist-Syndicalist faction within the Confederation urged the creation of a "united front" composed of all sections of the labor movement.[42]

Not all the Cenetistas were happy about the agreement, many of the more extreme Anarchosyndicalists believing strongly that the organization had been betrayed by Seguí and Quemades, who had talked Boal into signing. In a CNT plenum held at the request of the various regions late in October, the UGT-CNT pact became the subject of heated debate, as Buenacasa and other delegates made clear their opposition to the detente and their fears that it foreshadowed some type of electoral collaboration between Socialists and Syndicalists. In the face of the accusations they made, Seguí had once again to disclaim any electoral intentions and to reaffirm the orthodox antiparliamentary position of the CNT.[43]

Nevertheless, the plenum confirmed the pact, and even went on to approve a proposal that the CNT and the UGT work together in an effort to resolve the Río Tinto miners' strike, which had been in progress since June 26. This would be the first cooperative venture of the two organizations since August 1917. As always, the Cenetistas—or at least the more militant Anarchosyndicalists—wanted to push things further and faster than the Socialists wished to do. Their conception was that the Río Tinto conflict should be turned into a general strike of all miners in Spain, and that this should be followed by general strikes on the railways and in other industries until the British-owned Río Tinto Company capitulated. The plan bore a strong resemblance to the strategy that the French CGT had sought unsuccessfully to carry out the previous May, and thus had revolutionary overtones that cannot have been pleasing to Largo Caballero or the other Ugetista leaders—nor even, for that matter, to the moderate, Seguí-led Syndicalists. When Seguí traveled to Río Tinto with some UGT leaders (including Núñez Tomás), the only proposal that emerged from their inspection was entirely moderate and reasonable: namely, that a special levy of one peseta be imposed on each member of the UGT and CNT in order to help the Río Tinto miners carry their struggle forward to a successful conclusion.[44]

The division between reformist and revolutionary impulses within the CNT was revealed again in the course of a metalworkers' strike launched in Barcelona on October 21. This strike, in which Cenetistas and Libres cooperated for the first time, would prove to be the last major labor effort in Catalonia until 1923. The leadership of the movement was supplied by the moderate Cenetistas (notably Ramón Arín, the head of the Metalworkers' Union), who, conscious of the deepening recession in Spanish industry, sought to carry out only a partial strike confined to the metallurgical industry and having very limited objectives. However, the intransigent Anarchosyndicalists once more sought to turn the strike into a thoroughgoing revolutionary movement. Under their pressure the work stoppage became general, embracing, in the end, more than 23,000 workers in 844 enterprises.[45] Nor were they content with conventional strike action: on October 11, Anarchist pistoleros assassinated the metallurgical employer Tarrida, and on October 30 they dispatched the president of the Electrical Employers' Association. Needless to say, the militant Anarchosyndicalists were indignant when the moderates—chiefly Seguí, Quemades, and Arín—succeeded in bringing the strike to an end through a compromise settlement and reliance on a mixed commission. The extremists no doubt shared the view expressed by the young Communists of the PCE, who declared that the settlement of the strike clearly revealed the spread of "Syndicalist opportunism" and "collaboration of a vile sort."[46] It should be noted that the metalworkers of the Sindicatos Libres joined this strike, not, perhaps, with very great enthusiasm but largely from a desire to demonstrate their sincerity and willingness to cooperate with the Unicos in a purely syndical struggle.[47]

Martínez Anido and "Definitive Pacification"

The renewal of an openly repressive policy in Catalonia was signaled by a meeting convened by the mayor of Barcelona on November 5 and attended by the various interest groups of the city, most notably by the Employers' Federation. The problem of continuing violence in the port city was discussed— three more workers were shot that very day—and strong criticism was directed at Governor Bas, whose policy of conciliation toward the Syndicalists was held responsible for the continued bloodletting.[48] The employers keenly resented the fact that Bas's office door had been opened on more than one occasion to Seguí and to other Syndicalist leaders, including such labor allies and go-betweens as Francisco Layret and Luis Companys. The governor's efforts at fairmindedness only caused the employers to stigmatize him as "soft" on Syndicalism and as an obstacle to the total victory in the class war that they seemed to be seeking.[49]

Beyond their expressed concern about terrorism, the employers appear to have had compelling economic motives for wishing to be rid of Carlos Bas. By October or November it was clear that the Spanish economy was nearing the brink of the first major crisis of the postwar period. Exports had declined steadily through 1920, and an increasing quantity of foreign goods were entering the country, as in the period before 1914. Spanish producers, having failed to use their wartime profits to modernize, not only were losing the foreign markets gained during the halcyon days of the war but were surrendering the domestic market to cheaper (and often superior) goods manufactured abroad. By the autumn of 1920 prices began to drop, unemployment rose, consumption fell off, and bank credit became more and more restricted. The national balance of payments, which had stood at plus 381 million pesetas in 1918 and plus 227 million in 1919, fell to minus 424 million by the end of 1920 and would reach minus 500 million in 1921. Emigration, the unerring index of Spanish economic distress, climbed from 71,720 in 1919 to 147,918 in 1920. As always, the crisis hit Catalonia first and hardest. As early as November the textile industry—the backbone of the region's economy—began slowing down perceptibly. But the real collapse was signalled by the sudden failure of the prestigious Bank of Barcelona in December. Hundreds of industries and businesses began to reduce production and lay off workers, so that by 1921, for example, no less than half of Catalonia's metalworkers were out of work.[50]

In this situation the employers saw an irresistible opportunity to strike a decisive blow against the labor movement. Among them prevailed something more than mere fear of revolutionary upheaval. Choosing to ignore the fact that the most prominent leaders of the CRT were committed not to revolution but to *reivindicaciones* of a very material and negotiable kind, the capitalist class sought to realize a dream of somewhat primitive grandeur, which was nothing less than the complete liquidation of the autonomous labor movement in Catalonia.

The November 5 meeting, then, reflected the employers' exasperation at the government's failure to apply to the workers the iron hand they felt the situation demanded. Hence the conclave resulted in a strongly worded resolution of protest against Governor Bas that called for his resignation. The response of the Dato government was prompt and propitiatory: by telegram it hastened to assure the employers that "the government is taking under most serious consideration your legitimate protest and will not omit any effort to remedy such a painful situation."[51] At almost the same moment, the military governor, Martínez Anido, confronted Bas in his office, bluntly demanding that the latter take draconian measures against the Cenetistas or get out. This terse and angry dialogue was recalled by Bas:

> Anido: Señor Governor, the atentados continue, and the methods of pacification are useless. Peace will be restored if you order the shooting of—or let fall where they may—*gentes* like Eugenio d'Ors, ... Joaquín Montaner, Francisco Layret, Salvador Seguí, Luis Companys, Angel Pestaña, Mario Aguilar, Guerra del Río, the Ulled brothers, and others.
>
> Bas: Señor Military Governor, I am the civil governor, but I am not an assassin.
>
> A: Do not use explosive words. It is not a question of assassinating but of executing.
>
> B: I do not do that.
>
> A: Well then, give up your post and let me do it. . . .
>
> B: I will take it up with the Interior Minister.
>
> A: It is all the same to me. The day after tomorrow I will occupy your office.[52]

Martínez Anido's confidence was not ill founded. When Governor Bas telephoned Interior Minister Bugallal in Madrid, the latter appeared to be already apprised of the situation and urged the controversial governor to surrender his post—a step that Bas immediately took. On the afternoon of November 8, as the result of a telephone call from Prime Minister Dato, Martínez Anido was appointed governor of Barcelona province. To the reporters he said: "I am not a politician; I am a soldier. . . . The situation is critical, and we have to do everything to guide it for the good of Barcelona and of Spain. I love and respect this land [of Catalonia], which I consider my second homeland, and I feel real grief to see what ought to be a peaceful and prosperous city converted by the terrorists into a city of crimes."[53] On the following day Anido traveled to Madrid, where he held lengthy conferences with Dato and Bugallal, from whom he appears to have received carte blanche to deal with the situation in Barcelona as he thought best.[54]

The new governor confronted a variety of problems. He was aware of the increasing restlessness of the Army leaders in Catalonia regarding the social struggle and of the possibility that if the conflict were not soon moderated the military might take matters into its own hands.[55] There was also the question of the high cost of living, a subject with which Anido, as the ex officio president of the Junta de Subsistencias, had to be directly concerned. He had to assure, moreover, a definitive settlement of the recently ended metalworkers' strike, for which purpose he asked the government for the immediate appointment of a mixed commission. Above all else, there was the problem of terrorism, now endemic in Barcelona and seemingly rooted in the structure of the city's industrial life. Upon the suppression of this social plague his whole success depended, and he was clearly prepared to take the most drastic steps to put an end to the atentados and achieve what he termed a "definitive pacifica-tion."[56] He was convinced that the labor leaders—all of them—would have to be separated from the masses and the sindicatos closed down before this ob-jective could be reached. Thus in practice he would tend to ignore the distinc-tion, which he himself made, between the extreme Anarchosyndicalists who advocated and practiced terror and the moderate Syndicalists who had merely tolerated or even actively opposed the atentados.[57]

The Cenetistas themselves, especially the extremists among them, saw the new appointment as a provocation and were prepared to fight. Within a few days of the governor's appearance terrorist activity resumed, including attacks on members of the Guardia and the placing of dozens of bombs in various parts of the city. The Anarchosyndicalists sensed that they were fighting to keep the mass of workers loyal to the CRT, and they feared that any signs of weakness or passivity might start those workers drifting away.[58] Martínez Anido nevertheless bided his time, seemingly in no hurry to begin the crack-down that everyone expected. One day after another passed with no one jailed and no workers' centers closed; and the governor even publicly chided those distraught citizens who came to his office with panicky denunciations. Cer-tainly, the Catalan bourgeoisie were fearful, and in some cases close to hys-teria.* One prosperous citizen suggested to the journalist Francisco Madrid that all persons who had lost loved ones in the atentados should be seated in the Plaza de Cataluña with their faces covered; all the workers of the city would then be marched before them so that they could single out the men guilty—or suspected—of atentados for summary execution.[59]

When his plans were finally completed, Martínez Anido proceeded to act, using as his excuse the shooting of a company chauffeur by the Cenetistas in a dispute at the plant of the journal *La Publicidad*. Just hours after this epi-sode, on November 20, the general launched what was clearly a well-prepared assault on the leadership of the CRT. About midnight the police began knock-ing on the doors of Syndicalist leaders, and by dawn the Model Prison was filled, the sindicatos closed down, and the labor press proscribed. The arrests went on for several days, and when they were completed most of the high- and middle-level Cenetista officials were behind bars, including Seguí (who had

---

* A. del Castillo, writing in the fall of 1920, conveyed something of the atmosphere in Barcelona: "Not only the police and the army, but also the better class of citizens are taking active part in this struggle. The latter have armed and are drilling in military formations. These civic guards, like the police and the army, have unlimited authority to use arms, to arrest suspected persons, to search houses, and to inflict summary punishment. Even the rector of the University of Barcelona, a worthy old gentleman with a venerable beard, who, under ordinary conditions, would not harm a fly, has armed himself to the teeth and taken command of a company of young men, who, elegantly dressed and carry-ing brand-new rifles, have placed themselves at the service of 'the cause.' " Del Castillo, "Bolshevism in Spain," p. 763.

just returned from a trip to Río Tinto), Martín Barrera, Simón Piera, Antonio Amador, David Rey, the Vidal brothers, and Ramón Arín; the Republican lawyer Luis Companys, a long-time ally of the Cenetistas, was also detained. Altogether, about 64 leaders of note were imprisoned (though Evelio Boal, general secretary of the CNT, managed to avoid arrest until early in March 1921). In this same period Anido also imposed telephone and newspaper censorship and conducted energetic searches that turned up large quantities of weapons.

If the governor hoped that the arrest of the leading Syndicalists, among whom, he said, were "the most responsible leaders and directors" of the atentados,[60] would put a stop to terrorist activity, he must have been rudely disappointed. The attacks continued and even increased in number, suggesting that the real infrastructure of the Anarchist action groups had not been seriously impaired. During the first three weeks of Martínez Anido's tenure (November 9–30) 22 atentados were carried out, as the struggle between the Sindicatos Libres and the Sindicatos Unicos continued to mount.[61] On November 26 the president of the Libres of Reus, one Capdevila, was assassinated, and on the same day Sr. Albareda, owner of the Hotel Continental (whose waiters had been organized by the Libres), was accosted by Cenetista gunmen on the Rambla de las Flores and seriously wounded. The next day, in apparent retaliation, the moderate José Canela—like Seguí, a "pure" Syndicalist—was gunned down, and his companion Andrés Nin narrowly escaped death. A few days later Canela's friend Carlos Bort was also dispatched. The pattern here, as earlier, was one in which the Anarchist extremists of the CRT carried out atentados that frequently resulted in reprisals not so much against themselves, since they remained mostly anonymous, as against the more moderate—and more visible—leaders of their own organization. Shootings were also being carried out in this period by the bourgeois volunteers of the Somatenes, who, for example, assassinated a union delegate on November 20.[62]

Meanwhile, the Sindicatos Libres were achieving a rapprochement with Martínez Anido. On November 19, just one day before the mass arrest of the Cenetista leaders, a delegation from the Libres visited the governor's office in an effort to make clear to him their complete disagreement with the tactics of the Unicos. They told him that their organization was based on respect for the conscience of its individual members, and that their activity would always be within the law, using only the legal weapons of the strike and the boycott, and these only when all lesser means of overcoming the employers' resistance had failed. The delegates also informed Anido that they shared his desire to suppress terrorism, and that to that end they were placing themselves unconditionally on the side of the authorities. The governor responded congenially, emphasizing that he was not opposed to the workers' being organized, since he recognized unions as necessary to them, but only to their permitting themselves to be dominated by militant elements who would lead them into attacks on the public order. In the struggles between capital and labor, he said, he wished to remain neutral—so long as the workers maintained the principles of "good sense and peaceableness" that he recognized as guiding the labors of the Sindicatos Libres.[63]

There may well have been more to this informal understanding, but no testimony of it has survived; and in any case it was of little immediate help to the Libres, whose life continued to be a somewhat desperate one. Toward the end of November a secret meeting of all the Libres' committees was held in the San Andrés district and attended by representatives of the various trades in which the Libres had succeeded in getting a foothold during the year since their founding: waiters, cooks, rubber workers, chemical workers, printers, metalworkers, glaziers, masons, bakers, and leatherworkers. Also present were representatives of the Libres' committees from Badalona, Igualada, Manresa, Mataro, Tarrasa, and Reus. The tenor of the meeting was extremely somber, as each committee related its tribulations in the struggle against the Unicos and recited the lengthening list of its dead, which usually included a large percentage of the original founders.[64]

José Soler, a bank clerk, acknowledged the gloomy prospects of the organization but affirmed that as a man of ideals he was resolved never to retreat, adding that the struggle ought to be carried on to the death, since in this way the Libres could give an example to the whole region, which had been the victim of the most terrible clandestine power that history recorded. Villena, of the Sindicato Libre of Printers, was more pessimistic. He doubted that his own group could keep up the struggle against the Unicos much longer, since many of its early leaders were dead and perhaps 50 percent of its original members had been fired from their jobs owing to pressure applied by the CRT. In addition, he said, the governor had not approved the printers' *reglamento*, and they did not know which side to turn to.[65]

Other delegates rose with similar tales of assassination, attrition, and discouragement, and it was clear that the future of the Libres, at this moment, remained in doubt. But the consensus of those present was that the creation of the new unions and their preservation through a year of combat had cost too much blood and toil to allow of their being disbanded, which would in any case, they thought, be a cowardly betrayal of their ideals. The presiding officer summed up the prevailing sentiment by acknowledging that although all those present were doubtless under sentence of death, they ought not to fear the struggle, whatever happened, since it was the same to die tomorrow as in fifty years and often less painful to die in the street than in bed. He was sure, he said, that in the end the Libres would achieve a definitive victory over the Cenetistas and would thereby free the entire working class from the yoke of those "dishonorable killers." He ended by reminding the delegates of the

Libres' recent visit to Martínez Anido, observing that the governor had impressed them as a "very upright and just military man" who was determined to put an end to terrorism in Barcelona.[66]

A few days later, on December 2, Anido issued a manifesto making it clear that in view of the "shameful recrudescence of terrorist crimes" since his assumption of the civil governorship, he would exercise his authority with a severity appropriate

> to the gravity of the harm done Barcelona by the craven types who think it legitimate to resort to the most execrable excesses of violence in order to impose on the rest their plans of dissolution.... But I wish to declare that ... I shall not carry the punishment further than the excess demands; nor shall I ever neglect to make the necessary distinction between revolutionary intentions and the material demands that the workers, in their natural desire for betterment, can legally bring forward in social conflicts.... I must not forget that energy ought to be the sister of justice, [and that] for such a labor I require the assistance of all social classes in the territory of this governorship.[67]

These words, as it turned out, merely reflected the governor's resolve to use increasingly harsh measures in dealing with the unrest in his province, including the exile of troublemakers to remote provinces and a greater reliance on the Ley de Fugas.

Francisco Layret and the Workers' Candidature

Despite the arrest of their leaders and the suppression of their unions, the Cenetistas were no less prepared than the Libres to continue the struggle. On November 21, the day after the mass arrests, the underground Committee of the CRT proclaimed a general strike in Barcelona to protest Anido's policies. For several days the life of the city was nearly paralyzed: streets were silent and deserted, shipping in the harbor did not move, and the trains did not run. Anido, looking out from his balcony across deserted thoroughfares, was heard to mutter, "I don't know how we will get out of this one."[68]

On November 30 the situation in Barcelona took a sharp turn for the worse with the murder of the Republican politician Francisco Layret, who had long acted as a lawyer for the CNT. Layret, a close friend and associate of Salvador Seguí and Luís Companys, was a frail, half-crippled visionary whose painful gait, assisted by canes, gave him the appearance of a mechanical doll. As an ultra-Left Republican very sympathetic to the Cenetistas, he was hoping to draw them into an electoral coalition that might revolutionize Spanish politics. Like so many left-wing Republicans in Catalonia—one thinks of Eugenio d'Ors, Angel Samblancat, or Marcelino Domingo—his imagination had been fired by the Russian Revolution, and he had sought, along with Domingo and Gabriel Alomar, to have the Catalonian Republican Party enter the Third International.[69]

Layret was committed to the idea that the Syndicalist leaders should, as candidates, take part in the next elections—not, presumably, in order to go to the Cortes, but in order to win the privilege of parliamentary immunity.[70] After the arrests of November 20, he revived and extended this idea, even going so far as to make contact with the Socialists and to envision a broad electoral coalition of Cenetistas, Socialists, and Republicans. No doubt he hoped that in view of the extraordinary measures recently taken against it the Confederation would temporarily forgo its apolitical policy and help create a large, pro-labor parliamentary faction, which would help to discourage the establishment of the military dictatorship that many foresaw in the near future. At the very least Layret must have hoped that the Syndicalist leaders could be freed from jail, just as their Socialist counterparts had been freed in 1918.[71]

The Socialist response to the idea was favorable, especially that of the left-wing leaders. On November 29, the day before his death, Layret met in the Hotel España in Barcelona with the Terceristas García Quejido and Ramón Lamoneda, and some sort of electoral agreement was reached.[72] There is strong evidence that Salvador Seguí—from behind bars—expressed approval of this scheme (called the Unión Proletaria) and even made up a tentative slate of candidates, which is said to have included himself, Pestaña (still absent in Russia), Eugenio d'Ors, Gabriel Alomar, Andrés Ovejero, Layret, Marcelino Domingo, and others. Persistent rumors in the press hinted that Seguí, who had many contacts among the Left-Republicans and always viewed them as necessary intermediaries between the CNT and the government, contemplated leading the Confederation down the electoral path.[73] But precisely how serious he was about this, and whether even he could have carried the rank-and-file Cenetistas along with him, must remain in doubt.

On November 30 Layret, while on his way to visit Companys and Seguí in jail, was shot down on the Calle de Balmes by three gunmen who were not apprehended.[74] His grand vision—it had never been more than that—died with him. A few days later Seguí, Companys, and some 34 other CNT leaders, nearly all of them presidents or secretaries of unions, were marched in shackles aboard the dispatch boat *Giralda*, which took them to the Fortress of Isabella II, commonly called Castillo de Mola, located in Mahón on the island of Minorca. Here they would remain until the spring of 1922.[75]

Though it was never established who murdered Layret, the act deeply angered the Cenetistas, who now tried to expand the strike against Martínez Anido into a nationwide general strike against the whole Dato regime. Their feeling was that the various regional organizations of the CNT, which had grown so rapidly during the past two years, should now come to the aid of the Catalonian Syndicalists, and that the Socialists, with whom a pact had been signed on September 2, should also be required to give evidence of their solidarity and fighting spirit.[76] Thus, shortly after Layret's death, messengers were sent to Madrid to propose that the UGT join the CNT in a strike of indefinite duration. Without waiting for Socialist concurrence, however, the CNT unilaterally proclaimed the strike on December 12. The National Committee of the UGT took up the question on December 14—only five days before the national elections—and, under the influence of Largo Caballero and Besteiro, had no difficulty in deciding not to adhere to what was, in effect, a call for another revolutionary general strike like that of August 1917.[77]

The Socialist leaders resented the fact that the CNT had called the strike without first consulting its ally, and clearly felt that nothing in the pact obligated the UGT to join such a movement. Largo Caballero had already said, on December 9, that he did not feel that prevailing circumstances—above all, the continuing industrial crisis—made likely the success of a general strike, with its character of "mere protest." Such a strike, moreover, would threaten the workers with severe repression. Nor would the Socialists, he said, consider joining any strike until its organization was "the most perfect possible."[78] Perhaps most decisive was the nearness of the election and the ever-resurging hope of the Socialists that (providing there were no general strike) they would make substantial gains.

The withdrawal of Socialist support doomed the general strike to failure within a few days. The only aid it received in the Madrid area came from the PCE, which loyally called out its small union following and duly suffered in the fierce repression that ensued.[79] In Asturias and Vizcaya a few Ugetistas launched wildcat strikes in support of the Catalonian Anarchosyndicalists and against the orders of both the UGT and the Socialist Party.[80] The clandestine National Committee of the CNT now accused the Socialists of "treason" and of putting electoral interests ahead of united action. Indeed, the Committee charged that the UGT had entered into the September pact with no other object than to ensnare the Cenetistas in electoral action.[81] The short-lived alliance was broken.

The Socialists in the Elections of December 1920

On the eve of the elections it was evident that the PSOE's internal tensions, which had subsided somewhat after the Party's conditional adherence to the Comintern in June, were once again mounting. In particular, the news of the Twenty-one Conditions imposed by the Second Comintern Congress had slowed and even reversed the Party's leftward drift. A reaction against Moscow was soon apparent in the Madrid Socialist Group, which fell once again under the control of the right-centrists, who now put together an electoral slate composed entirely of anti-Comintern Socialists: Iglesias, de los Ríos, Besteiro, Largo Caballero, Prieto, and Llaneza. It also became clear that the voting bloc represented by the UGT would not be put at the disposal of Tercerista candidates, nor of anyone who did not declare his loyalty to the Amsterdam International, and that such persons would, in fact, be boycotted if they tried to run. Frozen out of the race, Terceristas like García Cortés and Ramón Lamoneda were placed in a difficult situation, torn between their enthusiasm for the Russian Revolution and their desires for higher office. The liaison with Layret and the Cenetistas—the abortive Unión Proletaria—had been designed precisely to salvage their electoral hopes. The hostility felt by the two wings of the Socialist Party toward each other began to rise alarmingly, and there was more and more talk of a possible schism.[82]

The December 1920 election marked rather clearly the ebbing of the revolutionary tide that had swept over Spain since the autumn of 1918. Only two months earlier the journal *España*, in attacking Dato, had spoken hopefully about the possibility of a revolutionary regeneration of the country:

> There are moments when revolution is an imperative ethic, in order to save the life of a people. Spain cannot continue to be lulled to sleep by Dato, lagging a century behind in the march of the world. She is full of problems, avaricious for solutions, ardent for creative darings. If there is logic in history, if Spain does not consider itself a dead nation, this decree [by Dato, dissolving the Cortes] is the revolutionary prelude.[83]

But in fact, the elections revealed that Spain, like the rest of Europe, had already traversed the summit of revolutionary expectation and was sliding into an era of reaction and political fatigue. The renovative portents of 1917 were being forgotten, and it even appeared as though the old system of the Turno would reemerge.[84] This was the third election in three years, and the progressive forces were showing signs of weariness, while their coffers were increasingly depleted. The political scene, as *España* commented on the eve of the voting, was characterized by an "absolute lack of passion" among the people,[85] a judgment that would be borne out by the high rate of abstention. The government had all the advantages of the situation. With its money it controlled the caciques and the masses of the rural regions, and it gained support from the growing fear of the Russian Revolution among the urban middle classes, as well as from their revulsion at the terrorist wave in Barcelona.

These two phenomena—the Revolution in Russia and the Red Terror in Catalonia—were increasingly linked together in the middle-class mind, mutually reinforcing one another and driving toward the Conservative Party large numbers of voters who, somewhat earlier, had been more liberal. As with anti-Bolshevik anxieties in the rest of Europe, the fear that Spain might recapitulate the Russian Revolution was probably never greater than at this moment, when in fact the Revolution had already passed its point of maximum influence in the West and was beginning to lose some of its attractive power among the masses. The editors of *España* complained that men who were called liberals and republicans now saw in Russia an "apocalyptic" threat and were beginning to forget their former principles and group themselves around the old State they had once scorned. They embraced their enemies of yesterday in order to save what they both valued above their differences: the regime of private property. "The phantasm of Bolshevism," said *España*, "has, sad to say, converted a quarter of Spain into Datistas." And that quarter, they knew, would be added to the other one-quarter who naturally followed the Conservatives.[86]

The Russian Revolution may have harmed the progressive forces in other ways as well. By radicalizing Socialist ideology, the Revolution had a year earlier motivated the breaking of the Republican-Socialist Alliance, with the result that the election of December 1920 would be the first to be fought by the PSOE without electoral allies, for which the Socialists would pay a high price. Moreover, the announcement of the Twenty-one Conditions, by aggravating relations between the Party's right and left wings, alienated the leftists from an electoral campaign featuring only anti-Comintern candidates. The leftists' consequent lack of enthusiasm for the campaign may well have contributed, as *España* alleged, to the Socialist losses in the election.[87] No less weighty a factor was the rupture of the pact between the UGT and the CNT on the very eve of the voting, and the harsh denunciation of the Socialists by the Cenetista leaders.

For whatever reasons, electoral apathy on the part of both Ugetistas and Cenetistas was very great in all parts of Spain, with the overall rate of abstention in this election reaching 40 percent.[88] The combined Socialist and republican vote tallies dropped by about 9,000 from what the two groups had jointly received the year before. Pablo Iglesias was again elected to the Cortes, but with 5,564 fewer votes than in 1919.[89] In Madrid, Dato's ministerial slate won decisively, and in Barcelona the Lliga Regionalista reaped the greatest gains. The "forces of movement" in Spain were plainly in disarray.

1921: El Año Trágico

Whereas 1920 had been marked by some impressive collective efforts by organized labor, the following year would see very few of these, as the deepening economic crisis drained the workers' vitality and eroded their solidarity. It would be a year mostly of isolated and individual actions, and would witness the apogee and decline of *pistolerismo* in Barcelona, the inauguration of the Ley de Fugas by the police of Martínez Anido, the assassination of Eduardo Dato in Madrid, the murder of Evelio Boal in Barcelona, the first exchanges of shots between Socialists and Communists in Vizcaya, and, finally, the supremely individualist action of General Manuel Fernández Silvestre, who led a Spanish army to disaster at Annual in Morocco. King Alfonso, who was a close friend of both Dato and Silvestre, would later say that 1921 had been "the saddest year of my life, only comparable to 1931 and the one that, in the last analysis, did most to accelerate the process that obliged me to abandon Spain."[90]

The harsh policies of Martínez Anido in Barcelona, which had swept from the scene all the regular leaders of the CRT and forced the unions underground, by no means immediately suppressed the terrorist activities of the Anarchist groups.* Indeed, the groups regarded the advent of Anido as both a challenge and an opportunity to give battle. "The moment had arrived," the terrorist Ricardo Sanz recalled, "to defend oneself and also to press the attack, with all its consequences."[91] For this purpose the Anarchists relied on the power of their action groups (grupos de afinidad), most of them formed since 1916, whose youthful cadres were regarded by many extremists as the "best and most active elements" within the CRT.[92] These groups, it should be noted, were not necessarily formed in parallel with the sindicatos but tended to coalesce according to the personal friendships and compatibilities of young Anarchists who might belong to various unions. The best of these militants were idealists firmly convinced they were nobly fighting a defensive war on behalf of the CNT, which they likened to an embattled Troy whose masses would otherwise be defenseless against the pistoleros of the employers and of the Sindicatos Libres.[93]

That the wave of terrorism had originally been triggered by the Anarchists' own resort to assassination of employers in wage disputes was, perhaps, not recalled. Reprisal had followed upon reprisal in a lengthening chain of violence, and the original casus belli was forgotten—along with any conception of how the social revolution had to be made under modern conditions. Energies that might have posed a revolutionary threat to the regime if coordinated were dissipated by the hopelessly individualistic efforts of the groups, who cherished above all else their independence and inner democracy. For the groups were, as Sanz has said, "without hierarchies, without chiefs, without mentors, with a discipline accepted voluntarily and respected because it emanated from agreements in meetings." The only central direction in this period was provided by the "committees of relations," which kept the groups in touch but exerted no coercion. The result was a self-gratifying and thoroughly un-Leninist decentralization, the lower groups having complete freedom to go their own way as the spirit moved them.[94]

---

* In fact, the peak was reached in January 1921, when 21 killings took place within a 36-hour period; Morato, Pablo Iglesias, p. 241. During the whole of 1921 the number of atentados would total 228: 18 against employers, 12 against managers, etc., 56 against the police, and 142 against workers; Pabón, II (1), 208. It should be stressed that not all of these attacks were the work of the Cenetistas, many of them being launched by the Sindicatos Libres. To place these figures in perspective, it would be well to recall that even among less febrile peoples terrorism flourished in this period. For example, in Germany during 1918–22 there were no fewer than 376 political murders; Henry Grosshans, The search for modern Europe (Boston, 1970), p. 329.

What most disturbed the authorities was the fact that the groups were composed in considerable measure of non-Catalans, whose ranks were continually being replenished from the outside. Workers from all over Spain—most of them extremely young—found their imaginations inflamed by the struggle in Barcelona, and offers of assistance were continually being made to the clandestine National Committee. Youthful militants from the provinces, and especially from the South, drifted into Barcelona in a steady stream.[95] As Sanz wrote: "It was incredible, inconceivable! In spite of constant bloodshed, the ranks of the [groups] remained intact. Where one fell another joined immediately. The police were astonished by this inexplicable phenomenon."[96] This constant replenishing of the ranks of the Anarchist gunmen was indeed a source of great concern to Martínez Anido, who wondered how a terrorism constantly revitalized from the outside could ever be extinguished. It was largely this concern that lay behind two of the governor's most controversial policies: the forcible repatriation to the provinces of non-Catalan militants, and the imposition of the Ley de Fugas.[97] The first repatriations were carried out in mid-December 1920, and during the next year hundreds of militants were marched, sometimes in shackles and in extremely inclement weather, along the roads leading out of Catalonia. Escorted by the Guardia Civil, they were conducted to remote villages—which might or might not be their original homes—in Valencia, Aragon, Murcia, Almería, or Extremadura.[98] The Ley de Fugas was inaugurated on January 20 in Barcelona by the shooting, presumably during an attempt to escape, of the militants Juan Vilanova, Julio Peris, Ramón Gomar, and Diego Parra, who, significantly, were all Valencians.[99] This method of extermination, despite criticism from the Socialist deputies in the Cortes, would be used with telling effect throughout 1921.

It is not surprising that for the Anarchist groups the struggle became personalized in the demonic figure of Martínez Anido, whose assassination became for them a matter of obsessive concern. "Among the men of the Confederation," says Sanz, "none doubted that so long as Martínez Anido was in the civil government of the province, the situation would not change; and therefore it was a question of *amour propre* and dignity to eliminate him."[100] "Everything conceivable" was contemplated: poison, the garrote, blowing up Anido's house, derailing his train, shooting him while he was at mass, and kidnapping a member of his family. It was even suggested that Martínez Domingo, the inoffensive mayor of Barcelona, be murdered—on the assumption that Anido would have to attend the burial service, where he could be shot down. But thanks to the indefatigable efforts of the municipal police, commanded by General Arleguí, nothing worked, and Martínez Anido continued as the nemesis of the CNT.[101]

Finally, unable to hunt down Martínez Anido, the action groups decided that they would direct their fire against those figures in the Ministry of the

Interior who, they thought, had "primary responsibility" for events in Catalonia because they had maintained Anido in office.[102] Thus in February 1921 three Anarchists associated with the Metalworkers' Union in Barcelona—Pedro Mateu, Luis Nicolau, and Ramón Casanellas—transferred their activities to Madrid. Their original target was Interior Minister Bugallal, whom they regarded as "a perverse man of low moral character."[103] But Bugallal seems to have been forewarned, and the pistoleros were never able to get within range of him. It was therefore decided to assassinate Prime Minister Dato himself—not, in fact, because he was regarded as chiefly responsible for the presence of Martínez Anido, but simply because he proved to be the most accessible target.[104] On March 8, the three Anarchists, speeding past on a single motorcycle (with a sidecar) and firing Mauser pistols, gunned down Eduardo Dato in his car in the Puerta de Alcalá, a task made easier by the Prime Minister's fatalistic reluctance to take the precautions that the situation in Barcelona would seem to have warranted. On March 14, Mateu was arrested in Madrid, proclaiming, "I did not fire against Dato but against the ruler who authorized the Ley de Fugas."[105]

The crackdown on the Left in the aftermath of Dato's assassination was far-reaching and severe. Jails were filled all over Spain, and in Madrid the whole National Committee of the Communist Party was arrested. Among the others incarcerated were such diverse figures as Salvador Quemades, Angel Samblancat, Mauro Bajatierra, and Francisco Miranda. The last two were among some 50 persons who were held nearly two years without being brought to trial.[106]

The new government of Allendesalazar, installed on March 12, decided to retain Martínez Anido as civil governor of Barcelona, despite the rising tide of criticism against him. On February 10, even before Dato's death, a debate on terrorism had been launched in the Cortes, and the Socialists, especially Besteiro and Prieto, had harshly criticized Anido's use of the Ley de Fugas. Prieto's attack was so severe that Anido challenged the portly labor leader to a duel, which the new Minister of War, Viscount de Eza, sternly forbade.[107]

The role of Martínez Anido as civil governor of Barcelona in the years 1920–22 has rarely been treated sympathetically. And indeed, he was a formidable figure: the prototype of the bullnecked, authoritarian policeman, hard, taciturn, self-righteous, and devoted to a remorseless concept of duty.[108] His duty, as he understood it, was to achieve the pacification of Barcelona by any means. Whether his means were, in fact, excessively harsh or whether gentler measures would have sufficed can never be known with certainty. What is certain is that violence had become organized and endemic in the province, representing in part a deformation of the revolutionary impulse of the Catalonian workers and in part a kind of purposeless chain reaction that fed mindlessly on itself, providing psychic satisfaction and/or profit to the terrorists, but accomplishing nothing of value for the working class. Whereas in 1909 the revolutionary discontents of the workers had been diverted into anti-clerical incendiarism, in 1919–21 they were channeled into a futile violence against individuals.

For the authentic Anarchists of the groups, this dispersed and bloody war carried on against their enemies—against employers, other workers, police, and politicians—was the moral equivalent of the revolution they wanted but did not know how to make. Like Martínez Anido—whom, in reality, they had themselves summoned to power—they were zealots of duty, men dedicated to an endless holy war against "bourgeois" Spain, even as the governor was bound to its defense. On behalf of the policies of Martínez Anido, it should be said that previous periods of conciliation had not appeased the Anarchists, even as the coming of the Republic ten years later would neither appease nor mellow them. For they lived always in a separate and impermeable world very different from that of the "pure" Syndicalists or the Socialists, a timeless world charged with millenarian expectancy, in which the revolutionary process could presumably be accelerated by something as small as the flash of a Star pistol.

To compound the problem, the atentados had also become good business, and a certain percentage of the terrorists were neither Anarchists nor visionaries in any real sense but simply journeymen pistoleros—proletarian mafiosi—who had found a profitable line of endeavor. The endeavor was profitable because it was nourished by the cash boxes of the unions, constantly replenished by the dues paid in by the workers, from which the Anarchist groups siphoned off the funds they needed. Though it was true, as the terrorists themselves acknowledged, that the Cenetista masses were involved neither materially nor emotionally in the atentados, they nevertheless financed them.[109] For the Anarchists had fastened an iron grip on the unions that was almost impossible to break, as the efforts of Seguí and Pestaña early in 1920 had revealed. Thus Anido's draconian measures might seem not wholly unjustified, since even the most legitimate syndical activity on behalf of the most moderate objectives contributed to the support of the pistoleros.

It should be reiterated, too, that the separation between terrorists and Syndicalists had been very blurred within the Confederation, since the action groups received substantial aid and comfort from the bona fide Syndicalists and, indeed, absolutely depended on it. Although it is clear that Martínez Anido in fact distinguished, at least in his own mind, between extremists and moderates within the CRT, he was very conscious of this dependence, and his strategy was ruthlessly simple: he would dissolve the whole union structure and forbid the payment of the dues upon which the terrorists lived and without which they could not indefinitely continue to function.[110]

Such a policy placed both workers and employers between two fires—between the Anarchist groups, who threatened their lives if they did not pay, and the governor, who threatened their liberty if they did. The collection of dues, then, was treated as a crime, and the fact that Anido was something more than a mere tool of the employers may be deduced from the harsh threats he leveled against those employers who succumbed to pressure from the Unicos and agreed to collect dues secretly from their workers on behalf of the clandestine unions.* The employers were placed in a most difficult situation, since, as the collection of dues began to drop dramatically, the action groups resorted to blackmail, threatening factory owners with assassination if they did not pay over certain sums of money.

Nevertheless, the Employers' Federation supported the governor whole-heartedly, encouraging its members to refuse aid to the Unicos and lamenting that there had been employers who cooperated with the clandestine Syndical-ists, thus displaying cowardice and a lack of both dignity and "masculinity."[111] That Martínez Anido's suppression of dues payments proved effective is sug-gested by the sudden upsurge, beginning in May and June, of armed robberies committed by the Anarchists in order to replenish their dwindling funds.[112] In an attempt to keep up the spirits of the clandestine militants, the Anarchist leaders also circulated stories to the effect that large sums of money would soon be arriving from "Russia, England, and Italy" to sustain the underground organization.[113]

Little by little, the efforts of the police to penetrate the terrorist organization proved successful. Captured terrorists were subjected to severe interrogations, and much information was elicited; bomb factories and weapon caches were discovered. Among the alleged terrorists apprehended or killed were: Pedro Vandellós, Juan Batllori Ventura, Francisco Peña Alvero, Rosario Segarra, Vicente Sales Moliner, Rosario Benavente, Juan Elías Saturnino, José Palau Requena, the brothers Asdrúbal and Aníbal Alvarez Galindo, Salvador Sal-sench, and José María Foix. The structure of the underground organization was, as Oller Piñol says, "complicated," but the terrorists could be divided into two general groups: those who planned the attacks without necessarily taking part in them, and those on the lowest level who carried out the assignments and often knew only the person who assigned their targets. The arrest of Vandellós, supposedly the author of some 70 atentados, along with that of the brothers Alvarez Galindo, was considered an especially crucial step in the progressive decimation of the terrorist infrastructure in Barcelona. The multi-plication of arrests, which often led to the implication of other activists, along with the use of numerous spies and informers, gradually gave the police a rather complete knowledge of the terrorist movement, and the committing of

---

* He announced in the newspapers: "If I learn that some employer, acceding to the demands of the Syndicalists, hands over money to them, I will at once order his arrest, and he will remain in jail until the last Syndicalist is freed." Oller Piñol, p. 100.

an atentado more and more frequently resulted in the arrest of those responsible within hours. "What produced the most fear among the pistoleros and their leaders," writes Oller Piñol, "was that as soon as an attack was committed, its authors were arrested the same day or evening in their own homes." This so disconcerted the groups that in the end many gunmen withdrew completely from terrorist activity.[114]

Above all, there was a continual slaughter of the militants of the underground unions and of the Anarchist groups—an attrition that gradually wore down the resistance of the Cenetistas and paved the way for pacification. In October the CNT published *Páginas de sangre*, a chilling account of the losses suffered by the organization between November 1920 and October 1921. The roster of deaths, which no doubt included both terrorists and innocents, totaled about fifty militants, and there were many wounded.[115] One of the most notorious assassinations carried out by the police was that of Evelio Boal, the general secretary of the CNT, whose hiding place was discovered on March 2. The frail Boal was bloodily beaten and carried off to jail, where he was tortured in an attempt—unsuccessful, it would appear—to extract from him the names of the other members of the National Committee. Finally, on June 12, he was released from prison at 2 A.M., unarmed in the dark streets, and was shot down less than 300 feet from the police station, in a modified application of the Ley de Fugas.[116]

Finally, there was a massive jailing of Cenetistas, which went on steadily through 1921, until in October of that year, according to the figures of the CNT, more than 3,000 militants were in the prisons of Catalonia.[117] This roundup was facilitated by the abolition of jury trials, and by the intimidation and even attempted assassination of lawyers partial to the CNT, who were often forced to flee the city. Thus the trajectory of the CNT during 1921 was inexorably downward. With its leaders imprisoned and its ranks depleted by assassination as well as by the steady withdrawal of workers from the outlawed sindicatos, it ceased to be a revolutionary or even a viable movement in Catalonia by the spring of the year.

Anarchosyndicalist efforts in the agrarian South suffered a comparable decline during 1920–21. After the military repression of mid-1919 and the failure of the expected "black repartition" to transpire, something went out of the rural movement, and it never recovered its early vitality. The small peasants and landless laborers of Andalusia proved unable to convert their millenarian excitement into revolutionary organization. The vast network of rural sindicatos, which, under the stimulus of the Russian Revolution, had burgeoned so quickly in 1918–19, fell apart with nearly equal rapidity. The revolutionary vision faded, the élan of the peasants drained away, and by mid-1921 the southern masses had reverted to the state of somnolence and disorganization in which the first news of the Bolshevik triumph had found them in November 1917.[118]

Ironically, it was only now, against this backdrop of proletarian and peasant failure and general revolutionary debilitation, that the Spanish Communist movement, in both its "political" and Syndicalist forms, began its struggle for life, vigor, and unity of purpose. Had the movement emerged in 1919, its task would have been easier; but it was, in fact, born late and would be condemned to ride a subsiding wave of popular enthusiasm and militancy. Not until April 1921 would the first major Communist schism occur in the Socialist Party, and only in that same month would the forces of Communist Syndicalism achieve cohesion in the Lérida plenum. But the beacon-light of the Bolshevik Revolution was already beginning to grow dim in the Peninsula, and Spanish workers were increasingly weary. Of critical importance was the fact that the emergence of the Communist movement was bracketed by two tragic events—the assassination of Dato in March and the military disaster at Annual in July—which ensured that early efforts toward unity and growth would take place in an atmosphere saturated by repressive measures.

CHAPTER TWELVE

Schism in the Socialist Party

Response to the Twenty-one Conditions

Having decided to summon a final extraordinary congress to consider the Twenty-one Conditions, the Socialists braced for a last struggle over the issue of the Party's international allegiance. Everyone sensed that this would be the climactic moment in a contest that had consumed nearly two years; that if the majority approved Moscow's terms, schism by the right wing, on the French pattern, was a certainty; and that if the Conditions were rejected, schism by the left wing, in the Italian manner, was probable. The mood of the Party was one of apprehension—colored, perhaps, by a feeling of relief that the long crisis was nearing its end. For some the entire conflict still had an air of unreality, and they could scarcely believe that the debate on the Internationals should have divided the Party as it had. Despite the rancors that two previous congresses dominated by this issue had aroused, many Socialists were as yet unable to see significant doctrinal differences between the contending factions. Beneath the clash of rhetoric they sensed only the underlying consensus, the inherent centrism, within the Party's ranks.

In an article poignantly titled "Let us not divide," Pablo Iglesias asked if there were "some fundamental reason" requiring Spanish Socialists to split their party, and could only conclude that there was none. So far as he could see, the majority and the minority concurred in all fundamentals: they were agreed "that the means of production and distribution must be socialized; that political power must be conquered in a revolutionary way; that the proletariat must exercise a dictatorship until the bourgeois elements do not constitute a danger to the new social order; and that we must enter parliament, municipal councils, and provincial assemblies." Since all these principles were accepted, wrote Iglesias, it was clear that the Socialist factions were separated only by "questions of shading." Why, then, must the Socialists divide and fight each other at a time when unity was more precious than ever?[1] Despite the fact that Iglesias was bedridden during the months preceding the 1921 Congress, he carried out an impressive labor of propaganda and persuasion on behalf of the Vienna International and against Moscow. He interviewed scores of militants, wrote letters, composed articles, and exerted a moral influence that in the end would prove to be decisive. García Venero is probably correct when he suggests that if Iglesias had died in 1920, the PSOE would have been incorporated without reservation into the Communist International.[2] His influence in 1921 may well have tipped the balance against the Comintern.

Oscar Pérez Solís, who, curiously enough, was about to switch sides in the struggle, expressed a view similar to that of Iglesias. Asking whether the Party was divided by a "substantive question," he answered: "No. In our appreciation of the truth of Socialism we are all agreed." The disparity within the Party, he thought, had to do with the "mode of action, the manner of operating, and, above all, the velocity of that action." But even the question of "velocity" —that is, of revolutionary temper—was not the heart of the matter. The real cause of the split, said Solís, was something less flattering, something "very national," which he described as an "incompatibility of characters," a matter of *personalismo*. In the present conflict, he thought, ideas were subordinated to personalities:

> Ideas are the least of it in this [arena]: what is craved is the cockfight, the slashing attack, the flying feathers, the struggle of rival champions; and the whole spectacle is disguised as an ideological combat, making use of ideas, as of loincloths, to cover the shame of personal idiosyncrasies.... [The militants] group themselves and struggle for their respective caliphs, not for this or that interpretation of the sacred text.[3]

The contrasting moods of the two factions were revealed in a series of debates on the Twenty-one Conditions held in April within the Madrid Socialist Group. Sentiment in this body, which had fervently supported the Comintern in 1919–20, had begun to turn against Moscow as soon as news arrived of the imposition of the Conditions in the late summer of 1920; and by the following April the balance of power had swung back to the right-centrists.[4] García Cortés and his pro-Comintern partisans were displaced from the leadership, and Largo Caballero took over as president, so that he, along with Besteiro, once more headed up the majority of Madrid Socialists. Besteiro, his confidence restored, aggressively carried the main burden of the anti-Comintern debates. He spoke out sharply against the Terceristas, denying that the country was on the eve of revolution and charging that the Russian events had been unconscionably used by the left-centrists to create a revolutionary "phantasm" whose only effect was to incite Socialists to fight among themselves. He reiterated, for the benefit of the partisans of Moscow, the central theme of Pablismo: the idea that evolution and revolution, far from being antithetical, actually went together. "We are," he said, "evolutionists and revolutionaries because, in good logic, evolution and revolution are the same thing: revolution is no more than the acceleration of evolution," and only "bourgeois ideology" could call them antithetical.[5]

Ramón Lamoneda, young, combative, and indignant, led the opposition to Besteiro. He vehemently denied that personalities had anything to do with the split in the Party, and suggested that even if the Third International had not been born, it would have been necessary for the PSOE to overhaul its principles and to develop a "revolutionary personality" in sharp contrast to the pale image of moderation that it had projected for so long. To this end he argued in favor of the Twenty-one Conditions, frankly advocating greater party discipline and centralization.[6]

When the International question was put to the test, the Madrid Group voted 243 to 147 for the Vienna International over the Comintern.[7] Given the leading role of the Madrid organization, the Terceristas could only view this result as an unfavorable portent for the approaching Party Congress. However, they were consoled by the fact that regardless of the Twenty-one Conditions, the Bolshevik fever continued to grip the mining districts of Asturias and Vizcaya, and that only a few days earlier a congress of the powerful Asturian Regional Confederation had voted 24 to 2 for entry into the Third International.[8]

It was not surprising that the right-centrist leaders of the PSOE should find the Twenty-one Conditions unacceptable, since those conditions, after all, had been framed precisely with the ideological frailties of the postwar centrist parties in mind. Iglesias's critique, in particular, could have been anticipated. Calling attention to Condition Three, which required Communist agitation among army troops, he pleaded that such a tactic would expose the Party to the most severe retribution; and, in view of the brutality with which the government already treated a lawfully conducted Party, what would be its fate, he asked, if it were to step outside the bounds of legality in the manner demanded by the Comintern? Iglesias was sure that the moment this was tried "the jails would fill with Socialists and the Party would dissolve." Of course the Party could go underground, but, he asked, "Could the Party, living in the shadows, realize its principal task—that of giving to the masses a consciousness of their interests, of uniting them in large numbers and obtaining the benefits that it is possible to attain for the workers in certain fields?" The Comintern's insistence on illegality would work a "special hardship" on the Spanish Socialist Party because of its smallness and relative weakness, said Iglesias; and he reminded his readers that the Law of Jurisdictions was still in effect in Spain.[9]

Iglesias was also disturbed by the Comintern's insistence that "reformists" of all shades be excluded from the Socialist parties; and he reiterated the distinction, so crucial to Pablismo, between "pure" reformists and (though he did not use the term) "revolutionary" reformists. If the Comintern meant by "reformists" those who thought it possible to move solely by means of reforms to the final Socialist order, then, he thought, "There are no such reformists in the Spanish Socialist Party," or at least, "We do not know of any." All Spanish Socialists, he insisted, were "revolutionary" rather than "pure" reformists, in the sense that without renouncing "violent action when the circumstances ... made it advisable" they nevertheless understood that they had to obtain from the present regime immediate benefits in order to give the workers "the knowledge and the vigor necessary to make the social revolution."[10] In thus seeking to deny the distinction between right-centrists and left-centrists Iglesias enunciated one of the central myths of his creed: the conviction that the winning of reforms and the gradual improvement of the workers' lives would sharpen rather than dull their desire for revolution.

The Conversion of Oscar Pérez Solís

On the eve of the 1921 Congress *El Socialista* published an article by Oscar Pérez Solís that can only have astonished his readers. Entitled "Blanquismo y Socialismo," it strongly hinted that Solís was about to transfer his allegiance from the Second to the Third International—that he was prepared to leap, in effect, from reformism to Leninism, from the far Right of his party to its far Left.[11] It will be recalled that at the two previous PSOE congresses, Pérez Solís had fought adherence to the Comintern with all the eloquence he possessed. More than a few times he had derided the Terceristas for permitting themselves to be dazzled by the "illusion" of the Russian Revolution; and he had frequently poured scorn on those who imagined that the Spanish proletariat, with its lack of *consciencia* and its "pusillanimity," could make a revolution. "I know the realities of my country," he said at the 1920 Congress, "and in spite of all the revolutionary verbalism here, I do not believe in the revolutionary capacity of the Spanish people."[12] Now, less than a year later, he was himself in the process of becoming a partisan of Moscow and would soon play a leading role in the formation of the Communist Labor Party of Spain. So remarkable was his transformation, and so vital was his role in the splitting of the Socialist Party in 1921, that it will be helpful to examine the circumstances that motivated his change of course.

In his article, Solís attempted to explain the change in ideological terms, as simply the result of his conversion to a more voluntarist creed. After writing more favorably of the Soviet regime than he had ever done before, he observed that the Soviet Republic offered "an example of Blanquism" in the sense that it had been born and sustained "through the action of a rash and audacious minority that is not concerned with parsimonious and systematic evolutions." The Bolsheviks, he said, believed that Socialism had reached "the height of its spiritual force, and they wish to give it to the world without delay, without the tedious wait that a slow awakening of the masses would require." With these words, the ex-reformist revealed that he had not altered his appraisal of the *inconsciencia* of the Spanish people, or even of the essentially un-Marxist character of the Russian Revolution. Instead, he had merely chosen to vault over the deterministic confines of his earlier creed in order to declare a new-found faith in the efficacy of purposeful, conscious minorities. "Will it not be necessary," he asked, "on top of all the rhetorical discussions and academic theses now inundating our [Party], that the Socialist movement fill itself with the spirit of Blanquism, and that we all be, practically speaking, a little bit Blanquist?" Of theories, Solís decided, "we have a surplus: what we lack is action. . . . I prefer action to scientific wordiness, and a revolutionary gun to scholarly discourses about liberty."[13]

Such a remarkable change of heart, of course, had not resulted merely from abstract reflection on the merits even of that "extraordinary agitator" Blanqui, but had to do, rather, with the complex character and adverse fortunes of Pérez Solís. A major key to his conversion lay in the fact that he had been on the far Right of his party less because of innate conservatism or moderation than because of a certain honesty and impressionability that made it difficult for him to separate his existence and his ideology. The Valladolid milieu had necessitated a slow, semi-Socialist labor of political education and organiza-tion among extremely backward masses; and Solís had accepted this, har-monizing his Socialist creed with the realities of his region. In his essential temper, however, he was far from conservative and had little in common with the solid, social-democratic types who dominated the PSOE and who habitually and comfortably combined verbal revolutionism and class intransigence with reformist practices. Pérez Solís was perhaps too intellectual, too rigorous in his thought processes, to be able to share comfortably in the consensual "revo-lutionary-reformism" of Pablismo. The most intellectually consistent posture for a Socialist in a country like Spain in the early twentieth century would seem to have been either the most patient reformism or the most voluntarist revolutionism, since the development of Socialist consciousness by the masses was clearly something for the remote future. A man with the critical capacity of Pérez Solís could be content, perhaps, in one camp or the other; but in the somewhat hypocritical middle ground of revolutionary-reformism he was bound to be uncomfortable.[14]

In the light of this, Solís's expulsion from the city of Valladolid in December 1919 was of primary importance in explaining his sudden leftward swing. This exile was closely related to the exceptionally vigorous campaign he had waged against caciquismo in Castile since the autumn of 1918, in the course of which he had published a series of very candid articles in *El Sol*. As this campaign began to gain momentum and to win popular support, the "liberal" cacique of the region, the Duke of Alba, took alarm and began to contemplate the removal of Pérez Solís from the scene. In November 1919 Solís was placed on trial for allegedly calling the Duke's honor into question, and was sentenced to three years, six months, and 21 days of exile at least 125 miles from the city of Valladolid.[15] Thus was his political career in Valladolid province ended and the labor of years, which now seemed on the verge of success, negated.[16] Solís's political views were not, however, immediately affected, and it will be recalled that in the PSOE Congresses of December 1919 and June 1920 he had continued to oppose the trend to Bolshevism within the Party. But some years later, looking back on his expulsion, he spoke of the anger he had felt when he discerned that his martyrdom was insufficiently appreciated by the liberal and Socialist forces in Spain, many of whom were reluctant to speak out against Albismo: "I wept with rage more than with pain upon seeing myself so abandoned. . . . I could hear the laughter of my enemies; and I felt for the first time the frenetic impulse to do evil, consciously and deliberately, in order to satisfy the thirst for violence with which the bitterness of defeat had filled my heart."[17]

Exiled from Valladolid, Pérez Solís was invited to come to Bilbao and take a place in the Socialist organization of Vizcaya, then headed by the tough, amiable, and rotund Indalecio Prieto. Prieto was a right-wing Socialist whose views had hitherto closely paralleled those of Solís, both men having refused to believe that a revolutionary situation existed in Spain. Both had been skeptical also of the Russian Revolution, and had made clear their impatience with revolutionary *palabrería* and their continued support for the Second International. Prieto must have regarded Solís as the ideal recruit—an extremely articulate spokesman for a sane and sensible Socialism. In recognition of the new arrival's talents, he was made editor of the Party newspaper in Vizcaya, *La Lucha de Clases,* and was obviously expected to sustain Prieto in his fierce factional contest with the dissident, pro-Comintern elements headed by the rough-hewn founder of Vizcayan Socialism, Facundo Perezagua.[18]

The contrast between the labor milieus of Valladolid and Bilbao was, of course, enormous, and played a part in the ideological transformation that Pérez Solís was shortly to undergo. The journey from Castile to the coast, he said, was like going "from the cold to the fire," from the village to the city. The drowsy ambience of Valladolid, where one could find "scarcely a dozen true bourgeois," had failed to generate either a numerous or a potent capitalist adversary, and the result had been to dilute Valladolid Socialism and cause it to "dissimulate its antibourgeois content in excessively broad, democratic formulas." It was only now that Solís recognized that ideologically he had been "nearer to radical petty-bourgeois and quasi-Socialist democracy than to the pure Marxist line." The backwardness of Valladolid, he realized, had eroded and diminished his Socialist convictions. Vizcaya, with its many mines and factories, its ports and foundries, its well-developed bourgeoisie and its tens of thousands of workers, was the beating heart of Spanish Socialism and caused Solís to feel "more virile, more intrepid, and more vigorous of spirit." The confrontation in Vizcaya between a relatively dynamic capitalism and an increasingly class-conscious proletariat resulted in far more severe social struggles than those he had experienced at home, and to this he attributed, in part, his drift toward a more doctrinaire and intransigent Socialism.[19]

Moreover, the atmosphere in Vizcaya was then greatly inflamed. The workers were passing through an extremist phase that had several causes: the decline of the region's industrial prosperity after the Armistice, and especially after the end of 1920; the intruding Syndicalist vogue; and above all the influence of the Russian Revolution, which, "surrounded with mystery and legend," found in the Vizcayan masses, as Solís observed, a people susceptible to messianic appeals and eager to reach the promised land as quickly as possible. Enthralled by the "revolutionary illusion" that followed the war, the Vizcayan workers were being steadily drawn away from the evolutionary and "parsimonious" Socialism with which Prieto was identified. They were embracing the cause of the Russian Revolution, and in many cases were even being converted to Anarchosyndicalism, which they equated with Bolshevism. This extremist current inevitably drew Solís along with it, his evolution to the Left beginning from the "first moment" of his contact with the pulsating life of Vizcaya. "The disenchantments of the peace," he later wrote, along with "the blow that made me leave Valladolid and the ambience of Vizcaya (which for the first time caused me to be an actor in the real class war—not the simulacrum of social war that I had experienced in Castile), opened a profound breach in my anti-Bolshevik opinions."[20]

For their part, the Vizcayan workers—or large numbers of them—fell almost immediately under the charismatic influence of Pérez Solís, succumbing to his vivid oratory and breezy manner. In fact, their feeling for him quickly became, as some of his detractors complained, a kind of "idolatry."[21] But at the same time, the workers, who were "mostly extremists," reproached him for his reformism, and above all for his opposition to the Third International, which they universally admired. The impressionable Solís now began to view the Bolshevik Revolution more favorably, seduced by the masses whom he sought to lead. "The masses," he later recalled, "were beginning to make me theirs, drawing my thinking and my will toward theirs.... Insensibly, in the heat of the affection of those masses, there reappeared the Socialist fervor of my earliest period." Thus, said Solís, "I began to slide toward Communism in the heated ambience of Vizcayan labor of 1920."[22]

Pérez Solís's rapid evolution toward the Left was also related to the factional situation in the Vizcayan Socialist Party. Between the followers of the clever, cultured, and immensely adroit Prieto—probably the greatest of all the Socialist parliamentary leaders—and the followers of the rude and vigorous agitator Facundo Perezagua there had been for some time a deep and bitter antagonism, amounting, as Solís said, to "a real civil war."[23] That the intellectual Solís should desert the polished Prieto in order to side with Perezagua the roughneck was, no doubt, ironic; but it made sense in light of the exile's new-found ambition to replace Prieto as the master of Vizcayan Socialism. He had been brought to Vizcaya and given the editorship of *La Lucha de Clases* precisely to strengthen Prieto's hand against his enemies. Too late did this leader discover that Solís, far from being a pliant tool, had resolved to seize power for himself and, to facilitate this, was gravitating toward the pro-Bolshevik Left.[24] Just how much Solís's desire to displace Prieto—which he never denied—figured in his remarkable turn to the Left is impossible to say. Certainly, a pro-Comintern and revolutionary posture, given the leftist mood of the masses, must have seemed a plausible weapon to use against the conservative Prieto. And no doubt the pro-Comintern stand of the whole Perezagua faction, of which Solís soon became the virtual leader, was also not without opportunistic overtones. Solís himself was cynical about Perezagua's support for the Communist International, being convinced that the old agitator supported Moscow only because Prieto was anti-Bolshevik, and that if Prieto had favored Moscow, Perezagua would have opposed it. The support of the Vizcayan masses for the Russian Revolution was, he thought, far more sincere than that manifested by their leaders.[25]

But the conversion of Pérez Solís to Bolshevism required one last wound of adversity before it was complete. This took the form of yet another defeat of his electoral ambitions when he stood for the Cortes in December 1920. Not only did he lose, but he collided once more with the ubiquitous forces of caciquismo and ended the election campaign by being dragged off to prison by the Guardia. When the "very gentlemanly" officer who accompanied him to jail expressed regret at seeing him in such a situation, Pérez Solís replied, somewhat impertinently, that Leon Trotsky had also been imprisoned many times—once in Spain—and was now Commissar of War in Russia. "That imprisonment," wrote Solís, "was the beginning of my revolt against all that did not carry the stamp of violence."[26]

By this time the pro-Comintern forces were in the ascendant in the Vizcayan Socialist Federation; and when the regional congress met shortly before the 1921 Party Congress, it voted for adherence to the Communist International by a large majority and chose Solís and Perezagua as its delegates to carry the pro-Comintern mandate to Madrid. On the train taking him toward the capital, Solís discovered that he was sharing a compartment with the Archbishop of Burgos. The encounter was an emotional one for him, since many years before, as a boy, he had been in the cleric's congregation in Oviedo. The Archbishop, affable and well informed, was delighted to find that he was traveling with an ex-parishioner who was none other than the notorious Pérez

Solís. After a long and pleasant conversation, the two men parted when the Archbishop left the train at Valladolid. Solís later recalled that it passed through his mind to ask the prelate to hear his confession, and that, unthinkingly, he had stepped forward to kiss the latter's ring. But suddenly remembering that he was, after all, the "delegate of the Socialist Party, who sympathized with the Third International," he distractedly doffed his hat instead. As he stood in the station watching the retreating figure of the Archbishop, the voice of God spoke to him, saying, "Why do you not return to Me?"[27]

The Asturian Scene

The other northern stronghold of the Socialist movement was Asturias, with its many mining towns and growing factory population. Here, too, the drift of the Socialists toward Communism was the result of economic recession, an inflamed popular mood, and factionalism. As in Vizcaya, the war had given a powerful stimulus to mining and industrial activity. Coal mining, the dominant interest, had expanded greatly in response to the growth of Spanish manufacturing and a decline in the importation of foreign coal. The war meant high production and high prices, and hence the well-organized miners were able to capitalize on the employers' desire to maintain production: along with the eight-hour day, they achieved wage gains that made Asturian miners among the best-paid workers in the country. In Spain as a whole the number of miners employed increased between 1914 and 1920 by about 110 percent; and the increase must have been at least this in Asturias, where half the coal in Spain was mined.

The Socialist-dominated Asturian Miners' Union, which had 19,000 members in 1914, doubled in size by 1917 and continued to grow thereafter, with workers flooding in from many regions of Spain, perhaps mostly from rural Castile.[28] This influx of "new workers" helped radicalize the labor scene, as it did elsewhere, and necessarily had an impact on the rapidly growing Asturian Socialist Party. The influx of masses of *inconscientes* workers into the Miners' Union was regarded by its reformist president Manuel Llaneza less as a boon than as a tribulation. "Few among this great multitude," he complained, "entered into frank communion with our ideals.... There came ... a new generation who neither knew nor wanted to know the history of our past, who neither taught themselves nor wished to be taught."[29] Llaneza was especially disturbed by the Asturian miners' enthusiasm for the Russian Revolution. The new masses, instead of devoting themselves to "the conquest of knowledge that must necessarily have raised [them] from an inferior condition," let themselves be blinded by the "glare" of the Bolshevik Revolution. Unlike the "slow and persistent flame" to which Llaneza likened Pablismo, the Revolution was a "destructive fire," dazzling the workers by its apparent promise of immediate redemption and weakening the patient virtues that had previously characterized them.[30]

This desire for a miraculous transformation played into the hands of the Anarchosyndicalists, who, beginning in the autumn of 1918, began to make inroads in both the Asturian and Vizcayan labor movements. The Cenetistas were, of course, greatly strengthened by their open support of the Russian Revolution, which had tended to fuse the images of Syndicalism and Bolshevism in the popular mind. In 1919 the CNT made significant conquests in the Asturian provinces, and the Asturian Regional Confederation, which claimed—with some exaggeration—18,000 members, was formed. The Syndicalists were especially strong in the port of Gijón and in the iron foundaries of Sama and La Felguera, as well as in the mining center of Mieres.[31]

Thus the moderate Socialists in Asturias had to struggle on several fronts: against the employers, who sought wage reductions; against the pro-Comintern Socialists, who sought to displace them from positions of leadership; and against the Syndicalists, who hoped to absorb all the workers into their ranks. Basic to the radicalization of Asturian labor was the economic crisis that began almost immediately after the Armistice and worsened more rapidly there than elsewhere in Spain. Coal mining was essential to the region's prosperity, and very soon after the Armistice the British began to discharge large quantities of coal, no longer needed for the war, in Spanish ports. Asturian industrialists had neither modernized their methods of extraction nor integrated their holdings; nor had they had the foresight even to increase their production of coke, which was more easily salable.[32] Consequently, the area fell into a prolonged depression, which explained in large measure the ability of the pro-Comintern Socialists and Anarchosyndicalists to win support among the workers.

The Reluctant Bolshevik: Isidoro Acevedo

As early as the summer of 1919 the Asturian Socialist Party had become a bastion of pro-Communist sentiment. Many young and enthusiastic exponents of Bolshevism—typified, perhaps, by José Calleja and José Cuesta—were prepared to utilize the economic crisis, the Bolshevik Revolution, and the Syndicalist threat in an attempt to unseat the conservative leaders gathered around Manuel Llaneza, José María Suárez, and Andrés Saborit and to push the Party to the Left. However, the militant who would play the crucial role in committing the Asturian Socialists to Communism was an older leader who had always appeared to be in the mainstream of Pablismo and who had not been precipitate in joining the march toward Moscow: Isidoro Acevedo.

Acevedo had been born in 1867 in Luango, a small fishing village on the edge of the Cantabrian Sea not far from Gijón. Trained as a printer, he had absorbed his Socialism from the primal source—that is, from the Printers' Association of Madrid, over which Pablo Iglesias had presided. Having joined the Madrid Socialist Group in 1886, he belonged to the heroic age of Spanish Socialism and was closely associated with Iglesias in the early efforts of the Party in Madrid. In 1900 he transferred his activities to the North, where he was, successively, editor of the Socialist organs of Santander and Bilbao. In 1914 the Socialists of his native region paid tribute to his political and literary abilities by offering him the editorship of *El Aurora Social* in Oviedo; and he became before long a major figure in the Asturian Socialist Party and in the Regional Federation of the UGT.[33]

Like so many Spanish printers, Acevedo had something vaguely aristocratic about him. With his greying beard, which gave him a resemblance to Karl Marx, his relatively extensive culture, and his distinguished manner, he was a patrician figure among the Socialists. His doctrinal grounding was more substantial than that of most militants, and he had gained a reputation as one of the ideologues of Spanish Socialism. Although a rather gentle personality, he was intensely anticlerical and antimilitary, and his unrestrained journalism had more than once led him through prison doors.[34] His polemical writings revealed him as an orthodox exponent of Pablismo. Prior to the schism of 1921 Acevedo had never questioned the central premise of Pablo Iglesias, namely, that all roads would somehow lead to the final revolutionary consummation. He had always urged that the Party be flexible and pluralistic in its methods, and no more than Iglesias himself had he feared that some roads, such as electoralism or the pursuit of small gains, might dampen or even extinguish the revolutionary impulse. In 1914 he wrote in *Acción Socialista*:

> The true Socialist does not waste time in disquisitions, largely metaphysical, about whether one should give preference to economic action ... to political action ... or to cooperativism and mutualism, etc. The true Socialist does not disdain any of these actions.... All action that tends to destroy privilege and to diminish the exploitation of man by man ... should be accepted and practiced by Socialism, which is not a doctrine of utopian dreamers, *revolucionarios inorgánicos*, or spirits tormented by passion, but rather a scientific doctrine that has to triumph by its own efficacy [*virtualidad*], employing a rational tactic based on the realities of life and the developments of society.[35]

Though concurring in all the essentials of Pablismo, Acevedo, like Andrés Saborit, had nevertheless not accepted the founder's pro-Allied position on the war, and had instead upheld the pacifist cause.

Personal factors may partly explain Acevedo's continuing alienation from the right-centrist leadership of the Party. A rift appears to have opened up between him and Besteiro around the time of the August Strike in 1917, in which he had played a vigorous and competent role. And in October 1920 he had not been nominated by the Asturian Socialists as a candidate for the Cortes, a slight that left him somewhat embittered.[36] He remained, nevertheless, essentially right-centrist in outlook, lagging appreciably behind the majority of Asturian Socialists in their enthusiasm for the Bolshevik Revolution and for the Communist International. It will be recalled that Acevedo had acted as a unifying agent in Party struggles over the question of the Internationals, being one of the authors of the compromise resolution adopted by the 1920 Congress. And if he now broke with Iglesias, Besteiro, Largo Caballero, Llaneza, Saborit, and the rest, this reflected less an uncontrolled enthusiasm for the Bolsheviks than a recognition that the drift of the Asturian workers since the Armistice had inexorably been toward Moscow. Like Pérez Solís in Vizcaya, Acevedo enjoyed great popularity among the workers; and, no less than the ex-artillery captain, he had to follow the masses whom he wished to lead.[37]

The European Context

Before we turn to the turbulent debates that marked the extraordinary congress of the Socialist Party in April 1921, it will be well to place that gathering in its European setting. The Twenty-one Conditions had had their first test at the Halle Congress of the German Independent Socialist Party in October 1920. There Zinoviev, with exhausting eloquence, achieved a tour de force: the majority of the German Party agreed to accept Moscow's conditions and looked forward to the creation of a united Communist Party in Germany.[38] At Tours, in late December, the French Socialist Party had likewise been won for Bolshevism almost en masse, with a small right wing seceding.[39] And at Livorno, in January, the Comintern, though not winning over the majority of the Italian Socialists, had at least achieved a secession by the Left that resulted in a substantial and viable Communist Party of some 50,000 members, led by Amadeo Bordiga.[40]

These successes helped create the last surge of revolutionary optimism that the Comintern forces would experience. Coming one after another, they conveyed the impression that the tide of world revolution was growing stronger, and that the final victory could not be long delayed. But this hopeful mood did not, in fact, survive the winter months; and after the suppression of the Kronstadt Mutiny and the failure of the Communist revolution in Germany, the apocalyptic expectations stirred all over Europe by the events of 1917 began to be extinguished.[41] In Spain, too, the revolutionary vitality that had sustained the workers since the spring of 1918 was visibly ebbing, and the severe repression that followed the assassination of Prime Minister Dato on March 8 could only further its demise. Thus the April Congress of the Socialist Party, called to discuss the Twenty-one Conditions, met not merely in the backwash of the German debacle (it had been only two weeks since the defeat of the "March Action") but amid the gloom of an unprecedentedly severe Spanish reaction.

Unlike the other congresses held in the winter of 1920–21, the Spanish gathering did not generate much interest among the Russian Bolsheviks. No Zinovievs, Zetkins, or Rákosis appeared to lend support to the cause of the Terceristas—and it cannot be supposed that the frightened ministers of Alfonso XIII would have spared any effort to bar Comintern agents from Spanish soil.

Nor is there any record of dramatic cablegrams from Moscow urging the Socialist delegates to rise to the historical occasion. The Comintern leaders appear to have been mostly absorbed in contemplating the ruins of their hopes for a German revolution. When so large a Communist Party in so industrially advanced a nation had failed to make a revolution, the Russian Bolsheviks could not henceforth be expected to be optimistic about Communist prospects elsewhere.[42]

In contrast to the French Congress of Tours, where the envoys sent to Russia—Cachin and Frossard—had both returned to urge adherence to the Communist International, the Spanish delegation, as we have seen, had returned from Moscow divided. Daniel Anguiano had urged acceptance of the Twenty-one Conditions but at the same time expressed reservations about the dictatorship of the Bolshevik Party; and Fernando de los Ríos had wasted no time in mounting an anti-Comintern campaign. What also distinguished the Spanish situation from both Tours and Halle was the greater weight of the anti-Comintern trade-union elements within the Party. The close link between the Party and the trade unions that characterized Spanish Socialism was a two-way street. In contrast to the French Socialists and the German Independents, Spanish Socialists had to deal with a union leadership that was not merely negative toward the Comintern—it was negative almost everywhere in the West—but was also unusually effective. Men like Iglesias, Besteiro, Largo Caballero, and Llaneza were as much leaders of the UGT as they were of the PSOE; and through them, as well as through a host of lesser labor functionaries, the conservative trade-union influence bore heavily on the Party.[43]

If comparison is made with the Italian Socialists, it is evident that the "center" elements in Italy were substantially to the left of the Spanish centrists; for at Livorno the Center had accepted all of the Twenty-one Conditions save the last, which provided for the expulsion of dissidents.[44] In Madrid, by contrast, the Center, or at least a majority of it, would find the Twenty-one Conditions unacceptable almost in their entirety. Clearly, anti-Comintern centrists such as Besteiro and de los Ríos could not be precisely equated with the Serratis and Lazzaris of Italian Socialism. Still, the final result of the Madrid Congress would resemble that of Livorno: the Center and Right would join to defeat the pro-Comintern Left. In Spain, of course, the Left that eventually split away to form the Communist Labor Party was not as large either absolutely or proportionally as the Left that Bordiga led out of the Italian Socialist Party; nor was the number of authentic revolutionaries within it so great.

Finally, there was a last basic resemblance between the April Congress and those of Halle, Tours, and Livorno: at bottom, the line of division between the pro- and anti-Comintern forces in all these meetings was one more of temper than of doctrine. This was the line that separated those who could believe in the imminence and reality of a Spanish revolution from those who could not. Whether belief one way or the other was influenced by ambition or by personalismo was, perhaps, beside the point. The lack of doctrinal difference between the two factions—to which Pablo Iglesias had called attention—reflected the fact that within the PSOE, as elsewhere, the dispute was between those who interpreted the common Marxist creed in a voluntarist way and those who sought to apply it in a more determinist manner. The right-centrists agreed with Kautsky that Socialists should not attempt to seize power in a backward country; the left-centrists proclaimed their readiness to leap over the stage of the bourgeois republic, seize power, and make the social revolution largely from above.[45]

The Socialist Party Congress of 1921

The last of the three Spanish Socialist congresses to deal with the Comintern question held its sessions April 9–13—only a month after the death of Dato—and was by far the most turbulent, being marked by numerous personal collisions and repeated interjections from crowded galleries. Partisan emotions surpassed anything the Party had experienced in its four decades of life. The plea of Iglesias on the eve of the Congress that the delegates should disappoint the Party's enemies, who hoped for schism, by setting an example of "elevated feeling" was largely ignored.[46]

Fernando de los Ríos, professorial with his trimmed black beard, pince-nez, and dulcet voice, launched the debate by recapitulating the critique of the Soviet regime that he had delivered following his return from Russia. In a long speech—begun only after all bourgeois reporters were cleared from the room—he reminded the delegates that freedom of thought and expression was "absolutely denied" by the Bolshevik government, and that the workers were not free to change their occupations. He observed that the factory councils were dying out, and that the legal food ration in Russia had been reduced to only "23 percent" of that necessary for life. At this point the interjections began, as a voice from the gallery called out, "But who are the guilty ones?" And Torralba Beci shouted, "What about Andalusia?" In stressing the low living standards in Russia, de los Ríos was using one of the more effective weapons that conservative Socialists in the West could deploy against the Russian Revolution, hoping to play on the workers' fears that a revolution, however desirable in the abstract, might cost them living standards won as the result of long and arduous labors. How effective this weapon would be in the Spanish context was perhaps open to question.[47]

Daniel Anguiano rose to speak in favor of accepting the Twenty-one Conditions. He did not challenge the facts presented by de los Ríos, only questioning the interpretation to be placed upon them. He reminded his listeners how many of the Revolution's difficulties had been caused by the Allied blockade and the hostility of the capitalist powers. The restriction of liberty, he thought, operated in any event mostly against those who, because of the "state of their consciousness," had to be regarded as bourgeois. But he also felt that the criticisms foreign Syndicalists had made of the Bolshevik regime should be given greater attention by the Russian leaders, since they could only benefit the Revolution. Anguiano nevertheless defended Bolshevik press restrictions, which, he felt, were intended to protect the Revolution and did not seem inappropriate to him. As for the anomalies pointed out by de los Ríos, he urged that these arose basically from the desire to sustain an economic order that, after all, had socialized all means of production. The rationing of essential goods to Soviet citizens, which de los Ríos complained of, actually signified a social equity hitherto unknown in any country, resulting from a revolution that for the first time in history had liquidated the bourgeoisie and abolished all class privilege. Yet to this favorable assessment Anguiano added a final observation that revealed his own "Syndicalist" deviation from Bolshevism: the "gravest error" of the Soviet system was the "exclusive preponderance" of the Communist Party! If such a system were applied in Spain, he said, in a somewhat surprising conclusion, he would not oppose it; but he would not himself join the Communist Party because of the "rigorous shackles" with which it limited freedom of thought.[48]

Far more orthodox support for the Bolshevik Revolution came from Virginia González, a plump, motherly, and emotional woman—a worker in a shoe factory—who had long served on the National Committee of the Party and had been one of the founders of the Nuestra Palabra Group. She reiterated the failures and "betrayals" of the Second International but seemed especially anxious to counter the charges of opportunism that had been brought against the Terceristas. She reminded the delegates of her own consistently "left" position within the movement, recalling her long-standing hostility to the Republican-Socialist Alliance—which she termed the "first deviation" of the Party—and her consistent opposition to the war. At the same time she accused those who had led the 1917 General Strike of having lost the revolutionary drive they had once possessed. She ended by urging acceptance of the Twenty-one Conditions, noting that they did not require, as some had claimed, that the revolution be made on a fixed date, but simply demanded that the Party be placed on the "terrain of action," so that when revolutionary circumstances arrived the proletariat would have an "effective instrument" at its disposal.[49]

The rejoinder to Virginia González was delivered by Andrés Saborit, the deputy from Oviedo, whose substantial girth, sober attire, and somewhat prim manner made him seem old beyond his 36 years. With weighty gallantry, he said that he lamented having to speak against a *compañera* with whom he had "always agreed." And it was indeed true that Saborit, who had only recently stepped down as president of the Federation of Young Socialists, had always been among the leftists of the Party, having opposed the prewar Revisionism of the intellectuals, the Republican-Socialist Alliance, and, during the war, the pro-Allied enthusiasms of the majority. His was, however, the dogmatic leftism of a sectarian temper rather than the voluntarist leftism of a revolutionary personality. A printer by profession, he personified the Pablista blend of intransigent verbalism and cautious procedure. Though a left-centrist before 1919, he had been deterred from supporting the Comintern, not merely because he lacked revolutionary passion—many of the Terceristas were not very revolutionary either—but also because of his personal devotion to Pablo Iglesias and his Boswell-like relationship to Julián Besteiro. He had had, moreover, the good fortune to be elected to the Cortes in 1918; and thus, despite his relative youth, he had an assured position in the Party, and little to gain by supporting the Communist International, which, it should be remembered, still bore antiparliamentary connotations for many Socialists. Extremely able and practical, the phlegmatic Saborit was not in the least susceptible to the millenarian appeals of the Russian Revolution. Preserving his intransigent creed in immaculate purity, above the battle, and devoting himself completely to day-to-day ameliorative labors, he resembled a good, serious-minded German Social Democratic municipal councillor.[50]

After pointing out that it was easy enough to draw praise by talking about "the traitors of the Second International," Saborit—a former Zimmerwalder—insisted that "in Spain one cannot speak in this manner, because here there have been no [traitors]." By this he meant, of course, that there had been no Socialist ministerial participation or voting of war credits. The Spanish Socialists, he might have added, had sinned only in thought and not in deed. Saborit was willing, however, to discuss the twistings and turnings of his Tercerista opponents, pointing out, for example, that the most prominent pro-Comintern militants in Spain were, *mirabile dictu*, those who during the war had maintained the most extreme pro-Allied position.[51] After dwelling for a suitable time on this inconvenient truth, Saborit then analyzed the consequences that acceptance of the Twenty-one Conditions would have for the PSOE. Here he echoed, in funereal tones, the gloomy analysis made by Pablo Iglesias: "The reality of the Spanish Socialist Party," he said, "is so sad, so flabby, that an acceptance of the principles of the Third International would bring no real change in the potential revolutionary action it could develop."

Beyond that, said Saborit, the truth was that there were no real differences between the elements approving the Comintern and those opposing it: both groups were, in fact, "collaborationists" who maintained contacts with ministers and had asked the government for such things as public works or had intervened on behalf of imprisoned militants. Saborit ended by reminding the delegates that he himself would always be in favor of "the class struggle and revolutionary Socialism," but that he had to warn against the dangers of following the path of the Third International. The greatest single danger, in view of the UGT's adherence to Amsterdam, was that "civil war" would be carried into the trade unions, dividing and splintering the labor movement still further. Finally, Saborit could not believe that the delegates really wanted to repudiate "industrial tribunals, social legislation, and the necessity of intervention regarding the tariff question."[52]

The Problem of Exclusions

Among the most difficult and sensitive issues raised by the Twenty-one Conditions was that relating to exclusions from the Party. There was almost unanimous resistance on both the Left and the Right to the idea that anti-Comintern leaders should be summarily expelled. However, the right-centrists utilized the issue with some skill—hoping, of course, to erode support for the Comintern—by suggesting that the adoption of the Conditions would inevitably mean the expulsion of all militants who had voted against these Conditions in the Congress. They evoked pathetic visions of the most illustrious leaders of Spanish Socialism, including even Pablo Iglesias, being driven from the shelter of the Party they had served so long. The problem for the left-centrists was to assure the delegates that refusal to vote for the Conditions would mean only displacement from the leadership and not ejection from the Party. This was perhaps a dubious textual interpretation of Conditions Seven and Twenty-one, but it seems to have accorded with the understanding that Anguiano had carried away from his discussions with the ECCI in Moscow.[53] Roberto Alvarez, one of the lesser-known Terceristas, denied that Moscow required the expulsion of any comrade, and he stressed the distinction between voting for the Conditions and complying with them. If, he said, Comrade Largo Caballero not only refused to vote for the Conditions but also refused to comply with them, then would it be "a case of his being expelled or of his simply leaving the Party?"[54]

This analysis, which seemed to the right-centrists not devoid of sophistry, brought the stocky, blunt-speaking Largo Caballero to the rostrum to deliver one of the key addresses of the Congress. Almost completely disinterested in, and even irritated by, theoretical questions, Largo oscillated between a frank recognition of his reformism and a feeling that in some sense he was a "revolutionary." On this occasion, conscious of the hostility he aroused among the assembled pro-Comintern delegates, he made no effort to placate them. "I have always been characterized in this organization as a reformist," he said, "and of this I am not ashamed; but I would be ashamed to make revolutionary declarations and then, in practice, be an opportunist or an *arrivista*." He was especially concerned, he said, with the Comintern requirement of clandestine organization, since it would place the Party and the trade unions in "a situation where they could not live." (Voices in the gallery: "You're afraid! You're afraid!") "We would not be able to resist," said Largo, "because of our slight strength."[55]

Largo professed to have no doubts that the Twenty-one Conditions required the expulsion of right-wing leaders from the Party. "I do not accept the Twenty-one Conditions; I will not vote for them," he said. And consequently, "Since I will not leave the Party, I will be expelled from the Party." He asked the Terceristas how they could wish "that we [anti-Comintern Socialists] should be obliged to vote to the effect that we are 'yellow' traitors." The Twenty-one Conditions, he said, necessarily implied the exclusion of those who voted against them, and the Terceristas could not keep dissenters in the Party and still comply with their duty. But Largo reminded the delegates that if, by contrast, the Party did not enter the Comintern, there would continue to be room enough in it for all tendencies.[56]

Largo also cleverly exploited the difficult issue raised for all European trade-unionists by the Comintern's demand (Condition Ten) for an implacable struggle against the Amsterdam Trade-Union International (IFTU). This was a sore point for many workers otherwise devoted to the Russian Revolution. For the IFTU had never had very close ties with the Second International and had not been tainted by the odor of betrayal that hung about the latter organization. The recent creation by the Bolsheviks of the Red International of Labor Unions (or Profintern)—whose first congress was three months away —raised the problem of divided loyalties, and hence the danger, to which workers everywhere were justifiably sensitive, that the European trade-union movement would be split into fragments, fatally weakening the workers' principal weapon against their capitalist enemies.[57] Thus Largo struck a sensitive nerve when he reminded his listeners that the Moscow Conditions required a Party adhering to the Comintern to attack the very organization to which the UGT belonged and to indulge in the "villainy" of branding as traitors those Ugetistas who participated in the labors of the IFTU. He left no room for doubt that approval of the Twenty-one Conditions would place the PSOE squarely in opposition to its historic ally, the UGT. In a rare display of emotion, Largo concluded by saying to the Terceristas that "to consider as traitors and reformists those of us who have served thirty or more years in the Party . . . is to forget that we were the founders of the Party, and that to the Party we have devoted the energies and enthusiasms of our whole lives."[58]

The rebuttal to this speech was delivered by Isidoro Acevedo, the bearded patrician of Asturian Socialism, who stood up to say that the "decisive moment" had arrived for the Spanish Socialist Party, and that the Asturian delegates would vote as their constituents wished them to vote: for the Third International. As for the exclusion question, Acevedo again reminded the Congress that Zinoviev had never indicated the need for any exclusions from the Spanish Party. "Where have you gotten the idea," he asked, "that we will throw you out of the Party?" And he added that "if you respect the decisions made here, then neither in Moscow nor anywhere else will your exclusion be demanded. . . . Such is my honorable conclusion." The differences within the

Party, he insisted, were merely tactical. If the anti-Comintern leaders would accept the decision of the present Congress, there need be no schism, and the Party would remain united within the Third International.[59]

Perhaps the most crucial address of the April Congress was delivered by Julián Besteiro—crucial not because of anything new or penetrating that it contained, but because of its unprecedented harshness and the peculiarly wounding nature of its accusations against the partisans of Moscow. No doubt Besteiro felt himself provoked; certainly he revealed his mounting irritation in the face of a Tercerista challenge that he increasingly regarded as wrong-headed and self-serving. This was a challenge, moreover, that had displaced him for a time from the leadership he was accustomed to exercise in the Party. But however motivated, his remarks would tear the last bonds of unity within the Party, making a schism nearly inevitable.

Besteiro began by once more denying that the division in the Socialist ranks was one between revolutionaries and nonrevolutionaries.

> The difference between revolution and evolution does not exist in Spanish Social-ism. "Revolutionary" is every moment of the development of the class struggle against the capitalist regime. And those who say that it is necessary to prepare the proletariat for the revolution by maintaining secret societies, in order to coddle [the workers], as in a nursery, ... do not know what they are talking about. The proletariat makes the revolution in all its actions.[60]

Above all, Besteiro sought to strip away all pretensions to revolutionary ideal-ism or doctrinal superiority that the Terceristas might assert. In a fateful phrase that would reverberate long after it was uttered, he said that in his judgment the division within the Party was nothing more than "a mutiny of sergeants who aspire to become generals." He observed that in other countries the dispute over the Third International was a matter of principles, ideals, and tactics, which explained the violence of the language often used in those de-bates. But in Spain there were no principles and no ideals; "here," he asserted, there remained "only the insults."[61]

Predictably, these words produced a storm of anger in the galleries and among the Tercerista delegates. As heated denials and expostulations rained down on the greying head of the Madrid professor, he looked up and said defiantly: "I, who am not a general nor aspire to generalship, in spite of your interruptions, will continue in that opinion." When an uncertain order had been restored, Besteiro went on to pursue the theme that the Moscow con-ditions would mean expulsion of the anti-Comintern militants, who, he in-sisted, would not be willing to continue as "slaves" within the Party, with the "sword of exclusion" hanging over their heads. "We warn you," he said, "that this means the dissolution of the Party." He conceded that the Terceris-tas might win the vote, and might be left with the Party name and with *El*

Socialista; but, he said, "the masses will desert you *muy pronto*." Not content with the blows already delivered, Besteiro had saved one insult to the last: the "logical thing," he said, would be for the Terceristas, if they insisted on going into the Comintern, to join the already-existing Communist Party, the PCE. "But you do not do this," he mocked, "because the truth is that the Communists do not want you." As the young Communists in the gallery sarcastically applauded this remark, Besteiro concluded: "And they do not want you because they think that you are insincere." Once again the chamber fell into disorder and angry confusion, amid which the long-cherished unity of the Party was rapidly dissolving.[62]

The Communist International Rejected

The last address of the 1921 Congress was delivered by the youthful Ramón Lamoneda. Like so many Terceristas, Lamoneda presented a peculiar blend of careerism and idealism. Born in Madrid about 1893, he became a printer, joined the Young Socialists in 1910 at the age of 17 or 18, and entered the Party in 1912. He was small in stature, compact, but with a certain elegance of bearing. His maturity and intelligence, coupled with superior forensic abilities, gave him a role in the Socialist movement that far exceeded his years. In the prewar period, impatient with the Sisyphean tactics and rigidifying power structure of the PSOE, he had associated himself with the disparate and discontented group of intellectuals and "outsiders" who had coalesced around the New School. By 1914 he was the leader of the left-wing current within the Madrid Young Socialists and took a strong stand against the war and, later, on behalf of the Zimmerwald movement; unlike many of the Young Socialists, he opposed the Party's pro-Allied stance throughout the war. He met Trotsky in Madrid in 1916, and two years later became one of the founders of *Nuestra Palabra*. In the December 1919 Congress it was he who framed the resolution dissolving the Republican-Socialist alliance.

In April 1920 Lamoneda had refused to follow the febrile youths who left the Party to form the PCE. Although there could be no doubt of the sincerity of his leftist views, it was characteristic of him to draw back from so rash a step, since he held a good opinion of his own abilities and had careerist aspirations of some scope. He wanted, in fact, to move up the hierarchy of the PSOE, not to pioneer a new party; and he hoped, in the not too distant future, to attain a seat in the Cortes. His radicalism, then, lacked the impetuous and eschatological quality apparent in such Terceristas as Daniel Anguiano, Torralba Beci, Ramón Merino Gracia, and Juan Andrade, and his enthusiasm was always under control.[63]

Conscious that he was speaking the last word of the Congress regarding the Comintern issue, Lamoneda again denied that the division within the Party had anything to do with *personalismo* or lust for office, and he dwelt at length on the sacrifices the Terceristas had made on behalf of the Socialist movement. He directed his fire less against the provocative Besteiro than against the imperturbable de los Ríos, complaining that the farther the latter had got from Spain, the more he had shed his character as a delegate of the Spanish Socialist Party; and that in the end, his ingrained "liberal prejudices" had caused him to bring back from Russia word of "everything disagreeable" that he had seen. The Andalusian deputy had forgotten that he was journeying to a country under full revolutionary dictatorship and had been "terrified" by the lack of liberty he observed there; what he had not understood was that the violence in Russia was no greater than that of the French Revolution, whose praises were still being sung by liberals like himself. As Lamoneda thus chided de los Ríos for his criticisms of Soviet Russia, noting that some of these had even been quoted in the bourgeois press, the Terceristas in the galleries, roused by this recollection of de los Ríos's "calumnies," began to chant "Viva Russia! Viva Russia!" and raise cheers for the Third International. Confusion reigned in the Casa del Pueblo for about fifteen minutes.[64]

When order had been restored, Lamoneda resumed his attack on the anti-Comintern leaders, realistically observing that for many of them, the Twenty-one Conditions were not the true cause of their hostility to a rapprochement with Moscow, since, after all, they had opposed the Comintern even before these Conditions had been formulated. As he questioned the accuracy of Pablo Iglesias's contention that adoption of the Conditions would justify persecutory actions by the government, the aroused anti-Comintern delegates, believing their founder abused, began to bawl loudly in their turn, "Viva Iglesias! Viva Iglesias!" and once again disorder descended on the chamber. When Lamoneda was able to make himself heard, he concluded his address by castigating the pro-Vienna "reconstructors" for threatening to abandon the Party, and for "making impossible" every conciliatory proposal that had been brought forward, as well as for their assertions that schism, by one side or the other, was inevitable. Finally, he said: "In the name of the Executive Committee I ask you to vote for entry into the Third International—for even more injurious than the retirement or exclusion of worthy comrades would be any separation of the Party from the masses."[65]

The voting—briefly delayed by a fight in the gallery—began immediately. The formal question posed was whether the Party should give its allegiance to the Vienna Union or whether it should accept the Twenty-one Conditions and thereby adhere to the Comintern. The atmosphere in the Casa del Pueblo during the voting, in contrast to that of previous congresses, was angry and explosive. The votes were gathered amid an unprecedented shower of epithets: "*Traidores!*," "*Farsantes!*," "*Canallas!*," and so on. Before the results were made known, Andrés Ovejero—a man of great idealism and disinterestedness —made a brief, emotional speech in which he said that however the voting went, he would neither stay in the old Party nor go with the Terceristas. His days as an active militant were over, even though he would continue to fight "in the streets" for the ideals of Socialism. Thus Ovejero reflected the disenchantment that a number of Socialist intellectuals felt in the presence of the harsh and not always elevated struggle that had been waged. He would be joined in his—as it turned out, temporary—abandonment of the Party by such distinguished figures as Luis Araquistáin and Verdes Montenegro, who also decided that although the Party might have lost its revolutionary vitality, the Terceristas were not altogether reliable guardians of the revolutionary flame.[66]

When the votes were finally tallied, 8,808 had been cast in favor of adherence to the Vienna Union and only 6,025 in favor of acceptance of the Twenty-one Conditions and entry into the Comintern. This was a hard blow for the Terceristas, though one not entirely unexpected, and it left them with the burden of decision: if the Party were to be split, it would have to be their doing.[67]

The Birth of the Communist Labor Party

In fact, the decision to split the Socialist Party in case of an adverse vote had already been taken by the leading Terceristas, who had met each evening in the confines of the New School to review the day's debates and plan their strategy. They believed that adherence to Moscow would win the support of a large but not necessarily decisive number of delegates, and they had frankly discussed the possibility of schism. At first most of the assembled leftists felt they should stay with the Party even if the Twenty-one Conditions were rejected, this being especially urged by Acevedo and by Facundo Perezagua. The leading role in engineering the rupture fell to Núñez de Arenas and to that recent convert to Blanquismo, Pérez Solís. These two were aided by the elderly and respected figure of García Quejido, who, as one of the founders of the Party, was enveloped in a mystique only a little less luminous than that surrounding Pablo Iglesias himself.

Pérez Solís argued that the Party had come to a point where the once-hallowed unity survived only as a fiction, and that it was therefore necessary to delimit sharply the two opposing groups; for unless this were done many Terceristas would be "confused in spirit," and would be subjected to further accusations that they had only been dissimulating Bolshevik attitudes that they had not really shared. This argument was especially compelling to Pérez Solís himself, who had been "pained" that the sincerity of his new-found convictions was doubted not only by the anti-Comintern forces but by the *muchachos* of the PCE. Having cast his lot with the Communist International, he seemed compelled to adopt an extremist position in order to dispel doubts about his revolutionary virility.[68]

Perezagua, who almost certainly felt that the whole thing was a mistake, allowed himself to be swept along by the eloquence of Pérez Solís. More difficult to persuade was Acevedo. But when the other Tercerista leaders were at last unanimous in their decision to split the Party, this militant, played upon by conflicting forces, finally consented to go along in order not to disrupt the harmony that had been achieved. Pérez Solís perceived that Acevedo agreed to the split "with a great deal of pain in his heart, in order to avoid being thought pusillanimous." Above all, the scales were tipped toward schism by the invective to which the Terceristas had been exposed at the Congress, and especially by that emanating from Besteiro. Their sincerity having been impugned and their dignity assailed, the pro-Comintern leaders now felt impelled to separate definitively from the Party of Pablo Iglesias.[69]

Even before the final voting, a manifesto had been prepared, chiefly by Pérez Solís, to justify the Terceristas' withdrawal. And as soon as the adverse vote was made known, this delegate, accompanied by a group of his armed Vizcayan partisans, elbowed his way through the confusion and climbed to the stage of the *teatro*, where he read a document in which appeals to dignity and to doctrine were strangely mingled:

> The ending of the debate over adherence to the Communist International imperatively demands of us a public declaration of our incompatibility with the elements who have pronounced in favor of [the Vienna Union]. We cannot and must not collaborate with them, nor even passively assist in their work, which we consider counterrevolutionary and anti-Socialist. Such collaboration would imply in us a lack of proper dignity, and above all a disloyalty to the ideological principles and tactics that we see represented in the Communist International.
>
> We cannot with dignity live [*convivir*] with those who, by the clear statements of some of their most representative leaders—lowering the level of discussion, which we had hoped to see based on doctrinal grounds—have thrown at us accusations of immorality and *arrivismo*, [suggesting] that we are dominated by despicable ambitions. To this we wish to respond only with our separation from the ranks, leaving behind those who try thus to impugn the rectitude of our intentions.

To stay in the Party, then, would mean an intolerable loss of dignity. But the manifesto asserted that in addition to the question of dignity, "which by itself could prevent our coexistence with these unjust and inflamed detractors," there loomed the commitment of the Terceristas to the Communist International and the fact that an "obvious and irremediable divorce" existed between the doctrines and tactics of the Vienna and Moscow Internationals. Thus

> we would be traitors to our most intimate convictions if, by rendering homage to a false unity of party, a unity that the Reconstructors were [themselves] resolved to break ... [and that] cannot be feigned if it does not exist in hearts and consciences ..., we were to sacrifice our duty to put the cause of revolutionary Communism before every other consideration.

With the serenity of those who obey an obligation of conscience, we leave this congress, in which there is no longer anything to be done. We wish to join ... that to which we already spiritually belong, the Communist International, which, in spite of all the subtleties and dialectical sophistries that try to distinguish one from the other, is inseparable from the Russian Revolution and intended to accelerate the overthrow of capitalist society. We do not wish to remain any longer among the lazy, tired legions who seem to expect from time alone the consummation of a labor of which they do not feel capable. We wish to be in the International of action, which does not fear the magnitude of the dangers or the harshness of the sacrifices on the road of social revolution.

Between you and us there is no longer a community of belief, and there cannot be a community of effort. One and all we are going to be summoned before the working class. It will judge us. ... And we believe, with unquenchable faith, that the Spanish proletariat will go not with you down the placid road to Vienna but along the hard path, the way of salvation that is called the Communist International, under whose colors we will gather from now on.[70]

With the reading of the manifesto completed, some 34 delegates, led by the venerable García Quejido, filed out of the chamber. In regional and numerical terms, this represented chiefly a withdrawal of the Asturian and Vizcayan Socialists; it also included the Young Socialists, who, under López y López, were led out of the Party for the second time in a year. The seceding delegates reassembled almost immediately at the New School, where they proclaimed the establishment of the Communist Labor Party (Partido Comunista Obrero,* PCO)[71] and selected a National Committee composed of García Quejido, Núñez de Arenas, Anguiano, Perezagua, and Virginia González.[72] An appeal was then issued asking all workers and all Socialist groups to send their adherences to the PCO without delay. The use of the word "labor" in the title of the new party reflected the influence it possessed—and sought to enlarge—within the trade unions of the UGT, as compared to the relative isolation of the year-old PCE. A new journal was also established, with the suitably menacing title La Guerra Social, and was placed under the editorship of Torralba Beci.[73]

The founders of the PCO hoped that the new party could ride to an early victory on the wave of pro-Bolshevik enthusiasm that had surged in the Peninsula since 1918. But in fact they had waited too long. Without their being aware of it, that wave had already crested and begun to lose momentum. The PCO, born perhaps a year too late and in hardly favorable circumstances, would be burdened from the start by various handicaps, some of which it would not have faced earlier, such as a collapsing economy, a steadily contracting labor movement, and an erosion of popular faith. In addition, the

* The formal title was Communist Labor Party of Spain (PCOE); but I have used the shorter form, which was more commonly employed by Spaniards.

party began without the cash reserves held by the Socialists, without a daily newspaper, and without any deputies in the Cortes;[74] nor was it overstocked with gifted leaders. Still, the ranks of the PCO were not inconsiderable by Spanish standards, and there remained among sectors of the working classes a reservoir of faith in Bolshevism—though in the end the new party would prove to be lacking in the kind of talent and charisma needed to mobilize the pro-Communist masses successfully. Finally, and not least among the handicaps faced by the PCO, there was the fact, as previously noted, that it appeared in the interval between two traumatic events in the national life of Spain, both of which seriously blighted the political atmosphere and created a climate of persecution that gravely affected the ability of the PCO to proselytize and to grow: the murder of Dato and the disaster of Annual.

Socialists Versus Communists

The schism was a hard blow to Pablo Iglesias. Spanish Socialism, with its impressive postwar growth, had at last seemed to be approaching maturity, and the UGT was becoming for the first time a formidable mass movement. With the breakdown of caciquismo, the Socialists were beginning to win electoral victories—always the focus of Iglesias's efforts—in various parts of the Peninsula, and still greater gains seemed to be in the offing.[75] Now, the old and ailing leader saw the work of nearly half a century suddenly falling, at the moment of its consummation, into ruin under the impact of the Russian Revolution—whose turbulent depths, one suspects, he had always feared.

Though nearly at the end of his life, Iglesias now had to wage a last fight to save what he could of his disintegrating party; and it must be said that he proved equal to the challenge. Without losing a moment, he summoned the Executive Committee of the shrunken PSOE to his home; and there, around his sickbed, they composed an anxious appeal to the Socialist rank and file, urging them "in this crucial moment," when "battle companions" were separating, to remain steadfast within the Party and to support the pro-Vienna resolution that had been adopted. In a new-found tone of conciliation, the Committee insisted that the vote of the Congress did not require the withdrawal of the defeated Terceristas, who would retain complete liberty to defend their views within the Party. Nor did the vote against the Twenty-one Conditions mean that the Socialists were rejecting the Russian Revolution:

> We are not in agreement with the [Conditions]; but we affirm today, as we have done since the first day of the Russian Revolution, that we are, indeed, fully identified with that Revolution, for with it begins the era of capitalist decay and of Socialist achievements. Because of it, by its efforts, and thanks to its sacrifice, other peoples will win benefits that will necessarily be translated into a renovation of their social institutions. We are with the Russian Revolution; and to our Party we say, as always, that we consider ourselves obliged to defend it.[76]

The Socialist leaders thus reaffirmed their support of the Revolution, but they remained certain that history would consider it an error—certainly understandable in view of the "noble impatience" of the Bolsheviks—to have crippled the spontaneity of the world proletariat's adherence by demanding "obeisance to a concrete theory and tactic," which thereby became in itself an obstacle to the solidarity of the movement. As always, the Socialist appeal concluded with a restatement of the revolutionary-reformist faith:

> Today, as always, our Party claims for itself a revolutionary character and affirms that it conceives the revolution to be identified with the class struggle, all of whose many requirements must be carefully and selflessly heeded; a struggle that today ... is taking on a sharper character; a struggle that demands responsibility every hour [but is careful not] to open an abyss between the promises of emancipation and the immediate possibilities, since this would be equivalent to encouraging sloth and smothering consciousness of the need for constant effort— just as it would stimulate, also, the ingenuous and miraculous faith so deeply rooted in our national tradition.[77]

The weeks and months following the withdrawal of the Tercerista leaders from the April Congress were filled with anxiety and confusion. It could not be doubted that the existence of the Socialist Party hung in the balance, as the rank-and-file militants—torn between their fervor for the Russian Revolution and their loyalty to Pablo Iglesias—decided whether or not to follow the secessionists out of the fold. The major Socialist-Communist struggles were waged in the two northern foci of the Socialist movement, that is, in the mining and industrial zones of Vizcaya and Asturias. The Party journals in these regions were filled with gloomy speculations about the possible magnitude of the schism and with poignant appeals for unity. Thus the Prieto organ in Bilbao, *La Lucha de Clases*, which had earlier been wrenched from the hands of Pérez Solís, reflected bitterly that at the very moment when the Socialist Party had come to predominate among the Vizcayan workers and the city of Bilbao was beginning to "turn Socialist," the schism had put everything in doubt.[78]

The greatest obstacle that the Socialists faced in their struggle for survival was the continuing extremist mood of most northern workers, which ultimately derived from the worsening economic situation. By mid-1921, as the result of a virtual cessation of exports, some 40 percent of the Vizcayan miners were unemployed, and the rest were restricted to a three-day work week. Much the same situation prevailed in Asturias, and also in the mining districts of the South—Peñarroya, Puertolano, and Río Tinto.[79] Whereas the miners had poured into the sindicatos at a great rate during 1918–20—by the latter year no fewer than 90 percent of them were organized—during 1921 they began to drop away in increasing numbers, so that Socialists and Communists found themselves struggling for a prize that grew smaller with each passing month.[80]

The economic decline put the Socialist leaders in an awkward situation.

During the boom years of the war they had extracted large wage increases from the employers, who were enjoying high profits, and had kept the industrial peace in the North. Now, in a period of recession, these leaders, ever sober and realistic, were even willing to contemplate wage reductions in order to help the owners lower their costs and thereby compensate for the steady fall of profits. Such reasonableness, of course, was a tempting target for the Communists in their campaign to assail conservative labor leaders and win over the mass of Ugetistas. The PCO's greatest appeal, it may be noted, would prove to be among the younger workers and the Socialist Youth; older militants were more likely to remain within the Socialist camp.[81]

An early victory for the PCO came at a congress of the Asturian Miners' Union held in Oviedo in August. Through the efforts of Enrique García, a Communist city councillor from Mieres, the reformist boss Manuel Llaneza, who had expressed willingness to open negotiation on wage reductions, was deposed as head of the union, and a new Committee composed chiefly of Communists was elected. This victory proved ephemeral, however, for when the matter was submitted to a referendum of all the miners, Llaneza was restored to power.[82] Communist influence in Asturias nevertheless continued to be significant, and the Asturian Regional Federation of the PCO, with a membership of about 1,500, was larger at birth than the Socialist Federation from which it sprang. (It was also larger than the only other regional federation established by the PCO in this period, that of Vizcaya.)[83]

The response to the schism in Vizcaya did not measure up to the hopes of Pérez Solís and his colleagues. Many Vizcayan Socialists who had ardently supported the Russian Revolution and the Communist International had nevertheless not bargained for a schism; and they were quick to point out that Solís and Perezagua had in fact been given no mandate to split the Party. When the Bilbao Socialists met to discuss the actions of their delegates to the recent congress, there were enough changes of heart and abstentions to give the anti-Comintern forces a slight edge, thus displacing Solís and restoring Prieto to leadership. This maneuver produced sessions so turbulent that the Bilbao police had to be called in to protect the supporters of Prieto. Pérez Solís and Perezagua were formally expelled from the Asturian Party, and a violent internecine struggle began within the Vizcayan labor movement. Communist strength in this region was second only to that in Asturias: about 500 militants gathered to form the Communist Group of Bilbao, which also gained many adherents from the mining and manufacturing towns of the region.[84]

Altogether, during the first year of its existence, the PCO grew to approximately 80 groups, located mainly in Asturias and Vizcaya. The Party claimed some fifty municipal councillors and three provincial deputies, but no deputies to the Cortes. Its total membership before the severe repression of the summer of 1921 was estimated, perhaps somewhat generously, at about 6,500.[85]

Despite the increasingly unfavorable political climate in the wake of Dato's assassination, which coincided with the initial organizational efforts of the PCO, the Communists were optimistic about their prospects. "Communism in Spain," wrote Torralba Beci, "appears to have a fine future";[86] and only a month after the secession the Terceristas felt able to assert that they had irrevocably "slain" the Socialist Party.[87] But the old Party had not been dealt a mortal blow, and its expected disintegration failed to occur. Instead, the followers of Iglesias fought back with their fabled toughness and tenacity, and the struggle flowed out of the union halls and Casas del Pueblo and into the streets, mines, and factories of Vizcaya and Asturias, bringing numerous clashes and confrontations in the years 1921–23.[88]

The PCE Confronts the PCO

There were now two Communist Parties in Spain: the newly formed Communist Labor Party and the year-old Spanish Communist Party. The statutes of the Comintern, to which they both adhered, required the merging of the two, and discussions aimed at this union were launched as soon as the PCO was formed. But the bringing together of two such spiritually disparate groups of militants would prove extraordinarily difficult and would never, in fact, be wholly accomplished.

During the first year of its existence the PCE had not grown as its young founders hoped it would. Nor had it penetrated the trade unions beyond its foothold among the woodworkers and metalworkers of Madrid. The Party's total membership almost certainly did not exceed 2,000 and may have been considerably less. Its strength lay chiefly in Madrid, but it also included a few isolated groups in Asturias, Vizcaya, and Andalusia.[89]

Despite its ultra-Left criticisms of Lenin and the Russian Bolsheviks, the PCE came closer to the Leninist model and the Bolshevik mood than any of the other revolutionary groups or parties in Spain in this period. In contrast to the Terceristas of the PCO, it was driven by an authentically revolutionary impulse; in contrast to the Anarchosyndicalists, it did not exaggerate the efficacy of the revolutionary spontaneity of the masses; and in contrast to the Communist-Syndicalists, it did not deviate toward the notion of Syndicalist supremacy. For the PCE the Party was all. Its leaders spoke again and again of the need for a *consciente* minority, given the "superlative incapacity and ignorance of the masses of workers," and of the need for organization, discipline, and proletarian ruthlessness.

Like the Bolsheviks, the PCE adopted an attitude toward the old order of "the worse the better"; and they refused, for example, to join the left-centrists in a campaign to combat an announced rise in rail fares, arguing that the increase would mean a higher cost of living and therefore a greater revolutionary propensity among the masses. For much the same reason they were opposed to industrial tribunals. In contrast to the left-centrists, then, they did not share the Pablista idea that better material conditions would strengthen the workers' revolutionary drive.[90] Of the worsening economic situation in Spain, the PCE remarked in November 1920: "Happily, the class struggle in Spain is acquiring the character of open and violent civil war. Happily, we say, because this sharpening of the struggle, which increases the grief of the working class, brings closer the moment of its definitive liberation from the capitalist yoke. ... It is civil war that is on the march."[91]

To the PCE, the capitalist counteroffensive appeared less as a threat of extermination than as a portent of the coming revolution. Against the violence of the capitalists the young Communists affirmed the necessity for labor itself to respond with "maximum violence." They admonished their followers that in the coming era of revolutionary struggle "no weapon can be disdained." And in the autumn of 1920, on the very eve of the labor movement's decline, they were certain that Spain was on the move and that things were happening: "For once we can say that Spain is marching in unison with the rest of the world. ... The rapid march of events in our country confirms us in our belief and hope that the Spanish proletariat will be among the first to break the chains of its economic slavery. ... The dawn of a new day already lights the horizon."[92]

To those Socialists who urged caution, the PCE militants replied with scorn, citing the example of the Russian Revolution. "Russia and Spain are spiritually much closer than [is realized by] the bourgeois writers and politicians, or by the traitorous leaders of our labor organizations. In the face of their impotence to retard the march of events, those miserable counterrevolutionary leaders ... can only say: We are not ready!" Against those who wished to wait for the masses to develop "culture" and consciousness, the young Communists opposed a voluntarist ethic. They conceded that the Spanish proletariat still lacked sufficient revolutionary consciousness and was guided more by "an instinct to free itself" than by a clear vision of its historical mission; but they insisted that since Russia had summoned the world proletariat to fulfill its historical mission, it was "impossible to wait any longer." They were sure, they said, that the Spanish proletariat had only to take control of society in order to rise to the task.[93]

In December 1920 the PCE had revealed its temper in two choices that it made. First, it decided, "as a matter of principle," not to participate in the parliamentary elections held that month—a choice that reflected both its strong antiparliamentary bias and a prudent recognition of its lack of mass support. Since Party Secretary Ramón Merino Gracia, who remained committed to the Comintern theses on parliamentarianism, was absent in Russia, the antielectoral current within the PCE easily predominated. Diatribes were composed against the prevailing "candidate fever" of the Socialists and against the tendency of thinly disguised bourgeois intellectuals to offer themselves as Socialist candidates. "For us," said *El Comunista*, "all that [electoral] activity is a useless and frenzied foolishness." Elections and any other activities that tended to strengthen the bourgeois system were in "manifest contradiction" to the PCE's revolutionary Marxist principles.[94]

The PCE's other decision—positive rather than negative—was to join in the revolutionary general strike proclaimed by the Catalonian Syndicalists in response to the assassination of Francisco Layret in December 1920. Willing to match their actions to their words, the youths of the PCE joined the Cenetistas and called out on strike the two small unions they influenced, this being the only syndical support the CNT received in the Madrid area. The consequence, of course, was that the Communists shared in the ensuing repression, suffered many arrests, and had their journal suspended until February 1921. The assassination of Dato in March 1921 resulted in further arrests of PCE leaders and in a renewed suspension of *El Comunista*. The impending First Congress of the PCE had to be indefinitely postponed.[95]

These adversities, along with the worsening climate of oppression in the country, necessarily discouraged even the overconfident PCE youths. When the publication of *El Comunista* was resumed in April—in time to greet the schism in the Socialist Party—the revolutionary optimism of the young militants had undergone a subtle diminution. They did not yet renounce the possibility of revolution in Spain; but, with the failure of the December general strike, they conceded that the government and the bourgeoisie seemed to be gaining new strength. Their journal now emphasized the excesses of the "White Terror," the sufferings of the proletariat, and the thrust of the capitalist counteroffensive, and less often proclaimed the imminence of a social upheaval. The PCE at last appeared to recognize that an era had ended.[96]

Even so, the fact that the Socialist Party, after its April schism, seemed on the verge of dissolution pleased the young men of the PCE and caused them to feel more than ever the gravity of their mission. They suspected that their tiny sect was about to come into its inheritance. Louis Portela wrote that the PCE was "now, more than ever, the only revolutionary hope of the Spanish proletariat." It formed, he was certain, the "revolutionary vanguard" of the Spanish labor movement, and this entailed a profound responsibility. The Party had to establish a "fierce discipline" and insist that adherence to its banner should not be a matter of vague, platonic idealism or of merely paying dues. What was needed, said the 20-year-old Portela, was "a dedication of all one's life to the revolution. It is a question of giving one's life day after day, hour after hour, minute after minute.... Adherence to our Party means the renunciation of tranquility, of the home, of liberty, of life. Only a party educated in this spirit can carry out so high a historical mission."[97]

In the last analysis, the messianic and revolutionary ardor of the youths of the PCE was inspired by the Russian Revolution, which they viewed as the great redemptive event of the modern period. Whenever discussion turned to the Revolution, a note of genuine reverence crept into the pages of *El Comunista*, contrasting oddly with that journal's usually harsh and irreverent tone. The Anarchosyndicalist Felipe Aláiz would accuse the young militants of "intoning homely paeans" to the Soviets "precisely the same" as those the Catholics intoned to their saints.[98] And in the period after Dato's death, as they sensed the ebbing vitality of the masses and the slow decline of faith in the miraculous transforming power of the Russian Revolution, the PCE militants fell to writing jeremiads about the growing "heedlessness" of a Spanish proletariat for whom the Russian revolutionaries had sacrificed so much.[99]

Yet the PCE's reverence for the Russian Revolution did not imply blind obeisance to Lenin or to the norms of the Communist International, and a majority of its members remained opposed to any kind of parliamentary activity. On this issue there continued to be two tendencies within the Party. That represented by Juan Andrade, Luis Portela, Eduardo Ugarte, Emeterio Chicharro, and Angel Cardona was opposed to electoralism partly on the grounds of principle and innate ultra-leftism but also for pragmatic reasons. As Cardona said, if the PCE members sought parliamentary office, the Spanish people, in their current "psychological state," would undoubtedly "receive us with fear and suspicion."[100] Supporters of this viewpoint sought to strengthen their position by calling attention to Moscow's Condition Sixteen, which affirmed that the Comintern would "bear in mind" the varying conditions in different countries, and to the thesis on parliamentarianism itself, which admitted the possibility of "special circumstances."[101] Time, of course, would reveal the unwillingness of the Comintern leaders to acknowledge that the ingrained apoliticism of the Spanish masses constituted a special situation.

The other tendency within the PCE was represented by Ramón Merino Gracia, Rafael Millá, and Rito Esteban, all of whom were somewhat older than the norm for their party. Merino Gracia, especially, returned from Moscow in the early part of 1921 as a faithful disciple of the Russian leaders, bringing with him the Comintern's renewed insistence that Spanish Communists participate in elections. Against the ultra-leftism of his younger colleagues, he preached the virtues of international discipline, and partly for this reason would begin to lose their favor. Millá, the oldest of the PCE militants, also proved more orthodox, arguing that antiparliamentarianism would make the Spanish Communist Party a "caricature of Anarchosyndicalism," thereby causing it to lose its essential, that is, its political, character. A cessation in parliamentary activity would only come, he thought, when the struggle had reached the point where it could be transferred into the streets, where one would then go, "weapon in hand."[102]

But despite these differences, the young Communists of the PCE were united in their distrust of the left-centrists, whom they regularly denounced for "fraudulent revolutionism" and inveterate "centrism." Fearful that a large Communist Party might emerge from the April Congress to displace them as the torchbearers of the Communist International, they had attacked the Terceristas with increasing shrillness. On the opening day of the Congress, *El Comunista* had declared that the pro-Comintern Socialists continued to exhibit all the defects that characterized the right-centrists: "vacillation, cowardliness, and calculation." The Terceristas were basically "as reformist [and] as treacherous as those who frankly call themselves right-wing Socialists."[103]

Thus the Jacobins of the PCE watched the division of the Socialist Party with mixed feelings. On the one hand, they were delighted by the impending breakup of the old party, congratulating themselves that their own secession had been the first "mortal blow" struck against it; and they urged the "real revolutionaries" of the PSOE to join the ranks of the PCE, leaving no doubt that this would not include most of the Tercerista leaders, who were considered incapable of regeneration.[104] On the other hand, the rapid formation of the PCO by the secessionists was viewed with undisguised ill-will, mixed with apprehension and jealousy. For a year the PCE militants had had the distinction of being the sole spokesmen for the Comintern in Spain; now they sensed the possibility of forced absorption into the larger PCO, with its more prestigious leaders, its greater mass following, and what they considered its spurious revolutionism. Merino Gracia set the polemical tone, referring to the new party as a band of "blackguards, fools, and connivers" whose false faith, he thought, would not long deceive the Communist International. The policy of the PCE, he said, would be one of union with the secessionist elements of the PSOE and exclusion of their "centrist" leaders.[105]

Despite the bitterness of these accusations, it was difficult to see real ideological differences between the two Communist Parties; and the whole record of the discussions and polemics that accompanied their unification efforts of 1921–22 may be searched in vain for substantive disagreements. Insofar as the conflict was not merely a matter of personalities, it arose mainly from the diverging temperaments of the two factions. The Marxist creed of the PCE ultras was orthodox enough in the abstract but contained Blanquist and voluntarist overtones, reflecting, no doubt, the optimism and impetuosity of youth. In contrast, most of the PCO leaders were in fact, as the young Communists insisted and as the Comintern agent Graziadei later discerned, somewhat "centrist" in their basic outlook.[106] This is to say that they were nearly a generation older, had absorbed the Pablista ideology, and had mostly ceased to believe in miracles. Perhaps for these reasons they would prove more servile to the commandments of the Comintern than the militants of the PCE. Where the PCE extremists, for example, intuitively sensed that parliamentary action was, at bottom, a tactic not wholly compatible with the primal urge to revolt and was more likely to sustain than to undermine the bourgeois system, the older leaders of the PCO—shaped by the social democratism of the PSOE—never sensed any incongruity between the parliamentary and the revolutionary impulses. They were entirely willing to follow Lenin on the electoral question, and were even ready themselves to undergo the rigors of parliamentary contests leading to seats in the Cortes.[107]

Apart from these temperamental differences, there remained the question of continuity—or rather, lack of continuity—between the prewar and wartime Left and the PCO of 1921. There was an awkward heterogeneity of origins among the Terceristas. The Spanish Socialist Left had not evolved in a gradual or coherent manner; it had not broadened down from precedent to precedent, nor had it been as a river steadily gathering strength. Rather, it had advanced with stops and starts, like a slow-moving train, changing its passengers and crew at various intervals and arriving finally at its destination—rapprochement with the Comintern—but with a rather different complement than that with which it had started.

This simile is not altogether fair, since some of the crew had in fact remained aboard for the whole trip. Militants like Virginia González, César González, Ramón Lamoneda, Facundo Perezagua, and José Caleja had been consistent in their leftism: they had not flirted with Revisionism; they had opposed the Republican-Socialist Alliance; they had abjured the pro-Allied obsession during the war; and they had acclaimed the Russian Revolution from the first moment, supporting, as well, the Comintern and the Twenty-one Conditions. But there were many who rode the "train" of leftism a considerable distance in these years, only to disembark at some point before the last station was reached: one thinks of such erstwhile leftists as Andrés Saborit, Manuel Cordero, Manuel Vigil, Gómez de Fabián, and Verdes Montenegro. Conversely, many of those who reached the end of the line and helped to form the PCO had, so to speak, boarded the train only at the last moment. García Quejido had been fervently pro-Allied and Wilsonian. Isidoro Acevedo, though an orthodox pacifist during the war, had during the 1920 Congress worked for a conditional, "reconstructionist" adherence to Moscow. Núñez de Arenas had been a Fabian and a Revisionist before the war, and then an antiwar Zimmerwalder; he had also supported the Republican-Socialist Alliance in 1918 and had been an admirer of Wilson immediately after the war. Daniel Anguiano had been pro-Allied during the war; and though he warmly greeted the Russian Revolution, he had declined to accept the role of the Bolshevik Party in the dictatorship of the proletariat. Torralba Beci, Manuel Pedroso, and Evaristo Gil had all been extreme partisans of the Allied cause and had supported the electoral alliance with the left-bourgeois parties. Mariano García Cortés, despite his leadership of the Left, had been feckless in the August Movement of 1917 and was tainted by corruption. Finally, there was Pérez Solís, whose ideological odyssey from the extreme Right to the extreme Left was notorious in the Socialist Party, and whose vividly phrased denunciations of the pro-Comintern forces in 1919 and 1920 still reverberated uncomfortably.*

Thus the PCE's lack of confidence in the Tercerista leaders was not without foundation. Indeed, there was something prophetic about it. García Cortés, within a year or two, would leave the ranks of Communism in order to enter the Liberal Party of Count Romanones, and would later find a place in Franco's Spain as an antilabor journalist. Núñez de Arenas would abandon the Communist Party in 1923, fleeing to France in order to escape a prison sentence in Spain. Ramón Lamoneda would quietly return to the Socialist fold within a few years. Daniel Anguiano would withdraw from the Party almost immediately. And Pérez Solís, after a few violent years as the leader of Vizcayan Communism, would revert to the Catholic Church in 1928 and would later command Francoist militia in the Civil War.

At the same time, the animosity that the PCE leaders felt for the Terceristas was not devoid of egoism, reflecting as it did an extreme reluctance to be absorbed in a larger and perhaps more viable Communist movement in which others would play the dominant roles. For all their idealism, the men of the PCE were far from free of the personalismo that afflicted the labor movement no less than the society of which it formed a part.

The Struggle for Communist Unity: First Phase

Owing to the barriers of mutual distrust that had arisen, the forging of Communist unity, which began in the spring of 1921, was certain to be a slow and painful process. The initiative for unification came almost entirely from the PCO, while the PCE drew on nearly inexhaustible reservoirs of self-righteous recalcitrance. Even though the PCO's position on some questions, such as that of parliamentarianism, was more in harmony with Comintern norms than that of the PCE, it was the smaller group that insisted on its moral and ideological superiority at every step.

At the first of the unification meetings, held in Madrid on May 11, the PCE representatives Juan Andrade, Luis Portela, and Emeterio Chicharro presented a set of conditions for unification whose unyielding sectarianism left the men of the PCO stunned and dismayed. The PCE opening statement was wholly devoid of conciliatory spirit, referring in martyred tones to the lonely struggle that their party had waged for the last year, having "as enemies" [both] the reformists and yourselves.... Today we congratulate ourselves that after a

---

* A little more than a year earlier Pérez Solís had called the Communist International "fiercely doctrinaire, unilateral, sectarian, and dogmatic"; *Nuestra Palabra*, 26.ii.20. It should be mentioned that in addition to the figures described above there were a few other intellectual, pro-Allied Socialists, such as Andrés Ovejero and Luis Araquistáin, who, having lost their faith in Wilson, went over to the Left in 1919–21 but debarked from the Communist "train" just before the PCO was founded.

year you have recognized your error and now refuse to contribute your presence to prolonging the life of the [PSOE], placing yourselves at our side to work sincerely for the Communist International. With your schism we see at last that our seed has flowered." There followed a long and uncharitable rehearsal of the Terceristas' transgressions, among which were a "lack of revolutionary audacity" and a failure to attack severely the "social democratic traitors" of the PSOE, including Pablo Iglesias.[108]

The major condition imposed by the PCE, and the biggest barrier to unity, was a demand for the exclusion of certain militants from the unified Party; this was based on Condition Seven of the Comintern statutes, which ordered Communist parties to break with reformism and centrism. The PCO representatives were told that their "first duty" was to eliminate from their ranks militants who were "openly centrist," since these "deceitful social traitors" could never be permitted to enter a unified party. The exclusion of no fewer than seven PCO leaders was demanded: Daniel Anguiano, Mariano García Cortés, Oscar Pérez Solís, Isidoro Acevedo, José López y López, Lázaro García, and Facundo Perezagua.[109]

Among the other conditions set forth by the PCE representatives, several promised to be severely disruptive. Two-thirds of the editorial staff of the unified Party's journals was to be made up of PCE members, and two-thirds of the Central Committee—as well as the regional and syndical committees— was to be similarly constituted. The Central Committee thus formed should have the power to exclude from the Party "those who do not carry out the obligations imposed by the Communist International" and should be explicitly allowed to carry out a "scrupulous purging" of all sections of the PCO. Finally, the name of the new party was to be Partido Comunista Español![110] Clearly, these conditions were intended to permit the PCE to purge the PCO of its most prestigious leaders and then absorb the leaderless Tercerista masses into its own ranks. That this was comparable to the fox swallowing the lion did not deter the young militants.

The representatives of the PCO—Núñez de Arenas, César González, and Torralba Beci—were shocked by the severity of the terms set forth. Núñez de Arenas, who was noted for his self-restraint, had to say that he found their tone "deplorable," and that they seemed calculated to wound and to make fusion impossible. Nevertheless, conscious of their greater numerical strength and maturity, the men of the PCO were prepared to be extremely conciliatory. They reminded their youthful adversaries of the many contributions PCO militants had made to the struggle on behalf of the Russian Revolution and the Comintern. They recalled the efforts of Lamoneda, Núñez de Arenas, and García Cortés on behalf of the Zimmerwald movement and pointed out the exertions of the *Nuestra Palabra* Group. They chided the PCE leaders about the hastiness and poor planning that had marked their schism from the PSOE in April 1920, reminding them that the Federation of Young Socialists had been able to reconstitute itself with an almost undiminished membership. By contrast, they noted, the PCO's own recent schism had actually "slain" the Socialist Party, so that within six months the PCO would have more members than the PSOE. This, said the PCO leaders, was a result "not to be disdained in a party that ought to be of the masses, not of small minorities more or less intelligent."[111]

Regarding the PCE demand for two-thirds of the seats on the unified Central Committee, the men of the PCO noted that the Comintern statutes themselves provided for representation in proportion to the numerical size of merging Communist factions, which would give the PCO a decided edge. They were nevertheless prepared, they said, to offer the PCE equal representation on all committees. On the crucial question of exclusions, they made no flat refusals, saying only that the question could not be turned over to a committee, but was something for the whole Party to decide. They refused to consider any "concrete cases," and they noted that even Moscow had not named any Spanish candidates for expulsion.

Finally, the PCO delegates proposed that there be an immediate fusion of the two existing Central Committees, who would then preside jointly over the Party, considered as a single entity, until a congress could be convened; or that there at least be a "pact" between the parties until the meeting of such a congress. The PCO statement closed with a gentle warning: "Now the members of both our parties, together with the workers who look with sympathy on the Communist movement, will judge; and on comparing the two sets of conditions and on examining our respective attitudes, they will decide who, in the final analysis, is really working for the unification of forces favoring the Third International."[112]

The delegates of the PCE were entirely unmoved by either the conciliatory tone or the compromise proposals of the PCO. Juan Andrade responded with a harsh speech, saying that the PCE could not accept anything less than two-thirds control of a unified Central Committee. This was necessary, he said, because the PCO contained nonrevolutionary elements who had to be "purged" before the holding of the first Party Congress. He explained that the PCE had the right to conduct such a purge of its rival because its grasp of revolutionary truth was far superior to the "petty-bourgeois" equivocations of the PCO. The PCO delegates should not think it strange, said Andrade, that the PCE militants considered themselves "superior as a group and as individuals," since they were, after all, "the best"—those who had known the proper moment to separate from the Socialist Party.[113]

Blended with the realistic fear of the PCE leaders that they would be personally displaced by the fusion process unless the PCO were first purged was a genuine conviction, most evident in Andrade, that the rival Party was in fact infested with heretics and "traitors"—actual or potential—who would betray the truths of revolutionary Marxism. Thus a PCE-dominated Committee would have to be able to exclude from the PCO "all those whom we should consider dangerous," since it was essential that "only the pure" should go to the first Congress. Andrade explained that there were PCO members "who may not obviously lack the principles of the Third International, but who in insignificant things, in a paragraph of a manifesto ... indicate their propensity to betrayal." The men of the PCO "would not see these little things because of your lack of doctrinal preparation." For Andrade, wickedness and betrayal were everywhere: in an obiter dictum on the French labor movement he observed that Cachin and Frossard had betrayed internationalism, that Loriot was a "vacillator," and that Souvarine was "completely weak"; all had "failed in their duty" and would have their conduct investigated at the next Comintern Congress. The PCE, though few in numbers, had the sacred obligation—even beyond Spanish frontiers, apparently—of "overseeing the application of the principles of the Third International."[114]

The PCO delegates reacted to these manifestations of hubris calmly enough, and Núñez de Arenas maintained his conciliatory tone. He refused to give in to the PCE demand for two-thirds control of all committees, but as a concession he now agreed to accept the idea of exclusions in principle, provided they were carried out by the whole Party acting through its congress. He searched patiently for other areas of agreement and sought to keep the discussions calm and rational.

> In this [unified] Party there does not have to be total mutual admiration.... In your past conduct, and in ours, there has not been a strict subordination to the spirit of Moscow; but the important thing is what Portela has said: that both of us have the will and desire to be correct.... Errors there have been—you have committed some—and there will be others, above all during the period of formation.[115]

Núñez reiterated the PCO's desire that a Central Committee be formed at once, giving equal representation to both parties, and that preparatory work for the unification congress be permitted to proceed. To the PCE delegates, he complained that their pretension to control two-thirds of the Committee seemed "dictated by a little bit of self-love, [and] by the desire to hold over us the fact that you were recognized by Moscow." In a last effort to stave off the failure of unification efforts, Núñez pleaded the good faith of the PCO:

> Placed on a footing of equality, we would carry out the work of preparation for the congress with complete loyalty. I guarantee that during this time we will not depart from Communist principles. But assuming, hypothetically, that we did so, you would be able to go to the congress with greater authority to accuse us, and you would triumph. We have confidence in the masses.[116]

In the end, the unification committee did fail in its purpose, and it became clear that the Spanish Communists would not be able to send a united delegation to the forthcoming Comintern Congress. The men of the PCE refused to accept unification on any terms but their own; and, in an article entitled "More firm and intransigent than ever," Andrade placed the entire blame for the failure on the PCO:

> The negotiations undertaken to try to unify all Spanish Communists have come to an end. This outcome was to be expected. . . . We knew that our desires for union were not shared by the leaders [of the PCO], that this was a [goal] they saw themselves forced to accept [only] by the pressure of the masses. We knew very well the intentions of the [PCO] leaders to sabotage in practice every true and sincere attempt at fusion of the Spanish Communists.[117]

Despite the failure to achieve unity, the two parties agreed that they would try to observe restraint in their relations with one another. More important, it was decided that a unification congress would be held in Madrid in September, following the sessions of the Third Congress of the Communist International in Moscow—from which both sides hoped, it is certain, to receive support. The leaders of the PCE soon revealed that they did not take the pledge of restraint very seriously; and that in the hope of enlarging their own and diminishing their opponents' forces prior to the September Congress, they intended to wage an all-out organizational and journalistic war against the "centrists" of the PCO. "We are going to the Congress," said Andrade, "to conquer the masses with our *criterio*" and to "indicate the betrayals, deviations, and compromises of the [PCO] leaders."[118] It was also evident that the PCE would not accept the decisions of the unification congress unless these harmonized completely with its own views, and that if such harmony were not achieved, it was prepared to continue the split indefinitely.[119]

The failure to unite the two Spanish Communist Parties in the spring of 1921 meant that each had to send its own delegation to the Third Comintern Congress in Moscow, whose sessions were scheduled to open on June 22. The PCE mission was headed by Ramón Merino Gracia and included Rafael Millá, Angel Pumarega, Gonzalo Sanz, and Joaquín Ramos; that of the PCO was headed by Torralba Beci and included César González, Virginia González, José Rojas, and Evaristo Gil.[120] Each delegation planned to appeal to the Executive Committee of the Comintern for aid in overcoming obstacles to unity, and each hoped to win favor for its own position.

These two parties would be joined by still a third group of Spanish Communists, who would participate not in the Comintern Congress but in the founding congress of the Red International of Labor Unions (RILU, or Profintern), which would hold its sessions in Moscow at about the same time.

This third element would be composed of representatives of the Communist-Syndicalist tendency within the CNT and would be led by Andrés Nin and Joaquín Maurín. Nin and Maurín—recent recruits to Syndicalism—were remarkably similar in their revolutionary psychology to the young militants of the PCE, sharing a comparable taste for action and violent rhetoric. They hoped, by taking the CNT into the Profintern, to draw upon the powerful appeal of the Russian Revolution in order to transform radically the spirit and tactics of the Confederation—curbing its spontaneity, centralizing and disciplining it, and making it a more effective instrument for revolution in Spain. Thus, in Moscow in the summer of 1921, the Comintern would grasp in its hand the three fragments of a potentially large and viable Spanish Communist movement. The question was whether these fragments could be brought together and harmoniously joined.

CHAPTER THIRTEEN

Communist Syndicalism

Communist Syndicalism was the fourth and last of the tendencies to appear within the CNT in this era. It was never more than that—a tendency—and cannot be compared in numbers and influence with the Anarchosyndicalist or "pure" Syndicalist currents. It owed its brief period of hegemony in the Confederation to the peculiar circumstances of the Catalonian labor movement during the repressive governorship of Martínez Anido, and to the exceptional ability of its principal leaders, the bourgeois intellectuals Andrés Nin and Joaquín Maurín. Led by these two militants, neither of whom had been shaped by Bakuninist influences, the Communist-Syndicalist movement represented the most radical effort to turn the CNT, under the influence of the Bolshevik Revolution, into a centralized and authentically revolutionary organization.

The Communist-Syndicalists shared with the Anarchosyndicalists an intense admiration for the Russian Bolsheviks; but they differed from the majority of Cenetistas in that they also held Leninist values, being greatly preoccupied with the need for centralized leadership and organizational discipline. The main advantage of the Communist-Syndicalists was the groundswell of popular sympathy for the Russian Revolution, and the question in 1921–22 was whether they would be able to utilize this powerful current—which was already beginning to slacken—to dislodge the CNT from its Anarchosyndicalist moorings and point it toward a more modern revolutionary ideology. For it is clear that despite its combative temper the CNT had not yet become an effective revolutionary instrument. Since about 1915, and especially in the postwar period, its unions had filled up with masses of peasant-proletarians who were capable of great surges of enthusiasm but were also undisciplined and little disposed to sustained, coordinated effort. The leadership of the CNT had remained divided, moreover, between Anarchosyndicalists committed to aggressive but essentially pseudorevolutionary tactics and "pure" Syndicalists whose revolutionary-reformist ideology did not differ from Pablismo as much as they supposed. The result had been much rhetoric, a plethora of uncoordinated strikes, many terrorist attacks against employers, police, and

Libres, and, finally, a chronic uncertainty about whether the purpose of syndical activity was to make the revolution or not.

Among the "pure" Anarchists, as we have seen, there had already spread by the summer of 1920 some despair over the possibility that a mass organization like the CNT could make a revolution worth having. And by mid-1921 even the Anarchosyndicalists would begin to question the relevance of the Bolshevik example to Spain and to Cenetista aspirations. The "pure" Syndicalists, exemplified by Salvador Seguí, had not been beguiled by the Russian Revolution in the first place, and their goal, which they could never articulate clearly, continued to be the creation of a powerful syndical organization that could achieve integration in the national community on favorable terms—this being obviously a labor of years and decades, and one lacking in apocalyptic appeal. Thus it was left to the Communist-Syndicalists to try to fuse the authentic revolutionary impulse of the Anarchosyndicalists with the more modern organizational spirit of the "pure" Syndicalists and to contemplate leading the CNT toward a revolutionary conquest in the near future. Repelled by both Anarchist individualism and Syndicalist "economism," the Communist-Syndicalists—not unlike Lenin in 1902—chose the road of revolutionary and organizational elitism. But like a flare lit at dusk, their revolutionary hopes perversely burned brightest just as the gloom of the repressive regime of Martínez Anido settled over the Catalonian labor movement and as the CNT was beginning to falter.

By the spring of 1921, the CNT in Catalonia was, as José Peirats has said, "decapitated."[1] The capitalist counteroffensive had succeeded in outlawing the CRT, suppressing its journals, and imprisoning its first-line leaders. The clandestine committees of the CNT and CRT continued to exist and to function, but sporadically and with grave difficulty. The loss of the older or more established militants made it necessary to coopt younger—or at least newer—men into the committees, and this gave the Communist-Syndicalists both opportunity and influence they would never otherwise have enjoyed.[2] Thus the irony of Martínez Anido's indiscriminate repression was that by removing the Confederation's top leaders—most of whom represented a Syndicalism that was nonterroristic and, beneath its rhetoric, actually "governmental"—it favored the rise of a Communist-Syndicalist tendency whose aim was to make the CNT a more formidable revolutionary movement than it had ever been before. For the new men looked to Moscow in a more emulative spirit than any of the other elements within the organization; and unlike the pro-Bolshevik Anarchosyndicalists, they would end by adopting a virtually Leninist conception of revolutionary organization. Capitalizing on the Confederation's disarray, they would reach the height of their influence in the period from spring 1921 to spring 1922—an epoch, unfortunately for their aspirations, that was marked by the rapid decay of the Sindicatos Unicos, as the masses who had earlier flooded into them now melted away like a defeated guerrilla army.[3] Nor did the Communist-Syndicalists have an uncontested influence within the decimated CNT, being obliged to carry on a struggle—generally nonviolent—with the Anarchosyndicalists and the action groups, and a more deadly struggle with the Sindicatos Libres.

Andrés Nin, "Fanatic of Revolution"

Two of the most rapid ascents within the clandestine structure of the CNT were experienced by Andrés Nin and Joaquín Maurín, both of them newcomers to the Confederation who always remained, in a sense, "outsiders." Nin was born in Vendrell in the province of Tarragona in 1892, the son of a small farmer who was determined to see his precocious offspring have an education and a career. After attending the local school and the normal school at Tarragona, Nin moved to Barcelona, where he took up residence in late 1914. He taught briefly at the Escola Horaciana, a lay institution of Anarchist coloration, though his own politics were republican, and then moved on to become a professional journalist. Like many young Catalans in this period, he found himself attracted by both the vital movements then undergoing a "renaissance" in his region, that is, by Catalanism (of the left-wing variety) and by Syndicalism. For a time he edited the Republican and Catalan journal *Poble Català*, from which he passed to *La Publicidad*, run by Amadeo Hurtado, and then to the Fabra Agency directed by Claudi Ametlla.[4]

Nin's political evolution was almost continuous during these years. Endowed with exceptional vitality, a keen and restless mind, and an authentically rebellious temperament, he moved across the spectrum of the Left in search of an appropriate revolutionary vehicle: beginning as a pro-Allied republican who greeted the Allied victory with messianic fervor, he would end as a Bolshevik. Inspired by the Russian Revolution, he first left the republican ranks to join the Socialist Party of Catalonia and to collaborate for a time with the not very revolutionary Fabra Ribas in editing *La Internacional*. But it was almost inevitable that he would gravitate toward the rising Syndicalist movement, which in the fall of 1919 was expanding so impetuously and which seemed to him the true bearer of the revolutionary spirit in the Peninsula. He had already organized the Sindicato of the Liberal Professions, which adhered to the CNT. But his final break with Socialism came during the December 1919 Congress of the PSOE. Nin was, indeed, one of the few links between that gathering and the simultaneously held sessions of the CNT in the Congress of the Comedia, at which he appeared as a delegate of the Liberal Professions. Angered by the Socialists' failure to adhere unequivocally to the Comintern and by what he termed the Party's "sickening reformism,"[5] he had walked out of the sessions in the Casa del Pueblo and, joining the Cenetistas, was permitted to speak briefly at the very close of the Congress of the Comedia. "I am a fanatic of action, of revolution," Nin confided to the delegates.

I believe in actions more than in remote ideologies and abstract questions. I am an admirer of the Russian Revolution because it is a reality. I am a partisan of the Third International because it is a reality—because over and above ideologies it represents a principle of action, the principle of the coexistence of all the truly revolutionary forces that seek an immediate establishment of Communism.[6]

Nin revealed, in his brief oration, several of the themes that would characterize his brand of revolutionary Syndicalism and that were the essence of the Communist-Syndicalist creed: an emphasis on activity, a sense of revolutionary urgency, an indifference to doctrinal problems, and a conviction that such problems should be subordinated to the overriding need for labor unity in the revolutionary struggle. What was not yet apparent was his intensely Jacobin spirit and the un-Syndicalist degree of revolutionary centralization he would later advocate.

Joaquín Maurín and Reflections on Violence

No less a revolutionary activist was the other major figure of Spanish Communist-Syndicalism, the young Aragonese schoolteacher and journalist Joaquín Maurín. Born in 1896 into a relatively prosperous farming family in the province of Huesca, Maurín had been intended by his parents for the priesthood. He studied Latin in the seminary at Barbastro, attended the normal school at Huesca, and took a baccalaureate degree in the Lérida Institute. Rejecting a priestly career, he became a teacher in the Liceo Escolar of Lérida and wrote for El Ideal, the organ of the Lérida Young Republicans. His literary flair was at once apparent, and he gained praise from Miguel Unamuno and an acquaintance with Pio Baroja. Maurín was an Aliadófilo during the war and enthusiastically supported the August Movement of 1917. His first contact with the forces of labor came in the winter of 1917–18, during the great amnesty campaign waged on behalf of those imprisoned during the general strike. For this campaign he composed a seres of articles entitled "España con honor," and was confirmed in his growing interest in the working class by a letter of gratitude received from the Socialist leaders imprisoned at Cartagena.[7]

The Russian Revolution evoked in Maurín "from the first moment" a profound sympathy and became the catalyst of his conversion to Syndicalism. For he believed that the revolutionary Syndicalism of the CNT embodied better than any other movement in the Peninsula the same regenerating forces to which the Revolution had given expression in Russia. He sensed that under the impact of the war and the Revolution Spain was stirring from her old lethargy, that the progressive forces were gaining momentum. The labor movement's rapid growth after 1918 suggested that it might soon become the major focus of opposition to the moribund Restoration system, and Maurín wanted to be identified with it in the renovative efforts that he believed lay ahead.[8]

Two antithetical figures symbolized for Maurín the competing tendencies within the Spanish labor movement: the Socialist Julián Besteiro, leader of the August Strike committee and a professorial Menshevik; and the Syndicalist Salvador Seguí, a proletarian agitator and organizer whose confident figure at the rostrum "irresistibly reminded" Maurín of Danton. Maurín had been attracted to Socialism, as he later recalled, "by history, continuity, and the sense of responsibility," but he was pulled decisively toward Syndicalism by its "revolutionary and combative spirit." He later wrote, "Doctrinally I found myself close to the Socialists"; but "in practical terms the Syndicalists seemed to me more realistic, more daring, younger." "Temperamentally," he felt himself to be "a man of action," and in 1919 he began to read Sorel's *Reflexions sur le violence*—he being one of the relatively few Spanish Syndicalists, it must be said, who did so. To Maurín, Sorelian Syndicalism embodied what was sound in Marxism and was, in addition, "pragmatic and creative."[9] Above all, he distilled from Sorel and from the depths of his own personality an exaltation of revolutionary violence that would run like a red thread through all his writings in this period. The violence that he eulogized, however, would not be the spontaneous, individualistic, and inchoate violence of the Anarchists but a purposive, collective, and organized popular violence, which, guided by an elite, would both destroy and regenerate. Which is to say that Maurín's revolutionary outlook was inherently more modern than that of most Cenetistas, emphasizing as it did elitist and organizational themes; and it brought him, even before his visit to Moscow, remarkably close to the Leninist conception.[10]

In June 1919 Maurín was conscripted into the Army and served a tour of duty at the Montaña Barracks in Madrid. Here he continued, in the midst of his military tasks, to ponder the implications of Sorel's *Reflexions* and to keep one eye on the burgeoning Syndicalist movement in Catalonia. While still in uniform he attended the 1919 CNT Congress in Madrid; and from the galleries of the Comedia he gazed down on all the great leaders of the CNT —Seguí, Pestaña, Boal, Buenacasa, Quintanilla, Carbó, and the rest—listening to the often tumultuous debates. Between sessions he frequented the cafés where the Aragonese and Catalan delegates gathered. In the Café Fornos he met the irrepressible Seguí, who smilingly told him, "Thanks to you, we are holding a congress of workers, peasants, and...one soldier." It was also at the Congress of the Comedia that Maurín for the first time met the genial and bespectacled Andrés Nin, whose revolutionary temper and didactic personality so closely matched his own and whose lifelong friend he would become. In little more than a year these two young men—both so marginal in the 1919 Congress—would dominate the two most important committees of the CNT.[11]

The discovery and arrest of the CNT's general secretary, Evelio Boal, in March 1921 gave the Communist-Syndicalists their opportunity. Nin, who himself had nearly been assassinated by the Libres the previous November, was now coopted into the clandestine National Committee, replacing Boal as acting general secretary and largely dominating that body. At about the same time Maurín was coopted into the Committee of the CRT, in which he soon became the preeminent figure. Nin and Maurín worked closely together, with the result that for the better part of a year the influence of the Communist-Syndicalists would be decisive within the CNT.[12]

The voice of Communist-Syndicalism in the spring of 1921 was the journal *Lucha Social* of Lérida, which, because of the suspension of *Solidaridad Obrera*, was also the chief organ of the CNT in Catalonia. The journal was edited by Maurín, who had as his principal associate the Lérida printer Pedro Bonet. Among the other representatives of Communist-Syndicalism in this era were: Eusebio Rodríguez (Tarragona), Hilario Arlandis (Valencia), Jesús Ibáñez (Asturias), José Roca (Bilbao), and José María Foix, who worked with Maurín in the Association of Municipal Employees.[13] In Barcelona the Communist-Syndicalists had a significant though by no means decisive influence among the metal, textile, transport, printing, and retail workers; but the influence of the Anarchosyndicalists proved invincible in the construction and woodworkers' unions. Nowhere in this period did the Communist-Syndicalists succeed in completely taking over a single union.[14] The history of the movement in Catalonia and in the rest of Spain remains poorly documented and, indeed, obscure. Its adherents, though some were highly placed, constituted only a relative handful among the legions of Cenetistas and remained, as we have suggested, more of a tendency than a faction. Not until the founding of the Grupos Rojos Sindicales in December 1922 would they acquire real cohesion.[15]

But the emphasis of the Communist-Syndicalists was unmistakable: more insistently than any other group of Cenetistas, they advocated the disciplining and centralizing of the CNT and the unification of all revolutionary movements and tendencies in Spain. Having grasped the connection between labor unity and revolutionary success, *Lucha Social* lamented: "The labor movement has been characterized these last years by a dispersed, atomistic, and undisciplined activity. What happened was very sad. When one of the great capitals [of Spain] was at white heat, the rest were cold....All [struggles] were isolated combats, impregnated with an excess of localism that made a unified [revolutionary] movement impossible." This dispersion of effort had been a great misfortune, since with a unification of forces it would have been possible to launch an assault that, if well led, would surely have "pulled to the ground the fortress of capitalism." What was needed to gain a revolutionary victory was "a proper selection of leading elements, the postponement of minor questions on behalf of our great objective, [and] fierce unification."[16]

In Madrid, the youthful Communists of the PCE greeted the emergence of the Communist-Syndicalist movement in Catalonia with approval as sincere as it was patronizing. They sensed in the followers of Nin and Maurín kindred revolutionary spirits who, like themselves, preached the need to strengthen centralized leadership and to deemphasize spontaneity and localism. Ramón Merino Gracia, who had recently returned from the Comintern Congress, wrote an article in *El Comunista* dedicated to the "intelligent minority that leads the revolutionary Syndicalist movement in Spain but still hesitates to enter the Partido Comunista Español." One of the major tasks of the PCE, said Merino, was to enlist the leading elements of revolutionary Syndicalism, first "divesting them of their theoretical errors." Having already accepted the need for the dictatorship of the proletariat, he said, it only remained for them to agree that this dictatorship be exercised by a political party, namely, by the PCE. It was not necessary that all Cenetistas join the Communist Party, since those who wished to devote themselves mainly to union work should be free to do so. All that was necessary, said Merino, was an "intimate and unifying interpenetration" of the two revolutionary internationals—that is, of the Comintern and the Red International of Labor Unions.[17]

Above all, the Madrid Communists hoped that the projected gathering of Syndicalist and Communist delegates in Moscow in the summer of 1921 would facilitate the unification of revolutionary forces in Spain; and they viewed as very promising the "change of outlook" that the CNT had presumably undergone. It seemed to them that the Spanish Syndicalists were daily "separating themselves from classic Anarchism." They were certain that the Cenetista delegation to Moscow would operate "on a practical and theoretical ground in frank approximation to Marxist Communism, forgetting the vacillating line ...of Angel Pestaña."[18]

But the subordination of Syndicalists to Communists was precisely the rub. For the truth was that despite the enthusiasm most Cenetistas felt for the Russian Revolution, their consciousness had as yet been little altered by Leninist ideas. The majority were still attached to the pleasures of local autonomy, to the right of the small unit to act spontaneously as the spirit moved it. Infused with a proud sectarianism and often unreconciled even to taking orders from their own regional, national, or local leaders, the mass of Cenetistas were very unlikely to accept subordination of the CNT to the Comintern, much less to the Communist Party of Spain. If it seemed otherwise in the spring and summer of 1921—that is, if it seemed that the Cenetistas were prepared to cooperate fully with the Russian Bolsheviks and accept their leadership—this was an illusion. But it was an illusion engendered by the fact that the CNT had indeed fallen under the control of a small minority of Communist-Syndicalists, who would be able to send to Moscow a delegation composed precisely of those who had been among the marginal minority at the Congress of the Comedia a year and a half earlier.

The Lérida Plenum and the Profintern

The question of Syndicalist participation in the new Red International of Labor Unions was first discussed by the European Syndicalist organizations at a meeting in Berlin in December 1920. Angel Pestaña, along with the German Anarchosyndicalists, had been among the instigators of this gathering; but his arrest immediately upon his arrival in Spain from the Comintern Congress, along with the clandestine status of the CNT, had prevented either his own return to Berlin or the sending of another Spanish representative. At the Berlin meeting the more Anarchist-oriented delegates, such as Rudolf Rocker and Augustin Souchy, urged the formation of a Syndicalist International entirely independent of Bolshevik influence. However, the Russian trade-union representative, one Belinsky, was able to discourage such an undertaking, and the majority of Syndicalists agreed to participate in the first Profintern Congress. But two issues especially preoccupied them: first, the precise relationship between the Profintern and the Comintern; second, the nature of the dictatorship of the proletariat that was being urged upon them. They agreed to go to Moscow only after adopting a seven-point resolution asserting the necessity of complete Syndicalist independence from all political parties and insisting that the revolutionary dictatorship be exercised by the unions rather than by the Communist parties of their respective countries. Although these reservations precisely matched the views of most Spanish Syndicalists, it would become apparent in Moscow that the Spanish delegation was by no means irrevocably wedded to them.

That delegation was chosen by a secret plenum of the CNT held in Lérida on April 28, just two weeks after the Communist schism in the Socialist Party.* Perhaps by chance, seven of the ten delegates present were of the Communist-Syndicalist persuasion: Andrés Nin (National Committee), Joaquín Maurín (Catalonian Regional Confederation), Hilario Arlandis (Levantine Regional Confederation), Jesús Ibáñez (Asturian Regional Confederation), Arenas from Galicia, Parera from Aragón, and Belloso of the Northern Region. For reasons that have never been clarified, most of the northern and central areas of Spain were not well represented; and the Andalusian delegates arrived

---

* According to Maurín, this plenum also discussed the repression to which Martínez Anido had subjected the CNT. Parera, the Anarchist delegate from Aragon, held that the Cenetistas should continue their terrorist tactics in response to Anido's harsh measures, whereas the National Committee (Nin) and the CRT Committee (Maurín) opposed the use of terror as a system. Maurín says that Parera advocated a "permanent and systematic terrorism." "La CNT y la III Internacional," *España Libre*, 21.x.60.

immediately after the close of the sessions, nevertheless giving their approval to the decisions taken by the plenum.[19] The Anarchosyndicalists, especially those outside Catalonia, soon complained that the Lérida plenum was, in effect, a Communist-Syndicalist conspiracy—little less than a coup d'etat. Not all the organizations of the CNT had received invitations, they said; and the fact that an unusually high percentage of those attending spoke French (and were thus available to go abroad as delegates) seemed to them suspicious. But the critics had to acknowledge that at least two bona fide Anarchists were present at the plenum, although it was claimed that these persons were "inexperienced."[20]

The truth would seem to be that the Lérida plenum was no more irregular than many another clandestine gathering of the CNT in this era of intense repression. But it is also certain that it represented a definite crystallization of the Communist-Syndicalist tendency (more or less coinciding with the formation of the PCO in Madrid and the North), and that, in the end, the plenum chose four of its own members as the CNT delegation to the approaching Moscow congress of the Profintern: Nin, Maurín, Arlandis, and Ibáñez. At the suggestion of Arlandis, the Federation of Anarchist Groups of Catalonia was approached and given the opportunity to name a delegate. This resulted in the presence in the delegation of the young printer and ideologue Gaston Leval, a Franco-Spaniard who had fled France in 1914. It should be noted, as well, that the mandate formulated by the Lérida plenum and carried by the delegates to Moscow contained a quite firm insistence on the preservation of Syndicalist autonomy.[21]

There is, in fact, little reason to doubt that prior to their departure for Moscow both Nin and Maurín continued to think in terms of the autonomy and self-sufficiency of Syndicalism. Thus Nin wrote:

> The Spanish Syndicalists understand that the dictatorship of the proletariat, which they accept as the inevitable transitional means, must be exercised not by a political party ... over and against the working class, but rather by the proletariat itself, by means of its syndical organizations. Revolutionary Syndicalism is sufficient in itself to carry out the prerevolutionary labor and, above all, to build upon firm foundations the free Communist society of tomorrow.[22]

Where Nin and the Communist-Syndicalists differed from other pro-Bolshevik Cenetistas, at this point, was that they were markedly nonsectarian, seeking not merely coexistence with other revolutionary elements but active collaboration. "We are going to Moscow," wrote Nin, "with the firm purpose of achieving the unification of all the revolutionary forces and of defending the doctrine and the spirit of revolutionary Syndicalism."[23] Finally, it should be stressed that the Communist-Syndicalists were not able to read before their departure the negative report on the First Comintern Congress that Angel Pestaña, locked up in Montjuich, would release only later in the year.[24]

The five delegates departed for Russia separately in order to avoid the rigorous police surveillance imposed by Martínez Anido. For Nin and Maurín, who traveled together and were being actively being sought by the Catalonian authorities, capture might have meant a quick death by the Ley de Fugas, which had been inaugurated three months earlier. Having no money or passports, the two militants timed their departure to coincide with the crowds and confusion of the Lérida festival, thereby eluding the police. They made their way, somewhat perilously, across the snow-covered Pyrenees on foot, groping through mists of low-flying clouds that drenched them and obscured the narrow trails. Crossing the principality of Andorra, they reached the French frontier and descended the north slope of the Pyrenees. Their arrival in Toulouse coincided with the Feast of Pentecost, and the young Spaniards were struck by the sharp contrast between the good spirits and well-being of the French people and the austerity and poverty of the nation they had left behind. They concluded that this contrast was the work not of nature but of history. France, they agreed, was what it was by virtue of the great Revolution, whereas Spain's deplorable condition resulted from its never having experienced such an upheaval. They were strengthened in their conviction that the Peninsula needed, above all else, a revolution, and that somehow the key to this regenerating event would be found in Moscow. Ironically, they arrived in Paris just in time to read reports of the suppression of the Kronstadt Mutiny, which, however, they largely discounted as calumnies of the bourgeois press. In Paris they conferred with French Communist-Syndicalist Pierre Monatte (since spring 1919 the editor of the influential *La Vie Ouvrière*), who aided them in their efforts to reach Moscow.[25]

Nin and Maurín then made their way to Berlin, where they joined Arlandis, Ibáñez, and Leval. Since this was in the immediate aftermath of the assassination of Dato, the German police—apprised of the large reward offered by the Spanish government for help in the capture of the assassins—were especially on the alert for suspicious-looking Spaniards. The delegates, therefore, had to observe extreme caution as they made contact with the German Anarchosyndicalists Rudolf Rocker and Fritz Katter, as well as with the young writer Theodor Plivier.[26] The Russian embassy supplied the Spaniards with money and with passports identifying them as "Russian repatriates"; and they continued on by train to Stettin, from there by ship to Revel, and from there, once more by train, to Petrograd.

Gaston Leval, the one authentic Anarchist in the group, discovered only now, as their train rolled through the German countryside, that his companions were "all Communists."[27] In the doctrinal discussions that inevitably ensued, tempers were aroused, and threats even of physical violence were made against the lone Anarchist delegate. With relations thus somewhat strained, the young Spaniards arrived in Moscow shortly before the opening session of the founding congress of the Profintern. Ecstatic at finding himself at last in the capital of the Revolution, Maurín wrote: "*La Internationale* breaks from our lips and from our hearts. A strong emotion takes possession of our souls. We enter the great *fratria*, that is to say, the land of brothers. Arriving from where the workers are persecuted, we come to where the workers have put an end to the exploiters. We have reached the Russia of the social revolution. Viva Russia!"[28]

The First Congress of the Profintern

Two congresses of revolutionaries met in Moscow in the summer of 1921, one composed of "political" Communists and the other of antipolitical revolutionary Syndicalists. Pride of place necessarily went to the Third Congress of the Communist International, which began on June 22 within the gilded halls of the Kremlin itself. The First Congress of the Red International of Labor Unions took a somewhat subordinate position, beginning its sessions on July 3 in the less elegant confines of the House of Trade Unions. The RILU—more commonly known as the Profintern—had emerged as the Syndicalist counterpart of the Communist International, having its origin chiefly in the Bolshevik desire to counter the reviving Amsterdam International. It was an effort to carry the Revolution rapidly forward by gathering all the "revolutionary" workers of the world into an organization separate from but closely related to the Comintern. By this means the Bolsheviks could salve the antipolitical sensibilities of European Syndicalists while harnessing them to Communist political purposes. Organized in Moscow in August 1920, the Profintern was born in an atmosphere of enthusiasm and faith, at a moment when the Bolshevik tide was flowing toward Warsaw and when it was difficult not to believe in the imminence of a general European revolution. Far from being a carefully calculated move, it was an impetuous effort—as Zinoviev later admitted—to break through the enemy's lines by frontal assault and quickly capture the trade unions of the West.[29]

Yet, within weeks of its birth, after the Red Army's retreat from Warsaw, the alluring revolutionary vistas had begun to fade. Born too late to catch the tide of history, the Profintern would be an even less successful demiurge of the revolutionary process than the Comintern itself. Unable to hold its first congress until the summer of 1921—after the Kronstadt Mutiny, the failure of the March Action, the start of the New Economic Policy, and the signing of the Anglo-Soviet Trade Agreement—the Profintern confronted a Europe from which the revolutionary floodwaters were rapidly receding. In fact, the offensive spirit of the Communist movement had been broken, and the leaders of the Third International would increasingly be urging the need for caution. But beyond that, the Profintern would also be confronted with the evident determination of the Bolsheviks to assert Communist political control over the Syndicalist movements of Europe—a resolve that placed the Syndicalists in a real dilemma, requiring them either to retreat or to be dominated. Like moths drawn to a flame, they were irresistibly attracted by the splendor of the Russian Revolution but faced the possibility that it might consume them.[30]

Indeed, all the assertions of Syndicalist autonomy and all the strong resolves to cooperate without being dominated that the Syndicalists carried with them to Moscow proved no match for the well-organized and implacable Bolshevik effort to subordinate the revolutionary trade unions to Communist political leadership. The course of the First Profintern Congress was almost entirely dominated by the Bolshevik-controlled Russian Federation of Trade Unions and by the presiding officer A. Lozovsky. Approval of each of the Bolshevik-inspired resolutions adopted here was assured by the large and essentially fictitious majority that the Russians were able to construct by their control of the credentials committee and by the admission of pro-Bolshevik minority groups from large, conservative European unions or from exotic smaller nations. The Congress, in fact, was run in an altogether high-handed manner. The American George Williams, representing the IWW, said:

> Regarding the rules governing the Congress, they were simple—there were none as far as I could discover. I asked about them but everyone pleaded ignorance, but by diligent observation I learned that Lozovsky was the fountainhead of all rules, and whatever he said could be depended upon as an established rule unless some situation, in his opinion, called for a reversal of former decisions.[31]

Among the 380 delegates from 41 nations, the Spanish delegation played an important and even a leading role in the Congress, but one that would be marked by ambiguity of purpose. Nin, Maurín, Arlandis, and Ibáñez remained a united team and continued to be dazzled by the Revolution and by the new Soviet order. In contrast to the obstructionist French delegation, they were regarded by Alfred Rosmer, who served as Lozovsky's chief whip during the sessions, as a source of "great support." Rosmer found the Spaniards "young, ardent, enthusiastic, and personally very sympathetic." Somewhat to his surprise, he discovered their ideological position to be essentially his own. Only Arlandis among these four—still somewhat influenced by his Anarchist past—caused the directors of the Congress "a certain amount of ennui."[32] The Anarchist Gaston Leval, on the other hand, separated himself almost immediately from the other Spanish delegates and made common cause with the Anarcho-syndicalists in their opposition to all efforts to subordinate the Profintern to the Comintern. Leval had apparently come to Moscow not ill-disposed toward the Bolsheviks and hopeful that some kind of "honorable collaboration" could be effected between Syndicalism and Bolshevism. Once in Russia, however, disenchantment had set in. This was partly owing to the general aspect of repression presented by the Soviet Republic, but perhaps more to what Leval discovered about the treatment of Russian Anarchists in conversations with such figures as A. M. Schapiro, V. M. Eikhenbaum, G. P. Maksimov, Emma Goldman, and Alexander Berkman.[33]

Nin and Maurín, by contrast, discovered in the Russian Bolsheviks a spiritual affinity that soon led them away from the pure revolutionary-Syndicalist principles they had carried with them across the Pyrenees. As left-bourgeois intellectuals they had never been immersed in the emotional world of Anarchism, and it now became clear that their power-oriented and pragmatic revolutionary outlook made them Leninists at heart. Earlier they had found a "refuge" in revolutionary Syndicalism in Catalonia because, as Nin said, it was the movement that most nearly satisfied their emotional needs: their desire for contact with the masses, their hunger for action, and their insistence on a more or less immediate revolution. But in Moscow they came to realize that "so-called revolutionary Syndicalism" was "obsolete in this century"; and it was increasingly apparent to them that a centralizing revolutionary discipline, whose necessity they instinctively understood, could only be supplied by the Communist Party.[34]

The bridge between revolutionary Syndicalism and Bolshevism was presented to the young Spaniards in the amiable figure of an Anarchist turned Comintern functionary—Victor Serge. Having lived in Catalonia in 1916–17, Serge had a special interest in the Spanish delegates and was impressed by their intelligence, austere character, and youthful idealism. With the sensuous eye of an artist, and convinced that a man's external appearance was the mirror of his soul, Serge saw in Maurín's "lofty, somewhat harsh profile, his long face and smiling gravity," the figure of a young knight. Andrés Nin, a "laughing young fellow," had, under his round gold spectacles, an intense expression that was relieved by a certain *joie de vivre*.[35] Accompanied by Serge, the two Spaniards absented themselves briefly from the Profintern Congress in order to pay a visit—perhaps symbolic of their shifting ideological perspective—to a session of the Comintern Congress, where Zinoviev presided in an atmosphere already touched with solemnity.[36]

The role of the Spanish delegation at the Profintern Congress was, as we have suggested, an ambiguous one. The Spaniards, far from being mere tools of the Bolsheviks, worked earnestly on behalf of Syndicalist autonomy, and, along with the German Anarchosyndicalists, even took the lead in this effort.[37] Yet in the end they would give their votes to Bolshevik-sponsored resolutions whose only result would be to make Syndicalist autonomy a fiction; and they would be the only representatives of a major Syndicalist organization to do so. The Bolshevik leaders, for their part, acknowledged the importance of the Spanish delegation, which was second only to the Russian Trade Union Federation in number of affiliates represented, and they spared no effort to win it over.[38]

The Spaniards were not unaware of the distorted pattern of representation imposed on the Congress by the Russians; and very early in the sessions they proposed, with the backing of several other delegations, a resolution protesting the prevailing "fictitious majority," which, they complained, was made up of obscure and unrepresentative delegations from "Palestine, Turkey, Bukhara, Khiva, Java, Korea, and India." In place of this they proposed that a "decisive vote" be given to the revolutionary Syndicalist delegations of the West. They spoke of the importance of Syndicalist independence and asserted that only the Western proletariat should determine the orientation of the RILU. But with the aid of the votes of complaisant delegates from Asia and elsewhere this resolution was easily defeated, and the Congress moved inexorably on to its appointed tasks.[39]

One victory, however, was gained by the Cenetista delegation when they defeated the efforts of the Spanish Communist Party, whose representatives were also in Moscow, to obtain a vote for one of their members in the Profintern Congress—an effort unquestionably encouraged by the Bolshevik-controlled credentials committee. That committee had in fact given the PCE delegation a deliberative vote, to be exercised by Gonzalo Sanz on the basis of his membership in the PCE-dominated Woodworkers' Union of Madrid. After a short, sharp struggle, the Communist-Syndicalists succeeded in having Sanz's prerogative reduced to a consultative vote. Thus the factional struggle between Spanish Communists in Moscow during the summer of 1921 was revealed as a three-way contest: to the rivalry between the PCO and the PCE had been added a dispute between the PCE and the Catalonian Communist-Syndicalists.[40]

The main thrust of Bolshevik efforts in the Congress was, of course, directed toward the subordination of the Profintern to the political guidance of the Communist International. Lozovsky made the Bolshevik position clear when he frankly said to the recalcitrant French delegates that the Charter of Amiens, with its assertion of Syndicalist autonomy and neutrality vis-à-vis all political parties, was both theoretically and practically an "error" that could have "disastrous" consequences. Syndicalists, he said, should be neutral with respect to bourgeois political institutions but not with respect to the Communist Party, which, after all, shared "a common ideal."[41]

Aside from Lozovsky, the chief protagonists of a close link between Syndicalist organizations and Communist parties were Alfred Rosmer and Tom Mann. Theirs was the difficult task of convincing the Syndicalist delegates that the proposed relationship between the Profintern and the Comintern would not result in Syndicalist subordination. The highly respected Rosmer reminded the delegates that the hallowed First International had actually encouraged the commingling of parties and labor organizations—a tradition ended only by the Second International. The Communists, he said, did not intend to sub-

ordinate the trade unions, but simply wished to win over to their ideas a majority within the unions, which every tendency had the right to do. As for
Comintern-Profintern relations, the important thing was the form that cooperation took. To see in the mere establishment of a relationship a danger to
Syndicalist independence was to yield to the arguments of Amsterdam and
the Second International. To imagine, for example, that the mere presence of
a Comintern representative on the Profintern committee would threaten subordination was to denigrate the force and power of the RILU. Anyway,
thought Rosmer, the facts already supported a contrary view, since during the
year of its embryonic existence the Profintern had been "completely free"
from Comintern pressure. It was a question, therefore, not of the "subordination" of the Syndicalists but rather of the "grouping" of revolutionary forces.[42]

During the discussion of this question in committee, the Spaniards presented
a moderately worded resolution urging that the revolutionary leadership be
given neither to Communists nor to Syndicalists exclusively but to whichever
force was the strongest in a particular country. They doubted the wisdom, they
said, of trying to establish a "uniform line of conduct" for the entire world
movement. In those nations where Syndicalism was weak, it was inevitable
that the Communist Party should seize the revolutionary leadership; but in
the "Syndicalist nations," where the trade-union movement was powerful
and pursued revolutionary goals, it should be not Communists but Syndicalists
who formed the vanguard of the revolution. In a country like Spain, where
the CNT had "one million members" and the two Communist parties only
"eleven thousand," the lead would necessarily be taken by the CNT. Nevertheless, they said, "We do not ask that ... only the revolutionary Syndicalists
be the revolutionary vanguard. What we ask is that it not be specified that this
will be exclusively the Communist Party. . . . We ask for a collaboration of all
the revolutionary forces, but we raise our voices against all exclusivism."[43]

But the chairman of the committee, the Russian trade-union chief Tsyperovich, refused to accept this amendment; and the Polish delegate Leder went
so far as to suggest that the strength of the CNT in mid-1921 might not be
what it once was, so that the Communist Party in Spain had perhaps gained
a corresponding importance. This was heatedly denied by the Spanish delegate, who, with questionable accuracy, insisted: "Revolutionary Syndicalism
in Spain ... has never had so much influence as at the present time." Leder
bluntly countered with the Bolshevik view of the matter, affirming that
whether or not the CNT had declined in strength, the leadership in Spain
necessarily had to belong "to the Communist Party as an international party,
[that is,] to the Communist International, since the struggle in Spain is no
more than a part of the world struggle."[44]

Just before the voting on the principal resolution of the Congress—that dealing with the relationship between Comintern and Profintern—Hilario Arlan-

dis offered a last apologia for Syndicalist autonomy, urging that the Communists treat the CNT as an equal and not as a "younger brother." He reminded his listeners of the historic origins of Syndicalist suspicion against political parties of all types and raised the question of whether the Comintern, since it was, after all, "political," might not some day turn opportunist and betray the cause of the workers' liberation. But all of this seems to have been essentially propitiatory, for in the next breath Arlandis disclosed that although his previous words were to be construed as a declaration of principle, "The Spanish delegation, in accord with its mandate, supports completely the . . . resolutions of Comrades Tom Mann and Rosmer in favor of a close relationship with the Communist International." In theory, then, the Spaniards defended the absolute autonomy of the Syndicalist movement. But in practice—and in the interests of revolutionary collaboration—they were willing to accede to a thinly veiled Syndicalist subordination.[45]

At this point, the obedient and essentially artificial majority of the Congress, over the protests of the Anarchosyndicalist minority, including Gaston Leval, voted a series of resolutions that gave the Bolsheviks the victory they desired in the Congress—at the same time undermining any possibility of successful revolutionary collaboration between the Comintern and the mass Syndicalist organizations of the West. The most important of these, entitled "On the question of relations between the [RILU] and the Communist International," asserted in its preamble that

> The logic of the existing class struggle demands the most complete unification of the proletarian forces in their revolutionary struggle, and requires as a consequence close contact and organic union between the various forms of the revolutionary labor movement, above all between the Communist International and the [RILU]. It is thus highly desirable that all efforts be made in the national field toward the establishment of similar relations between Communist parties and Red labor unions.[46]

The resolution went on to call for, first, the unification of the revolutionary Syndicalist unions under the Profintern and, second, the maintenance by that body of the "closest possible ties" with the Communist International, which alone was identified as the "vanguard" of the revolutionary world labor movement. These ties were to be effected by means of a "reciprocal representation" between the Comintern and Profintern executive bodies. As if to ensure that the point were not missed, the resolution repeated that the link between the two organizations had to be "organic and technical," and that there should be a "close and real tie between Red labor unions and the Communist Party in the application of the directives of the two congresses." This centralizing resolution, which would prove repugnant to all major Syndicalist organizations, was passed by a margin of 282 to 25, Andrés Nin and Joaquín Maurín signing for the Spanish delegation.[47]

In itself, the resolution merely strongly implied the subordination of the Profintern to the Comintern, and hence that of all the national Syndicalist organizations to their respective Communist parties. That such a subordination was indeed the intention of the Bolsheviks may be deduced from the fact that not even lip service was paid to the concept of Syndicalist autonomy, as well as from the nature of the Profintern Constitution approved by the Congress at this time. Especially significant was Article Four, which gave to the pro-Bolshevik Syndicalist minorities in various countries representation proportionate to the size of the labor organizations they claimed to represent—despite the fact that those organizations might be affiliated with the Amsterdam International. Article Ten provided that the governing body of the Profintern should send three members to the Executive Committee of the Comintern with decisive votes; and in the same manner, three Comintern representatives would sit on the Executive Committee of the Profintern. This exchange, plus the Bolshevik-controlled majorities in each organization, would, of course, ensure the complete docility of the Profintern executive.[48]

Although its Bolshevik mentors communicated to the outside world a picture of serene unanimity within the Profintern Congress, there was, in reality, a sharp division between the Communist majority (not all of whose mandates could withstand close scrutiny) and the revolutionary Syndicalist minority that in fact represented the only mass organizations in attendance. The Syndicalists, confronted by the Bolsheviks' iron grip on the Congress, were forced into clandestine opposition. Meeting in their hotel rooms after the daily sessions, they tried to formulate a program to counter the one being imposed upon them. They were not pleased by the necessity of a semisecret opposition, but they were incensed by Bolshevik efforts to sabotage the concept of a purely economic, purely Syndicalist International, and they resented Bolshevik press releases suggesting that harmony and unity reigned in the Congress. They could see no alternative but to formulate their own position and advertise it to the world.[49]

The meetings of the opposition delegates, however, showed a striking lack of accomplishment. This was partly a result of the babel of tongues with which they had to contend, but in a larger sense it derived from the doctrinal and tactical differences by which the minority itself was riven. The delegates from the smaller Syndicalist organizations—those of Germany, Sweden, Norway, Holland, and the United States—advocated, in general, complete withdrawal from the Profintern and the formation of a new and purely Syndicalist International. They did so not only because of their distaste for Communist political control but also because of the Bolshevik insistence that they "liquidate" themselves in the larger, conservative trade-union organizations of their respective countries and pursue the "boring from within" tactic upon which the Bolsheviks relied. The representatives of the major Syndicalist organizations—

those of Spain, Italy, and France—did not face the prospect of having to merge with larger organizations and were concerned primarily with the problem of Syndicalist autonomy from their Communist parties. For this reason, and because they deplored the prospect of still further fragmentation of the revolutionary forces, they strongly urged staying within the Profintern and waging a minority struggle against Communist political control. The Spanish delegation attended the secret meetings and urged the latter policy.[50]

The Bolsheviks had some knowledge of these opposition gatherings and of the division within the Syndicalist ranks, and they dispatched "persuasive emissaries" to work upon the Spanish, French, and Italian delegates. Only with the Spaniards did they succeed; and this, indeed, explains the ambiguity of Spanish participation in the Profintern Congress: that is, its association with both the subordinating tendencies of the Communist majority and the rebellious spirit of the Syndicalist minority. It seems certain that the Spanish delegates had no intention of covertly betraying the concept of Syndicalist autonomy; rather, they were sincerely convinced that they could defend that concept by working within the Profintern.[51]

That this is a just verdict is suggested by the adherence of the Spanish delegation to some of the oppositional statements clandestinely circulated during the closing stages of the Congress. The Syndicalist minority, frustrated as much in its efforts to unite the Syndicalist forces as in its attempts to influence the inexorable march of the Congress, futilely issued a variety of manifestos—upon no one of which, unfortunately, was there general agreement. These had in common sharply voiced criticism of the fictitious majority by which the Bolsheviks had worked their will and proposals to set up a formal opposition within the Profintern; one paper even suggested the creation of an opposition "bureau" in Paris.[52] The manifesto to which Joaquín Maurín (along with many others) affixed his signature was phrased as follows:

> Although [we are] a minority at the constituent Congress of the [RILU], because of a representation that deviates from true forms of representation for a trade-union movement, we wish to state that we believe . . . that we represent the real power of the workers. . . . Without desiring to minimize the power and prestige of the Communist International . . . we have the deepest conviction that the power and prestige of the [RILU] will not be increased but, on the contrary, decreased if it stands under the moral influence of the Third International or is subordinated to it. Partly for this reason, partly for other reasons . . . it is absolutely necessary that we create a defense organization of elements within—and for the moment even outside—the [RILU] in order to thus battle for complete independence of and complete autonomy from every political organization.[53]

Another act of Syndicalist insubordination at the Profintern Congress had to do with the plight of a group of Russian Anarchists who had been incarcerated in Taganka Prison in Moscow. With the intention of forcing the

Bolsheviks to explain publicly the reasons for their detention, they began a hunger strike timed to coincide with the arrival of the Profintern representatives in Russia. This produced protests by several delegates on the floor of the Congress, among whom was Hilario Arlandis. Indeed, the speech that the Spanish ex-Anarchist made on behalf of the imprisoned Russians so enraged Trotsky, who happened to be present, that he is said to have hurled himself on the Spaniard, seizing him by the lapels and shouting, "I should certainly like to see that happening to you, petty-bourgeois that you people are!"[54] But the protests were nevertheless effective, and the Soviets agreed, in the end, to release the imprisoned Anarchists on the condition that they leave Russia.[55]

News of the "organic link" resolution reached Spain rather quickly and produced an immediate adverse reaction in Anarchosyndicalist centers. Even as the members of the Nin-Maurín delegation were trying to make their way back from Russia to Spain, Cenetista opinion was turning against the Bolsheviks; and the delegates would come back to find the climate of opinion in the CNT very much changed and increasingly hostile to themselves. But before considering the Anarchist revival that the Profintern resolutions helped touch off within the CNT, it will be well to examine the role of the "political" Communists, who were also in Moscow during this summer, and to trace their struggle to achieve unification of all the Communist forces in Spain.

CHAPTER FOURTEEN

The Struggle for Communist Unity

The Third Congress of the Comintern

Simultaneously with the sessions of the Profintern, the Third Congress of the Communist International assembled in the Kremlin (June 22 to July 12). The temper of this gathering differed greatly from that of the 1920 Congress. As a result of the imposition of the Twenty-one Conditions, the essential nature of the Comintern had been clarified and its authoritarian modus operandi defined. Hence those exotic or dissident revolutionaries—the Pestañas, Souchys, Serratis, and Borghis—who had lent diversity to the Second Congress were missing, and the majority of those present had at least tacitly accepted Moscow's discipline. Beyond this, the delegates were conscious that Europe had entered a period of revolutionary lassitude. Ambitious strike movements in France, England, and Czechoslovakia had been defeated; quasi-revolutionary movements in Italy and in Spain had come to nothing; and the bloody suppression of the Kronstadt Mutiny suggested that an era had ended in Russia as well. The proclamation of the New Economic Policy—a partial reversion to capitalism—signaled the Soviet regime's capitulation to the growing unrest of the peasants, who had refused, in effect, to bear further burdens. Most serious, perhaps, was the recent humiliating collapse of the ill-advised "March Action" staged by the German Communists.[1]

Not surprisingly, the constantly reiterated theme of the 1921 Comintern Congress was the assertion that the postwar era of revolutionary spontaneity and instability had ended, requiring Communist parties to switch from assault tactics to the tactics of siege. Instead of continuing preparations for an immediately impending revolution in Europe, the Comintern leaders now conceded that the majority of workers were not yet under Communist sway; and they began to emphasize the need for organizational and agitational work based on the assumption that the revolution was now only a long-term prospect. This change in tactical outlook required, as Radek said, the direct involvement of the Communists in trade-union struggles, the creation of "experienced, large, revolutionary mass Communist parties," and the avoidance of premature uprisings. The German March Action, a major subject of debate at the Congress, was not precisely denounced as a putsch by the Bolsheviks; but it was clear that they did not wish to see such an enterprise repeated, and they condemned as "dangerous adventurism" the attempts of "impatient and politically inexperienced revolutionary elements to resort to the most extreme methods" on the assumption that the revolution was imminent.[2]

The whole emphasis of the Third Congress, then, was on the fact that the capitalist adversary had everywhere regained his equilibrium and was, for the time being, stronger than the proletarian forces. The need for intense preparation and propaganda within the trade unions was urged, not with the idea—stressed at the 1920 Congress—of making the revolution as soon as possible, but rather with the purpose of improving the material conditions of the workers while winning them to Communism and strengthening their long-range revolutionary potential. Above all, the isolation of the Communists would have to be overcome by a tactical reconciliation with their despised Socialist rivals; and the Third Congress would thus foreshadow the inauguration of the United Front policy, which would be announced not long after the close of the sessions. Like the Russian Bolsheviks who inaugurated the New Economic Policy, the Western Communists would face the painful necessity of taking one step back in order to take two steps forward.[3]

The Spanish Question

The two Spanish delegations to the Third Comintern Congress were virtually swallowed up in a gathering that numbered 509 delegates from 48 countries. The tiny combined membership they represented was completely overshadowed by the claimed membership of many other European Communist parties. According to figures released by Mátyás Rákosi at the time, the Communist International had 51 sections with a total membership of 2,800,000; of this total the Russian Party had 550,000, the German and Czechoslovak parties 300,000 each, the French 130,000, the Norwegians 97,000, the Yugoslavians 85,000, and the Italians 70,000.[4] It is not surprising that the Spanish Communists, representing at most about 6,500 members,[5] did not play a role comparable to that played by the Spanish Communist-Syndicalists at the neighboring Profintern Congress, and that the Executive Committee of the Comintern continued to show little interest in the Spanish situation.

The debates of the Third Congress centered mainly on the problem of the German Communist Party and its March Action, and on the question of the Italian Communists. In a long survey of the world scene, during which he lamented that history had "deceived us so badly" on the matter of the imminence of the European revolution, Trotsky, though ranging far, made no reference to Spain.[6]

Of the two Spanish Communist factions, the leadership of the Congress appeared to favor the larger PCO, whose delegation was headed by Torralba Beci, over the PCE, led by Merino Gracia, and only Torralba was permitted to address the gathering. This partiality—if partiality it was—was consistent with the whole tenor of the Third Congress, which emphasized conformity to the Comintern theses and discouraged ultra-Left tendencies. It harmonized, for example, with the Bolsheviks' rejection of the concept (advanced at the Congress especially by the German KAPD) of the small, pure, sectarian party, a concept so attractive to the doctrinaire youths of the PCE. Still, it is not certain that the ECCI had at this point actually identified the PCE as ultra-Left, and the better treatment of the PCO may only have reflected the fact that the PCE delegation arrived in Moscow after the sessions had begun.[7]

In his necessarily very brief address, Torralba Beci revealed his dismay at the swing of the Congress away from the more revolutionary theses of 1920. He felt that the shift in trade-union work—from an emphasis on revolutionary preparation to a concern with amelioration and long-range organizational activity—would be "detrimental to the Communist Party of Spain and to the entire Communist movement." Spanish workers, he said, were "already accustomed to the slogans contained in the guidelines of the Second Congress." Should these now be changed, the Communists would certainly be viewed with suspicion, and the Communist cells "would be driven from the labor unions." The Spanish Communists had been working in complete accord with the theses of the Second Congress, and it was "vitally necessary" that they be permitted to continue in this way "for some time longer."[8]

Torralba also remarked on the chastisement administered to the German KAPD (whose ultra-Left and sectarian tendencies somewhat resembled those of the PCE, though going beyond them), observing that he did not see how the PCE delegates could now "return home with the same slogans" they had previously used. He expressed optimism about the possibility of unifying the PCO and the PCE in the near future, saying he was hopeful "that we will be able to obtain a certain amount of time from the [ECCI], here in Moscow in order to undertake the solution of this question in Spain." In discussing the other labor movements of the Peninsula, Torralba considerably minimized the strength of the UGT, which he set at 100,000, and exalted the Communists, whom he vaguely described as controlling "the metalworkers, the miners, and a large majority of the labor unions of Madrid." He did not, however, give a specific figure for the numerical strength of the Communists in Spain.[9]

The delegates of the PCE, not permitted to take the floor, had to listen in irate silence to Torralba's speech. Despite a previous agreement to avoid polemics, they consoled themselves by publishing, in the pages of the Third Congress's journal *Moscou*, denunciations of their rivals and complaints that the role of the PCE was not better appreciated. Merino Gracia observed:

"Among the countries of Europe, Spain is the only one [whose] revolutionary activity is almost completely unknown, especially in Russia." Hoping to undermine Comintern confidence in the men of the PCO, Merino accused them of having been "inveterate enemies" of Zimmerwald and Kienthal, and of having been unconscionably tardy in giving their support to the Bolshevik Revolution. He was anxious to reveal that the PCO had been in existence only two months, and he denied, incorrectly, that it had any trade-union support. The leading figures of the PCO were all "centrists," he said, and it was they who posed the major obstacle to unification. Above all, Merino was angered by Torralba's assertion that the differences between the PCO and the PCE were only superficial. On the contrary, he declared, the differences were very great—nothing less, in fact than the "abyss" that separated "a centrist and opportunist party from a revolutionary Communist Party."[10]

The three Spanish Communist factions, then, did not present a picture of reconciliation in Moscow in the summer of 1921. Despite the great distance they had traveled in order to reach the capital of the Revolution, they had moved no closer to one another. Separated by temperamental and/or regional barriers, they entirely lacked fellow feeling, and their mutual recriminations cannot have been reassuring to the leaders of the Comintern. Nevertheless, at the conclusion of the Third Congress, representatives of the PCO and the PCE were brought together in a meeting held under the auspices of the Latin section of the Comintern and chaired by Jules Humbert-Droz.

Both sides again set forth their views, and in the course of the discussions the representatives of the PCE were induced to limit the number of exclusions of PCO militants that they demanded. The list was now shortened to include only Acevedo, García Cortés, Anguiano, and Pérez Solís. Humbert-Droz and the other members of the Latin section, after listening to statements by Torralba Beci and Merino Gracia, announced that in their opinion differences between the two parties were not fundamental, and that fusion should be undertaken without delay. To facilitate this, it was decided, on the advice of Zinoviev, to send a Comintern emissary to Madrid to mediate between the two factions. Although Niccola Bombacci was considered, the choice fell on Count Antonio Graziadei, a professor of economics and long-time Socialist who had been one of the founders of the Italian Communist Party. That Graziadei would arrive in Madrid somewhat predisposed to the PCE possibly owed to the conversations he held in Rome with one of the PCE delegates, Rafael Millá, after the dispersal of the Congress.[11]

The Moroccan Disaster

In the aftermath of the Moscow Congress, the news from Spain inspired in some Comintern leaders, for the first time since the autumn of 1919, a certain optimism about revolutionary prospects in the Peninsula. At Annual in Morocco, on July 21, a Spanish army, ill-equipped and exceedingly deficient in morale, was led by General Fernández Silvestre into one of the most humiliating defeats ever suffered by Spanish land forces.[12] Failed by their officers, who could not organize an orderly withdrawal in the face of an attack by several thousand Berber tribesmen, the raw Spanish troops broke formation and fled in disarray, with the result that more than 8,000 of them were slaughtered and a whole chain of positions rolled up. The catastrophe immediately raised the political temperature in Spain and engendered a violent debate on the question of where "responsibility" for it should be fixed. This debate, which gained great intensity over the next two years, had almost necessarily to lead in one of two directions: either toward a liberalizing, and perhaps even a revolutionizing, of the regime, or toward some kind of preemptive coup d'etat by the military.[13]

From Moscow, it looked at first as though Spain might be thrown, as in 1909, into a revolutionary crisis from which the Communists could gain advantage. On September 14, in a meeting of the Enlarged Executive Committee of the Comintern, Karl Radek observed that "important events" were occurring in Spain, including the "complete defeat of Spanish imperialism," and the return of Maura to power "in the capacity of savior." "It would be well," he said, "if we looked over this question," since "there appears to be arising ... a most revolutionary situation."[14] Radek proposed the drafting of a manifesto to the Spanish people. But this document, when it appeared, fell short of being a revolutionary appeal, and it must have become clear to Comintern observers that the immediate effect of Annual had been to unify rather than to divide the country. No doubt the authority of the throne was, in the long run, irreparably undermined by the growing popular conviction that King Alfonso had incited Silvestre to his rash action; but despite ever more strident demands for "responsibilities," the nation as a whole seemed ready to unite behind the national government formed by Antonio Maura on August 13.[15]

The most concerted labor action at this time was a general strike declared by the Vizcayan Communists in late July with the purpose of preventing the embarkation of troops to Morocco. The Communists also sent a message to the Ugetista leaders in Madrid, urging a joint meeting to discuss the use of proletarian forces to end the Moroccan war, to which the Socialists did not reply.[16] In Catalonia, the pacification carried out by General Martínez Anido was sufficiently complete that the government, despite disturbances elsewhere, was able to embark troops for Morocco in the aftermath of Annual without the least interference from the Cenetistas.[17]

The opportunity presented by the Annual disaster was too tempting to be ignored by the youthful Communists of the PCE, whose bias toward insurrectional tactics had been revealed earlier. Immediately after the defeat, and while such cooler heads as Merino Gracia and Rafael Millá were still in Moscow, the firebrands of the PCE—Ugarte, Andrade, and Portela, among others—became absorbed with the possibility of organizing an armed uprising. This revolt was to center among the tough and chronically rebellious miners and metalworkers of Vizcaya, where the PCE controlled several small Communist groups. In July or August Ugarte traveled through Vizcaya, meeting conspiratorially with groups of workers, issuing insurrectional instructions, and encouraging the stockpiling of weapons and explosives.* Under the prompting of Ugarte and his fellows, who were apparently undeterred by the recent debacle of the March Action in Germany, the Vizcayan miners gathered weapons and manufactured bombs, awaiting each day the signal to rise in revolt. But the signal never came; instead, there finally arrived an order to cancel all plans and dispose of the weapons that had been accumulated. In fact, the PCE leaders in Madrid had not been able to gain the support of the newly formed PCO in Vizcaya, whose leader, Pérez Solís, turned down Ugarte's request for aid with amused disbelief. The return from Moscow of Merino Gracia and Rafael Millá also dampened the revolutionary plans of Ugarte, Andrade, and Portela, who were accused by their enemies in the labor movement of "Anarchist tendencies."[18]

It nevertheless remained true that of all the political parties in Spain, the most forceful protest against the Moroccan war was made by the Communists, who also suffered the most severe persecution as a consequence, including the imprisonment of their leaders, the temporary outlawing of the Party, and the suspension of their journals.[19]

The Graziadei Mission

Early in November, in the aftermath of the crisis produced by Annual, the Comintern agent Antonio Graziadei arrived secretly in Madrid. His intention was to oversee the unification of the PCE and PCO, but also to survey the general situation of the Communist Party in the various regions. However, the intensification of repressive measures in Spain, caused by the resumption of the government's offensive in Morocco, severely hindered his movements. The entire two weeks of his stay had to be spent clandestinely in Madrid, with

---

* One of the groups contacted was that of the iron miners of Somorrostro, whose militants had joined the PCE shortly after its formation. The mood of the group has been described by one of its members, a young miner's wife named Dolores Ibarruri: "In our revolutionary infantilism we thought everything was possible, and so we devoted all our efforts to organizing the insurrection.... Our party might well have served as the model for the kind of errors Lenin described in *"Left-wing" Communism, an infantile disorder*, the errors of Communist parties which, isolated from the masses, were not able to work out strategy and tactics that took into account their countries' specific situations. If ever there was a party capable of making any sacrifice, it was our party. But in spite of its capacity for struggle and sacrifice, its sectarianism rendered its good qualities sterile and ineffectual, isolated it from the masses, and reduced its influence." Ibarruri, pp. 69–70.

contacts necessarily limited to a few leaders of the two factions in the capital. Many of the Communist leaders were in prison as a result of the large-scale arrests made after Annual, and some militants, including Merino Gracia, had not yet returned from Moscow.[20]

Fusion negotiations were thus carried on with the greatest possible secrecy, in the home of a minor Party member and only during the hours from sunset to dawn every night from November 5 to 15. In order to avoid the attentions of the police and to facilitate negotiations, only one representative from each of the two parties was chosen to meet with Graziadei. The PCE sent Gonzalo Sanz, a diminutive but vigorous young leader of the Madrid Woodworkers' Union; and the PCO was represented by the suave and cerebral Núñez de Arenas. The bulk of the discussions involved these three men, with Graziadei calling in and consulting other members of the PCE and PCO as the necessity arose.[21]

The Comintern delegate developed great respect for both Sanz and Núñez de Arenas. Of Sanz he said, with the intelligentsia's somewhat patronizing admiration for the noble proletarian, "It was wonderful to hear that worker talk on equal terms, especially regarding the fusion question, with an intellectual as forceful as Núñez de Arenas." His assessment of Núñez was that he possessed a "very remarkable intelligence and a culture of the first order," but, like most PCO leaders, was perhaps "a little bit centrist."

> He is the type of *universitaire* nourished on French traditions. By virtue of his origins and his temperament, he is perhaps more under the influence of Jaurès than of Marx. Only recent reading and a reasoning process—slightly forced— have been able to make him a Communist. Since at heart he verges on a centrism of the Left, he is a man who will be able to do the new party much good or much ill. In any case, he is a force one must take into account.[22]

Graziadei was less impressed by the old militant Antonio García Quejido, who irresistibly reminded him of the Italian Socialist Lazzari. He decided that Quejido—the titular head of the PCO—because of his age and "modest" intelligence could not "thoroughly comprehend the regenerating idea of Communism."[23]

Though somewhat predisposed toward the PCE, Graziadei was not unsympathetic to the men of the PCO, in whose defense he occasionally spoke out. Thus he reminded the PCE leaders that their rivals had, after all, issued a pro-Comintern manifesto in January 1920, in which they had defended their remaining in the Socialist Party on purely tactical grounds, that is, in order to bring a mass party into the Communist International.[24] Moreover, although many PCO leaders were undoubtedly somewhat centrist, Graziadei had to recognize that among the members of the PCE there were those (like Andrade and Ugarte) of a "somewhat ultra-Left tendency." However, he acknowledged the extensive doctrinal preparation of the young Communists, and he satisfied himself that their electoral abstentionism was a matter of tactics rather than of principles. He passed on to the ECCI a sympathetic summary of the PCE view of the parliamentary question:

> Spain not being a democratic country, the masses have little regard for deputies or local councillors. And the opinion of these comrades was that perhaps it would be more useful to conduct a political action with a view to forming a proletarian party entirely outside the political and administrative powers of the country. It is therefore an opinion that is not at all contrary to the fundamental principle of the conquest of political power, but which, in view of the national circumstances, will require that the question be posed in a completely special manner.[25]

Thus Graziadei did not necessarily dissociate himself from the belief of the PCE's left wing that because of the unique depth of antiparliamentary feeling among the Peninsular masses, Spanish Communists, without forsaking the conquest of political power, should be permitted to renounce electoral and parliamentary activity.

After prolonged and exhausting negotiations, fusion terms were agreed upon; and although both sides made concessions, the PCE seemed to emerge with a perceptible advantage. The most crucial question, that of the makeup of the new Central Committee, was resolved by giving the PCE what it had demanded all along: two-thirds of the seats during the interval before the first congress of the unified Party. Thus nine Committee positions went to the PCE and six to the PCO. The PCO representatives were reconciled to this division by the fact that it was temporary and by Graziadei's assertion that according to the Comintern statutes the PCE could have laid claim to even more seats. In return for this concession, the PCE, acceding to the ECCI's dictum that the conduct of the members of the PCO should be judged only from the moment that Party had detached itself from the Socialist Party, dropped their demands for exclusions.

Graziadei was inclined to believe that the PCE's criticisms of those it sought to exclude were "in general well founded"; but he also realized that fusion would simply be impossible unless the demands were dropped. He recognized not only that the PCO maintained too strong a spirit of solidarity and "chivalry" to submit to exclusions, but that the hostility of the young Communists toward the PCO leaders obviously stemmed—except in the case of García Cortés—from political rather than moral considerations. Thus Graziadei was able to convince the PCE leaders that "the fundamental question was not that of the exclusion of four comrades, so difficult for them to obtain, but that of assuring to the Left of the united Party (that is to say, to themselves) the majority in the Central Committee and control over all the presses of the Party, from the moment of fusion until the first congress."[26]

The question of editorial control of the Party newspaper was a difficult one. The first candidates put forward—Andrade for the PCE and Núñez de Arenas for the PCO—were each unacceptable to one party or the other, Andrade because of his harsh polemicizing and Núñez de Arenas because of his "centrist" tendencies. The solution to this problem again favored the PCE in that it placed the moderate PCE leader Rafael Millá as editor in chief over both Andrade and Núñez de Arenas, who would serve together on the editorial board. Editorial control was considered vital by the PCE representatives, and the desire for it explains their willingness to drop the matter of exclusions. Such was their faith in the power of the printed word that with the Party journal in their hands they confidently expected to be able to convert their rather artificial majority on the Central Committee into an authentic majority within the Party by the time of the first congress. Isidoro Acevedo was left in charge of the Communist journal *Aurora Roja* in Asturias with a PCE man to watch over him. But in Vizcaya, Pérez Solís—since "even the comrades of his own party recognize that he tends to pass too easily from one political attitude to another"—was relieved of his editorship of *Bandera Roja* of Bilbao, which caused him some pain. For the title of the principal Communist newspaper Graziadei, perhaps somewhat pointedly, favored the name *Claridad*, whereas the Spaniards, with what may have been a truer appreciation of their temper and of their task, decided upon the name *La Antorcha*.[27]

Rather wisely, Graziadei did not attempt to draw up a declaration of principles to which the two parties would agree. Instead, it was decided that the theory and practice of the new Party could be "none other than those of the Third International," especially with respect to the principles called into question by the Spanish Anarchist tradition of individual action and anti-electoralism.[28] On these terms unification of the PCE and the PCO was achieved on November 14, and the skill of Graziadei had seemingly accomplished in ten days what the Spanish Communists had not been able to achieve in months of negotiation and recrimination. Each side felt, moreover, that it had won a victory—the PCE with regard to control of the Central Committee and the Party journal, and the PCO with regard to the question of exclusions.

Though not able to travel to the various regions of Spain, Graziadei quickly perceived the "very modest" level of activity of both Communist parties in the autumn of 1921; and he noted that the severity of police measures in the Peninsula had caused the Communists' never very large membership to decline still further. The numerical strength of the PCO he estimated at only 4,500, though he acknowledged its influence in the unions of the UGT. He estimated PCE strength at 2,000 and observed that by itself that party "had never been able to exercise an appreciable influence over the unions or the masses." Nevertheless, it was clear that the Comintern, through Graziadei, had to a degree thrown its weight on the side of the miniscule PCE, favoring it because it had been the first to adhere to Moscow and because it was felt, as Graziadei said, to be possessed of a purer revolutionary faith.[29]

The Revolt of the Ultra-Left

As it turned out, the painfully negotiated unity of the Communists lasted scarcely longer than it took Graziadei to make a circuitous return via Paris to Italy. It was almost immediately threatened by an unexpected shift in the balance of power within the new Central Committee that rendered the victory of the PCE illusory. The shift was due to a change in the outlook of Merino Gracia, who after two visits to Moscow had become a wholly orthodox disciple of the Bolshevik leaders and could be counted on to support the theses of the Comintern, whatever they might be at any given time. When Merino returned to Spain shortly after Graziadei's departure, it became apparent that he was no longer in accord with his former comrades, the ultra-leftists Andrade, Ugarte, Portela, and the rest. Upholding the essentially conservative, anti-adventurist line enunciated by the Third Congress, Merino proceeded to lecture these militants on their "putschism" and "sectarianism"—allegations by no means unfounded—which he considered responsible for the fact that the membership of the PCE had actually declined since its birth. Joined by one or two other ex-PCE militants on the Central Committee, Merino Gracia now achieved an understanding with his old enemies of the PCO, thereby creating a new majority within that body. The ultra-leftists suddenly found themselves a minority within the committee they had expected to dominate, and their disillusionment with Merino Gracia was very great.[30]

Thus it was soon clear that the fusion so laboriously worked out by Graziadei had wrought no miracles. Under a fictitious unity the divergent currents of Spanish Communism continued to flow in separate channels, thus ensuring that the greater part of their energies would continue to be consumed in internecine struggles. Indeed, the history of the Communist Party of Spain up to the coming of the Dictatorship is essentially a study of factionalism.

Open conflict was renewed on December 4, when the Central Committee, after lengthy discussion, decided to enter candidates in the municipal elections shortly to be held throughout Spain. The opposition of the ultra-leftists to this was based on the anti-electoral principles they had previously espoused, but also on the tactical ground that the Party simply was not sufficiently prepared to enter the contest on such brief notice. With somewhat heavy irony they accused the majority of "putschisme électorale."[31] The majority, for their part, were determined to convince Moscow of their fealty and orthodoxy by waging an election campaign, however hopeless it might prove to be.

The precarious unity of the Party was further weakened by a strongly worded and impolitic article published by Merino Gracia in the first issue of *La Antorcha*, in which he harshly indicted the leftist errors of the PCE militants in the light of the theses of the Third Comintern Congress. It was this ill-timed and somewhat ex post facto attack, coupled with the refusal of *La Antorcha* to permit the minority to publish a rebuttal, that now goaded the ultra-Left into rebellion. Stopping just short of open schism, its leaders formed an entity called the "Spanish Communist Group" (GCE) and published, on January 1, 1922, a defiant manifesto against the Party leadership, in which they nevertheless insisted on their loyalty to the directives of the Comintern. Their only purpose, they said, was to place the Party in a better position to "conquer the laboring masses," something that could be achieved only by purging its "semireformist, *arriviste*, and inactive elements." The recent fusion, they complained, had turned out to be a step backward, since it had "suffocated the only voice" that since April 1920 had consistently propagated the principles of the Communist International.[32]

Clearly, the leaders of the old PCE had never reconciled themselves, despite Graziadei's efforts, to the absorption and disappearance of their beloved Party within the united Communist Party of Spain. Half religious sect and half adolescent in-group, the little Party remained the vessel of their faith and the repository of their devotion. They had fully expected, they confessed, that its adherents would continue to operate as an "organic and homogenous group" within the new Party, thereby ensuring the ultra-Left's cohesiveness and control; and their manifesto was frankly directed "principally to the comrades who fought at our side in the [PCE]."[33] Unable to articulate really substantive criticisms, the dissidents continued obsessively to attack the vague heresy of "centrism"—a preoccupation, as we have seen, that was no longer in fashion in Moscow and that Lenin himself had denounced at the Third Congress.[34]

When news of the formation of this faction reached Moscow, the ECCI responded with a blunt telegram invoking the statutes of the Comintern and ordering the dissolution of the Communist Group without delay. The dissidents replied with a letter to Zinoviev, trying to justify their oppositional stand and complaining that the Central Committee of the Spanish Party was seeking to "strangle" all efforts at Communist discussion. The issue they emphasized was the one that came closest to being a substantive question in their dispute with the majority, namely, the matter of electoral tactics. They argued against the "absurd decision" of the Spanish Communists to participate in elections despite "the hostility and abstention of the great masses of workers" and against the wishes of many local sections of the Party. But they were careful to insist, again, that their opposition to electoral participation was in no way inspired by Anarchist principles, and they urged the ECCI to study the whole question seriously and to intervene in Spain in a way that would uphold the principles of "revolutionary Communism."[35] In a separate letter sent to Antonio Graziadei the dissidents charged that their foes within the Party were turning away "little by little from the revolutionary goal" and reducing the role of the Central Committee to "ordinary bureaucratic tasks."[36]

Meanwhile, the Central Committee itself had responded to the formation of the Communist Group by suspending from party office all who had signed the opposition manifesto, leaving their final fate to be decided by the impending First Congress of the unified Party. That Congress was held secretly in Madrid in March 1922 and had as the central theme of its debates precisely the conflict between the orthodox majority and the ultra-Left minority, with the latter strongly urging tactical antiparliamentarianism. The majority inevitably prevailed, and the Congress decreed the expulsion of the dissidents— save for those who agreed to recant—for a period of one year. The Spanish Communist Group was ordered dissolved.[37]

The minority leaders who refused to recant were Eduardo Ugarte, Juan Andrade, Luis Portela, Emeterio Chicharro, and the ex-Anarchist Angel Pumarega. These now resigned from the Party and were followed out by most of the Young Communists. In a meeting held in Retiro Park on March 19, the ultra-leftists voted to dissolve the Communist Group, as they had been ordered to do. But they immediately formed another entity, the "Union of Proletarian Culture"—a name that apparently seemed less factional to them and with which they hoped to avoid any charge of seeking to split the Party even as they maintained their continuity with the old PCE. They appealed to the ECCI to nullify their suspension from the Party; and, rather unrealistically, they continued to hope that the Comintern would once more intervene, as it had done with Graziadei, and restore them to the preeminent position to which they felt their revolutionary purity and intransigence entitled them.[38]

The Humbert-Droz Mission

This proved a vain hope, as the Comintern indeed intervened, but not on the dissidents' behalf. In April 1922 the ECCI sent Jules Humbert-Droz, Comintern Secretary for the Latin Countries, to Spain with full authority to resolve the factional problems that had so absorbed the energies of the Spanish Communists. In Madrid the Frenchman held conversations with the various protagonists and—like Graziadei before him—came to the conclusion that there was nothing fundamental or "organic" about the division within the Spanish Party. "I have searched in vain," he said, "for a political source of the conflict. . . . I have not found anything beyond the question of participation in elections."[39]

More important than any of the issues raised by the opposition, thought Humbert-Droz, was the problem of *personalismo* that so sorely afflicted the Party and was especially evident in the hostility of the dissidents toward their erstwhile comrade Merino Gracia and toward the PCO militants whose exclusion they had vainly sought. The whole desire of the ultra-leftists to continue to operate as a cohesive, self-conscious element within the new PCE seemed to him a reflection of that same tendency. The Spanish Party was the victim of an unfortunate Spanish tradition: "the very dangerous survival of individualist methods."[40] It was chiefly an ingrained Spanish individualism, he believed, that had prompted the young malcontents to various acts of indiscipline and kept them from submitting with good grace to the decisions of their Central Committee. Their criticisms of the Party leaders seemed to him only an echo of the pre-fusion polemics of 1920–21—vague and insubstantial charges never accompanied by concrete policy alternatives.[41]

With respect to the main issue raised by the ultra-Left, that of tactical abstention from electoral activity, Humbert-Droz had to confess that in the Spanish context the dissidents' opposition to taking part in elections was not unreasonable. The question of whether the circumstances in Spain were opportune for parliamentary participation by Communists was, he admitted, "debatable"; and he acknowledged to the ECCI that the position of the protesters had nothing in common with the dogmatic antiparliamentarianism of the Anarchists. Both points of view—electoral participation or abstention—could be argued in Spain, he said, and he himself was making no recommendation to the Comintern on this score.[42]

What could not be argued, Humbert-Droz felt, was the need for greater discipline within the Spanish Party. Obviously irritated by the individualism of the Spanish Communists, the Comintern agent was resolved to settle the festering Spanish question once and for all by a stern "leçon de discipline." He severely lectured the youthful dissidents on the responsibilities of being Communists, telling them that whatever their particular views, their "elementary duty" had been to submit to Party discipline and exert every effort to make the Graziadei settlement work out successfully. Though not denying their devotion to the Communist cause, he stressed that this devotion had to be "inseparable from an absolute and constant discipline." If they were to avoid permanent expulsion from the Comintern, they had to agree to permanently disband their faction within the Party, to dissolve the Union of Proletarian Culture, to abstain from personal and insulting polemics, to apologize for their latest accusations, and finally, to abandon their "purely negative [and] critical attitude." The five rebels (Andrade, Ugarte, Portela, Chicharro, and Pumarega) were given 24 hours to accept or reject these terms; and, after much soul-searching, all but Pumarega accepted them and were retained in the Party, though under suspension. For nearly a year the role of the ultra-leftists within the Spanish Communist movement was greatly reduced.[43]

Humbert-Droz did not come away with an entirely negative view of the Communist Party of Spain. On the contrary, he generously observed, it had made a "good impression" on him, largely because it was composed "almost exclusively" of workers.[44] He optimistically reported that the Central Committee of the PCE was determined, once the internal conflict was resolved, to be much more active than before, and he expected that great progress would be made. He had hoped to spend a week or more visiting other industrial centers in the Peninsula, but after only a few days in Madrid he received an urgent telegram from Zinoviev calling him back to Paris and to problems of greater concern to the Comintern than the fate of the small and faltering Spanish section. Thus he left Spain after only the briefest of visits.

Had Humbert-Droz been able to complete his tour of the Spanish regions, he would probably have felt less optimistic about the Party's future. For in the early part of 1922 the PCE was, in fact, still extremely deficient in organizational unity, having no regular communication and coordination between the Central Committee and the local sections.[45] To the charge of *personalismo*, Humbert-Droz would have had to add that of *localismo* as well, since the Communists in various parts of Spain seemed mainly to be going their separate ways during this period. In part, this simply reflected the variety of labor milieus in the Peninsula and the instinctive adjustment by local Communists to the mentality peculiar to the workers in their region. But two other factors also discouraged coordination: first, the severity of the government's somewhat selective repression, which was directed more against Communists than against Socialists and kept a great many Communist militants behind bars at any given moment; second, the Party's chronic shortage of money and its inability to obtain adequate funds from the Comintern. Together, these two disabilities sharply restricted the propaganda and organizational activity that alone could have solidified the Party on a national basis.[46]

The Revival of Anarchosyndicalism

Another source of Communist disunity was the continuing aloofness of the Communist-Syndicalists headquartered in Catalonia, to whose struggles we must now turn. Although the Nin-Maurín group had voted for the "organic link" resolution in Moscow and had preached the unity of all revolutionary forces, its members did not seem greatly interested, in the aftermath of the Profintern Congress, in achieving unity in Spain or in accepting the leadership of the Madrid-based Communist Party. Both regional pride and a sense of Syndicalist superiority to mere "politicals" no doubt played a part in this; but perhaps equally important was the Communist-Syndicalists' increasing preoccupation with the mounting factional struggle within the CNT, marked by the resurgence of Anarchist attitudes among many Cenetistas who had been half won over to the Bolshevik idea of revolutionary centralism.

The members of the CNT delegation encountered many difficulties in making their way back to Spain after the close of the First Profintern Congress. Andrés Nin traveled as far as Berlin, but was there arrested and imprisoned for a time. After his release he gave up the effort to return to Spain and made his way back to Moscow, where he joined the Russian Communist Party and became a Profintern functionary. Joaquín Maurín reached Paris in the early autumn but remained there for some months, apparently judging it unsafe to return to Catalonia. From a distance he composed occasional articles for *Lucha Social*, which continued to be published in Lérida under the direction of Pedro Bonet. Arlandis and Gaston Leval were arrested in Berlin, but ultimately succeeded in making their way back to Spain. Ibáñez was able to cross the Spanish frontier safely but was arrested almost immediately thereafter.[47]

The Profintern delegates returned to a country experiencing the full force of the post-Annual repression, and to a Catalonia in which the CNT, having lost its violent struggle with Martínez Anido, had ceased to exist as a mass organization. The severity of Anido's measures had achieved their purpose, at least temporarily. The Sindicatos Unicos had mostly ceased to function, and dues were no longer being collected in significant sums; the regular Cenetista leaders remained in exile in Minorca or imprisoned in Catalonia, and the terrorists of the action groups were in jail, in hiding, or dead. The terrorist attacks had at last been extinguished, and the new year of 1922, as Oller Piñol has said, dawned in peace and with a greater feeling of security among all social classes in Catalonia than had been known for a long time.[48]

As for the Communist-Syndicalists, their fortunes began to ebb from the moment news of the organic link resolution arrived in Spain. The disclosure of this centralizing measure in the late summer of 1921 coincided with an already evident decline in the élan vital of Spanish workers, and with a certain dimming of the luster of the Bolshevik Revolution, after nearly three years of millenarian expectation. The capitalist counteroffensive was now in full flood, and police repression following the Dato assassination and the disaster at Annual reached its highest pitch. In fact, the time had clearly arrived for the Cenetistas to give up the revolutionary hopes they had nourished since late 1918 and to make the doctrinal and tactical reevaluations their increasingly unfavorable situation demanded. The organic link resolution was the catalyst of this process, helping to accelerate the repudiation of the Bolshevik heresies to which the Cenetistas had partially succumbed under the spell of the Russian Revolution. Bolshevism, with its connotations of revolutionary audacity and centralizing proletarian dictatorship had been a congenial mystique in a period when the labor movement was growing rapidly and when the faith and combativeness of the workers were at their height; and, as we have seen, many Cenetistas had become half Bolshevized. But in the face of evident and overwhelming defeat, and with the Catalonian labor movement in shambles, the tendency of many militants was to forsake action, along with doctrinal novelties, and to take refuge in the consolations of old, established dogma. Thus the period 1921–23 would see a revival of Anarchist ideology and rhetoric and a growing rejection of all "statist" and authoritarian deviations.

But if the old themes returned, they were played in a lower key. It was a chastened Anarchism that revived, in which the emphasis was no longer on the possibility of an imminent revolution but on the unreadiness of the workers to make any revolution worth having. Increasingly, the Anarchosyndicalists adopted the themes that the "pure" Anarchists had been purveying since 1919, namely, the necessity to educate and uplift the ignorant and materialistic masses before courting social upheaval. Among the ideologues of the CNT there was an ever-greater stress on the need not for audacious minorities and putschist actions but for an intensive "educational" and propagandistic campaign designed to cultivate "consciousness" and "culture" among the proletarians.[49] The Communist-Syndicalists satirically referred to this tendency as "Anarchoreformism" and denigrated its educationist emphasis in their press.[50] Still, it would seem to have been a natural response to the decisiveness of labor's defeat. An increasing number of militants showed signs of having been sobered by the experience through which they had passed under the rule of Martínez Anido; and there was a growing willingness to concede that terror tactics had had a great deal to do with bringing disaster down on the CNT.[51]

Thus a divided state of mind emerged: on one hand, there was a desire to return to the old libertarian values; on the other, there was a new willingness to coexist with the capitalist adversary and pursue the peaceful pathways of syndical action. The leaders of the once-powerful Barcelona Federation of Sindicatos Unicos confessed publicly that the "unanimous" desire of the Syndicalists was for an "era of peace," for a "respite." The workers' organizations, they said, felt an "irresistible desire" to regain legal status, and even to "collaborate" in the solution of the industrial crisis disrupting the life of the country.[52] This mood clearly favored the cause of the "pure" Syndicalists within the CNT. And it would, in fact, pave the way for the last phase of ascendency they would enjoy before the coming of the Dictatorship—indeed, the last such phase they would ever enjoy.

In this context the Profintern resolutions, especially the one providing for the subordination of Syndicalist movements to Communist parties, jolted and dismayed the great majority of Cenetistas, and their doubts regarding the Bolsheviks, which, because of their great need to believe, they had so far suppressed, suddenly crystallized into overt hostility. They continued to admire the Russian Revolution as a historic event, but they more and more regarded the Bolsheviks as perverters of this great, redemptive movement of the Russian masses. Far from carrying the Confederation toward an acceptance of Communist leadership and political tactics, the Profintern resolutions gave added momentum to the Anarchist revival. The spearhead of this resurgence was the newly founded journal *Nueva Senda* of Madrid, which began to publish in the summer of 1921 at about the same time as news of the Profintern resolutions arrived in Spain. The first accusations against the Nin-Maurín delegation appeared in the pages of this journal in August, under the name of Francisco Durán. Durán was soon joined by Manuel Buenacasa—now as intemperately against the Bolsheviks as he had once been for them—and Gaston Leval, who had returned from Moscow to continue the battle against domination of the CNT by the Comintern-Profintern.[53]

The CNT now began a renewed phase of introspection and debate regarding its fundamental nature and purposes. "What is the Confederation?," asked *Nueva Senda*. "What does it represent in the movement of the Spanish proletariat, and what special characteristics justify its existence as an organization distinct from the UGT?"[54] The consensus of the contributors to the new journal was that the CNT, following the Bakuninist resolution of the 1919 congress, was ineluctably a libertarian movement and had to reassert its Anarchosyndicalist nature against the "statist" and dictatorial innovations associated with the Bolsheviks. Thus *Nueva Senda* was filled with renewed evocations of absolute liberty and spontaneity, along with old-fashioned denunciations of authority in all its various forms. The Vizcayan Anarchist José Ortega reminded his fellow Cenetistas that "all power is synonymous with tyranny." The dictatorship of the proletariat was a Russian importation, he said, and whether it was exercised by Russian Communists or Spanish Anarchists, it, too, was tyrannical and therefore unacceptable. Bringing full circle the whole debate on revolutionary power that the Bolshevik Revolution had touched off, Ortega suggested that the revolution in Spain, though no longer an immediate prospect, was nevertheless necessary and would doubtless be bloody and violent when it did come. But he was anxious to stress, in a reversion to pre-1917 rhetoric, that there would be no need for a dictatorship, since the people in their righteous anger could make the revolution unaided by elitist parties.[55]

The resuscitation of the Anarchist spirit was especially evident in the attacks leveled by *Nueva Senda* against the Nin-Maurín delegation for its "betrayal" in Moscow. In trying to defend the organic link resolution, said March Fivall, these traitors had tried to defend the indefensible, and in Moscow they had "frittered away the accumulated labor of years."[56] The very legitimacy of the delegation was called into question, and the Communist-Syndicalists were accused of packing the Lérida Plenum of April 1921.[57] The "treason" of the delegation lay in its failure to wage a last-ditch fight against the statist and party concepts put forward by the Bolsheviks. Every Syndicalist, affirmed Eduardo Cancho, "should prefer to die" before submitting to any political party whatever.[58] The Communist-Syndicalists were also condemned for their advocacy of centralization within the CNT, and for their alleged infatuation with the "materialist concept of history." Their addiction to the false determinism of Marx, said *Nueva Senda*, had led them to neglect the potent influence of both Anarchist ideals and moral values.[59]

The resistance to Communist-Syndicalism was strongest among the Vizcayan Cenetistas. Syndicalism in this region had expanded rapidly after the middle of 1918 and had passed through its own phase of infatuation with the Russian Revolution. Enthusiasm for the Soviets had been greatly stimulated, moreover, by the founding of *Solidaridad Obrera* of Bilbao early in 1920, under the editorship of the ardently pro-Bolshevik Manuel Buenacasa.[60] Even so, not all Vizcayan Syndicalists had been unrestrained in their praise of the Soviet regime, and there were always some who cautioned against the "excessive suggestion" of the Revolution and against the idea of any sort of political control over the sindicatos. Communist-Syndicalism, in fact, never had much strength in Vizcaya, and after the First Profintern Congress disenchantment with Bolshevism seems to have been rapid and thoroughgoing. Under the leadership of the doctrinaire Galo Díez the Vizcayans would emerge as perhaps the CNT's most vocal defenders of a pure, pristine Anarchosyndicalism.[61]

At the urging of Díez and the Northern Syndicalists, the anti-Bolshevik elements in the CNT held a secret "national" plenum in Madrid on August 14, 1921, less than a month after the close of the Profintern Congress and shortly after the disaster at Annual. The resolution approved here was extremely hostile to the Nin-Maurín group and may be considered the opening salvo in a battle to restore orthodox Anarchosyndicalist ideology within the CNT. Though not actually "disavowing" the Profintern delegation, as some have supposed, the Madrid resolution did seek to reaffirm the Anarchist orientation of the Confederation, as set forth in the resolutions adopted by the Congress of the Comedia in 1919. It asserted the CNT's "absolute independence" of all political parties, on the ground that the Confederation—whose final goal was declared to be "Communist Anarchism"—was "sufficient in itself to prepare, direct, and carry out the social revolution."[62] Feeling against the Nin-Maurín delegation ran very high at this meeting, and the majority evidently favored an open disavowal, from which they were dissuaded only by leaders conscious of the impropriety of taking such an action before the delegates themselves had been heard from.[63]

In October, even though most of the Profintern delegates had not returned to Spain, the Communist-Syndicalists retaliated by holding a "national" plenum of their own to review the delegates' conduct in Moscow. Held in the more sympathetic atmosphere of Lérida during October 15–16, this gathering proved more favorably disposed toward the Profintern. It decided that the choosing of the delegation had been "regular," and that no judgment regarding its conduct in Moscow should be made until the members of the CNT had had a chance to familiarize themselves with the Profintern resolutions.[64]

This plenum was promptly labeled "illegal" by the Anarchosyndicalists of the Northern Region—not, as they admitted, because of its composition but because it had departed, in their view, from the sacred Anarchist principles of the Congress of the Comedia.[65] Coupled with this denunciation was a demand, emanating from the non-Catalan Cenetistas, that the headquarters of the CNT National Committee be moved from Barcelona to Zaragoza. Since the statutes of the Confederation provided that the Committee be composed of militants from whatever city it happened to be located in, this was tantamount to removing it from the control of the Communist-Syndicalists, whose strength lay mainly in Barcelona, and placing it in the hands of the Anarchosyndicalists, who were stronger in the provinces. Alarmed by this prospect, the Communist-Syndicalists published an impassioned plea in *Lucha Social*, urging that the Committee not be removed from the heart and center of the Syndicalist struggle in Catalonia and calling attention to the fact that "despite the most savage repression in the history of the class struggle," the National and Catalonian Committees had never ceased to function.[66]

What was more surprising, perhaps, was the unflagging revolutionary optimism of the pro-Comintern Syndicalists. Despite irrefutable evidence that Martínez Anido had won his war with the CNT, and that the morale and numbers of the Cenetistas were declining daily, *Lucha Social* continued to exhort its readers in Sorelian and slightly didactic tones on the necessity for "an implacable class struggle" and an "idealization of the doctrine of collective violence." Amid the silent desolation of the once-great Catalonian labor movement, the Communist-Syndicalists continued to talk of revolution and to affirm that violence was the "very heart" of proletarian action.[67]

The Ideological Evolution of Nin and Maurín

This raises the question of precisely what it was that the Communist-Syndicalists believed during this phase of the social struggle in Spain. By early 1922 it was evident that Andrés Nin had crossed over the somewhat hazy line separating a highly elitist revolutionary Syndicalist creed from Bolshevism. For him, the trip to Moscow had been decisive, and everything in his makeup —his need to surrender to the revolutionary mystique, his thirst for action, his appreciation of power, and his indifference to dogma—combined to ensure that his capitulation to Leninism would be complete. After his futile attempt to return to Spain, he came back to Moscow, as we have seen, and joined the Russian Communist Party. He had already made a great impression on the leaders of the Profintern, and especially on Lozovsky, who, recognizing the young Spaniard's exceptional qualities, brought him into the secretariat of the International, where he virtually became an assistant Secretary General of the Profintern. Nin married a Russian woman, mastered the Russian language with remarkable facility, and became an indefatigable functionary of the Communist International. His energy and remarkable linguistic ability would evoke the admiration of the delegates to the Second Profintern Congress, where he seemed able to communicate fluently in all languages. His choice, then, was to remain in Moscow and labor at the heart of the world revolutionary movement rather than languish in exile in Paris or in prison in Spain.[68]

On the anniversary of the Kronstadt Mutiny, Nin revealed how far his conversion to Leninism had gone by warmly defending the Bolsheviks' bloody suppression of the Kronstadt sailors, insisting that the sailors' demand for "soviets without Bolsheviks" would have eliminated the only force able to preserve the Revolution and keep it on its proper course. Like the ex-revolutionary Syndicalist—or converted Bolshevik—that he was, he affirmed the vital importance of strong-willed elites, noting that although the great social revolutions had all been achieved by the masses, they had always required "an able and audacious minority, with concrete objectives and an unbreakable will ... to guide and lead them." For Nin, this heroic minority was no longer a cluster of Syndicalist militants. Power, he said, properly belonged in the hands of the Communist Party, for despite all that might be said by "those who try to make the revolution by sentimental declamations," the Party was the only entity that knew what it wanted and where it was going. With all its faults, the Party was "the only force capable of governing the destinies of Russia and preventing the return to Tsarism." Nin justified all Bolshevik repressions in the holy name of the Revolution:

> The Russian Communist Party is the only guarantor of the Revolution; and, just as the Jacobins saw themselves obliged to guillotine the Hébertists even though they represented a tendency to the Left, just as we ourselves have eliminated those who constituted an obstacle to the realization of the objectives we pursued, so our Russian comrades see themselves inevitably obliged to smother implacably every attempt to break their power. It is not only their right but their duty. The health of the Revolution is the supreme law.[69]

Although Joaquín Maurín, as we have seen, possessed a revolutionary temperament very similar to that of Andrés Nin, he held to a peculiar middle ground between revolutionary Syndicalism and Leninism throughout 1921–22. His own temper, along with his exposure to Sorelian thought, had given him a very elitist and voluntarist perspective on the problem of revolution. Yet, like his French counterparts, Georges Sorel and Edouard Berth, he hesitated to join the Communist Party. Whether this was merely a tactical delay, as Nin suggested,[70] or was based on theoretical reservations or on *personalismo*, is not clear. Certainly, there was little to distinguish the fundamentals of Maurín's thought from Leninism, for he exalted in his writings what Lenin exemplified in action: the supremacy of will over the inertia of historical and social forces. For Maurín, as for Lenin, the revolution was a moral imperative rather than a historico-economic necessity. Perhaps more explicitly than Lenin, he repudiated what he called the "formulistic fatalism" that he felt Marx had distilled from the fact of the growing concentration of capital. Maurín was quite sure that that concentration would never produce the revolution automatically. Revolutions, he said, "do not come by themselves; it is necessary to force them." Opportune moments might appear, but it was necessary to have in readiness a "revolutionary apparatus" that was filled with an audacious spirit and could determine the precise moment for the revolutionary assault.[71]

With respect to Russia, Maurín did not hesitate to affirm that the Party was "vital to the salvation of the Revolution," and his observation that there was "nothing democratic" about its organization was not intended as a reproof. The Bolshevik Party, he remarked, had the characteristics of "an instrument of war" and was "eminently centralist and authoritarian." At the same time, he felt that the Party had admitted too many new members and had become "polluted," losing its revolutionary purity and even, to some degree, its contact with the masses. He saw the Workers' Opposition of A. Kollontai and A. G. Shlyapnikov as a natural response to the degeneration and bureaucratization of the Party. Yet, Syndicalist though he claimed to be, Maurín felt only a qualified sympathy for that quasi-Syndicalist opposition movement, being too convinced of the Party's importance to the success of the Revolution. The paradox of the Bolshevik Party, he said, was that "without it the Revolution would not have sustained itself so long" but that "one of the great dangers" threatening it nevertheless lay within its own ranks.[72]

In the ultra-leftist articles that he published in *Lucha Social*, Maurín clearly felt unable to call the Party by its name, yet this seemed to be exactly what he was trying to sell to the Catalonian workers. It was necessary, he said,

> to create a union of combat, a league of revolutionaries, achieving a union of all the elements who wish to commit their hearts to the flames of revolutionary torment. Such a clandestine organization, operating within the masses, would so sustain their expectations that they would be ready at the propitious moment. ... The revolution will not occur by itself; it must be incubated by means of a systematic labor carried out by men of resolute temper. ... It is necessary to form a legion of revolutionaries; it is necessary to create a school of revolution. It is not enough to have audacity and to be rebellious; it is necessary to be revolutionaries *por sistema*, professional revolutionaries.[73]

This voluntarism was reinforced by a kind of vulgar pragmatism—by a depreciation of theories and a skepticism about man's ability to reduce to theory the infinite complexity of reality. All theories, Maurín believed, were ultimately broken and betrayed by the facts. In history, there was "only one thing" that never failed, and that was "action." Though ideologues might pretend that events transpired in accord with the demands of their doctrine, revolutionary

Syndicalism drew its ideas "from its own persistent action." The empirical and "eminently pragmatic" character of Syndicalism freed it from all the "residues of rationalist philosophy" and meant, Maurín boldly asserted, that it could never be mistaken in its activity.[74]

Curiously mingled with this emphasis on the role of conscious elites and on the importance of "action" in the prerevolutionary phase was a certain fatalism about the period following the revolutionary upheaval. Whether from expediency or from conviction, Maurín refused to speculate on the shape of the postrevolutionary society. Though scorning the "fatalistic determinism" of the Marxists, he nonetheless stood in awe of the revolutionary phenomenon itself: "Men and ideas are the playthings of great events. Revolutions are creative in themselves, and the direction they take depends on the complexity of the circumstances confronting them in their development, which no one can foretell. The Revolution will be as it shall be."[75] It was useless to speculate, then, about the course the revolution would take, and Maurín observed that the Bolsheviks themselves had been tossed every which way by the stormy seas of the Revolution. Lenin's great value was precisely his flexibility, without which, Maurín was certain, the Bolsheviks could never have retained power. Time spent in speculating on the postrevolutionary period would be better spent in preparation for the revolution. "This is not the time to waste one's breath," wrote Maurín, "It is the time for action." All of which is to say that Maurín could not doubt that the revolution, when it came, would be redemptive. It might be elemental, turbulent, and unchartable, he seemed to say, but it could not possibly fail to be beneficent; and, in a curious aside, he questioned whether there could ever be such a thing as a "crime" during a period of social revolution.[76]

Maurín was no less captivated than Nin by the new Soviet order. Where an Anarchist or a social democrat might see nothing but regimentation, emerging authoritarianism, and the death of liberty, the young Maurín was mesmerized by the power of the Soviet state. That power—symbolized by the "magnificent spectacle" of militarized masses marching in endless columns through Red Square and by the muscular bodies of 6,000 young athletes moving in the rhythmic unison of mass calisthenics—made an overwhelming impression on him, stirring visions of invincible proletarian power. "Russia, within a few years—if the proletarians of Europe have not already learned how to destroy their own states—will issue forth from its frontiers, its youth filled with energy and singing, and will carry out the great liberating revolution, the war that will put an end to all wars and all injustice."[77]

Still, Maurín held back from joining the Communist Party until 1923, and the precise nature of his activity until that time remains unclear. Apart from his journalistic labors and his continuing exhortations to revolution, he seems mainly to have sought to survive and to keep alive the idea of a pro-Bolshevik

Syndicalism against the mounting and frequently violent opposition of the Anarchosyndicalists, the Sindicatos Libres, and the police agents of Martínez Anido.

Maurín and the Communist-Syndicalists of Catalonia never achieved a close relationship with the "political" Communists centered in Madrid and the North. In part, this simply reflected geographical separation and the force of regional differences, as well as residual feelings of Syndicalist self-sufficiency and amour propre. But the restraint of the Communist-Syndicalists in regard to the Communist Party also stemmed from serious doubts about the capacity of that party's leaders. The seemingly endless factional struggles of the Communists had made a poor impression, and the men of *Lucha Social* felt little confidence in either the PCO or the old PCE. The schism of the Terceristas from the Socialist Party in April 1921 was viewed without great enthusiasm in Catalonia, and doubts were expressed that the men of the PCO, merely by a change of name, would acquire revolutionary qualities they had not hitherto possessed. The "opiate of Socialism," it was feared, had been in their blood for too many years.[78]

Thus in Moscow, during the sessions of the Profintern and Comintern congresses, the members of the Nin-Maurín delegation had appeared less than eager to fraternize with the representatives of the PCO or the PCE and had revealed a certain hauteur as the representatives of a "million-man" Syndicalist organization confronting tiny Communist splinter groups. In November *Lucha Social* complained that despite its desire for rapprochement with the Communists, it found the fusion squabbles of the two Communist factions "not very edifying." The PCO was criticized for a lack of dignity in writing to Prime Minister Maura on behalf of the freedom of political parties; and the PCE was chided for apparently having no other thought than its struggle with the PCO, and for its excessive concern with posts and positions. Though declaring the urgent need for a unification of all the authentically revolutionary forces in Spain, the Communist-Syndicalists left little doubt that they would prefer to unite with the followers rather than the leaders of Spanish Communism.[79]

The Communist-Syndicalists, then, maintained a nearly complete independence of the Communist Party. There was full autonomy on both sides, accompanied by occasional liaisons for specific purposes—for example, in the implementation of the United Front and in the campaign against the Moroccan War. Maurín, with some exaggeration, has described the relationship in the years 1921–23 as "always excellent" but without any merging of the two groups. The principal liaison figure among the Communists was César González, and among the Communist-Syndicalists Maurín himself.[80] But news of Communist-Syndicalist activity rarely appeared in *La Antorcha*, and news from the North was equally scarce in *Lucha Social*. There continued to be, in fact, two Communist movements in the Peninsula: one political and centered in Madrid and the North, and one Syndicalist, centered in Catalonia and Valencia. Not until December 1922 would there be created, at the Comintern's request, a true organizational linkage between them. The two movements remained, then, separate and distinct, without much rapport or mutual trust. And as the Comintern agent, Humbert-Droz, correctly discerned, this "duality of origins," which continued to be revealed in the work of the two organizations, created "many sources of conflict and mutual incomprehension."[81]

CHAPTER FIFTEEN

The Failure of the Comintern in Spain, 1922-1923

With the arrival of 1922 the Spanish Communist movement—so recently and precariously unified—entered upon its year of decision and its time of troubles. Whereas 1920-21 had been a phase of birth, preparation and the welding of factions, the new year would usher in an era of defeat and debilitation that would not be reversed for a decade. Nevertheless, the Communists, spared the knowledge that the tide of history was running irreversibly against them, entered the new year with undiminished enthusiasm. They were deterred neither by the deepening economic crisis, which was steadily draining the strength from the sindicatos, nor by the waning vitality of the workers, which they were sure would soon revive. Yet, in fact, the period from January 1922 to the advent of the Dictatorship in September 1923 would be marked by an almost unbroken series of defeats. Virtually all Communist endeavors would fail during these 21 months: the effort to preempt the Socialists in Vizcaya and Asturias; the attempt to bring Socialists and Cenetistas into a united front with the Communists; the struggle in the Zaragoza Conference to keep the CNT within the Comintern; the bid to dominate or disrupt the November Congress of the UGT; the decision to participate in the elections of April 1923; and, finally, the use of terrorist tactics in Vizcaya. Nothing worked, and it became apparent even before the Dictatorship, that the Communists would not in this era capture the Spanish labor movement, or even become a significant political force in the life of the nation. Both the Socialists and the Anarchosyndicalists would decisively turn back the Communist challenge in 1922-23 and reaffirm the ideological positions they had held before the coming of the Bolshevik Revolution. The Communists' numerical strength would melt away, and by the mid-1920's the Communist Party of Spain would be little more than a small bureau of exiles plotting in Paris.

Socialists Versus Communists in the North

During 1918-21 labor agitation had been most intense in Catalonia and the South, where the Cenetistas led the struggle against the forces of order and privilege. But by the end of 1921, with the pacification of both Barcelona and Andalusia, the "hour of Syndicalist lassitude," as García Venero calls it, had begun.[1] The center of labor unrest now shifted to the North, to Asturias and Vizcaya, where the capitalist counteroffensive ignited a series of major strike actions designed to prevent wage cuts demanded by employers who themselves faced steadily falling profits. Superimposed on the struggle of the northern miners and metalworkers against their employers was the struggle of Socialists against Communists for control of a region that had always been the heartland of Spanish Socialism. The competition between the two labor movements—one struggling to survive and the other to be born—was only partially mitigated by the Communists' sudden switch to the United Front tactic early in 1922 and continued to be punctuated by melees and shootings wherever Socialists and Communists rubbed shoulders. The labor struggle of this period was essentially a defensive, rearguard action by a divided working class against a revitalized and resolute capitalist adversary who seemed, at times, determined not merely to reduce wages but actually to liquidate the trade unions, whose existence, in an era of retrenchment, had become an inconvenience.

The struggle between Socialists and Communists in the North was especially severe in Vizcaya, where the partisans of Indalecio Prieto encountered the exalted followers of Oscar Pérez Solís. The forces on which the Communists could initially count in this region were not inconsiderable, among both the Socialist militants and the workers in the sindicatos. Pérez Solís himself confessed the advantages with which the Communists began their endeavors in the aftermath of the April schism, and also suggested two reasons for the ultimate debacle of Vizcayan Communism: the lack of a sufficient number of leaders competent to guide the pro-Comintern masses, and the plethora of violent youths, yearning for direct action, who attached themselves to the Party. These younger militants, "contaminated with Syndicalist methods," were prone to call too many ill-timed strikes for extreme demands and to conduct them with excessive violence. The chief result of this, thought Solís, was to frighten away many potential Communist recruits and make easier the reconquest of various organizations by the Socialists, "who did not boast like us, but had more skill in maneuvering."[2]

The shock troops whom Pérez Solís half led and half followed—and whose virile revolutionism he more than half admired—were the former Young Socialists, who went over to the Communist Party almost en masse and who, as Solís ironically noted, had received their training from the very Socialists they now threatened. Partly because these extremists were so numerous in the movement, and partly because there was so little sober and farsighted leadership at the top, the activity of the Communist Party in Vizcaya during 1921–23 was characterized neither by careful planning nor by patient organizational efforts. Rather, there appeared to be an impetuous desire to give battle and to try to build the party and bring the revolution by storming tactics.[3] Despite the overall decline of the Vizcayan labor movement, a somewhat apocalyptic mood prevailed among many younger workers and contributed greatly to the wave of violence that engulfed the Basque Provinces. Many atentados were initiated by the "action groups" of the young Communists in this era—though never, as Prieto ruefully observed, against employers but only against other workers.[4] Since the struggle in Vizcaya was often a three-way conflict between Socialists, Communists, and Syndicalists, it is not surprising that Bilbao ranked first in the number of atentados per capita and was second only to Barcelona in absolute terms.[5]

It cannot be said that Pérez Solís was himself without blame for the violence that erupted in the Vizcayan capital. Certainly, his transformation had been remarkable, the ex-monarchist and reformist Socialist giving himself over, gun in hand, to the politics of the street. Later he would complain about the "retarded adolescents... who abounded among us";[6] but it was, after all, Solís himself who frequently led them in assaults on Socialist meetings, and even in armed attacks on the Casa del Pueblo of Bilbao, which for a time the Communists occupied. It was Solís, too, who developed so strong an animosity against Prieto that he tried on at least one occasion to arrange the Socialist leader's assassination.[7] When the Anarchist terrorist Ramón Casanellas, one of the assassins of Premier Dato, arrived in Bilbao in the course of his flight from the police, Solís unhesitatingly gave him shelter in the printing plant of his journal *Las Noticias*. Here he and Casanellas spent many evenings together over a period of perhaps two months before Casanellas, escorted to the frontier by the audacious Solís, was able to make his way to France and ultimately to Russia, where he was soon converted to Bolshevism.[8]

But terrorism was never an end in itself, and the main preoccupation of Solís and the Vizcayan Communists continued to be the defeat of their Socialist rivals and control of the unions of the UGT. Late in November 1921, at a congress of the Vizcayan Miners' Federation, the Communists were actually able to seize control of that organization, a coup that led, in turn, to a secession of pro-Socialist miners in La Arboleda and to increased friction between the two tendencies in all of Vizcaya. The early months of 1922 witnessed an upsurge in clashes between Socialists and Communists, in which there were numerous shootings and several deaths.[9] The immediate dispute between the two groups was over the proper method of dealing with the wage reductions that employers were then seeking to impose. The Communists, hoping to win the workers to their side by an inflexible stand, were in favor of a strong counterattack carried out by means of aggressive strikes. The Socialist leaders, willing to recognize the legitimate difficulties of the mine operators, favored compromise agreements that would enable workers to remain on the job and pay their union dues. The numerical strength of the miners' unions had already dropped over the previous two or three years, as many mines had closed, and the Socialists wanted to avoid a further decline.[10]

At a secret meeting in Vigo, early in 1922, the employers decided on a general lowering of wages but resolved to develop their attack gradually, shifting from one region and one industry to another.[11] The disunity of the northern workers—split mainly between Socialists and Communists, but with some adhering to the CNT—was clearly a handicap in meeting this capitalist offensive, and it was in this context that the United Front policy, inaugurated by the Comintern late in 1921, obviously had some utility in Spain. Although the original split, precipitated by the Comintern, might be regretted, a rapprochement now seemed in order and would have the blessing of the Moscow leaders.

The United Front

The United Front tactic, which had been hinted at in the theses of the Third Comintern Congress, involved a dramatic reversal of the Comintern line regarding the social democratic parties of Europe. So far, the policy had been to impose upon Communists a ruthless separation from the Socialists; and in pursuit of this goal, virtually all the Socialist parties of the West had experienced disruptive schisms, some, like the Spanish, being left almost shattered. This approach, however, had reflected a basic optimism about the proximity of the European Revolution and had stemmed from the conviction that the European masses were, in fact, revolutionary in spirit and had only to be separated from reformist social democratic leaders in order to be led to a final assault on the capitalist regime.

But the revolution did not materialize, and as early as the autumn of 1920, after the failure of the Red Army outside Warsaw and as the forces of order in Europe regained their equilibrium, it became clear that it was not coming in the near future. The workers' obvious loss of spirit, more apparent every day, suggested that the time for revolutionary optimism had passed. This recognition, in turn, led almost inevitably toward a policy of rapprochement with the social-democratic forces from which the Communists had so recently split and upon whom so much opprobrium had been heaped. Unpleasant and even embarrassing as it might be, realism—that vaunted Bolshevik quality—demanded such a tactical swerve if the Communists were to retain any influence on the European labor movement. As Zinoviev said in the 1924 Comintern Congress, "The tactics of the united front were in reality ... an expression of our consciousness, first, that we have not yet a majority of the working class, secondly, that social democracy is still very strong, thirdly, that we occupy defensive positions, and ... fourthly, that the decisive battles are still not yet on the immediate agenda."[12]

This policy change set off an uproar in the European Communist parties and tested to the limit their capacity for obedience to the revolutionary high command. For it meant that there were, in effect, no longer any objective criteria for determining Communist orthodoxy. The concept of "deviation" was born, so that "Left" and "Right," as Jane Degras has said, ceased to be actual positions and became merely errors in timing. As an inherently unrevolutionary policy, the United Front tactic meant that adherence to Comintern dictates rather than to Communist doctrine became the standard of Party discipline and loyalty.[13] For revolutionary purists this was hard to swallow. It was all very well for Radek to say that the Communists were entering upon this course "not because we want to merge with the social democrats, but in the knowledge that we shall stifle them in our embrace."[14] Yet it was not easy to call back the harsh rhetoric hurled against the Socialist enemy, or to collaborate with those so recently denounced as "social traitors."

Possibly from a Latin sense of dignity, it was the French, Italian, and Spanish Communist parties that refused, for a time, to give their assent to the United Front tactic. At a meeting of the Enlarged Executive Committee of the Comintern, held in Moscow from February 21 to March 4, 1922, the Spanish delegate joined with the French and Italian representatives to vote against the theses in question. The main argument advanced was that since the Communists had declared the social democrats to be the worst enemy of the working class, the sudden switch to a policy of cooperation would produce confusion and uncertainty in the workers' ranks.[15] Nevertheless, having been outvoted in the ECCI, the Spanish delegate submissively said to the Comintern leaders: "You may be assured that on this question, as on all others, we will remain faithful to the resolutions of the Third International."[16] Such complaisance, then and later, would cause García Venero to describe the Spanish Party as one of the most servile sections of the Comintern.[17]

There was some opposition to the United Front in the Central Committee of the newly unified Communist Party of Spain; but the disagreement appears not to have followed factional lines, since some of the ex-PCE leaders proved more willing to accept the new policy than some of the PCO supporters.[18] At the Party's first congress, held in Madrid in March 1922, the United Front issue was overshadowed by the factional problem of the ex-PCE dissidents and their antiparliamentary heresy. Thus the issue had, in general, less impact in the Spanish Party than in the French PCF; and in spite of the resistance shown by a few delegates, in whom, as the official history says, "sectarian tendencies were very strong," the United Front was adopted by the congress without serious opposition.[19]

The Communist-Syndicalists in Barcelona, with whatever secret misgivings, also accepted the new tactic with docility and tried to make the best of it. In the still rancorous aftermath of the UGT-CNT Pact, ruptured by the Socialists in December 1920, this was not easy or popular. *Lucha Social* defended the policy no more often than necessary, and always in rather general terms. The new tactic was described simply as a "great grouping" of the masses, with only the barest suggestion that it would involve cooperation between the CNT and the despised reformist trade-union leaders who followed Pablo Iglesias and Largo Caballero. The Communist-Syndicalists had, of course, always advocated a "united front" of all revolutionary elements in the labor movement; but the Comintern's new policy went well beyond that in demanding liaison with reformists as well as revolutionaries.[20]

The United Front in Spain

The first attempt to put the United Front tactic into practice was made by the Communists in Vizcaya, where labor unity was, indeed, vital owing to the intensifying capitalist counteroffensive. Spanish mine owners had by then begun to orchestrate their campaign of wage reductions, cutting salaries first in Peñarroya, where, after a two month strike, the Ugetista leaders accepted the reductions; then in Asturias, where small cuts were agreed to by the Socialists (led by Manuel Llaneza) without much resistance; and finally in Vizcaya. In this last region Socialists and Communists split violently over the advisability of striking in order to combat the imposed reduction.[21] In the face of falling prices and out of a desire to maintain production the Vizcayan Socialists were inclined to accede, at least in part, to the owners' demands. The Communists, however, hoped to expand their following by capitalizing on the angry mood of the rank and file of the workers. On April 10, they set up what purported to be a United Front Committee—without the concurrence of the Socialist leaders—and proclaimed a strike.

This immediately touched off a series of collisions between Communists and Socialists in the Vizcayan mining zone, the most serious of which occurred that same night in the town of Gallarta, where the Secretary of the Communist Miners' Union, José Bullejos, was shot and severely wounded and a Communist gunman killed.[22] The authorities immediately proclaimed a state of siege, and Communist militants were assiduously tracked down and arrested by the police.[23] Six days after the Communist-initiated strike began, the committee of the Socialist union, whose workers had continued on the job, undertook to sign a contract with the employers providing for a wage reduction of one and a half pesetas per day. The Communists, through their United Front Committee, attempted to regain the initiative and to counter this appeasement of the employers by proclaiming a general strike, which failed to materialize.[24] The aggressive tactics of the Communists were supported by the few workers who adhered to the CNT in this region.[25]

In May the center of agitation shifted to Asturias, where the mineowners announced that they intended to reduce wages once again, this time by 20 percent. Manuel Llaneza, acknowledging that the owners had some justice on their side, countered by proposing that instead of a cut one hour be added to the working day. He asked for a temporary delay, and said that if the idea of wage cuts were abandoned, the workers would agree to do all they could to increase productivity in the mines. The employers immediately rejected this suggestion, and continued a policy of calculated stubbornness apparently designed to precipitate rather than prevent a strike. Perceiving that the owners might actually welcome a fight, the Socialists strongly urged the Asturian miners not to accept the conflict that the owners seemed so eager to provoke.[26] But the rank and file of the workers, who were being subjected to an intense agitational campaign by the Communists, were in an increasingly radical frame of mind and ill-disposed to listen to moderate leaders. In a referendum they made clear that they wanted neither the reduction in wages nor the extra hour added to their day. The journal *El Sol* observed that in Spain, as in the rest of the world, the leaders of the masses appeared to be "de-authorized"; and its editors lamented the probability that a mining strike in Asturias, at a time when postwar strains were being added to the "chronic disorganization" of Spain, would gravely dislocate the national economy.[27]

In the end, the Asturian Socialist leaders, caught between the obduracy of the employers and that of the workers, reluctantly declared a strike in mid-June; this involved 25,000 to 35,000 workers and was waged until early August, when, aided by the good offices of the Sánchez Guerra government, a compromise settlement considerably less unfavorable to the workers was arrived at. In the course of this bitterly fought strike, Llaneza drove some 13 Communist-led sections out of his union; and these reluctantly formed a new miners' union, the Sindicato Único de Mineros, which remained for some time as a small splinter union in opposition to the much larger Socialist-dominated Sindicato Minero Asturiano.[28]

Almost simultaneously with the Asturian strike there began a strike by the Vizcayan metalworkers, accompanied by further pleas from the Communists for the establishment of a United Front.[29] By June 10 the Communist campaign on behalf of this tactic had rolled into high gear. On that date the Central Committee of the Communist Party (urged on by Humbert-Droz) sent to the committees of all other labor organizations in the Peninsula—not excluding the Anarchists—an open letter urging that all join in a united front in order to work for the following objectives: an end to wage reductions; the removal of Martínez Anido from power in Barcelona and of Governor Fernando González Regueral in Vizcaya; a broad amnesty for all political and social prisoners; the abolition of the death penalty; an end to the Moroccan War and the abandonment of Morocco; the prohibition of lockouts and state aid for all those whom such tactics had forced out of work.[30]

Only two days earlier, Largo Caballero had spoken, in the Casa del Pueblo of Madrid, in such a way as to suggest that he was not opposed to the idea of a "united front" among the workers—something that he in fact regarded as essential in view of the danger that the employers' offensive might soon spread from Asturias and Vizcaya to Madrid. Yet it was not at all certain that he meant by the term what the Communists did, and he would shortly back away from any suggestion that the UGT enter into a liaison with the Communists.[31]

On June 15, in the midst of the hard-fought Vizcayan metalworkers' strike, a meeting of some 1,600 workers was held in the Casa del Pueblo of Bilbao in which Pérez Solís delivered an eloquent plea for the United Front. Two days later the Communist leader spoke again at a turbulent assembly in Madrid, at which there also appeared Acevedo (representing the Asturian workers), Virginia González, Ramón Lamoneda, and Tiburicio Pico. But all suggestions that the United Front be transferred to Madrid from Asturias and Vizcaya, where it was allegedly in operation, produced only protests and derisive exclamations from the Socialist audience. Lamoneda, placed on the defensive, insisted that the "power"—he did not say numerical strength—of the Communist Party was growing, and that in any case this power "should not be measured by its national numerical importance, since it is with an international organization that one deals." Besides, he asked, was it not always minorities who contributed the most to the political life of a nation?[32]

Meanwhile, the news from the North suggested that what little harmony had been achieved between Socialists and Communists under the slogan of the United Front was breaking down badly. The entire scene in Vizcaya and Asturias was very agitated in the early summer of 1922. The Communists were active, and there were many meetings and many clashes between workers and the Guardia or between Socialists and Communists. To control the situation, the government of Sánchez Guerra felt compelled to send extra troops into the Asturian mining zone.[33]

Both the Socialists and the Anarchosyndicalists responded negatively and even somewhat contemptuously to the Communist proposal that they enter into a United Front. The National Committee of the UGT replied that it did not wish to participate in such an arrangement, since it did not wish to acknowledge or dignify a party "that until now has done nothing other than divide and weaken the forces of organized labor, [and which] by its conduct offers no guarantee of the seriousness and loyalty indispensable in the struggle against capitalism."[34] The Committee of the CNT replied in a similar vein, refusing even to consider a United Front for the reason that the Communist party "neither can nor should represent the Spanish proletariat in any way."[35] Both *El Socialista* and *Solidaridad Obrera* of Valencia began an intensive campaign against the United Front idea. When the Communists set up a United Front Committee in Madrid during a woodworkers' strike there, the UGT replied by suspending from its ranks all organizations that participated in it, including the Woodworkers' Union, and by threatening the complete expulsion of all UGT unions that might contemplate a liaison with the Communists.[36]

Largo Caballero was the ceaselessly active and implacable foe of any alliance with the Communists, and the severity of his measures would cause them to liken him to the German Noske and the Italian Mussolini.[37] On July 7 Largo delivered an inflammatory address that emphasized the determination of the Socialist leadership to abstain from the United Front. In a speech suffused with *schadenfreude* he taunted the Communists with the inadequacy of their growth and their relative inactivity since the April schism. He recalled for them the faith they had once had in the efficacy of heroic minorities, and he sought to enhance whatever embarrassment they might feel over the Comintern's sudden change of policy and the fact that Communists were now required to demand not the revolution but only a minimum program and "cheap bread." His answer to all demands for a United Front was simply that the Communist Party was "wounded unto death," and that Communists should return "to the bosom of the [Socialist] Party, which they should never have left."[38] The Communists, angered by this, tried two days later to disrupt another meeting at which Largo was to speak by walking ostentatiously out of the hall as the "Spanish Noske" advanced to the rostrum.[39]

In August the capitalist counteroffensive spread to Madrid when employers in the woodworking industry staged a lockout against their recalcitrant employees. This was a Communist-dominated union, and there followed a rash of protest meetings sponsored by the Communist Party and usually presided over by Vicente Arroyo. The Madrid Communists saw the lockout as an opportunity to win the Socialist rank and file over to the United Front tactic. Manuel Núñez de Arenas, general secretary of the Party, chided the Socialist leaders for not permitting free discussion of the United Front within the ranks of their presumably democratic organization and for trying to decide the matter by fiat.[40] But to the Communist suggestion that a plebiscite be conducted among the UGT membership, the Socialists responded negatively.[41]

Although the Communists would continue their efforts on behalf of the United Front for several years, they would never succeed in drawing either the UGT or CNT into such an alliance. Indeed, in place of unity there emerged still more divisions within the ranks of labor, as the Communist unions expelled from the UGT uniformly failed in their efforts to gain readmission and were required to come together in the Grupos Sindicales Rojos (GSR), organized in December 1922.[42] Following Comintern policy, this organization resolutely refused to put itself forward as a third Spanish labor organization competitive with the UGT and the CNT; yet it was obviously the nucleus of such an organization and could only divide the workers still further. Indeed, the spectacle of the Spanish labor movement early in 1922 mocked all talk of a "united front": in the North Communists and Socialists continued to exchange blows and pistol shots; in Madrid organized workers collided with the unorganized;[43] in Catalonia Anarchosyndicalists still clashed violently with the Sindicatos Libres; in Alicante Syndicalists and Catholic-Syndicalists fought;[44] and everywhere in the Peninsula Socialists and Anarchosyndicalists regarded each other with renewed hostility and deepening suspicion.

The Campaign Against the Moroccan War

One of the few things that Socialists, Communists, and Anarchosyndicalists could agree on in this period was their opposition to the Moroccan War and their belief that it should be terminated and the Protectorate abandoned. Agitation against the war had resumed in the aftermath of the Armistice, with the Socialists taking the initiative. In March 1919 they registered their first major postwar protest against the continued Spanish presence in Morocco and the revival of military activity there under the Liberal Government of Romanones. The Executive Committee of the Party declared it "intolerable" that the pro-German Spanish ruling class, who had been "ultra-pacifists and ultra-neutrals while Europe and America were struggling to liberate the world from Germanic tyranny," were now "animated by warlike fervor against the Berbers of Morocco." After the colonial disaster of 1898, the domestic disaster of 1909, and the "disaster of Germanophile neutrality" during the war, the Spanish people, the Socialists asserted, wanted not an endless colonial war but only "peace, labor, liberty, and regeneration."[45] In November 1921, following the Spanish debacle at Annual, the Socialists in the Cortes laid down still another barrage of criticism against the whole policy that had made the defeat possible. In a restrained yet devastating critique of the war's rationale, Julián Besteiro urged the ruling classes to provide some compelling reason why the conflict should go on.

> And if you do not speak clearly, if you do not give the country a convincing reason on behalf of which Spain's youth should go freely to Morocco, knowing that they have a noble and worthy mission to carry out, ... I say to you that we will have the right to declare that it is an illegitimate cause, not made in the defense of Spain ... and I have the right to say to you that [this cause] does not merit a war under such conditions, nor a single drop of blood of one son of Spain, nor a single tear of a Spanish mother.[46]

Agitation against the war was especially intense during the spring and summer of 1922, when it was spearheaded by the Socialist and Communist youth organizations. Toward the end of April the Young Socialists, who had been reconstituted after two Communist schisms, issued a somewhat sweeping manifesto which, besides calling for an end to the war, also demanded a reduction of military service to one year, hygienic improvements in all military barracks, an end to the Law of Jurisdictions, a reduction of the Army by 50 percent, and the closing of the military academies.[47] Oddly enough, these radical demands do not seem to have unduly aroused the officer corps or the authorities. But when the Young Communists published several antimilitary articles in *La Antorcha* in late July, a severe retribution was in store for them. Admittedly, their language was provocative:

> Our thesis is *abandonista*. By virtue of doctrine, interest, and morality, we believe that there is no other solution than abandonment of Morocco pure and simple. We are in this matter more definitive than Abd-el-Krim himself. We also believe that the time has come to pass from purely verbal and rhetorical protest to action that may put an end to the campaign. After the proposals of the Rif there cannot be fired one more shot. Each million that is spent [is] useless payment to a military bureaucracy discredited and crushed in the dust of its own ineptitude.[48]

These bellicose words did not fail to enrage the military establishment. Almost immediately there descended on the Young Communists—who happened to be gathered at the New School—a squad of policemen led by an irate military judge, one Comandante Pita, who personally arrested all those present, including the Juventud's General Secretary Tiburicio Pico, who was conducted to the Model Prison at 3 A.M.[49] Other arrests came the next day; and since many of the Young Communists fled the country to avoid long prison terms, the Madrid group was largely decimated. The New School hastened to send a note to the press explaining that it was merely a nonpartisan organization "constituted by intellectual elements of the Left—liberals, reformists, Socialists, Communists"—and not affiliated with a particular party.[50] In any event, the Communists, under orders from the Comintern to vigorously oppose Spain's colonial war in Morocco, were clearly carrying out this mandate with more zeal than discretion. A very large percentage of the arrests of Party members in this period were occasioned by antiwar protests, so that the Communist Party was nearly as much a victim of the Moroccan conflict as the army of General Fernández Silvestre.

The Zaragoza Conference

The social scene in Catalonia early in 1922 was far more tranquil than that in Vizcaya or Asturias; but it was a tranquility imposed by force and signifying the absence of syndical life. The Cenetistas were too oppressed and too weakened to take much part in the campaign against the Moroccan War, let alone contemplate a resumption of their anticapitalist offensive. Nevertheless, there were signs of recovery. While Socialists and Communists struggled for ascendancy in the troubled mining and industrial zones of the North, the Cenetistas were taking the first steps toward a revival of their almost wholly defunct organization in Catalonia, a process greatly aided by the coming to power of the Conservative leader Sánchez Guerra on March 30. This personage, who became head of the Conservatives after the death of Dato, had long been considered the bête noire of the labor movement, chiefly because of his role in aborting the 1917 general strike; but he now emerged as a conciliator. Convinced that further repression would be counterproductive, he undertook on April 1 to reestablish constitutional guarantees everywhere in Spain, including Catalonia. This resulted in the freeing of all the Cenetista notables imprisoned in Catalonia and Minorca, and it opened up the possibility of reviving the CNT under a moderate leadership—although it should be noted that the Confederation was still banned as an illegal organization.[51]

Shortly after his return from exile in April, Salvador Seguí traveled to Madrid, where he held conversations with various political figures and gave his support to the formation of a future Liberal government in which Alejandro Lerroux would have a place. It appears to have been understood that the Syndicalists would observe a certain benevolence toward such a government in return for a normalization of the trade-union situation and a maintenance of constitutional guarantees.[52] For this Seguí was immediately and publicly condemned by the extreme Anarchosyndicalists within the CNT.[53]

The feud between Libres and Cenetistas continued in Catalonia, with shots still occasionally being exchanged; but now it appeared to be the Libres who were more aggressive, whereas the Cenetistas issued somewhat plaintive protests about the threats to which they were subjected and indicated their desire to return to a condition of normality.[54] In the brief "general strike" that flared up in Spain on May 1, 1922, the work stoppage in Barcelona was organized chiefly by the Libres.[55]

At the same time, paradoxically, efforts were being made to achieve a unification of Unicos and Libres, with the initiative apparently coming from the latter. Early in June the first fusion of the two groups took place, in the Waterworkers' Union. The head of the Libres, Ramón Sales, expressed the hope that the "fratricidal struggle" between the two organizations would come to an end; and the Socialist journalist Luis Araquistáin, observing that the Spanish public received news of this fusion with "great emotion," viewed it as the beginning of a reconciliation important not only to the working class but to Spain as a civilized country. Later in the same month the Libres sent messages of fraternal support to the workers of Vizcaya and Asturias.[56]

Within the reviving CNT the struggle between Communist-Syndicalists and Anarchosyndicalists continued, but it was clear that the partisans of Moscow were slowly losing out. Everything worked against them at this time: the exhaustion of the workers; the dissolution of the Sindicatos Unicos (which had lost, according to García Venero, more than 90 percent of their members[57]); the dimming of the luster of the Russian Revolution; the impact of the organic link resolution; and, above all, the reestablishment of constitutional guarantees and the return from exile or jail of the regular Cenetista leaders. The committees of the CNT and CRT were once again filled with the old militants of the Confederation, and the Communist-Syndicalists were increasingly displaced.

The movement to take the CNT out of the Comintern immediately gained strength, and was, in fact, one of the principal motives behind the decision that was now taken to summon a major plenum of the battered organization. Preparations for the conference were carried out in secret, since the CNT was still banned, and with a rapidity that the Communist-Syndicalists found distressing, since they feared there would be too little time for Cenetista leaders to familiarize themselves with the activities of the Nin-Maurín delegation in Moscow and to discuss the resolutions adopted there.[58] One of the guiding spirits behind the summoning of the new conference was Manuel Buenacasa, and his haste was explained in part by his desire that the CNT should send a delegation to the founding congress of the Anarchosyndicalist International (or International Association of Workers), which was scheduled to begin meeting in Berlin on June 16. Using an assumed name, Buenacasa approached the authorities in Zaragosa and obtained permission to hold "a meeting of workers from different localities," not mentioning that it would be a gathering of the dreaded CNT. When the Zaragosa Conference began its sessions in the Centro Obrero, on June 11, the authorities were dismayed to discover that it was nothing less than a plenum of the entire CNT leadership. After hearing the provocative opening speech of Acting General Secretary Juan Peiró, the police tried to stop the sessions but were deterred by the threat of a general strike of all Zaragosa workers and were forced to leave the conference in peace.[59]

At Zaragoza the CNT, as Buenacasa said, rose "phoenixlike" from its own ashes, seeking an orientation that would permit its revival and reconstruction.[60] The contrast with the mood of the 1919 Congress of the Comedia could scarcely have been greater. Revolutionary optimism and sectarian hubris had given way to sobered prudence and a desire for peaceful coexistence with other social forces. The delegates were almost uniformly in a chastened mood, few desiring to see more years like those from 1919 to 1921.[61] Among the Anarchosyndicalists there was, above all, a desire to rectify the ideological error they had made in December 1919, when, in hot haste and partly to "dish" the Socialists, they had forced through the resolution of adherence to the Comintern. In the grip of a reviving libertarian orthodoxy, they found the continued presence of the CNT in that organization—now revealed in all its intrinsic authoritarianism—virtually intolerable. Thus the question of international affiliation would be the main item on the agenda of the Zaragoza Conference. Nearly two years of crisis and clandestine existence had passed without an opportunity to examine the reports of the CNT's delegations to Moscow in 1920 and 1921, and all factions within the Confederation wanted the matter settled definitively.

The first session of the Conference, presided over by the arch anti-Bolshevik Galo Díez, had as its principal item of business the naming of delegates to the Berlin Congress and the formulating of the instructions they were to take with them. The opening address was delivered by Angel Pestaña. Aware that the reports he had published in November 1921 and March 1922 had been read by most of the delegates, he spoke only briefly, summarizing the main points he had made earlier.[62] He explained the circumstances under which he had gone to Russia and did not deny that he had signed the by now notorious founding manifesto of the Profintern, saying only that the majority of the Moscow Congress had "imposed" it on him and that in any case he had felt that the CNT's decision to adhere to the Comintern had left him no choice but to sign. Moreover, he reminded the delegates, Lozovsky had assured him that if he signed, rectifications and changes in the Profintern statutes could always be made later—something that he discovered not to be the case. Pestaña concluded with the observation that the Profintern was, in fact, only a "standin" for the Bolshevik Party, having been created merely to serve Russian interests; the CNT, therefore, should withdraw from it provisionally (a definitive separation, he pointed out, could only be made by another congress, not by a plenum).[63]

Although the Conference had not yet heard from the other delegates who had traveled to Moscow, it was decided, on the afternoon of June 12, to choose delegates who would leave immediately for the Anarchosyndicalist Congress in Berlin, with the understanding that the results of the Zaragoza deliberations would be mailed to them later. The two men chosen were Avelino González and Galo Díez, who left the following day.

The only member of the Nin-Maurín delegation to speak at the Zaragoza Conference was Hilario Arlandis: Andrés Nin remained in Moscow; Joaquín Maurín had been wounded by the Libres and was in the hospital; Jesús Ibáñez was apparently not invited to attend; and Gaston Leval sent a report but did not appear personally. Arlandis insisted that the delegation had been legitimately constituted and had impeccably observed its mandate to defend the autonomy of the CNT. The independence of the CNT, he said, was not compromised by the resolutions adopted at the RILU Congress, but was, in fact, "absolutely guaranteed." The Comintern and the Profintern, he assured the skeptical delegates, were "two distinct organizations" and would operate in complete independence of one another.[64]

There now ensued one of the more impassioned debates in the history of the CNT, during which all the wrath of the Anarchosyndicalists, built up since the previous July, descended on the hapless Arlandis. Buenacasa, representing the region of Aragon, Rioja, and Navarre, presented a resolution that reflected his new-found bitterness toward the Bolsheviks. Like a disillusioned suitor, he demanded an "absolute, immediate, and radical separation" from the Communist International and the immediate adherence of the CNT to the new International then being formed at Berlin.[65] Thus his proposal went beyond that of Pestaña, who, along with the more moderate Syndicalists such as Seguí, Peiró, and Viadiu, questioned whether the Zaragoza Conference—technically a plenum—had the authority to break definitively with the Comintern. In this, as in other matters, the Anarchosyndicalists showed themselves to be not overly concerned with the strict observance of due process.

The international question was finally referred to a committee, which struggled for three days to draft a resolution on the Comintern-Profintern issue. The final document, though hardly a masterpiece of brevity or clarity, had the virtue of being a compromise acceptable to most of the delegates. In a lengthy preamble it was asserted that the original adherence of the CNT to the Comintern had reflected less an affinity of principles than a feeling of sympathy for the Russian Revolution and could not be considered binding on the future actions of the CNT. However, it was recognized that since the decisions of a national congress could only be modified by a similar congress, any declaration made by the Zaragoza Conference would have to be construed merely as "orientation and counsel" and could not be final. The heart of the resolution, therefore, provided that the Zaragoza Conference should accept "in principle" the separation of the CNT from the Profintern, and that, in view of the difficulty of quickly assembling a congress, a referendum should be held on this question within one month's time. Also to be submitted to referendum was the advisability of the CNT's joining the new Anarchosyndicalist International. When presented to the entire Conference, this resolution was approved without difficulty, though the referendum would never actually be carried out, and the departure of the CNT from the orbit of Moscow was, in fact, final and definitive at this time.[66]

The "Political" Resolution

Other important matters decided by the Zaragoza Conference, though apparently less vital to the delegates than the international question, nevertheless cast light on the divided spirit and changing power relations within the CNT. The uneasy coexistence of the two major tendencies that had for so long divided the organization was apparent even to outside observers.[67] The Anarchosyndicalists, weakened in power and prestige, defensively confronted the "pure" Syndicalists, whose position had been strengthened as a result of the ordeal through which the Confederation had passed. Where the Congress of the Comedia had been "Anarchist" and intransigent, the Conference of Zaragoza, dominated by the Seguí-led moderates, was "Syndicalist" and, on the whole, conciliatory.

In the afternoon session of the 13th, the Anarchosyndicalists launched accusations against both Seguí and Pestaña for their past deviations from Anarchosyndicalist orthodoxy. But the two militants defended themselves in long speeches justifying their support for the Mixed Commission and for the UGT-CNT Pact of September 1920, as well as their wholly moderate intervention in the Río Tinto strike. Finally, in the late evening, the delegates voted to approve the conduct of both militants, who were now declared "rehabilitated." The approval of the Mixed Commission expressed here contrasted sharply with the denunciations heaped upon it at the Congress of the Comedia and greatly displeased the orthodox Anarchosyndicalists, who, of course, were less interested in improving the material lot of the workers than in abolishing the capitalist system.[68]

Other decisions that reflected the ascendancy of the "pure" Syndicalists included: an agreement (for the first time) to pay salaries to Cenetista officials (this step, urged especially by Seguí, looked toward the creation of a paid corps of functionaries and of course outraged Anarchists like Galo Díez); a refusal to remove the headquarters of the CNT from Barcelona to more Anarchist Zaragoza; and the selection of a new National Committee dominated by moderates, the new body being composed by Juan Peiró (general secretary), Salvador Seguí, Angel Pestaña, José María Martínez, Eusebio Carbó, and Galo Díez.[69]

But the measure that most clearly revealed the decline of the extremists at Zaragoza was the so-called "political" resolution. This document, truly delphic in its vagueness, may be described as the manifesto of the moderates and appeared to be an attempt to convey a message of conciliation to the people of Spain without at the same time wholly alienating the Anarchosyndicalists within the organization. Worked out and sponsored by the moderates Seguí, Pestaña, Viadiu, and Peiró, the resolution declared the "political" nature of the CNT and insisted that the organization could not "withdraw itself" from any of the problems of national life. The interpretation hitherto given to political action, it was asserted, had been too narrow and arbitrary. Although the CNT was, of course, a "thoroughly revolutionary" organization that absolutely rejected parliamentary action and collaboration with political parties, the Cenetistas were nevertheless "obliged to reach certain solutions and to realize certain moral values [regarding] all moral, economic, social, and political problems." Thus the CNT was, to the astonishment of many, declared to be "wholly and absolutely political, since its mission is to conquer the rights of [intervention and surveillance] with respect to the evolving values [*valores evolutivos*] of the national life; and, to such end, its duty is to exercise positive action by means of coercion derived from the resources and manifestations of strength of the CNT."[70]

The meaning of this opaque and ill-drafted statement was obscure from the moment of its conception. Its wording, as *El Sol* charitably remarked, was "not very clear," and it immediately gave rise to speculations in the bourgeois press that the Cenetistas would before long be seeking seats in the Cortes.[71] *El Sol* believed, briefly, that there had been a "profound modification" in the modus operandi of the Syndicalists, and that they would now abandon direct action and utilize parliamentary tactics.[72] *La Libertad* said, "We must regard with great satisfaction the decisions taken by the Zaragoza Assembly, which will reintegrate the working masses into ... national politics"; and *La Voz* exaggeratedly announced, "Soon we'll be seeing Pestaña and Seguí as deputies." At the same time, the Anarchist press launched a series of bitter attacks on the resolution.[73]

But it appeared that the meaning of the moderates had been misunderstood, for on the following day *El Sol* received a terse and emphatic telegram from Peiró stating that the affirmations made by *El Sol* regarding the entry of the Cenetistas into politics were "absolutely incorrect," and that the antiparliamentary stand of the CNT had not been changed.[74] Nevertheless, García Venero is probably correct when he suggests that the resolution was intended to indicate the CNT's willingness, when constitutional liberties were endangered, to recommend to its militants in the future that they vote for political parties committed to sustaining those liberties. In particular, the resolution (which was inspired chiefly by Seguí) was probably intended to clear the way for Cenetistas to vote for the Liberal Bloc then shaping up, with which Seguí had had contact only two months earlier in Madrid.

Whatever its precise meaning, the "political" resolution signified one thing clearly, and that was the supremacy of the moderates within the CNT. Had the doctrinaire Anarchosyndicalists been in control, as in December 1919, it is certain that no resolution couched in these terms would have been conceivable. What the moderates seemed to be saying was that the CNT, having passed through a violent ordeal partly as a result of its own excesses, was now willing to regard itself as only one part of a pluralistic society in which there were many kinds of problems that affected the well-being of the workers. Rather than focusing obsessively on the goal of a revolution designed to usher in "libertarian Communism," the CNT was prepared to concede a degree of legitimacy to existing Spanish society and to interests outside of itself. As opposed to the Anarchists' total critique and absolute moral rejection of "bourgeois" society, the moderate Syndicalists sought to proclaim that although the CNT was "revolutionary," antiparliamentary, and opposed to all political parties, it was nevertheless a part of the nation and involved in the nation's political life, broadly defined. The resolution would thus seem to have been an attempt, muffled and almost incoherent, to hold out the olive branch and begin the normalization of the CNT's relations. The Socialist deputy Fernando de los Ríos, viewed the "political" resolution essentially in this light, and described it as "an obvious evolution" of Spanish Syndicalism, marking a transition from the "dictatorial" and "messianic" vision that had so far dominated the CNT to the more constructive path of "contrition." This, he felt, held out the promise of a future unification of the two great labor organizations of Spain.[75]

The relative eclipse of the doctrinaire Anarchosyndicalists at Zaragoza was also suggested by the defeat of a counterresolution proposed by them. This somewhat poignantly worded measure insisted that the CNT's troubles had arisen chiefly because the Cenetista leaders had forgotten that Anarchism was still the *razón de ser* of the CNT, whereas Syndicalism was nothing more than "a body of which Anarchism is the soul." Unwilling to concede that their own hubris had contributed to the failure of the Confederation, the Anarchosyndicalists attributed the debacle to the unwillingness of the moderate Syndicalists to propagate Anarchist doctrines among the workers, who therefore suffered from *inconsciencia*. The Syndicalist movement, they thought, had crumbled because its leaders, caught up in the struggle for material gains, had let the resplendent Anarchist vision of a just and egalitarian society be supplanted by the mere desire to raise wages and shorten the working day. The great error, indeed, had been to urge the raising of wages rather than insisting upon the abolition of the wage system. What was needed, above all else, was a powerful propaganda effort designed to create an authentic Anarchist consciousness among the workers, without which the revolution would be, in the end, a destructive rather than a creative thing.[76]

The Anarchosyndicalists' rejected resolution revealed the same retreat into esoteric realms observed earlier among the "pure" Anarchists. Now that the revolution had failed, they etherealized it, asserting a new-found conviction that the destructive side of the revolutionary process had received too much emphasis. It was necessary, instead, to "paint" the revolution in its more lustrous and Anarchist form, in which it was "beautiful and always smiling." Finally, the Anarchosyndicalists reaffirmed the belief they had temporarily abandoned under the spell of Bolshevism: Anarchist consciousness, they now insisted, was more important than organization, and the open and frank propagation of Anarchist ideals should take precedence over organizational and tactical themes. Without the creation of *hombres conscientes*, they said, organization and tactics would be of little avail. Thus the thinking of the Anarchosyndicalists had returned to its beginning, discarding the revolutionary optimism and greater absorption with power and organization that had been encouraged by the Bolshevik Revolution.[77]

But if the Anarchosyndicalists lost the fight to determine the ideological line of the CNT, they had at least won the struggle over international affiliation. They had not gained the absolute and unqualified separation from Moscow they demanded; but the proposed referendum on the international question was never held, and the withdrawal of the Confederation from the Comintern-Profintern was, as we have said, final. The new International Association of Workers (AIT) held its first congress in Berlin (December 25, 1922, to January 2, 1923) under the auspices of the German Anarchosyndicalists associated with Rocker and Souchy, and with the two Spanish Anarchosyndicalist delegates in faithful attendance. The declaration issued by this gathering reaffirmed Anarchosyndicalist principles in their purity and made explicit the break with Bolshevism and with the statist heresy of the proletarian dictatorship.[78] With this manifesto, as Rocker wrote, "the breach with Bolshevism and its adherents in the various countries was completed," and Anarchosyndicalism now "traveled its own road."[79] Bolshevik efforts to create a unified revolutionary Syndicalist international under the domination of the Comintern had failed, and the European labor movement was now more fragmented than ever.

The victory of the Anarchosyndicalists on this issue necessarily meant the defeat of the Communist-Syndicalists, who had clearly failed in their efforts to transform the ideology of the CNT and to make it the strong right arm of Bolshevism in the Spanish Peninsula. The activities of the pro-Bolshevik Syndicalists are poorly documented in the period immediately before and after the Zaragoza Conference; but their leaders, certainly, had returned from Moscow fired with zeal to convert the CNT from Anarchism and to harness its revolutionary energies in a more constructive manner than ever before. As apostles, however, they had proved ineffective. Struggling against the police, the Libres, the Anarchosyndicalists, and the ebbing enthusiasm of the masses, they found that their revolutionary and centralizing rhetoric lacked appeal among the rank-and-file Cenetistas. Maurín (still holding back from joining the Party) labored mightily in Catalonia, Arlandis in Valencia, and Ibáñez in Asturias. But the whole tendency of the Confederation at this time—toward Anarchism on the theoretical level and accommodation in practice—was unfavorable to them.[80]

The Permanent Crisis of the Communist Party

Meanwhile, the "political" Communists of Madrid and the North continued, under equally unfavorable circumstances, their struggle to forge Party unity and achieve a coherent collective identity. This was a difficult task, since the several tendencies within the movement had little more in common than the fact that all had worshipped at the shrine of the Bolshevik Revolution. But precisely what "Bolshevism" meant in the Spanish context remained a matter of dispute, despite the very great willingness of the Comintern to lay down guidelines. There were, broadly speaking, two basic schools of thought during 1922 as to what the Communist Party should be, one "political" and the other "Syndicalist." The activity of the Party through most of the year was, in fact, more syndical than political, chiefly because of the need to combat the capitalist counteroffensive in Asturias and Vizcaya and also because the trade unions were the immediate ground on which the Socialists had to be beaten if the Communist Party were to survive as anything more than a mere sect.

The "Syndicalist" tendency in the Party was strengthened by the weight of the "new workers" who, especially in Vizcaya and Asturias, were swept into the Party (or the unions under Communist control) during 1921–22 under the spell of the Bolshevik Revolution. A large percentage of these adherents were young workers new to the organized labor movement. Some were recruited from the UGT, and even from the CNT, but the majority had been roused to political consciousness for the first time by the Revolution and by the postwar struggles in the North.[81] They tended to be spontaneous, undisciplined, prone to violence, and instinctively apolitical. Their anti-electoral attitudes, however, stemmed less from doctrinal sources than from the psychology of the peasant masses who had streamed into the northern industrial zones during the boom years of the war. Just as their counterparts in Barcelona were drawn toward the extremist tendency within the CNT, so these workers gravitated toward the most radical form of protest available—in this case Communism. They wished, as Ramón Lamoneda said, to view the Communist movement as something other than a political party. To them, Communism connoted "radicalism" in labor affairs, and radicalism, in turn, could only mean hostility to political action. Accustomed to the fact that elsewhere Syndicalism was the traditional enemy of Socialism, the new workers imagined that the Communists were essentially "Bolshevik Syndicalists." The very limited political activity of the Party in this period—along with the continuing "antiparliamentary prurience," as Lamoneda called it, of the ex-PCE dissidents—inevitably reinforced this impression.[82]

There was, of course, no direct link between these apolitical masses and the Madrid Left-Communists associated with Andrade, Ugarte, and Portela; but the leftists' numerous anti-electoral statements were considered by the Communist majoritarians to be a source of encouragement to "Anarchosyndicalist" tendencies within the Party. Such tendencies were also encouraged, in no small measure, by one of the leading Communist militants in Vizcaya, José Bullejos. Bullejos, though not denying the need for an organized party and a certain amount of parliamentary activity, felt that the Communists' major emphasis should be on syndical activity, which he described as "primary" and "constructive," something that molded the revolutionary mentality of the masses more decisively than parliamentary action. Bullejos's chief complaint, in fact, was that the Party had concentrated not too much but too little on syndical activity.[83] Antipolitical tendencies among the Communist rank and file were encouraged in other regions as well by those who were preoccupied with the need to win the Cenetista masses to Communism (Hilario Arlandis in Valencia would be an example). In general, those militants who operated in areas where the Socialists had predominated were electoral-minded, while those active in zones previously committed to the CNT were anti-electoral.[84]

Needless to say, this antiparliamentary line was opposed by the left-centrists, who, during the course of 1922, attempted to indoctrinate the Party's rank and file with the idea that the political struggle had to take precedence over the campaign within the trade unions. Lamoneda, as Party Secretary of the Interior, spoke out almost petulantly, insisting that "we are a *political* and *parliamentary* party that aspires to the possession of political power and does not disdain the parliamentary forum." Opposing the "apolitical debilities of infantile radicalism," Lamoneda urged that the Party derive "as much profit as possible from the great electoral agitations that are approaching." The Communist Party of Spain, he said, must acquire "the physiognomy, the personality, and the belligerency that the Communist parties of other countries have."[85]

Manuel Núñez de Arenas, the Party's general secretary, was no less willing than Lamoneda to sacrifice himself in parliamentary contests, and he also lamented what he thought were Anarchist tendencies within the movement. The Party, he said, contained many "excellent comrades who, for fear of the sin of falling into reformism, become ill with infantile radicalism and believe themselves to be stronger and more sincere Bolsheviks by virtue of rejecting every political action." The outlook of these elements (who, he acknowledged, were full of enthusiasm and self-abnegation) contained residues of "Anarchism" that reflected the weakness of the Communist education among them. Concealing his exasperation behind praise, Núñez de Arenas spoke of those "magnificent people, [noted for] generosity and decisiveness in the terrain of Syndicalism," who nevertheless lacked a foundation in Communist doctrine and an orientation toward political activity.[86]

Something that all militants could agree on was the fact that the Communist Party, since its first congress in March 1922, had suffered from a lack of coordination, having remained inchoate, poorly organized, and without close ties between the leaders in Madrid and those who led in the provinces. The Party's sections, as José Bullejos complained, had acted "inorganically, in an isolated manner, independently, without an overall plan [or] common, guiding programs."[87] But there were a number of reasons for this, quite apart from any spirit of *localismo*. Subventions from the Comintern in this period—and their amount is not known—were never adequate to the difficult tasks confronting the Party and were overbalanced by the drain on the Party's funds resulting from the intensive strike activity in Asturias and Vizcaya. For in these regions, which were the principal arena of the Party, the striking—and nearly starving—workers ceased to pay dues or make donations to the Party and, indeed, had to draw on Party funds to help them survive.[88] Hard upon the strikes, moreover, came a growing unemployment crisis that deprived the Party of still more of the funds essential to vigorous activity.[89]

To compound their difficulties, the Communists were dealing with an entrenched and cunning Socialist adversary who revealed little naiveté, indecision, or softness in confronting the threat that the Party posed. The Socialists showed themselves to be ruthless, resourceful, and, as Lamoneda complained, well versed in the arts of labor caciquismo.[90] They received, moreover, considerable indirect assistance from the government, which molested them relatively little in this era but concentrated its repressive efforts on the Communists, who were systematically hunted down and jailed. The result was that the Socialists, sheltered by a relative immunity and more united than ever because of the withdrawal of their pro-Bolshevik dissidents, were able to rebuild their unions with considerable success, while the Communists frequently languished in prison.[91]

Finally, there was the continuing factional discord within the Communist Party, the main polarities of which continued to be the left-centrist majority and the ultra-Left minority. This dispute went well beyond what might have been merely a healthy tension between two tendencies, and was, rather, a rancorous and exhausting feud, charged with personal animosities, that paralyzed the will and obscured the purpose of the Party until the summer of 1923. The most serious result of Communist factionalism was that it dismayed and drove away from the Party substantial numbers of potential recruits who wished to belong to a revolutionary party but who came to doubt the capacity of the movement's leaders.[92]

The Fourth Comintern Congress

In the midst of its campaign on behalf of the United Front and against the war in Morocco, and while its internal divisions remained unresolved, the Communist Party had to choose a delegation to attend the approaching Fourth Congress of the Comintern, scheduled to meet in Moscow beginning on November 7, 1922. This congress, as *La Antorcha* observed, would be the first in which Spanish Communism presented itself with a "normal face," that is, as a united party. The Spanish delegation was composed of Isidoro Acevedo, César González, Vicente Calaza, and Gabriel León Trilla, all of whom were able to make the trip to Moscow without incident.[93] Their role in the Congress would be, however, a limited one.

The Spanish Party had by now acquired a minor notoriety among the Bolshevik leaders for its dissensions and leftist tendencies. Since the number of votes allotted to the various parties depended not merely on their actual membership but also on their "political importance... in the present stage of the revolutionary struggle,"[94] the Spaniards, with a claimed membership of about 5,000, were given three votes, whereas the British, with the same membership, were allotted seven. Nevertheless, the Spanish delegates would later stress the cordiality with which they had been received by the Bolshevik leaders. Zinoviev revealed, they thought, more than a merely casual interest in the Spanish Party and made a point of requesting an interview with the delegation. Bukharin greeted Acevedo with warm *abrazos*, and the Spanish delegates had the impression—almost certainly erroneous—that the "credit" of the Communist Party of Spain was rising in the estimation of the Russian leaders.[95]

Acevedo was permitted to speak briefly to the Congress, though, since he knew no language other than Spanish, it was necessary for the German delegate Stirner to serve as translator. The gray-bearded Asturian, apparently eager to emphasize the zeal with which the Spanish Communists were prepared to obey the commandments of the Comintern, remarked, perhaps a little self-righteously, that although the United Front tactic had been "systematically sabotaged" in France, the Spanish Party—despite the greater difficulties inherent in its situation—had done "everything possible in order faithfully to uphold it." Although expressing reservations about the Comintern's stand on the question of workers' control, Acevedo concluded by saying, "Let the resolutions and decisions of the Congress be what they may, the Spanish Party will in every case and in every way remain loyal to the Communist International and preserve international discipline." At this point, Zinoviev—no doubt recalling the ultra-Left tendencies within the Communist ranks in Spain—broke in, remarking to Stirner, "What did he say about Lenin's statements regarding the developmental diseases of [Communist parties]?" But Acevedo's time was up, and he made no substantive response to what was, in effect, a mild reproach.[96]

Zinoviev's interjection called attention to the fact that since the autumn of 1921 the ECCI had been involved in efforts to bring unity to the Spanish Party and to cope with the ultra-Left tendency that had emerged within it. The most substantive issue raised by the youthful dissidents had been their claim that in the Spanish context parliamentary action by Communists was counterproductive and should be abandoned. This was in part, no doubt, an ideological rationale for an irrepressible factional impulse; but it nevertheless stemmed from a sincere conviction, and, as both Graziadei and Humbert-Droz had conceded, it was not an unreasonable position. The Spanish delegation in Moscow once more revived the whole matter of the Left opposition within their party, with Acevedo, González, and Calaza supporting the electoral stand of the left-centrists and Trilla the anti-electoral position of the dissidents. Trilla complained about the sanctions that had been imposed by the majority on his colleagues—Andrade, Ugarte, Portela, and the rest—and he protested so vigorously against the report made by his fellow delegates to the Congress that he would later find himself censured by his party.[97] The whole matter was turned over to the Spanish Commission of the Comintern, which took testimony and rendered its report to the Congress at the very end of the sessions, following a long debate on the French party.

The report of the Spanish Commission was delivered by Jules Humbert-Droz, who made a broad but somewhat superficial survey of the Peninsular labor scene as viewed from Moscow. He noted the dissolution of the CNT and the adoption of reformist tactics by its leaders, and he advised that the moment was favorable for the Communists to encompass the presumably revolutionary masses who were thus being "abandoned" by their increasingly conservative leaders. This raised the question of the Spanish dissidents' demand that their Party give up electoral propaganda and activity in order not to alienate the apolitical workers of the Peninsula and to win them over more quickly. But it is clear that the Spanish Commission did not decide this issue on its merits as a tactical proposition; and indeed, there were few in that body with enough knowledge of Spain to do so.

The main concerns of the Commission appear to have been, first, to adhere to the theses of the Comintern and, second, to minimize factional conflict within the Spanish Party. The majority correctly discerned that the electoral question, though not unimportant, was, in the final analysis, mainly a screen for factional behavior; and they recognized that to decide in favor of the Spanish minority would simply lead to the disaffection of the pro-electoral majority and therefore create still greater factional problems. Thus Humbert-Droz advised the Congress of the Commission's decision that it would be better for the Spanish Party to win over the Cenetista masses at a somewhat slower rate than to "ruin" them by a departure from Communist principles— a course that would in any case lead only to "renewed and embarrassing crises" in the near future. Instead, the Spanish Party had an obligation to "clarify and make comprehensible" to the Anarchosyndicalist workers the nature of the "revolutionary tactics of parliamentarianism" as defined by the Second Comintern Congress, emphasizing that for Communists electoral activities were a means of revolutionary struggle and not "an asylum for ambitious reformists or petty-bourgeois careerists."

As for the rest of Humbert-Droz's lengthy report, the burden of it was that the Spanish Communists had, with all their strength, to continue the struggle for the United Front and for the unification of the UGT and the CNT. Any thought of setting up a separate Communist labor organization was to be sternly repressed. Spanish workers had to be shown that only the "personal ambitions and interests" of Ugetista leaders stood in the way of labor unity, and that, by contrast, the Communists supported such unity steadfastly. Humbert-Droz also urged cooperation between Communists and Communist-Syndicalists in Spain, suggesting the formation of a "mixed committee for the unity of Spanish labor unions"—a suggestion that, as previously noted, would lead José Bullejos the following month to found in Bilbao the Grupos Sindicales Rojos. The report of the Spanish Commission was accepted unanimously and without debate by delegates doubtless eager to begin the long journey home.[98]

Little need be said about the Second Profintern Congress, which met at the same time as the Fourth Comintern Congress, since the CNT was not officially represented. Andrés Nin and Joaquín Maurín were present, along with delegates representing Communist unions in Spain (Acevedo, González, Calaza, and Trillo), but in contrast to the 1921 Congress, the Spanish delegates, representing only a few thousand workers, were distinguished mainly by their unobtrusiveness (though Nin, as a Profintern functionary, was quite active). Lozovsky spoke at length, devoting much time to the nature of the Anarcho-syndicalist offensive against the Profintern and confiding to the delegates that the Anarchist attacks on Communist-Syndicalism represented merely a "repercussion" of the world capitalist counteroffensive, since Anarchism, he thought, had always been the ally of reformism. On the Executive Bureau of the Profintern there was now but one representative for all the Spanish-speaking countries: Andrés Nin.[99]

The UGT Congress of November 1922

Simultaneously with the sessions of the Fourth Comintern Congress there met in Madrid (November 19–21) an unprecedentedly turbulent congress of the UGT. Just as the Zaragoza Conference in June had witnessed the climactic confrontation between Communist-Syndicalists and Anarchosyndicalists, so this assembly would be the culminating moment in the postwar struggle between Communists and Socialists. Everything since the April schism of the Socialist Party had been building toward this encounter. The Ugetista leaders did not fear any Communist takeover of the UGT, since this was beyond the realm of possibility; but they were afraid that the Congress would be disrupted, and that the Communists would try to split the trade-union organization just as they had split the Party the year before. The Communists, for their part, categorically denied any divisive intentions, pointing out that the theses of both the Comintern and the Profintern forbade the splitting of national labor movements.

Precisely what the Communists did hope to accomplish at this assembly is not clear. Adherence of the UGT to the Profintern, which they of course desired, was obviously unobtainable. Bullejos, writing from the Larriñaga jail, complained that the Communists were going to the UGT Congress "without a program of action, without a serious and thoughtful plan."[100] It was characteristic of the Communists in this period that they were indeed going to the November Congress without a strategy—mainly, it would seem, in order to make trouble for the Socialists, and perhaps merely to disrupt the sessions. The Ugetistas for their part, were determined that this should not occur, and they let it be known that disturbances would be severely dealt with. Beyond this, they were resolved to prevent any Communist-sponsored inquiry into the functioning of the UGT National Committee, as well as any discussion of the UGT's refusal to join in the general strike proclaimed by the Cenetistas in December 1920.[101]

The Congress, attended by some 160 delegates, opened in the salon of the Casa del Pueblo on November 19, with Remigio Cabello of Valladolid presiding. Cabello made a plea for peace and order but warned that disruptions would not be tolerated. "We have the coercive force to maintain peace," he said, "because violence is not the exclusive weapon of a few; it is a two-edged sword, and can be turned against those who first employ it."[102] The debates were thus launched in an extremely tense atmosphere. The 24 Communist delegates were greatly outnumbered by the Socialist representatives, and three of them had their credentials successfully challenged and were excluded from voting. This in turn led to the challenge of the credentials of some Socialist delegates, but in each case the Communists were voted down by majorities of more than 80 votes. Outside, pro-Communist workers, singing La Internationale, were trying to force their way past the guards carefully posted by Largo Caballero and gain entry to the visitors' gallery. Their unavailing efforts set off a commotion within the chamber, for a time drowning out the presiding officer.[103]

The chief spokesman for the Communist minority in the Congress was Núñez de Arenas, who was aided by Facundo Perezagua, Pérez Solís, and Juan Pozas. Acknowledging the great disparity between the numerical strength of the majority and that of the Communist minority, Núñez urged that the Communists nevertheless be given representation as Communists on the various committees of the Congress simply as a matter of fairness to a minority that had a right to be heard. Largo Caballero, as general secretary, stubbornly resisted giving the pro-Comintern forces a foothold and accused them of trying to form "a union within the union." In the UGT, he piously observed, there was neither a majority nor a minority: there were only Ugetistas. Because of the "organic nature" of this particular minority, said Largo, to consent to their request—that is, to officially recognize them as a minority and concede them representation in all committees on that basis—would be to consent to the creation of an extra-UGT organization. Despite arguments in its favor by the moderate Asturian delegate Teodomiro Menéndez, the Núñez de Arenas proposal was easily voted down, 80 to 19.[104]

The Communists also protested the exclusion of their partisans, who were being held outside the doors despite the fact that there were still empty seats. Largo defended this policy on the grounds that two foreign representatives,

Léon Jouhaux and J. Oudegeest, were going to address the Congress and deserved some protection from disruptors. This news touched off a loud chorus of protests and of cheers for Russia. Unable to get his supporters admitted, Núñez next proposed that the Congress vote a formal salutation to the Soviet Republic on its fifth anniversary. This was immediately countered by a delegate from Santander, who proposed to add to Núñez's resolution a protest against Bolshevik persecution of the Socialist Revolutionaries in Russia. In the brief but acrimonious debate that ensued, Núñez explained that in fact the Socialist Revolutionaries were neither Socialists nor revolutionaries but only representatives of the Russian bourgeoisie. Unconvinced by this exposé, the Congress passed the amended resolution 114 to 16.[105]

Tempers were rising now, and interjections from the half-filled galleries were becoming more numerous and more violent, especially those from a small nucleus of Communist supporters high in the nearly empty second tier. The presiding officer, Menéndez, appeared visibly shaken by the tension and tumult in the chamber as he tried vainly to maintain order. The climactic moment came at the start of the fourth session when Largo Caballero proposed the naming of a UGT delegation to the International Peace Conference, to be held in the Hague the following month. Pérez Solís rose to ask whether it was not true that this conference would be attended by "bourgeois elements"; and when Largo conceded that this would indeed be the case, Communist spectators began to shout denunciations of his "collaborationist policy."[106] The naming of the delegation was nevertheless approved over violent objections; and it was at this point of maximum tension that Menéndez undertook to introduce the two foreign labor leaders to the Congress.

As the Socialist majority accorded the visitors a tumultuous ovation, the Communists—who, of course, viewed Jouhaux and Oudegeest as "enemies of Soviet Russia"—began what was, no doubt, a preplanned counterdemonstration. When Oudegeest started to speak, they shouted protests and threw onto the stage various placards bearing messages denouncing the Amsterdam International for its opposition to the United Front. This, in turn, was the signal for Largo's security guards to go into action. Armed with clubs, they advanced up the aisles toward what appeared to be the center of the disturbances, in the second tier. At this moment shots were fired, and one of the advancing Ugetista guards, the Young Socialist and *hombre de choque* Manuel González Portillo, fell dead, while another Young Socialist was wounded. Pandemonium reigned in the chamber as Largo Caballero and Besteiro pointed accusingly from the stage at the left-wing Communist Mariano García,* shout-

* This man should not be confused with either Ramón Merino Gracia or Mariano García Cortéz. Mariano García had belonged to the PCE and had been one of the left-wing dissidents associated with Andrade and Ugarte. If García was, in fact, the assassin of González Portillo, then the responsibility of the ultra-Left for the debacle of Spanish Communism would appear very great.

ing above the uproar, "That's the one! That's the one!" The police quickly entered the building and arrested García (upon whom no gun was found), Núñez de Arenas, Virginia González, Joaquín Ramos, Fernández Mula, and several others.[107]

Although the actual assassin of González Portillo was never identified, the Socialist leaders moved with great rapidity to take advantage of an incident that could only redound to their benefit. As the fifth session opened, several hours later, the Ugetistas voted to expel all Communist delegations from the Congress—that is to say, all those who had a mandate to vote for adherence of the UGT to the Profintern. They also quickly voted a resolution condemning the Communist Party and holding it responsible for the shooting of González Portillo. Fifteen unions that refused to agree to this were summarily expelled from the UGT, the number of workers represented by them being estimated at about 15,000.[108]

The shooting of González Portillo was the culminating disaster for the Communists in 1922. In every part of Spain the Socialist press began a campaign to achieve maximum exploitation of the killing, endeavoring to discredit the Communist leaders by holding them personally responsible for the murder. Thus Manuel Cordero wrote: "It should be clear that for us the ones responsible for this crime are not those who carried it out but those who plotted it: Oscar Pérez Solís, Ramón Lamoneda, Virginia González, Núñez de Arenas, Perezagua...." In this manner the Communists were placed fatally on the defensive, trying again and again to defend themselves from the charge, to which they were far from invulnerable, of being excessively addicted to violence.[109]

CHAPTER SIXTEEN

Labor and the Dictatorship

The Revival of the Terror in Catalonia

While the Socialist moderates, capitalizing on the mistakes of their enemies, were winning the struggle for control within the UGT, the opposite process was taking place within the CNT, where the supremacy of the moderate Syndicalists (which lasted only some ten months after the Zaragoza Conference) was being seriously challenged. Although the rank-and-file Cenetistas, along with their leaders, had been sobered by the repression under Martínez Anido, this was less true of the Anarchist groups, who were only waiting for the opportunity to stage a comeback. Almost as soon as constitutional guarantees were restored by Sánchez Guerra in April 1922, the *grupos de afinidad* began to revive and reorganize, and by summer a resurgence of terrorist attacks in Barcelona attested to their renewed vitality.[1] The editors of *El Sol* continued to be baffled by a terror that involved the assassination of workers by workers:

> In that sinister contest in Barcelona, in which so many have already fallen, without glory for the dead and without the satisfaction of an ideal fulfilled for the killers, since no one knows exactly for what he kills or for what he dies, all have failed—police, governors, tribunals, public opinion. All tactics have failed, conciliation no less than terror. It is a profound illness that permeates every natural and wholesome conception of social life; it is a pathological convulsion, like an epidemic.[2]

Most of the new shootings in fact involved members of the action groups and the Libres and seemed to have to do with the settling of old scores between pistoleros.[3]

Martínez Anido remained as civil governor of Barcelona, along with his right-hand man Arleguí, who continued as chief of police. Anido's popularity with the Catalonian bourgeoisie had grown steadily since his assumption of power in November 1920, and he was increasingly viewed as a savior. His harsh methods had brought peace to Barcelona, and the industrial and propertied classes showed their gratitude with banquets and eulogies. "One might discuss the orientation of [Anido's] policy," said *El Sol*, "but not his personal success." The Madrid journal likened the governor to Mussolini, observing that he had taken power in Catalonia in a situation comparable to that created in Italy by the Communist threat and had acted in an "analogous manner" to the Italian dictator, gaining a similar popularity with the forces of order.[4] In Madrid, nevertheless, the government of Sánchez Guerra increasingly felt that Martínez Anido had outlived his usefulness, and that the only hope for a permanent pacification of Catalonia would lie in the removal of the man whose stern measures had first broken the back of terrorism in the region. Anido, however, enjoying the full support of the Army and the bourgeoisie, was not disposed to leave his post.[5]

The Cenetista revival continued to gain momentum. Many militants who had been jailed or driven underground by the repression now resumed their organizational and propagandistic labors. *Solidaridad Obrera* began to publish again in Barcelona, and eight or ten weeklies appeared in other parts of Spain. The organ of the Anarchist groups, *Tierra y Libertad*, also resumed publication. Salvador Seguí and Angel Pestaña were especially active. Seguí, speaking in Seville and in Jerez de la Frontera, emphasized that the Cenetistas rejected both violence and parliamentarianism and were aware that the hour of the revolution had not yet arrived.[6] Early in August Pestaña spoke to a crowd in Alcoy, assuring them that the CNT had entered on a period of cooperation. Like Seguí, he was careful to stress—probably in order to counteract the effect of the Zaragoza "political" resolution—that the Cenetistas were resolutely anti-parliamentarian and would never become councillors, deputies, or ministers. As usual, Pestaña prefaced his speeches with a few words of populistic self-depreciation calculated to win over his plebeian audiences, identifying himself as a "mediocre" speaker and lamenting that his "only university" had been the factory.[7]

On the night of August 25 Pestaña was the victim of a sensational atentado carried out in the industrial town of Manresa shortly before he was to address local Syndicalists regarding the Comintern. Wounded four times, he was taken, on the verge of death, to a hospital in the same city. Public opinion was shocked by the fact that pistoleros, evidently on the orders of Martínez Anido, were seen loitering outside the hospital, waiting to finish their assignment.[8] Whatever Anido's intention—if indeed he was behind this attack—the episode backfired badly, for it was the final straw that broke the patience of Sánchez Guerra and Interior Minister Bugallal, who now began seriously contemplating the governor's dismissal.

On October 23, in a desperate attempt to recoup his position and get public opinion on his side, Anido engineered a simulated attack against himself.

An agent provocateur was sent to the Anarchists of the action groups and had little difficulty interesting them in a plot to assassinate the man who, above all others, they desired to eliminate. The resulting affray involved little danger for Anido but caused the deaths of three Anarchist pistoleros and one policeman. The ministers in Madrid quickly learned of the plot's origin, and the fate of Anido was sealed. In an angry telephone conversation Sánchez Guerra notified Anido of the removal of Arleguí as police chief, and left no doubt that he would welcome the governor's resignation. The following day, October 25, Martínez Anido surrendered his office, after almost two years as the virtual dictator of Barcelona province.[9]

At first it seemed that labor relations might enter a new and peaceful era after Anido's fall. On November 24, Pestaña, by then recovered from his wounds, assured the Ateneo of Barcelona that the CNT intended to live within the law. Similar assertions were made by the Sindicatos Libres, and there appeared to be some chance for a labor rapprochement.[10] But the revival and renewed belligerence of the Anarchist action groups, which were achieving greater coordination than ever before, cast serious doubt on the ability of the moderates to retain control of the Syndicalist organization they were so assiduously rebuilding. From December 1922 to May 1923 in Barcelona alone 34 deaths and 76 injuries resulted from atentados. Anarchist propaganda reappeared in full force, and in September 1922 the National Committee of the CNT was moved from Barcelona, where it was controlled by the moderates, to Zaragoza, where the extreme Anarchosyndicalists were stronger.[11]

Because the drastically shrunken unions no longer had funds that could be requisitioned, the Anarchist groups continued a tactic they had initiated in mid-1921, namely, that of social brigandage. Thus in October they staged a sensational train robbery, stealing 500,000 pesetas and engaging in a heavy exchange of gunfire with government troops.[12] Robbery now began to replace terrorism as an outlet for the energies of the action groups, ostensibly with the intention of providing financial aid to the CNT. But Angel Pestaña later denied vehemently that any significant part of the money from these crimes had gone to the Confederation. On the contrary, he insisted, the robberies cost the CNT far more than it gained from them, mostly in court expenses. The CNT committee set up to aid prisoners had orders not to accept money obtained from robberies, though Pestaña acknowledged that behind the back of the National Committee "a few pesetas" were taken.[13]

Above all, there was an organizational transformation among the Anarchist groups. Possibly taking a page from the Bolsheviks, the groups began to centralize their leadership: the Catalonian Federation of Anarchist Groups set up a Regional Committee of Relations, which became a kind of politburo for Spanish Anarchosyndicalism, organizing and coordinating Anarchist groups all over Spain. The guiding spirit of this body was the Los Solidarios action group, led by Buenaventura Durruti, Francisco Ascaso, Juan García Oliver, Rafael Escartín, and Ricardo Sanz. These men were the avant-garde of the Anarchist revival within the CNT, and later on, in 1927, they would be the founders of the Federación de Anarquistas Ibéricos (FAI).[14] Relations between the terrorists and the moderates within the CNT were far from cordial at this time. Pestaña—perhaps having learned a lesson from his earlier acquiescence in the atentados—publicly denounced the robberies and thereby incurred the hostility of the groups, so that, as he said, "the atmosphere that formed against me ... was unbreathable." When the tension between moderates and extremists had nearly reached 'the point of explosion," however, the dictatorship of Primo de Rivera put an end to a situation that had become insupportable.[15]

The Death of Salvador Seguí

By about March of 1923 the Anarchist elements seem to have regained the upper hand within the Catalonian sindicatos.[16] The supremacy of the extremists was further assured by the assassination of Salvador Seguí, presumably by gunmen of the Sindicatos Libres, on March 10, 1923. The background to Seguí's murder was a revival of strike activity in Barcelona during the winter of 1922-23, when strikes occurred among the glass, transport, and rail workers, as well as among employees of the Metro. These strikes—especially the last— had been marked by a recurrence of atentados and a renewed cycle of reprisals between Unicos and Libres. The mass firings of Metro workers in retaliation for their strike, along with the shooting of three workers in two days (including a certain Jiménez of the Libres), had poisoned the atmosphere.

The ebullient Seguí—who had just returned from a meeting of the National Committee in Zaragoza—and his friend Pedro Comas were shot down without warning on a Sunday evening on the crowded Calle de la Cadena in one of the most populous districts of Barcelona. The apparent motive was retaliation for the murder of members of the Libres—most recently the shooting of Jiménez—by Anarchist pistoleros. Thus once again a moderate and antiterrorist leader paid the price for atentados committed by members of the action groups. The murder came in the midst of an amnesty campaign being carried on by the Cenetistas, and the news of it, as the militant Alberto Pérez wrote, "fell like a bomb" among the workers of Barcelona. On Monday morning they went to work as usual; but when they heard that the authorities, fearful of disturbances, had already ordered Seguí's body to be buried, spontaneous work stoppages began. The Barcelona Local Federation met and decided to second the workers' protest movement by decreeing a general strike of 24 hours and the holding of a demonstration in the Plaza de Cataluña.[17]

Relations between Seguí and the Anarchists within the Confederation had been extremely bad during the months preceding his death, and there were many members of the action groups who were not sorry to see him removed from the scene. There is no certainty, of course, that Seguí—either then or during the period of the Republic—could have turned back the Anarchist tide within the CNT, yet there can be no doubt that his death removed the major obstacle to the re-radicalizing of the movement.[18] No other Cenetista leader had the personal force and constructive talents necessary to lead the CNT out of the morass of terrorism and into a positive role in national life.*

Labor and the Elections of April 1923

The elections of April 1923—the last to be held before Primo de Rivera's coup d'etat—clearly revealed the apolitical indifference of the Cenetistas, the growing conservatism of the Socialists, and the continued impotence of the Communists. The major influence on the elections themselves was, of course, the still-reverberating disaster of Annual, which only a few months earlier had forced the resignation of Bugallal (who was implicated in Crown decisions leading up to the disaster) and brought down the Conservative Sánchez Guerra government. A new Liberal ministry under García Prieto, the first since 1919, came to power, quickly deciding to dissolve the Cortes and schedule new elections for April 29.

The dominant coalition in these elections was the Liberal Bloc, whose formation had been suggested as early as 1920 by the left-wing Liberal Santiago Alba but was not complete until the spring of 1922. The Bloc was committed to a reform program broadly designed to democratize Spanish political and social life, pledging, in effect, a "New Deal" for the Spanish people. It may not unfairly be regarded as the last effort of the old Canovite system to regenerate Spain and save itself. Its program was wide-ranging and involved a partial democratization of the Senate, the obligatory convening of the Cortes for a certain period during each fiscal year, suffrage reform, land reform, the restoration of constitutional guarantees, the legalization of all labor organizations, and rehabilitative economic and budgetary policies. Most controversial,

---

* The best obituary was written several years later by Pérez Solís, who observed that Seguí had seen "better than anyone the extremely grave dangers hovering over the Catalan labor organization because of the possessed and visionary men who had carried it into the blind alley of terrorism. Seguí, who perhaps had very little faith in the chimerical theories of Anarchism, which earned him violent attacks . . . from the cave-Anarchists . . . confronted with presence of mind the tragic situation that [Anarchist] experiments created in Catalonia; and in the end, having been the only syndical leader who sustained opposition to a suicidal tactic with exemplary firmness, he ended as a victim of the barbarous struggle he had tried to stop. Those who killed him . . . surely saw in Seguí the only balanced man who might have been able to give the [Catalonian proletariat] a serious, disciplined organization without revolutionary deliriums or criminal violence. . . . [The murder] was an unpardonable error. For Seguí, although he might have had moments when his spirit weakened before the blindness and brutality of many of his comrades, had the makings of a leader of masses, who knew how to confront them when it seemed to him they were wrong." Pérez Solís, *Memorias*, p. 236.

perhaps, were the Liberal Bloc's views regarding Morocco; for it looked toward a deemphasis of military hegemony in favor of civilian rule, and it was firmly committed to the punishment of those responsible for the Annual Disaster.[19]

The Communist Party was at an exceedingly low ebb during the early months of 1923, with its membership depleted, many of its leaders imprisoned, and its ranks divided by internal quarrels, especially the continuing struggle between electoral and anti-electoral tendencies. In January General Secretary Núñez de Arenas was charged with lese majesty as the result of an article on Morocco published in *La Guerra Social*. Confronted by the prospect of an eight-year prison sentence, he chose to flee to France—where he would permanently remain, so that the Party was deprived of one of its most able leaders at this critical moment. César González, upon his return from Moscow, was chosen to replace Núñez as acting general secretary.[20]

On March 9 the ECCI dispatched from Moscow a radiogram informing the Spanish Communists that they "absolutely must take part" in the approaching elections.[21] The Central Committee had already resolved upon such a step and had drawn up a list of 25 Communist candidates, who would be assigned to electoral districts in various parts of the Peninsula. In Madrid the Party's candidates were the recently departed Núñez de Arenas, Ramón Lamoneda, Isidoro Acevedo, Oscar Pérez Solís, Antonio García Quejido, and José María Viñuela (a militant still in prison as a result of the August Strike of 1917). This slate, though containing the most prestigious names the Communists had to offer, was easily outpolled by the Socialist slate, which included Pablo Iglesias, Julián Besteiro, Manuel Cordero, Francisco Largo Caballero, Andrés Saborit, and Fernando de los Ríos. The highest Socialist vote obtained was Besteiro's 21,417, which compared with the highest Communist vote (excluding the sympathy vote for Viñuela) of 1,392, won by Lamoneda. The only consolation for the Communists in the Madrid campaign was that their nemesis Largo Caballero, who received 18,260 votes, was not elected.[22]

In Barcelona, where the Cenetistas sulked on the sidelines, there was considerable abstentionism, the Socialists polling only 3,000 votes and winning no seats. Even this was significantly better than the performance of the Communist slate, composed of Juan Pozas, Gonzalo Sanz, and Leandro Carro, who received little help from the Maurín-led Communist-Syndicalists. In Seville the Communist candidate José Rojas was decisively crushed by the electoral expertise of his Andalusian opponents, though he claimed to have received 1,000 votes "with little notice and only three meetings."[23] In Asturias the Communist slate was headed by Torralba Beci, who gained a total of 321 votes while losing to the Socialist candidate Manuel Llaneza (who, regarded as the lesser of two evils, is said to have received some support from the industrial interests). In Bilbao the Socialist incumbent, Indalecio Prieto, was awarded election under the terms of Article 29 of the Electoral Code, so that no contest ensued for his office. However, in the Bilbao district of Ensanche the unsuccessful Communist candidate, who was aided in his electioneering by the Young Communists, claimed to have won more than 1,000 votes, while having to overcome a certain amount of apolitical feeling among the workers.[24]

Altogether, the Communists—who as yet had no permanent campaign machinery—held more than 100 meetings in the 15 days preceding the elections. Despite the fact that some sections of the Party (e.g., in Valencia and Catalonia) either refused to carry out orders to participate in the elections or revealed a marked lack of enthusiasm, the Communist leaders professed satisfaction with the results, believing that the campaign had produced the best propaganda effort yet put forth by the Party. Although no Communist candidate came remotely close to winning a seat in the Cortes, it was claimed that the election was salutary in that it had "dissipated" the anti-electoral prejudices within the Party and affirmed its personality as a "class political party" rather than an "apolitical sect."[25]

In actual fact, the elections of 1923 were little less than a disaster for the Communist Party and clearly reflected its failure to grow at the expense of the Socialist rival it imagined it had "slain" as a result of the April schism. The Socialists had won seven seats in the Cortes, their highest total yet, and the Communists themselves had to admit—in a moment of candor—that the election had been a "failure" for them, since the great mass of workers in the contested regions remained loyal to Socialism, and since even many middle-class voters had supported the party of Pablo Iglesias.[26] Gómez de Baquero, writing in El Sol, confirmed the impression that the more than 20,000 who had voted for Socialist candidates in Madrid had not all been conquered by Socialist ideology but, rather, had voted for the Socialists as a "clean" party— and above all as one that pursued the "responsibilities" for Annual. As for the Communists, Gómez de Baquero observed that the brief moment when it appeared that—under the spell of the Bolshevik Revolution—they would carry the Spanish masses along with them, had passed. The workers, he remarked, had swung decisively in favor of the Socialists, thus showing their basic "good sense and equilibrium" as well as the enduring effects of Socialist educational efforts.[27]

The Communists, looking for the silver lining, held the view that the Socialists were moving steadily to the right and becoming simply the "extreme left wing of bourgeois liberalism."[28] They accused the Liberal Bloc, which won 223 seats in the election, of having "stolen" the Socialists' agrarian program— specifically, that elaborated by Fernando de los Ríos, which involved "drawing to the life of law and property one million proletarians of the countryside," through land reform. To Santiago Alba, the Communists attributed the assertion that this program would constitute a "major obstacle to the possible triumph of a Communist revolution"; and they could not refrain from calling attention to the irony that the Liberals, "in order to prevent a revolution, draw upon the agrarian program of the Socialist Party, which claims to be revolutionary."[29]

Thus the ray of light that the Communists discovered amid the general gloom was their conviction that the rightward drift of the Socialists—whom they saw moving toward a republicanism concerned only with the "minimum desires" of the working class—had created a political vacuum on the Left, which could be "splendidly filled" by their own Party as the true partisan of the revolutionary working class in Spain.[30] From the standpoint of the rest of the country, of course, the most crucial thing about the election was that it had given the Liberal Bloc, headed by García Prieto, a majority in the Cortes with which it could govern the country. It appeared that the parliamentary system, as Madariaga said, was "rapidly ceasing to be a puppet show" and was becoming a reality.[31]

The triumph of the parties most closely associated with the demand for fixing "responsibilities" for Annual was, of course, not well received in military circles. The officer corps felt, with some justice, that the true responsibility for the Annual Disaster rested not with the Army but with the civilian politicians who had refused to vote the monies needed to maintain the military establishment at the necessary level of efficiency. The Cortes, opened on April 6, witnessed until its closure on July 24 continuous and dramatic debates on the Moroccan Question. Meanwhile, Spanish forces in the Protectorate were still under attack, and the García Prieto government was subjected to much pressure to send reinforcements—something it was reluctant to do for obvious political reasons. Indeed, it not only refused to send more troops, but also appointed the first civilian ever to hold the post of High Commissioner in Morocco, Luis Silvela.[32]

In this context, the notion of establishing a military dictatorship to solve Spain's problems and ensure fulfillment of the Army's "mission" in Morocco gained considerable ground during the summer of 1923. The center of military conspiracy at this time, as Stanley Payne has shown, was located in Madrid, among the group of officers surrounding General José Cavalcanti. The principal desire of these men was that the campaign in Morocco be aggressively waged until Spanish hegemony was assured. Whether this was done under civilian or military rule was a somewhat secondary consideration for them, but they had come to the conclusion that the task could best be achieved under a military caudillo. The problem was to find the right man for the job.[33]

The Second Congress of the Communist Party

In the midst of this political ferment, and in an atmosphere thick with rumors of an impending military takeover, the Spanish Communist Party—preparing for its Second Congress—was still engaged in violent internal debate about its methods and objectives. It was, in fact, in serious trouble and nearly on the verge of dissolution. Most of the militants would have agreed with Ramón Lamoneda's rueful admission that "it is not so easy as it might seem to create, recruit, organize, and discipline a political party."[34]

The Central Committee remained in the hands of the Madrid left-centrists, whose leading figures, since the flight of Núñez de Arenas, were César González, Ramón Lamoneda, and Torralba Beci. These militants were committed to electoral activity, as well as to an absolute and rather unimaginative obedience to the dictates of the Comintern. They had so far given the party a reasonably competent, though not brilliant, leadership. Their interests lay primarily in the regions where Socialism had hitherto prevailed, that is, chiefly in Castille, Vizcaya, and Asturias. Like the Socialists before them, they seem to have concluded that the Cenetista masses could only be won over at the cost of altering the political character of their party. They were accused, with some justice, of a lack of concern about the regions where Anarchosyndicalist ideology had held sway, that is, Catalonia, the Levant, Aragon, and Andalusia.[35]

But the charge—so frequently made in this period—that the Communist Central Committee was insufficiently active was, though true, somewhat unfair. For the Party had no paid offices, and the general secretary, the editor of *La Antorcha*, and the others had to work eight hours a day at their trades, leaving party work for off hours. Efforts by the left-centrists to remedy this situation were opposed by the ultra-leftists, who feared that an entrenched bureaucracy like that of the Socialists would result.[36] The Party was also starved for funds for such necessary activities as propaganda, trade-union work, and electoral campaigning. The Comintern had been a somewhat censorious step-parent, frequently nagging the infant party while denying it the material aid that might have helped it to grow in a most difficult environment.

The Party was also handicapped by its smallness and by the consequent lack of effective organizers and propagandists. In some areas there was not a single Communist militant who could effectively address crowds and persuasively explain Communist ideas. Here, too, the ultra-Left opposed the use of full-time "professional" propagandists. Although there was doubtless, even during 1921-22, a sizable potential clientele for Communism in Spain, the Party—whatever its other failings—simply lacked the men and the means to place itself in contact with susceptible workers and to win them over. As late as the summer of 1923 it was admitted that there were important labor concentrations in Spain where the Communist voice had never been heard.[37]

The conflict between left-centrists and ultra-leftists in the Party, which both Graziadei and Humbert-Droz had sought to resolve, had not diminished, but in fact reached its climax in the summer of 1923, on the eve of the Party's Second Congress. Juan Andrade led the attack on the majority, and, as in the past, it was extremely difficult to find substance in his charges. Silenced for many months as a result of the sanctions imposed on him in March 1922, he was permitted to publish critical articles in *La Antorcha* just prior to the Second Congress. This resulted in little more than an exhumation of all his old charges against the left-centrist leaders, whom he ritually accused of having a "petty-bourgeois spirit" and of suffering from a "terrifying mental confusion." Sectarian as ever, Andrade insisted that reformist "deformations" abounded in the Party, and that it would be necessary to "extirpate" them.[38]

But concrete differences between the factions were, in truth, difficult to bring forward, since in this period all the ex-PCE dissidents for whom Andrade spoke had at least formally accepted the Comintern position on all issues, including electoral participation, the United Front, and work within conservative trade unions. They, too, celebrated the need for centralization and for submission to the norms of the Communist International, asking only that the application of those norms not be "mechanical." In effect, Andrade's charges added up to a deep personal dislike for the Party's leaders, a jealous resentment of their monopoly of power and position within the Party, and a vague feeling that things ought to be going better. This, in reality, is what he meant when he said that the crisis of the Party was preeminently a "crisis of leadership."[39]

From Valencia, Hilario Arlandis launched criticisms not dissimilar to those made by the Madrid ultra-Left. Almost entirely absorbed with the possibility of winning the CNT for Communism, Arlandis regarded that body as both more revolutionary and more important than the UGT, whose penetration did not seem to interest him greatly. He was willing to acknowledge the Confederation's ideological shortcomings, but he felt that these were more than offset by the revolutionary character of the masses over which it held sway, whose "habit" of violence offered the Communists an "excellent field of action." Arlandis also lacked interest in electoral politics and refused to participate in the April elections, convinced that electioneering was no way to win the confidence of the Valencian workers.[40]

The antipolitical critique was heard from still another quarter when the Andalusian Communist Alfonso Mejías made explicit something that Arlandis had only hinted at: his belief that the Party should abandon parliamentary efforts altogether when approaching the apolitical masses of the South. Electoral activity could not possibly prosper in Andalusia, he said, for the reason that parliamentarianism in that region had in the past been "so negative and ineffective," and had so "disgusted" the masses that they did not wish to hear —and would in fact repudiate—anyone who tried to justify it. Mejías could not believe that the Comintern really meant to insist on parliamentary action in Spain; and he seemed to regard it as a needless rigidity that the Central Committee should ordain this policy in Andalusia, where it could only be counterproductive. Parliament, said Mejías, leaving no doubt about his personal views, was the "maximal bourgeois organization," involving an absolutely unacceptable collaboration with the propertied classes.[41] Carlos Romero added to these reflections the accusation that the Party had almost completely neglected the agrarian problem in Spain, with the result that Communist influence among the peasantry was "almost nil."[42]

The Central Committee defended itself as best it could, noting that "when a party does not find itself in favorable circumstances for growing, it is very easy to charge it with errors of leadership." In addition to calling attention to the lack of Party funds and the greatly changed atmosphere in Spain, reflected in a growing depression and lethargy among the workers, the Committee also suggested that the Communists' melancholy record was due to "internal resistances" and even deliberate "sabotage." Against Andrade's charge of a crisis of leadership, the leaders themselves called attention to the "crisis of indiscipline" within the Party's ranks, lamenting the "internal confusion" that resulted from a multitude of "small insubordinations."[43] César González struck a more hopeful note. He acknowledged that the Communist Party of Spain had been slow to find unity; but he felt sure that the approaching congress, which he regarded as having a "constituent" character, would bring to an end the "formative period" of Spanish Communism.[44]

All the long-accumulating tensions within the Party found explosive release in the Congress that began in Madrid on July 8, with Comintern Secretary Jules Humbert-Droz and the French Communist Jacques Doriot in attendance. An opening message from the ECCI acknowledged the "particularly grave circumstances" under which the Party was meeting and the dangers that confronted a Spanish working class "pursued by the bourgeoisie, betrayed by the reformists, and disoriented by Anarchist confusionism." In view of the danger that a "pseudo-Fascist regime or military dictatorship" might be established in Spain, the ECCI delivered a sermon on the undiminished necessity for the United Front. This tactic, it was suggested, was more important in Spain than in any other country because of the uniquely schismatic tendencies of the labor movement there. The ECCI also candidly observed that, judging from the April elections, the Communist Party still had no "formal influence" on the working class—in contrast to the Socialists, whose hold on the masses was conceded to be far from negligible. The ECCI's remedy for this was a somewhat general prescription: an intensification of propaganda and the imposition of a more severe Party discipline.[45]

The initial debates of the Congress, during which Lamoneda tried to defend the policies of the Central Committee against the violent assaults of its numerous critics from the various regions, were so agitated that the alarmed Humbert-Droz felt compelled to come forward and address the tumultuous assembly much earlier than he had planned. Acknowledging that he was departing from Comintern practice, he made it clear that he intended to intervene actively in the labors of the Congress. Yet he was at some pains to advise the delegates that the Comintern was not without an understanding of the special handicaps under which Spanish Communists had to labor, the greatest being the necessity of fighting on two fronts. Whereas the other European Communists had to confront chiefly the reformist social democrats, in Spain the Party was caught between the reformism of the Socialists and the ultra-Left tendencies of the Anarchosyndicalists. This added burden, said Humbert-Droz, posed a "terrible task" for Spanish Communists, who would perform an "enormous service" for the Comintern if they succeeded in transforming the Anarchosyndicalist mentality of a great portion of the Spanish proletariat.[46]

As for the crisis of the Spanish Party, Humbert-Droz observed that Party membership was, in fact, stationary; and that for this to be the case in a period "so rich in happenings" in the political and social realm there must be "some grave defect in its procedure." This defect lay not in the Party line, which seemed to him correct, but simply in the relative inactivity of the Central Committee. This had kept the Communist Party enveloped in a "conspiracy of silence," and the only cure, Humbert-Droz believed, was the establishment of a permanent secretariat. At the same time, he rejected Lamoneda's complaint that there was no money, saying that the working class would render assistance quickly enough when they saw the Communists working actively on their behalf. Finally, Humbert-Droz professed optimism about the Party's future. In Spain, he said, both social reformism and Anarchism had borne all their evil fruits, with the result that there were now "great possibilities" for Communist penetration of the masses.[47]

Torralba Beci immediately tried to capitalize on the favorable impression made by Humbert-Droz by proposing a conciliatory resolution, which declared that errors had been made on both sides, that all diverging viewpoints should be reconciled, and that the Party should march toward the future united. The Congress should render no judgment, Torralba believed, either on the activities of the Central Committee or on the criticisms that had been made of it. This pacific gesture, however, was quickly submerged by a renewed torrent of criticism and mutual recrimination, which rolled on as though neither the Comintern secretary nor Torralba had spoken.

Delegates from various regions jumped up to reiterate their criticisms of the Committee for its alleged slothfulness and for its failure to understand the problems peculiar to their respective areas. They also vented their irritation with one another. Thus Eduardo Castro of the Asturian-Leonese Federation stood up to accuse Hilario Arlandis of the Valencian Federation of trying to infiltrate Anarchosyndicalist ideas into Asturias and Vizcaya, saying that the vital need was to reduce rather than augment such influences in the Communist Party. He, in turn, was attacked by Rito Esteban, who spoke of the need to attract Syndicalists to the Party. Oscar Pérez Solís seconded this assertion by declaring that the UGT was, after all, only a "fossilized" organism, "petrified" by its own reformism, whereas the CNT, despite its errors, was still the "central" labor organization in Spain, grouping together the most restless and revolutionary elements. Castro rose again to renew his attack on ultra-Left and "Syndicalist" elements in the Party, proposing in this connection a censure of Gabriel León Trilla (who was not present) for his ultra-leftist posture at the Fourth Comintern Congress. Castro also took the opportunity to attack Juan Andrade for his "sinister labor" in the Party. Andrade angrily counterattacked, and the Congress—indeed, the Party—seemed again on the verge of dissolution.[48]

But as the debate reached this dangerous pitch, Humbert-Droz intervened once more. In an eloquent and surprisingly effective address, he succeeded— this was an authentic tour de force—in somehow gathering all the threads of the conflict together, explicating them to the aroused Spaniards, and to a considerable degree reconciling the delegates of the various regions to one another. His central theme was the "dualism" of the Party's origins and the need to overcome it lest the movement perish. As a solution to the crisis he advocated a central committee of "concentration" that would bring all the opposition elements into the circle of power and let them share in the sobering responsibilities of leadership and Party work. By thus urging that power no longer be concentrated in the hands of a few militants in Madrid but instead be divided among the regions and the factions, Humbert-Droz was clearly getting to the heart of the problem—which, as he himself had earlier suspected, had less to do with principles than with *personalismo*. The enthusiastic ovation given the Comintern delegate as he retired from the rostrum after his long speech strongly suggested that the Party had reached and—almost miraculously—passed through its moment of maximum crisis, and that the factional tensions that had so drained its energies were suddenly close to being resolved. Above all, Humbert-Droz had made it clear that the life of the Party was hanging in the balance, and it was evident that the delegates had taken this assessment seriously.[49]

A resolution much like the one Torralba had proposed earlier was now unanimously passed, declaring the period of divergencies within the Party "definitively terminated" and proclaiming "the necessity, the urgency, that the Party, by concentrating its forces, pass to the period of Communist construction...." The Central Committee was now broadened to include Eduardo Castro, Torralba Beci, Pérez Solís, Hilario Arlandis, Feliciano Alonso, Juan Andrade, and Manuel Pereira. Both César González and Pérez Solís were nominated for the post of general secretary. Solís, who probably wanted the office, felt compelled to refuse, saying that his "spiritual condition" was inadequate, and that in addition his presence in Bilbao was useful to the Party.

The job was finally given to González, though it was clear to all that the dominant personality in the Congress, and the real *caudillo* of Spanish Communism, was none other than the brilliant Solís.[50]

It was Solís who composed and read the principal resolution placed before the Congress, entitled "The immediate political tasks of the Party." This essentially revolutionary document bore the stamp of Solís's audacity and reflected the crisis atmosphere prevailing in Spain on the eve of the military coup d'etat that nearly everyone expected. Aside from lending its support to the campaign for "responsibilities," the Communist Party, it was asserted, should have as its immediate task the struggle against the impending dictatorship. Nor was this to be necessarily a pacific resistance, for Pérez Solís suggested not only the creation of *centurias obreras* (that is, of paramilitary workers' formations on the German model) but active agitation among the rank and file of the Army. In a somewhat delphic but carefully worded passage of unmistakable intent, Solís urged the need

> to spread actively and at the same time with all possible discretion, among certain involuntary servants of the pretended bourgeois legality the idea that the coup d'etat would mean an intensification of the war in Morocco, a fierce persecution of the workers, and a bourgeois reaction that, because it would come about violently, thereby creating a truly revolutionary situation, should be taken advantage of by the working class in order to [guide] the abnormalities of the bourgeois state toward the most transcendent objectives of the proletariat.[51]

With this allusive language Pérez Solís seemed to express the hope that would later sustain the Communists of Weimar Germany; namely, that a revolution of the Right would be only the signal for a redeeming proletarian revolution of the Left. In this form the resolution was approved unanimously, and the Second Congress adjourned in an atmosphere of fraternal good feeling in sharp contrast to its mood at the start.[52]

Unfortunately for the ill-starred Communist Party of Spain, this unexpected resolution of its internal difficulties came only on the eve of a military coup that would render illusory all hopes that the Party could achieve numerical growth and viability in the near future. Ironically, the Communists themselves, by virtue of a bold and violent action carried out in late August, may well have hastened the military down the road to dictatorship.

The Climax of Vizcayan Communism

That Pérez Solís took seriously the bold program he had enunciated at the July Congress became clear the following month, when he endeavored to launch a general strike in Bilbao, timed to coincide with an uprising of Basque troops embarking from the port of Málaga for Mellila in Morocco. What is not clear is the precise motive behind this incredible plan. Possibly it was related to the resolutions on imperialism and colonialism adopted at the Fourth

Comintern Congress the previous November, which made clear the determination of the Communist International to undermine Western imperialism by supporting in every possible way colonial "national" movements.[53] And conceivably the presence of the French Communist Jacques Doriot in Madrid at the time of the Second Congress of the Spanish Party was in some way connected with the scheme. Certainly the Comintern wished to embarrass French and Spanish imperialism in Morocco; and, as the events of the mid-1920's would make clear, it was not averse to placing excessive burdens on the ailing Spanish Party in order to achieve that end.[54] Whether this was the motive for the events of August 23, 1923, is, without further evidence, impossible to say.

On the night of August 22, Solís held a meeting in the mining zone with all Vizcayan Communist leaders in which he announced that the Party would declare a general strike for the following day. Since most workers in Bilbao and its environs were not enrolled in Communist unions and would not willingly obey such an order even if they received it in time, it was clear that the strike would have to be imposed at gunpoint by a few Communist action groups. The operation could only be described, then, as a reckless gamble almost certain to end in violence. This sudden and quite arbitrary declaration of a general strike was linked to the fact that the Communists had succeeded to some degree in infiltrating the Garellano Regiment, whose barracks were on the Calle de San Francisco not far from the Casa del Pueblo. Communist cells had been formed among the soldiers, and some of them had agreed to rebel at the time of their embarkation from Málaga, scheduled for August 23. Other cells had been formed among soldiers of the garrison in San Sebastián, and these had agreed to rebel at the same time. The general strike in Bilbao, then, was timed to coincide with these military mutinies.[55]

But precisely what Pérez Solís expected all of this to accomplish remains uncertain. Possibly, he felt that from this spark the latent revolutionary movement in Spain could be ignited—with Morocco as the catalyst. More likely, if his report to the July Congress is to be credited, he hoped that some sort of dialectical process would ensue whereby the Communist coup would trigger the impending coup of the military, which, in turn, would touch off the awaited proletarian uprising. The belief that a military takeover would be brief and abortive seems to have been fairly widespread among labor leaders (being held, for example, by Angel Pestaña).[56]

On the morning of August 23, Communist gunmen met the early shift workers arriving by tram at Bilbao's great steel plant Altos Hornos and told them that the strike had been decreed. When some of the workers refused to take this edict seriously, the Communists fired their weapons into the air to emphasize their resolve to close the steel complex down. The shock of surprise gave the followers of Pérez Solís a momentary victory, as the bewildered workers now began to return to the city. But at this point the Socialists sent out orders to their militants forbidding them to join the Communist effort and ordering them, in effect, to report for work. So, as the morning advanced, more and more workers converged on Altos Hornos, and the Communist edict was increasingly called into question. In a desperate effort to salvage their plan, the Communist gunmen began to fire at the trams, at first in warning and then more seriously. Several workers were shot and a few were killed. One witness observed a blond youth—who turned out to be Jesús Iribarren, one of Solís's personal guards—jump on the rear platform of a tram where, "quite tranquilly," he fired a single pistol shot into the head of the conductor, killing him instantly.[57]

Meanwhile, in the center of Bilbao, the police had been mobilizing to deal with the Communist threat. As they converged on the Communist-controlled Casa del Pueblo, a fierce fire-fight broke out in the Plaza de la Cantera, with perhaps 100 armed Communists exchanging shots with the police and Guardia. As the Communists retreated into the Casa del Pueblo, the firing grew in intensity, and finally police and Guardia stormed the building, killing and wounding perhaps a score of those within, so that blood could be observed running down the front steps of the building. Inside, some 70 Communist militants were disarmed and lined up against the stage of the auditorium with hands upraised. The initiator of the day's events, Pérez Solís, was not among them, but lay on the floor unconscious, shot through the chest and seemingly on the verge of death. A Civil Guard, discovering the Communist leader, was about to administer the coup de grace and desisted only when told by a police agent that the man was already dead. But the durable Solís soon revived; and when his old antagonist, Captain Alegría, came up and said, "What, you here too?" the Communist caudillo replied with his customary composure, saying, "Are you not at the head of your men? Well, I also."[58]

Meanwhile, in Málaga, some 50 or 60 soldiers of the Garellano Regiment, led by Corporal Sánchez Barroso and faithful to their understanding with Pérez Solís, mutinied as they were being embarked for Morocco. Refusing to board their troopships, they resisted all efforts to coerce them, killing their sergeant and wounding some other noncommissioned officers. In the end, the rebels were subdued, and Corporal Barroso was immediately tried by a military court and sentenced to death. But popular feeling against the Moroccan War had grown greatly during the course of 1923, and the Barroso affair became a cause célèbre, receiving wide publicity and triggering an intensive press campaign on his behalf. Thus the government of García Prieto was placed between two fires, liable to incur the wrath of an aroused public if Barroso were executed and the wrath of the Africanistas if he were not. In the end, the sentence was commuted, and the government simultaneously announced that there would be no further movement of troops to Morocco.[59]

In the face of these decisions, the anger of the officer corps against the García

Prieto government passed all bounds, and the Barroso affair may well have been the final consideration that broke their irresolution and turned them toward rebellion.[60] To a degree, then, Pérez Solís would seem to have succeeded in his apparent plan: the military coup d'etat was in fact precipitated. He was even correct in his prediction that the swing of the pendulum away from a military dictatorship would be, in Spain, very great, and that the monarchy, undermined by its acceptance of that dictatorship, would give way to a "mass" regime of the Left. What he had not anticipated was the length of time the dialectical process would require and the fact that when the monarchy finally fell, in 1931, he would find himself once more in the arms of the Church and on the side of the forces of order.

The Labor Response to Primo de Rivera

The military uprising on September 13 received either active or passive support from a surprisingly broad spectrum of groups and interests in Spain. There was widespread recognition that the parliamentary regime was not dealing adequately with the country's problems, and an ingenuous belief prevailed that a new political upheaval would be desirable in order that out of chaos might come renovation.[61] The Catalan Regionalists and many bourgeois liberals (including Ortega y Gasset), as well as more conservative sectors of public opinion, welcomed the Dictatorship, at least initially, hoping that it would, among other things, extinguish the wave of terrorism that was once more engulfing Barcelona. The great mass of the people, though not openly enthusiastic about the new military regime,[62] were not ill disposed toward it and awaited its initiatives. Even within the labor movement there was something less than a unanimous determination to combat the Dictatorship at all costs.

Despite its small size and lack of cohesion, the Communist Party succeeded in raising the most active protest against the establishment of the new regime. As early as August 31, the Communists had sought to meet the impending coup by forming a united front with the Madrid Cenetistas and with the local federation of Anarchist groups—to which the Socialists and the Catalonian Syndicalists refused to give their adherence. On the day of the coup d'etat, the groups joined in this front issued a manifesto proclaiming the formation of an "action committee" to struggle against the Dictatorship and against the war in Morocco, which they assumed would be intensified as a result of the military takeover. The Socialists and the Catalonian Syndicalists, though they had often enough in the past threatened general strikes in order to thwart a coup by the military, again refused to join in any concerted effort.[63]

The Communists, seeking cooperation wherever they could find it, dispatched César González to Barcelona to meet with a plenum organized by the separatist Colonel Macía and including Anarchists, Syndicalists, republicans, and other dissidents. Not content merely to confer, the Communists launched, in Bilbao, a one-day general strike, in which some Socialists participated—this being, in fact, the only overt labor reaction in Spain to the military coup.[64] Although the Communists were hardly in a position to oppose really serious resistance to Primo de Rivera, this leader nevertheless found it convenient to exaggerate the Communist threat and to justify, at least in part, his seizure of power on that basis. Shortly after the coup he asserted, "I have come to fight against Communism."[65] As early as November 1923 several members of the Party's National Committee were arrested, and the following month numerous arrests of Communist leaders were made in various cities, these being justified by the supposed discovery of a "Communist plan" for a simultaneous uprising in Spain and Portugal on December 28. All the local headquarters of the Party were raided, sacked, and closed. From this time on, the Party, even though its journal *La Antorcha* was legally allowed to publish, lived a hunted existence, caught between the certainty of numerous arrests if it became too active and the insistence of the Comintern that it not be passive and "opportunistic." One Central Committee after another would be either arrested by the police of Primo de Rivera or pushed from office by the machinations of the Comintern.[66]

In Catalonia, the coming of the Dictatorship found the CNT still too weak to put up any resistance. In the year since the departure of Martínez Anido (who would shortly reemerge as Primo's Minister of the Interior) the work of syndical reorganization had gone forward; but it was still in its initial stages, and the mounting of a serious labor offensive against the new regime was not something the Cenetistas could undertake single-handed. They were resolved not to commit themselves without the support of the Socialists, and to this end Manuel Buenacasa went to Madrid on September 14 to see Pablo Iglesias and to propose, as a first step, a joint strike by Socialists and Syndicalists in the capital.

Though initiated by the arch-Anarchosyndicalist Buenacasa, this proposal had a distinctly political purpose, being intended to save the Restoration party system from destruction at the hands of Primo de Rivera. The plan was for the UGT and the CNT to mobilize the people of the capital in a massive demonstration timed to coincide with the arrival of the king in Madrid from his summer capital in San Sebastián, thus conveying to Alfonso the united opposition of the working class to the Dictatorship. It was generally known that Prime Minister García Prieto was prepared to ask the king for full power to liquidate the military coup in Barcelona, and Buenacasa hoped that pressure by the Madrid workers, applied at this delicate moment, might facilitate such a solution. Both Iglesias and Largo Caballero listened courteously to Buenacasa, and he gained the impression that they were close to agreeing with him. But as on so many previous occasions, the two Socialists argued instead that the UGT could not act so precipitately, and that they would have to consult with representatives of the PSOE and with Ugetistas in the provinces. Time, however, was running out, and in the end no united stand was taken by the UGT-CNT against the military coup. Within a day or two the king formally entrusted the government to Primo de Rivera.[67]

Within the CNT, the coming of the Dictatorship seems to have hastened a process that was already under way, namely, the resurgence of the more extreme Anarchosyndicalist elements. The changing power relationship between the Syndicalist factions was evident in the meeting of the Catalonian Regional Confederation held at Granollers on December 30, which, in contrast to the Zaragoza plenum 18 months earlier, was distinctly Anarchist in tone. This was revealed by the conference's rather truculent reaffirmation of those Bakuninist principles proclaimed by the Congress of the Comedia in December 1919—a step opposed only by a handful of Communist-Syndicalists, led by Joaquín Maurín. The anti-Comintern mood of the Anarchosyndicalists was revealed by their use of force to prevent attendance at Granollers by a delegation of the Metalworkers' Union, in which the Communist-Syndicalists were strongly represented. A few days later the Anarchosyndicalists carried the battle into that union itself, intervening—by force, according to Maurín—to elect a new, anti-Communist committee. The coming of the Dictatorship, then, coincided with a continuing struggle between the Anarchosyndicalists and their rivals for control of the union committees and with the growing ascendancy of the Bakuninists. The bitterness of the contest was revealed by occasional exchanges of gunfire between Cenetista militants, and by such uncomradely acts as the sending of several sticks of dynamite through the mails to the headquarters of the Communist-Syndicalist organ *La Batalla* in March 1924.[68]

The most critical issue within the CNT at this time was whether the Confederation should continue to operate legally, as the "pure" Syndicalists and Communist-Syndicalists desired, or whether, in response to the Dictatorship, it should dissolve itself and operate clandestinely, as the more zealous Anarchosyndicalists wished. Angel Pestaña, concerned as always to preserve the organizational structure, urged that the CNT remain in the open and continue building up its depleted ranks. Pestaña would even advocate Cenetista participation in the mixed arbitration committees soon to be established by Primo de Rivera, and he seemed prepared to play a collaborative role not wholly dissimilar to the one that Largo Caballero would undertake on the Socialist side, even supporting the formation of a "bloc des gauches" with the left-bourgeoisie in order to defend constitutional liberties.[69]

But as early as October 1923 the extremist elements were able to gain control of the Barcelona Local Federation of Sindicatos Unicos, whereupon they immediately ordered the closing of the sindicatos and the suspension of *Soli-*

daridad Obrera. The moderates, however, were able to regain the initiative temporarily; and by means of the new journal *Lucha Obrera* they succeeded in winning over the majority of the workers to their conviction that the unions should continue to function openly. The extreme Anarchosyndicalists, seeing that they had moved too rapidly, and perhaps fearful of being displaced from leadership, now revived *Solidaridad Obrera* and reopened the unions, which continued to function for some months longer. Nevertheless, the CRT plenum held in Sabadell on May 4, 1924, was even more Anarchist in spirit than that of Granollers, and the one Communist-Syndicalist who dared make an appearance was simply refused the right to speak.

A few days after the Sabadell meeting the whole issue of clandestinity versus legality was suddenly rendered academic when, in response to the murder of a Barcelona official by the Anarchists, the civil governor ordered the closing of the sindicatos and the suspension of *Solidaridad Obrera*. Once more the government had intervened in the labor movement in such a way as to strengthen extremist elements. For the next seven years the CNT would virtually cease to exist, its stunted, underground committees increasingly dominated by the more extreme Anarchosyndicalists. The birth of the Second Republic in the early 1930's would find the Confederation more than ever under the control of Anarchist elements and fully prepared to subvert rather than to sustain the new republic and the "bourgeois" liberties it would bring.[70]

The Socialist response to the military coup was, as I have suggested, peculiarly passive. Though only they, of all labor groups in the Peninsula, were at this moment sufficiently strong and organized to have any hope of impeding the establishment of the Dictatorship, the Socialists refused to let Buenacasa tempt them into hasty action. On the day of the coup they issued a cautious manifesto that deplored in rather harsh terms the "sedition" of the "praetorian minority" and the complaisance of the monarch, but nevertheless ended by urging the Spanish people to "take no initiatives" without receiving instructions from the committees of the PSOE or UGT. After observing the developing situation for two more days, the Socialists issued another statement on October 15, reiterating to the workers "the necessity of abstaining from any action to which they may be urged by impatient persons of good faith or by elements who wish by deceitful means to hurl the proletariat into sterile movements that can offer a pretext for repressive measures."[71]

In fact, the Socialists were far from united on how best to deal with the military coup. The "political" Socialists, with their interests and aspirations focused on the parliamentary arena, were clearly more incensed by the suppression of politics under Primo than were the Ugetistas, who quickly discerned that the Dictatorship would not necessarily be incompatible with the workers' continuing struggle for material gains. This split was not surprising. During the previous decade the Party leaders had shown themselves to be, on the whole, more doctrinaire, more idealistic, and more concerned with the nature of the political regime than those figures—symbolized by Largo Caballero—who identified mainly with the sindicatos. Whether it was the question of the war, the possible overthrow of the monarchy, or the significance of the Russian Revolution, the trade-union leaders had been consistently more cautious and less susceptible to ideological appeals. So it was that now the Ugetista chieftains confronted the end of the parliamentary system with considerably more sangfroid than did the Party leaders. Whereas the Socialist parliamentary minority anxiously appealed to Melquíades Alvarez, the president of the Congress of Deputies, to "take some initiative" toward restoring constitutional guarantees and, by implication, reviving the parliamentary system, the Ugetistas, by contrast, were quite prepared to undertake negotiations with the country's new dictator.[72]

These negotiations were initially conducted by Manuel Llaneza, head of the Asturian miners and the second most powerful figure in the UGT. Over the past several years Llaneza had established a remarkably cordial relationship with General Bermúdez de Castro, the military governor of Oviedo, and through this officer he received, in late September, an invitation to come to Madrid and talk with Primo de Rivera about the possibilities of a rapprochement between the Socialists and the Dictatorship. Primo, for his part, had been urged to this conciliatory gesture by General Marva, who now directed the Institute of Social Reforms. Beyond that, Primo had already sized up the Socialists as an essentially constructive and "national" group within Spanish society, and his famed "intuition" told him that he could work with them.[73]

It was characteristic of Llaneza that although he cleared his decision to make the trip with the committee of the Asturian Miners' Union, he did not undertake any prior consultation with the committees of the PSOE or the UGT. On October 1 he traveled to Madrid, where he was met at the North Station by military officers who took him directly—without any stop at the Casa del Pueblo—to see Primo de Rivera. The ensuing discussions were officially described as dealing merely with the Asturian mining zone; but it is certain that much broader issues were involved, and that Primo and Llaneza both emerged convinced that the Socialists and the military could cooperate effectively. In a public statement Llaneza told the workers that there was "nothing to fear"; and only after this interview did he deign to consult with the committees of the PSOE and UGT. One month later the military governor of Madrid, the Duke of Tetuán, paid a well-publicized visit to the Casa del Pueblo, and, as Tuñón de Lara says, a kind of mutual nonaggression pact between the Army and the Socialists was confirmed, despite the misgivings of the parliamentary leaders.[74]

This rapprochement notwithstanding, the position of most Socialists was that there should be no "political" collaboration with the Dictatorship; and on January 9, 1924, the National Committee of the PSOE unanimously agreed that Socialists should not accept any political office under the new regime that was not the result of free elections or contingent on a representative post held in a labor organization. On this basis the Socialists refused to take part in the National Assembly shortly created by Primo de Rivera. But when Primo renovated the old Council of State as a kind of corporativist body and invited the Ugetistas to participate in it, Largo Caballero and the other trade-union leaders were ready to do so, Largo being selected (technically by his labor colleagues in the Institute of Social Reforms) to sit as a paid councillor. Prieto and de los Ríos regarded this as a grave error, and raised the question in a meeting of the PSOE National Committee on December 10, 1924, being defeated 14 to 5. This vote so disgusted Prieto that he resigned his seat on the Executive Committee of the Party. But to no avail. It was clear that power and influence were steadily draining away from the Party to the UGT, from parliamentarians to trade-unionists.

Thus Largo Caballero would be the preeminent figure of Spanish Socialism during the 1920's, cleverly using his official position to build Socialist strength in virtually every part of Spain; and the fall of the Dictatorship in 1930 would find the UGT emerging for the first time as a mass organization, thanks largely to this collaboration. What could not be foreseen was that in the stormy new period opened by the Republic, and in the face of an amazing revival of the Anarchosyndicalist movement in the early 1930's, the Socialists would be forced to make a sharp turn to the left so that Largo, unwilling to see Ugetista workers swallowed by the CNT, would be compelled to become, for the first time in his career, an authentic leftist—the so-called "Spanish Lenin."[75]

By the end of the decade surveyed in this study the revolutionary Left had come nearly full circle. As in 1914, the organized working class was reduced in numbers, defeated, apathetic, and divided between Socialists, operating within the law, and Anarchosyndicalists, once more condemned (after May 1924) to a clandestine existence. The years from 1914 to 1923 had been years of ideological excitement, growth, conflict, and rising expectations; but now that the tumult was stilled and the Dictatorship established, it was difficult to see that labor had made any enduring gains. From the standpoint of the working class, the era of the World War and the Russian Revolution was remarkable chiefly for its failures: the regime had been neither revolutionized nor renovated; the country's economic base, despite the war boom, had not been transformed; neither the Socialists nor the Anarchosyndicalists had undergone any significant doctrinal evolution; and the Peninsular working class had not been unified or permanently strengthened.

Perhaps the most revealing failure of this era was the fact that the intense ferment generated by the war and the Bolshevik Revolution did not give rise to a viable Communist movement—a failure that provides a convenient theme with which to conclude this study of the revolutionary Left in the early twentieth century. In a sense, perhaps, all the European Communist parties born in the postwar period were failures, at least in terms of the expectations that the Comintern and their own partisans held for them. But failure, like success, is usually a matter of degree. In France and Italy, for example, the Communist parties of this era, though something less than mass organizations, were at least viable at birth and would later become effective mobilizers of a variety of popular discontents. The Communist Party of Spain, by contrast, virtually succumbed in infancy. By the mid-1920's one was confronted less with a party than with a paradox: how was it possible that from a popular response to the Russian Revolution not exceeded in any other country, and in the context of a thoroughly radicalized working class, so little should have resulted? Of all the European Communist parties, that of Spain remained perhaps the weakest and most ill-starred until the early 1930's, when it "arrived" under somewhat unusual circumstances. Even before Primo de Rivera's takeover, and despite the exertions of Humbert-Droz, the Communist movement was nearly moribund; and by 1925 it could claim only about 500 militants in all of Spain and almost no influence in the trade unions.[76]

Many things had seemed to favor the emergence of a Communist Party at this time. Spain shared nearly all of the social, economic, and political weaknesses usually considered to have nourished Communism in her Latin neighbors: extremes of wealth and poverty, sluggish economic growth, alienation of the urban and rural masses, the continuing failure of liberal institutions, and a more or less chronic social crisis, aggravated by the war. In view of the excitement generated in Spain by the Bolshevik Revolution, there was reason to believe that revolutionary elements drawn away from both the Socialists and the Syndicalists would join together, as in other countries, to form a Communist movement of sufficient vitality to become a factor—perhaps an important force—in the life of the country. The collapse or transformation of both the Socialist and the Anarchosyndicalist movements was anticipated by many, and the emergence of a new and revolutionary Marxist party was awaited. Looking back from the perspective of the 1930's, Joaquín Maurín said of this period that "a whole series of circumstances had contributed to favor the development... of a great revolutionary socialist party, that is, a true Communist party." The country was in "a revolutionary era in which the masses were receptive and events [were favorable].... Amid the general tumult, Russia appeared like a beacon. The darkness was dispelled by the light from the East.... Communism represented the future."[77]

The failure of this great Leninist party to appear was due in some measure to purely contingent causes. Parties, like Napoleonic generals, have the need to be lucky, and this was something the Communist Party of Spain clearly was not. Its greatest misfortune was the fact that (chiefly because of the skillful delaying tactics of the anti-Comintern Socialists) it was born late (April–November 1921), and thus came on the scene after the postwar wave of revolutionary and pro-Bolshevik enthusiasm had passed its peak. Among other things, this tardy arrival meant that the new party would encounter while still in its formative phase the full force of the repressive measures resulting from the death of Dato and the disaster at Annual—two events with which the Communists had no connection but for which they would pay a high price. The Party suffered severely as the result of governmental measures, and the repeated imprisonment of party workers was a formidable obstacle to organizational and recruiting activity.[78] Equally unlucky was the shooting of the Young Socialist González Portillo at the 1922 UGT congress—a stroke that did much to discredit the Communist Party and discourage potential adherents.

No less unfortunate for the new party was the relative indifference of the Comintern toward its fate and the reluctance of the Moscow leaders to supply it with adequate funds. There is little question that the Comintern got about what it paid for in Spain in 1919–23, and that more generous funding would have produced a somewhat larger and more viable party. A further reflection of the Comintern's essential disinterest in the Party's fate was its insistence that the Spanish Communists sustain an active and inevitably dangerous opposition to the Moroccan War. Such a policy, though it would further Soviet foreign policy by embarrassing Western imperialism, could only result in intense pressure on the young party and a consequent thinning of its already reduced ranks.

Finally, the Comintern's equally stubborn insistence on electoral and parliamentary tactics in Spain—to be rigidly applied here as everywhere else in the world—could hardly enhance the popularity of the Party among the masses of revolutionary-minded but antiparliamentary workers and peasants. These masses could probably have been won in significant numbers from Anarchosyndicalism to a revolutionary movement of the Leninist sort, but never to one advocating electoral tactics. The great "revolutionary Communist Party" that Maurín awaited had to be built, if it were to be built at all, out of essentially the same human materials and on the basis of many of the same impulses that had sustained the CNT. The Communist-Syndicalists and the ex-PCE ultra-leftists instinctively understood this: they grasped that the formula for Communist success in Spain had to be an appeal to the workers on the basis of both antiparliamentarianism *and* the seizure of political power by a revolutionary party. But the leaders of the Comintern, increasingly committed to centralization and uniformity in the world Communist movement, opted for the more orthodox parliamentary faction within the Spanish Party, preferring a smaller, slower-growing, but more docile movement to one that would be larger and more dynamic but also more Iberian.

Yet poor timing, governmental repression, and Comintern rigidity do not entirely explain the failure of Spanish Communism. Such contingent factors would have weighed less heavily if the original strength of the Party had been greater; and the reason for this numerical inadequacy must be sought chiefly in underlying structural causes. The most important of these was the slow pace of Spanish industrial development, which resulted in a labor movement both materially and ideologically retarded with respect to similar movements elsewhere in Western Europe. This retardation was most clearly reflected in the sharp and seemingly unbridgeable dichotomy between a primitive Socialist movement on the one hand and an equally underdeveloped, albeit vigorous, Syndicalist movement on the other. Though we are often told that Communism is a disease of incipient industrialization, it must be said that for Spain in this era the Russian Revolution came, in effect, too soon, catching the labor movement in a stage of development not yet favorable for the launching of a Leninist party. Spanish Socialism and Syndicalism were on a different time track from their counterparts in France and Italy. It was ironic but true that precisely because of their retarded evolution, which reflected Spain's general economic backwardness, they continued in the postwar period to represent for the great majority of workers essentially viable "revolutionary" alternatives to Communism.

In France, by way of contrast, both Socialists and Syndicalists had evolved farther and experienced more, so that much of their pristine self-confidence and élan had been dissipated. The defeat of the great strikes of 1909–13, the collapse of proletarian solidarity in the face of the war, the dilemmas of patriotic collaboration in the Union Sacreé, the industrial transformation of France during the war, the erosion of the myth of the state-as-enemy—all of these developments had in some degree sapped the faith of both Socialists and Syndicalists, calling into question the vital myths that sustained them. Increasingly, there existed, as Robert Wohl has said, a "malaise" at the heart of both movements.[79]

The case was very different in Spain, where both Socialists and Syndicalists emerged morally unscathed from the war, uncompromised by ministerial collaboration and untouched by economic transformations that in any case had not yet affected the Peninsula. Thus for most Socialists the rhetorical revolutionary-reformism of Pablismo still appeared as a radical and respectable creed. Despite the great enthusiasm for the Bolshevik Revolution that swept over Spain in the postwar period, the Pablista synthesis retained its credibility, and the mystique of party unity its compelling force. The majority of militants—typified by such dogmatic leftists as Andrés Saborit, Manuel Cordero, or Verdes Montenegro—could see no revolutionary advantage in joining the Comintern nor, after the split, in joining the Communist Party.

To them, the choice did not appear to be between revolution and reform, but between two ways of revolution.

Crucial was the fact that the delayed development of Spanish Socialism, along with the continuing aloofness of the intelligentsia from the labor movement, had inhibited the appearance of a large and militant left wing whose conversion to Bolshevism might have ensured the success of the Communist Party. Although a few intellectuals did enter the Socialist Party after 1909, it continued to be a small and predominantly plebeian movement with an uncomplicated ideology and relatively little internal differentiation. Largely for this reason, its myths remained basically unchallenged and its self-image as a revolutionary party still believable. Had Spain actually participated in the war, and had the Socialists been forced to vote war credits and sit in war cabinets, the credibility of Pablismo might well have been eroded and the door opened for the emergence of a left-wing successor party. The Socialists' strong pro-Allied stand, though embarrassing in the post-Versailles context, could not by itself have such an effect. In light of this, the shrewdness of Besteiro's decision to reject all suggestions of Socialist ministerial participation in the aftermath of the war becomes more apparent, since it helped preserve the revolutionary image of the PSOE and thereby narrowed the appeal of the Communists.

It should be remembered, too, that the severity of the social struggle in the Peninsula served to clothe the Socialist Party, despite its reformist practice, in an aura of revolutionary oppositionism and martyrdom that, again, could only weaken the appeal of Bolshevism. Thus the division between pro- and anti-Comintern factions in the PSOE, though it generated much heat, remained primarily a debate over timing, with neither the Terceristas nor their opponents being conscious of any doctrinal abyss between the two groups. The most revealing indication of this was the fact that the Communist schism of April 1921 was obviously something less than historically inevitable, and, indeed, almost did not happen at all. What finally produced the split were not irreconcilable doctrinal differences, but rather the rhetorical excesses of the anti-Comintern forces, the injured pride of the Terceristas, and an intense effort of persuasion by two gifted but somewhat marginal figures in the party, Oscar Pérez Solís and Manuel Núñez de Arenas. The schism resulted, then, less from a crisis of Pablista ideology than from pique and *personalismo*; and it was for this reason that the great majority of Socialists either stayed with or returned to the old party, with fatal consequences for the strength and viability of the new PCO. Certainly, the personal role of Pablo Iglesias as tribal patriarch also had a restraining influence. Had Iglesias, like Jaurès, died in 1914—or even in 1920—the history of Spanish Socialism might have been very different.

The Syndicalists of the CNT were in a similar condition of retarded evolution. Organized only in 1911 and not really launched until 1914, the Confederation was still in its adolescent phase, unbroken, idealistic, and filled with optimism about the future. The war had not transformed its economic base or called into question its hostility to the state and its belief in "direct action." Above all, the men of the CNT retained their faith in the central myth of a "class" revolution to be made spontaneously by the great mass of the workers, and this despite the elitist and organizational challenge posed by Leninist ideas and by the success of the Bolshevik Revolution. By contrast, French Syndicalism had lost the rapturous expectancy of its younger days and was confronting, in the postwar period, the uncertainties and ambiguities of middle age. For Syndicalism was always and everywhere a transitional creed, which could only exert its hold through a Sorelian suspension of disbelief by the masses. Under the impact of prewar failures and wartime compromises, the faith of French Syndicalists had weakened; they had begun to appreciate the complexity of the industrial order, and even to discern the uses of the bureaucratic state. By 1919 there were "signs of fatigue and of waning enthusiasm" and a widespread feeling that Syndicalism was in decline.[80]

Postwar French Syndicalism differed from the Spanish movement in another important respect: it had dropped virtually all the Anarchist ballast it once possessed. Those militants who had not evolved toward plain reformism moved toward an authentic revolutionary Syndicalism, which, by virtue of its rejection of Anarchist individualism and its acceptance of an organizational ethic, placed them remarkably close to the Leninist position—as the Bolsheviks were always ready to point out. This ideological affinity, conjoined with the crisis of French Syndicalism, helps to explain the movement into the Communist Party (though their sojourn might be brief) of such Syndicalist leaders as Pierre Monatte, Gaston Monmousseau, and Alfred Rosmer, as well as the creation of a significant Communist-Syndicalist movement, the Confédération Général du Travail Unitaire.

By contrast, the peculiarity of Spanish Syndicalism was that there were so few Monattes, Monmousseaus, and Rosmers. The reigning ideology of this somewhat retarded movement continued to be an authentic *Anarcho*syndicalism that harmonized remarkably well with the character and mentality of large numbers of workers, especially in Catalonia and the South. Although there were, as we have seen, competing tendencies within the movement, this unique synthesis of Anarchist and Syndicalist impulses continued to command the loyalty of the great mass of Cenetistas. In the crucial period 1919–21 there simply was no widespread feeling that this hybrid ideology had lost its revolutionary credibility or been historically superseded; and even during the decline of 1921–23 the prevailing belief was that the movement had been materially but not morally defeated. The stability of the Anarchosyndicalist ideology was, of course, encouraged by the lack of any dramatic industrial transformation in Catalonia—by the continued prevalence of small factories, intransigent employers, unassimilated peasants, and hostile state authority.

Thus the Anarchist motif in Spanish Syndicalism retained its vitality, and the "reach" of the Anarchosyndicalist synthesis would prove no less compelling among the Cenetistas than that of Pablismo among the Socialists. Above all, the movement retained its revolutionary self-image. If overt reformism had managed to conquer the CNT, no doubt the Communist ranks would have been correspondingly enlarged. Spanish participation in the war would also doubtless have had a disruptive effect. But in fact the blows needed to defeat and morally discredit Spanish Anarchosyndicalism would not come until the 1930's, during the Civil War, when nearly all Cenetista myths would be shattered against the harsh imperatives of large-scale military action. The war of 1936–39 would do with a vengeance to the CNT what the war of 1914–18 did to the French CGT.

The Communist appeal in Spain in 1919–23, then, fell into what is best described as an ideological vacuum. This was the void that existed between an underdeveloped Socialist Party, most of whose adherents remained steadfastly enthralled by the Guesdist vision of a historically inevitable but rather distant revolution, and a retarded Syndicalist movement that was genuinely revolutionary but oriented toward the Anarchist ultra-Left and committed to a vision of revolutionary spontaneity more appropriate to the nineteenth than to the twentieth century. There were, of course, fragments derived from both movements that (under the impulse of the Bolshevik Revolution) had detached themselves and sought to come together in a new, revolutionary Marxist party: plebeian antiwar left-centrists, disillusioned pro-Allied intellectuals, Young Socialists, Socialist Students, and Communist-Syndicalists. But the fragments were too few, the milieu too challenging, and the gravitational attraction of the existing labor subcultures too commanding. Communism in Spain would have to await better days and changed circumstances.

Notes

Notes

Complete authors' names, titles, and publishing information for the works cited here will be found in the Bibliography, pp. 539–48. The following abbreviations have been used in the Notes:

AGC Andrade-Geers Correspondence (collected at the International Institute for Social History, Amsterdam)
INE Instituto Nacional de Estadistica (Madrid)
IRS Instituto de Reformas Sociales (Madrid)
HDA Humbert-Droz Archives (bracketed numbers refer to individual documents in the Archives, as listed in the Bibliography)

Chapter One

1. The best general survey of Spanish labor in the nineteenth and twentieth centuries, and one well integrated with the economic history of Spain, is the Catalan scholar Tuñón de Lara's *Introducció a la història del moviment obrer*. Also useful is García Venero's *Historia de los movimientos sindicalistas españoles*. For the early twentieth century, see Fernanda Romeu Alfaro, *Las clases trabajadores en España (1898–1930)*.

2. On the origins and early history of the anarchist movement in Spain see: Brenan, Chapter 7; Cole, Pt. II, Chapter 20; Martí, Chapter 4; Termes Ardevol, *El movimiento obrero en España*; Tuñón de Lara, *Introducció*, pp. 92–162; González, *Istoria ispanskikh sektsii Mezhdunarodnogo Tovarishchestva Rabochikh;* Abad de Santillán, Vol. I; Lorenzo, Chapter 1; Jackson, "The origins of Spanish Anarchism"; Clara E. Lida, "Agrarian Anarchism in Andalusia: Documents on the Mano Negra," *International Review of Social History*, XIV (1969), Pt. 3, pp. 315–52; Glen A. Waggoner, "The Black Hand mystery: Rural unrest and social violence in southern Spain, 1881–1883," in Robert J. Bezucha, *Modern European social history* (New York, 1972), pp. 161–91.

3. The uniqueness of Spanish Syndicalism will only become fully apparent when more monographic research has been carried out, and when systematic comparison with similar movements in France, Italy, and Latin America has become possible. The best survey of the Anarchosyndicalist movement in Spain appears in Brenan, Chapter 8. On the comparative question see Marvaud, pp. 56ff.

4. Maurín, *Révolution et contre-révolution*, pp. 113–15. On the dialectical interplay between Socialism and Anarchism in the European context, see Rosenberg, pp. 222–25, and Wohl, pp. 29–33.

5. See, for example, Cánovas Cervantes, pp. 15–16, 19–26.

6. Feuer, p. 135.

7. Tamames, Chapter 28; Vicens Vives, *Economic history*, Chapter 46; "Spain's interest in the war," *American Review of Reviews*, LIV (July–Dec. 1916), 99. For economic and political comparisons between Spain and Italy see Linz, "The party system in Spain." That the economic development of Giolittian Italy provided a more favorable context for organized labor than that of Restoration Spain appears evident. See Clough, pp. 132, 170; Horowitz, p. 60. For a nationalist critique of Spain's semicolonial status see Eloy Luis André, "Los problemas de España y la guerra europea," *Nuestro Tiempo*, Apr. 1916, pp. 17–32.

8. Ulam, pp. 129–30. By far the most thorough treatment of the agrarian problem is found in Malefakis, *Agrarian reform and peasant revolution*, Chapters 1–5. For the symbiotic relationship between agriculture and industry see Raymond Carr, pp. 397–413.

9. Raymond Carr, pp. 413–14. The exodus from the land has been studied chiefly in terms of its impact on emigration overseas, and the sources, numbers, and impact of peasants migrating to the urban-industrial zones in Spain have received less attention. See IRS, *Información sobre emigración*. For a discussion of prewar emigration see "Commerce and manufacture in Spain," *Economist*, 18.x.13, p. 748.

10. An excellent description of the Catalonian labor milieu is given in Ullman, pp. 61ff. For a discussion of the sources of the distinctive revolutionary mentality of the southern peasants see Malefakis, "Peasants, politics, and civil war in Spain." An interesting descriptive account of the Vizcayan industrial scene on the eve of the war is presented in Valdour, II, Chapter 50.

11. Raymond Carr, Chapters 9–12. For a succinct sociological analysis of Restoration parties and pressure groups, see Tuñón de Lara, *Historia y realidad del poder*.

12. Ortega y Gasset, *Obras completas*, I, 273, 274, 280. A fine social history of the Restoration era is found in Miguel Martínez Cuadrado, *La burguesía conservadora (1874–1931)*.

13. Equally stultifying to the system, as Juan Linz points out, was the fact that the challenge to the caciquismo of the major parties did not, as in Italy, come from political parties that could expand over the whole country and offer a national alternative to the existing system. Rather, it came from Carlism and from regional nationalism. Linz, p. 20.

14. Some measures were: an employers' liability act (1900); the regulation of female and child labor (1900); the establishment of the Institute of Social Reforms (1904); factory inspection (1906); a Committee for Internal Colonization (1907); a National Thrift Bureau to supervise old age insurance (1908); maximum hours for labor in mines (1910); construction of workers' housing (1911). On this subject see: Leger, "La législation du travail en Espagne"; Coman, "Insurance for the superannuated worker in Spain"; Baldasano, "The real position of Spain."

15. Juan José Morato in *El Heraldo de Madrid*, 30.vi.08; Clarence Perkins, "The social and economic problems of modern Spain," *Political Science Quarterly*, XXVII (Mar. 1912), 92–98; "Recent wage changes in various countries: Spain," *International Labor Review*, Aug. 1928, pp. 256–60.

16. Payne, *Spanish Revolution*, p. 23.

17. Vicens Vives, *Els Catalans*, pp. 162–64, 167.

18. *Ibid.*, p. 165.

19. *Ibid.*

20. Valdour, I, 84.

21. Vicens Vives, *Els Catalans*, p. 166. In 1913 Jacques Valdour estimated that

95 percent of the skilled workers in Barcelona were Catalan and the remaining 5 percent, though from other provinces, had been "Catalanized" by a lengthy sojourn in the province. Recent immigrants from other provinces, he noted, made up the great mass of unskilled workers in the Catalan factories and mixed very little with the general Catalan population. They did not learn the language, and often returned to their native provinces after six months. Valdour, I, 78.

22. Vicens Vives, *Els Catalans*, p. 169.

23. Díaz del Moral, pp. 168–69; Ullman, Chapters 5, 15.

24. Maitron, pp. 288ff; García Venero, *Historia de los movimientos sindicalistas*, p. 338; Montseny, *Anselmo Lorenzo*.

25. García Venero, *Historia de los movimientos sindicalistas*, pp. 338–43; García Venero, *Historia de las internacionales*, I, 448ff; Ullman, pp. 109–10.

26. Ullman, pp. 307–8, 322–28; Munilla, p. 110.

27. Ullman, pp. 317–18.

28. The transcript of this congress is reprinted in Díaz del Moral, pp. 528–32.

29. Joll, *The Anarchists*, pp. 212ff.

30. Peirats, *Los anarquistas*, p. 14.

31. Tuñón de Lara, *Introducció*, p. 233; García Venero, *Historia de las internacionales*, I, 458ff.

32. On the early history of the Socialist Party see: Mora, *Historia del socialismo obrero español*; Morato, *El partido socialista*. A good survey of Spanish Socialism from its origins to 1930 is presented in Payne, *Spanish revolution*, pp. 62–81. See also Arbeloa, *Orígines del partido socialista obrero español (1873–1880)*.

33. See "El partido socialista"; Lichtheim, p. 9.

34. Saborit, *Julián Besteiro*, p. 76; Iglesias, *Exhortaciones a los trabajadores*.

35. See "El partido socialista." For Vera's marxism see T. Jiménez Araya, "La introducción del marxismo en España: el Informe a la Comisión de Reformas Sociales de Jaime Vera." *Anales de Economía*, 15 (July–Sept. 1972), pp. 107–49.

36. On this theme, see Nettl, "The German Social Democratic Party, 1890–1914, as a political model"; Roth, *The Social Democrats in Imperial Germany*, Chapter 9.

37. del Rosal, p. 15.

38. Tuñón de Lara (*Introducció*, p. 197) blames the Socialist defeat in Catalonia on the "eccentric" leadership of the UGT in that region; but the distinctive mentality of the labor force there would seem to have been more important. See Jesús Pinilla Fornell in *El Sol*, 21.iv.18.

39. Díaz del Moral, p. 162.

40. Díaz-Plaja, p. 55; Morato, *El partido socialista*, pp. 240–41.

41. Díaz del Moral, p. 162; Morato, *El partido socialista*, p. 262.

42. Auburn, "Manuel Núñez de Arenas y de la Escosura (1886–1951)"; Morato, *El partido socialista*, pp. 269–71.

43. On the role of intellectuals in the Socialist Party, see: Ramos Oliveira, *Nosotros los marxistas*, Chapter 16; Zugazagoitia, pp. 56–57; Maurín, *Révolution et contre-révolution*, pp. 100–101; Araquistáin, *España en el crisol*, pp. 51–53; "Los intelectuales y el socialismo," *El Comunista*, 16.v.20.

44. Saborit, *Julián Besteiro*, pp. 67–70.

45. *Ibid.*, p. 69.

46. Tuñón de Lara, *Introducció*, p. 208.

47. For a journalistic but useful comparison of the Socialist and Syndicalist mentalities, see Conze, pp. 37–71.

48. Pérez, p. 21; Olivar Bertrand, "Repercusiones."

49. Aunós Pérez, pp. 322–28; Seco Serrano, pp. 102, 105.

50. Mousset, pp. 174–80; on the views of Lerroux, see Laborde, p. 187.

51. On the indifference of the masses to the war see also: Luis Araquistáin in *Hispania*, 1.vii.15; and "La prensa española y la guerra," *Bulletin Hispanique*, XIX (1917), 125.

52. Mayer, pp. 4ff.   53. Hardinge, pp. 256–66.

54. Francés, p. 344.   55. Romanones, *Notas*, III, 100.

56. Mousset, pp. 179–83.   57. Pijoan, p. 668.

58. Madariaga, "The future of Spanish neutrality," p. 144.

59. "La situation en Espagne," Introduction, p. 13.

60. Hardinge, pp. 259–60.

61. Griffith, pp. 364–65; Peter, Bishop of Southwark, pp. 209–19; Bolin, p. 135; Hardinge, pp. 257–58.

62. Bolin, p. 147; Madariaga, "Dark forces," p. 182; Cunningham, pp. 437–38.

63. Madariaga, "Spain's home war," pp. 380ff. Miguel de Unamuno wrote: "The idea that Spain was neutral during the war was a fiction. There was a war here—a war that was civil and bloodless, but a war." *España*, 6.xi.19, p. 5.

64. "La prensa española y la guerra," p. 123.

65. Breton, p. 860; Lantier, "L'attitude des intellectuels," p. 46.

66. *El Socialista*, 2.viii.14.

67. *Ibid.*, 6.xii.14; *Nuestra Palabra*, 10.viii.18.

68. *El Socialista*, 30.viii.14. The rapid switch of the Spanish Socialists from pacifism to "defensism" contrasted with the behavior of the Italian Socialist Party. Italian Socialists, especially after May 1915, would seem to have had as much reason as the French and more reason than the Spaniards to jettison their pacifist doctrines and support the war as a struggle of democracy against autocracy. That they did not do so is explicable at least partly in terms of the domestic situation they confronted, in which virtually all elements of Italian society felt a historic animosity for the Habsburg monarchy—a fact that paradoxically left the Socialists freer to follow a pacifist line. By the same token, the Spanish Socialists could more easily have followed an orthodox pacifist policy if the forces of order in Spain had not been so strongly committed to the Central Powers. But, in view of this commitment, to have expected them to opt for a cool pacifism in the European war was to expect what was psychologically impossible. Given the intense pro-German mood in Spain, indifference to the Allied cause was simply not a tenable platform for men of the political Left. In Italy this dialectical factor was muted because of an almost universally shared Austrophobia. Had the Italian forces of order revealed themselves as determined supporters of the Central Powers, the Socialists might well have had to become non-pacifist defenders of the Allied cause. Indeed, at the outset of the war, when they assumed their government was going to honor its treaty commitments to the Central Powers, Italian Socialists adopted a pro-Allied posture. Only when they discovered the cabinet's intentions did they swing over to neutralism. It was, perhaps, only the enthusiasm of many middle-class Italians for the Allies that permitted essentially francophile Italian Socialists to indulge in the luxury of prewar pacifist orthodoxy. Spanish Socialists could not afford this luxury. As Carl Landauer has said, the stress that the neutral Socialists laid on the general, "imperialist" causes of the war "was effective only in those countries where the governments were leaning toward the Allied side." Landauer, I, 521–23.

69. *El Socialista*, 6.xii.14.

70. Walling, pp. 410–11; Fainsod, p. 68.

71. *El Socialista*, 25–26.vii.15.
72. *Acción Socialista*, 5.ix.14.
73. Interview with Ramón Lamoneda, 23.vi.66; *El Comunista*, 11.v.21. In response to the Zimmerwald Manifesto *El Socialista* said that the judgment of this document was correct insofar as other wars were concerned, such as the Boer War, the Russo-Japanese War, or the Balkan Wars. But the present conflict was not between capitalist nations but between two worlds: that of democracy and that of tyranny. Socialism, "the essence of democracy," knew that its destiny and future were at stake. If the Central Powers were to win the war, the "purveyors of pacifism at all costs" would have "a grave responsibility before history." *El Socialista*, 17.x.15.
74. Rosmer, *Le mouvement ouvrier*, pp. 554–57; *Acción Socialista*, 18.x.15.
75. Rosmer, p. 411.
76. *El Socialista*, 31.x.15.
77. *Ibid.*
78. There is no real biography of Besteiro, though Saborit's *Julián Besteiro* contains much useful information, including excerpts from many speeches. Don Niceto Alcalá-Zamora expressed the opinion that Besteiro's stay in Paris made less of an impression on him than his sojourn in Germany, where he spent brief terms at the universities of Munich, Berlin, and Leipzig, emerging from this experience as a "formed and convinced Marxist." See Besteiro, p. 122.
79. *El Socialista*, 31.x.15.
80. Morato, *El partido socialista*, pp. 286–87.
81. Tuñón de Lara, *Introducció*, pp. 254–55.
82. *Solidaridad Obrera*, 6.viii.14; Díaz del Moral, p. 277.
83. Comín Colomer, *Historia del anarquismo*, I, 291–92.
84. Pestaña, *Lo que aprendí*, p. 49.
85. *Ibid.*, pp. 67–68.
86. *España*, 7.iii.18.
87. See, for example, *Solidaridad Obrera*, 25.v.17.
88. *Ibid.*, 5.ix.14.

Chapter Two

1. For an analysis of some of the difficulties that arise in the use of Spanish statistics, see Baelen, pp. 10–12 (footnote).
2. Vicens Vives, *Historia*, Tome IV, Vol. II, p. 37.
3. Baelen, p. 13; Bruguera, p. 334.
4. INE, *Principales actividades*, p. 10.   5. *Ibid.*, p. 9; Giner, p. 20.
6. *Informes de los inspectores*, I, 148.   7. Bruguera, p. 334.
8. *Report presented by the National Federation*, p. 2.
9. INE, *Principales actividades*, p. 93.   10. Baelen, p. 10.
11. Laborde, p. 164.   12. Baelen, p. 12.
13. Laborde, pp. 134ff.   14. Baelen, p. 15.
15. Pabón, I, 458–68.
16. Vicens Vives, *Historia*, Tome IV, Vol. II, p. 165; Lacomba, *Crisi i revolució*, pp. 21–22. On this theme see José Luis García Delgado, "Datos para una historia de la estrategía patronal en España: Frente al Proyecto de Ley estableciendo una contribución directa sobre los beneficios extraordinarios ocasionados por la I Guerra Mundial." *Anales de Economía*, 13 (Jan.–Mar. 1972), 39–132.
17. Baelen, p. 20.

18. Lacomba, *Crisi i revolució*, pp. 119ff; *Informes de los inspectores*, p. 148.
19. *Resumen de las informaciones*, p. 35.
20. *Informes de los inspectores*, pp. 89–126.
21. *Nuestra Palabra*, 14.ix.18.
22. *El Sol*, 19.vi.18.
23. *Nuestra Palabra*, 14.ix.18.
24. *Informes de los inspectores*, p. 91.
25. *Report presented by the National Federation*, p. 4.
26. *Informes de los inspectores*, p. 129.
27. de los Ríos, "The agrarian problem in Spain," p. 832.
28. Laborde, pp. 163ff.
29. Baelen, p. 13.
30. Laborde, pp. 164–65.
31. IRS, *Información sobre emigración*, pp. 37, 51.
32. *Ibid.*, p. 14.   33. Cunningham, pp. 421ff.
34. Laborde, p. 140.   35. Cunningham, p. 422.
36. IRS, *Encarecimiento*, p. 82.   37. *Ibid.*
38. Juan José Morato in *El Heraldo de Madrid*, 30.vi.08.
39. IRS, *Encarecimiento*, pp. 84–85.
40. Laborde, p. 135; INE, *Principales actividades*, p. 12.
41. *El Sol*, 18.iii.19; Laborde, p. 135.
42. Saborit, *Julián Besteiro*, p. 121. According to Largo Caballero this congress was held one month earlier than originally planned, apparently because of the seriousness of the economic crisis and perhaps also in order that it might coincide with the Valencia meeting of the CNT, discussed below. *La huelga de agosto en el parlamento*, p. 13.
43. Romanones, *Las responsabilidades*, p. 204.
44. *El Socialista*, 24 v.16. The Congress elected a new National Committee composed of the following figures: President, Pablo Iglesias; Vice-President, Francisco Largo Caballero; Secretary-Treasurer, Vicente Barrio; Vice-Secretary, Daniel Anguiano; members, Julián Besteiro, Virginia González, Andrés Saborit, Modesto Aragonés, Eduardo Torralba Beci, Manuel Cordero, and José Maeso. Saborit, *La huelga*, p. 46.
45. Nettlau MS, p. 232A.
46. *Ibid.*, p. 233A.
47. Saborit, *Julián Besteiro*, p. 125; Saborit, *La huelga*, p. 50.
48. Soldevilla, *Un segle de vida catalana*, II, 1325–26.
49. Saborit, *Julián Besteiro*, p. 123. During the June interview with Romanones, the Minister of Development, Rafael Gasset, assured Largo Caballero that the government's pending budget allotted large sums to public works and construction, and that "by October" there would be no unemployed and would, indeed, be more jobs than workers. The budget, of course, was not passed by the Cortes. *La huelga de agosto*, p. 14.
50. Pestaña, *Lo que aprendí*, p. 57.
51. "La situation en Espagne," Introduction, p. 13.
52. Serge, *Memoirs*, p. 52.
53. Breton, "En mai a Madrid," pp. 856–57.
54. Trotsky, *Mis peripecias*, p. 13.
55. *Ibid.*, pp. 28–29.   56. *Ibid.*, pp. 27–39 *passim*.

57. *Ibid.*, p. 47.

58. *Ibid.*, p. 92.

59. *Ibid.*, p. 6; Trotsky, *My life*, p. 266.

60. Trotsky, *Mis peripecias*, p. 10.

61. *Ibid.*, pp. 132–34.

62. Quoted in Elorietta y Artaza, p. 33.

63. *Solidaridad Obrera*, 6.i.17; Deutscher, p. 246.

64. Chamberlain, I, Chapter 5.

65. García Venero, *Historia de las internacionales*, II, 149.

66. *Tierra y Libertad*, 21.iii.17.

67. *Ibid.*, 28.iii.17; *Solidaridad Obrera*, 22.iii.17.

68. Serge, *Memoirs*, p. 53.

69. Madariaga, "Dark forces," p. 180.

70. Araquistáin, *Entre la guerra y la revolución*, pp. 83–87; Díaz del Moral, pp. 283–84.

71. *Bulletin Periodique des Presses Espagnoles* (Paris), 31.iii.17.

72. The connections between the war, the Russian Revolution, and the revolutionary mood in Spain emerge most clearly in Araquistáin, *Entre la guerra y la revolución*.

73. *El Socialista*, 1.v.17. For an assertion that Iglesias experienced "joy" upon hearing of the March Revolution, see Saborit, *La huelga*, p. 51.

74. *El Socialista*, 1.v.17.

75. Kennan, pp. 5–6, 13.

76. *El Socialista*, 1.v.17.

77. *Solidaridad Obrera*, 20.v.17.

78. The complete manifesto is reprinted in Saborit, *La huelga*, pp. 52–55.

79. *España*, 3.iv.17.

80. Pestaña, *Lo que aprendí*, p. 58.

81. *El Sol*, 6.x.18.

82. Pestaña, *Lo que aprendí*, p. 59.

83. *Los sucesos*, pp. 192–93, 204–5.

84. Lacomba, *Crisi i revolució*, pp. 123–35; Mousset, p. 183.

85. *España*, 15.iii.17; *Bulletin Periodique des Presses Espagnoles*, 31.iii.17; "La situation en Espagne," VII, 11. Nettlau suggests that the Socialists may have moved closer to intervention after the March Revolution in order to counteract the Revolution's impact on the Allied war effort. Nettlau MS, p. 235.

86. Fernández Almagro, pp. 285–88; Heredero, "Crises políticas durante la guerra."

87. Araquistáin, *Entre la guerra y la revolución*, pp. 70–83; "La situation en Espagne," Introduction, p. 13. For Maura's speech see Maura Gamazo and Fernández Almagro, pp. 293–97.

88. García Venero, *Melquíades Alvarez* (1954), pp. 296–99; Herold, p. 49.

89. Araquistáin, *Entre la guerra y la revolución*, pp. 19–20.

90. Nettlau wrote: "Since March 1917 the Russian Revolution has been known; however, before the summer of 1918 it seems not to have influenced the movements I have discussed. That is, the activities of all [types], the politicians, the Socialists, the Syndicalists, and the Anarchists, from spring to August 1917 are only to a small degree motivated by the possibilities for the overthrow of the regime that the fall of the Tsardom in Russia revealed; but they are to a much greater degree the results of a condition caused by the war." Nettlau MS, p. 241.

91. *El Socialista*, 27.v.17.

92. *Ibid.*

93. *Ibid.* A summary of the speeches in the Plaza de Toros, made by *El Liberal*, is found in Díaz-Plaja, V, 352–64.

94. *El Socialista*, 27.v.17.

95. *Ibid.*, 28.v.17; Portela MS, IV, 11–25.

96. *El Socialista*, 28.v.17.   97. *Ibid.*
98. *Ibid.*   99. *Ibid.*
100. *Solidaridad Obrera*, 1.v.17.   101. *Ibid.*, 11.v.17.
102. *Ibid.*, 25.v.17.
103. *Ibid.*, 10.vi.17; Nettlau MS, p. 233.
104. *Solidaridad Obrera*, 25.v.17.   105. *Ibid.*, 9.vi.17.
106. *Ibid.*, 11.vi.17.   107. *Ibid.*
108. *Ibid.*, 26.ix.18.

Chapter Three

1. Baelen, p. 5.

2. "If Spain had been a belligerent, there would be today in Madrid a Provisional Government with a Spanish Kerensky at its head," Madariaga, "Spain and Russia," p. 198.

3. The most thorough study of the revolutionary movement of 1917 is Lacomba, *La crisis española de 1917*, to which my account is indebted.

4. For a Marxist interpretation of the Spanish revolutionary movement of 1917, see Rapp-Lantaron, pp. 72–112.

5. For a perceptive, critical statement of the Army's role in modern Spain, see Aunós Pérez, pp. 330–36.

6. On the impact of the Moroccan War, Ortega y Gasset wrote: "The Moroccan affair was not big enough to temper the spirit of a militia like ours, but small as it was, it was sufficient to reawaken professional pride. The army's group consciousness was then reformed, it concentrated on itself, it united within itself. But this by no means meant that it rejoined the other social classes. On the contrary, this act of cohesion within the army took place around the core of those same bitter feelings. . . . Morocco made the broken soul of our army into a clenched fist, morally prepared for attack. From that time on, the military group has been a loaded rifle with no mark to shoot at." *Invertebrate Spain*, p. 49.

7. Lacomba, *La crisis*, p. 107.

8. Payne, *Politics and the military*, pp. 123–24.

9. Lacomba, *La crisis*, p. 106.

10. *La Correspondencia Militar* said: "Ah! But there is a Spain, there is a *patria* that many thousands of men have sworn to defend to the last drop of blood; and it is impermissible that either in Barcelona or anywhere in Catalonia the land that is ours, that of our fathers, that of our sons, should, for any reason, continue to be insulted and ridiculed; and if, to make it respected, we must spill blood, that of our enemies will be spilled to the last drop." Quoted in *El Sol*, 27.i.19.

11. Díaz-Plaja, V, 299. For vivid journalistic accounts of the events of the summer of 1917, see José Buxadé, *España en crisis: La bullanga misteriosa de 1917*, and Augusto de Castro, *O que eu vi e ouvi em Hespanha, junho a agosto de 1917* (Lisbon, 1917).

12. Payne, *Politics and the military*, p. 127. For a partial dissent from Payne's critique see Seco Serrano, p. 110n.

13. Lacomba, *La crisis*, p. 113; Aunós Pérez, p. 334.

14. Lacomba, *La crisis*, p. 117.

15. *Ibid.*, p. 112.

16. Payne, *Politics and the military*, p. 127.

17. Lacomba, *La crisis*, pp. 111–12.

18. "The Spanish crisis," *New Statesman*, 30.vi.17, pp. 294–95.

19. Pabón, I (2), 498.
20. Burgos y Mazo, *Páginas*, pp. 24–25.
21. Balcells, pp. 24–25.
22. Madariaga, "Spain and Russia," pp. 201–2.
23. Pabón, I (2), 448ff.
24. Lacomba, *La crisis*, pp. 168–71.
25. Aunós Pérez, p. 337.
26. García Venero, *Historia de las internacionales*, II, 164.
27. Pabón, I (2), 503–6; Lacomba, p. 177.
28. Burgos y Mazo, *Páginas*, pp. 109–10.
29. Pabón, I (2), 508.
30. Soldevilla, *Tres revoluciones*, pp. 109–10.
31. Pabón, I (2), 507–10.   32. *Solidaridad Obrera*, 6.vii.17.
33. Pabón, I (2), 513.   34. *Ibid.*
35. *Ibid.*, pp. 513–14; Soldevilla, *Tres revoluciones*, p. 121.
36. García Venero, *Historia de las internacionales*, II, 159.
37. The members were Melquíades Alvarez, Francisco Cambó, H. Giner, Pablo Iglesias, Alejandro Lerroux, Felipe Rodés, José Roíg y Bergadá, and José Zulueta.
38. Soldevilla, *Tres revoluciones*, pp. 121–22.
39. Pabón, I (2), 517.
40. Soldevilla, *Tres revoluciones*, pp. 124–28.
41. Pabón, I (2), 519.
42. Serge, *Memoirs*, p. 57. Besteiro later said that the UGT had intended to declare a general strike at once, even though they were not prepared, if the government had tried to dissolve the Assembly "violently." *Los sucesos*, p. 191.
43. Pabón, I (2), 525–26; Seco Serrano, p. 112.
44. Aunós Pérez (pp. 337–39) comments on Cambó's ambivalence as a revolutionary. See also Besteiro's judgments of Cambó in *Los sucesos*, pp. 193–95; Pabón, I (2), 526.
45. Madariaga, *Spain*, p. 319.
46. Some estimated that the strike would finally have come in October or November. See "La situation en Espagne," Pt. VII, p. 7.
47. Quoted in Soldevilla, *Tres revoluciones*, p. 45.
48. Buxadé, pp. 61–62.   49. Soldevilla, *Tres revoluciones*, p. 24.
50. *Ibid.*, pp. 88–89.   51. *Ibid.*, pp. 90–91.
52. Morato, *Pablo Iglesias*, p. 221.   53. *Ibid.*, pp. 221–22.
54. Saborit, *Julián Besteiro*, p. 175; Morato, *Pablo Iglesias*, p. 223.
55. Araquistáin, *Entre la guerra y la revolución*, p. 174.
56. The assumptions that governed Socialist planning for the strike were candidly set forth by Besteiro, Largo Caballero, and Andrés Saborit in the Cortes in 1918. See *Los sucesos*.
57. Pestaña, *Lo que aprendí*, pp. 62–63. The remark ascribed to Iglesias seems less than characteristic, and Andrés Saborit, *La huelga*, p. 64, expresses doubt that the meeting ever took place.
58. Ibarruri, p. 64.
59. Largo Caballero, *Mis recuerdos*, pp. 52–54; see also Pestaña, *Lo que aprendí*, pp. 59–61.
60. *Solidaridad Obrera*, 17.vii.17.
61. García Venero, *Historia de las internacionales*, II, 165–66.
62. Quoted in Lacomba, *La crisis*, p. 238; Saborit, *La huelga*, p. 68.

63. Lacomba, *La crisis*, pp. 274ff.

64. *Los sucesos*, p. 192.

65. Manuel Cordero wrote (pp. 30–31): "We did not pay attention to the *abuelo*. His opinion did not receive a single favorable vote. Such was the optimism that dominated us in those times."

66. *Ibid.*, p. 32.

67. Saborit, *La huelga*, pp. 8–9, 52–55.

68. *Ibid.*, p. 74. For the official version see *La Epoca*, 15.viii.18.

69. Largo Caballero, in *El Sol*, 6.x.18.

70. Cordero, p. 32.

71. Díaz del Moral, p. 283.

72. Acevedo, "La huelga," pp. 570–71.

73. *Los sucesos*, pp. 218, 221ff; Acevedo, "La huelga," pp. 570–72.

74. Lacomba, *La crisis*, pp. 256–57.

75. Gabriel Alomar, "La huelga en Barcelona," *España*, 8.xi.17; Pardo de Tavera, "Spain and the Great War," pp. 362–63.

76. Pestaña, *Lo que aprendí*, pp. 63–65.

77. Pabón, I (2), 545.

78. Pestaña, *Lo que aprendí*, p. 65.

79. Francisco Villanueva, "La huelga en Bilbao," *España*, 25.xi.17; Acevedo, "La huelga," 572–73; *Los sucesos*, p. 112.

80. Llaneza, "La huelga de agosto en Asturias," *España*, 1.xi.17. See also Llaneza's remarks in *Nuestra Palabra*, 21.ix.18 and 12.x.18.

81. Acevedo, pp. 573–77.

82. Unamuno, "En Salamanca: Notas de un testigo," *España*, 25.x.17.

83. Araquistáin, "Orígenes y proceso de la huelga general," *España*, 25.x.17. Thus the French journalist Jules Laborde, resident in Spain, viewed the ferment of 1917 as Germanophile. "[Germany] has given a lot of money to induce [Cambó, Maura, Lerroux] to provoke, as if it were their own movement, the events of 1917.... Whatever may be one's judgment of the means used, or the harshness of their effect, M. Dato has helped Spain get through a dangerous moment. The country will probably do him justice when more is known about the role of German intrigue in the political malaise of the Peninsula." Laborde, pp. 197, 220.

84. *Los sucesos*, p. 241; Saborit, *La huelga*, p. 75.

85. Saborit, *La huelga*, pp. 77–78. For the defense presented by the committee's military lawyers, see *La condena del comité de huelga*.

86. Saborit, *La huelga*, pp. 76–77.   87. *Ibid.*, p. 82.

88. *Ibid.*, p. 83.   89. *Nuestra Palabra*, 24.viii.18.

90. Romanones, *Las responsabilidades*, p. 204.

91. Salaya, p. 23.   92. Pérez Solís, *Memorias*, p. 175.

93. *El Sol*, 8.x.18.   94. *Los sucesos*, p. 203.

95. See, for example, Unamuno's speech in the Plaza de Toros in May 1917; Díaz-Plaja, V, 355.

96. Ortega y Gasset, *Invertebrate Spain*, pp. 55–56.

97. Alvarez del Vayo, p. 210. Andrés Saborit has sought to deny that Besteiro lost his revolutionary fervor as the result of the events of 1917; see *Julián Besteiro*, pp. 41, 116. Pérez Solís, however, concurs with Alvarez del Vayo; *Memorias*, p. 328.

98. *El Sol*, 9.iii.19.

99. As late as 1961 this version of the general strike was still being advanced. Mauricio Carlavilla wrote that the purpose of the strike was "to drag Spain into the war and to sacrifice hundreds of thousands of Spanish lives to the greater glory

of Albion and, even worse, in order to save the Russian Revolution.... With the failure of Romanones to carry us into the war by Royal decree, the Spanish revolution of 1917 was a desperate attempt to do away with the King." (See Largo Caballero, *Correspondencia secreta*, p. 69n.) García Venero says, more moderately, that the defeat of the attack on the monarchy in 1917 was also a defeat of the idea that Spain should enter the war, toward which it was being pulled by the "pro-Allied vehemence of the leftists"; *Historia de las internacionales*, II, 268.

100. *El Socialista*, 27.v.17.
101. Burgos y Mazo, *Páginas*, p. 309.
102. Fernández Almagro, p. 327; Balcells, p. 35.
103. Lacomba, *La crisis*, p. 292.
104. Quoted in *ibid.*, p. 288.
105. Pabón, I (2), pp. 555ff.
106. Soldevilla, *Tres revoluciones*, pp. 83–84.
107. Lacomba, *La crisis*, p. 303.
108. Cierva y Peñafiel, pp. 202–8.
109. Lacomba, *La crisis*, p. 317; Fernández Almagro, pp. 316–18.

Chapter Four

1. Clarkson, p. 482.
2. Especially among young middle-class intellectuals, the August Strike and its repression produced an upsurge of interest in the problems of the working class and a desire for closer contact. See, for example, Balbontín, pp. 137ff.
3. Fernández Almagro, p. 320. Gerald Brenan (p. 221) wrote: "Every revolutionary movement, every strike that fails after courageously defying authority, is a moral success in Spain and leads to an increase in the numbers of the defeated party. That is a measure of the difference of psychological climate between Spain and other European countries."
4. Vicente Barrio in *El Sol*, iv.x.18.   5. *Solidaridad Obrera*, 5.xi.17.
6. *Tierra y Libertad*, 28.xi.17.   7. *Ibid.*
8. *Ibid.*, 14.xi.17.   9. Hennessy, pp. 81, 253–54.
10. Balcells, p. 173. On these themes see: López and Santillán, *El anarquismo en el movimiento obrero*; Jordán, *La dictadura del proletariado*; and "Dionysius," *Almanaque de Tierra y Libertad para 1921*.
11. The spirit of the Anarchist groups is best revealed in Sanz, *El sindicalismo y la política*.
12. A contrast between the Spanish and French labor movements lay in the fact that the Jacobin-Blanquist tradition of dictatorial elitism was attenuated in Spain, so that Spanish receptivity to Leninism (which was partly shaped by Blanquist influences) would in the post-1917 period be correspondingly diminished. In contrast, French Marxism had never entirely lost its original Blanquist admixture, and it was this that formed the counterpart to the antidemocratic, elitist elements in Leninism. Thus the Blanquist sources of Bolshevism helped account for the relatively wide appeal of the Communist Party in France (Lichtheim, pp. 7ff). In Spain, by contrast, the Marxists eschewed Blanquism in favor of democratic tactics, whereas the Anarchosyndicalists were inclined to reject it in favor of a populist spontaneity combined with only a vague sort of ideological guidance by "conscious" anarchists. On the weakness of Jacobinism in Spain see Ramos Oliveira, p. 41. It is of course true that Bakunin's own writings contain Leninist-like passages denigrating spontaneity and urging the need for an "invisible dictatorship" of professional revolutionaries; but this aspect of his thought seems not to have had much impact

in Spain, where Anarchism continued to connote either putschist uprisings by small groups or, on the other hand, mass spontaneity in the revolutionary process. See Pyziur, pp. 128ff. Only in 1927, with the founding of the Federación Anarquista Ibérica (FAI), did the "invisible dictatorship" come into existence.

13. Even the Russian Anarchist Alexander Schapiro, who visited Spain in 1933, was shocked by the Anarchosyndicalists' addiction to spontaneity: "Si l'esprit de la révolution inévitable régne en maître dans l'Espagne prolétarienne et paysanne, on ne peut pas en dire de même de l'esprit d'organisation de cette révolution. *L'instinct de la spontanéité révolutionnaire continue encore à primer toutes autres considérations chez les militants. L'idée que l'action révolutionnaire destructive contient en elle-même les germes de l'activité révolutionnaire reconstructive est encore profondément enracinée chez nos camarades et est un obstacle constant à l'inoculation du virus organisateur dans l'activité de la CNT.*" Quoted in Brenan, p. 264.

14. Prat, pp. 23ff; Fabri, p. 3; López and Santillán, pp. 44ff; Jordan, pp. 5–7, 17ff.

15. *Tierra y Libertad*, 14.xi.17.   16. *Ibid.*, 21.xi.17 and 26.xii.17.

17. *Ibid.*, 9.i.18.   18. *Ibid.*, 2.i.18.

19. Manuel Buenacasa in *Solidaridad Obrera*, 12.xi.17.

20. *Tierra y Libertad*, 26.xii.17.

21. Angel Pestaña later acknowledged the existence of this dualism in the anarchist psyche when he wrote: "On the level of the exposition and criticism of ideas, the Spanish Anarchist maintains an unsurpassable correctness; but ... on the level of the real and the possible there is, in Anarchist circles ... an unequaled fervor on behalf of the *atentado* against men and things." *Lo que aprendí*, p. 165.

22. *Tierra y Libertad*, 26.xii.17.

23. *Ibid.*   24. *Ibid.*

25. *Ibid.*   26. Nettlau MS, p. 244.

27. Maurín, "De España a Moscu sin pasaporte."

28. Lenin, *State and revolution*, pp. 74–75.

29. "This [suppression of the bourgeoisie] is compatible with the diffusion of democracy among such an overwhelming majority of the population that the need for *special machinery* of suppression will begin to disappear.... The people can suppress the exploiters even with very simple 'machinery,' almost without any 'machinery,' without any special apparatus, by the *simple organization* of the *armed masses.*" *Ibid.*, p. 79.

30. Collinet, pp. 79–87.

31. See Daniels, pp. 27ff. Daniel Bell (p. 374) points out that this pamphlet, which was almost the only Bolshevik tract available abroad in the early days of the Revolution, was a more or less calculated attempt to cater to the primitive egalitarianism and instinctive Anarchosyndicalism of the Russian masses. For the impact of *State and revolution* on Spanish intellectuals, see Balbontín, p. 145.

32. *Solidaridad Obrera*, 11.xi.17.   33. *Ibid.*, 11.i.18.

34. *Ibid.*   35. *Ibid.*, 11.vii.18.

36. *Solidaridad Obrera*, 12.xi.17.   37. *Ibid.*

38. Morato, *Pablo Iglesias*, p. 234.

39. *El Socialista*, 10.xi.17. A month later the Socialist journal was of the opinion that the recent revolution in Portugal would be, perhaps, a more "fertile" source of lessons for Spain than the Russian Revolution. *Ibid.*, 10.xii.17.

40. *Ibid.*, 1.iii.18.

41. Saborit, *La huelga*, pp. 87–88.

42. Madariaga, "The danger of militarism," p. 307.

43. Besteiro later sought to justify this aloofness by saying that those French and

British Socialists who had joined their governments during the war had done so in a more promising context. The Spanish Socialists, he said, were not so well organized, nor was the political situation in Spain promising. Besteiro denied that the Maura government had any renovating possibilities and called it a "government of mystery." *El Sol*, 15.ix.18. For the Socialist veto of Maura, see *ibid.*, 3.v.18.

44. *Ibid.*, 21.v.18; de los Ríos, "The labor movement in Barcelona," p. 472.

45. *El Sol*, 1.v.18.

46. *Ibid.*, 17.vi.18.

47. *El Socialista*, 12.xii.18; *El Sol*, 17.vi.18 and 24.i.19.

48. *El Sol*, 15.vi.18.   49. *El Socialista*, 9.iv.12.

50. *Nuestra Palabra*, 6.viii.18.   51. *Ibid.*

52. *Ibid.*, 17.viii.18.   53. *Ibid.*, 31.viii.18.

54. *Ibid.*, 14.xii.18.   55. *Ibid.*, 7.xii.18.

56. *Ibid.*, 31.viii.18.   57. *Ibid.*, 7.ix.18.

58. *Ibid.*, 14.xii.18.   59. *Ibid.*, 23.xi.18.

60. *Ibid.*, 6.viii.18.   61. *Ibid.*, 12.x.18.

62. *Ibid.*, 14.xii.18.   63. *Ibid.*, 7.xii.18.

64. *Ibid.*, 14.ix.18.   65. *Ibid.*, 6.viii.18.

66. *Ibid.*, 12.x.18.   67. *Ibid.*, 21.ix.18 and 12.x.18.

68. *Ibid.*, 30.x.18.   69. *Ibid.*, 7.ix.18 and 15.xi.18.

70. *El Sol*, 9.ix.18.   71. *Ibid.*, 16.vii.18.

72. *Ibid.*, 24.xi.18; see also the article by Mario Cavio, 1.xii.18.

73. *Ibid.*, 25.x.18.   74. *Nuestra Palabra*, 7.ix.18.

75. *Solidaridad Obrera*, 15.viii.18. 76. *Nuestra Palabra*, 28.ix.18.

77. *El Socialista*, 27.viii.18.   78. *Nuestra Palabra*, 7.ix.18.

79. *El Sol*, 3.iv.18.   80. *Ibid.*, 28.ix.18.

81. *Ibid.*, 7.x.18.

82. Romanones, *Notas*, III, 156ff; Mousset, Chapter 15; Hurtado, II, 63ff.

83. Pérez Solís, *El partido socialista*, p. 67.

84. Hardinge, p. 265.

85. *El Sol*, 14.vii.18. Jaime Brossa wrote that the victory of the Allied powers "planted in the mind of the population the idea of the King's abdication," but that by April 1919 these feelings had dissipated. Brossa, "The domestic and foreign policy of Spain," *The Nation*, 5.iv.19, p. 519.

86. *El Sol.*, 7.x.18.   87. *Ibid.*, 6.xi.18.

88. *Ibid.*, 14.xi.18.   89. *Ibid.*, 13.xii.18.

90. *El Socialista*, 9.i.19.   91. *Tierra y Libertad*, 26.vi.18.

92. *El Socialista*, 8.ix.18.   93. *Ibid.*, 23.xi.18.

94. *El Sol*, 11.xi.18.   95. *El Socialista*, 20.xi.18.

96. *Nuestra Palabra*, 24.viii.18.   97. *Solidaridad Obrera*, 12.xi.18.

98. *El Sol*, 11.xi.18; *Solidaridad Obrera*, 13.xi.18.

99. *El Sol*, 11.xi.18.

100. Díaz del Moral, Chapter 10. On the eve of the Armistice (9.xi.18), *Nuestra Palabra* observed: "Although the Spanish people do not know the heroic Bolsheviks, they begin to concern themselves with the fate of the Russian Revolution and with the imminent possibility of an analogous revolution in Spain."

101. *El Sol*, 11.xi.18.

102. Portela MS, III, 1.

103. *Solidaridad Obrera*, 11.xii.18.

104. Baelen, Chapter 2. Reminiscences of life in the Vizcayan mining region in the postwar period are found in Ibarruri, pp. 67ff.

105. Baratech Alfaro, p. 46.
106. *El Socialista*, 26.i.19.
107. *Ibid.*, 18.iii.19.
108. *El Maximalista*, 2.xi.18.
109. *Ibid.*
110. *Ibid.*
111. *Solidaridad Obrera*, 3.xii.18.
112. *El Soviet*, 19.xii.18.
113. *Ibid.*
114. *El Debate*: "La dictadura ... y pronto!"; *La Acción*: "Se necesita un dicta-dor"; *La Correspondencia Militar*: "La dictadura es la salvación." Quoted in *El Sol*, 1.iii.19. See also *El Sol*, 15.i.19.
115. Burgos y Mazo, *El verano de 1919*, p. 181.
116. Ortega y Gasset, *Invertebrate Spain*, p. 71.
117. Quoted in "The class war in Spain," p. 742.
118. Quoted in *Solidaridad Obrera*, 8.vii.18.
119. "The class war in Spain," p. 739.
120. Denjean, p. 181.
121. *Nuestra Palabra*, 9.xi.18.
122. *El Sol*, 16.i.19.
123. Fernández Almagro, p. 328n.
124. Bernaldo de Quirós, *El espartaquismo agrario andaluz*; Calleja, *Rusia: Espejo saludable para uso de pobres y ricos*; Elorietta y Artaza, *El movimiento bolchevista*; Corréas, *El bolchevismo en España*; Rafael Gasset, *La humanidad insumisa*; Carlos Pereyra, *La Tercera internacional*; Royo Villanova, *Bolchevismo y sindicalismo.*
125. *El Sol*, 14–18.i.19.
126. *Ibid.*, 1.xii.18.
127. Saborit, quoted in *El Sol*, 6.i.19.
128. Besteiro in *El Sol*, 18.i.19.
129. *El Sol*, 19.v.19.
130. *Ibid.*, 4.x.18.
131. García Venero, *Historia de las internacionales*, II, 267–70.
132. *El Sol*, 8.x.18.
133. *Ibid.*, 11.x.18.
134. Largo Caballero, *Mis recuerdos*, p. 57.
135. García Venero, *Historia de las internacionales*, II, 229–30.
136. *Rasgos históricos de la Unión General de Trabajadores de España*, pp. 7–9. According to *El Sol* (9.vii.19) the UGT, in October 1918, had 468 sections and 89,601 members; but according to *Nuestra Palabra* (12.x.18) the Thirteenth UGT Congress was attended by 125 delegates representing 237 sections and 83,259 members.
137. Thus Núñez de Arenas remarked: "This congress, which has not aroused polemics, which has not provoked violent articles, has been stronger, more important than the previous ones." *España*, 12.xii.18.
138. *El Sol*, 26.xi.18.
139. Saborit, *Julián Besteiro*, pp. 174–76; see also Sukhanov, pp. 6–14.
140. Morato, *El partido socialista*, p. 35.
141. See especially the critique by José Sánchez Rojas in *El Sol*, 9.xi.18.
142. "Evolución del socialismo español," pp. 44–45.
143. *El Socialista*, 17.x.18.
144. *Ibid.*, 30.xi.18 and 1.xii.18.
145. *Ibid.*, 1.xii.18.
146. *Ibid.*
147. *Ibid.*
148. *España*, 12.xii.18.
149. Saborit, *Julián Besteiro*, p. 177.
150. *Nuestra Palabra*, 7.xii.18; *El Socialista*, 8.i.19.

Chapter Five

1. Angel Pestaña was among the Cenetista leaders who were hopeful that a revolutionary coordination of urban and rural workers could be achieved in the

postwar period; Rosmer, *Moscou sous Lénine*, p. 54; Díaz del Moral, p. xiii. Inevitably, this chapter is greatly influenced by Díaz del Moral's superb study of the Trienio Bolchevista in Córdoba province—an investigation conducted in the Thucydidean manner, on the scene as the events were unfolding. Edward Malefakis's study *Agrarian reform and peasant revolution in Spain* contains a perceptive summary and analysis of the Trienio, as well as a helpful section on rural Socialism (pp. 145–61). The best primary source on the Trienio is IRS, *Información sobre el problema agrario*, which is filled with diverse testimonials on the origins of the movement.

2. Díaz del Moral, p. 171.

3. IRS, *Información sobre el problema agrario*, pp. 36, 73, 74, 98; Baelen, p. 33.

4. Bernaldo de Quirós, p. 36.

5. Díaz del Moral, p. 326.

6. Malefakis (pp. 145–47) stresses the conjunction of inflation, the Restoration political crisis, and the Bolshevik Revolution in the genesis of the Trienio, whereas I place somewhat greater emphasis on the power that the Bolshevik myth, more or less unaided, revealed in arousing rural workers who clearly had not been aroused by the political crisis of 1917 and who, at the outset of the Trienio, were economically better off than they had ever been before. This is not to say, of course, that once begun the Trienio may not have been fed by inflationary pressures. In general, the witnesses interviewed by the investigators of the IRS were divided on this question, with some seeing the strike as "economic" in its origin and others viewing it as the result of "political" events—chiefly the Bolshevik Revolution—on the outside. IRS, *Información sobre el problema agrario*, pp. 13ff. The issue perhaps reduces itself to whether the war (with the inflationary pressures it generated) or the Russian Revolution (with its mythos of soil repartition) was the primary causal factor in triggering the agrarian agitations of the Trienio.

7. Díaz del Moral, pp. 276–79.　　8. *Ibid.*, p. 279.

9. Bernaldo de Quirós, p. 37.　　10. Brenan, p. 118.

11. Díaz del Moral, p. 385.　　12. Bernaldo de Quirós, p. 38.

13. IRS, *Información sobre el problema agrario,* p. 15. Other noted Anarchist preachers were Sánchez Rosa, Diego Alonso, Hijinio Noja, Antonio Amador, and Aquilino Medina.

14. Díaz del Moral, p. 299; according to Pascual Carrión (pp. 80–81, 86f), in Andalusia Córdoba province was second only to Huelva in the amount of land possessed by small proprietors (22.85% as compared to 36.6%). In total number of small proprietors, Córdoba ranked second only to Jaen province (68,741 to 95,582). Figures are for 1930.

15. Díaz del Moral, pp. 295–96.　　16. Brenan, p. 181.

17. Díaz del Moral, p. 290.　　18. *Ibid.*, p. 371.

19. Both remarks quoted *ibid.*, pp. 283–84.

20. Bernaldo de Quirós, p. 39.

21. Costedoat-Lamarque, p. 39.

22. IRS, *Información sobre el problema agrario*, p. 19.

23. Denjean, pp. 166–67.

24. IRS, *Encarecimiento de la vida*, p. 82. The mayor of Puente Genil insisted that the disturbances in that region began before there had been any significant rise in the price of essential goods; IRS, *Información sobre el problema agrario*, p. 35.

25. The statement of the Farmhands' and Herders' Association of Córdoba

asserted that the wages of rural workers had begun to rise in 1917 and had more than doubled by harvesttime of 1918; IRS, *Información sobre el problema agrario,* p. 73. Costedoat-Lamarque (p. 85) believes that wages had trebled.

26. *El Sol,* 30.iii.19; IRS, *Información sobre el problema agrario,* p. 39. Referring to the Andalusian peasants, Madariaga wrote: "Today, their grievance is not one of salary. The are 'up against' the landlord. They have heard of the emancipation of the Russian peasant, and they want to taste the pleasure of working for themselves on their own land." Madariaga, "Spain in transition," p. 708.

27. *El Sol,* 25.x.19.

28. *Ibid.,* 9.vii.19. Granada was the main Socialist stronghold in Andalusia.

29. *Ibid.,* 10.ii.19 and 1.v.19.   30. Díaz del Moral, pp. 306–7.

31. *Ibid.,* pp. 290, 307.   32. *Ibid.,* pp. 310–11.

33. Buenacasa, pp. 166–67.   34. *El Sol,* 10.ii.19.

35. Dos Passos, *Rosinante to the road again* (New York, 1922), pp. 109–11.

36. Costedoat-Lamarque, p. 24; Buenacasa, p. 164; Anice L. Whitney, "Labor unrest in Spain," *Monthly Labor Review,* XII, No. 5, p. 159.

37. Denjean, p. 167.

38. Díaz del Moral, pp. 393–97.

39. Burgos y Mazo, *El verano de 1919,* pp. 172–77.

40. Hernández, *Negro y rojo,* p. 32.

41. Denjean, p. 168.

42. *El Sol,* 4.ix.20.

43. Burgos y Mazo, *El verano de 1919,* p. 355.

44. Tyler Dennett, "Blessed chaos in Spain," *Fortnightly Review,* 17.v.19, p. 86; *El Sol,* 1.iii.19.

45. *El Socialista,* 11.v.19.

46. Cuadrado, II, 817–26. They were not, however, the same seats: Anguiano was not returned, but this loss was made up by the election of Fernando de los Ríos from Granada.

47. *Ibid.,* p. 825.

48. *El Sol,* 22.i.19.

Chapter Six

1. Balcells, p. 159; *El Sol,* 21.ii.19.

2. See the remarks of a Syndicalist from Alicante, quoted in *El Sol,* 23.x.19.

3. Pérez Solís, *Memorias,* p. 193; *El Sol,* 21.ii.19.

4. See Baelen, Chapter 2.

5. See "Una magnífica visión constructiva de Salvador Seguí," in Madrid, *Ocho meses,* pp. 93–98.

6. Buenacasa, p. 68; Brenan, p. 224.

7. Buenacasa, pp. 54, 127; Díaz del Moral, p. 321.

8. See *Memoria del congreso celebrado en Barcelona.*

9. Solano, pp. 31, 32; Peiró, Chapter 3.

10. Buenacasa, pp. 214–15.

11. Pabón, II(1), 100–102.

12. The decisions of the Congress with respect to the Sindicatos Unicos are summarized in *Memoria del congreso,* pp. 71–79. The complete *reglamento* of the new industrial unions is reproduced in Solá Cañizares, pp. 33–36. See also on this Congress Baratech Alfaro, pp. 48ff.

13. Buenacasa, pp. 64–65, 253–54.   14. *Ibid.,* pp. 7–9.

15. *Ibid.*, p. 64.
16. *Ibid.*, pp. 251–56.
17. Nettlau MS, p. 251.
18. Pestaña, *Lo que aprendí*, p. 161.
19. Buenacasa, p. 65.
20. See Chapter 11.
21. Buenacasa, p. 66.
22. Francés, p. 424.
23. Pabón, II(1), 67, 71.
24. *Ibid.*, pp. 15–17.
25. Francés, p. 424.
26. *El Sol*, 11.ii.19.
27. Burgos y Mazo, *El verano de 1919*, p. 171.
28. Denjean, pp. 164ff.
29. *El Sol*, 10.ii.19; Díaz del Moral, p. 325.
30. Denjean, p. 166.
31. *El Sol*, 15.ii.19; Denjean, p. 167.
32. *El Sol*, 23.i.19.
33. *Ibid.*, 15.i.19. There were also rumors that workers in the Vizcayan industrial zones were stockpiling weapons; *ibid.*, 16.i.19.
34. On the question of Catalanism, Seguí said: "The policy sponsored by the Lliga has tried, and in part succeeded, in announcing to all Spain that there exists in Catalonia no other problem than their own: regionalism. This is a falsehood; in Catalonia, in addition to the social problem, which is not Catalan but universal, there exists the problem that other peoples in Europe have posed: the problem of liberty and of administrative decentralization that all liberal men accept. Now, then, the Lliga does not represent this problem, since if it did . . . Cambó would not have been a minister . . . in a centralist government." *Salvador Seguí: Su vida, su obra*, pp. 46–47.
35. *El Sol*, 23.i.19.
36. *Ibid.*, 26.iii.19.
37. *Ibid.*, 23.i.19.
38. Buenacasa, p. 67.
39. Balcells, p. 71.
40. Hurtado, p. 79.
41. Madrid, pp. 14–20, contains a lengthy statement by Pestaña on the strike. Balcell's summary of the strike is excellent, pp. 73–99. For a good synthesis of this era, see Payne, *Spanish revolution*, pp. 37–61.
42. Madrid, *Ocho meses*, p. 14.
43. *Ibid.*, pp. 15–16.
44. Madrid, *Ocho meses*, p. 17; Fernández Almagro, p. 352.
45. Balcells, p. 82.
46. Baratech Alfaro, pp. 56–57.
47. *Ibid.*, p. 57.
48. The best source on Seguí's early life is Viadiu, *Salvador Seguí* ("*Noy del Sucre*"). Pere Foix, *Apòstols i mercaders*, indulges in literary license and should be used with care. See also the essays in *Salvador Seguí: Su vida, su obra*. A rather fictionalized but not wholly misleading portrait of Seguí ("Dario") as revolutionary activist will be found in Victor Serge's novel *Naissance de notre force*.
49. Viadiu, pp. 10–22; Foix, pp. 57–60.
50. Viadiu, pp. 25–28.
51. Foix, pp. 57–58 (footnote).
52. Viadiu, pp. 31–32.
53. *Ibid.*, p. 11.
54. Buenacasa, p. 79; Pérez Solís, *Memorias*, p. 236.
55. Viadiu, p. 40.
56. Germinal Esgleas (in *Salvador Seguí: Si vida, su obra*, pp. 89–92) has insisted that Seguí was an Anarchist, and Buenacasa (pp. 261–62) has asserted the same. But it is certain that Nettlau is correct when he says that Seguí "never was" an Anarchist (Nettlau MS, p. 232). Viadiu has confirmed Seguí's almost constant quarrels with the Anarchists, and Joaquín Maurín, writing in 1923, acknowledged

that Seguí "signified in Spain the passage [of the Catalonian labor movement] from Anarchism to Syndicalism" (*El Socialista*, 3.ix.23). See, finally, "Le possibilisme de Salvador Seguí," in Lorenzo, pp. 55–58.

57. Raymond Carr, p. 510.

58. Viadiu, p. 37; Baratech Alfaro, p. 50.

59. *El Comunista*, 20.xi.20.

60. See the discussion of possible Cenetista electoral participation in *El Sol*, 24.iv.19.

61. Viadiu, pp. 44–45.

62. Baratech Alfaro, p. 57; Alvarez del Vayo, p. 188; Balcells, p. 83. Francés (p. 429) speaks of the "miracle" of Seguí's "persuading of the wisdom of returning to work 25,000 men who did not want to." Foix (p. 72) claims that there were 35,000 present. See also pp. 23–24. For a brief, verbatim excerpt from Seguí's speech, see Soldevilla, *Un segle de vida*, II, 1328–29.

63. Buenacasa, p. 216.   64. Balcells, pp. 97–98.

65. Pestaña, *Lo que aprendí*, p. 194.   66. Baratech Alfaro, pp. 57–58.

67. Balcells, p. 88.

68. I regret that I have never been able to obtain a copy of Pla y Armengol's *Impresiones de la huelga general*. Solano has considerable documentary material on the strike, pp. 84–113.

69. *El Sol*, 25.x.19.

70. Baratech Alfaro, p. 59.

71. Burgos y Mazo, *El verano de 1919*, pp. 169–70.

72. Balcells, p. 96.   73. Peirats, *Los anarquistas*, p. 17.

74. Balcells, pp. 99–100.   75. *Ibid.*, p. 111.

76. *Ibid.*, pp. 100–101.   77. Díaz del Moral, p. 315.

78. Quoted in *Kommunisticheskii Internatsional*, No. 5 (1919), col. 764.

79. Nettlau MS, p. 280.   80. *Ibid.*, p. 231A.

81. *Solidaridad Obrera*, 3.iv.17.   82. *Ibid.*, 27.iv.17.

83. Nettlau MS, p. 231b.

84. See Albert Camus, *The Rebel* (New York, 1956), pp. 158–72.

85. Among the more prominent militants, Manuel Buenacasa and Eusebio Carbó perhaps best exemplified the ambivalencies of the Anarchosyndicalist temper. On Carbó, see Foix, pp. 201–39.

86. For the psychology of the second, or *arriviste*, group, see Sanz, *El Sindicalismo y la política*.

87. Buenacasa, p. 68.

88. Pestaña, *Lo que aprendí*, p. 92.

89. *Ibid.*, pp. 165–67, 182; Sanz, p. 99.

90. J. Romero Maura, "Terrorism in Barcelona and its impact on Spanish politics 1904–1909," *Past and Present*, No. 41 (Dec. 1968), pp. 130–83.

91. *Ibid.*, pp. 137, 147–56.

92. Farré Moregó, p. 111. This was the assassination of the employer José Antonio Barret (see p. 176).

93. Pestaña, *Lo que aprendí*, p. 170.   94. Baratech Alfaro, p. 61.

95. Pestaña, *Lo que aprendí*, p. 174.   96. *Ibid.*, p. 180.

97. D. Quintiliano Saldaña, in the Prologue to Farré Moregó, pp. x–xii; Baratech Alfaro, p. 63.

98. Baratech Alfaro, pp. 60–61.

99. Pestaña, *Lo que aprendí*, p. 176.

100. Buenacasa, p. 68.

101. Maurín, *L'anarchosyndicalisme en Espagne*, p. 31. The number of "social crimes" committed both by the workers and by their opponents in 1917–21 was distributed among Spain's major cities as follows: Barcelona, 809; Bilbao, 152; Valencia, 151; Zaragoza, 129; Seville, 104. The total number of *atentados* for all of Spain in this period was 1,756. In Barcelona the number of such crimes rose after 1916: 43 in 1917; 93 in 1918; 109 in 1919; 304 in 1920; and 254 in 1921. Of these attacks, the number against workers (many of whom belonged to unions hostile to the CNT) was 440; against employers and foremen, 218; against the police and the Somatén, 88. The total killed in Barcelona (1917–21) was 255, with 733 wounded. García Venero, *Historia de los movimientos*, pp. 365–66. A statistical breakdown of political crimes in several Spanish cities during 1917–21 (adapted from Farré Moregó) is presented in Payne, *Spanish revolution*, pp. 59–61.

102. Pestaña, *Lo que aprendí*, p. 177. Baratech Alfaro (pp. 59–60) says that the fees ranged from 500 to 1,000 pesetas, depending on the importance of the individual to be liquidated and the risk involved.

103. Pestaña, *Lo que aprendí*, pp. 171ff.

104. Balcells, pp. 104ff.

105. This schema was advanced by General Martínez Anido in an interview in *El Sol*, 15.ii.22.

106. Pestaña's book *Lo que aprendí en la vida* is largely given over to an agonized effort to explain the origins of terrorism in Catalonia and Pestaña's long-term association with many militants who were terrorists; and it suggests that the CRT had become, by the time of the Dictatorship, a kind of moral morass: "We all know...that it has been publicly denied...that the [CNT] knew anything [about the atentados]. This is a half truth, one of those truths that covers a lie. The organization, it is certain, knew nothing of the atentados that were being committed. Neither the organization nor its militants [knew of them].... One did not meet or discuss or organize them.... But if the organization never in fact met to plan the atentados, everyone knew that the authors of the atentados were sustained and paid by the organization, and that victims fell after having been pointed out to the executioners by those who had an interest in their fall." *Lo que aprendí*, p. 79. Further on (p. 113), Pestaña writes: "However hard, violent, and painful for us to confess it, it must be said that the men who killed, the moral authors, those who executed [terrorist acts]...were in our midst, they lived in Anarchist and Syndicalist circles, they were visible members of the organization and of the groups, and they enjoyed in the general opinion and in the working class [all] the respect and consideration that any man could deserve and enjoy."

107. *Ibid.*, p. 175.

108. Balcells, p. 114.

109. Fernández Almagro, pp. 360–61.

110. Burgos y Mazo, *El verano de 1919*, p. 191.

111. Madrid, *Ocho meses*, pp. 35–37.

112. *Ibid.*

113. Buenacasa, pp. 70–71.

114. In mid-November (18.xi.19), *Solidaridad Obrera* took note of these internecine disturbances, protesting against attacks by certain *compañeros* on other *compañeros*. The Syndicalist journal complained that these "revolutionaries of the coffee table" could attack other Cenetistas because they enjoyed immunity.

115. Buenacasa, p. 72.

116. Burgos y Mazo, *El verano de 1919*, pp. 355–57.

117. Madrid, *Ocho meses*, p. 41.

118. *España*, 16.x.19.

119. Burgos y Mazo, *El verano de 1919*, p. 352.

120. Pestaña and Seguí, p. 7.

121. Even though he mentioned the possibility of a union of the CNT and the UGT, Seguí labeled the Socialist Party as "nothing but a prolongation or extension of the radical parties of the bourgeoisie, of which it is the latest expression." Pestaña and Seguí, p.23.

122. *Ibid.*, p. 21.

123. *Ibid.*, pp. 21–22.

124. *Ibid.*, pp. 18–24.

125. *Espartaco*, 31.x.19.

126. *Ibid.*

127. Burgos y Mazo, *El verano de 1919*, pp. 354–55.

128. Balcells, p. 120.

129. Madrid, *Ocho meses*, pp. 39–40.

130. The discussions are summarized by Balcells, pp. 122–23.

131. *Ibid.*, p. 121.

132. Madrid, *Ocho meses*, pp. 34–35.

133. *Ibid.*, p. 42.

134. *Ibid.*, p. 39.

135. Burgos y Mazo, *El verano de 1919*, p. 451.

136. Balcells, p. 129.

137. Buenacasa, p. 72.

138. *Ibid.*, pp. 73–74.

139. *Ibid.*, p. 74.

140. *Espartaco*, 22.ii.20.

Chapter Seven

1. Degras, *The Communist International*, I, 2–4.

2. *Ibid.*; Portela MS, I, 62; Hulse, pp. 1–16. Although the text of the Bolsheviks' radiogram was not printed in *Nuestra Palabra*, it did appear in *El Socialista*, 25.i.19.

3. Renaudel, pp. 7–21.

4. Degras, *The Communist International*, I, 28.

5. Renaudel, pp. 35–60.

6. *Ibid.*, pp. 133–35.

7. *Ibid.*, pp. 135–37; *El Socialista*, 10.xii.19.

8. *Nuestra Palabra*, 15.ii.19.

9. Degras, *The Communist International*, I, 3.

10. Hulse, pp. 3, 17–35; Degras, *The Communist International*, I, 16.

11. Hulse, pp. 21–22; Degras, *The Communist International*, I, 16.

12. Degras, *The Communist International*, I, 19–26, 41.

13. Maurín, *Révolution et contre-révolution*, p. 131.

14. See, for example, the exchanges recorded in *Los sucesos de agosto*.

15. Aron, "The impact of Marxism in the twentieth century," in Drachkovitch, p. 7; Joll, *The Second International*, p. 104.

16. See p. 110.

17. *El Sol*, 15.ix.18.

18. *Ibid.*, 2.ii.19. Largo Caballero, in a similar manner, after calling for the overthrow of the monarchy, reiterated that the Socialists would not participate in power because of their determination to preserve the "purity" of their creed and to avoid becoming corrupted "like some republicans and like the Lliga Regionalista," which had accepted the monarchy's offer to collaborate. *Ibid.*, 14.xi.18.

19. *Ibid.*, 20.iii.19.

20. Gay, pp. 243–44.

21. Kautsky, p. 93. Kautsky's ideas on this subject were explicated by the Russian Menshevik Tasin in *El Sol*, 25.vi.19.

22. Saborit, *Julián Besteiro*, pp. 177–84, 361–64; *El Socialista*, 1.v.19. Some years later Besteiro said, "Comrades, I always had respect and enormous admiration for the Bolsheviks; don't misjudge me. And I once said that if I had been Russian in 1918, I would probably have been at the side of Lenin. At that moment, the Russians could not have done more than they did, and they have had to face enormous realities that overwhelmed them." Quoted in Saborit, *Asturias*, p. 286.

23. *El Socialista*, 20.ix.19.

24. *Renovación*, 15.xi.19.

25. *Ibid.*

26. In dealing with factional tendencies in the PSOE I have gained insight from Guenther Roth's *The Social Democrats in Imperial Germany*, which treats the rise of right- and left-wing factions within the SPD as intimately related to the retention of a deterministic Marxist ideology and the pursuit of reformist policies.

27. *El Sol*, 17.ix.19 and 17.xii.19.

28. Pérez Solís, *Memorias*, pp. 56–80.

29. *Ibid.*, pp. 83–91.

30. For a perceptive portrait of Cabello and a discussion of Valladolid Socialism, see *ibid.*, pp. 97–103, 116–27.

31. *Ibid.*, pp. 148, 204.

32. *Ibid.*, pp. 136, 151.

33. *Ibid.*, p. 151.

34. *Ibid.*, p. 152.

35. *Ibid.*, p. 173.

36. *Ibid.*, pp. 175–78.

37. *Ibid.*, p. 201.

38. *Ibid.*, pp. 183–89. For Pérez Solís's stand on the regionalist question, see also *El Sol*, 16.ii.19 (his speech to the Atheneum) and 2.xii.18.

39. *Diario de Sesiones*, 28.i.15.

40. Pérez Solís's first article appeared on September 3, 1918, and the series was published later the same year as *El partido socialista y la acción de las izquierdas*.

41. Pérez Solís nevertheless described himself as having been "intoxicated with *aliadofilia*, inflamed with the stupid pretension that the victory of the Allies was going to be the universal triumph of Justice, Right, Liberty, and other things equally beautiful." *Ibid.*, p. 232. For Solís's critiques of caciquismo, see: *Memorias*, pp. 120ff; *El Sol*, 26.i.19 and 17.ii.19.

42. Pérez Solís, *El partido socialista*, p. 33.

43. *Ibid.*, p. 49; *España*, 12.iv.17.

44. *El partido socialista*, pp. 36, 43.

45. *El Sol*, 17.xi.18. Indalecio Prieto had made a similar point a few months earlier, saying that he did not believe the Socialists would feel impelled to overthrow a liberal, renovating monarchy. *El Sol*, 14.vii.18.

46. *El partido socialista*, pp. 49–51.

47. *El Sol*, 17.xi.18.

48. *El partido socialista*, pp. 4, 9.

49. *El Sol*, 17.xi.18.

50. The issues of *Nuestra Palabra* from March 15, 1919, to February 5, 1920, have apparently been lost.

51. See pp. 114–15.

52. Portela MS, I, 65; Burgos y Mazo, *El verano de 1919*, p. 328.

53. *Nuestra Palabra*, 15.ii.19 and 22.ii.19.

54. Pro-Bolshevik meetings in the period before and after the Armistice were numerous. See *El Sol*, 4.xi.18, 11.xi.18, 6.i.19, 25.i.19, 10.ii.19, 20.iii.19, 15.vi.19, and 25.vi.19. For pro-Bolshevik meetings in the provinces, see *El Socialista*,

25.xi.18 (Santander), 13.i.19 (Bilbao), 17.i.19 (La Multa), 24.i.19 (Eibar), 11.ii.19 (Granada), and *Solidaridad Obrera*, 10.xi.18 (Valencia).

55. Portela MS, I, 66–67.

56. *El Sol*, 17.xi.18. The ideological evolution of Núñez de Arenas presents certain problems. Though he served on the editorial staff of the strongly pro-Allied journal *España* during the war, he seems—at least at Party gatherings—to have maintained an anti-Aliadophile stance and to have backed the Zimmerwald movement. Yet his education, his university background, and his Francophile antecedents suggest a mentality similar in many ways to that of such passionate Aliadófilos as Andrés Ovejero, Luis Araquistáin, or, indeed, Julián Besteiro. Within the Socialist Party, the anti-Aliadófilos were generally doctrinaire plebeians rather than intellectuals—men like Saborit, César González, Manuel Cordero, or Ramón Lamoneda. Núñez de Arenas, with his essentially liberal idealism, should have been the prototypical Aliadófilo but was not. Yet in the period of the Armistice he acted like one, for he was swayed by Wilsonianism and became a member of the Spanish section of the Society for the League of Nations (see *El Sol*, 8.xi.18). At the Party Congress of November–December 1918 he supported the Republican-Socialist Alliance, as well as the resolution committing the Party to a bourgeois-democratic republic. And he revealed a complacent acceptance of the Party's minimum program, acknowledging without disapproval: "There has been drawn up a program that a merely liberal government could make its own. To such an extreme have we arrived in Spain that the most radical party has to struggle to defend the program of the European parties of the Right." *España*, 12.xii.18. Yet within a few months Núñez de Arenas opted for Bolshevism.

57. *El Sol*, 20.i.19.

58. *España*, 1.xi.19.

59. *El Sol*, 25.i.19.

60. *Ibid.*, 10.ii.19.

61. *El Socialista*, 1.vii.19. See also "Fin de ensueño Wilsoniano," *El Sol*, 9.v.19.

62. *El Sol*, 21.vii.19.

63. *Ibid.*

64. *El Sol*, 14.vii.19. The failure of the Lucerne Conference to reestablish the Second International during the first week of August no doubt also strengthened the move toward the Comintern. Hulse, p. 96.

65. *El Sol*, 30.vii.19.

66. Burgos y Mazo, *El verano de 1919*, pp. 184, 328.

67. *El Socialista*, 2.viii.19.

68. Saborit, *Julián Besteiro*, pp. 173–74.

69. Rapp-Lantaron, p. 86.

70. Saborit, *Julián Besteiro*, p. 172.

71. *El Socialista*, 30.viii.19.

72. *Ibid.*, 25.x.19.

73. *Ibid.*, 6.ix.19.

74. Of all the members of the Executive Committee of the PSOE, only Daniel Anguiano and Virginia González voted for immediate adherence to the Communist International; Rapp-Lantaron, p. 86n.

75. Tuñón de Lara, *Introducció*, pp. 220–21.

76. Interview with Luis Portela, 17.v.64.

77. "Evolución del socialismo español," p. 44.

78. Rapp-Lantaron, p. 90.

79. Pérez Solís, *Memorias*, p. 263.

80. *Nuestra Palabra*, 28.ix.18.

81. *Ibid.*

82. Pérez Solís, *Memorias*, pp. 262–63.

83. *España Nueva*, 10.i.18.

84. *El Socialista*, 11.i.18; *España Nueva*, 13.ii.18.

85. Portela MS, I, p. 62.

86. The GES was formed in April 1917 and held its first congress in December 1918, with groups from five cities represented. *El Socialista*, 23.xii.18.

87. Balbontín, pp. 119, 142.

88. See Chapter IV, Note 2.

89. *El Socialista*, 3.iv.17.

90. *Ibid.*

91. *España Nueva*, 27.iv.18.

92. *Ibid.*

93. Balbontín, p. 143.

94. *Ibid.*, pp. 143–44.

95. *Ibid.*, pp. 144–45.

96. *Ibid.*, p. 143.

97. *Ibid.*, p. 145. For another youthful and essentially religious response to the Russian Revolution see Castro Delgado, *Hombres made in Moscu*, pp. 55–57: "Enrique thought less about God. The 'social revolution' had replaced God in the world of his daily preoccupations.... Now he thought about Lenin. When his father said grace to God at the dinner table, Enrique thought about his own god: Lenin. 'Yes! God exists! Lenin! Lenin! Lenin!' "

98. Balbontín, p. 146. Balbontín acknowledged that not all of his comrades in the GES interpreted Marxism as he did. Eduardo Ugarte, for example, "laughed frequently at my mystical dreams and judged that the goal of Socialism did not consist in bringing to the world evangelical love, or even Proudhonian equality, full of apostolic asceticism, but rather a kind of perpetual Dionysian orgy" (p. 147).

99. *Ibid.*, pp. 149–50.

100. *El Socialista*, 1.xi.19; *España Nueva*, 30.xii.17; *Renovación*, 10.i.20. Interview with Juan Andrade, Paris, 9.iv.64. Interview with Luis Portela, Barcelona, 17.v.64.

101. *El Socialista*, 6.ix.19; Burgos y Mazo, *El verano de 1919*, p. 35; "José de Cataluña," "El Socialismo en Cataluña," *El Socialista*, 23.viii.20.

102. *El Sol*, 8.xii.18; *España*, 23.x.19.

103. See p. 335.

104. *El Socialista*, 2.ix.19. See also Juan de los Toyos, "Estamos más cerca que nunca," *ibid.*, 17.iii.19.

105. *El Socialista*, 18.ix.19. See also the interview given by Eleuterio Quintanilla, *ibid.*, 1.x.20.

106. The attitude of the Anarchosyndicalists was clearly revealed in a remark by the journal *El Comunista* of La Felguera (19.vi.20): "Maximalists, Bolsheviks, Libertarian-Communists, Spartacists—what does the name matter if the important thing is the principles! We were the first to support the Russian Revolution, to worship it in its beginnings.... Impenitent revolutionaries, we defend the Russian comrades even in their mistakes."

107. The evolution of Anarchist and Anarchosyndicalist attitudes toward the Bolshevik Revolution and the dictatorship of the proletariat is discussed in Chapter 11.

Chapter Eight

1. "Evolución del socialismo español," p. 44. During the first four months of 1919, the PSOE increased its membership by 50 percent, with most of the new recruits coming from the *campos* of Andalusia, Extremadura, and Castile. *El Sol*, 30.iv.19.

2. See Kautsky, Chapter 2; Roth, p. 189.

3. *El Socialista*, 12.xii.19.

4. *Ibid.*, 13.xii.19.

5. *Ibid.*, 12.xii.19.

6. *Ibid.*; Acevedo, *Impresiones*, p. 197.

7. *El Socialista*, 10.xii.19.

8. *Ibid.*

9. *Ibid.*, 13.xii.19.

10. *Ibid.*

11. *Ibid.*, 10.xii.19.

12. *Ibid.*

13. *Ibid.*, 13.xii.19.

14. *Ibid.*, 11.xii.19; *El Sol*, 15.xii.19. The new Executive Committee of the Party, selected at this time, included: Iglesias (president); Besteiro (vice-president);

Anguiano (secretary); Núñez Tomás (vice-secretary); Saborit (secretary of meetings); Largo Caballero, Ovejero, Fabra Ribas, Núñez de Arenas, Lucio Martínez, and Lamoneda (members).

15. *El Socialista,* 18.xii.19.
16. See *HDA,* [4], "Les Jeunesses Espagnols et le Parti Socialiste."
17. See Chapter 9.
18. See "Acerca de la Tercera Internacional," in *El Socialista,* 1.x.20.
19. *Espartaco,* 19.i.20.
20. Burgos y Mazo, *El verano de 1919,* pp. 356–57.
21. Buenacasa, pp. 74, 76.
22. Samblancat wrote about the convening of the "Red Congress," calling it "the soviet of the workers." It was meeting, he said, "amid sabers and police helmets, amid bared teeth and closed fists, amid political crises, strikes, lockouts, and threats of impending repression and devastating martial law." *El Comunista* (Zaragoza), 2.i.20. Buenacasa, p. 89.
23. Buenacasa, p. 89.
24. *Ibid.,* pp. 77–80.
25. *Ibid.,* pp. 81–82.
26. *Memoria del congreso de 1919,* pp. 9–34.
27. Buenacasa, p. 82.
28. Nettlau MS, p. 257; Maitron, p. 299.
29. *Memoria del congreso de 1919,* p. 84.
30. *Ibid.,* p. 91.
31. *Ibid.,* pp. 93–94.
32. *Ibid.,* pp. 95–98, 102–4.
33. *Ibid.,* pp. 105–7.
34. *Ibid.,* pp. 107–9.
35. *Ibid.,* pp. 109–10.
36. *Ibid.,* pp. 116–17.
37. *Ibid.,* pp. 117–19.
38. *Ibid.,* pp. 120–21.
39. *Ibid.,* pp. 121–23.
40. *Ibid.,* p. 125.
41. *Ibid.,* pp. 125–30.
42. *Ibid.,* pp. 132–33.
43. *Ibid.,* pp. 140–42.
44. *Ibid.,* pp. 134–37.
45. Buenacasa, p. 85.
46. *Memoria del congreso de 1919,* pp. 139–41.
47. *Ibid.,* pp. 156–57.
48. *Ibid.,* p. 158.
49. *Ibid.,* p. 167.
50. *Ibid.,* p. 168.
51. *Ibid.,* p. 172.
52. *Ibid.,* pp. 346–52.
53. *Ibid.,* pp. 368–71.
54. *Ibid.,* p. 357.
55. *Ibid.,* pp. 359–62.
56. *Ibid.,* p. 367.
57. *Ibid.,* p. 344.
58. *Ibid.,* pp. 363–66.
59. Peirats, *Los anarquistas,* p. 28.
60. The resolution appears in *Memoria del congreso de 1919,* p. 373.
61. The significance of this resolution was that it formulated what had previously been implicit: the interdependence of Anarchism and Syndicalism within the CNT. Thus Rafael Vidiella says that "Anarchosyndicalism was born" in the Congress of the Comedia. The complaint of the "pure" Syndicalists was that by officially committing the CNT to Anarchist norms the resolution confounded Anarchism and Syndicalism and narrowed the area within which the organization could maneuver. The explicit commitment to Anarchism was regarded as a retreat from Syndicalist apoliticism and a kind of declaration of war against all other parties, implying the exclusion from the CNT of those workers who were republicans or Socialists. Thus, it was felt, the resolution prevented the CNT from achieving alliances or understandings with various political organizations for the purpose of broadening those

political freedoms that the "pure" Syndicalists viewed as essential to the growth and success of the trade-union movement. See Vidiella, "Causas del desarrollo, apogeo y decadencia de la CNT," *Leviatán*, No. 10 (Feb. 1935), p. 30. The Anarchist Ricardo Sanz concurred, in effect, with Vidiella, saying that "alongside the old energizers and creators of militant Syndicalism, one found in the Congress of the Comedia, as delegates, a series of new *valores* with an exuberant quantity of ideas, new conceptions of the class struggle that were a surprise and a revelation. Anarchosyndicalism revealed itself for the first time without equivocations or [disguises] as a constructive thing." Sanz, *El sindicalismo*, p. 40.

Chapter Nine

1. Lenin's *Notebooks on imperialism* reveal only the most perfunctory interest in Spain and little real knowledge. Though noting Spain's dependence on France for investment capital, Lenin does not specifically identify Spain as a "semicolonial" country, nor does he seem to be aware of the extent of British and Belgian investment. He discusses peasant uprisings among the Rumanians and the Hottentots, but reveals no awareness of the agrarian problem in Spain. He quotes with approval, however, Engels's comment that "the Bakuninists in Spain have given us an incomparable example how *not* to make a revolution." Lenin, *Collected works*, XXXIX, 493ff, 555, 562, 566, 680, 682.
2. Maurín, *Révolution et contre-révolution*, p. 132; Pestaña, *Memoria*, p. 22.
3. *Kommunisticheskii Internatsional*, No. 5 (Sept. 1919), pp. 763–64.
4. *L'Internationale Communiste*, No. 9 (Apr. 1920), col. 1484.
5. E. H. Carr, III(4), 175–76.
6. Gómez, pp. 34–41; *Bolshaia Sovietskaia Entsiklopediia*, 1st ed. (1926), p. 182; letter from Manuel Gómez to the author, 16.v.65; letter from Luis Portela to the author, 29.iv.65. For a more extensive treatment of Borodin's mission to Latin America, see Draper, III, 236–41. I have found the account of Borodin's mission to Spain presented in M. N. Roy's *Memoirs* (Bombay, 1964) almost wholly fictional, especially where it suggests that Roy played a part in Borodin's contacts with the Spaniards, which he did not (pp. 223–36). See also Arthur N. Holcombe, *The spirit of the Chinese Revolution* (New York, 1930), pp. 47–48.
7. Letter from Manuel Gómez, 16.v.65.
8. *Ibid.*; Gómez, p. 41; *El Sol*, 25.iv.20.
9. Gómez, pp. 35–36. The English Communist J. T. Murphy, who met the Russian emissary a few weeks later in Amsterdam, wrote: "I was especially attracted to Borodin. He was a tall, well-built, black-haired, swarthy-complected man, an excellent linguist, thoroughly acquainted with the general literature and history of many countries and a professional revolutionary to boot.... Of all the so-called 'emissaries' of Lenin I have known, I know of none more expert and capable than he in winning the confidence and regard of the people to whom he was sent." Murphy, pp. 88–89. Borodin was extremely serious and was reputed to have a "passion for equality." In Russia, in the presence of the beautiful English sculptress Clare Sheridan he was capable of asking, "What is your economic position in the world?" Sheridan wrote: "We had supper together, of cabbage soup and tepid rice, and talked until 2 A.M. Michael always says that the food is eatable even if it is not. He never complains, he just pretends to eat it.... He wants me to think about a statue interpreting the Soviet idea, and told me a good deal about the III International, as representing a world brotherhood of workers. The plan of the International is very fine: 'Workmen of the world unite.' If they did unite they could hold

the peace of the world forever. . . . He has encouraged and cheered and tolerated me. He reminds me sometimes of Munthe, in his adhesion to his convictions and his demands that one should live up to one's idealism." Sheridan, pp. 87, 104, 121–22.

10. Cole, IV(1), 318–20.

11. *El Comunista*, 18–21.v.21.

12. Merino Gracia in *El Sol*, 25.iv.20. See also Merino's article "Un año de vida," in *El Comunista*, 16.iv.21, and Portela's article, *ibid.*, 21.v.21.

13. *HDA*, [10], "Rapport de A. Graziadei," 18.i.22.

14. "Como juzga Borodin el socialismo español," *El Comunista*, 1.iv.20. For the left-centrists' version of Borodin's visit see "Declaraciones de Borodin," *Nuestra Palabra*, 12.ii.20. The left-centrist leaders responded to Borodin with a certain amount of humility: "The deficiency of our doctrinal culture, the prolonged alliance with the radical bourgeois factions, the *fobias* and *filias* of the war, have created among Spanish workers a series of confusions that at times prevented us from appreciating the principles of class struggle. . . . Borodin's words open before our eyes new horizons, and dissipate many of the nebulosities that weaken our revolutionary action. [Borodin also reveals] to many comrades . . . that the Third International is not a fantasy, that it is an organization with existence in reality." *Ibid.*, 19.ii.20.

15. *El Sol*, 25.iv.20; letter from Manuel Gómez, 16.v.65. Borodin's next appearance was at the Conference of the Amsterdam Bureau, which met early in February. From there he returned to Russia, where he attended the Second Congress of the Comintern in Moscow in the summer of 1920. When Borodin left Russia in October 1920, he announced that he was returning to Madrid; and, indeed, the Spanish Communists were expecting him. But he never returned to Spain, and the men of the PCE last heard of him in Berlin. They felt somewhat betrayed by him, since he was supposed to be bringing them money. Sheridan, p. 120; Andrade to Geers, 29.xii.20, *AGC*.

16. Portela MS, I, 78–82.

17. *Renovación*, 17.iii.20.

18. *Ibid*. The assertion of García Venero (*Historia de las internacionales*, II, 326) that García Cortés engineered the schism of the Young Socialists does not correspond to the facts. García Cortés was, in fact, the *bête noire* of the Madrid group, who disliked him for the corrupt electoralism that they felt he represented. Nor did García Cortés approve of the split. Portela MS, IV, 11–25; *El Comunista*, i.v.20.

19. Portela MS, I, 83–86. The members of the FJS National Committee who organized the coup were José Illescas (vice-president), Ramón Merino Gracia (secretary), Luis Portela (vice-secretary), Tiburicio Pico (director of *Renovación*), Vicente Pozuelo (secretary of meetings), Emilio Agudo (*vocal*), Eduardo Ugarte (*vocal*), Rito Esteban (*vocal*), and Eleuterio Rodríguez (*vocal*). The one member who refused to go along with the plan was José López y López, the president. Merino Gracia (p. 178) explained the decision to found the PCE in the following terms: "Upon the return of [Besteiro and Anguiano] from the Rotterdam Conference, the Socialist Party kept silent for quite some time, all the while working against the Communists. We Young Socialists were quite convinced that the members of the Party would never become true Communists and would never dream of a basic reorganization. What they want is simply a verbal adherence to the Third International." See Ramón Merino Gracia, "Le parti socialiste ouvrier," in *Le mouvement communiste international*, p. 178.

20. *Renovación*, 15.iv.20.

21. *El Comunista*, 4.v.21. It was, in fact, charged that such an influx had occurred, and Rafael Millá wrote a long article seeking to distinguish the Communism of the PCE from the "Communist Anarchism" of the Cenetistas; *ibid.*, 1.vi.20.

22. *Renovación*, 15.iv.20.

23. Portela MS, I, 84–92; *El Comunista*, 16.iv.20.

24. Portela MS, I, 91–92; *ibid.*, IV, 50; *El Comunista*, 21.v.21. Merino Gracia (p. 178) would later claim that 100 sections of the FJS adhered to the PCE, and that the total membership of the FJS had stood at 10,000. There were two Young Socialists, in particular, whom the schismatics had expected to follow them in the creation of the PCE and toward whom some bitterness was felt: José López y López and Ramón Lamoneda. *El Comunista*, 6.xi.20. The figure of 50–60 Madrid youths is mentioned by Juan Andrade; Andrade to Geers, Oct. [?] 1920, *AGC*.

25. *El Comunista*, 16.iv.21. By June, the headquarters of the PCE had been moved to Calle Mendizábal 87, the premises of the New School.

26. Portela MS, III, 1–3. For Merino Gracia's views on progressive education, see *El Socialista*, 12.v.17.

27. *HDA*, [10], "Rapport de A. Graziadei."

28. Interview with Luis Portela, 17.v.64.

29. Andrade to Geers, [June 1920?], *AGC*.

30. Andrade to Geers, 28.vii.20, *ibid*.

31. *Ibid.*; Castro Delgado, p. 62.

32. *El Comunista*, 16.iv.21.

33. Portela MS, III, 4; Balbontín, pp. 147–49, 154–55. Graziadei regarded Ugarte as extremely intelligent but not quite mature intellectually and as suffering from the "malade d'infantilisme"; *HDA*, [10].

34. Portela MS, III, 8–9; Andrade to Geers, 9.vi.20, *AGC*.

35. Portela MS, IV, 7–9.   36. *Ibid.*, III, 6–8.

37. *Ibid.*, 14–15.   38. *Ibid.*, 11–12.

39. *Ibid.*, 9–15.   40. Hulse, pp. 152–60.

41. Andrade to Geers, 20.v.20, 9.vi.20, and 3.vii.20, *AGC*; *El Comunista*, 16.v.20.

42. *El Comunista*, 1.v.20.

43. Andrade to Geers, [May 1920?], *AGC*.

44. *El Comunista*, 9.iv.20.

45. *Ibid.*, 20.iv.21.

46. *Ibid.*, 9.iv.21.

47. Andrade to Geers, 20.v.20 and 29.xii.20, *AGC*. The disaffiliation of the Amsterdam Bureau is discussed in *El Comunista*, 1.vi.20.

48. Andrade to Geers, [1920], *AGC*. Andrade wrote: "I have *en cartera* an article against the opportunism of [Lenin and Radek]. I have taken it from *Kommunismus* of Vienna. It seems to me very correct. [The Bolsheviks] are doing things in a very centrist way. The last *folleto* of Lenin against the extremists is abominable. How the Spanish centrists will read it! Lenin is giving his arm to our enemies. With this work in hand, the Spanish centrists, if they were not so brutish and uncultured, could discredit us with the working class. But the situation is not so bad as it might be, since as of now they do not even know that it has been published." Andrade to Geers, 4.vi.20, *AGC*.

49. *El Comunista*, 27.xi.20.

50. Andrade to Geers, 28.viii.20, *AGC*.

51. *Renovación*, 15.iv.20.
52. Andrade to Geers, 28.viii.20, *AGC*.
53. *Ibid.*   54. *El Comunista*, 20.xi.20.
55. *Ibid.*, 27.xi.20.   56. *Ibid.*
57. Andrade to Geers, [winter 1921–22], *AGC*.
58. *El Comunista*, 5.iii.21.
59. Andrade to Geers, 29.xii.20, *AGC*.
60. The commitment to elitist purity was given frankest expression in an article entitled "The chosen," *El Comunista*, 3.vii.20. In November 1921 the men of the PCE would deny the accusation made by rival Communists that their goal was to form "a reduced nucleus of pure Communists," but at the same time they would admit that "many people have been expelled from our Party who were in error. We do not regret this. The Communists will now see, when the fusion is made [with the PCO], the magnificent results of purifying the Party. . . . The masses must conquer, yes; but in order to make of each worker an excellent Communist militant." *El Nuevo Orden*, 9.xi.21.
61. *Nuestra Palabra*, 12.ii.20.
62. The PCE militants rejected the idea that the revolution would not come for twenty or thirty years: "On the contrary, the Communists consider that the social regime for which we are fighting will come into our hands without much delay— a question of three or four years at the most. As a result, it is necessary to change our attitude, laying aside all reformist feeling in order to expend all our energy in preparing *la lucha final*." *El Comunista*, 1.v.20.
63. This manifesto, which was said to have been drawn up in the presence of Borodin, was clearly antischismatic in intent, being premised on the need to take a united party into the Comintern. It was signed by Virginia González, Daniel Anguiano, Mariano García Cortés, José González de Ubieta, Ramón Lamoneda, Ramón Merino Gracia, Manuel Núñez de Arenas, and César González. *Nuestra Palabra*, 12.ii.20; *El Comunista*, 21.v.21. The document is summarized in Callejas, pp. 445–46.
64. *El Socialista*, 12.ii.20. The postponement of the Geneva Conference and the report brought back from Rotterdam by Besteiro finally converted the Asturian leader Isidoro Acevedo to the belief that the PSOE had no alternative but to enter the Third International; *ibid.*, 12.iv.21.
65. *Ibid.*, 24.ii.20.
66. *Ibid.*, 25.vi.20. In the Ramírez letter, Besteiro was referred to as a "radical Menshevik"; *El Sol*, 23.iv.20.
67. Rapp-Lantaron, pp. 92–93. For an account of the debate over Anguiano's misdemeanor, see Comín Colomer, *Historia del partido comunista*, pp. 51–52.
68. Rapp-Lantaron, p. 94; Merino Gracia, p. 178.
69. *El Sol*, 25.iv.20; *El Comunista*, 1.v.20. Torralba Beci was strongly opposed to the expulsion of Merino Gracia, and spoke of "the signal cowardice of expelling a comrade for the crime of having created the Communist Party but giving as the reason for his expulsioin that he had calumniated another comrade." *El Comunista*, 1.v.20.
70. *Ibid.*   71. *Ibid.*, 22.iv.20.
72. Cole, IV(1), 324.   73. *El Socialista*, 15.vi.20.
74. *Ibid.*, 11.vi.20.   75. Borkenau, p. 184.
76. *El Socialista*, 11.vi.20.   77. *Ibid.*, 14.vi.20.
78. Saborit, *Julián Besteiro*, p. 183. The journal *España*, expressing the views of

Luis Araquistáin and the left-wing intelligentsia, made this comment on the attitude of the Socialist leaders: "From Russia sounds a voice of historical duty; from the bosom of the Executive Committee of the [PSOE] responds a voice of utilitarianism, of opportunism, of possibilism.... We say frankly: taking into account the responsibilities that weigh on the leaders of Spanish Socialism and agreeing that it is necessary to proceed with caution, we would have liked to see in the majority report a little more boldness, idealism, and historical feeling." *España*, 26.vi.20.

79. *El Socialista*, 11.vi.20.

80. *España*, 26.vi.20.

81. *El Socialista*, 19.vi.20. Pérez Solís later denigrated the ideological content of the dispute over the Comintern: "In reality, under the appearance of the struggle for and against Bolshevism, what caused the ferment was the profound discontent of the laboring masses of those days. One part of them, whether the most balanced or the most inert I do not know, did not wish to change the slow pace marked out from Madrid by the leaders of Spanish Socialism for another more lively; the other part, in contrast, either because they felt the necessity of going faster or because they were influenced by the convulsive social phenomena then occurring in and outside of Spain, believed that the Spanish labor movement needed to step up the pace. At bottom, the dispute reduced to this, although the addicts of each side said that the motive was Bolshevism. [But] so little was known of Bolshevism, though its friends as well as its enemies could intuitively divine something of it, that the Bolshevism of the one side and the anti-Bolshevism of the other were scarcely more than labels hastily chosen to distinguish oneself from one's opponent." Pérez Solís, *Memorias*, pp. 273–74.

82. *El Socialista*, 19.vi.20.

83. Pérez Solís, *Memorias*, pp. 224ff.

84. *El Socialista*, 18.vi.20.

85. *Ibid.*, 22.vi.20; Denjean, p. 147.

86. *El Socialista*, 22.vi.20 and 24.vi.20.

87. *Ibid.*, 23.vi.20.

88. *Ibid.*

89. *Ibid.*

90. *Ibid.*

91. *Ibid.*, 25.vi.20.

92. Andrade to Geers, 3.vii.20, *AGC*.

93. *El Socialista*, 26.vi.20.

94. *L'Humanité*, 2.vii.20.

95. See Chapter 10.

96. Saborit, *Julián Besteiro*, p. 184.

97. García Venero, *Historia de las internacionales*, II, 252; *El Socialista*, 8.vii.20.

98. Rapp-Lantaron, p. 95.

99. For a somewhat harsh indictment of bureaucratic tendencies within the PSOE-UGT, see Andrade, pp. 204–73. For a more general treatment of the same problem see Michels, *Political parties*.

100. On the theme of "amateurism" in the CNT see Pestaña, *Normas orgánicas*.

101. Largo Caballero, *Mis recuerdos*, pp. 28–33.

102. *Ibid.*, p. 34.

103. *Ibid.*, p. 37.

104. *Ibid.*, p. 34.

105. *Ibid.*, p. 35.

106. *Ibid.*, p. 53; Madariaga, *Spain*, p. 450.

107. Largo Caballero, *Mis recuerdos*, pp. 40–42; Burgos y Mazo, *El verano de 1919*, p. 327.

108. *El Comunista*, 1.vi.20. Similar criticism of the bureaucratic tendencies of the UGT appeared in *Nuestra Palabra*, 10.viii.18.

109. The complete Communist program at this time is found in *El Comunista*, May 1, 1920.

110. For biographical information on Llaneza, see Saborit, *Asturias*, pp. 137–222.

111. *Ibid.*, pp. 182–83; *El Socialista*, 2.vii.20.
112. Saborit, *Asturias*, pp. 182–83; *España*, 17.vii.20.
113. García Venero, *Historia de los movimientos*, p. 405. For the complete statutes of the UGT, adopted at this Congress, see *ibid.*, pp. 441–61.
114. See pp. 39ff.

Chapter Ten

1. E. H. Carr, III, 161–69, 181–86.
2. Lenin, *"Left-wing" Communism*, pp. 7–8, 10.
3. Trotsky, pp. 22–23.
4. Rosmer, *Moscou sous Lénine*, pp. 75–88.
5. Pestaña, *Setenta días: Lo que yo ví*, p. 8. Quemades was considered to be somewhat anti-Comintern; *El Socialista*, 13.vii.21.
6. Pestaña, *Setenta días: Lo que yo ví*, pp. 5–14; Pestaña, *Memoria*, p. 18.
7. Pestaña, *Setenta días: Lo que yo ví*, p. 19.
8. Pestaña, *Lo que aprendí*, p. 109.
9. *Ibid.*, pp. 13, 109.
10. *Ibid.*, p. 14.
11. *Ibid.*, pp. 111–13. Pestaña went on to remark: "My attention was drawn to the 'racial' hatred that [seethed] all around. The Navarros and Aragoneses, for example, did not mix with the Vizcainos or Asturianos.... The same was true between the Vizcainos and men from other regions. The Riojanos also kept to themselves. But one most noted this race hatred between the Gallegos and all the rest; for all were united against the Gallegos, who were the butt of all jokes." *Ibid.*
12. *Ibid.*, pp. 24–25.
13. *Ibid.*, pp. 26–27. Pestaña's visage often seemed overcast with melancholy, and Salvador Seguí would refer to him as the "Knight of the Woeful Countenance." Foix, p. 127.
14. Pestaña, *Lo que aprendí*, pp. 117–18.
15. *Ibid.*, pp. 119–20.
16. *Ibid.*, p. 120.
17. *Ibid.*, pp. 29–33.
18. *Ibid.*, pp. 37–40.
19. *Ibid.*, pp. 40, 45–46.
20. *Ibid.*, pp. 46–47.
21. *Ibid.*, pp. 66–73.
22. Nettlau MS, p. 264. Pere Foix believes that up to 1922 Pestaña actually constituted the "Anarchist opposition" to Seguí. He describes Pestaña as the Cenetista leader who was "most often" opposed to Seguí's policies, and he suggests that Anarchist resentment toward Seguí might have taken more violent form had not Pestaña acted as a mediator. Yet he also asserts that after Seguí's death (1923) Pestaña evolved toward the very position that Seguí had maintained. Foix, p. 128. My belief is that even before 1922 the disagreement between the two men was more verbal than substantive—something most clearly demonstrated, perhaps, by the essential similarity of their views on the Bolshevik Revolution.
23. Burgos y Mazo, *El verano de 1919*, p. 353.
24. Rosmer, *Moscou sous Lénine*, p. 59; Serge, *Memoirs*, p. 104.
25. Murphy, pp. 160–61; Degras, *The Communist International*, I, 187–88.
26. Pestaña, *Memoria*, pp. 34–39. Peirats errs when he says that Pestaña did not sign this document (*Los anarquistas*, p. 25). For an Anarchist defense of Pestaña in this connection, see *Le Libertaire*, 10–17.vi.21.
27. Rosmer, *Moscou sous Lénine*, p. 61.
28. *Vtoroi Kongress*, pp. 43–50.

29. *Ibid.*

30. *Ibid.*, pp. 58–59; Pestaña, *Memoria*, pp. 52–54.

31. Pestaña, *Memoria*, pp. 52–54.

32. *Ibid.*; Rosmer, *Moscou sous Lénine*, pp. 101–2. Rosmer recorded that Pestaña spoke in "un ton plus trenchant" than either Tanner or Souchy. Curiously enough, in an article he published at this time Pestaña spoke of the need for cooperation between the CNT and the new Spanish Communist Party, saying that "all the actively revolutionary forces in Spain—the [CNT] and the new Communist Party—must go arm in arm in the struggle for the liberation of the Spanish proletariat." "Professional'noe i politicheskoe dvizhenie v Ispanii," *Pravda*, 25.vii.20. Whether Pestaña actually wrote this or whether it was a phrase contributed by the editors of *Pravda* is difficult to say, though the latter seems more likely.

33. *Vtoroi Kongress*, p. 68. So far as I can determine, Lenin never made reference to Spain in any of his Comintern speeches.

34. *Ibid.*, p. 71.

35. *Ibid.*, p. 73.

36. *Ibid.*, p. 85.

37. Pestaña, *Memoria*, p. 64.

38. *Ibid.* Radek was not, in fact, well disposed toward the Anarchosyndicalists and did not hide his belief that they should be excluded from the Comintern. Rosmer, *Moscou sous Lénine*, p. 117. For Radek's attitude toward the Anarchists, see his *Anarkhisty i sovetskaia Rossiia*.

39. Pestaña, *Memoria*, pp. 65–66.

40. *Ibid.*, p. 67.

41. Albert Resis, "Comintern policy toward the world trade-union movement," in John Shelton Curtis, ed., *Essays in Russian and Soviet history in honor of Geroid Tanquary Robinson* (New York, 1963), p. 238.

42. Tsyperovich, "Internatsional professional'niykh soiuzov," *Kommunisticheskii Internatsional*, Nos. 7–8 (Nov.–Dec. 1919), pp. 983–88.

43. Lenin, *What is to be done*, pp. 40–41; Collinet, pp. 79–87; Zinoviev, pp. 10–11.

44. Pestaña, *Memoria*, p. 70.

45. *Ibid.*, p. 77. Pestaña was opposed to having the first congress of the RILU in Moscow, saying that such a meeting would have "no utility at all," since the excessive influence of the Russian Communist Party would be "as prejudicial to the conference as the Manzanilla tree is to those who sleep in its shade"; *ibid.*, pp. 40–41. He was, of course, overruled by Lozovsky.

46. Goldman, pp. 799–800.

47. Pestaña, *Consideraciones*, pp. 31–34.

48. Pestaña, *Setenta días: Lo que yo pienso*, pp. 257–62.

49. Pestaña, *Setenta días: Lo que yo vi*, pp. 192–93.

50. *Ibid.*, p. 193.

51. *Ibid.*, p. 194.

52. Quoted in Maurín, "La CNT y la III Internacional," *España Libre*, 21.x.60.

53. Pestaña, *Setenta días: Lo que yo vi*, p. 198.

54. *Le Libertaire*, 10–17.ii.22.

55. *Solidaridad Obrera*, 31.xii.20; *La Vie Ouvrière*, 4.ii.21. For the reign of Martínez Anido, see Chapter 11.

56. *El Comunista*, 27.xi.20.

57. Andrade to Geers, 29.xi.20, *AGC*.

58. *El Comunista*, 5.iii.21.

59. *Ibid.*

60. *Ibid.*

61. *El Socialista*, 18.i.21. For the text of the Twenty-one Conditions, see Degras, *The Communist International*, I, 166–72.

62. *El Socialista*, 8.i.21.

63. De los Ríos, *Mi viaje*, pp. 1–22; *El Socialista*, 10.i.21.

64. Pritchet, pp. 164–65. For the Socialist humanism of de los Ríos, see his *El sentido humanista del socialismo* (Madrid, 1926). See also Morton Kroll, "Spanish Socialism and the Spanish political environment" (unpubl. doctoral dissertation, UCLA, 1952), and Darío Pérez, *Figuras de España* (Madrid, 1930), pp. 255–68.

65. *Protokoll des Vierten Kongresses*, p. 902.

66. Anguiano was born in Haro, in Logroño province, in 1882, the son of a railroad worker. He grew up in Las Caldas in Santander province but soon moved with his father to Catarroja in Valencia. Here Anguiano became a partisan of Blasco Ibáñez and absorbed the ideas of Valencian republicanism. However, in 1905, as the result of a long correspondence-polemic with a Socialist friend in Santander over the respective merits of Socialism and Republicanism, Anguiano, characteristically, acknowledged the superiority of his friend's arguments and converted to Socialism. *Los sucesos de agosto*, pp. 25–26.

67. *El Socialista*, 18.i.21.   68. *Ibid.*

69. *Ibid.*   70. *Ibid.*

71. *Ibid.*

72. De los Ríos later reported that after this declaration, and during his subsequent stay in Russia, an attitude of "reserve and coldness" was most evident on the part of Zinoviev and Radek, whereas Bukharin and the other Bolsheviks remained entirely cordial. *Mi viaje*, p. xv.

73. *El Socialista*, 18.i.21.

74. "Au parti ouvrier socialiste espagnol," *L'Internationale Communiste*, No. 15 (Jan. 1921), cols. 3345–48.

75. *El Socialista*, 18.i.21.   76. *Ibid.*

77. *Ibid.*   78. *Ibid.*

79. *Ibid.*, 29.xii.20.   80. *Ibid.*, 19.i.21.

81. *Ibid.*

82. *Ibid.*, 17.i.21. The members of the National Committee at this time were Pablo Iglesias (presiding), Isidoro Acevedo (Asturias), Francisco Azorín (Andalusia), Remigio Cabello (Castilla la Vieja), José López Darriba (Galicia), Tomás Giner (Aragon), and the various members of the Executive Committee—Anguiano, de los Ríos, Fabra Ribas, García Quejido, Núñez de Arenas, Ovejero, and César González.

83. *Almanaque de Tierra y Libertad*, p. 196.

84. *Ibid.*, p. 3.

85. Jordán, *La dictadura del proletariado*, p. 5. This pamphlet was published by the anti-Seguí *Espartaco* group in Madrid and reflected its point of view.

86. *Almanaque de Tierra y Libertad*, p. 5.

87. *Ibid.*, p. 206. See also José Prat's pamphlet *Herejías?*

88. *Almanaque de Tierra y Libertad*, p. 186.

89. *Solidaridad Obrera* (Bilbao), 3.xii.20. The Anarchosyndicalist writer "Hector" agreed with this and observed that although the revolutionary spirit of the CNT always put it "a priori" on the side of the revolutionary forces of the world, the Cenetistas would not accept dictation. The CNT would adhere to the Third International only so long as that International conceded "autonomy to each nation to employ the tactics that it believes pertinent for the overthrow of the capitalist regime." *Ibid.*, 29.x.20.

90. Quoted in Rocker, pp. 95–96.

91. *Solidaridad Obrera* (Bilbao), 27.viii.20.

Chapter Eleven

1. Baelen, Chapter 2; Payne, *Spanish revolution*, pp. 44, 59. The number of strikes increased from 403 in 1919 (198,733 strikers) to 424 in 1920 (244,684 strikers); Balcells, p. 181.

2. The Anarchist journal *Espartaco* (22.ii.20) complained bitterly about the failure of the moderate Syndicalist leaders to meet the lockout with a revolutionary strike: "If the general strike had been declared against the lockout, even supposing that it had not taken on a revolutionary aspect, [with] shooting, fires, assaults, barricades, [in view of the then-existing cohesion] of the workers' forces, the bourgeoisie would have had to yield through hunger before us, since we are used to hunger and the bourgeoisie are not; but since bread was available [because of the failure to strike], those who could buy [bread] ate it, and there was left to the locked-out workers no way to avoid starving to death other than to be shot or to surrender."

3. Fernández Almagro, pp. 369–70.

4. Francés, p. 441. Nine of the rebellious soldiers fled the barracks and escaped. There was no response to the coup in the city of Zaragoza, and the Syndicalist organization there was at some pains to inform the authorities that the plot had been a "purely personal" effort by Chueca, of which they had no knowledge. Díaz-Plaja, V, 449–52. There were no further uprisings among the soldiers, but there continued to be some cause for concern. In the summer of 1920 a correspondent for *La Vie Ouvrière* reported that the inscriptions "Long Live the Soviets" and "Long Live the Revolution" appeared on the walls of barracks at the main staff headquarters; Rapp-Lantaron, p. 81.

5. Quoted in *El Comunista* (Zaragoza), 6.ii.20.

6. Salaya, pp. 26–27, notes: "The measures of the government amount to no more than a mere change of governors. Formidable strategy, that of the men who control the destiny of Spain! Half a turn to the right, half a turn to the left. Did the departing governor defend the employers? Then the entering governor protected the sindicatos. A charming way to achieve political and economic equilibrium!"

7. Buenacasa, p. 217.

8. Soldevilla, *Un segle de vida*, p. 1331.

9. Pestaña, *Lo que aprendí*, p. 187.

10. *Ibid.*, p. 188. It may be noted that the Barcelona Local Federation apparently continued to make efforts to curtail the terrorists within its ranks. On November 17, 1920, it caused to have published in the journal *España Nueva* (ostensibly in the name of the so-called Juventud Sindicalista of Barcelona) an article that gave the names and addresses of terrorists within the CRT. Buenacasa (p. 100) could not decide whether this was an ingenuous error or a calculated move; the latter seems more probable.

11. Peirats, *Los anarquistas*, p. 29.

12. Francés, p. 420.

13. Two of the best sources on the Libres are F. Baratech Alfaro, *Los Sindicatos Libres en España*, and J. Oller Piñol, *Martínez Anido*. For a hostile impression, stressing the terrorist side of the Libres, see Peirats, *La CNT*, I, 25–28.

14. Baratech Alfaro, p. 65. Angel Pestaña acknowledged that there were many workers in the unions of the CNT who were there to defend economic rather than ideological interests. His estimate was that only 30 percent were ideological Syndicalists. *El Sol*, 19.i.21.

15. Pestaña, *Lo que aprendí*, p. 186.
16. García Venero, *Historia de los movimientos*, pp. 382–83.
17. Salaya, p. 28.   18. Baratech Alfaro, p. 68.
19. *Ibid.*, p. 70.   20. *Ibid.*, pp. 77–80.
21. Oller Piñol, pp. 40–41.
22. Baratech Alfaro (pp. 71, 76) says that the Libres attracted "important nuclei" from the following factories, among others: Girona, Fabra y Coats, Hispano-Suiza, Lainiere Española, Portabella y Compañía, Fenicada Hartman, Xarxa-nova, España Industrial, and Cascante Hermanos. Outside Barcelona, Sindicatos Libres were formed in such towns as Mataró, Manresa, Badalona, Igualada, Tárrega, Reus, Sabadell, and Rubí. *Los Sindicatos Libres*, pp. 71, 76. Nowhere does Alfaro give a precise figure for the number enrolled in the Libres in Barcelona.
23. *Ibid.*, p. 74.   24. Oller Piñol, p. 38.
25. Baratech Alfaro, pp. 73–75.   26. *Ibid.*, pp. 74–77.
27. Balcells, pp. 138–39.   28. *Ibid.*, p. 143.
29. Among others, the Valencian Syndicalist leader Eusebio Carbó was accused of complicity in this murder and was for a time imprisoned. *La Antorcha*, 7.vii.22.
30. Balcells, p. 138. On April 30, 1923, the Libres published a lengthy statement exonerating themselves and blaming the Unicos for all terrorist activity; see Baratech Alfaro, pp. 133–41.
31. See Chapter 9.
32. Gasset, pp. 6–8.
33. *Ibid.*, p. 170. On the conservative identification of Syndicalism and Bolshevism in this period, see A. del Castillo, "Bolshevism in Spain," *Living Age*, XX (Oct.–Dec. 1920), 762–64.
34. Gasset, pp. 248–55.   35. Seco Serrano, p. 131.
36. *Ibid.*, p. 133.   37. Balcells, p. 145.
38. Díaz-Plaja, V, 457; Tuñón de Lara, *Introducció*, p. 298.
39. Díaz-Plaja, V, 458.
40. Balcells, p. 149. The signatories for the UGT were Largo Caballero, Manuel Cordero, Luis Fernández, Juan de los Toyos, and Lucio Martínez Gil.
41. Such, at least, was the conviction of *El Comunista*, 6.xi.20.
42. *El Socialista*, 5.x.20.
43. *El Comunista*, 6.xi.20; Buenacasa, p. 98.
44. Buenacasa, p. 99.   45. Oller Piñol, pp. 43–44.
46. *El Comunista*, 20.xi.20.   47. Baratech Alfaro, p. 81.
48. Oller Piñol, pp. 45–47.
49. A lengthy statement by Bas on the problems and perils of his governorship is recorded in Madrid, *Ocho meses*, 79–93. The outlook of the capitalist class during the Restoration era is discussed in Antoni Jutglar, *Actitudes conservadores ante la realidad obrera: la etapa de la Restauración*. (Madrid, 1970).
50. Baelen, pp. 26–27; Balcells, pp. 159ff. The price drop was especially severe for textiles and metal products. Thus for woolen textiles the price index fell from 362.9 in 1919 to 330.1 in 1920 and to 200.3 at the end of 1921; INE, *Principales actividades*, p. 147. For the period from September 1919 to March 1921 the overall movement of prices, taken at six-month intervals, was as follows: in the countryside, 190.9, 208.1, 220.3, and 185.7; in the cities, 180, 192.3, 202.6, and 173.5. See Tusell, p. 159.
51. Oller Piñol, pp. 51–52.
52. Madrid, *Las últimas veinticuatro horas*, pp. 29–30.

53. Oller Piñol, pp. 51–52.
54. *Ibid.*, pp. 52–53.
55. *Ibid.*, p. 51.
56. Baratech Alfaro, p. 62.
57. *El Sol*, 15.ii.22.
58. Oller Piñol, pp. 54–55; Baratech Alfaro, p. 85.
59. Madrid, *Las últimas veinticuatro horas*, pp. 31–32.
60. Oller Piñol, p. 57.
61. Balcells, p. 155.
62. *Ibid.*, p. 154.
63. Baratech Alfaro, pp. 90–91.
64. *Ibid.*, pp. 87–88.
65. *Ibid.*, p. 90.
66. *Ibid.*
67. *Ibid.*, p. 86.
68. Oller Piñol, p. 55.
69. *España*, 9.x.20; Madrid, *Las últimas veinticuatro horas*, pp. 42–43; Balcells, p. 164.
70. *España*, 13.xi.20.
71. Madrid, *Las últimas veinticuatro horas*, p. 66.
72. *Ibid.*, p. 54.
73. *Ibid.*, pp. 54–55. See also *El Comunista*, 6.xi.20. The young Communists of the PCE spoke of the "monstrous marriage" between the Seguistas and the bourgeois republicans; *ibid.*, 20.xi.20.
74. Madrid, *Las últimas veinticuatro horas*, pp. 64–65.
75. *Ibid.*, p. 68.
76. *Solidaridad Obrera* (Bilbao), 17.xii.20.
77. Tuñón de Lara, *Introducció*, p. 301.
78. *Solidaridad Obrera* (Bilbao), 17.xii.20.
79. *Ibid.*
80. García Venero, *Historia de los movimientos*, p. 406.
81. Buenacasa, pp. 101–2.
82. *España*, 25.xii.20.
83. *Ibid.*, 9.x.20.
84. Martínez Cuadrado, II, 829.
85. *España*, 18.xii.20.
86. *Ibid.*, 25.xii.20.
87. *Ibid.*
88. Martínez Cuadrado, II, footnote on pp. 830–31.
89. García Venero, *Historia de los movimientos*, pp. 406–7; Tusell, pp. 158–69.
90. Seco Serrano, p. 129. Strike activity was at a low ebb in this period, dropping from 424 strikes in 1920 to 233 strikes in 1921. The number of strikers dropped by 66 percent. Balcells, p. 181.
91. R. Sanz, p. 53.
92. *Ibid.*
93. *Ibid.*
94. *Ibid.*, pp. 87–88.
95. Oller Piñol (p. 106) confirms the extreme youthfulness of many of the pistoleros, noting the "curious fact" that the majority of those arrested were between the ages of 15 and 20. Ricardo Sanz (pp. 97–98, 103–4) remarks that almost all the members of the action groups were between the ages of 18 and 25, with very few over that age.
96. R. Sanz, p. 59.
97. Anido himself seems never to have acknowledged his reliance on these two policies; and his biographer devotes only one sentence to the repatriations; Oller Piñol, p. 66. For an otherwise rather frank discussion of the Barcelona social scene and the nature of the Anarchosyndicalist movement, see the interview of Anido in *El Sol*, 15.ii.22.
98. Leval, pp. 50–51; *España*, 4.xii.20.
99. Nin, "Pourquoi Dato fut assassiné," p. 6.
100. R. Sanz, p. 61.

101. *Ibid.*; Baratech Alfaro, p. 95; Oller Piñol, pp. 96–98.
102. R. Sanz, p. 67.
103. *Ibid.*, p. 73.
104. *Ibid.*
105. Pabón, II(1), 211–12. Andrés Nin said, regarding Dato's death: "The terrorist attack cannot be justified at all; its revolutionary value is more than doubtful, but it is providential. Dato's politics inevitably led to his tragic end. He was not assassinated: he committed suicide." Nin, "Pourquoi Dato fut assassiné," p. 7.
106. *El Comunista*, 2.iv.21; *La Antorcha*, 11.v.23.
107. Prieto, *De mi vida*, p. 309. For the protest of the Communist International against the repression in Spain, see "La terreur blanche en Espagne," *L'International Communiste*, No. 16 (Mar. 1921), cols. 3717–20.
108. Oller Piñol's *Martínez Anido* is a very sympathetic and rather biased treatment of the subject but supplies a useful corrective to the views of the Syndicalists and their sympathizers.

109. R. Sanz, p. 58.
110. *El Sol*, 15.ii.22.
111. Oller Piñol, p. 101.
112. Baratech Alfaro, p. 95.
113. Oller Piñol, p. 106.
114. *Ibid.*, pp. 104–8.

115. Nin, pp. 6–7. The names of these militants are listed in Peirats, *Los anarquistas*, I, 24–25. In 1923 the CRT published a folleto, *Ideas y Tragedia*, listing 106 Cenetista militants dead and 41 wounded. Gómez Casas, p. 143.
116. Nin, p. 7.
117. *Ibid.*
118. Díaz del Moral, p. 391.

Chapter Twelve

1. *El Socialista*, 28.iii.21.
2. García Venero, *Historia de las internacionales*, II, 354.
3. *El Socialista*, 5.iv.21.
4. For example, the pro-Bolshevik intellectual Luis Araquistaín, under the impact of the Twenty-one Conditions, turned against the Communist International, fearing that the "etc." following Moscow's published list of exclusions would almost certainly include not only such Spanish leaders as Besteiro, Prieto, and Largo Caballero, but even Pablo Iglesias himself. He declared that the Conditions were "Napoleonic" in conception and would place the whole world movement under the control of a few men in Moscow. *El Socialista*, 15.x.20 and 20.x.20.

5. *Ibid.*, 1.iv.21.
6. *Ibid.*
7. *Ibid.*
8. *Ibid.*
9. *Ibid.*, 6.iv.21.
10. *Ibid.*, 9.iv.21.
11. *Ibid.*, 12.iv.21.
12. *Ibid.*, 22.vi.20; Denjean, p. 151.
13. *El Socialista*, 12.iv.21.

14. The tendency for bourgeois intellectuals to take their place at either one extreme or the other of Socialist movements is both suggested by Michels and discounted by him; Michels, pp. 293–304.
15. *El Sol*, 19.xi.19 and 23.xi.19. In understanding the expulsion of Pérez Solís, it should be kept in mind that the elections of June 1919 went very well for the Valladolid Socialists, and that the movement was spreading into the countryside with mounting success. Almost certainly, Alba sensed a threat to his control of the province, hence his desire to expel the most talented and articulate Socialist in the region. Pérez Solís, *Memorias*, pp. 204, 210.
16. Pérez Solís, *Memorias*, pp. 205–8.

17. *Ibid.*, p. 217.

18. *Ibid.*, pp. 221, 224.

19. *Ibid.*, pp. 219ff.

20. *Ibid.*, pp. 232, 261.

21. *El Comunista*, 25.v.21.

22. Pérez Solís, *Memorias*, p. 227.

23. *Ibid.*, p. 229.

24. Solís received support not only from the Perezagua faction but also from the Basque Nationalists, who were the bitter enemies of Prieto and who, indeed, had clashed with the Socialists on many occasions. He gained the editorship of the journal *Las Noticias*, which Prieto called "the first Bolshevik newspaper in Spain"—which was printed in the same plant as the Nationalist paper *Euzkadi* and may have been subsidized by the Nationalists. *El Socialista* (Toulouse), 25.xii.52.

25. Pérez Solís, *Memorias*, p. 262.

26. *Ibid.*, pp. 250–51.

27. *Ibid.*, pp. 266–69.

28. "Report presented by the National Federation of Spanish Miners," pp. 1–2; Saborit, *Asturias*, p. 196. Saborit says that along with the Railworkers' Federation, the Asturian Miners' Union formed the "keystone" of the UGT; *ibid.*, p. 161. The Asturian Socialist Party numbered only 1,144 members in 1919 but grew rapidly thereafter; "Evolución del socialismo español," p. 45.

29. Saborit, *Asturias*, p. 196.

30. *Ibid.* Prieto, in Vizcaya, likewise asserted that it was the newest and most *inconscientes* workers who favored the Comintern. *El Socialista*, 11.iv.21.

31. Brenan, p. 224; Saborit, *Asturias*, p. 206. *Memoria del Congreso de 1919*, p. 36. One sign of Syndicalist growth in this area was the establishment in 1920 of *Solidaridad Obrera* of Gijón, with Manuel Buenacasa as editor; *El movimiento obrero*, p. 97.

32. Saborit, *Asturias*, p. 183.

33. Acevedo, *Impresiones*, pp. 14–15.

34. *Ibid.*, p. 16.

35. Quoted in Saborit, *Asturias*, p. 111.

36. *Ibid.*, pp. 109–10.

37. *El Comunista*, 25.v.21.

38. E. H. Carr, III, 221–24.

39. Wohl, pp. 197–201.

40. E. H. Carr, III, 228.

41. *Ibid.*, III, 231.

42. *Ibid.*, III, 337–38.

43. *Ibid.*

44. *Ibid.*, III, 228.

45. *Ibid.*, III, 223–24.

46. The 1921 Congress began with the reading of a letter from Iglesias in which he said that a vote for the Twenty-one Conditions would be a "great error" and would immediately result in a schism in the Party's ranks. He urged acceptance of the de los Ríos proposal that the PSOE enter the Vienna Union. Morato, *Pablo Iglesias*, p. 237; *El Socialista*, 12.iv.21.

47. *El Socialista*, 11.iv.21; E. H. Carr, III, 224.

48. *El Socialista*, 11.iv.21.

49. *Ibid.*

50. *Ibid.*

51. *Ibid.*

52. *Ibid.*

53. Condition Twenty-one stated: "Those members of the party who reject in principle the conditions and theses put forward by the Communist International are to be expelled from the party.... The same applies in particular to delegates to the extraordinary congresses." Degras, *The Communist International*, I, 172.

54. *El Socialista*, 12.iv.21.

55. *Ibid.*

56. *Ibid.*

57. E. H. Carr, III, 207, 211–12.

58. *El Socialista*, 12.iv.21.

59. *Ibid.*

60. *Ibid.*, 13.iv.21.

61. *Ibid.*

62. *Ibid.*

63. The youths of the PCE had apparently felt that Lamoneda was one of them,

and they made frequent references to his "betrayal" in the pages of *El Comunista*; see, for example, the issues of 6.xi.20 and 16.iv.21.

64. *El Socialista*, 13.iv.21.

65. *Ibid*.

66. Comín Colomer, *Historia del Partido*, p. 68; *El Socialista*, 14.iv.21.

67. *Ibid*. This represented, according to Saborit, a loss of 2,244 votes for the Comintern position, as compared with the congress of June 1920; *Julián Besteiro*, p. 188.

68. Pérez Solís, *Memorias*, pp. 275–77.

69. Pérez Solís later wrote: "It took more effort to convince Isidoro Acevedo, whose vote was extremely important, since it represented the whole Socialist Federation of Asturias. This extremely good man, for whom the Socialist and later the Communist allegiance was but a Calvary of punishments, borne with stoic firmness at a time closer to old age than to middle age, resisted taking a step that seemed imprudent; but finally, in order not to be the discordant note in the unanimity I had succeeded in establishing among the rest of the delegates... he lent his signature to the declaration." *Memorias*, p. 277. *El Comunista* (16.iv.21) observed: "The inflamed and violent attacks of the reformists put the centrists in a difficult situation. In spite of their sincere intentions not to attack the sacrosanct unity of the Party, they saw themselves forced to break it."

70. *El Socialista*, 14.iv.21. The signers of the manifesto (dated April 13) were: Oscar Pérez Solís, Facundo Perezagua, Isidoro Acevedo, Lázaro García, Virginia González, Pedro García, Mariano García Cortés, Eduardo Torralba Beci, Exoristo Salmerón, José López Darriba, José Luis Martínez Ponce, Luis Mancebo, Lorenzo Luzuriaga, José López y López, Gonzalo Morenas de Trejada, Roberto Alvarez, Severino Chacón, Manuel Pedroso, Antonio Fernández de Velasco, Carlos Carbonell, Marcelino Pascua, Manuel Martín, Evaristo Gil, Feliciano López, Luis Hernández, Eduardo Vicente, Francisco Villar, Angel Bartol, Vicente Calaza, and José Rojas (listed in Saborit, *Julián Besteiro*, p. 190). It will be noted that two names are absent from this list: Ramón Lamoneda and César González. Noting that it was Acevedo who had the deepest reservations about the schism, Pérez Solís admits: "Nevertheless, it was not he but I who in a few days, comprehending that we had gone farther than we should have, tried to put myself in touch with Acevedo —who had already returned to Asturias, as had I to Vizcaya—to find a way to rectify the mistake that had been made. But it was already too late. The declaration read by me at the Socialist Congress... could no longer be amended; the schism was consummated." Pérez Solís, *Memorias*, p. 278.

71. The organizing committee of the PCO included Virginia González, Antonio García Quejido, Daniel Anguiano, Eduardo Torralba Beci, Manuel Núñez de Arenas, Luis Mancebo, and Evaristo Gil. Comín Colomer, *Historia del Partido Comunista*, p. 106.

72. *Historia abreviada*, p. 32.

73. García Venero, *Historia de las internacionales*, II, 395.

74. *Ibid.*, p. 391.

75. Zugazagoitia, p. 62. The numerical strength of the UGT at this time was 240,114. The strength of the PSOE before the schism of 1921 was 45,477. Immediately after the schism it was 23,010. Martínez Cuadrado, II, 487.

76. *El Socialista*, 15.iv.21.   77. *Ibid*.

78. Quoted in *ibid*., 19.iv.21.   79. Bullejos, "Le mouvement," p. 323.

80. By 1925 only 10 percent of the miners would be organized; *ibid*., p. 325.

81. Manuel Vigil, quoted in *El Socialista*, 23.iv.21.

82. Saborit, *Asturias*, pp. 185–86; *El Comunista*, 23.iv.21 and 8.vi.21.

83. Torralba Beci, in *L'Humanité*, 13.vi.21.

84. Pérez Solís, *Memorias*, pp. 278–79; *Historia abreviada*, p. 35. On the labor crisis in Vizcaya, see *El Comunista*, 20.vii.21.

85. Juan Andrade in *El Comunista*, 21.v.21.

86. Quoted in *L'Humanité*, 13.vi.21.

87. Quoted in *El Comunista*, 14.iv.21.

88. Zugazagoitia, p. 62; Pérez Solís, *Memorias*, p. 278.

89. See *HDA*, [10], "Rapport de A. Graziadei." Not only had the PCE not grown since its founding, but the intense sectarianism that characterized it had resulted in numerous exclusions of the "impure" and the doctrinally inadequate. *El Nuevo orden*, 9.xi.21.

90. *La Antorcha*, 20.vii.23.

91. *El Comunista*, 27.xi.20.

92. *Ibid.*

93. *Ibid.*

94. *El Comunista*, 27.xi.20.

95. *Solidaridad Obrera* (Bilbao), 17.xii.20; *El Comunista*, 2.iv.20.

96. See *El Comunista*, 26.ii.21.

97. *Ibid.*, 16.iv.21.

98. *Lucha Social*, 9.vii.21.

99. *El Comunista*, 6.xi.20.

100. *Ibid.*, 8.vi.21.

101. *El Comunista*, 4.v.21. The theses on parliamentarianism stated in part: "It does not at all follow from the theoretical admission of parliamentary activity that participation in actual elections and in actual parliamentary sessions is *in all circumstances* absolutely necessary. That depends on a whole series of specific conditions. In certain circumstances it may be necessary to walk out of parliament.... In certain circumstances it may be necessary to boycott elections and to remove by force ... the entire bourgeois State apparatus." Degras, *The Communist International*, I, 154.

102. *El Comunista*, 8.vi.21.

103. *Ibid.*, 9.iv.21.

104. *Ibid.*, 16.iv.21 and 26.ii.21.

105. *Ibid.*, 20.iv.21.

106. See *HDA*, [10].

107. Unfortunately, I have never been able to locate any copies of the PCO organ *La Guerra Social*. Thus this discussion of PCE-PCO relations inevitably reflects the fact that the PCE point of view is far better documented, since copies of nearly all issues of *El Comunista* are still extant.

108. *El Comunista*, 14.v.21.

109. *Ibid.*

110. *Ibid.*

111. *Ibid.*

112. *Ibid.*, 18.v.21.

113. *Ibid.*, 25.v.21.

114. *Ibid.*, 21.v.21.

115. *Ibid.*

116. *Ibid.*, 25.v.21.

117. *Ibid.* But in reality, it was the PCE that had hoped to sabotage fusion efforts. In a letter to the Dutch Communist Geers, written some years later, Andrade confessed that the PCE had "waged a war to the death with the PCO" and lamented that "in spite of the efforts we made not to arrive at fusion, this came about under the coercion of the International." Andrade to Geers, 20.iii.28, *AGC*.

118. *El Comunista*, 25.v.21.

119. *Ibid.*, 25.v.21.

120. Comín Colomer, *Historia del Partido Comunista*, p. 113. The ECCI invitation to the Third Congress was sent out in May and called for the Congress to meet two months earlier than provided for in the Comintern statutes. The Communist

parties were asked to send delegations as large as possible and composed of one-third members of the Central Committee and two-thirds members who represented the local organizations of the Party and who were closely linked with the "working masses." Special importance was attached to the last point. Degras, *The Communist International*, I, 222, 224.

Chapter Thirteen

1. Peirats, *Los anarquistas*, p. 31.
2. Nettlau MS, p. 272.
3. See p. 439.
4. The journalistic world in which Nin moved is described by Claudi Ametlla, Chapters 30–33. See also the prologue by Oriol Puigvert and the biographical essay by Wilebaldo Solano in Nin, *Els moviments*, pp. 9–65.
5. Hurtado II, 62; Nin, "Pridisloviem," p. 6.
6. *Memoria del congreso de 1919*, p. 374.
7. Maurín, "Hombres e historia."
8. Maurín, "De España a Moscu."
9. Maurín, "Hombres e historia" and "La derrota"; letter to the author from Maurín, 9.viii.65.
10. See, for example, *Lucha Social*, 29.iv.22.
11. Maurín, "El II Congreso de la CNT."
12. Peirats, *Los anarquistas*, pp. 32–33.
13. Jose María Foix, a white-collar worker, expressed a characteristic Communist-Syndicalist viewpoint when he said: "Well, then, it seems to me that when the revolution has triumphed, in order to guide the economy and establish the new order it will be necessary to launch a system that without being dictatorial will have enough power to discipline the multitudes and not throw away our victories. The fear of discipline must not lead to renunciation of *la revolució salvadora*. Will the unions have enough understanding and the necessary strength to consolidate the revolution? This I doubt; and if this makes me a Communist, so be it." Pere Foix, p. 49.
14. Letter to the author from Joaquín Maurín, 9.viii.65; Bullejos, *Europa*, pp. 63–64.
15. See pp. 451–52.
16. *Lucha Social*, 21.v.21.
17. *El Comunista*, 7.v.21 and 22.vi.21.
18. *Ibid.*
19. Maurín, "La derrota."
20. *Nueva Senda*, 10.xi.21. The names of the two Anarchists are not known.
21. Maurín MS, p. 2; *Lucha Social*, 27.v.22.
22. *El Comunista*, 18.vi.21.   23. *Ibid.*
24. See Chapter 15, Note 62.   25. Maurín, "De España a Moscu."
26. Nin, *Els moviments*, pp. 27–29.
27. Interview with Gaston Leval, 29.v.64.
28. *Lucha Social*, 30.vii.21.
29. Degras, "United-front tactics," p. 10.
30. Humbert-Droz stated the dilemma of the Syndicalists: "They have retained from the old Syndicalist tradition the idea that Syndicalism is all-sufficing, and, while they take the existence of a revolutionary party into account, they are greatly embarrassed by its presence, they do not know what role to give it in the common

struggle and consider it almost as a kind of rival." *Communist International*, III, No. 19 [1921], p. 373. On the question of Profintern relations, see: A. Lozovsky, *Internatsional professional'nykh soyuzov* and "Les anarcho-syndicalistes"; Krasnyi Internatsional Profsoyuzov, *Profintern i Komintern*.

31. Williams, p. 16. The debates are summarized in *Moscu*, the journal of the First Profintern and Third Comintern Congresses. For the full stenographic text of the proceedings, see *Iyi Mezhdunarodnyi Kongress*.

32. Rosmer, *Moscou sous Lénine*, p. 192.

33. Interview with Gaston Leval, 29.v.64.

34. Nin, "Pridisloviem," p. 7.

35. Serge, *Mémoirs*, p. 157; Serge, *From Lenin to Stalin*, p. 37.

36. Victor Serge in the Preface to Maurín, *Révolution et contre-révolution*, pp. v–ix.

37. Murphy, p. 174.

38. Williams, p. 30.

39. *Lucha Social*, 3.v.22.

40. *Ibid.*, 24.vi.22.

41. *Moscou*, 10.vii.21.

42. *Ibid.*, 12.vii.21.

43. *Lucha Social*, 24.vi.22.

44. *Ibid.*

45. *Ibid.*

46. *Moscou*, 13.vii.21.

47. For the full texts of this resolution and Nin's speech on behalf of it, see *Iyi Mezhdunarodnyi Kongress*, Pt. 7, pp. 14–15.

48. Williams, p. 8.

49. The minority resolutions are printed in Williams, pp. 28–38.

50. *Ibid.*, pp. 28–30.

51. Arlandis seemed to have the greatest concern for Syndicalist autonomy, and even Nin paid lip service to the concept; *Moscou*, 13.vii.21.

52. Williams, p. 34.

53. *Ibid.*, pp. 35–37.

54. Serge, *Mémoirs*, p. 142.

55. Peirats, *Los anarquistas*, p. 28.

Chapter Fourteen

1. Page, p. 186.

2. Degras, *The Communist International*, I, 243, 246.

3. See "Theses on the structure of Communist parties," *ibid.*, I, 256–71.

4. *Ibid.*, I, 222, 224.

5. See *HDA*, [10].

6. Degras, *The Communist International*, I, 229.

7. G. Sanz, p. 20.

8. *Tretii Bsemirnyi Kongress*, p. 406. Enrique Castro Delgado has given a graphic description of this idealistic and dedicated militant: Torralba Beci was "a very tall man, somewhat bent over as though twisted by the tempestuous winds of a life longer even than his own. When he walked... his body gave the impression that all its joints had been loosened and that any moment it might fall to pieces. He wore an old black homburg bearing the sweat stains of many years. And dark suits much too large for his body, which made him appear like a large and curious puppet. By virtue of years of wear his clothes had an almost blinding sheen; and his lapels were covered with a kind of lacquer composed of spilled drinks and the ashes of many cigarettes... He shaved infrequently, and one supposes that he bathed from time to time, more from tradition than from hygiene. [He had] a long, thin face, with a color such as one sees in old houses on seacoasts; and the fingers of his left hand appeared to be made of old gold. He was neither young nor old, perhaps about 45; but he gave the impression of

one advancing rather rapidly toward old age. His wife María, always in mourning and always beautiful, was the one striking thing in that human misery; for her that man was only the guarantee of hunger and the source of many burdensome things. And [there were] two young children, whom he frequently embraced, silently, with those immensely long arms that seemed like two withered branches of an ancient tree. They lived on a narrow street near Glorieta de San Bernardino, in a sordid and depressing house, with cobwebs, dust, and mountains of books and magazines piled everywhere. But he was a great man by virtue of his sincerity, a good journalist, and a magnificent revolutionary, with or without Marx, because for him the revolution was like a mistress of whom he was eternally enamored." *Hombres made in Moscu*, p. 61.

9. *Tretii Bsemirnyi Kongress*, p. 407. It is said that the KAPD delegates, hearing that Torralba was going to speak on behalf of the "Communist Labor Party," imagined from the similarity of names that the PCO, like the KAPD, was an ultra-Left party. The tone of his speech, however, supposedly caused them to turn away, remarking, "*These* people are as Right as the German Independents"; *El Nuevo Orden*, 9.xi.21.

10. *Moscou*, 12.vii.21 and 14.vii.21. Merino, like Torralba, took liberties in describing the strength of the various movements in Spain. In an apparent slap at the Cenetista delegation led by Nin and Maurín, he informed his readers that the CNT had no more than 100,000 members, whereas the UGT enrolled better than 250,000. With respect to the Socialist Party, Merino claimed that since the April schism it had included no more than 15,000 members. For his own PCE, he boldly claimed 5,000 members and a circulation for *El Comunista* of 10 to 12 thousand. To his rival the PCO he assigned a numerical strength of less than 5,000.

11. G. Sanz, p. 20; *HDA*, [10]; *Deiatel'nost'*, pp. 9, 23, 68.

12. Raymond Carr, pp. 516–17.

13. See Payne, *Politics and the Military*, 166–70.

14. *Deiatel'nost'*, pp. 213–14.

15. "K ispanskomu proletariatu," *Deiatel'nost'*, pp. 214–16; *Lucha Social*, 29.x.21; Seco Serrano, pp. 141ff.

16. *La Antorcha*, 19.i.23. This strike was effective only in Vizcaya, where Facundo Perezagua took the lead. In Bilbao the strike was total, and when Perezagua spoke in the *ayuntamiento* against the prosecution of the war, he and some 40 other Communists were immediately arrested. Nevertheless, the Miners' Union continued the strike in the whole zone until Bilbao was occupied by the army in the first days of August. Tuñón de Lara, in Núñez de Arenas, *Historia del movimiento*, p. 221.

17. Oller Piñol, pp. 109–10.

18. *Ibid.*, p. 69; Pérez Solís, *Memorias*, p. 275.

19. *La Antorcha*, 15.xii.22.

20. *El Nuevo Orden*, 3.ix.21. This journal, which appeared for only a few issues, replaced *El Comunista* and was, in turn, replaced by *La Antorcha*, the organ of the unified Communist Party.

21. *HDA*, [10].

22. *Ibid.*

23. *Ibid.*

24. See p. 264.

25. *HDA*, [10].

26. *Ibid.*

27. *Ibid.*

28. *HDA*, [1], "Document consacrant la fusion."

29. *HDA*, [10].

30. Interview with Luis Portela, 17–22.v.64; *HDA*, [8], "Platform de l'opposition."

31. *HDA*, [8].

32. *HDA*, [3], "'Group Communiste' à Zinoviev"; *HDA*, [11], "Rapport-mémoire de Humbert-Droz."

33. *HDA*, [8].

34. Page, p. 194.

35. *HDA*, [3].

36. *HDA*, [2], "Les exclus du Comité Central."

37. *HDA*, [7], Merino Gracia to Humbert-Droz; *HDA*, [11].

38. Portela MS, IV, p. 3.

39. *HDA*, [11]; *HDA*, [5], "Lettre d'Humbert-Droz au Presidium de l'Internationale Communiste."

40. *Ibid.*

41. *Ibid.*

42. *HDA*, [11].

43. *Ibid.*; *HDA*, [5].

44. *HDA*, [11].

45. *La Antorcha*, 24.xi.22.

46. *Ibid.*, 8.vi.23.

47. Regarding the problems of the returning delegates, see *Lucha Social*, 26.xi.21.

48. Oller Piñol, p. 111.

49. Another aspect of the Anarchist revival of this period was the urging by some militants that the CNT return to craft-unionism; *Lucha Social*, 26.xi.21.

50. *Lucha Social*, 12.xi.21.

51. Nettlau MS, p. 277; *Lucha Social*, 26.xi.21.

52. *Lucha Social*, 8.iv.22.

53. For references to the Durán charges, see *Nueva Senda*, 10.xi.21.

54. *Ibid.*

55. *Ibid.*, 26.i.22.

56. *Ibid.*, 19.x.21.

57. *Ibid.*, 10.xi.21.

58. *Ibid.*, 26.i.22.

59. *Ibid.*

60. Buenacasa also edited, for a time, *Solidaridad Obrera* in Gijón; *El movimiento obrero*, p. 77.

61. *Solidaridad Obrera* (Bilbao), 3.xii.20.

62. *Lucha Social*, 27.viii.21.

63. *Nueva Senda*, 10.xi.21.

64. *Lucha Social*, 19.xi.21.

65. *Ibid.*

66. *Ibid.*

67. *Ibid.*, 12.xi.21 and 8.iv.22.

68. Nin, *Els moviments*, pp. 31–32; Maurín MS, pp. 4–5.

69. *Lucha Social*, 29.iv.22.

70. Nin, "Pridisloviem," p. 7.

71. *Lucha Social*, 29.iv.22.

72. *Ibid.*, 22.iv.22.

73. *Ibid.*, 29.iv.22.

74. *Ibid.*, 4.iii.22.

75. *Ibid.*

76. *Ibid.*

77. *Ibid.*, 6.viii.21.

78. *Ibid.*, 23.iv.21.

79. *Ibid.*, 19.xi.21.

80. Letter from Joaquín Maurín, 9.viii.65.

81. *HDA*, [9], "Rapport au Comité Executif."

Chapter Fifteen

1. García Venero, *Historia de los movimientos*, p. 412.

2. Pérez Solís, *Memorias*, p. 280. The unwisdom of many of the Communist strikes in this region would later be remarked by the Comintern delegate Jules Humbert-Droz; *HDA*, [9].

3. Pérez Solís, *Memorias*, pp. 279–80.

4. Prieto, *Yo y Moscu*, pp. 310ff. 5. Farré Moregó, p. 283.

6. Pérez Solís, *Memorias*, p. 280. 7. Prieto, *Entre sijos*, p. 75.

8. Pérez Solís, *Memorias*, pp. 296–305. Solís's major polemical effort in this period—perhaps reflecting his conversations with Casanellas—was a lengthy and vigorous tract, *Cartas a un anarquista* (Madrid, 1923), which appeared serially in *La Antorcha* and was an effort to convert the Cenetistas to an appreciation of the need for political leadership and tactics. On Casanellas's conversion to Bolshevism, see Acevedo, *Impresiones*, pp. 70–75.

9. *El Sol*, 11.i.22, 13.i.22, 19.ii.22, and 11.iv.22; *La Antorcha*, 24.xi.22.

10. Saborit, *Asturias*, pp. 186–97.

11. Bullejos, "Le mouvement," p. 323.

12. Degras, *The Communist International*, I, 308.

13. Degras, "United-front tactics," p. 13.

14. Degras, *The Communist International*, I, 308.

15. *Ibid*.

16. Rosmer, *Moscou sous Lénine*, p. 207.

17. García Venero, *Historia de las internacionales*, II, 393.

18. *La Antorcha*, 6.vi.23.

19. *Historia abreviada*, p. 34. On the role of the Comintern agent Humbert-Droz in bringing this congress to an acceptance of the United Front, see *HDA*, [6], "Lettre d'Humbert-Droz au Secretariat."

20. *Lucha Social*, 4.ii.22 and 11.ii.22.

21. Bullejos, "Le mouvement," p. 323.

22. *El Sol*, 11.iv.22; Ibarruri, p. 72. The employers issued a statement seeking to explain the economic plight of the mining industry and to justify on the basis of prices, costs, and productivity the step they were taking; it is quoted in part in Baelen, pp. 102–3.

23. *El Sol*, 11.iv.22; Ibarruri, p. 72.

24. Bullejos, "Le mouvement," pp. 323–24.

25. *La Antorcha*, 15.vi.23.

26. *El Sol*, 16.v.22.

27. *Ibid*.

28. Bullejos, "Le mouvement," p. 324; *La Antorcha*, 22.ix.22. The settlement—worked out with the help of the Minister of Labor, Sr. Calderón, and with the aid of Llaneza, Suárez, Saborit, and others—was clearly designed to encourage greater productivity in the mines. Work resumed on August 9, with no reprisals and with a 5 percent reduction in wages. The workers agreed to work more intensively and to increase production by 10 percent over the prestrike level. Their performance would be assessed by a mixed commission early in November, and if production had by then increased by at least 20 percent, wages would return to their former level. Baelen, pp. 103–4. This August settlement was the third reduction the miners had accepted in the postwar period. *La Antorcha* (11.viii.22), in the aftermath of this settlement, spoke bitterly of the "criminal complicity" of the Socialists, and called the agreement the "Himalayas of treason" of the Socialist Party.

29. *El Sol*, 17.v.22.

30. *Ibid*., 10.vi.22; Comín Colomer, *Historia del partido comunista*, p. 128.

31. *El Sol*, 9.vi.22.

32. *Ibid*., 18.vi.22.

33. *Ibid*.

34. Quoted in *La Antorcha*, 15.vi.23. Nevertheless, the Cenetistas called attention to their "very federalist" organization and conceded, in effect, the right of local sindicatos or regional organizations to make pacts with other workers' forces in their respective locales or regions, provided such agreements were for concrete purposes not in violation of the CNT's principles.

35. *Ibid.*

36. *Ibid.*, 15.xii.22.

37. *Ibid.*, 11.iv.23.

38. *El Socialista*, 7.vii.22. For the Communist reply to Largo's attack and a justification of the United Front tactic in Spain, see *La Antorcha*, 14.vii.22.

39. *El Sol*, 9.vii.22.

40. *Ibid.*, 18.viii.22.

41. *El Socialista*, 17.vi.22.

42. See the article by José Bullejos in *La Antorcha*, 18.vii.22.

43. *El Sol*, 30.vii.22.

44. *Ibid.*, 21.vii.22. The process of mitosis was seen even within the Catholic Miners' Union in Asturias, which split as one group of miners decided to affiliate with the Sindicatos Libres of Catalonia. *La Antorcha*, 29.vi.23.

45. *El Socialista*, 21.iii.19.

46. *Diario de Sesiones*, 4.xi.21.

47. *El Sol*, 23.iv.22.

48. *La Antorcha*, 21.vii.22.

49. *El Sol*, 3.viii.22.

50. *Ibid.*

51. *Buenacasa*, p. 106.

52. *Partido socialista obrero español: Convocatoria y ordén del dia para el XII congreso ordinario del partido* (Madrid, 1927), p. 62. A Socialist chronicler commented regarding this episode that Seguí had a "very outstanding political spirit," and that he "wished to evolve, might have accepted going to parliament, and in his speeches did not renounce the [discussion of] political themes." Seguí, he wrote, had an "understanding" with Lerroux and was on "speaking terms" with the Republican Soriano, who had ties with García Prieto; *ibid.*

53. *El Sol*, 25.iv.22.

54. *Ibid.*, 24.v.22.

55. Salaya, pp. 39–40.

56. *El Sol*, 2.vi.22 and 6.vi.22.

57. García Venero, *Historia de los movimientos*, p. 413.

58. Hilario Arlandis, "La conférence de Saragosse," *La Lutte de Classes*, 5.vii.22.

59. Buenacasa, pp. 107–8.

60. *Ibid.*, p. 106.

61. *Lucha Social*, 11.iii.22; Nettlau MS, p. 277.

62. These reports were *Memoria al comité* and *Consideraciones y juícios*.

63. *Lucha Social*, 24.vi.22. Salvador Seguí also believed that the CNT should leave the Comintern, and he spoke of "the abyss dividing us both ideologically and tactically" from the Communist International. Nevertheless, Andrés Nin, in reviewing the debates at Zaragoza, acknowledged the restraint that characterized the speeches of the moderate leaders, in contrast to those of the Anarchosyndicalist delegates; *Internationale Presse-Korrespondenz*, 12.viii.22.

64. *Ibid.*; *Lucha Social*, 14.x.22.

65. *El movimiento obrero*, p. 111.

66. The complete text of the resolution on the Comintern will be found in *La Lutte de Classes*, 5.vii.22.

67. *El Sol*, 13.vi.22.

68. *Ibid.*, 14.vi.22.

69. Buenacasa, pp. 142–43.

70. The text of the "political resolution" reads as follows: "La Ponencia encargada de dictaminar sobre nuestra posición ante la política nacional declara que: Considerando que, a deducir por la Historia, los partidos políticos sin excepción no suponer valor moral alguno en ninguno de los ordenes de sus actuaciones; Considerando que en la pasada represión, como en todas las represiones, los partidos políticos han sido responsables directos, ya sea por acción, ya sea por omisión, la Ponencia expone su pensamiento de que entre unos y otros partidos políticos no pueden ni deben establecerse distingos de ninguna clase y que la conducta de la CNT debe ajustarse a la de los partidos políticos. Por otra parte, la ponencia declara que: Considerando que, por la razón misma de llamarlos apolíticos, la CNT no puede inhibirse de ningún de las problemas que con vida nacional se plantean; Considerando que la interpretación dada a la palabra 'política' es arbitraria, ya que ella no puede ni debe interpretarse en el solo sentido de 'arte de gobernar a los pueblos,' sino que su acepción universal quiere expresar la denominación común de las actuaciones de todo orden en absoluto de los individuos y de todas las colectividades; Considerando que, para ser lógicos con nosotros mismos, estamos obligados a aportar soluciones y a ser valores determinantes a todos y en todos los problemas morales, culturales, económicos, políticos y sociales, la Ponencia propone; Que la CNT declare que, siendo un organismo netamente revolucionario que rechaza franca y expresamente la acción parlamentaria y de colaboración con los partidos políticos, es, a la vez, integral y absolutamente política, puesto que su misión es la de conquistar sus derechos de revisión y fiscalización de todos los valores de evolución de la vida nacional, y a tal fin, su deber es el de ejercer la acción determinante por medio de la coacción derivada de las manifestaciones de fuerza y de dispositivos de la CNT.—J. Peiró, Angel Pestaña, Salvador Seguí y José Viadiu." *El Sol*, 16.vi.22.

71. *Ibid.*

72. *Ibid.*, 14.vi.22.

73. Buenacasa, pp. 138–40.

74. *El Sol*, 17.vi.22.

75. *Ibid.*, 21.vi.22.

76. The complete text of the counterresolution is in Buenacasa, pp. 155–56.

77. *Ibid.*, p. 156.

78. Rocker, pp. 383–84. The principles of the AIT are discussed in García Venero, *Historia de las internacionales*, pp. 381–85.

79. Rocker, p. 384.

80. Nin, "Pridisloviem," pp. 5–7. See also Maurín, "Armonia sindicalo-comunista," *El Socialista*, 3.ix.23.

81. Miguel García in *La Antorcha*, 5.i.23.

82. *La Antorcha*, 29.xii.22.

83. *Ibid.*, 24.xi.22.

84. *HDA*, [9], "Rapport au Comité Executif."

85. *La Antorcha*, 11.viii.22.

86. *Ibid.*, 29.ix.22.

87. *Ibid.*, 24.xi.22.

88. *Ibid.*, 8.vi.23.

89. *Ibid.*, 5.i.23.

90. *Ibid.*, 29.xii.22.

91. G. Sanz, *ibid.*, 17.xi.22.

92. Díaz del Moral, p. 165.

93. *La Antorcha*, 29.ix.22, 1.xii.22, and 2.ii.23.

94. *Communist International: Fourth Congress*, pp. 288–94.

95. *La Antorcha*, 16.iii.23; Acevedo, *Impresiones*, pp. 23ff.

96. *Protokoll des Vierten Kongresses*, pp. 163–64. Because of either inadequate translation or faulty transcription, Acevedo's speech was not recorded fully in the

Protokoll. The complete text is given in *La Antorcha*, 15.xii.22. It reveals rather sharp criticism of the French party for noncompliance with the United Front and suggests—rightly or wrongly—that Spain's propinquity to France caused this attitude to spread among the Spanish masses, thus making the task of the Spanish Communists more difficult. Nevertheless, in his original speech Acevedo himself made it clear that he regarded the United Front as only a temporary policy, appropriate to a transitional period.

97. *La Antorcha*, 27.vii.23.
98. *Protokoll des Vierten Kongresses*, pp. 884–88.
99. *Rapports*, pp. 70–103.
100. *La Antorcha*, 3.xi.22 and 24.xi.22.
101. *Ibid.*, 12.i.23.
102. Quoted in *ibid.*, 8.xii.22.
103. *Ibid.*
104. *Ibid.*, 24.xi.22.
105. *Ibid.*, 8.xii.22.
106. *Ibid.*
107. *Ibid.*, 24.xi.22 and 8.xii.22.

108. García Venero, *Historia de los movimientos*, p. 406. The expelled Communist unions followed the emphatic orders of the Comintern Congress and made every effort to gain readmission to the UGT; at the same time, they joined with the already excluded Asturian unions and with the Communist-Syndicalists in the Bilbao meeting of December 1922 to form the Grupos Rojos Sindicales, whose total membership was estimated, perhaps rather generously, at 40,000. *La Vanguardia Mercantil*, 29.xii.22.

109. *La Antorcha*, 22.xii.22.

Chapter Sixteen

1. *El Sol*, 26.vii.22 and 3.viii.22.
2. *Ibid.*, 27.vii.22.
3. R. Sanz, pp. 95ff.
4. *El Sol*, 13.viii.22.
5. Oller Piñol, Chapter 13.
6. R. Sanz, p. 95; *El Sol*, 27.vi.22.
7. *El Sol*, 3.viii.22.
8. *Ibid.*, 26.viii.22 and 27.viii.22. Indalecio Prieto, who had clashed with Martínez Anido earlier over the Ley de Fugas, now claimed that the attempted assassination of Pestaña had in fact been carried out by the Libres at the instigation of Anido. Oller Piñol, pp. 145–46.
9. Peirats, *Los anarquistas*, p. 35.
10. García Venero, *Historia de los movimientos*, p. 419.
11. *Cultura y acción*, 7.x.22.
12. Maurín, *L'anarchosyndicalisme*, p. 34.
13. Pestaña, *Lo que aprendí*, p. 90.
14. R. Sanz, pp. 111, 124.
15. Pestaña, *Lo que aprendí*, pp. 100–101.
16. García Venero, *Historia de los movimientos*, p. 420.

17. *La Antorcha*, 23.iii.23. The murder of Seguí led to the retaliatory slaying of Cardinal Soldevila, the Archbishop of Zaragoza, by Francisco Ascaso; Buenacasa, pp. 232–33.

18. On Seguí's relations with the extreme Anarchosyndicalists, see the columns of *Cultura y Acción* and *Páginas Libres* for 1922–23. The republican leader Félix Azzati was addressing a meeting of republicans early in February 1923, as Seguí entered the hall. Azzati said to his audience, "As you see, Sr. Seguí has come to hear republican propaganda, and this proof of tolerance speaks very well in his favor. It demonstrates that our differences of ideal are only momentary and cir-

cumstantial. We are both looking for something similar; and, perhaps, marching by different roads, we will someday meet." *El Socialista*, 6.ii.23. On the theme of Seguí's moderation, see also Gómez Casas, pp. 141–42.

19. García Venero, *Santiago Alba*, pp. 172–73.

20. Portela MS, II, 13–16.

21. *La Antorcha*, 23.iii.23.

22. *Ibid.*, 11.v.23; Saborit, *Julián Besteiro*, p. 70; Núñez de Arenas, in Tuñón de Lara, *Historia*, p. 224. On Viñuela, see *Nuestra Palabra*, 25.i.19. The votes for all the Madrid candidates are listed in Gonzalo Redondo, *Las empresas políticas de José Ortega y Gasset* (Madrid, 1970), I, 379. See also Tusell, pp. 170–85.

23. *La Antorcha*, 6.vii.23.

24. *Ibid.*, 22.vi.23.

25. *Ibid.*, 8.vi.23.

26. *Ibid.*, 30.iii.23 and 13.vii.23. The ECCI, too, would speak freely of the "failure" of the Spanish Communists in the 1923 elections; *ibid.*, 13.vii.23. The seven Socialist deputies were: Pablo Iglesias, Julián Besteiro, Fernando de los Ríos, Indalecio Prieto, Manuel Cordero, and Andrés Saborit.

27. *El Sol*, 2.v.23.

28. *La Antorcha*, 11.v.23.

29. *Ibid.*, 18.v.23.

30. *Ibid.*, 8.vi.23.

31. Madariaga, *Spain*, p. 336.

32. Raymond Carr, p. 571; Payne, *Politics and the military*, p. 193.

33. Payne, *Politics and the military*, pp. 192–93.

34. *La Antorcha*, 29.xii.22.

35. *HDA*, [9].

36. *La Antorcha*, 8.vi.23.

37. *Ibid.*

38. *Ibid.*, 1.vi.23 and 15.vi.23; *El Joven Comunista*, 20.vii.23.

39. *La Antorcha*, 1.vi.23.

40. *Ibid.*, 22.vi.23.

41. *Ibid.*, 15.vi.23.

42. *Ibid.*, 29.vi.23.

43. *Ibid.*, 8.vi.23.

44. *Ibid.*, 20.vii.23.

45. *Ibid.*, 13.vii.23.

46. *Ibid.*, 20.vii.23.

47. *Ibid.*

48. *Ibid.*, 27.vii.23.

49. *Ibid.*; *HDA*, [9].

50. *La Antorcha*, 27.vii.23. The Party officers were: secretary general, César González; secretary for international affairs, José Baena; secretary for the interior, Luis Portela; administrative secretary, Joaquín Ramos; secretary of agriculture, Feliciano Alonso; syndical secretary, Ramón Lamoneda; secretary for women, María Mayorga; *vocales*, Juan Andrade, Vicente Arroyo, José Rojas, Torralba Beci, Vicente Calaza, Gonzalo Sanz, Carlos Romero, José Baron. *Ibid.*

51. *Ibid.*

52. *HDA*, [9].

53. Degras, *The Communist International*, I, 382–92.

54. García Palacios, pp. 12–13.

55. Hernández, *Yo, ministro de Stalin*, pp. 5–7.

56. Buenacasa, p. 301.

57. Hernández, *Yo, ministro de Stalin*, p. 8.

58. *Ibid.*, p. 10.

59. Tuñón de Lara, in Núñez de Arenas, pp. 224–25; José García, *Diktadura Primo de Rivera* (Moscow, 1963), pp. 98–99.

60. Payne, *Politics and the military*, p. 194. The timing of the military coup would also be influenced by the fact that the Picasso Commission on Responsi-

bilities (named by the Cortes to inquire into the causes of the Annual disaster) was scheduled to present on September 20 a report certain to be damaging to the Army.

61. *El Sol*, 14.i.23.

62. García Venero, quoted in Gonzalo Redondo, I, 11.

63. *La Antorcha*, 31.viii.23.

64. Tuñón de Lara, in Núñez de Arenas, p. 226; *Historia abreviada*, p. 41.

65. Ratcliff, p. 37; *Historia abreviada*, p. 42.

66. *Historia abreviada*, p. 42; *The Communist International between the Fifth and Sixth Congresses*, pp. 273–74.

67. Buenacasa, pp. 300–302.

68. Maurín, *L'anarchosyndicalisme*, p. 40.

69. *Ibid.*, pp. 36–37.

70. *Ibid.*, p. 40. Writing in May 1924, Joaquín Maurín estimated Cenetista strength in Barcelona at about 25,000. *Solidaridad Obrera*, which had once published 50,000 copies, was now selling only 6,000 in all of Spain and only 2,000 in Barcelona. *Ibid.*, p. 41. The split between the extreme Anarchosyndicalists and the "pure" Syndicalists continued underground during the Dictatorship. It surfaced again during the Republic as the conflict between the intransigent *Faistas*, most of whom were younger and terrorist-oriented, and the older and more moderate *Treintistas*, whose ranks contained such organizationally minded leaders as Pestaña, Peiró, Quemades, and Viadiu, who continued to argue against revolutionary precipitance, especially in view of the coming of the democratic Republic. The revival of the CNT after 1929 is discussed in Rama, pp. 145–68. See also John Brademas, "Revolution and social revolution: a contribution to the history of the Anarchosyndicalist movement in Spain, 1930–1937" (unpubl. Oxford dissertation, 1956).

71. Cordero, pp. 44–47; Navas, p. 10.

72. Navas, pp. 11–12.

73. Saborit, *Asturias*, p. 124.

74. *Ibid.*, p. 215; Raymond Carr, *Spain*, p. 571; Tuñón de Lara, in Núñez de Arenas, *Historia*, p. 231.

75. Jackson, pp. 204, 206–10.

76. According to *La Vie Ouvrière* (16.i.25), by the end of 1924, the Communist opposition within the UGT was extremely weak and incohesive in Madrid and virtually "nonexistent" in the provinces. Only in the Madrid Woodworkers' Union was there any significant Communist activity, and everywhere the Communists suffered from a lack of coordination and discipline. A Comintern statement in 1928 acknowledged that "the great weakness" of the Spanish Communist Party was "inadequate contact" with the masses. *The Communist International between the Fifth and Sixth Congresses*, p. 273.

77. Maurín, *Révolution et contrerévolution*, p. 131.

78. Letter to the author from José Bullejos, 21.vii.66.

79. Wohl, pp. 39–41.

80. *Ibid.*, p. 41.

Bibliography

Bibliography

Abad de Santillán, D. Historia del movimiento obrero español. Madrid, 1967.
Acevedo, Isidoro. La huelga de agosto. *Nuestra Bandera*, No. 19 (1947), pp. 567–77.
———. Impresiones de un viaje a Rusia. Oviedo, 1923.
Alomar, Gabriel. La huelga en Barcelona. *España*, 25.x.17.
Alvarez del Vayo, Julio. The last optimist. New York, 1950.
Andrade, Juan. La burocracía reformista en el movimiento obrero. Madrid, 1935.
Araquistáin, Luis. Entre la guerra y la revolución. Madrid, 1917.
———. España en el crisol. Barcelona, [1920].
———. Orígenes y proceso de la huelga general. *España*, 25.x.17.
Arbeloa, Victor Manuel. Orígenes del partido socialista obrero español 1873–1880. Madrid, 1972.
Auburn, Charles V. Manuel Núñez de Arenas y de la Escosura (1886–1951). *Bulletin Hispanique*, LIII, no. 4, pp. 459–60.
Aunós Pérez, Eduardo. Itinerario histórico de la España contemporanea. Barcelona, 1940.
Baelen, Jean. Principaux traits du développement économique de l'Espagne de 1914 à l'avènement du Directoire Militaire. Paris, 1924.
Balbontín, José Antonio. La España de mi experiencia. Mexico City, 1952.
Balcells, Alberto. El sindicalismo en Barcelona, 1916–1923. 2d ed. Barcelona, 1968.
Baldasano, Tomás. The real position of Spain. *Fortnightly Review*, CX, new series (July 1921), 91–97.
Baratech Alfaro, F. Los Sindicatos Libres en España: Su origen, su actuación, su ideario. Barcelona, 1927.
Bell, Daniel. The end of ideology. New York, 1960.
Bernaldo de Quirós y Pérez, Constancio. El espartaquismo agrario andaluz. Madrid, 1919.
Besteiro, Julián. Marxismo y antimarxismo. Mexico City, 1966.
Bolin, Luis. Spain and the war. *Edinburgh Review*, CCXXVI (July 1917), 135–52.
Brenan, Gerald. The Spanish labyrinth. Cambridge, Eng., 1962.
Breton, Jean. En mai a Madrid. *Revue de Paris*, 15.vi.17.
Bruguera, F. G. Histoire contemporaine d'Espagne, 1789–1950. [Paris], 1953.
Buenacasa, Manuel. El movimiento obrero español, historia y crítica, 1886–1926. 2d ed. Paris, 1966.
Bullejos, José. Europa entre dos guerras. Mexico City, 1945.
———. Le mouvement des mineurs espagnoles. *L'International Syndicale Rouge*, Apr. 1925, pp. 322–25.

Burgos y Mazo, Manuel de. Páginas históricas de 1917. Madrid, 1917.
——. El verano de 1919 en gobernación. [Madrid], 1921.
Buxadé, José. España en crisis: La bullanga misteriosa de 1917. Barcelona, 1917.
Calleja, Rafael. Rusia: Espejo saludable para uso de pobres y de ricos. Madrid, 1920.
Cánovas Cervantes, Salvador. Rutas de la revolución española. Madrid, n.d.
Carr, E. H. The Bolshevik Revolution. Macmillan, 1951–53.
Carr, Raymond. Spain, 1808–1939. Oxford, 1966.
Carrión, Pascual. Los latifundios de España. Madrid, 1932.
Castro Delgado, Enrique. Hombres made in Moscu. Madrid, 1960.
Chamberlain, William Henry. The Russian Revolution, 1917–1921. Vol. I. New
    York, 1935.
Cierva y Peñafiel, Juan de la. Notas de mi vida. Madrid, 1955.
Clarkson, Jesse D. A history of Russia. New York, 1961.
The class war in Spain. Fortnightly Review, LXXXIII (May 1921), 738–44.
Clough, Shepherd B. The economic history of modern Italy. New York, 1964.
Cole, G. D. H. Communism and Social Democracy, 1914–1931. London, 1958.
Collinet, Michel. L'ouvrier français: Esprit du syndicalisme. Paris, 1951.
Coman, Katherine. Insurance for the superannuated worker in Spain. The Survey,
    28.ii.14.
Comín Colomer, Eduardo. Historia del anarquismo español. 2 vols. Barcelona, 1956.
——. Historia del partido comunista. Madrid, 1965.
Communist International. Fourth Congress: Abridged report. London, 1923.
The Communist International between the Fifth and the Sixth World Congresses,
    1924–1928: A report on the position in all sections of the World Communist
    Party. London, 1928.
La condena del comité de huelga. Mexico City, n.d.
Conze, Edward. Spain today. London, 1936.
Cordero, Manuel. Los socialistas en la revolución. Madrid, 1932.
Costedoat-Lamarque, Jean. La question agraire en Andalousie. Paris, 1923.
Cunningham, Charles H. Spain and the war. American Political Science Review,
    XI (Aug. 1917), 421–47.
Daniels, Robert V. The state and revolution: A case study in the genesis and trans-
    formation of Communist ideology. American Slavic and East European Review,
    XII (1953), 22–43.
Degras, Jane. United front tactics in the Comintern, 1921–1928. In David Footman,
    International Communism, pp. 9–22. London, 1960.
Degras, Jane, ed. The Communist International, 1919–1943: Documents. 2 vols.
    London, 1956.
Deiatel'nost', ispolnitel'nogo komiteta i prezidiuma I.K. Komunisticheskogo Inter-
    natsionala. Petrograd, 1923.
de los Ríos, Fernando. The agrarian problem in Spain. International Labor Review,
    June 1925, pp. 830–51.
——. Mi viaje a la Rusia sovietista. 2d ed. Madrid, 1922.
del Rosal, Amaro. Los congresos obreros internacionales en el siglo XX. Mexico
    City, 1963.
Denjean, François. Le mouvement révolutionnaire en Espagne. Revue de Paris,
    XXVIII (Nov.–Dec. 1921), 158–84.
Deutscher, Isaac. The prophet armed. Oxford, 1954.
Díaz del Moral, Juan. Historia de las agitaciónes campesinas andaluzas: Córdoba.
    Madrid, 1929.

Díaz-Plaja, Fernando. La historia de España en sus documentos (nueva serie): El siglo XX. Madrid, 1960.

"Dionysios" [José Antonio Birlán], ed. Almanaque de Tierra y Libertad para 1921. Barcelona, 1920.

Drachkovitch, M. M., ed. Marxism in the modern world. Stanford, 1965.

Elorietta y Artaza, Tomás. El movimiento bolcheviste. Madrid, 1919.

Evolución del socialismo español. La Lectura, XX (Jan. 1920), Pt. I, pp. 44–47.

Fabri, Luigi. La crisis del anarquismo. Buenos Aires, 1921.

Fainsod, Merle. International socialism and the World War. Garden City, 1969.

Farré Moregó, José M. Los atentados sociales en España. Madrid, 1922.

Fernández Almagro, Melchor. Historia del reinado de Don Alfonso XIII. Barcelona, 1936.

Feuer, Louis, ed. Basic writings on politics and philosophy: Karl Marx and Friedrich Engels. Garden City, N.Y., 1959.

Foix, Pere. Apòstols i mercaders: Quaranta anys de lluita social a Catalunya. Mexico City, 1949.

Francés, José María. Memorias de un cero a la izquierda. Mexico City, 1962.

Francisco Corréas, Juan. El bolchevismo en España. Madrid, 1920.

García Palacios, Luis. Los dirigentes del partido comunista al desnudo. Madrid, 1931.

García Venero, Maximiliano. Historia de las internacionales en España. 3 vols. Madrid, 1956.

———. Historia de los movimientos sindicalistas españoles (1840–1933). Madrid, 1961.

———. Melquíades Alvarez. Madrid, 1954.

———. Santiago Alba, monárquico de razón. Madrid, 1963.

Gasset, Rafael. La humanidad insumisa: La revolución rusa, el problema social en España. Madrid, 1920.

Gay, Peter. The dilemma of democratic socialism. New York, 1962.

Giner, Salvador. Continuity and change: The social stratification of Spain. Reading, Eng., 1968.

Goldman, Emma. Living my life. New York, 1931.

Gómez, Manuel. From Mexico to Moscow. Survey, Oct. 1964, pp. 34–41.

Gómez Casas, Juan. Historia del anarcosindicalismo español. Madrid, 1968.

González, A. Istoria ispanskikh sektsii Mezhdunarodnogo Tovarishchestvo Rabochikh, 1868–1873 gg. Moscow, 1964.

Griffith, Sanford. The German myth in Spain. Outlook, CXVI (May–Aug. 1917), 364–65.

Hardinge, Arthur. A diplomatist in Europe. London, 1927.

Hennessy, C. A. M. The Federal Republic in Spain. Oxford, 1962.

Heredero, Antonio. Crises políticas durante la guerra europea de los años 1914 al 1918. El Español, 10.iv.43.

Hernández, Jesús. Negro y roja: Los anarquistas en la revolución española. Mexico City, 1946.

———. Yo, ministro de Stalin en España. 2d ed., Prologue and Notes by Mauricio Carlavilla. Madrid, 1954.

Harold, A. Ferdinand. L'Espagne en 1917. Mercure de France, 3.iii.17.

Historia del partido comunista de España (versión abreviada). Paris, 1960.

Horowitz, Daniel C. The Italian labor movement. Cambridge, Mass., 1963.

La huelga de agosto en el parlamento. Barcelona, 1917.

542   BIBLIOGRAPHY

Hulse, James W. The forming of the Communist International. Stanford, 1964.
Humbert-Droz Archives [*HDA*]. Original documents held by the International Institute of Social History, Amsterdam; microfilm copies available at Harvard University and at the Hoover Institution, Stanford.
———. [1] Document consacrant la fusion entre le parti communiste espagnol et le parti communiste ouvrier d'Espagne. n.d. (no. 89).
———. [2] Les exclus du Comite Central s'adressent à Graziadei. 27.i.22.
———. [3] Groupe communiste espagnol à Zinoviev, Moscou. n.d. (no. 33).
———. [4] Les Jeunesses Espagnols et le Parti Socialiste. Communication du Bureau auxiliaire d'Amsterdam de la IIIieme Internationale, 16.iii.20.
———. [5] Lettre d'Humbert-Droz au Presidium XX de l'Internationale Communiste sur la situation du parti espagnol. 18.v.22.
———. [6] Lettre d'Humbert-Droz au Secretariat de l'Internationale Communiste. 6.vii.22.
———. [7] Merino Gracia to Humbert-Droz, 4.iv.22.
———. [8] Platform de l'opposition du parti communiste espagnol. Jan. 1922.
———. [9] Rapport au Comité Executif sur le congrès du parti communiste espagnol. 18.vii.23.
———. [10] Rapport de A. Graziadei. 18.i.22.
———. [11] Rapport-mémoire de Humbert-Droz sur le conflit intérieur du parti communiste espagnol. [May 1922].
Hurtado, Amadeo. Quaranta anys d'advocat. 2 vols. Barcelona, 1964.
Ibarruri, Dolores. They shall not pass. New York, 1966.
Iglesias, Pablo. Exhortaciones a los trabajadores. Madrid, 1926.
Informes de los inspectores del trabajo sobre la influencia de la guerra europea en las industrias españolas. Madrid, 1918.
Instituto de Reformas Sociales [IRS]. Encarecimiento de la vida durante la guerra: Precios de las subsistencias en España y en el extranjero, 1914–1918. Madrid, 1918.
———. Información sobre el problema agrario en la provincia de Córdoba. Madrid, 1919.
———. Información sobre emigración española a los países de Europa durante la guerra. Madrid, 1919.
Instituto Nacional de Estadística [INE]. Principales actividades de la vida española en la primera mitad del siglo XX. Madrid, 1952.
Iyi mezhdunarodnyi kongress revolyutsionnykh professional'nykh i proizvodstvennykh soyuzov: Stenograficheskii otchet. [Moscow, n.d.].
Jackson, Gabriel. The origins of Spanish anarchism. *Southwestern Social Science Quarterly*, XXXVI (1955), 135–49.
Joll, James. The anarchists. New York, 1964.
———. The Second International, 1889–1914. New York, 1966.
Jordán, F. La dictadura del proletariado. Madrid, 1920.
Kautsky, Karl. The dictatorship of the proletariat. Ann Arbor, 1964.
Kennan, George. Russia and the West under Lenin and Stalin. Boston, 1961.
Krasnyi Internatsional Profsoyuzov. Profintern i Komintern. Moscow, 1921.
Laborde, Jules. Il y a toujours des pyrénées. Paris, 1918.
Lacomba, Juan Antonio. Crisi i revolució al país Valencia. N.p., 1917.
———. La crisis española de 1917. Madrid, 1970.
Landauer, Carl. European socialism. Vol. 1. Berkeley, 1959.
Lantier, Raymond. L'attitude des intellectuels espagnols dans le conflit actuel. *Mercure de France*, 1.i.16.

————. Quelques points de vue espagnols sur la guerre. *Mercure de France,* 1.vii.18.
Largo Caballero, Francisco. Correspondencia secreta. Mauricio Carlavilla, ed. Madrid, 1961.
————. Mis recuerdos. Mexico City, 1954.
Leger, Robert. La législation du travail en Espagne. *Annales des Sciences Politiques,* XXI (1906), 495–515.
Lenin, V. I. Collected works. Moscow, 1968.
————. "Left-wing" Communism: An infantile disorder. New York, 1940.
————. State and revolution. New York, 1932.
————. What is to be done? New York, 1943.
Leval, Gaston. Ni Franco ni Stalin. Milan, n.d.
Lichtheim, George. Marxism in France. New York, 1966.
Linz, Juan L. "The party system in Spain: Past and future." Unpub. paper, 1966.
Llaneza, Manuel. La huelga de agosto en Asturias. *España,* 1.xi.17.
López Arango, E., and D. A. de Santillán. El anarquismo en el movimiento obrero. Barcelona, 1925.
Lorenzo, César M. Les anarchistes espagnols et le pouvoir, 1868–1969. Paris, 1969.
Lozovsky, A. Les anarcho-syndicalistes et l'Internationale syndicale rouge. *L'Internationale Communiste,* July 1922.
————. Internatsional professional'nykh soyuzov. Moscow, 1921.
Luis André, Eloy. Los problemas de España y la guerra europea. *Nuestro Tiempo,* Apr. 1916, pp. 17–32.
Madariaga, Salvador de. The danger of militarism. *New Europe,* 21.iii.18.
————. Dark forces in Spain. *New Europe,* 24.v.17.
————. The future of Spanish neutrality. *New Europe,* 15.ii.17.
————. Spain: A modern history. New York, 1958.
————. Spain and Russia: A parallel. *New Europe,* 30.viii.17.
————. Spain in transition. *Living Age,* 21.vi.19.
————. Spain's home war. *Contemporary Review,* CXIV (Oct. 1918), 381.
Madrid, Francisco. Ocho meses y un día en el gobierno civil de Barcelona. Barcelona, 1932.
————. Las últimas veinticuatro horas de Francisco Layret. Buenos Aires, n.d.
Maitron, Jean. Histoire du mouvement anarchiste en France, 1880–1914. Paris, 1952.
Malefakis, Edward. Agrarian reform and peasant revolution in Spain: Origins of the Civil War. New Haven, 1970.
————. Peasants, politics, and civil war in Spain. *In* Robert J. Bezucha, Modern European social history, pp. 192–204. Lexington, Mass., 1972.
Martí, Casimiro. Orígenes del anarquismo en Barcelona. Barcelona, 1959.
Martínez Cuadrado, Miguel. La burguesía conservadora (1874–1931). Madrid, 1973.
Martínez Cuadrado, Miguel. Elecciones y partidos políticos de España, 1868–1931. Madrid, 1969.
Marvaud, Angel. La question sociale en Espagne. Paris, 1910.
Maura Gamazo, Gabriel, and Melchor Fernández Almagro. Por qué cayó Alfonso XIII. Madrid, 1948.
Maurín, Joaquín. L'anarchosyndicalisme en Espagne. Paris, 1924.
————. Anarkhosindikalizm v Ispanii. Moscow, 1925.
————. La derrota. *España Libre,* 3.vi.60.
————. De España a Moscu sin pasaporte. *España Libre,* 20.x.61.

————. Hombres e historia. *España Libre*, 19.ii.60.

————. Unpublished MS in possession of the present author. (Cited as Maurín MS.)

————. Révolution et contre-révolution en Espagne. Paris, 1937.

————. El II Congreso de la CNT. *España Libre*, 1.iv.60.

Mayer, Arno J. Wilson vs. Lenin: Political origins of the new diplomacy, 1917–1918. Cleveland, 1959.

Memoria del congreso celebrado en Barcelona los días 28, 29, 30 de junio y el 1 de julio del año 1918. Pub. by Confederación Regional del Trabajo de Cataluña. Barcelona, 1918.

Memoria del congreso celebrado en el teatro de la Comedia de Madrid los días 10 al 18 de diciembre de 1919. Pub. by Confederación Nacional del Trabajo. Barcelona, 1932.

Merino Gracia, Ramón. Le parti socialiste ouvrier. *In* Le mouvement communiste international: Rapports, addressés au deuxième congrès de l'International communiste. Petrograd, 1921.

Michels, Robert. Political parties: A sociological study of the oligarchical tendencies of modern democracy. New York, 1962.

Mora, Francisco. Historia del socialismo obrero español: Desde sus primeras manifestaciones hasta nuestros días. Madrid, 1902.

Morato, Juan José. Pablo Iglesias, educador de muchedumbres. Madrid, 1928.

————. El partido socialista. Madrid, [1918].

Mountseny, Federico. Anselmo Lorenzo: El hombre y la obra. Toulouse, 1970.

Mousset, Albert. L'Espagne dans la politique mondiale. Paris, 1923.

Munilla, Gil. Historia de la evolución social española durante los siglos XIX y XX. Madrid, 1961.

Murphy, J. T. New horizons. London, 1941.

Navas, Miguel. Los socialistas españoles y la dictadura militar. Buenos Aires, 1929.

Nettl, J. P. The German Social Democratic Party 1890–1914 as a political model. *Past and Present*, Jan. 1965, pp. 65–95.

Nettlau, Max. Unpublished manuscript (Die Jahre 1915 ... bis 1923). International Institute for Social History, Amsterdam.

Nin, Andrés. Els moviments d'emancipació nacional. Paris, 1970.

————. Pourquoi Dato fut assassiné. *La Lutte de Classes*, 5.vii.22.

————. Pridisloviem. *In* Joaquín Maurín, Anarkhosindikalizm v Ispanii.

Núñez de Arenas, Manuel, and Manuel Tuñón de Lara. Historia del movimiento obrero español. Barcelona, 1970.

Olivar Bertrand, Rafael. Repercusiones en España de la primera guerra mundial. *Cuadernos de Historia Diplomática*, III (1956), 3–49.

Oller Piñol, J. Martínez Anido. Madrid, 1943.

Ortega y Gasset, José. Invertebrate Spain. London, 1937.

————. Obras completas. New York, 1950.

Pabón, Jesús. Cambó, 1876–1930. Barcelona, 1952.

Page, Stanley W. Lenin and the world revolution. New York, 1959.

Pardo de Tavera, T. H. Spain and the Great War. *Century Magazine*, XCV (1918), 360–65.

El partido socialista: Notas y recuerdas sobre su constitución y desarollo. *El Sol*, 30.iv.19.

Payne, Stanley G. Politics and the military in modern Spain. Stanford, 1967.

————. The Spanish revolution. New York, 1970.

Peirats, José. Los anarquistas en la crisis política española. Buenos Aires, 1964.
———. La CNT en la revolución española, Vol. I. Buenos Aires, 1955.
Peiró, Juan. Problemas del sindicalismo y del anarquismo. Toulouse, 1945.
Pereyra, Carlos. La Tercera Internacional: Doctrinas y controversias. Madrid, [1920?].
Pérez, Dario. Figuras de España. Madrid, 1930.
Pérez, Dionisio. España ante la guerra. Madrid, 1914.
Pérez Solís, Oscar. Memorias de mi amigo Oscar Perea. Madrid, 1929.
———. El partido socialista y la acción de las izquierdas. Valladolid, 1918.
Pestaña, Angel. Consideraciones y juicios acerca de la Tercera Internacional (Segunda parte de la Memoria presentada al Comité de la Confederación Nacional del Trabajo). Barcelona, 1922.
———. Lo que aprendí en la vida. Madrid, 1933.
———. Memoria que el comité de la Confederación Nacional del Trabajo presenta de su gestión en II Congreso de la III Internacional. Madrid, 1922.
———. Normas orgánicas. Barcelona, 1930.
———. Rapport de la Confédération Nationale du Travail. *In* Le mouvement communiste internationale: Rapports, adressés au deuxième congrès de l'Internationale communiste.
———. Setenta días en Rusia: Lo que yo pienso. Barcelona, n.d.
———. Setenta días en Rusia: Lo que yo ví. Barcelona, 1924.
———. El terrorismo en Barcelona. Barcelona, 1920.
Pestaña, Angel, and Salvador Seguí. El sindicalismo libertario en Cataluña. [Madrid], n.d.
Peter, Bishop of Southwark. Spain and the war. *Dublin Review*, CLVIII (Apr. 1916), 209–19.
Pijoan, J. Spain: Before, during, and after the war. *The Nineteenth Century*, XC (Oct. 1921), 667–82.
Portela, Luis. Unpublished MS in the possession of the present author.
[Prat, José]. Herejías? Barcelona, [1922].
La prensa española y la guerra. *Bulletin Hispanique*, XIX (1917), 123–33.
Prieto, Indalecio. De mi vida. Mexico, 1965.
———. Entre sijos de la guerra de España. 2d ed. Buenos Aires, 1956.
Pritchet, V. S. The Spanish temper. London, 1954.
Protokoll des Vierten Kongresses der Kommunistischen Internationale. Petrograd-Moskau, vom 5 November bis 5. Dezember, 1922 (Hamburg, 1923).
Pyziur, Eugene. The doctrine of Anarchism of Michael A. Bakunin. Milwaukee, 1955.
Radek, Karl. Anarkhisty i sovetskaia Rossiia. Petrograd, 1918.
Ramos Oliveira, Antonio. Nosotros los marxistas. Madrid, 1932.
———. Politics, economics, and men of modern Spain: 1808–1946. New York, 1948.
Rapp-Lantaron, E. Vliyanie velikoe oktiabrskaia sotsialisticheskoi revoliutsii podem v Ispanii v 1918–1920 gg. *In* Problemiyi rabochego i antifashistkogo dvishenie v Ispanii. Moscow, 1960.
Rapports de l'I.S.R. et d l'I.C. Paris, [1922?].
Rasgos históricos de la Unión General de Trabajadores de España. Toulouse, 1953.
Ratcliff, Dillwyn F. Prelude to Franco. New York, 1957.
Redondo, Gonzalo. Las empresas políticas de José Ortega y Gasset. 2 vols. Madrid, 1970.

Renaudel, Pierre. L'Internationale à Berne: Faits et documents. Paris, 1919.

Report presented by the National Federation of Spanish Miners to the Miners' International Federation, giving a resumé of the development of the mining industry in Spain during the year 1923. N.p., 1924.

Resumen de las informaciones de los inspectores del trabajo acerca de las consecuencias sufridas por las industrias en España con motivo del actual estado de guerra. Madrid, 1914.

Rocker, Rudolph, Anarchism and Anarchosyndicalism. In Feliks Gross, ed., European ideologies: A survey of twentieth-century political ideas. New York, 1948.

——. Anarcho-syndicalism. London, 1938.

Romanones, Count (Alvaro Figuroa y Torres). Notas de una vida (1912–1931). Madrid, 1947.

——. Las responsabilidades políticas del antiguo régimen. Madrid, n.d.

Romeu Alfaro, Fernanda. Las clases trabajadores en España (1898–1930). Madrid, 1970.

Rosenberg, Arthur. Democracy and socialism. Boston, 1965.

Rosmer, Alfred. Moscou sous Lénine. Paris, 1953.

——. Le mouvement ouvrier pendant la guerre: De l'union sacrée á Zimmerwald. Paris, 1936.

Roth, Guenther. The Social Democrats in Imperial Germany: A study in working-class isolation and national integration. Totowa, N.J., 1963.

Royo Villanova, A. Bolchevismo y sindicalismo. Madrid, 1920.

Russell, Bertrand. German social democracy. 2d ed. New York, 1965.

Saborit, Andrés. Asturias y sus hombres. Toulouse, 1964.

——. La huelga de agosto de 1917. Mexico City, 1967.

——. Julián Besteiro. Mexico City, 1961.

Salaya, Guillén. Historia del sindicalismo español. 2d ed. Madrid, 1943.

Salvador Seguí: Su vida, su obra. Paris, 1960.

Sanz, Gonzalo. Recuerdos de aquellos días. Mundo Obrero, 13.iv.50.

Sanz, Ricardo. El sindicalismo y la política. Toulouse, 1966.

Schorske, Carl E. German social democracy. New York, 1955.

Schumpeter, Joseph. Capitalism, socialism, and democracy. 3d ed. New York, 1942.

Seco Serrano, Carlos. Alfonso XIII y la crisis de la restauración. Barcelona, 1969.

Serge, Victor. From Lenin to Stalin. New York, 1937.

——. Mémoires d'un révolutionnaire. Paris, 1951.

——. Memoirs of a revolutionary. London, 1963.

Sheridan, Clare. Russian portraits. London, 1921.

Société des Amis de l'Espagne. La situation en Espagne. Mimeographed MS dated 12.xii.17. In Hoover Institution, Stanford, California.

Solá Cañizares, F. de. Luchas sociales en Cataluña, 1812–1934. Madrid, 1970.

Solano, E. G. El sindicalismo en la teoría y en la práctica. 2d ed. Barcelona, [1920?].

Soldevilla, Fernando. Un segle de vida catalana: 1814–1930. Barcelona, 1961.

——. Tres revoluciones. Madrid, 1917.

Spain's interest in the war. American Review of Reviews, LIV (Jul.–Dec. 1916), 99.

Los sucesos de agosto ante el parlamento. Madrid, 1918.

Sukhanov, N. N. The Russian Revolution, 1917. Oxford, 1955.

Tamames, Ramón. Estructura económica de España. Madrid, 1960.

Termes Ardevol, José. El movimiento obrero en España: La Primera Internacional (1864–1881). Barcelona, 1965.

Tretii Bsemirnyi Kongres Komunisticheskogo Internatsionala. Petrograd, 1922.

Trotsky, Leon. Mis peripecias en España. Madrid, 1929.
———. My life. New York, 1930.
———. Terrorism and Communism: A reply to Karl Kautsky. Ann Arbor, 1961.
Tuñón de Lara, Manuel. Historia y realidad del poder. Madrid, 1967.
———. Introducció a la història del moviment obrer. Barcelona, 1966.
Tusell, Javier. Sociología electoral de Madrid, 1903–1931. Madrid, 1969.
Ulam, Adam. The unfinished revolution. New York, 1960.
Ullman, Joan Connelly. The Tragic Week: Anticlericalism in Spain, 1876–1912. Cambridge, Mass., 1968.
Unamuno, Miguel de. En Salamanca: Notas de un testigo. España, 25.x.17.
Valdour, Jacques. L'ouvrier espagnol. 2 vols. Lille, 1919.
Viadiu, José. Salvador Seguí ("Noy del Sucre"): El hombre y sus ideas. Valencia, 1930.
Vicens Vives, Jaime. Els Catalans en el segle XIX. Barcelona, 1959.
———. Coyuntura económica y reformismo burgués. Barcelona, 1968.
———. An economic history of Spain. Princeton, N.J., 1969.
———. Historia social y económica de España y América, Tome IV, Vol. II: Burguesía, industrialización, obrerismo. Barcelona, 1959.
Villanueva, Francisco. La huelga en Bilbao. España, 25.x.17.
Vtoroi Kongress Kommunisticheskogo Internatsionala. Moscow, 1934.
Walling, William E. The socialists and the war. New York, 1915.
Williams, George. The First Congress of the Red Trade Union International at Moscow, 1921. Chicago, [1922].
Wohl, Robert. French Communism in the making. Stanford, 1966.
Zinoviev, G. The Communist Party and industrial unionism. London, n.d.
Zugazagoitia, Julián. Pablo Iglesias. Madrid, 1935.

Index

Index